the BUSINESS ENVIRONMENT

themes and issues in a globalizing world

the BUSINESS ENVIRONMENT

themes and issues in a globalizing world

fourth edition

PAUL WETHERLY AND DORRON OTTER

Great Clarendon Street, Oxford, OX2 6DP,
United Kingdom

Oxford University Press is a department of the University of Oxford.
It furthers the University's objective of excellence in research, scholarship,
and education by publishing worldwide. Oxford is a registered trade mark of
Oxford University Press in the UK and in certain other countries

First edition 2008
Second edition 2011
Third edition 2014

Impression: 2

Published in the United States of America by Oxford University Press
198 Madison Avenue, New York, NY 10016, United States of America

British Library Cataloguing in Publication Data
Data available

Library of Congress Control Number: 2017958455

ISBN 978–0–19–873992–0

Printed in Great Britain by
CPI Group (UK) Ltd, Croydon, CR0 4YY

To Barbara, Laura, and Becky (PW)

To Ingrid, Søren, Fredie, and Ferdy (DO)

CONTENTS

DETAILED CONTENTS

LIST OF CASES

ABOUT THE AUTHORS

Paul Wetherly is currently reader in politics in the School of Social Sciences at Leeds Beckett University, and has worked in higher education as a teacher, researcher, and manager for more than twenty-five years. He studied economics and public policy as an undergraduate before obtaining an MA in political sociology and a PhD in political theory. Paul's teaching and research have spanned discipline boundaries including economics, business, and politics. He spent many years in the business faculty of the university where he was responsible for leading a large business environment module. Paul's other publications include a range of articles and books on British politics, the state, and political theory.

Dorron Otter studied politics, philosophy, and economics at Oxford University and he worked in fields as diverse as youth and community work, retailing, tourism, and insurance. In 1984, he undertook a PGCE and spent five years teaching economics and business at Queen Mary's Sixth Form College in Basingstoke. He completed his postgraduate studies in the political economy of development at the University of Leeds and then was the first British Petroleum Fellow in Economic Awareness at the University of Durham. He worked at Leeds Beckett University from 1991 to 2017 where he combined a range of teaching and senior academic management roles and although recently retired he remains active in terms of academic consultancy and writing. As well as his contributions to the editing and writing of this book, his most recent publications have been a chapter on the ecological environment of business in L. Hamilton and P. Webster (eds.), *The International Business Environment* (2018) and on environmental thinking in P. Wetherly (ed.), *Political Ideologies* (2017) both published by Oxford University Press.

Contributors

David Amos is a law lecturer and solicitor. He qualified as a solicitor in 1993. He continued in practice until 1999 when he became a senior lecturer at Leeds Metropolitan University. He moved to Manchester Metropolitan University in March 2005 before becoming head of department at the University of Westminster. He is now Associate Dean (External Engagement) at City, University of London. He was a member of the Solicitors Regulation Authority's Working Party on the Written Standards for the Legal Practice Course (LPC) and is an LPC panel assessor for the Solicitors Regulation Authority.

Mike Franco is Associate Dean for Quality and Programme Leader for Accounting and Finance at Liverpool John Moores University. His principal research interests are in the field of quality assurance and enhancement within higher education. As programme leader for accounting and finance his teaching interests include leadership, economics, and strategic management.

Geoff Gregson is the JR Shaw Research Chair in New Venture and Entrepreneurship and the Associate Dean (Research) at the JR Shaw School of Business, Northern Alberta Institute of

Technology (NAIT) in Canada. He holds degrees from the University of Edinburgh (PhD, LLM, and MSc), University of Calgary (MBA), and University of Alberta (BPE). As an entrepreneur, Geoff has started up three ventures and continues to support entrepreneurs in building successful businesses; in his role at NAIT, as chairman of Axienta Ltd, a Malaysian-based enterprise mobility company and as a board member of JB Equity, a Hong Kong-based private equity firm focused on agri-businesses. Geoff's research interests include new venture creation, SME growth, risk capital, and angel investment, technology commercialization and intellectual property exploitation, innovation systems, innovation policy and enterprise support programmes and their evaluation. He has managed research projects from funders which include the Economic and Social Research Council, British Academy, Technology Strategy Board, Scottish Executive, Marie Curie (European Commission), Santander Bank, and government of Alberta.

Eamonn Judge is Professor Emeritus in the Faculty of Business and Law, Leeds Beckett University, and was, until recent retirement, professor at the Polish Open University, Warsaw, and Professor at Vistula University, Warsaw (where his students kindly acted as guinea pigs for trying out the new main case study of Chapter 8). His principal teaching and research interests, where he has published extensively, are in the field of transport, environment, and business development, particularly in relation to the UK and Poland.

Stratis Koutsoukos is a principal lecturer at Leeds Business School. Formerly deputy director of the European Regional Business and Economic Development Unit, Stratis is a course director for the BA in International Business and a Senior Fellow of the Higher Education Academy. His main areas of research and consultancy are European regional policy, economic regeneration, and European enlargement. Stratis has undertaken assignments for the European Commission, European Parliament, and the Czech ministries for industry and trade and regional development. He teaches European business strategy and international business across various levels of study.

Chris Mulhearn is reader in economics at Liverpool John Moores University. His work has appeared in a range of journals including: *World Economy*, *Journal of Economic Perspectives*, *World Economics*, *Industrial Relations Journal*, and *Local Economy*. His most recent books include: (with Howard Vane) *The Nobel Memorial Laureates in Economics: An Introduction to Their Careers and Main Published Works* (Edward Elgar, 2005); *The Euro: Its Origins, Development and Prospects* (Edward Elgar, 2008); *The Pioneering Papers of the Nobel Memorial Laureates in Economics*, vols. 1–5 (Edward Elgar, 2009), vols. 6–10 (Edward Elgar, 2010), vols. 11–14 (Edward Elgar, 2011). The third edition of his bestselling textbook, *Economics for Business*, widely used in the UK and abroad, was published in 2016.

Simon Raby is Professor in Entrepreneurship and Innovation at the Bissett School of Business, Mount Royal University in Canada, and a Director of Business Improvement and Growth Associates Ltd, a business founded in the UK that supports business schools in their quest to research and work with entrepreneurs and small and medium-sized enterprises (SMEs) in their regions. Simon has helped to create a multidisciplinary applied research programme 'Promoting Sustainable Performance' to challenge the way SMEs achieve growth and has developed leadership tools and programmes so that SMEs can apply this new thinking. Simon serves on the Board of the Institute for Small Business and Entrepreneurship, is educated to doctoral level and is an accredited and practising coach and facilitator. Simon is on the editorial board of the *International Journal of Entrepreneurial Behavior and Research*; a guest editor for the online journal of the Association for Management Education and Development (AMED) *Organisations and People*; and continues to write for academic, business, and policy audiences on topics central to SMEs' growth and success.

Simon Robinson FRSA, SFHEA is Professor of Applied and Professional Ethics, Leeds Business School. He has written and researched extensively in business ethics, corporate social responsibility, leadership, the nature and dynamics of responsibility, equality, integrity, shame and guilt, spirituality and ethics, and ethics and care. Books include: *Agape, Moral Meaning and Pastoral Counselling*; *Case Histories in Business Ethics*; *Spirituality and the Practice of Healthcare*; *Values in Higher Education*; *Ethics and Employability*; *The Teaching and Practice of Professional Ethics*; *Spirituality, Ethics and Care*; *Engineering, Professional and Business Ethics*; *Ethics and the Alcohol Industry*; *Leadership Responsibility*; *Business Ethics in Practice*; *Islam and The West*; *Business Ethics: Contemporary Global and Regional Issues Co-charismatic Leadership*; *Integrity and the Practice of Business*; *A Spirituality of Responsibility: An Islamic Perspective.* Chapters and articles include on applied ethics, integrity and dialogue, peacebuilding, responsibility, responsibility–pedagogy. He is director of the Centre for Governance, Leadership and Global Responsibility, senior editor of the new Palgrave book series on governance, leadership and responsibility, and editor-in-chief of the *Journal of Global Responsibility.*

ACKNOWLEDGEMENTS

We are again indebted to all at OUP for their terrific support, especially our editors Becci Curtis and Kate Gilks for keeping us on track with our writing schedule. We would like to thank all of the authors, both those who have been part of the team on the previous editions and those who have joined us for this fourth edition—Mike Franco, Geoff Gregson, and Simon Raby. We would also like to extend thanks to John Meehan, Martyn Robertson, Carol Langston, Alison Price, and Richard Rooke for their contributions to previous editions. We would also like to extend our thanks to all the reviewers who have commented upon revised draft chapters and reflected on their experiences of using the book with their students.

As always, we would like to thank colleagues and students at Leeds Beckett who have helped us in developing our approach to exploring the Business Environment.

The authors and publisher are grateful to all organizations who kindly granted permission to reproduce copyright materials within this edition. Crown copyright is reproduced under Class Licence Number C2006010631.

Every effort has been made to trace and contact copyright holders, but this has not been possible in every case. If notified, the publisher will undertake to rectify any errors or omissions at the earliest opportunity.

ABOUT THE BOOK

This book is designed primarily for students taking their first undergraduate module in the business environment or similar introductory modules on a range of related business degree, foundation degree, or vocational programmes. The book will also be a useful resource for more advanced studies. The editors both have considerable experience of teaching business environment, and the approach of this book is based on this experience and the comments of successive generations of students and reviewers. In addition to the editors' own chapters in the book, a team of contributing authors has been brought together to write specialist chapters based on their own areas of expertise.

All of the chapters are written in an accessible and engaging style and follow a standard layout with common pedagogical features. A key feature of the approach taken throughout the book is to introduce readers to debates and controversies surrounding the role of business in modern society, and to help them to think critically. In this way it is the intention of the book to provoke lively discussion and debate.

Themes and issues

There are two parts to the book: Part One introduces the core political, legal, economic, social-cultural, technological, and other environments of business, and their interrelationships, following the STEEPLE framework. Part Two, however, goes beyond these topics and invites readers to analyse a range of contemporary issues in the business environment such as the financial crisis and austerity, globalization, corporate power, equal opportunity, and entrepreneurship. These issues have been selected due to their prominence in discussions within business and the wider society, and their importance in shaping the future of business.

The book utilizes an innovative thematic approach to provide a consistent framework for analysis of business and the business environment. The eight themes are intended to help the reader to organize their own thinking about business. Each chapter begins with an overview of how the relevant themes relate to the particular chapter and the themes are then signposted by the use of markers in the margin, as shown here:

- **DIVERSITY** OF BUSINESS Business is a diverse category.
- **INTERNAL/EXTERNAL** The environment is both inside and outside organizations.
- **COMPLEXITY** OF THE ENVIRONMENT The external environment is multi-dimensional or complex.
- **LOCAL TO GLOBAL** SPATIAL LEVELS Spatial levels vary from the local to the global.
- **DYNAMIC** ENVIRONMENT The environment of business does not stand still.
- **INTERACTION** BETWEEN BUSINESS AND THE ENVIRONMENT There is interaction between business organizations and their environments.

- **STAKEHOLDERS** Individuals and groups that are affected by business decisions.
- **VALUES** Business decisions involve ethical questions.

The themes are introduced fully at the start of Chapter 1.

Format and pedagogical features

Each chapter follows a consistent format, providing a wide range of pedagogical features including 'Stop and Think' exercises, Mini-Cases, highlighted key terms, review and discussion questions, and assignments. These features, combined with this innovative structure and analytical approach to the subject matter, will encourage readers to fully engage with the issues raised and develop their interest in critical debate.

Real-world cases

The book is packed with examples, mini-cases, and end of chapter case studies looking at UK, European, and international business, illustrating each topic in real-life contexts. Careful attention has been paid to select cases and examples to which the intended student audience will be able to relate. Examples include Facebook, Cadbury, Samsung, Starbucks, Google, and the football industry.

NEW TO THIS EDITION

This edition has been updated throughout, with a large proportion of new case and illustrative material added. Major changes in the environment of business such as the UK referendum vote to leave the European Union ('Brexit') and the subsequent vote in Parliament to trigger Article 50 and start the process of withdrawal, and the changing attitudes to globalization that this vote seemed in part to reflect, have been taken into account in the text. The basic structure of the book has been retained but in the second part the chapters on the role of the public sector and on SMEs are completely new and a new chapter on inequality has been added to reflect the increasing debate about this issue.

HOW TO USE THIS BOOK

Learning objectives

Clear, concise learning objectives serve as helpful signposts to what you can expect to learn from each chapter.

Learning objectives

When you have completed this chapter, you will be able to:

- Recognize different uses of the term **business**, and distinguish between different forms, such as private, public, and not-for-profit organizations.
- Examine the controversy concerning the nature and purpose of private sector business.
- Describe the complexity of the **external environment** in which business operates and explain the idea of **environmental uniqueness**.
- Explore how businesses must respond to changing environmental factors in order to operate successfully, and how they seek to influence the environment.
- Use analysis tools such as PEST or SWOT to examine the business environment.
- Identify the themes and issues used in our approach to the business environment in this book, and how you can use them in your studies.

Themes

Key themes, introduced in Chapter 1, are described at the beginning of each chapter to show how each theme is relevant to the topic being covered. Markers in the text indicate where one or more of the themes are illustrated, helping to contextualize businesses and the environments in which they operate.

THEMES

The following themes of the book are especially relevant to this chapter

INTERNAL/EXTERNAL Businesses face contrasting market conditions and the nature of these markets fundamentally shapes business strategy.

COMPLEXITY The nature of the economic environment is a complex mix of economic, social, and political factors.

DYNAMIC Change and uncertainty are at the heart of the economic environment and this has been seen in the dynamic changes that have occurred in both the domestic and global economic environments over time.

VALUES Economics is centrally concerned with values; in the sense of the prices and costs of goods and services, in the sense of 'value for money', and in the sense of who benefits from the use of the resources.

Mini-Cases

The book is packed with varied, real-life examples to show how organizations have been influenced by, reacted to, or shaped the business environment in which they operate.

Mini-Case 1.1 Guiding the 'hidden hand'—the minimum wage and the 'livin

VALUES **STAKEHOLDERS** The idea of the 'hidden hand' is a metaphor for the way the market system, though based on millions of independent decisions and not subject to an overall plan or control by any actual hand, does not degenerate into chaos but operates in a highly coordinated way. It is *as if* a hidden hand is guiding it.

Adam Smith argued in the eighteenth century that even though businesses may be concerned only with their self-interest (profit) they would be guided, by and large, to serve the public good. This seems like a paradox—promoting the common good by acting selfishly. Smith's argument was that it would only be by serving the needs of others (customers) that

'employees with decent minimum standard the workplace' and to help business 'by ens will be able to compete on the basis of qua and services they provide and not on low p dominantly on low rates of pay' (*National* webarchive.nationalarchives.gov.uk/20 http://www.dti.gov.uk/er/nmw/index.htm

There are different levels of NMW, depen these rates are reviewed annually by the L sion which makes recommendations to go account of economic circumstances. This m lar, trying to balance improvements to NMW

Stop and Think boxes

Pause your reading and reflect on a question, implication, or consequence relating to the material being discussed. This feature will help you develop your reflection and critical thinking skills, and encourage you to draw on your own experiences.

Stop and Think

Use your knowledge of business and current events in the world of business to think o that highlight each of the themes.

What is business?

INTERACTION This is a book about the 'business environment' in a 'globalizing purpose of this introduction is to help you get to grips with what the business envi why it is important to study and understand it, and the particular approach taken

Key terms

Key terms are highlighted in chapters and collated in the end-of-book glossary, which defines subject-specific terms and concepts to aid your understanding.

Business is a diverse category. It does not refer only to private sector, profit-making companies. Public and voluntary (or third) sector organizations may also be regarded as businesses. The boundaries between these sectors are blurred, contested, and shift over time, for example, as a result of the policy of privatization initiated by Conservative governments in the UK in the 1980s. Within the dominant private sector, businesses vary in a number of ways, such as legal structure, industry, size and market power, and geographical reach. This diversity also means that, although there are common elements in the business environment, each business operates in an environment that is, to some extent, unique.

INTERNAL/EXTERNAL

This book mainly deals with the external environment, the surrounding conditions, and processes in the world outside the organization. However, it is useful to think of the environment as also having an internal dimension. This is because a business organization is not really a single, unified entity but is internally differentiated. In other words, it is a complex system. Managers within business, to be effective, have to deal with this internal environment as well as the external one. In addition, the ability of an organization to operate successfully within its external environment depends,

Case studies

Apply what you have learned by analysing real-life, contemporary business practices in these longer, end-of-chapter case studies with accompanying questions.

Case Study: Tax avoidance in a globalizing world—managing costs efficientl or acting immorally?

VALUES Tax avoidance: 'using tax law to gain a tax advantage not intended by Parliament' (House of Commons Committee of Public Accounts 2013: 3).

It may be argued that it is rational for profit-seeking companies to take steps to limit their tax liabilities, and tax avoidance may be seen as an obligation to their shareholders. Minimizing the tax bill enables companies to protect shareholder interests through paying a higher dividend or investing retained earnings in the business in order to sustain its competitiveness. Why pay more taxes than you have to? This is the logic of tax planning or legal tax avoidance measures

profit). The tax rate is one of a range of facto the locational advantage companies may g countries. For this reason, national govern set corporation tax at a 'competitive' (i.e. l to advertise their country as the 'best plac and thereby attract and retain investmen has been adopted quite vigorously by the (Chapter 4), and the UK is not alone. The a trend of reducing corporation tax from investment. This had slowed following th in 2008 but picked up again in 2015 (B

Review and discussion questions

Reinforce your learning and aid your revision with end-of-chapter review and discussion questions, which cover the main themes and issues raised in the chapter.

Review and discussion questions

1. How does the idea of a 'globalizing world' help us to understand the business environment?
2. To what extent do you agree that the only social responsibility of private sector business is to maximize profits?
3. 'There is no such thing as a free market.' Explain what is meant by this statement.
4. What is the rationale f cluding the public secto trast the characteristics
5. Give examples of the wa affects business decisi which businesses may i

Assignments

Designed to test the knowledge you have gained from studying each chapter and further your understanding, these assignments feature practical exercises and tasks for you to try.

Assignments

1. Investigate annual reports for two FTSE companies and analyse the extent to which they incorporate non-profit objectives and measures of performance.
2. Prepare a briefing for the vice chancellor of your university outlining the business case for the university to become a living wage employer.
3. Imagine you report to zon who has been calle Committee of the Hous to provide arguments j pany to avoid UK corp

Further reading and online resources

Take your learning further by exploring the key academic literature associated with a topic, using the annotated further reading and online resource lists at the end of every chapter to guide you. These will also point you towards useful sources to help you prepare for exams, essays, and research projects.

Further reading

Lawrence (2016) *looks ahead to the 'wave of economic, social and technological change' that will reshape Britain in the 2020s.*

World Economic Forum (2017) *provides an analysis of the global environment and global risks.*

Chang (2013) *provides a highly readable and challenging account of the nature of modern capitalism, confronting a number of 'myths'.*

Hutton (2015) *provides a c model of capitalism in reform.*

Raworth (2017) *offers a cr the economic model it h native approach focused environmental limits.*

HOW TO USE THE ONLINE RESOURCES

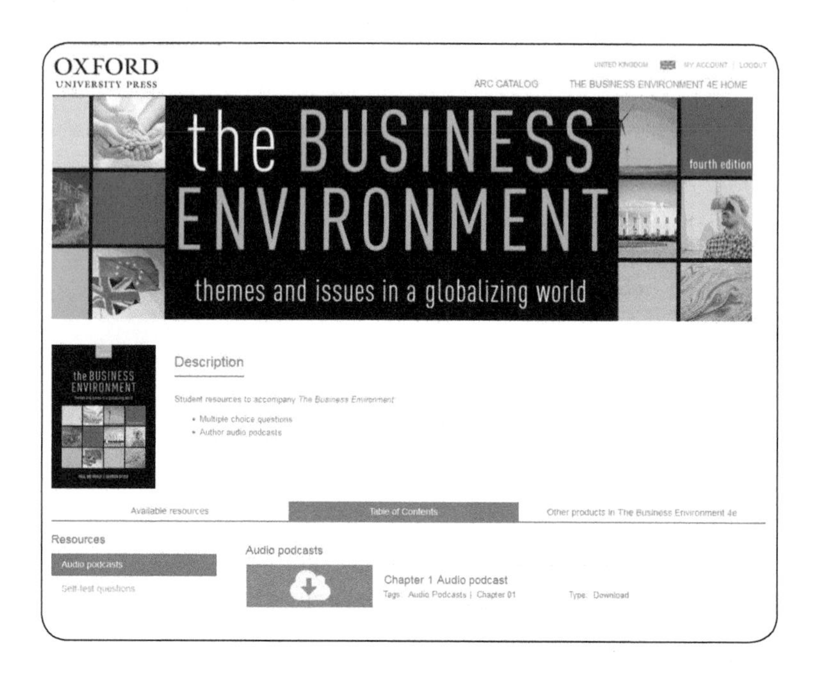

The online resources that accompany this book provide students and lecturers with ready-to-use teaching and learning resources. Students can benefit from multiple-choice questions to test their understanding and audio podcasts to learn on the go, while lecturers can make use of a test bank, PowerPoint slides, answers to the book's review questions, and a full lecturer guide for each chapter. Visit www.oup.com/uk/wetherly_otter4e/ to find out more.

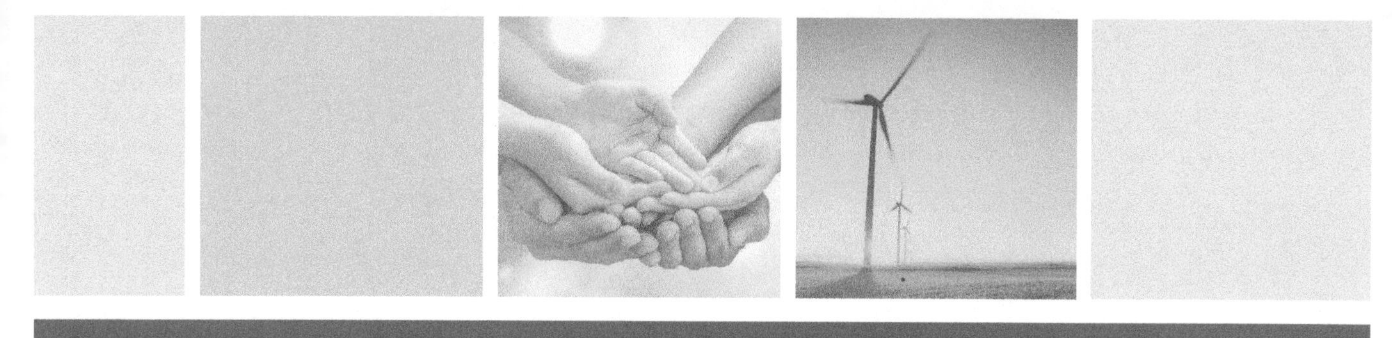

INTRODUCTION

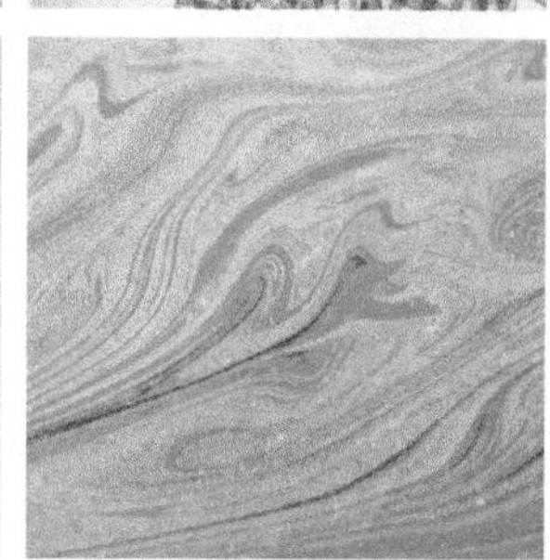

Chapter 1

Introduction: 'Business' and its 'environment' in a 'globalizing world'

Paul Wetherly and Dorron Otter

Learning objectives

When you have completed this chapter, you will be able to:

- Recognize different uses of the term **business**, and distinguish between different forms, such as private, public, and not-for-profit organizations.
- Examine the controversy concerning the nature and purpose of private sector business.
- Describe the complexity of the **external environment** in which business operates and explain the idea of **environmental uniqueness**.
- Explore how businesses must respond to changing environmental factors in order to operate successfully, and how they seek to influence the environment.
- Use analysis tools such as PEST or SWOT to examine the business environment.
- Identify the themes and issues used in our approach to the business environment in this book, and how you can use them in your studies.

THE APPROACH OF THIS BOOK–THEMES AND ISSUES

Eight key themes that will help you to understand and analyse the business environment run through this book. You will encounter these themes in this introduction and in each of the subsequent chapters as you examine a range of issues in the business environment. The themes will be signposted by the use of markers at the beginning of relevant paragraphs:

DIVERSITY Business is a diverse category.

INTERNAL/EXTERNAL The business environment is both inside and outside of organizations.

COMPLEXITY The external environment is multidimensional.

LOCAL TO GLOBAL The business environment can be analysed at a variety of spatial levels or scales.

DYNAMIC The environment of business does not stand still, the future is uncertain.

INTERACTION There is a two-way interaction between business organizations and their environments.

STAKEHOLDERS Individuals and groups that are affected by business decisions.

VALUES Business decisions involve ethical questions.

The themes are ways of conceptualizing business and the environment in which it operates. You will master these themes increasingly as you work through the book, but it is useful to begin with a brief introduction to each one.

DIVERSITY

Business is a diverse category. It does not refer only to **private sector**, profit-making companies. Public and voluntary (or third) sector organizations may also be regarded as businesses. The boundaries between these sectors are blurred, contested, and shift over time, for example, as a result of the policy of **privatization** initiated by Conservative governments in the UK in the 1980s. Within the dominant private sector, businesses vary in a number of ways, such as legal structure, industry, size and **market** power, and geographical reach. This diversity also means that, although there are common elements in the business environment, each business operates in an environment that is, to some extent, unique.

INTERNAL/EXTERNAL

This book mainly deals with the external environment, the surrounding conditions, and processes in the world outside the organization. However, it is useful to think of the environment as also having an internal dimension. This is because a business organization is not really a single, unified entity but is internally differentiated. In other words, it is a complex system. Managers within business, to be effective, have to deal with this **internal environment** as well as the external one. In addition, the ability of an organization to operate successfully within its external environment depends, in large part, on the effectiveness of internal systems and procedures. The internal environment has to be managed and adapted to the demands and opportunities of the external environment.

COMPLEXITY

We might think of the external environment primarily in terms of economic conditions and trends, to do with the behaviour of competitors and customers. The economy is, of course, of major importance. However, a moment's thought makes it clear that the external environment in which business operates is more complex and needs to be analysed also in terms of its political-legal, social-cultural, technological, and other aspects. These aspects are interrelated, as we can see if we think of the role that political decisions made in government have in shaping the economic environment. We will also see that many issues facing business have economic, social, political, and technological aspects. This way of conceptualizing a complex environment of business is captured by the analytical framework of PEST (Political–Economic–Social–Technological). In the first part of this book the chapters reflect an elaboration of the PEST model in which seven interrelated environments are identified: Economic, Technological, Political, Legal, Social-cultural, Ethical, and Natural.

LOCAL TO GLOBAL

Spatial level or scale refers to the geographical or territorial unit of analysis that we use to conceptualize and analyse the business environment. As citizens we live within the territory of a nation state, such as the UK, and we tend to think of our identities at least partly in terms of nationality. Similarly, the business environment tends to be discussed primarily at national level. For example, in the media we come across references to British business, the British economy, British society, and the British government. However, sometimes it is more appropriate to think of business and its environment at a more local level, perhaps in terms of an urban area or region. On the other hand, it has become increasingly important to think of business and the environment on a much larger spatial level, such as European or global. There is much debate about the nature, extent, and implications of globalization. In a 'globalizing world' there is a tendency for business and other economic, social, and political processes and relationships to move across or beyond the borders of nation states. One of the most important manifestations of this is the growth of multinational businesses.

DYNAMIC

We live in a fast-changing world, especially in the advanced or rich societies such as Western Europe. We have come to expect that the society in which we live and the way we live our lives will change over time, even within fairly short periods. This is a characteristic feature of modernity. This can be seen most clearly in relation to technological innovation and its impact in all areas of our lives. Today we are facing a near-term transformation of work brought about by automation and the 'robot revolution'. Because of this, businesses have to respond and adapt to changes in their environment, and deal with uncertainty about the future. But, at the same time, business organizations are themselves powerful agents of change, as shown by the example of technological innovation which is driven largely by business (see Chapter 3). Indeed, the dynamism of western societies is deeply rooted in basic features of their market economies—competition and the **profit** motive. This is often discussed in terms of entrepreneurial behaviour, which involves risk-taking and innovation, rather than relying on tried-and-tested approaches (see Chapter 15). Competitive markets place emphasis on innovation as the means of keeping up or getting ahead.

INTERACTION

There is two-way interaction between business organizations and their environment. Businesses influence and are influenced by their environments. Business organizations are not passive but seek to shape environmental factors to their own advantage. For example, business is an important actor in the political arena where it uses its connections, resources, and influence to shape policy decisions in its favour (see Chapter 11). Advertising is another obvious example of environment-shaping behaviour. Firms do not simply respond to changes in lifestyles and consumer behaviour that are happening automatically 'out there' in society but seek to influence and even create such changes through persuasive advertising. It is often difficult to disentangle this two-way interaction: firms may influence consumer behaviour but they also have to stay in tune with changing lifestyles and preferences.

STAKEHOLDERS

Business decisions have to be made in a context of multiple stakeholder interests and demands. A stakeholder is any individual or group that is affected by, and thus has a stake in, business decisions, and can be defined very widely to include society as a whole. This is because business decisions can have consequential effects for all members of society. For example, with the unfolding of the financial crisis since 2008 we have come to realize that we are all stakeholders in the banks. Stakeholders have the capacity to affect business performance through their decisions and behaviour. Satisfied customers will demonstrate loyalty in the form of repeat purchases, but dissatisfied ones will take the option to 'exit'. The same can be said of shareholders and employees. Furthermore, stakeholders may organize to apply pressure in order to influence business decisions. Consumers may support boycotts of businesses judged to be unethical; shareholders may campaign to influence the remuneration of board members; and employees may negotiate with employers through trade unions. It can be argued, in a stakeholder model of business, that the best businesses actively seek to engage with stakeholders. In any event, businesses now operate in an environment of greater public scepticism and, more than before, have to work to retain public trust.

VALUES

There are competing perspectives and values concerning the nature and purpose of business in society—relating to its power, responsibilities, performance, and ethics. For most of the twentieth century the western business model or capitalist system—based on private enterprise, competition, and profit—was challenged by socialism as an alternative model of economic organization based on state control and planning. It was argued that the capitalist values of individualism and self-interest had a downside in the persistence within these societies of poverty and inequality.

This was an argument about values: in favour of capitalism its supporters argued that it promoted individual freedom and choice, while its critics valued solidarity and equality more highly. Although the appeal of socialism may have faded, arguments about the acceptable extent of inequality have not gone away, as we can see from controversy surrounding the pay of chief executives and bankers' bonuses in recent years. And business finds itself at the centre of many other value-based debates in contemporary society concerned with issues such as environmental protection and climate change, fair trade, the responsibility of western companies for working conditions in developing countries, discrimination, and the social usefulness of some business activities and products (e.g. unhealthy foods). These debates are part of everyday political discussion and dialogue in which business must engage.

Stop and Think

Use your knowledge of business and current events in the world of business to think of examples that highlight each of the themes.

What is business?

INTERACTION This is a book about the 'business environment' in a 'globalizing world'. The purpose of this introduction is to help you get to grips with what the business environment is, why it is important to study and understand it, and the particular approach taken in this book. All businesses operate in a changing and, in some ways, unique environment that is the source of both *threats* and *opportunities*, and business decisions are concerned with striving to operate successfully in this environment given the *strengths* and *weaknesses* of the organization. This way of thinking about business decisions is the basis of the well-known SWOT analysis (see the SWOT section towards the end of this chapter). For example, businesses may have to respond to changing market conditions affecting the demand for their products, the behaviour of competitors, or changes in government policy. For example, all businesses must think carefully about the opportunities and threats presented by the UK's decision to leave the EU (Brexit). Whether a business manages to operate successfully within its environment depends on the criteria used to judge 'success'. We will see that this is a contested idea because success as judged by a business in its own terms (e.g. profitability) might be quite different from success as judged by others or from the point of view of society as a whole. For example, a reduction in corporation tax might be welcomed by business but opposed by others on the grounds that it would mean business not being required to contribute to society as it should. There are fundamental questions here about the nature and role of business and what we expect in terms of the performance of the economy. The answers involve rival models of business and the economic system.

We will look more closely at the meaning of 'business' and its 'environment', but we will begin with the idea that we live in a 'globalizing world'.

A globalizing world?

LOCAL TO GLOBAL From around the last quarter of the twentieth century, globalization has come to be widely seen and experienced as a key feature of life in the modern world, and even as an inexorable process of becoming more and more globalized. This is particularly the case in the rich countries of the West, but the very nature of a globalizing world means that the number of countries and people who are affected continually increases.

One of the ways we can gain an insight into the set of processes that are constitutive of a globalizing world is by considering the growth in international tourism. Foreign travel is made possible by rising living standards which mean that people have more money for leisure activities after they have paid for food, housing, and other necessities. More specifically, international tourism has been facilitated by technological developments lowering the cost of travel. Along with communications technologies, it can be argued that transportation is one of the principal facilitators of globalization. In the nineteenth century, British people took advantage of the new technology of steam trains to go on excursions to the seaside. In the late twentieth century, they took advantage of the new technology of passenger airlines to holiday overseas. Mass foreign travel is a fairly recent phenomenon in rich countries like the UK—we might think of the growth of package holidays to European destinations, such as Spain, in the 1960s and 1970s as a watershed. Since then foreign travel has become a more normal experience of British people and they are travelling further afield: destinations that were once 'exotic' become normal. Citizens of the rich countries are now being joined in rapidly growing numbers by people from fast-developing BRIC economies (Brazil, Russia, India, and China).

Hence the world is 'globalizing' in the sense that European, and now Russian and Chinese, people have increasingly global horizons when it comes to tourism. Tourism, in other words, is increasingly international or cross-border and creates interconnections and interdependence between the world's economies. The most obvious way it does this is through the dependence of the many and diverse companies and their employees that are part of the tourism sector on revenues generated by foreign visitors. Thus, UK economic performance is dependent in part on the country's success in attracting foreign tourists. The payments they make are equivalent, in terms of the balance of payments, to revenues earned by the export of goods. This interconnectedness is the essence of what we mean by a 'globalizing world'.

VALUES International tourism is not new, but the *volume* of cross-border movement is increasing. It is also still confined largely to travel between the rich countries of the world, yet people from the rich countries are travelling to more destinations and foreign visits from developing BRIC countries are growing fast. Hence, globalization is extending in geographical *reach* as well. (Still, we are a very long way from foreign travel being part of the lifestyle of all people in the world, and it is questionable whether such an outcome would be feasible or desirable. Again, what counts as success from a business point of view—more customers, revenue and profit—and from the point of view of individual customers—more affordable foreign travel—might be undesirable from the viewpoint of societal or environmental impact, such as damaging areas of natural beauty or contributing to global warming.)

If people are increasingly taking part in a globalizing world, then the same can be said of business. Indeed, it can be argued that globalization is fundamentally an economic phenomenon, driven by the profit motive and competitive pressures in the market. We can see this from the tourism example: although companies cannot make people undertake foreign visits against their will, the rise of international tourism has been powered by companies continually seeking new products and markets and promoting them through marketing.

A globalizing world involves the increasing volume and reach of cross-border movement and consequent interconnectedness. These movements include people, trade, and international investment. Globalization is both driven by business and constitutes the environment in which it operates. Thus, it is essential to our understanding of 'business' in its 'environments'.

However, globalization is not, in fact, an inexorable process. Although economic globalization can be seen as part and parcel of the inherent dynamism of markets as firms search for new markets and new locations for profitable production, it is also facilitated by political decisions and agreements on international trade, foreign investment, and migration. Western governments have tended to frame globalization both as an economic reality to which countries must adapt and as a desirable policy to pursue. There has been a consensus on globalization. However, in so far as globalization is a policy choice, it is dependent upon continued popular support and democratic legitimacy. It is important to recognize that globalization has always been contested and the focus of vocal protest in the shape of the 'anti-globalization movement' which has raised questions about who benefits and has claimed, in particular, that the policy is largely driven by the interests of western multinational corporations (MNCs). Anti-globalization has generally been a movement of the left with its demands for global justice and environmental protection. However, in recent years the growth in forms of right-wing, anti-establishment, politics has been interpreted as, in part, a backlash against globalization, driven by the feeling that many people are 'left behind'. The UK referendum vote in 2016 to leave the European Union (Brexit) and the election of Donald Trump as US President have both been seen as expressions of this backlash. For example, the director general of the International Labour Organization (ILO) characterized these two political shocks as 'the revolt of the dispossessed' in response to the benefits of globalization having been distributed 'extraordinarily unfairly' and people feeling that they are getting a 'raw deal' (Allen 2016). Similarly, the head of the International Monetary Fund, Christine Lagarde, argued that the benefits of globalization have to be more evenly spread and action taken to reduce inequality (Elliott 2017), and UK Prime Minister Theresa May has pointed to 'downsides to globalization' especially for 'people . . . on modest to low incomes' who 'see the emergence of a new global elite who sometimes seem to play by a different set of rules and whose lives are far removed from their everyday existence' (Merrick 2016). Lagarde and May are not, of course, siding with the anti-globalizers and they emphasize the benefits of globalization. Their argument is really that those benefits need to be more widely shared in order to maintain the legitimacy of globalization. However, some commentators have talked of an era of 'deglobalization' (Sharma 2016).

Stop and Think

What does the idea of 'living in a globalizing world' mean to you?

What is business? Broad and narrow definitions

DIVERSITY One way in which it is common to think about business is in terms of *a specific business organization* with which we are familiar, such as Amazon.com. It is this meaning that is being used when we refer to 'starting a business' or 'managing the business'. But there are a number of other, related, ways in which we might answer the question 'what is business?' To pursue the Amazon example a little further, we can see that two other answers are implied. One is to think of business in terms of *a specific activity*, which is what we refer to in answer to the question what 'line of business' an individual or organization is in. In this sense, Amazon can be described as an 'e-commerce and cloud computing company' which started out as an Internet bookseller and has since diversified. (It is worth noting here that large global corporations are often conglomerates, engaged in several business activities.) Amazon is also an example of a *specific legal form* of business—it is a 'public company' owned by its shareholders and part of the 'private sector' of the economy. As a private sector business, Amazon strives to operate profitably through sales of its products in competition with other companies in the same market. For example, Amazon competes not only with other Internet retailers but also businesses engaged in retail sales of books, music, consumer electronics, etc. in specialized stores and supermarkets. The particular market in which a business operates is clearly a key aspect of its environment, the arena in which businesses compete.

LOCAL TO GLOBAL But it is also important to think more broadly in terms of the character of *the business system* as a whole. We might refer to this, using terms such as 'the market system' or 'capitalism', but we should think of it not just in terms of economic organizations such as businesses but the whole range of organizations that interact to shape the pattern of economic activity, including trade unions, professional bodies, consumer groups, regulatory agencies, and other governmental bodies. It is customary to think of the business system in terms of a national economy, such as the UK, but in a globalizing world we need to recognize the ways in which the system operates across borders and creates the interconnectedness of nations. Thus, we may refer to the international (or even global) business system.

A further meaning of business is invoked when we refer to the 'business community' or perhaps 'business class'. This suggests that businesses constitute a distinctive group within society and that, for some purposes, individual business organizations may find it advantageous to work together to pursue shared interests or goals. For example, there may be a desire within the business community to present a common position in order to influence some aspect of government economic policy, such as a decision on taxation, interest rates, or business regulation. Such a common position might be presented by a collective business organization like the Confederation of British Industry (CBI). The business community may also now be thought of as spanning national borders, such as in the form of the annual meetings of the World Economic Forum (WEF) at Davos. However, there are often conflicting interests within the business community, for example, between renewable energy companies and oil producers in relation to carbon pricing.

Ways of thinking about 'business':

- a specific business organization or firm;
- type of economic activity engaged in—type of goods or services produced;
- legal form;
- the business system; and
- the business community.

Everybody would agree that Amazon is an example of a business organization, but there would be much less agreement on whether the term applies also to the police force, which is part of the state or 'public sector'. Thinking about these two examples can help us to clarify the meaning of business and to distinguish narrow and broad definitions. The reason for thinking that the police force is not a business arises from the common association between business, private ownership, paying customers, competition, and the profit motive. Citizens do not pay for policing services in the form of a market price that is set at a level to yield a profit, and the police do not face any competitors for customers (indeed the direct recipients of police services, crime suspects, are not really 'customers' at all in the sense of choosing to use the service). But this is a narrow view of business that equates it with a specific legal form and the private sector.

A broad view of business is based on thinking of business as an activity. If we step back from the particular line of business that Amazon is in, we can describe business in general terms as the activity of production—the transformation of various inputs (or 'factors of production') into diverse outputs in the form of goods and services to meet particular wants or needs of people in society. Amazon and the police are both engaged in this generic activity, using particular inputs (employees with particular skills and knowledge, particular types of equipment and technology) to produce particular services. They are both, in this broad sense, business organizations, and it is not relevant to this definition that Amazon is part of the private sector and the police service is part of the state or public sector.

DIVERSITY A key advantage of this broad definition is that it reminds us that there is more than one business model available, more than one way to organize an economy, and the advantages and disadvantages of different models are at the centre of controversy about the nature of business and its role in society. Why is Amazon in the private sector and the police service in the public sector? In the latter case, a large part of the answer is that we regard protection of the public as a primary duty of government and a right of citizens rather than something that should depend on their ability to pay, whereas in the former case, we are generally happy that consumption of books and DVDs can be left to individual choice and ability to pay. But, if we look a little more closely, we can see that even these apparently straightforward cases involve some degree of controversy. It is clear that governments cannot guarantee to protect their citizens from threats to their lives and property, and there is a large range of private sector businesses operating in the field of security. Many large stores employ their own security guards, so the protection of their property does depend, to some extent, on ability to pay. Indeed, in many countries the private sector is larger than the state in the security business: 'At least half the world's population lives in countries where there are more private security workers than public police officers' (Provost 2017). Although the market is very good at meeting most people's wants for books and DVDs, if you are poor and cannot afford to buy books, Amazon will not respond to your wants or needs. That is a large part of the argument for public libraries and a reason why there is concern over their future in the context of austerity-driven funding cuts (Kean 2016). So, in both of these cases there is a mix of public and private provision, and a broad definition of business allows us to analyse this mix (see Chapter 14).

Stop and Think

Distinguish between a 'broad' and 'narrow' conception of business.

Dealing with the problem of scarcity

This broad definition of business in terms of production can be related to the need of all societies to decide how to allocate the available productive resources between all the possible types of production of goods and services for which they can be used. What economists call the basic economic problem is scarcity—resources are limited and the large, and even open-ended, set of wants, needs, and goals that make demands on those resources can't all be satisfied at once (see Chapter 2). The broad definition of business recognizes that there is more than one way of dealing with this problem.

VALUES All societies have to develop and agree rules and institutions which provide the framework or system within which resources are allocated: that is, rules governing the operation of business in the broad sense. In any society such rules and institutions are likely to remain a constant focus of controversy and debate, because they might work more to the advantage of some members of society than others, and because there are competing values at stake. There is never likely to be unanimous agreement, hence the nature of the business system is always an intensely political issue. For example, the global economic recession, initially triggered by problems in the financial sector in 2008, reignited fierce political controversy over whether the crisis demonstrated the failure of the 'neoliberal' economic model that had been in place since the 1980s, and the need for government intervention to limit the recession and to regulate the market, particularly the banking sector. This has been bound up with controversy about austerity, the slow recovery and stagnating living standards, growing inequality and, as we have seen, a backlash against globalization. In other words, the business model is now open to question.

DIVERSITY What alternatives are available to society in deciding a framework of rules and institutions within which business operates? In the real world societies differ from each other in complex ways, but it is possible to identify some broad principles and mechanisms. To start with we can distinguish between centralized and decentralized systems. Centralized allocation of resources is undertaken by government or the state, whereas the market is a decentralized mechanism. Other decentralized mechanisms are: voluntary agencies and charities (third sector), and the 'informal economy'. These alternatives can be illustrated through the example of healthcare.

The market or capitalist system operates on the basis of private property, voluntary exchange, competition, and the profit motive. In a market for healthcare, services are offered by private companies which compete with one another for sales to paying customers, and the main purpose of business is to make a profit. In a pure market, individuals have to be self-reliant in meeting their own needs for healthcare through their ability to pay, e.g. through private insurance. The level of resources allocated to healthcare and the mix of services is determined by the decentralized interaction of buyers and sellers.

Government or the state provides an alternative mechanism to the market for allocating resources. Government can use its tax-raising powers to provide public services to citizens on the basis of criteria other than ability to pay and profitability. For example, the UK National Health Service (NHS) is essentially a tax-funded system that operates on the basis of equal treatment for equal need, and medical need replaces profit as the purpose of the business. In effect, taxpayers contribute to a common fund and all citizens are able to draw on the fund in the form of medical treatment on the basis of need, irrespective of the amount they have paid in. The level of resources allocated to healthcare is determined in a centralized way through government budget decisions, and the mix of services is determined by a central regulatory body coupled with decentralized assessments of clinical need by medical practitioners.

The voluntary, or **third**, sector provides an alternative decentralized mechanism for allocating resources where the purpose is to meet certain categories of need rather than to make a profit, though it is small in comparison with the private and public sectors. Funding is provided by voluntary donations and sometimes by government grants, and services are provided often on a last resort basis where individuals have no access to services provided through the market or government. For example, MSF (Médecins Sans Frontières) provides emergency medical assistance in circumstances of civil conflict or natural disaster, usually in poor countries. However, there is a role for the voluntary provision of health services even in one of the richest countries in the world, the US, because of the shortcomings of both the market and government in meeting the needs of the poor in that society.

Charities and private sector companies also operate in partnership with the public sector, entering into contractual arrangements to deliver public services in areas such as social care, homelessness, welfare-to-work, prison services, and drug addiction. This model is often referred to as the 'enabling state': the state funds the service but delivery is delegated to third sector or private organizations (a purchaser–provider split). There may be advantages in terms of harnessing expertise available to improve public services or reducing costs. However, such arrangements, particularly with private companies, have been controversial on a number of grounds including: opposition to introducing the profit motive into public services such as healthcare; whether the contracts offer value for money for taxpayers; negative impacts on employment terms and conditions; and the risk falling on the public sector which has to step in if a private or third sector operator fails or walks away from a contract.

The **informal** economy includes both paid and unpaid work. Informal paid work can be defined as 'the paid production and sale of goods or services which are unregistered by, or hidden from the state for tax, benefit and/or labour law purposes, but which are legal in all other respects' (Katungi, Neal, and Barbour 2006), such as businesses supplying goods and services and/or hiring workers on a cash-in-hand basis. Informal unpaid work includes informal care provided within the household or community. Although the informal sector is not included in government measures of economic activity, and therefore its size is difficult to determine, it is clear that it encompasses important areas of production of goods and services and constitutes a significant element of social and economic life. For example, it has been calculated that the total value of 'home production' in the UK in 2014 was over £1 trillion, equivalent to 56 per cent of the measured output (GDP) of the UK economy—most of this production being undertaken by women (Collinson 2016; Office for National Statistics 2016).

STAKEHOLDERS We can see that, aside from the informal economy, there are three basic models of business: the market, government, and the third sector, and these can be combined in different 'mixes'. Remember that we are including these in our broad definition of business because they are all engaged in the activity of production of goods and services of some kind. We can add to this that in each model of business, outputs are produced for 'consumers' (customers, users, or clients) and in response to their requirements, wants, or needs; and this is an intrinsic aspect of business. The important point is that the success of business is always bound up to some degree with consumers' requirements and expectations. These three models never exist in a pure form but may be combined or interact in various ways that shape the overall character of the business system within society. On an international level, there are important differences between countries in the ways these models combine and interact. Most obviously, these differences can be seen in the size of the public sector and the role played by government in economic life. The boundaries between these sectors are not fixed but shift as a result, most notably, of government policy. For example, the scope of the private sector and market has been expanded in the UK since the 1970s through a policy of privatization, as part of a move towards a more 'free market' business model. However, outside the pages of economics textbooks there is no such thing as a pure market system or free market, because markets everywhere have developed in conjunction with government, the third sector, and, more generally, the wider society.

A broad definition of business

Business is a mechanism for deciding the allocation of the resources available to society between various possible uses (or competing wants and needs), the methods of production, and the distribution of the output (who gets what), in a situation of scarcity where not all wants can be satisfied. The three basic forms of business are the market (private sector), government (public sector), and the third sector. In each case business success is bound up with meeting the requirements of consumers (though these are not the only stakeholders). The character of the business system is determined by the changing way in which the three forms are combined and interact.

The private sector of business

STAKEHOLDERS **DIVERSITY** The private sector is made up of business organizations that are owned and controlled as forms of private property. 'Private property' is a legal concept and, since laws are created though a political process, 'private sector' business is intrinsically political. This is an important point: politics does not 'interfere' with business from the outside but is key to its very constitution. As a society we have to decide the nature of private property rights and the legal framework for corporate governance. Private ownership includes a variety of legal forms. The largest businesses take the form of public limited companies (PLCs) which are owned by their shareholders (Office for National Statistics 2015). Private sector businesses can take other legal forms, such as sole traders, partnerships, mutual organizations, and private limited companies (see Chapter 5). Private ownership is the thread connecting all these types. However, the private sector is characterized by further specific features:

- production of goods and services for sale;
- the profit motive; and
- competition.

Private sector businesses produce goods and services for sale to customers in a context of competition with other firms in the market and with the principal purpose of making a profit. We will examine in more detail how markets operate in Chapter 2, but here we can look more closely at these features and see that they are not straightforward.

Free market vs. regulation?

The basic idea of private business is that firms are free to manage their own affairs and use their own resources as they choose. In this way, private ownership of business may be likened to other forms of private property where the whole point of owning something is to use it as we please and, usually, for our own benefit or self-interest. In business terms this means that businesses should be managed in the interests of their owners, and this means making a profit. It might be added to this that businesses are best able to judge for themselves how to manage their affairs efficiently, and that by being left to do this there is benefit for the wider public through the resulting innovation and economic growth. However, in reality there is no such thing as a **free market** in the sense of businesses being left entirely free to make decisions for themselves. In all market systems the law is used more or less extensively to regulate various aspects of business decisions and behaviour (see Chapters 4 and 5).

VALUES One of the prime reasons for using the law to regulate business is a recognition that a free market would have undesirable consequences for certain groups in society, including some of the stakeholders within firms. Consumers and employees would be at a disadvantage in their dealings with business without various protections afforded by law. In other words, although business pursuing its self-interest produces substantial public benefit such as greater prosperity, there are many ways in which business self-interest and the public interest clash. What is good for business is not always good for society.

For example, the National Minimum Wage Act (1998) and subsequent introduction of a national living wage in 2016, requiring all businesses in the UK to pay a **minimum or living wage**, ensures that profit-seeking businesses facing competitive pressures do not harm vulnerable groups of employees by forcing wages down below a decent level. Paying a minimum wage may be seen as a social obligation that business must fulfil. More fundamentally, this example raises the question of how we define business and what is good for business. If we equate a business that was paying below the minimum wage (e.g. a contract cleaning company) solely with the managers and shareholders, then the minimum wage might be seen as bad for business by raising costs and therefore potentially squeezing the profit margin. However, the office cleaners are stakeholders within the business so the increase in pay resulting from the minimum wage means the company is operating more successfully from their point of view. Thus, the example reveals the conflicts of interest between the different stakeholders that make up a business (Chang 2013: 190–8) (see Mini-Case 1.1).

It is clear that although we refer to private ownership of business, decisions about managing those businesses are never purely private ones since they involve certain restrictions and obligations defined by law. And law is the outcome of a political process that involves collective decision-making and reflects, in some way, values within society. Thus, the operation of business in the market involves an interaction of private and public decisions.

Mini-Case 1.1 Guiding the 'hidden hand'—the minimum wage and the 'living wage'

VALUES **STAKEHOLDERS** The idea of the 'hidden hand' is a metaphor for the way the market system, though based on millions of independent decisions and not subject to an overall plan or control by any actual hand, does not degenerate into chaos but operates in a highly coordinated way. It is *as if* a hidden hand is guiding it.

Adam Smith argued in the eighteenth century that even though businesses may be concerned only with their self-interest (profit) they would be guided, by and large, to serve the public good. This seems like a paradox—promoting the common good by acting selfishly. Smith's argument was that it would only be by serving the needs of others (customers) that businesses would be able to make a profit. When businesses throughout the economy act in this way the result is that the supply of goods and services matches consumer demand.

The hidden hand of the market operates through the price mechanism. The price adjusts until balance is achieved between supply and demand. For example, if supply exceeds demand the price will tend to fall, and vice versa.

The problem of low pay

However, the hidden hand can produce outcomes that are not socially desirable or fair. In labour markets, price is the wage or salary that people receive for the jobs they perform. The problem is that variations in this price are at the heart of income inequality and, more particularly, for some low-paid occupations this price might not be sufficient to enable people to have a decent standard of life.

One solution to this problem is to use the law to guide the hidden hand through price controls. The UK Labour government introduced a National Minimum Wage (NMW) in 1999, establishing 'hourly rates below which pay must not be allowed to fall'. The rationale for the NMW was to provide 'employees with decent minimum standards and fairness in the workplace' and to help business 'by ensuring companies will be able to compete on the basis of quality of the goods and services they provide and not on low prices based predominantly on low rates of pay' (*National Archives* http://webarchive.nationalarchives.gov.uk/20060213213640/http://www.dti.gov.uk/er/nmw/index.htm).

There are different levels of NMW, depending on age, and these rates are reviewed annually by the Low Pay Commission which makes recommendations to government, taking account of economic circumstances. This means, in particular, trying to balance improvements to NMW against possible negative effects in the form of job losses.

VALUES Although controversial when first introduced, being supported by the trade unions and opposed by the Conservative party and business, the minimum wage has now become an accepted part of the business landscape in the UK supported by all the main political parties. It has since been joined by a voluntary 'living wage' and, somewhat confusingly, a statutory 'national living wage'.

The 'national living wage'—step forward or gamble?

Reflecting the strength of the consensus achieved on minimum wage legislation since 1999, in 2015 the UK Conservative government announced the introduction of a 'national living wage' (NLW), which came into effect in April 2016. This was, in effect, an increase in the NMW for employees aged over 25, raising the rate from £6.50 to £7.20 per hour and with the aim of a progressive increase to 60 per cent of median earnings by 2020 (projected at the time to be £9) (BBC 2015a). Workers aged 25 and below would continue to be entitled to the lower NMW.

The Office for Budget Responsibility estimated that the increase would benefit 6 million workers who were either on the NMW or a higher rate but less than the new NLW (Stewart 2015). According to the Resolution Foundation (2016), the NLW 'represents the most significant step forward in the battle against low pay since the introduction of the National Minimum Wage in 1999', and it was welcomed by trade unions and campaigners. However, the reaction from business was mixed, with some questioning of whether the rise could be afforded or would threaten jobs, particularly in certain sectors such as retail (BBC 2015b).

A voluntary approach—the real 'living wage'

In styling their reform to the NMW the national living wage, the Conservatives seemed to echo the campaign for a voluntary living wage to be adopted by employers, but at the same time perhaps created some confusion. For this reason, the voluntary living wage is sometimes referred to as the *real* living wage. It is important to recognize that the NMW does not, by itself, protect against poverty. There are different definitions of poverty which lead to different measures of the incidence of poverty. However, all measures show that poverty is substantially a problem for households with at least one member in work, not just for workless households. For example, using a relative low-income measure (households with income below 60 per cent of the median in that year), over half of working-age adults (and two-thirds of children) in poverty in 2015/16 were living in households with at least one person in work (McGuinness 2016). Because the NMW is not calculated using the relative low-income measure it is not designed to lift people out of poverty. In contrast the NLW is intended to provide a floor of 60 per cent of median earnings for employees aged over 25 by 2020. Does fairness in the job market require something more? The living wage differs from the NMW/NLW in that: it is set independently of government and with no statutory force; it applies to all employees aged 18 years and above; and it is calculated on a different basis and at a higher rate, as 'the minimum pay rate required for a worker to provide their family with the essentials of life' (see Table 1.1).

The campaign for a living wage started in London in 2001 and has since become national in scope, with more than 3,000 employers accredited by 2017. The living wage is calculated independently of the government by the Centre for Research in Social Policy (CRSP) with a separate rate for London to reflect higher costs of living. The rates are calculated on the basis of 'what households need in order to have a minimum acceptable standard of living' in Britain today, and this standard is set in consultation with members of the public to ensure that it is grounded in a 'social consensus' (CRSP http://www.lboro.ac.uk/research/crsp/mis/thelivingwage).

The Living Wage Foundation (https://www.livingwage.org.uk) campaigns for the living wage and accredits employers who pay it. The main case for paying the living wage is that it is the right thing to do. However, the Foundation argues that, far from being a worthy burden, the real living wage benefits business as well as the individuals who are paid the wage and society as a whole. The benefits to business can be: improved recruitment and retention; reduced absenteeism; enhanced staff morale and work quality; and improved consumer awareness and reputation.

It seems that not all employers see it this way and there is still some way to go in the campaign: in 2016 5.6 million people in the UK (22 per cent of all employees) were paid

Table 1.1 The National Living Wage, National Minimum Wage, and the UK Living Wage, October 2016

Name	National Minimum Wage and National Living Wage		UK Living Wage and London Living Wage
Rates	16–17 yrs old, 18–20 yrs old, 21–24 yrs old, and apprentice rates	National Living Wage (25+)	18+
Basis	Based on affordability: rates negotiated to 'help as many low-paid workers as possible without damaging their employment prospects'.	Partly based on affordability: rate agreed to meet ambition of 60% of median earnings by 2020, 'subject to sustained economic growth'.	Based on need: calculation made according to the cost of living, averaged for household type.
Legal status	Legally binding, enforced by HMRC.		Voluntary, not enforced.
Level	£4.00, £5.55, £6.95, and £3.40 (Oct. 2016–March 2017).	£7.20 (to March 2017).	UK rate: £8.45; London rate: £9.75
Set by	Government, on advice from the Low Pay Commission.		Resolution Foundation overseen by the Living Wage Commission.

Source: Low Pay Commission 2016: viii, table 1.

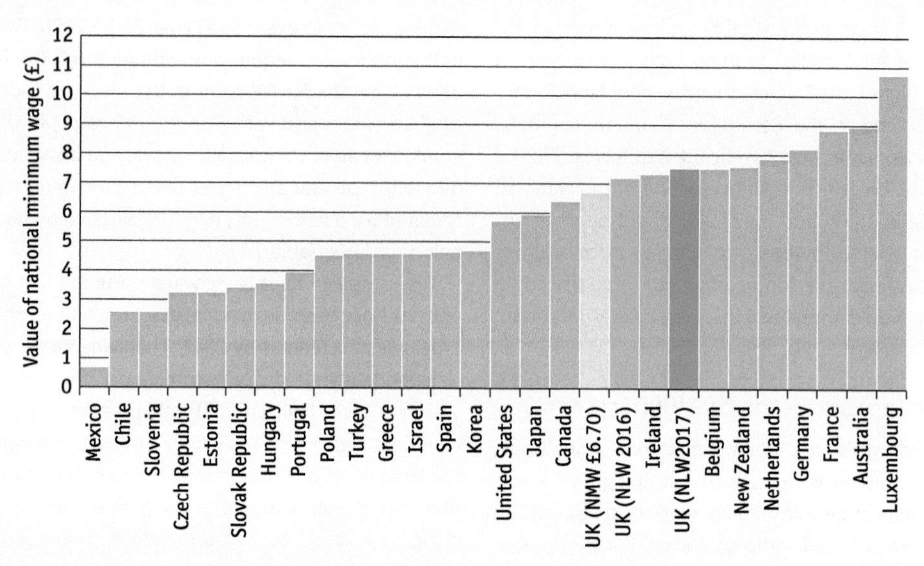

Figure 1.1 Comparison of minimum wages, by country, in £ based on PPP, July 2016.

Source: Low Pay Commission (2016), Fig. A4.3, p.228.

less than the voluntary Living Wage. The low-pay problem is concentrated among part-time workers, 43 per cent of whom earn less than the voluntary Living Wage, compared with 14 per cent of full-time workers. Partly reflecting the fact that women are more likely to work part-time than men (see Chapter 12), about 27 per cent of females earn less than the Living Wage, compared with 17 per cent of males (IHS Markit 2016; KPMG 2016).

How does the UK minimum wage compare to other nations?

LOCAL TO GLOBAL Minimum wage policies have been implemented in many other countries, including developing countries such as Brazil, India, and China (International Labour Organization 2016). Figure 1.1. shows how the UK NMW/NLW compares with a number of other developed countries, showing the improvement in the UK's ranking as a result of the NLW uprating in 2017. The calculation, using purchasing power parities (PPPs), is designed to be a more realistic comparison of what the minimum wage can purchase in the different countries. In broad terms, it might be expected that the minimum wage would reflect the level of average income (gross national income, or GNI, per capita) in particular countries (because richer countries are able to pay a higher minimum wage), but Figure 1.1. shows, for example, that the US has a relatively low minimum wage (ranking 12 of 26) despite being one of the world's richest countries. This shows that the minimum wage also reflects national political judgements about the appropriate level, which can be more or less generous.

Questions

1. **How does the NMW/NLW affect the private ownership of business?**
2. **Is it good for business, or bad for business? If you were an employer, would you support the NMW/NLW or the real living wage?**

Competition vs. market power?

So, private ownership turns out not to be a straightforward idea. The same can be said of competition and profit. Competition is a key aspect of the environment in which businesses in a market system operate, and we will look at it more closely in Chapter 2. It is competition that keeps businesses responsive to consumers since they have the option of going elsewhere if they are not satisfied. This reasoning is behind the claim that consumers are 'sovereign', meaning that they exercise power in markets since it is their preferences to which firms must respond. The other side of this is the idea that firms have little or no power in the market themselves. However, it seems clear that firms do not all face the same amount of competitive pressure and that some firms exercise more market power than others, particularly in the case of 'big business'.

VALUES **LOCAL TO GLOBAL** It seems clear that firms have more power when they face no or few competitors and less power when they face a large number of rivals. In particular, they may be able to engage in anti-competitive behaviour, most notably in the form of price-fixing. Such concerns are often raised in relation to prices in markets dominated by a small number of producers or suppliers. Giant corporations, especially MNCs that have created powerful global brands, may exercise power over consumers through persuasive advertising. Concern is sometimes also expressed about the political influence of such companies (see Chapter 11).

Profit vs. social responsibility?

VALUES **STAKEHOLDERS** At the start of this chapter it was stated that whether a business manages to operate successfully within its environment depends on the criteria used to judge success. We have also seen that, for all forms of business, success is bound up with meeting the requirements of consumers. The performance of business in the private sector is conventionally measured in terms of profitability (and, relatedly, share value) because this is seen as the prime motive—why else put money into a business if not to make more money? As we have seen, meeting the requirements of consumers is really a means to an end—businesses that do not produce goods or services that customers want (or can be persuaded) to buy are not profitable. However, the notion of business 'success' is not quite so straightforward, and this goes to the heart of debates about the role of private sector business in society.

First, it can be argued that the idea of the single-minded profit-maximizing business is an oversimplification that ignores the possibility that businesses may themselves have other **non-profit objectives**. There is no doubt that private sector businesses exist to make profits, but the question here is whether this primary motive is the only purpose that they do or should set for themselves. Indeed, John Kay has argued that there is a 'profit-seeking paradox: the most profitable companies are not the most profit-oriented' (2004a). The claim is that profitability arises indirectly from pursuing other goals, such as managing a pharmaceutical company with a mission that 'medicine is for the people'. Thus, in this view, the goal of making a profit is best approached obliquely. Second, in any case, other groups in society increasingly demand or expect business performance and success to be measured by criteria other than just profit. These groups—including employees, customers, suppliers, the wider community, or society—may be seen as **stakeholders** who are affected by, and therefore have an interest or 'stake' in, business decisions.

Thus, thinking about the success of business requires us to think about the criteria that are used as a basis for judgement, and this raises questions about whose interests are taken into account and who makes these judgements. If we see profit as the sole criterion, this involves, on the face of it, only taking into account the self-interest of business owners and might therefore ignore the interests of other stakeholders. Thus, the profit motive may be counterposed to some notion of wider social responsibility, which involves the argument that business success needs to be judged in terms of a wider set of social benefits and obligations (see Mini-Case 1.2 and Chapter 7).

Mini-Case 1.2 What is business for?

VALUES The profit-maximizing view of business may be defended on the following grounds:

1. It can be argued that private property is a basic principle of western societies and the whole point is that private property brings benefits to its owners. It is, therefore, not reasonable to expect people to use their private property other than for their own benefit.
2. Of course, individuals may choose to use some of their own property to benefit others by donations to charity or other means. But there are two reasons why it might not be reasonable to expect a business to act like this. First, the purpose of business is to make profit, whereas decisions about charitable giving should be left to the owners of the business in deciding for themselves how they use the distributed profits. Second, it can be argued that in a competitive market environment firms are under continual pressure to maximize profit in order to secure long-term survival. This is because profit can be used for reinvestment in the business to sustain or improve competitiveness, and because profitability is key to the ability of a firm to raise external finance. Firms which are less profitable than their rivals will tend to fall behind in the competitive struggle.
3. Third, it can be argued that through the single-minded pursuit of profit businesses simultaneously create benefit for society and thereby, far from ignoring the interests of other stakeholders, fully discharge their social responsibility. This is the 'hidden hand' argument, and the key idea is that firms only make profit by serving the needs and wants of customers. At the same time, profit-seeking businesses create employment and generate economic growth.

However, all of these arguments can be contested. As we have already seen, a problem with the hidden hand argument is that, even if customers are well served by business, the good deals that they enjoy might rely upon low-paid jobs. How do we balance the interests of consumers with those of low-paid workers? The NMW and arguments for a living wage can be seen as attempts to strike such a balance. The hidden hand also tends to create social costs or externalities such as environmental pollution (see Chapter 2).

INTERNAL/EXTERNAL The argument that firms are forced by competition to maximize profit in order to secure long-term survival is questionable because it suggests that businesses have no discretion in terms of their conduct. This is a simplistic model of the market and is contradicted by observations of business decisions, as can be seen from companies signing up as living wage employers (see Mini-Case 1.1).

It is true that private property is a basic principle or value of western societies for which there is strong public support. But private property is a legal arrangement which can be judged on the basis of whether it serves the common good of society as a whole. On this basis all western societies impose certain restrictions on private property. There are some things that people are not allowed to own (e.g. harmful drugs or guns) and restrictions on how property may be used (such as not being allowed to drive my car as fast as I like). Very few people would say that individuals should be able to drive their cars just as they please because that is the whole point of owning your own car. Most would agree that the likely harms to the community in the shape of road accidents from such a free-for-all outweigh the benefits to the car owners. Similarly, it is reasonable to say that we should judge the private ownership of business on the basis of the common good and not just that it allows the owners to do what they want with their own property.

Questions

1. **Do you think that the sole purpose of business is, or should be, to make as much profit as possible?**
2. **If your answer is 'no', would you think differently if you were a shareholder?**
3. **If your answer is 'yes', do you think that the pursuit of profit leads business to serve the public interest or common good?**

Other sectors of business—the public sector and the third sector

DIVERSITY The private sector is the dominant element within the UK and other capitalist or market economies—most of the goods and services that we consume on a daily basis are purchased from private sector businesses, and most employees work in the private sector. Yet if we think in terms of our broad definition—transforming inputs into outputs of goods and services to meet the needs and wants of consumers—it is clear that other types of organization are also involved in business. These are not-for-profit organizations operating in both:

- the **public sector**; and
- the 'third' sector of voluntary organizations.

DYNAMIC Although these organizations make up a relatively small part of the business or economic life of the country, they are involved in the production of some key services, such as healthcare and education. It is also important to note that the boundaries between these sectors are not fixed but can, and do, shift, largely as a result of political decisions. For example, in the recent past in the UK, mainly under Conservative governments in the 1980s and 1990s, a programme of **privatization** transferred businesses that had operated for many years as parts of the public sector—such as British Telecommunications, British Gas, and British Rail—into the private sector. Within these sectors business organizations are also diverse when considered, for example, in terms of the type of output they produce, their legal status, and size.

Differences between the private and public sectors

Public and private sector organizations differ in important respects. However, there is disagreement over how far these differences are real and whether the two sectors ought to be more alike. For example, reforms of the public sector since the 1980s—often referred to under the label 'new public management' (e.g. see Flynn 2012)—have attempted to make the public sector more like the private sector in some important respects.

- *Revenue.* Public sector organizations like schools and NHS hospitals are largely financed through taxation rather than sales revenue generated by customers paying a price in a market. Whereas in the market the principle is that you get what you pay for, as when you purchase a book from Amazon, the system of taxation and public spending disconnects what individuals pay in and what they get out. For example, a progressive system of income tax means that high earners pay a higher proportion of their income in tax than low earners. On the other hand, public spending decisions may involve a range of distributive principles and effects. Jobseeker's Allowance is paid to the unemployed and benefits lower earners disproportionately because their jobs tend to be less secure. We expect policing services to protect all citizens from crime. Education spending benefits higher earners disproportionately because a higher proportion of children from middle class families participate in higher education. The overall distributive effects of the various forms of taxation and public spending are complex. Who pays and who benefits are always highly contentious political issues.

STAKEHOLDERS

- *Accountability.* Private sector organizations are accountable to customers and shareholders. If they are not responsive to their customers they risk losing business to their more customer-focused competitors, and PLCs are legally required to safeguard the interests of their shareholders. Public sector organizations do not have shareholders. Some of them do have users who may be thought of (and think of themselves) as customers (such as hospital patients), and they are expected to be more responsive to them than perhaps they were in the past. But some parts of the public sector deal with people who do not choose to be users of the service and are therefore not customers in this sense, for example the prison service. In general, political rather than market-based forms of accountability are more important in the public sector, meaning accountability to politicians and, through a democratic process of election, to citizens.

- *Competition*. Consumers in the private sector can 'shop around' because firms operate in competitive markets. It is this that keeps businesses customer-focused and is the basis of **consumer sovereignty**. Of course, the amount of competition and consumer choice varies between markets and an important question concerns the operation of markets dominated by a small number of large businesses, known as oligopolies (e.g. supermarkets). Some public sector organizations also face competition in 'internal markets' where 'customers' have some ability to exercise choice (i.e. to 'shop around') between alternative service providers such as schools, universities, or hospitals. However, in general such choices are constrained and these organizations operate in less volatile, if not captive, markets.

VALUES

- *Motivation and ethos*. It can be argued that the public sector is, or should be, characterized by a distinctive **public service ethic**, meaning a commitment to public service. This sounds a bit like the customer orientation of the private sector, but it is very different. We expect teachers in state schools to be committed to their work and care about their students, whereas in the private sector serving customers is just a means to an end, a way of making money. However, it can be argued that this distinction is not so clear-cut. Some teachers might not be as committed as we would like and regard their job just as a way of paying the bills. On the other hand, Kay argues that successful firms in the private sector are not highly instrumental (Kay 2004b).

Stop and Think

What difference does it make whether a business is in the public or private sector? (For example, providing healthcare, operating train services, making cars.)

Conceptualizing the environment of business

Just as the term 'business' in reality refers not to a single type of organization but to a diverse range, so the environment of business is similarly diverse. Different types of business organization operate in different environmental settings or contexts. Here we will focus on the private sector.

Spatial level

LOCAL TO GLOBAL The environment is usually thought of as the world 'out there', the external context, comprising the wider social, cultural, economic, political, legal, technological, and other systems in which businesses operate. In the context of debates about 'globalization' (see Chapter 10) we may think of this external environment in terms of 'the world' in the sense that businesses may be affected by, and in turn influence, events on a global scale. This is particularly true in the case of companies that have a global reach or span of operations, especially MNCs that undertake production in more than one country. However, because of the way nations are connected through cross-border trade and financial transactions, economic events in one country can affect many others. For example, although the 2007–8 financial crisis may have originated in the US subprime mortgage market, it quickly spread to other countries, especially Europe, through the interconnected financial system. All businesses were affected by the ensuing 'credit crunch' and economic recession.

However, we can think of the environment in terms of different levels of analysis ranging from the small-scale and local environment at one end of a spectrum through to global systems and events at the other. We might think of small and medium-sized enterprises (SMEs) as operating in a more localized environment, such as within the local economy of a town or city, and giant corporations operating in a more national or global environment. However, even small businesses may be affected by events at a national or global level because of the way they are often linked in with supply chains spanning several countries. For example, they may depend on imported raw materials or components. At the other end of the spectrum even the largest companies also have to deal with local issues and concerns. Indeed, the term **glocalization** has been coined to draw attention to the need for global businesses to remain sensitive to the peculiarities of the local contexts in which they operate.

An important issue concerns the apparent discrepancy between the global reach of giant corporations and the political environment of business, which is still primarily managed at a national level. Put simply, there is no world government to manage the political environment of business at a global level. This discrepancy creates a difficulty because markets require a framework of rules in order to function effectively and so that they can be regulated for social benefit, and institutions to create and enforce such rules. However, although political authority still resides principally in the hands of national governments, there is an evolving framework of 'multilevel governance' (see Chapter 4). The most developed example of this is the European Union which has established a single market allowing free movement of goods, services, capital, and people between member states (the 'four freedoms') but also provides a framework for agreeing social protections on a Europe-wide scale (see Chapter 13).

Immediate and general environments

The 'immediate' environment involves those aspects which may require day-to-day or regular decisions and actions (e.g. relations with suppliers), while the 'general' environment is concerned with more distant or remote, but nevertheless consequential, issues (e.g. macroeconomic trends). On the whole, the general environment concerns events and systems that operate on a large scale and form a backdrop to day-to-day business decisions. The general environment also contains issues and events which are beyond the capacity of individual organizations to influence or control. For example, the onset of global recession in 2008 triggered by problems in the financial sector, the subsequent policy decisions by governments to rescue financial institutions, and the austerity programme that has been followed in an attempt to deal with government deficits and debt have been highly consequential aspects of the general environment of business in this period. More recently, the process of UK withdrawal from the EU following the referendum in 2016 and the triggering of Article 50 in March 2017 created immense uncertainty for business concerning future trading relationships and the economic impact of Brexit in the UK and the EU27. These are macroeconomic phenomena and decisions (operating at the level of the economy as a whole) affecting all businesses in the economy, and over which no individual business has much (if any) influence or control. On the other hand, the decision by a particular components manufacturer to raise its prices is part of the **immediate environment** only directly affecting other businesses which it supplies. This will affect day-to-day decisions by those businesses (e.g. to switch suppliers) and they may have some ability to influence the price change through negotiation.

Environmental uniqueness

The idea of 'environmental uniqueness' tells us that each business organization operates within an environment that is, to some extent, unique to it, and no two organizations operate in exactly the same environment. This idea warns against over-generalization in analysing the business environment. It reminds us that for **environmental analysis** to be useful to an organization it must be sensitive to the particular aspects of the environment that affect it and to which it must respond.

But we shouldn't take this idea too far—at its extreme it would suggest that a business environment textbook is required for every business organization in the economy! The absurdity of that idea shows us that **generalization**—meaning to make a statement with general application, about how things are in general terms, or that is intended to be true in most cases—is a necessary and useful approach in business and management. There are, in other words, general aspects of the environment that affect most businesses, so a firm should find useful environmental analysis that deals both with the general and the particular.

Stop and Think

Use your knowledge of business and current events in the world of business to think of examples that illustrate different spatial levels, the distinction between the immediate and general environment, and the concept of environmental uniqueness.

Interaction between business and the environment—responding, influencing, and choosing

Responsiveness

INTERACTION **INTERNAL/EXTERNAL** In order to operate successfully, businesses must be able to respond effectively to factors in their environment that affect them. The environment may be seen as presenting a range of threats and opportunities. A successful business will be one that is able to deal effectively with threats and take advantage of opportunities or, at least, is able to do so as well as or better than its competitors.

Influence

However, success may also depend on the ability of business to influence the environment in which it operates to its own advantage. Advertising is a clear example of business activity that is intended to influence the environment. Shifts in consumer preferences and spending patterns may pose threats or opportunities to which businesses must respond. Such shifts may occur for a variety of reasons, such as:

- changes in values and lifestyles in society;
- variations in affluence resulting from economic growth or stagnant living standards during 'austerity'; and
- changes in the age structure of the population.

Some of these shifts result from large-scale social changes over which business has little or no influence, and which constitute aspects of the general environment. For example, the ageing of the population has implications for the pattern of consumer spending as older people have wants and needs that differ from those of younger people (see Chapter 6).

However, businesses do not simply respond to shifts in preferences and spending patterns among consumers but are active in seeking to influence these shifts to their own advantage. Through advertising and branding strategies businesses may be able to create new tastes and fashions in society to which they then apparently respond. Ageing is a good example of this. As people get older their wants and needs change, but the lifestyles of older people today have also changed compared to previous generations. Older people now want to have a more active lifestyle than in the past. This is in part due to higher incomes and improved health, but we can also see how businesses may play a powerful role in influencing these changing lifestyles as they develop and promote new types of goods and services, such as in the field of leisure and tourism.

This example of interaction between business and the environment—responding to and seeking to influence consumer preferences—has implications for how we understand the working of a market system. The term 'consumer sovereignty' expresses the idea that consumers are ultimately in charge of the economic system because it is their preferences which drive business decisions about what to produce.

VALUES On the other hand the power of advertising leads us to question how far consumers really are in charge. The purpose of advertising is, after all, not merely to inform but to persuade. How far do we as consumers make decisions for ourselves, and how far are our decisions influenced by sophisticated advertising methods? In recent years this debate has been conducted in relation to 'healthy lifestyles'. Amid concern about rates of obesity, particularly among children (Boseley 2017; Obesity Health Alliance: **http://obesityhealthalliance.org.uk**), some have blamed the food industry for marketing foods with high fat and sugar content, but businesses respond by arguing that it is up to consumers to decide for themselves what they eat.

The business community is also actively engaged in the political arena at both national and international levels, seeking to ensure that legislators and policymakers are sensitive to business interests, for example in relation to food labelling (Chapter 11).

Stop and Think

You make choices about the music you listen to and the food you eat. We all like to think of ourselves as making our own decisions. But what factors in your environment have influenced your choices? How far has business shaped your lifestyle choices?

Choice of environment

Beyond responding to or influencing the environment, businesses may be able to choose a favourable environment in which to operate by deciding the location of their production activities. In searching for favourable environments in which to carry on production, firms are said to seek **locational advantage**. This applies to the establishment of new businesses, or new offices or factories on the part of existing firms; but it can also involve transferring operations from one location to another. Locational advantage may derive from factors such as:

- the availability of skilled labour;
- the cost of labour;
- a favourable tax or regulatory environment;
- the proximity of suppliers or consumers; and
- the quality of infrastructure, such as transport.

MNCs are often truly global in the sense that the production facilities they control are spread throughout the world, and it is sometimes argued that these companies are increasingly 'footloose' in the pursuit of their global business strategies. This means that they have no particular attachment to any country in which they operate but will shift production in search of favourable environments for their business (see Chapter 10). They may also be able to take advantage of their multinational structures to minimize their tax liabilities (see Case Study:

Tax avoidance in a globalizing world—managing costs efficiently or acting immorally?). The UK has offered a locational advantage to MNCs from outside the EU seeking access to the EU single market and has attracted a favourable share of foreign direct investment (FDI). The decision of the UK to withdraw from the EU in the 2016 referendum has stimulated public announcements by many businesses, not just in the financial sector, to relocate operations and jobs from the UK to other EU member states in order to ensure continued single market access and the ability to recruit skilled workers from within the EU. For example, two out of five firms in the UK games industry considered relocation largely due to concern over the ability to recruit skilled workers from the EU (BBC 2017).

Stop and Think

Can you think of other examples of how business is able to respond to, influence, or choose its external environment?

Environmental analysis

DYNAMIC As we have seen, businesses have to understand the 'surrounding conditions and circumstances' in which they operate in order to be successful. Environmental analysis is needed because the environment does not stay the same—it is dynamic—and, so, businesses must operate under a general assumption that the future will be different from the past. Technological change (Chapter 3) is a continuous source of disruption of existing business models. For example, the music industry has struggled to respond to the rise of downloading and, more recently, the rapid growth of streaming (British Phonographic Industry 2017; Fildes 2017). Much uncertainty surrounds the impact of automation—the so-called 'robot revolution'—in coming decades, with the potential to replace humans in the performance of tasks in many industries and occupations. It has been predicted that, as soon as the 2030s, around three in ten existing UK jobs could be at potential risk of automation, especially in the retail and wholesale, transport and storage, and manufacturing sectors (Elliott 2015; PWC 2017). Less certain is the extent to which job destruction will be accompanied and offset by job creation and the impact on inequality.

Markets and uncertainty

Businesses can never have complete knowledge of how the environment will change and therefore must operate in a somewhat uncertain environment. Indeed, the nature of the market system is that no one is able to direct its development or foresee the future. This is because market competition involves a continual process of experimentation and innovation in which most experiments fail, but it is not possible to say in advance which will succeed. For example, this is how personal computers were developed, through a process of trial and error involving many companies and in which 'no one saw for more than a few months ahead how the personal computer industry would evolve' (Kay 2004a: 104). Who can tell what the music industry will look like in ten years' time? Nevertheless, some level of understanding of the environment is essential to business and this requires some form of environmental analysis. In this section we will outline briefly some of the more familiar approaches.

PEST

COMPLEXITY The external environment is not just made up of markets but also includes political, legal, social, cultural, technological, and other factors and influences. It is, in other words, multifaceted and complex.

PEST is a simple framework for environmental analysis that distinguishes four categories or areas:

- political;
- economic;
- social; and
- technological.

There are variations on this basic type, such as STEEPLE (social, technological, economic, environmental, political, legal, ethical), and the first part of this book uses this elaboration of the basic PEST approach.

SWOT

INTERNAL/EXTERNAL **SWOT analysis** combines internal and external analyses—the strengths and weaknesses of the organization coupled with the opportunities and threats in the external environment. The capacity of a business to take advantage of opportunities and resist threats will depend on its internal strengths and weaknesses. An opportunity only really exists if an organization has the necessary skills or resources. Thus, an opportunity is not simply a feature of the external environment. Like PEST, SWOT is a simple framework (see Table 1.2), but its sophistication depends on the quality of the analysis under each heading.

Stakeholder analysis

STAKEHOLDERS A stakeholder is any individual, group, or organization that is affected by, and therefore has an interest in, the decisions and behaviour of the business. This might not be a direct effect as some stakeholders have public interest motivations. For example, an environmental pressure group has an interest in a business on account of the perceived harm its actions cause to the environment rather than any direct effect on the group's members. Other stakeholders have a direct interest because of the benefits or harm of the firm's actions to them. All the internal members of a business are stakeholders, including employees, directors, and shareholders. External stakeholders include customers, suppliers, competitors, politicians, policymakers, and the community or general public.

VALUES As well as being affected by a business, stakeholders may seek to influence business decisions in their own interests. There is a debate about how far businesses ought to be accountable to a wide range of stakeholders, and a stakeholder model of business may be contrasted with the traditional view of the firm as primarily or solely concerned with profit. Firms may themselves have different views about the desirability of

Table 1.2 The SWOT Framework

Strengths	Weaknesses
Opportunities	Threats

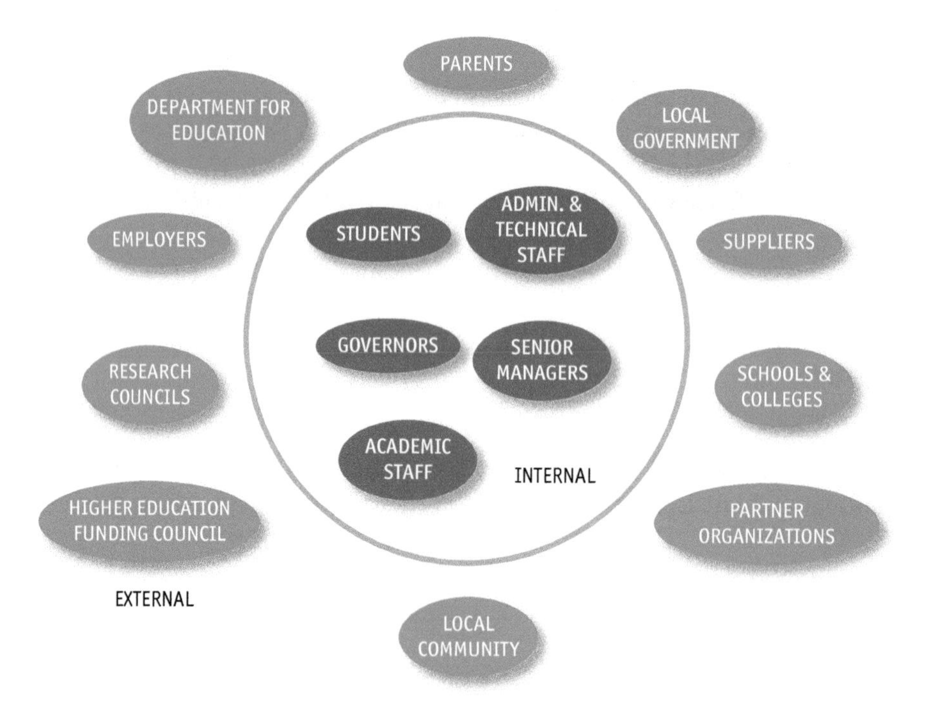

Figure 1.2 Stakeholder analysis—key university stakeholders

stakeholder engagement. In terms of environmental analysis, businesses need to have an understanding of:

- who their stakeholders are;
- the nature and level of their interest in the business; and
- their power to exert influence.

A stakeholder map is shown in Figure 1.2.

For each of the internal and external stakeholders shown:

(a) Identify the nature of their interests (e.g. the interests of students might include high-quality teaching).

(b) Consider whether there are any conflicts between the interests of different stakeholders (e.g. Do students and academics have the same interests?).

(c) Consider in what way, and to what extent, each stakeholder exercises power or influence (e.g. Do you have any influence over university decisions? Should you have?).

Stop and Think

Can you explain what is meant by each of the four terms that constitute the PEST framework: political, economic, social, technological?

Summary

- Business as an activity can be defined broadly as the transformation of inputs (or factors of production) into diverse outputs (goods and services) to meet the needs and wants of consumers. Business is a mechanism for deciding the allocation of the scarce resources available to society between various possible uses (or competing wants) in a situation of scarcity where not all wants can be satisfied.
- In a narrow sense, business is often used to refer to the private sector and the key characteristics of private ownership, competition, and profit. The broad meaning of business includes organizations in the public and third sectors.
- Market or capitalist economic systems, such as the UK, are dominated by the private sector. However, the boundary between the private, public, and third sectors is not fixed. The private sector is very diverse.
- The primary motivation of business in the private sector is profit. However, this is not the only measure of the purpose or success of business. In particular, it can be argued that business should fulfil wider obligations to society.
- Businesses can be understood as open systems interacting with their environments. Each business operates within an environment that is, to some extent, unique.
- The external environment is complex or multifaceted, dynamic, and must be analysed in terms of a variety of spatial levels or scales, from the local to the global.
- We live in a globalizing world, but globalization is not an inexorable process. Recent years have seen something of a backlash and recognition of the need to ensure that the benefits of globalization are shared more widely.
- It is important for business to engage in monitoring and analysis of the environment. A variety of techniques is available. However, business can never have complete knowledge of the environment or how it will change.

Case Study: Tax avoidance in a globalizing world—managing costs efficiently or acting immorally?

VALUES Tax avoidance: 'using tax law to gain a tax advantage not intended by Parliament' (House of Commons Committee of Public Accounts 2013: 3).

It may be argued that it is rational for profit-seeking companies to take steps to limit their tax liabilities, and tax avoidance may be seen as an obligation to their shareholders. Minimizing the tax bill enables companies to protect shareholder interests through paying a higher dividend or investing retained earnings in the business in order to sustain its competitiveness. Why pay more taxes than you have to? This is the logic of tax planning or legal tax avoidance measures (as contrasted with illegal tax evasion). In this view, the limit of a company's obligation to society is to obey the tax laws.

LOCAL TO GLOBAL One way in which MNCs can manage their tax liabilities is by locating production facilities in countries which have low rates of corporation tax (i.e. tax on profit). The tax rate is one of a range of factors that determine the locational advantage companies may gain from different countries. For this reason, national governments may try to set corporation tax at a 'competitive' (i.e. low) rate in order to advertise their country as the 'best place to do business' and thereby attract and retain investment. This approach has been adopted quite vigorously by the UK government (Chapter 4), and the UK is not alone. The OECD reported a trend of reducing corporation tax from 2000 to attract investment. This had slowed following the financial crisis in 2008 but picked up again in 2015 (Bowers 2016). Tax competition seems to show that the globalization of business enables large corporations to play governments off against each other in a competition to attract investment and, therefore, makes it hard for governments to tax business effectively. However, it is important to recognize that tax competition is a policy choice and not an inevitable result of globalization. The policy became a focus of disagreement between the political parties in the 2017 general election, with Labour proposing to increase corporation tax, and it has been criticized by campaigners such as the New Economics Foundation (NEF) and the Tax Justice Network as lacking evidence, redistributing wealth 'upwards' to the wealthy minority and so increasing inequality, and involving a dangerous 'race to the bottom' (Shaxson and O'Hagan 2013). This phenomenon, it can be argued, reveals the global tax system as 'dysfunctional' and in need of reform to ensure that taxes on profits are based on the actual business operations that take place in each country (Ocampo and Carmona 2015)

If governments want to attract business through low taxes, it makes it hard for them to state that they are going to 'get tough' on tax avoidance since this might be interpreted as hostile to business and unreasonable (since the avoidance is not illegal). Yet the UK and other governments have found themselves facing in both directions at once, and tackling tax avoidance has moved up the political agenda in the context of low public trust in business and concern that the benefits of globalization and economic growth are not being shared widely, leaving many people to feel 'left behind'. UK Prime Minister Theresa May emphasized tackling tax avoidance by wealthy individuals and businesses as part of her aspiration to create an economy that 'works for everyone' (Walker and Stewart 2016). Addressing the WEF in 2017, May urged the need to ensure businesses 'play . . . by the same rules as everyone else' and 'pay . . . their fair share of tax' (Elliott and Wearden 2017). This was not a new suggestion. Previously, Chancellor George Osborne had committed the UK government to 'ensuring multinational companies pay their proper share of taxes' and preventing 'artificial transfers of profits to tax havens' (HM Treasury 2012). Similarly, the previous Prime Minister David Cameron had identified 'aggressive' tax avoidance as raising 'ethical issues' and stated that 'businesses who think they can carry on dodging that fair share [of tax] . . . need to wake up and smell the coffee, because the public who buy from them have had enough' (Cameron 2013).

These statements followed a report by the House of Commons Public Accounts Committee which highlighted tax avoidance by MNCs with business activities located in the UK. Cameron's reference to 'smelling the coffee' appears to be directed at Starbucks, which was one of three US companies (the others being Google and Amazon) investigated by the Committee. The report states that

international companies are able to exploit national and international tax structures to minimise corporation tax on the economic activity they conduct in the UK. The outcome is that they do not pay their fair share (House of Commons Public Accounts Committee 2012).

MNCs are able to exploit tax laws by shifting profits to low-tax jurisdictions. They can do this by locating part of the business in a country with a low rate of corporation tax and by making transfers to that unit through devices such as royalty payments and internal prices. In this way, the profit is declared in the low-tax jurisdiction, away from the country where the economic activity took place. Starbucks claimed that it had made a loss in every year of its fifteen years of UK operations, except for one taxable year of profitability, despite reporting its UK business as successful to its shareholders. It had paid £8.6 million in tax from revenue of £3.1 billion. The Committee did not believe that Starbucks was making a loss in the UK (why would it carry on these operations if that were the case?) and claimed that UK profits were being shifted to the Netherlands and Switzerland where they were subject to a much lower rate of tax. Similarly, the Committee's investigation showed how Google and Amazon avoid UK tax by shifting profits to low-tax jurisdictions, respectively in Ireland and Luxembourg. These are not isolated cases, and the chair of the Committee claimed that they are widespread.

Such practices may be seen as pervasive among MNCs, and it is not just rich countries like the UK which are losing out on tax revenues. According to an 'extremely conservative' estimate by the OECD the erosion of tax receipts due to large global businesses shifting profits amounts to £65–160 billion a year on a global scale, and this is equivalent to between 4 per cent and 10 per cent of global corporation tax revenues (Bowers 2015).

The problem for governments in the UK and elsewhere is that corporate tax avoidance involves erosion of the tax base and creates a 'tax gap' between the revenues that are expected and those that are actually collected. This compromises the ability of the government to finance public services (including those that are important for business). It means that other taxpayers have to pay more, giving tax avoiders an unfair competitive advantage over firms that do pay their taxes, and this can undermine public confidence in the tax system and the willingness to pay tax. The head of the OECD has stated:

Companies have a responsibility to pay corporation tax in the jurisdictions where they operate. Citizens are already losing faith in their banks and the financial system. If big corporations fail to pay tax and leave it to SMEs and middle income groups, it will undermine democracy. This is about the survival of democracy (Gurria, quoted in Inman 2013; see also OECD 2013).

In this case, what's good for individual businesses is not good for government, business as a whole, or society. But is it 'unfair' or 'immoral'? In evidence to the House of Commons Public Accounts Committee, Google's Vice President for Sales and Operations in Northern and Central Europe stated that companies 'are required to do two things. One is to play by the rules . . . Secondly, we are required to manage our costs efficiently in order to satisfy our shareholders.' In this view minimizing tax through avoidance is 'not unfair to British taxpayers. We pay all the tax you require us to pay in the UK.' Against this view the chair of the Committee stated, 'We are not accusing you of being illegal; we are accusing you of being immoral' (House of Commons Public Accounts Committee 2012).

Google's view appears to be that morality stretches no further than obeying the law—a company's duty is to satisfy its shareholders within the law and nothing more should be asked of it. Donald Trump expressed this view during the 2016 presidential election campaign when he responded to a claim that he had avoided federal income taxes by saying 'That makes me smart' (Diaz 2016). However, this view does not appear to be shared among the wider public. In a 2015 UK survey 59 per cent of respondents agreed with the statement 'It is unacceptable to legally avoid tax' as against 32 per cent who think it is acceptable (Stone 2015). This suggests that 'managing costs efficiently' through tax avoidance might have the potential to backfire through reputational damage and even loss of sales. Indeed, there is some evidence that the fear of such damage might have shifted business attitudes to 'aggressive tax planning' towards a more 'compliant mind set' (Houlder 2016).

Google's view has also been challenged by the CBI, which lobbies on behalf of the business community as a whole. The director-general of the CBI supported action against tax avoidance: 'The majority of businesses pay the right amount of tax, and for the small minority which do not, times are getting tougher, and rightly so' (quoted in Elliott and Stewart 2013). Against Google's view it can be argued that acting morally requires us not merely to obey the letter of the law while looking for loopholes in it, but to behave in a way consistent with the spirit of the law, in other words paying the taxes that Parliament intended.

Questions

1. **To what extent is tax avoidance an inevitable consequence of a globalizing world?**
2. **Is corporate tax avoidance moral, or do companies have a moral obligation to pay the taxes intended by lawmakers? (If you were in charge of Starbucks what would you do?)**
3. **To what extent is the problem of companies 'gaming' tax regimes merely a consequence of governments playing a game of tax competition?**

Review and discussion questions

1. How does the idea of a 'globalizing world' help us to understand the business environment?
2. To what extent do you agree that the only social responsibility of private sector business is to maximize profits?
3. 'There is no such thing as a free market.' Explain what is meant by this statement.
4. What is the rationale for a broad definition of business, including the public sector and third sector? Compare and contrast the characteristics of the public and private sectors.
5. Give examples of the ways in which the external environment affects business decisions and behaviour, and the ways in which businesses may influence their environments.

Assignments

1. Investigate annual reports for two FTSE companies and analyse the extent to which they incorporate non-profit objectives and measures of performance.
2. Prepare a briefing for the vice chancellor of your university outlining the business case for the university to become a living wage employer.
3. Imagine you report to a senior executive of Google or Amazon who has been called to appear before the Public Accounts Committee of the House of Commons. Write a briefing paper to provide arguments justifying measures taken by the company to avoid UK corporation tax.

Further reading

Lawrence (2016) *looks ahead to the 'wave of economic, social and technological change' that will reshape Britain in the 2020s.*

World Economic Forum (2017) *provides an analysis of the global environment and global risks.*

Chang (2013) *provides a highly readable and challenging account of the nature of modern capitalism, confronting a number of 'myths'.*

Hutton (2015) *provides a critique of the current 'dysfunctional' model of capitalism in the UK and sets out proposals for reform.*

Raworth (2017) *offers a critique of mainstream economics and the economic model it has supported, and sets out an alternative approach focused on meeting all human needs within environmental limits.*

Test your understanding of this chapter with online questions and answers, explore the subject further through web exercises, and use the weblinks to provide a quick resource for further research. Visit the online resources at www.oup.com/uk/wetherly_otter4e/

Useful websites

Confederation of British Industry (CBI)
http://www.cbi.org.uk

Trades Union Congress (TUC)
http://www.tuc.org.uk

Department for Business, Energy & Industrial Strategy
https://www.gov.uk/government/organisations/department-for-business-energy-and-industrial-strategy

Office for National Statistics (ONS) (the UK's largest independent producer of official statistics and its recognized national statistical institute)
https://www.ons.gov.uk

Institute for Fiscal Studies (IFS)
http://www.ifs.org.uk

Organisation for Economic Co-operation and Development (OECD)
http://www.oecd.org

Eurostat (the statistical office of the European Union)
http://ec.europa.eu/eurostat/web/main/home

Full Fact ('the UK's independent fact-checking charity')
https://fullfact.org

References

Allen, K. (2016) 'Economic frustration has spawned Trump and Brexit, warns UN labour chief', *Guardian*, 14 November **https://www.theguardian.com/business/2016/nov/14/economic-frustration-spawned-trump-brexit-warns-ilo-chief**

BBC (2015a) 'Budget 2015: Osborne unveils National Living Wage' **http://www.bbc.co.uk/news/uk-politics-33437115**

BBC (2015b) 'Budget 2015: Business worries over cost of living wage' **http://www.bbc.co.uk/news/business-33447107**

BBC (2017) 'Two-fifths of gaming firms "could relocate over Brexit"' **http://www.bbc.co.uk/news/technology-39443169**

Boseley, S. (2017) 'Obesity on rise as quarter of European teens eat sweets daily', *Guardian*, 17 May **https://www.theguardian.com/society/2017/may/17/obesity-on-rise-25-european-teenagers-consume-sweets-daily**

Bowers, S. (2015) 'OECD hopes tax reforms will end era of aggressive avoidance', *Guardian*, 5 October **https://www.theguardian.com/business/2015/oct/05/oecd-hopes-reforms-will-end-era-of-aggressive-tax-avoidance**

Bowers, S. (2016) 'Corporation tax is on a downward trend, says OECD report', *Guardian*, 22 September **https://www.theguardian.com/business/2016/sep/22/corporation-tax-downward-trend-oecd-gdp-growth**

British Phonographic Industry (2017) *BPI Official UK Recorded Music Market Report For 2016* **https://www.bpi.co.uk/home/**

bpi-official-uk-recorded-music-market-report-for-2016.aspx

Cameron, D. (2013) 'Prime Minister David Cameron's speech to the World Economic Forum', 24 January, Davos-Klosters, Switzerland **http://www.number10.gov.uk/news/prime-minister-david-camerons-speech-to-the-world-economic-forum-in-davos**

Chang, H.-J. (2013) *23 Things They Don't Tell You About Capitalism* (Harmondsworth: Penguin)

Collinson, P. (2016) 'Home production economy worth £1tn a year', *Guardian*, 7 April **https://www.theguardian.com/uk-news/2016/apr/07/home-production-economy-worth-1tn-a-year**

Diaz, D. (2016) 'Trump: "I'm smart" for not paying taxes', CNN, 27 September **http://edition.cnn.com/2016/09/26/politics/donald-trump-federal-income-taxes-smart-debate/index.html**

Elliott, L. (2015) 'Robots threaten 15m UK jobs, says Bank of England's chief economist', *Guardian*, 12 November **https://www.theguardian.com/business/2015/nov/12/robots-threaten-low-paid-jobs-says-bank-of-england-chief-economist**

Elliott, L. (2017) 'Middle classes in crisis, IMF's Christine Lagarde tells Davos 2017', *Guardian*, 18 January **https://www.theguardian.com/business/2017/jan/18/middle-classes-imf-christine-lagarde-davos-2017-joe-biden**

Elliott, L. and Stewart, H. (2013) 'David Cameron makes swipe at Starbucks as he promises focus on tax', *Guardian*, 24 January **http://www.guardian.co.uk/politics/2013/jan/24/david-cameron-starbucks-focus-tax?INTCMP=SRCH**

Elliott, L. and Wearden, G. (2017) 'Companies must share benefits of globalization, Theresa May tells Davos', *Guardian*, 19 January **https://www.theguardian.com/business/2017/jan/19/companies-must-share-benefits-of-globalization-theresa-may-tells-davos**

Fildes, N. (2017) 'Streaming set to overtake physical music sales in UK', *Financial Times*, 13 April **https://www.ft.com/content/9e19d6d8-1f95-11e7-b7d3-163f5a7f229c?mhq5j=e1**

Flynn, N. (2012) *Public Sector Management* (London: Sage)

HM Treasury (2012) 'Autumn Statement 2012 to the House of Commons by the Rt Hon. George Osborne, MP, Chancellor of the Exchequer', 5 December **http://www.hm-treasury.gov.uk/as2012_statement.htm**

Houlder, V. (2016) 'Public opinion brings shift in business attitudes to tax planning', *Financial Times*, 29 August **https://www.ft.com/content/bca9bb20-6aca-11e6-ae5b-a7cc5dd5a28c?mhq5j=e1**

House of Commons Committee of Public Accounts (2013) *29th Report: Tax avoidance: tackling marketed avoidance schemes* (London: House of Commons) **http://www.publications.parliament.uk/pa/cm201213/cmselect/cmpubacc/788/788.pdf**

House of Commons Public Accounts Committee (2012) *Nineteenth Report—HM Revenue and Customs: Annual Report and Accounts* (London: House of Commons) **http://www.publications.parliament.uk/pa/cm201213/cmselect/cmpubacc/716/71602.htm**

Hutton, W. (2015) *How Good We Can be: Ending the Mercenary Society and Building a Great Country.* (London: Little, Brown)

IHS Markit (2016) *Living Wage Research for KPMG: 2016 Report* **https://assets.kpmg.com/content/dam/kpmg/uk/pdf/2016/11/living-wage-research-for-kpmg-october-2016.pdf**

Inman, P. (2013) 'OECD calls for crackdown on tax avoidance by multinationals', *Guardian*, 12 February **http://www.guardian.co.uk/business/2013/feb/12/oecd-crackdown-tax-avoidance-multinationals**

Katungi, D., Neal, E., and Barbour, A. (2006) *People in Low-paid Informal Work* (Joseph Rowntree Foundation) **http://www.jrf.org.uk/publications/people-low-paid-informal-work**

Kay, J. (2004) *The Truth About Markets* (London: Penguin)

Kay, J. (2004a) 'Obliquity', *Financial Times*, 17 January **http://www.johnkay.com/2004/01/17/obliquity**

Kean, D. (2016) 'Library closures "will double unless immediate action is taken"', *Guardian*, 12 December **https://www.theguardian.com/books/2016/dec/12/library-closures-will-double-unless-immediate-action-is-taken**

KPMG (2016) 'More than 5 million of UK's working population still being paid less than the voluntary Living Wage' **https://home.kpmg.com/uk/en/home/media/press-releases/2016/10/more-than-5-million-of-uks-working-population-still-being-paid-l.html**

International Labour Organization (2016) *Global Wage Report 2016/17* **http://www.ilo.org/wcmsp5/groups/public/---dgreports/---dcomm/---publ/documents/publication/wcms_537846.pdf**

Lawrence, M. (2016) *Future Proof: Britain in the 2020s* (London: Institute for Public Policy Research) **https://www.ippr.org/files/publications/pdf/future-proof_Dec2016.pdf**

Low Pay Commission (2016) *National Minimum Wage: Low Pay Commission Report Autumn 2016* **https://www.gov.uk/government/uploads/system/uploads/attachment_data/file/575634/10583-LPC-National_Living_Wage_WEB.pdf**

McGuinness, F. (2016) *Poverty in the UK: Statistics*, House of Commons Library Briefing Paper Number 7096, 16 June **http://researchbriefings.parliament.uk/ResearchBriefing/Summary/SN07096#fullreport**

Merrick, R. (2016) 'Theresa May uses major speech to attack new global elite that has "changed communities"', *The Independent*, 14 November **http://www.independent.co.uk/news/uk/politics/theresa-may-some-company-bosses-believe-i-am-anti-business-a7417241.html**

Ocampo, J. A. and Carmona, M. S. (2015) 'Tax avoidance by corporations is out of control: the United Nations must step in', *Guardian*, 30 September **https://www.theguardian.com/commentisfree/2015/sep/30/tax-avoidance-corporations-impacts-the-poor-united-nations-step-in**

OECD (2013) 'Action plan on base erosion and profit shifting' **http://www.oecd.org/tax/beps.htm**

Office for National Statistics (2015) *Ownership of UK Quoted Shares, 2014* **https://www.ons.gov.uk/economy/investmentspensionsandtrusts/bulletins/ownershipofukquotedshares/2015-09-02**

Office for National Statistics (2016) *Women Shoulder the Responsibility of 'Unpaid Work'* **http://visual.ons.gov.uk/the-value-of-your-unpaid-work**

Provost, C. (2017) 'The industry of inequality: why the world is obsessed with private security', *Guardian*, 12 May. **https://www.theguardian.com/inequality/2017/may/12/industry-of-inequality-why-world-is-obsessed-with-private-security**

PWC (2017) *UK Economic Outlook March 2017* **http://www.pwc.co.uk/economic-services/ukeo/pwc-uk-economic-outlook-full-report-march-2017-v2.pdf**

Raworth, K. (2017) *Doughnut Economics: Seven Ways to Think Like a Twenty-First Century Economist* (London: Random House)

Resolution Foundation (2016) *Low Pay Britain 2016* **http://www.resolutionfoundation.org/app/uploads/2016/10/Low-Pay-Britain-2016.pdf**

Sharma, R. (2016) 'Globalization as we know it is over—and Brexit is the biggest sign yet', *Guardian*, 28 July **https://www.theguardian.com/commentisfree/2016/jul/28/era-globalization-brexit-eu-britain-economic-frustration**

Shaxson, N. and O'Hagan, E. M. (2013) 'A competitive tax system is a better tax system' **http://www.taxjustice.net/cms/upload/pdf/TJN_NEF_130418_Tax_competition.pdf**

Stewart, H. (2015) 'Has George Osborne really introduced a living wage?', *Guardian*, 8 July **https://www.theguardian.com/society/reality-check/2015/jul/08/george-osborne-budget-national-living-wage**

Stone, J. (2015) 'Most people think legal tax avoidance is just as wrong as illegal tax evasion, poll suggests', *The Independent*, 1 March **http://www.independent.co.uk/news/uk/politics/most-people-think-legal-tax-avoidance-is-just-as-wrong-as-illegal-tax-evasion-10077934.html**

Walker, P. and Stewart, H. (2016) 'May promises her "party of workers" will govern for whole nation', *Guardian*, 5 October **https://www.theguardian.com/politics/2016/oct/05/theresa-may-conference-interventionist-government-for-workers**

World Economic Forum (2017) *The Global Risks Report 2017* (12th edn) **http://www3.weforum.org/docs/GRR17_Report_web.pdf**

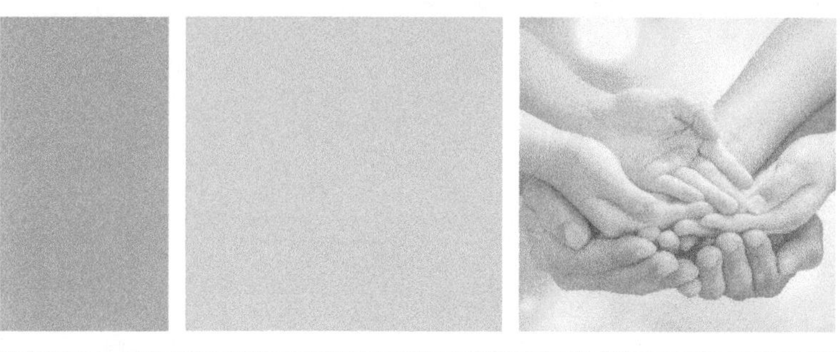

PART ONE ENVIRONMENTS

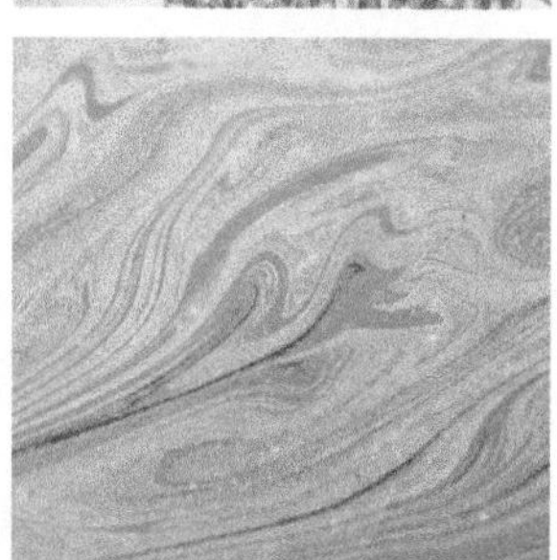

Chapter 2
The economic environment

Dorron Otter

Learning objectives

When you have completed this chapter, you will be able to:

- Explain the essential characteristics of the economic environment.
- Critically assess the way in which markets work and their role in creating a favourable economic environment.
- Analyse the competing perspectives about the role of markets in capitalist systems and the role of governments in providing essential institutional support.

THEMES

The following themes of the book are especially relevant to this chapter

- INTERNAL/EXTERNAL Businesses face contrasting market conditions and the nature of these markets fundamentally shapes business strategy.
- COMPLEXITY The nature of the economic environment is a complex mix of economic, social, and political factors.
- DYNAMIC Change and uncertainty are at the heart of the economic environment and this has been seen in the dynamic changes that have occurred in both the domestic and global economic environments over time.
- VALUES Economics is centrally concerned with values; in the sense of the prices and costs of goods and services, in the sense of 'value for money', and in the sense of who benefits from the use of the resources.

Introduction

Studying the economic environment is essential to identify the efficiency criteria by which we can assess the impact of business, and enables us to investigate the relative advantages and disadvantages of different economic systems. The defining characteristic of a capitalist economy is that privately owned business is primarily conducted through the market system and we will explore what this means and how businesses need to be aware of changing market conditions. However, as we will see, there are many cases where markets fail to achieve efficient outcomes and so governments need to intervene either through direct interference or regulation in markets or through providing or encouraging a range of market supporting institutions. There are a range of competing theoretical approaches to balancing the role of the state and markets and we will explore the development of these ideas in theory and practice.

Scarcity–the heart of the economic environment?

The starting point of most introductory economics textbooks is that human beings have no limit to their needs, wants, and desires but at any one moment in time there is a limit to the resources available to produce the goods and services to satisfy our demands. Resources can be grouped as follows:

Labour is that proportion of the population engaged in production whether this work is paid or unpaid. It is not just the quantity of labour available (the labour supply) that is important, but also its quality. The major influence on this is the extent to which education and training can improve labour productivity.

Land refers to all natural resources whether they are above the land (e.g. the air we breathe), below the land, or in the sea.

Capital is machinery, tools, and factories. Capital goods are required to produce the final goods/services that people want.

Enterprise: The entrepreneur is the key person without whom production would not take place. Entrepreneurs mobilize and decide how to use resources to produce goods and services.

Business and the economic problem

Commodities

Anything that satisfies a need, desire, or want is defined as a commodity. To produce commodities, resources are combined in the production process transforming inputs (resources) into outputs (commodities).

Stop and Think

VALUES Do you agree that we live in a world of scarcity? Is there a possibility that you personally could ever be satisfied with what you have?

Three problems necessarily flow from this central problem of scarcity and we need to consider how well a particular economic environment tackles them.

What makes for an efficient economic environment?

The allocation problem

COMPLEXITY If there are insufficient resources to satisfy every need or want, then decisions have to be made as to what to produce. The limited resources are shown in the box in Figure 2.1. Outside in the vortex of economic space lie the infinite needs and wants which, just like the real universe, keep on expanding. How can the resource-poor economy decide which voices to listen to out of the insatiable demands which we put upon it?

Stop and Think—the real cost of a resource decision is its opportunity cost

Imagine a certain quantity of labourers, raw materials, production, decision-makers, and machinery which together cost £1 million. You can decide what you want these resources to do for the next six months. Here are three ideas for you to consider:

1. These resources could be used to modernize private student houses with grants of up to £5,000 per house. Potentially 200 houses could be improved.
2. A new state-of-the-art lecture theatre complex could be built for £1 million.
3. Four luxury 5-bedroomed detached houses in an affluent suburb of the city could be built at a cost of £250,000 each.

Whichever decision you make costs £1 million but it is the owners of the resources and the users of whatever is built who will benefit from it. There are, however, other real costs in your decision without corresponding benefits. Let's say option 3 is chosen. The real cost to the economy is not £1 million but the lost opportunities of options 1 and 2. Once 3 is chosen then the chance of employing these resources to build 1 and 2 in the next six months is lost forever. Now, of course, we are unreasonable if we say that the real cost of the four houses is option 1 and 2 because you couldn't do both of these. Instead we define this cost, this **opportunity cost**, as the cost of the next most desired alternative. There are opportunities that have been lost as a result of deciding that resources should be used in a particular way.

What do you think would be the most efficient decision in this case? On what basis are you making this decision?

Whenever a business decision is made there is an opportunity cost in terms of the opportunities that have been lost as a result of this decision. So how can we judge whether allocative decisions are taken correctly? How can we construct an economic environment that ensures that the 'right' commodities are produced? In other words, how can we ensure that we achieve 'allocative efficiency'?

The production problem

How does the economy organize the production of the chosen commodity? If resources are scarce, businesses should produce the maximum output of the highest quality for the minimum input. This is referred to as productive efficiency. If resource costs are minimized, so must be the opportunity costs. Any firm is being productively efficient if it produces a level of output at which the average cost of inputs is minimized.

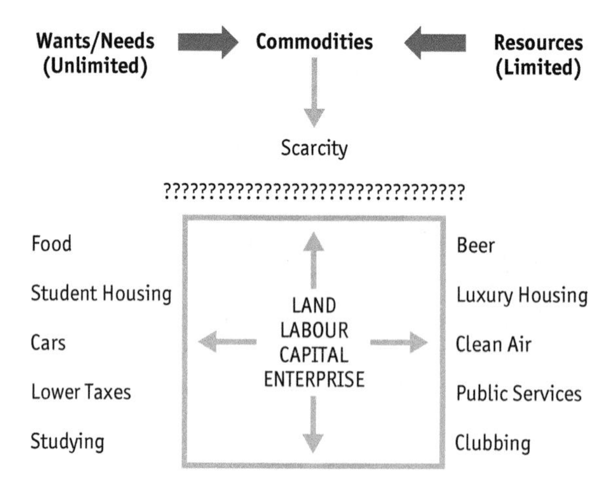

Figure 2.1 The business in its environment

The distribution problem

VALUES When the economy has decided what to produce, and how, it must decide who gets it.

This means that we ought to have a clear set of criteria for judging distributive efficiency or what can be variously described as equity, fairness, or justice and this is influenced by our value judgements. There can appear to be a conflict between efficiency in allocation and production and people's views as to appropriate distributive justice.

COMPLEXITY If we are to judge business efficiency in its wider context, we must relate it to these three aspects of efficiency, and it is likely that businesses operating in different environments will have different goals which may conflict with certain aspects of efficiency.

In an economic environment in which businesses are predominately privately owned the emphasis may be placed on customer satisfaction and cutting costs to maximize profits but there may well be a conflict between how the business views its efficient operation and how society judges it. 'People before profit' is a cry often heard from critics of business with popular campaigns against the perceived irresponsible behaviour of businesses. Chapter 6 explores this in more detail. The public sector will have goals other than profit but the lack of a profit motive may lead to a lack of incentives to cut costs and encourage wasteful use of resources.

Every day millions of economic decisions have to be made regarding allocation, production, and distribution, so what is the best way to organize economic activity?

Perspectives on the economic environment

VALUES The conventional view is that the starting point of economics is scarcity, but to what extent do we all agree with what is meant by scarcity? There are competing views as to the ideal way of creating an economic environment that will allow businesses to operate efficiently and these views can be derived from the differing conceptions of scarcity.

Consider Figure 2.2: What do you see? Some of you will see a young woman, some an old one. Some will see both. Some of you will wonder why this image has been included. The same picture but four different responses: those of you that see the young woman will not be able to

Figure 2.2 Young/old woman
This famous figure was published in 1915 in *Puck*, an American humour magazine, and is credited to British cartoonist W. E. Hill. It is likely though that he adapted this from an image that was popularly used on trading cards in the eighteenth and nineteenth centuries.
Source: Hill, W. E., 'My wife and my mother-in-law'. *Puck*, 10 (11) Nov. 1915.

immediately understand why people are seeing an old woman and vice versa; those of you that see both will smile knowingly; and those of you who can't see the point will wonder what this has to do with the economic environment! The same factual information is presented, and yet we have four different perspectives! (See also Mini-Case 2.1).

Mini-Case 2.1 Costs and benefits of higher education

Education can be seen as benefiting the individual, business performance, and the wider society. For society, there are clear links between rates of economic growth and educational attainment. For individuals, future earning potential and promotion prospects are higher, and they are likely to live longer and have more healthy lives. Businesses benefit from the increased productivity of the future workforces. Provision of early years education and seeking to ensure that schools have mixed social backgrounds have the biggest impact in terms of reducing social inequality, and the more educated that people are, the more likely they are to be active citizens in terms of voting and other forms of civic engagement. In September 2015 the Sustainable Development Goals were agreed at the United Nations, and Goal 4 of this states that globally education is vital to ensure 'inclusive and equitable quality education and promote lifelong opportunities for all'.

The shape of higher education funding has been changing in recent years, as some governments have sought to reduce levels of public sector funding relative to private funding. Within the countries that comprise the OECD (Organisation of Economic Co-operation and Development) there are varying approaches taken to the charging of private fees and the provision of public loans and grants. After 2002 the UK dramatically shifted to a much higher level of private fees supported by the provision of a student loans system. The argument was that while there is indeed a wider social benefit of having more students in higher education, an individual graduate's lifetime premium, compared to a non-graduate, was very high and students should be prepared to pay a private cost to match this substantial private benefit they receive, which was estimated at an average of approximately £400,000 in 2002. This figure is disputed and in a paper published in 2016 it was argued that the graduate premium had in fact dropped to only £100,000, which over a working life of 45 years would yield a benefit of only £2,222 per year before taxes and national insurance were calculated, which would not in any way cover the burden of the considerable debts that students would now have incurred.

This report was criticized for being too pessimistic and for too narrowly focusing on private costs and benefits. In 2016, the OECD estimated that the average male graduate premium was $258,400 in 2012 and for women it was $167,600. In relation to the private rate of return on income earned over a lifetime compared to the costs incurred, it estimated that this would be 14 per cent for men and 12 per cent for women. However, there are also wider social benefits that must be taken into consideration and it estimated these as being a social benefit over social cost of $143,700 for men and $74,100 for women.

Sources: OECD (2016), Kemp-King, S. (2016)

Questions

1. **What are the arguments for and against charging students fees to attend university?**
2. **What are the private benefits and costs and the social benefits and costs of higher education to an economy?**
3. **Given the constraints on the amount of public money going into universities, what measures can be taken to ensure that all those who can benefit from higher education are able to access it?**

Consider the following definitions of scarcity:

Definition 1

- We will never satisfy all our wants and needs because they are infinite and resources are finite.

Definition 2

- Given that resources are scarce, the aim of the economic environment is to ensure that we minimize the amount of resources used in production while ensuring high-quality outputs.

Definition 3

- Even if we accept that at the global level there is scarcity, the real pressing problem is that inequality means that resources are used to satisfy the needs of the rich at the expense of the poor. We thus have a world where there is abundance for the few and poverty for the majority.

Definition 4

- We must never forget that resources are finite. If there is economic growth, then this must be environmentally sustainable, and we need to live within the resource constraints of the planet.

Stop and Think

With which of these statements do you most agree?

For many people there is a healthy disregard for economics and economists. In the nineteenth century the political philosopher Thomas Carlyle referred to economics as 'the dismal science'. Today an echo of this is found in the opinions of many, reflected in the belief that all economic policy is destined to end in failure (Definition 1).

We can broadly distinguish four main schools of economic thought:

- a neoclassical or neoliberal view
- an institutionalist or structuralist view
- a socialist or Marxist view
- a green or environmentalist view

In the neoclassical/neoliberal school the environment in which businesses can flourish is one based on free markets where businesses are free of government interference.

For institutionalists or structuralists the way markets operate depends on the supporting institutional framework and structures which are vital for markets to work and, indeed, might be needed in cases where they don't work. These schools of thought tend to highlight the role of the government or state in ensuring that markets operate in a way that balances private with social goals. Despite their differences with neoclassical economists they share the view of scarcity outlined in Definition 2.

Socialists and Marxists see a fundamental problem in capitalist economic systems. Too high a reliance on markets alone tends to create high degrees of inequality and businesses work in such a way as to exploit consumers and employees (Definition 3).

An increasing concern in the latter part of the twentieth century and now into the twenty-first has been the effect of continued economic growth on the ability of the planet to sustain growth in terms of natural resource use. For the green movement resources are finite and businesses need to use them responsibly—and consumers, especially those of us living in prosperous countries should limit our demands (Definition 4).

Adam Smith and the birth of classical political economy

INTERACTION The modern economic system of market capitalism first took root in Britain. Prior to the development of modern market capitalism, the main form of business was agriculture. Producers were largely peasant farmers whose chief motivation was to produce enough food to survive. Given the risk and uncertainty of farming as a result of the inability to predict climate and the constant threat of pests and other crop diseases, farmers tended to spread the risk by growing a variety of different things. The decision as to what to produce was determined largely by natural resource availability and geographical conditions such as soil quality, access to water, and climate. How to produce was determined by the overriding desire to spread risk and thus diversify production as well as by traditional farming methods handed down through the generations. In this subsistence form of production, the use of technology was very limited and most production was very labour intensive. The distribution system though was largely determined by the political system. In all countries ownership of the land was concentrated in the hands of a tiny elite of powerful landlords ruled by an autocratic monarch. The landlords would retain their titles to the land as long as they supported the king through the provision of tribute in the form of taxes and in kind through military support. This system of economic production and political organization is referred to as **feudalism**.

Farmers worked the land but every year they had to give a proportion of what they produced to the landlords and/or monarch. This meant that the motivation for peasants to boost production was undermined by the knowledge that their ability to keep it for their own use depended simply on how much the landlord would want to take. In these conditions production levels tended to fall to the minimum subsistence level. The maximum that the landlord could take would only be determined by the minimum amount that peasant families would need to survive. Landlords would effectively then tax each household through the levying of rents in kind and they would exchange this produce in markets and purchase a much greater range of commodities than would be available to subsistence farmers. Even if the amount that the landlord was able to take from each farmer was low, since it was likely that he controlled the lives of many, he would be able to take a little from a lot of farmers and thus enjoy a very privileged lifestyle. It was the richer members of society who would use markets, buying goods from artisans who lived in the towns and also seeking to buy such luxury imports as were available from the trading routes to the East.

> ***Stop and Think***
>
> In this feudal system how are the three parts of the economic system resolved? Why might the rate of economic growth be slow and why might that not matter so much to those with political power?

Adam Smith is widely regarded as the first person to rigorously explore the emergence of what we now call market capitalism, which he saw as the best system in which to organize economic activity so as to increase the economic growth of a country or 'the wealth of nations', which was the title of his most famous book (Smith 1776).

Smith's central concern was to explain the rise in economic growth in Britain in the eighteenth century. For Smith the answer lay in the change in the basis of the economy away from one of wealth being generated for the small elite by exploiting peasants and using markets only in a limited way, to a system where wealth is created through the exploitation of markets themselves. Smith showed how an economic system based on widespread use of markets would result in a harmonious society. The key to this system is that in making money from markets, businesses will choose to specialize in terms of what they produce and the operation of the price mechanism will enable this market system to work efficiently (see Mini-Case 2.2)

There was money to be made by deliberately targeting production for sale in markets rather than simply using markets as a way of selling surplus goods extracted from the peasantry. This happened in two ways. First, enlightened landlords began to think about ways in which production could be increased so they could have access to more and more traded goods and, second, they began to think about the types of goods that would have the greatest market value.

The basis of the Industrial Revolution in Britain was the widespread production of wool and then cotton and the development of the ancillary processes of the textile industry. One big obstacle that could prevent these ideas from taking root would have been the continuation of the rigidly hierarchical system based on the monarch being able to increase the taxes he or she felt entitled to as incomes increased. It was in Britain that the consolidation of the monarchy up until the seventeenth century had the advantage of building a strong and unified country without too many internal power struggles. And yet by the end of the seventeenth century a profound political revolution had occurred resulting in a shift of power away from the monarch and to the landlord classes. The arbitrary power of the state to exact penal levels of taxation was abolished, patents were granted to enable innovation to occur, state monopolies for valuable areas of economic activity were abolished, and a legal system was established that meant that property rights were guaranteed so that contracts could be honoured, and profits generated could be kept by those that earned them. Finally, the growing military strength of Britain, especially through naval power, meant that international trade could occur without the constant threat of piracy on the high seas. Potential business activity was now freed from the power of the state, business people were free to enrich themselves, and a spirit of capitalism was born.

How do market systems work?

Specialization and the division of labour

The Wealth of Nations describes how productivity can be dramatically improved by developing a process of production based on the division of labour. Before the Industrial Revolution most clothing was either homemade or made by individual artisan tailors producing for the wealthier members of society. Smith uses the example of pins, used in the making of clothes, to illustrate the efficiency gains of specialization. Traditionally these were produced as a sideline in blacksmiths' shops whose primary purpose was making the goods for horse-drawn technologies (e.g. ploughing and transportation).

The expansion of textile manufacture meant the need for greater numbers of pins and this provided a market opportunity for enterprising capitalists. Now businesses would specialize in pin manufacture and in so doing could organize production in such a way as to dramatically increase production and lower costs. Smith describes how the manufacture of each pin is broken down into many individual tasks performed by specialist labourers and how this results in a huge increase in productivity.

The basis of modern production is in mass production techniques utilizing the division of labour. Once products have been made they need to be sold in markets. So, how do markets work and how might these markets in theory resolve the economic problems we have highlighted in this chapter? For Smith it was 'the invisible hand' of the price mechanism that explained how the system worked.

Mini-Case 2.2 The hidden source of the *Wealth of Nations*—'the invisible hand' or 'greed is good'?

Smith argued that it is markets that allow businesses to specialize and thus improve efficiency through the division of labour and reaping the benefits of economies of scale.

He emphasized three main elements key to this process: the expansion of the free market; the benefits of the increased division of labour that trade and specialization brings; and the continual need to accumulate capital/surplus and reinvest it in the production process.

The role of the price mechanism is then seen as being a vital ingredient. The invisible hand of the price mechanism drives the self-interested profit-seeking entrepreneur to continually expand production for the benefit of all.

Or in Smith's own words:

[Every individual] intends only his own gain, and he is in this, as in many other cases, led by an invisible hand to promote an end which was no part of his intention. Nor is it always the worse for the society that it was no part of it. By pursuing his own interest he frequently promotes that of the society more effectually than when he really intends to promote it.

Or, again he writes:

It is not from the benevolence of the butcher, the brewer, or the baker that we expect our dinner, but from their regard to their own interest. We address ourselves, not to their humanity but to their self-love.

As we will see in the end of chapter case, the financial sector is one of the most profitable specialized market operations today. The financial services industry congratulates itself on being the vital sector that enables the efficient allocation of resources as well as being a way of enabling businesses in other sectors to cut costs ensuring that productivity as a whole rises. Critics argue that such claims are merely self-serving, and they baulk at the incredibly high rewards that top 'City' financiers award themselves. In the 1987 novel *Bonfire of the Vanities* Tom Wolfe profiled what he saw as the arrogant excesses of the financial class in New York who saw themselves as being the 'masters of the universe', and in the same year the film *Wall Street* tried to capture the essence of the heart of the global finance industry, immortalized by the quotation of its anti-hero, the ruthless banker Gordon Gekko, that 'greed, for lack of a better word, is good'.

Questions

1. **Why does Smith argue that it is self-interest that is at the heart of the capitalist business environment?**
2. **Is self-interest the same as 'greed' and under what circumstances might it be legitimate for governments to reduce the profits earned by businesses?**

The price mechanism

Allocative efficiency

In a market system, consumers have the ultimate power over the use of resources because they signal their desire as to what should be produced by their willingness to pay the price. Producers respond to consumer demand through the operation of prices. If consumers do not want the product, the price will fall and demand will fall. If demand is high, then prices will rise and more resources will be used by the entrepreneur to produce that commodity. In this way resources are allocated 'in accordance with consumers' preferences'. Economists refer to this as consumer sovereignty.

Productive efficiency

DYNAMIC While specialization and the division of labour are vital for growth in modern economics there is a focus on the development of technology and the possibility of growing markets, allowing an increase in the scale of production and thus the ability to exploit **economies of scale.**

Smith's economic ideas were grounded in the political philosophy of liberalism. It is vital that the business owners have the freedom to own property and to earn and keep their hard-earned profits free from government intervention. While it is indeed the business community that is the engine of growth workers too are free in the market system. They must be free to work wherever they want and while they will not have anywhere near as great a share in the wealth of the nation they do benefit from the employment opportunities.

Smith was not a naive optimist in the spirit of human nature naturally operating for the good of society. He did though believe that the power of the market would curb any tendency for self-interest to operate against the common good. The primary drive for that success depended on giving the customers what they demand but Smith argued there was another market pressure on business. Competition is vital to prevent producers gaining monopoly power and exploiting consumers. Competition ensures that costs are always held low and combines with the profit motive to ensure that producers have the incentive to produce what consumers want and to produce quality and at the lowest cost. Consumers are guaranteed choice and variety. Free markets provide natural checks on the power of business over consumers.

There is a restless dynamism to capitalism in that businesses are always looking to cut costs and innovate and are driven by a competitive struggle. They will seek to invest their profits in new technologies.

Finally, neither under- nor overproduction of commodities can exist because prices will either rise or fall in response, matching supply and demand. Smith's description of the operation of markets through changes in supply and demand resulted in his belief that not only will markets bring about efficiency, they will also always be stable. It is the operation of the price mechanism as if by 'an invisible hand' that guides the overall economy.

Distributive efficiency

Distribution of commodities is strictly on the basis of ability to pay. In order to improve, people now have an incentive to work hard and develop the skills needed in the labour market, or even become entrepreneurs themselves. Potentially, the rewards for enterprise can be very high but, of course, many businesses fail. For most people income is derived from labour, so, if you want more from the market, you have to secure a more rewarding job. Owners of land and capital will seek to deploy these resources to get the best return. Incentives are the fuel that powers the economy. They are vital if capitalism is to grow.

The circle is complete. In order to better yourself you have the incentive to engage in the activities dictated by the needs of commodity markets. The highest rewards are where demand is strongest and where businesses and resource owners are able to gain a competitive advantage.

All of this is achieved without any conscious intervention by an external agency. The market system is a brilliant coordinating device, bringing together millions of consumers and producers.

Neoclassical and Marxist political economy

As the eighteenth century gave way to the nineteenth, other economies most notably in Western Europe and the US began to develop fully-fledged market economies and the Industrial Revolution boomed. However, Smith's optimistic view that this new market economy would lead to uninterrupted and continual growth encountered two major problems. First, economic growth rates were not stable, but economies moved through periods of growth followed by periods when growth fell. As urbanization increased, huge disparities between the rich and poor occurred, focusing attention on the appalling living conditions experienced by the new urban masses. Thomas Malthus argued that economic success, in allowing people to live longer, caused a problem in that population growth rates would exceed the growth rate of food production over time, leading to periodic crises and the prospect that growth would inevitably slow down to a 'stationary state'. His friend but intellectual opponent David Ricardo argued that it was not the growth of the population that was the problem but that as growth occurred more and more marginal land would have to be brought into production to feed urban populations and that this would lead to 'diminishing returns'. He challenged the pessimism of Malthus in arguing that the answer to diminishing returns was to expand trade internationally and that problems of food supply would be eradicated by encouraging free trade, and we will explore his arguments for this in Chapter 10. However, the main critique of the optimistic view of free market capitalism came from Karl Marx and the rise of the socialist movements across Europe in the later nineteenth and early twentieth centuries as well as from social liberal reformers who began to recognize that there was a role for the provision of essential public services.

Marx sought to develop a robust theory to challenge classical political economy. He was an ardent admirer of the potential for capitalism to indeed deliver the prosperity that Smith predicted, and he was a keen reader of the works of Smith, Malthus, and Ricardo. For Marx though there was a central contradiction in capitalism. Marx focused on the role of the workers in the production process. After all, if the key to wealth depended on specialization and the division of labour, then this implied that the source of wealth was indeed labour. Capitalists owned property, or in Marx's words, the means of production, and with this came the ability to control the hiring and firing and use of labour. In the process of production workers were paid the 'exchange value' of their labour or a wage and this was determined by the level of wages that would guarantee the minimum subsistence level. The reason for this being the minimum subsistence was that capitalists were able to drive down this wage, given the abundance of labour at their disposal. However, during the working day workers produced a 'use value' in the form of commodities which when sold were at a price much greater than the cost of the labour that went into them. In Marx's view profit is nothing other than the extraction of a 'surplus value' from workers by capitalists. For Marx, the answer was relatively simple in theory but fraught with practical difficulties. Since the power to extract surplus value came from private ownership, what if the means of production were commonly owned and then the surplus could be equitably shared? What was needed then was a political revolution and once this was achieved a new form of economic system based on socialism could be constructed. As we will see in Chapter 10, Marx's ideas while influential in western capitalist systems did not in fact lead to revolution and in Britain and America, which by the twentieth century were in the economic ascendancy in terms of global economic powers, there was a reformulation of classical political economy in the form of what came to be called neoclassical economics.

These ideas were developed in the early twentieth century and laid down the principles that to this day are the fundamental ones on which most textbook economic theory is founded. The challenge of neoclassical economics was to divert attention away from the focus on political struggles to one which seeks to show that free markets can bring about a frictionless world where the needs of consumers, producers, and workers are all brought into harmony through the operation of natural economic laws.

Modern day neoclassical economics focuses on quantifying and modelling the economic behaviour that underpins the effective functioning of the price mechanism. The main developments in economic analysis in the nineteenth century involved the work of Alfred Marshall who laid down the framework of equilibrium analysis which we explore below, that showed how market forces would enable markets to function in such a way as to produce efficient market outcomes. Theories of consumer, producer, and labour market behaviour were developed to show how individual consumption and production decisions were made and how income and wealth were naturally distributed between owners of labour, capital, and land. In this way the determinants of demand and supply could be identified and then, using market forecasting techniques, predictions could be made as to how changes in economic conditions could affect markets. These analytical tools are the basis of modern **microeconomics**, which is the study of how individual markets operate.

Markets and how they operate

COMPLEXITY **DYNAMIC** **LOCAL TO GLOBAL** It is vital for businesses to be able to understand the nature of the market for their products so that they can use this information to their commercial advantage. **Microeconomics** is fundamentally concerned with developing techniques to understand the operation on individual markets. To build a picture of the individual characteristics of each one would be an impossible task but by using a technique called **equilibrium analysis** we only need build a model surrounding one commodity and see how that market operates. Then using the same techniques we can apply this to other markets to see how they behave.

Let us build a simple equilibrium model to look at one market, the market for one brand of jeans.

Demand and supply

In a market there are consumers who demand the product and suppliers who would like to supply it. The first two questions are:

What influences a consumer's decision to demand the product (the determinants of demand)?

What influences a producer to supply the product (the determinants of supply)?

What are the most likely influences on you if you considered buying a pair of jeans?

Obviously, the price of the jeans is the key one but so would be your spending power or **disposable income**, fashion tastes and comfort, the prices and attributes of other types of jeans or trousers in general (or **substitute commodities**), the cost of going out to socialize (and other such **complementary** activities), and your general confidence in the future and expectations of the future course of prices.

What about the motives of the producer of the jeans? Well, for the private business its primary aim is to make a profit and so its willingness to supply will depend on the price it can get for each pair sold. However, this is not the only influence on supply. The business could supply other types of jeans or different types of product entirely. Profits depend on the costs of the resources that go into production and costs often depend on the state of existing technology. The business may not be a private one and/or may have goals other than simply profit maximization and this will affect its production decision. Government policies can also affect business decisions.

We can formalize these guesses in the form of demand and supply functions. These simply encompass all of the possible influences that might affect consumers' decisions to buy a particular commodity or a producer's decision as to whether to supply. Obviously, the influences that affect demand and supply will vary from commodity to commodity, person to person, business to business, and time period to time period. Nevertheless, it is possible to derive a general model that can apply in varying degrees to all commodities.

There is one important influence or variable that is common to both producers and consumers and this is the price of the product itself. Study the general demand function shown in the box below. This is *not* a mathematical statement but a shorthand summary of influences on demand.

The demand function

Da = f (Pa . . . Ps . . . Pc . . . Yd . . . T . . . SF . . . EPs)

where:

Da	the demand for commodity a
f	is a function of, depends on
Pa	the price of commodity a
Ps	the price of substitutes for commodity a
Pc	the price of complements for commodity a
Yd	disposable income
T	tastes
SF	sociological factors: age composition of population, culture
EPs	expectations about future prices, incomes

There are many things that affect demand, and with equilibrium analysis we assume a world in which we could isolate each factor in turn and then have a best guess as to how demand would be affected if it were to change and assume that we can freeze the other determinants.

Just as with demand we can draw up a list of possible influences on supply as shown in the box below.

The supply function

Sa = f (Pa . . . Pbcd . . . Pr . . . Tech . . . Goals . . . GP)

Sa	the supply of commodity a
f	depends on, is a function of
Pa	the price of commodity a
Pbcd	the prices of other goods that the firm produces
Pr	price of resources, inputs, costs (labour, denim)
Tech	technology
Goals	goals of the firm
GP	government policy

COMPLEXITY In the real world economic events are constantly changing and so are the variables in both the demand and supply functions. Using **equilibrium analysis**, we isolate each variable in turn and see how demand and supply would be affected if it were to change, and predict market changes. In this way, having established the relationship in isolation, we can then alter other things one at a time to see how our original analysis would be affected. However, as with weather forecasting, the strength of the forecast depends on correctly identifying the likely changes. Provided that these occur in the predicted way, the forecast will be correct. Contrary to popular prejudice most weather forecasts are mostly correct as the meteorological offices have become very sophisticated in terms of gathering information and using their computer models. Forecasts can go wrong. This may not be because the models built were wrong but that an unexpected change occurred. If only that could have been predicted, then the forecast would be right. This is the same in economics. We can do our best to try to look at all the influences on a market but all too often the unexpected happens and blows our forecast off course. Businesses have to deal with this uncertainty caused by the economic environment.

Demand and price

Let us start with the price of the commodity itself. How would a change in this affect both the demand and supply?

You could, in theory, ask every potential consumer how many pairs of jeans they might buy in a given time period. In reality it would be impossible, and even if it were possible, by the time you had gathered in all your responses, so many other things would have changed that you could not be sure that all consumers were responding to the same set of constant other factors.

Equilibrium analysis doesn't do this. Assume that you could ask all consumers at the same time and that as you ask all consumers, all other influences on the demand for jeans will stay the same! Then add up all the responses and you have the market demand curve. Well, Table 2.1 saves you the bother—and you can imagine that the research has been done for you.

Table 2.1 Price and demand sample data

Price (£ per pair)	Demand (000s per month)
20	80
25	70
30	60
35	50
40	40
45	30
50	20
55	10

We could illustrate this data diagrammatically. Since we are seeking to look at the effect on demand of a change in price we plot demand on the horizontal axis and price on the vertical one. What does this table or demand schedule show us? Simply that, other things being equal, if prices are low, then the demand for jeans will be high and that if prices are high, the demand for jeans will be low. Now, of course the figures are hypothetical, but wouldn't this at the very least be a good hunch as to what would happen? Economists do often have to proceed like this. They want to investigate economic behaviour. They make a guess what would be most likely to happen and make assumptions to isolate the dependent variables, and then theorize what might happen. If possible, they can then test this theory. You could do so if you want. Take a sample of people entering all jeans shops and ask them the question above. While your figures would be mere estimates, you would come up with the same trend. If people say they will buy a certain amount at a relatively high price, they will say that they are going to buy more when prices are lower. They would be odd indeed if they rushed out and bought fewer pairs if prices were to be less, assuming that all the other influences on demand were the same.

Demand curves

The information in the demand schedule above can be plotted on a graph. Figure 2.3 shows this. The demand curve is downward sloping from left to right.

If the original price were £50, the demand would be 20,000 per month. If the price fell to £20, then the demand would *increase from 20,000 to 80,000.*

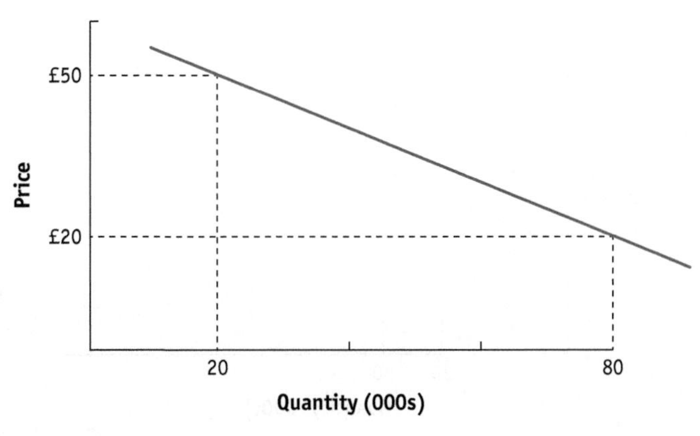

Figure 2.3 The demand curve

Table 2.2 Price and supply sample data

Price	Supply (000s of pairs per month)
20	0
25	10
30	20
35	30
40	40
45	50
50	60
55	70

Supply and price

Just as with demand, it is likely that a significant variable will be the price that the firm can get for its jeans. Other things being equal, and here an important other is the firm's costs, if price rises, this will mean two things:

1. The reason that price is rising is because demand is rising.
2. Rising prices should mean rising profits if more are produced.

The hypothesis is that supply will rise when price rises. On the other hand, what if price falls? Here you need to be cautious. A common response is to believe that a business might here try to increase sales to protect revenue.

However, consider this. The reason that price is falling is because consumers are deserting the product. Falling prices mean that profit margins are squeezed. Increasing supply would only make the situation worse!

Let us assume that you have done the other half of your market research. You ask the producer what they would supply at the following prices, other things remaining the same, and the information is displayed in Table 2.2.

Plotting the data given in Table 2.2 will produce Figure 2.4.

We are now in a position to put the two halves of the market together and analyse market movements. Demand and supply analysis is a very powerful economic technique for making sense of economic changes.

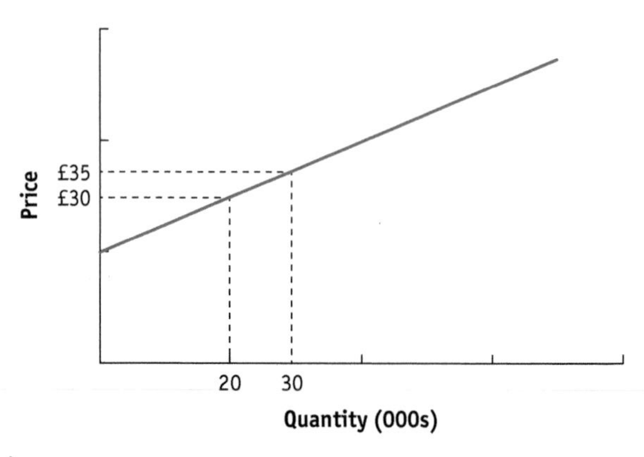

Figure 2.4 The supply curve

Table 2.3 Price, demand, and supply sample data

Price (£ per pair)	Demand (000s per month)	Supply (000s per month)
20	80	0
25	70	10
30	60	20
35	50	30
40	40	40
45	30	50
50	20	60
55	10	70

Let us return to the original demand and supply schedules. Table 2.3 combines the demand and supply functions.

We have plotted the separate halves of the market. Now let us put them together as in Figure 2.5.

Remember, the demand curve shows us what consumers will buy at various prices per month. It shows us their preferences, not what they actually buy.

The supply curve shows how many producers will produce per month at various prices. It doesn't tell us what they actually produce.

How then do the suppliers know what to do to match consumer preferences? In reality, they do not have the information as displayed above. They never ring us up at home to ask us what we are going to do!

In order to understand how the invisible hand of Adam Smith works the formal framework of demand and supply was developed in the late nineteenth century.

Imagine that the following happens.

Surplus in the market

The producers take a risk and initially decide to produce 60,000 pairs of jeans. In order for them to maximize their profits they want a price of £50 so this is what they charge. However, at that price how many will consumers buy per month?

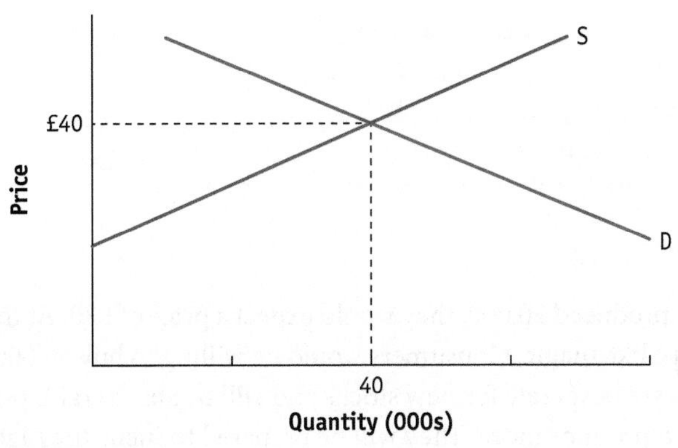

Figure 2.5 The equilibrium position

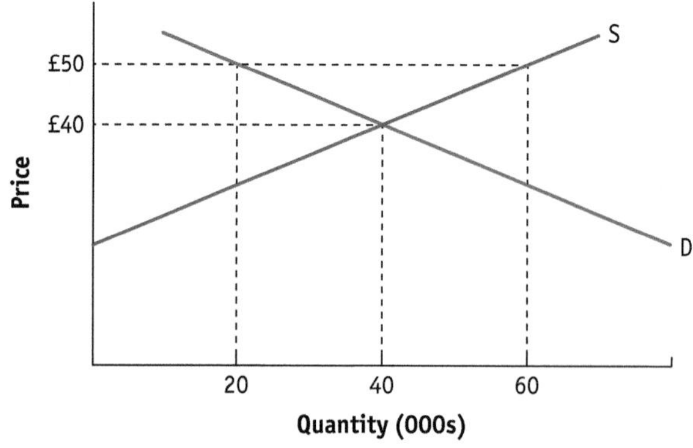

Figure 2.6 Market forces—dealing with a surplus

At a price of £50, consumers want 20,000. In Figure 2.6 we can see that there is a surplus of 40,000 being offered for sale every month.

Producers don't need to ask consumers what is going on. The surplus is immediately registered. To get rid of this surplus, retailers will have to lower prices and will be unwilling to give the same price as before to the manufacturers. Thus, the price begins to fall on the market. This signals to producers to produce less. If prices fall profits are squeezed and so firms cut back on production. They are hardly going to increase production given the fact that consumers are saying they will not buy so much. Producing such quantities will probably entail high costs per unit. If prices are falling, producers will have to reduce output to cut costs.

Now of course the producers will not immediately produce the right amount next time. Even if they cut production to 50,000 and charge a price of £45 they still are faced with a surplus production relative to the demand if prices are £45.

As long as there is a surplus, pressures will lead to falling prices. As prices fall, suppliers progressively cut back on production and consumers will be prepared to start buying more per month. Eventually, in theory prices will fall to £40. At £40 consumers are willing and able to purchase 40,000 and producers are willing to supply 40,000 as long as they get £40. In this position both consumers and producers are happy. Economists say the market is in equilibrium.

Stop and Think

Before reading on, try to answer the following:

What would happen if producers initially produced too little? For instance, say they initially produce only 20,000 at a price of £30.

What would be the imbalance in the market?

What effect do you think this would have on price?

How would this affect suppliers and why?

How will the market rectify this imbalance?

Shortages in the market

If producers initially produced 20,000, they would expect a price of £30. At this price the goods vanish from the shops like magic. Consumers would be willing to buy 60,000 at that price (see Figure 2.7). Retailers are desperate for new stocks and will be able to raise prices. Rising prices signal to producers to produce more. They will be prepared to incur the higher costs involved because of the higher prices.

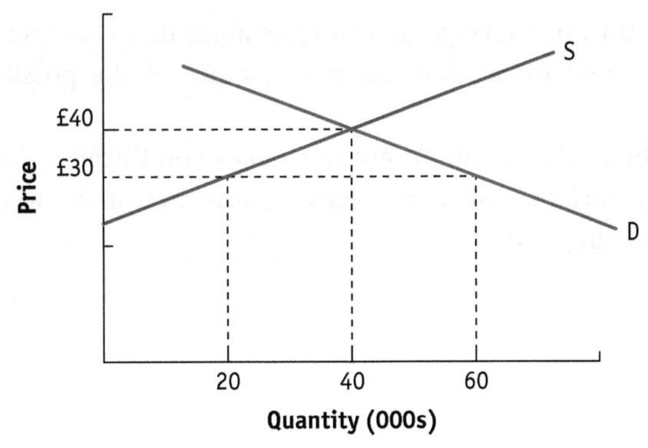

Figure 2.7 Market forces—dealing with a shortage

INTERNAL/EXTERNAL Any shortages of goods will result in prices rising and this process will continue until the decisions of producers are in accord with the wishes of consumers, i.e. at the equilibrium point.

Analysing market changes: the significance of equilibrium

Remember that while this theoretical adjustment process is taking place step by step we are assuming that all other things remain constant for both demand and supply. Given the original demand and supply preferences of the market, as long as nothing changes to alter this then equilibrium will be reached. This is a theoretical possibility. The market will have cleared.

In the real world, markets never reach this equilibrium as things are always changing. It is akin to the artist trying to paint the beautifully still millpond. Unfortunately, fish keep jumping and little children keep lobbing in stones. The artist knows that if he waits long enough the millpond will be still, but it never quite gets there. The artist gives up and then paints from his imagination, and no one is the wiser.

Economists do the same. By assuming that a particular market is in equilibrium, we can then use this possibility to predict the likely effect of dropping stones into the market. This enables us to predict the effect of any change in market conditions. In the real world it is difficult to unravel the effects of one change in isolation, as lots of things are changing. Equilibrium analysis allows us to do this. Use of this technique can provide you with an invaluable aid to making decisions. All too often decisions are made on the basis of insufficient attention to the many factors that could affect the outcome of the decision. Equilibrium analysis can help you avoid this.

Equilibrium analysis explained

Demand and supply curves show what happens to demand and supply if price changes. Whenever a market is in equilibrium, the only reason for the price to change is if something changes to alter either the demand or supply curves. If this happens, then one or other of the curves will shift and we will move towards a new equilibrium. The demand and supply functions show us all the possible causes of these shifts. Using the concept of equilibrium enables you to isolate any possible market change and predict what its effect would be if it alone were to change. It is a powerful tool if used correctly.

Proceeding like this, one change at a time, enables us to analyse the effect of individual changes and then build up a more complex picture of the possible combined effects of these changes.

The guidelines box below is important as it takes you through the steps that you need to follow to apply equilibrium analysis correctly. Follow these and you have at your fingertips a most powerful marketing tool!

Equilibrium analysis—guidelines for use

Imagine that you want to predict the effect of a change in any market, anywhere, any time.

- Assume that market is initially in equilibrium.
- Introduce the change. The key thing to decide is if it is a change on the demand side or the supply side.
- If it is a change in one of the determinants of demand, then the demand curve will shift, and we move along the supply curve.
- Will it increase (and shift the demand curve outwards) or decrease (and shift it inwards)?
- If it is a change in one of the determinants of supply, then the supply curve will shift, and we move along the demand curve.
- Will it increase (and shift upwards) or decrease (and shift downwards)?
- What will now happen to the price and how will the market readjust?
- Compare the new equilibrium to the old. What has been the effect of the change? Will this change now reverberate and affect other markets?

INTERACTION **COMPLEXITY** The use of equilibrium analysis can enable you to investigate the likely changes in the external economic environment on any business—see Mini-Case 2.3.

Mini-Case 2.3 The global smart phone market

Global sales of smart phones have been slowing down to single digit figures in recent years, but in 2016 worldwide sales still exceeded 1 billion. Growth is sluggish in developed countries but there is much higher growth in the emerging markets of South East Asia and Africa. The top two global companies are Samsung and Apple, but the fastest growing producers are now the Chinese companies, Huawei, Oppo, and Vivo who tend to sell less sophisticated brands in terms of the range and specification of features but are still styled to match the appearance of the more sophisticated brands.

In 2016, Samsung suffered a severe reversal of its profits as it had to recall its Note 7 handset because of problems with its battery catching fire. In the third quarter of 2016 the share of the global market between the leading companies was:

Samsung 21.8%

Apple 12.5%

Huawei 9.3%

Oppo 7.1%

Vivo 5.1%

However, in terms of the overall global profit, Apple's share was 91 per cent: $8.5 billion out of total profits of $9.3 billion. The iPhone remains one of the most popular brands in the world, which allows Apple to charge a premium price for its phones greatly exceeding the cost of manufacture, thus enabling the company to increase profits even in areas where sales growth is slow.

Sources: Sui (2016), International Data Corporation (2016)

Questions

1. **Use equilibrium analysis to illustrate the differences between the demand and supply conditions in developed and developing countries that might explain the different growth patterns of smart phones.**
2. **What effect would the problems faced by Samsung have had on the demand for iPhones? Use a diagram to illustrate.**
3. **What are the differences in the determinants of demand and supply for Apple phones and those of the Chinese companies?**
4. **How might these differences explain the different market positions and strategies pursued by these companies?**

Market power

In the neoclassical view of the economy it is market power that drives the economy and no one producer can have more than another if there is competition—but is this always the case?

So far, we have developed a model that will enable us to predict with confidence the effect of any individual change in any market on the price and output of the firm in question.

However, what we cannot yet say is whether the change is a significant one for the business. When measuring the extent of these changes we must define 'lot' or 'little' to get a sense of proportion. Thus when measuring the extent of the changes in the market we use percentages. Price elasticity is the measure we use to assess the extent of market changes.

Going back to our market model, if there is a given shift in the supply curve the impact of this on price and output will depend on the slope of the demand curve. Study the small shift in supply in Figures 2.8 and 2.9; both are drawn to the same scale.

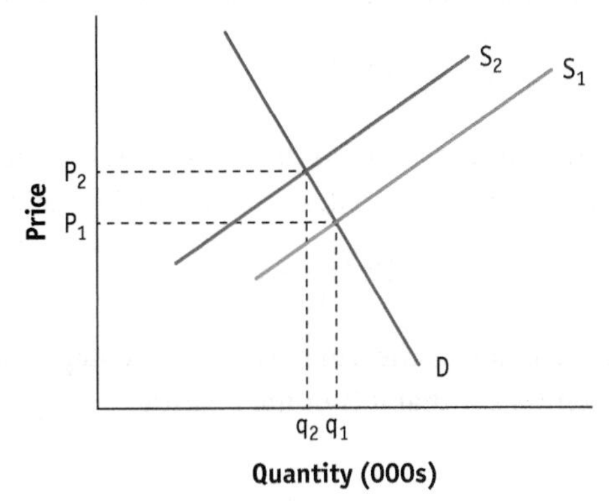

Figure 2.8 Shift in supply with a relatively inelastic demand curve

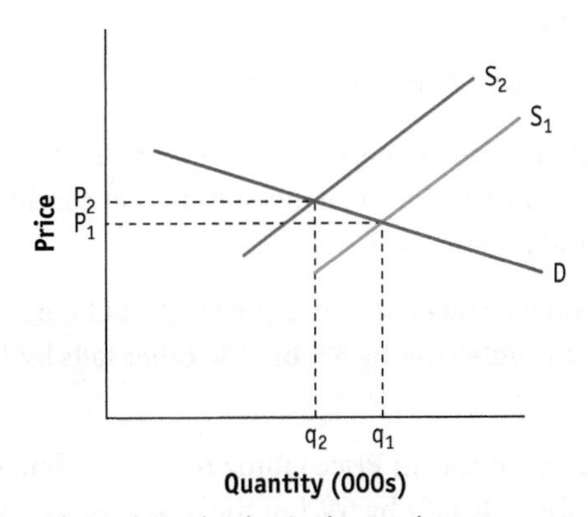

Figure 2.9 Shift in supply with a relatively elastic demand curve

In Figure 2.8 there is a relatively large rise in price but a relatively small fall in demand, as a result of the shift in supply from S1 to S2. The same shift in Figure 2.9 produces the same change in direction of price and quantity, but here there is relatively small rise in price and a relatively large fall in demand.

> *Stop and Think*
>
> If you were a manager of a company in these markets, which market would you prefer to be operating in if, for example, there was a rise in costs?

The reason for the different outcomes of the same market change in the above is because there is a different elasticity of demand in each case. Elasticity of demand measures the responsiveness of demand to changes in price. Does demand stretch by a relatively large amount or a little?

To calculate the elasticity of demand the following formula is used

$$\frac{\text{Percentage change in the quantity demanded}}{\text{Percentage change in price}}$$

For example, if price changes by 1 per cent does demand change by more than 1 per cent, less than 1 per cent, or is there a 0 per cent change? The possibilities can be summarized as follows.

The three degrees of price elasticity of demand

If the percentage change in demand is greater than the percentage change in price, i.e. price elasticity of demand (Ped) is greater than 1, then we say that it is relatively elastic:

$$\text{Ped} => -1$$

If the percentage change in demand is less than the percentage change in price, i.e. price elasticity of demand is less than 1, then we say that it is relatively inelastic:

$$\text{Ped} =< -1$$

If the percentage change in demand is the same as the percentage change in price, i.e. price elasticity of demand is 1, then we say that it is unitary elastic:

$$\text{Ped} = -1$$

NB: the sign is −1 because of the inverse relationship between price and demand. The revenue of a firm is calculated as follows:

$$\text{Revenue} = \text{Price} \times \text{units sold}$$

Let us see why the elasticity of demand facing a product is very important and will have a great effect on determining the effect on revenue of changes in market conditions. Consider the following cases where the demand is *elastic*, e.g. −2

Imagine that a market change results in Price rising by 5% but demand falling by 10%. If one half of our revenue formula rises by 5% but the other falls by 10% then overall revenue will have fallen.

Imagine that a market change results in Price falling by 5% but demand rising by 10%. If one half of our revenue formula falls by 5% but the other rises by 10% then overall revenue will have risen.

Table 2.4 Relationship of price elasticity of demand to revenue

Price	Elasticity	Revenue
rises	elastic	falls
rises	inelastic	rises
falls	elastic	rises
falls	inelastic	falls

In both these cases the demand is elastic but when price rises revenue falls and when price falls revenue rises. Consider the following cases where the demand is *inelastic*, e.g. −0.2

> Imagine that the price rises by 5% but demand falls by 1%—in this case revenue will rise.
> Imagine that price falls by 5% but demand rises by 1%—in this case revenue falls.

Of course, if elasticity of demand was unitary, then a small change in price would have no effect on revenue. Table 2.4 summarizes the effect of elasticity on revenue.

One of the main determinants on elasticity of demand is the number of substitutes available for the product or the degree of competition that the product faces. If a business is operating in a market in which there is little or no competition, then the elasticity of demand will be highly inelastic. If, on the other hand there is a high degree of competition, then the elasticity of demand will be relatively elastic. The degree of elasticity of demand is thus hugely important for businesses.

If markets are competitive, as is assumed by the neoclassical perspective, the behaviour of firms will be to try to cut prices and costs so as to increase revenue and profits. It is likely that this economic environment will encourage businesses to be allocatively and productively efficient. If the existing number of firms is too few and each one is making considerable profits, then providing that there are no barriers to entry other firms will enter the market and drive down prices. If resource markets are competitive, the same thing should happen with owners of resources receiving fair incomes and so equity should be achieved.

However, if markets are not competitive the reverse will happen. Businesses will seek to push prices up and restrict their outputs. In so doing they will earn more revenue and higher profits. They will not be so interested in cutting costs as they can simply raise prices. It is likely that profits will be excessive and so allocative and productive efficiency will not be attained even though the firm is highly profitable. There will be a clear conflict here between the goals of the firm and the wishes of the wider stakeholders. In resource markets owners of resources can exploit their monopoly power to raise their incomes leading to income inequality.

Therefore, a major characteristic of the economic environment is the degree to which it is a competitive environment and where it is not the government may have to play a role in ensuring that business does not exploit its potential monopoly power.

Stop and Think

How and in what ways might governments seek to curb the power of monopoly?

(See http://www.europarl.europa.eu/RegData/bibliotheque/briefing/2014/140779/LDM-BRI(2014)140779_REV1_EN.pdf)

Income elasticity of demand

While changes in prices can exert short-term changes on the profits of businesses, long-term effects can be felt depending on the way in which consumers in a market react to changes in incomes. In the long term, incomes in developing countries tend to rise. Income elasticity of demand measures the sensitivity of demand to changes in income. If as income rises demand rises by a greater percentage, then the income elasticity of demand is elastic. If it rises, but by a lower percentage, then the income elasticity of demand is inelastic.

Another influence on firms, apart from the nature of the competitive environment which they are in, is the nature of the product that they produce. We can distinguish between three main types of business activity:

Primary: mining, fuel extraction, farming, forestry

Secondary: manufacturing

Services: retailing, marketing, finance, travel

In general, as economies grow, the proportion of income spent on primary incomes tends to decrease and that spent on manufacturing and especially services tends to increase. This can make life difficult for primary producers unless they can find ways of increasing market power through restricting competition. In the case of farming it is very difficult for agricultural suppliers to gain market control, and across the globe agriculture is recognized as a sector that needs government support.

When do markets not work? Market failures and the case for government intervention

If markets are competitive then the invisible hand as conceived by Adam Smith will be sufficient to bring about economic efficiency. For many businesses it should be markets alone that determine the external economic environment, and their role is to be left free to determine their strategic response to the market environment.

However, even within the neoclassical view of the world a simple blind faith in markets being the key to economic efficiency needs to be treated with caution, as there are a range of **market failures** that can occur which require government intervention. Structuralists or institutional economists argue that in fact these can be extensive and that for successful economies it is imperative that due attention is paid to how markets can either be reformed, replaced, or supported in other ways through institutional reform. Marxists and socialists will always seek to train the spotlight on examples of abuse of market power in relation to employees; consumers and greens will seek to hold business to account on their environmental record.

Allocation

Merit goods: these are goods that you might argue all people should have irrespective of their income. There is a consensus in the modern world that all people should have shelter, heating, clean water, adequate nutrition, law and order, education, and health. If we leave such things to the market many people may be priced out of the markets for these goods. Thus, it is argued that the state should ensure that everyone has some basic access to these. We will explore in Chapter 10 the global commitment made in 2015 for all countries across the world to achieve the Sustainable Development Goals by 2030.

Public goods: some goods cannot be supplied via markets because it is impossible to provide one person with them while excluding others, e.g. street lighting, defence, fire services. Here, if people were allowed to opt out of paying, then they would still benefit from those who did pay; and it would be unfair if this was so or, indeed, may endanger anyone wanting to pay.

Adam Smith was aware that some vital areas of economic activity required large amounts of long-term investment that might be out of the reach of private businesses in terms of the capital required, or in which businesses would be unwilling to invest given the prospect of profits not being achieved in the foreseeable future. Such public works programmes would need to be provided through the government. In recent years there have indeed been growing calls for more spending on infrastructure projects as a way of boosting economic growth.

Externalities: market prices reflect the individual cost to the business and the benefit gained from the product. However, many economic activities have social benefits above the benefit to the user, e.g. in the case of health and education. A healthy and educated population benefits society as a whole, as healthy and educated people are more productive workers and demand less spending by the state. On the other hand, many activities have social costs beyond the user or producer, e.g. cigarettes and cars. Since the Rio Earth Summit of 1992 increasing attention has been paid globally to the concept of sustainable development, which we explore in Chapter 8.

Stop and Think

If merit and public goods are to be provided, what institutional reforms will governments need to make?

How might governments ensure that wider social benefits are provided? Can you give examples of commodities that provide these?

How might social costs such as pollution be curbed?

Production

INTERNAL/EXTERNAL There are a range of possible problems that can occur in production in a market system.

Degrees of competition

We have explored the danger of monopoly power. If markets are dominated by firms with a high degree of monopoly power, there will be a real possibility of exploitation of the consumer, suppliers, and employees as well as a wasteful or environmentally damaging use of resources as firms seek to minimize direct costs. At the very least, there is a general acceptance of the need for governments to take responsibility for ensuring that competition is free and fair and to take action against the abuse of monopoly power. This means that all countries need to have rigorous competition and anti-monopoly policies.

LOCAL TO GLOBAL However, as we shall see in Chapters 10 and 13, the move to greater economic cooperation at the regional and global levels means that the focus of this regulation needs to be at the appropriate spatial level.

Natural monopoly

Often such monopoly power is attained by using unfair anti-competitive practices but sometimes there are industries in which the most efficient scale of organization would be to have just one or a few large companies. These industries are referred to as natural monopolies and have the characteristic of involving such high initial outlays of capital expenditure that it makes sense for only big companies to operate in the industry so as to fully exploit the potential economies of scale. Examples of such industries would be: power generation; rail and road infrastructure supply; and water and sewer provision. There are a range of other companies where research and development costs might be very large and where the only way of recouping these outlays is if the eventual successfully tested products can be sold without competition.

Destructive competition

INTERACTION Competition can sometimes be highly damaging, e.g. if it leads to diminishing safety standards, and this is referred to as destructive competition. In the airline industry for example, it is vital that health and safety standards are upheld, and this requires both national and global air safety bodies to monitor adherence to these standards.

Microeconomic instability

Individual markets can be very unstable and create uncertainty. As we have seen, one source of this lies in the nature of the way market demand changes as a result of price changes and this is particularly problematic in primary commodity markets.

Stop and Think

We have seen that the price elasticity of demand for primary commodities is relatively inelastic. Why then does this explain why prices are likely to fluctuate to a large extent as a result of shifts in supply?

Why and in what ways do so many governments seek to intervene in agricultural markets?

Distribution

VALUES Perhaps the greatest problem of all in market systems is that, if left alone, they tend to lead to great inequalities of income and wealth. The reasons for this are hotly contested. For those with a belief in the innate capacity of markets to bring about prosperity this is the result of the natural distribution of skills and ability in the population. It is inevitable that rewards will be heavily skewed, with some people gaining vast incomes as a result of their exceptional skills and ability to have correctly anticipated risks and uncertainty. While the argument for provision of merit and public goods is accepted, this world view insists that such social provision must be kept to a minimum to avoid the need for high taxes which will undermine the incentives for risk taking and enterprise.

However, these inequalities may not reflect the rewards earned by people in their productive capacity but may reflect self-perpetuating social inequalities and barriers. As we have seen, Marxists and socialists root this in a class system which gives the power of distribution decisions to the owners of capital. Institutionalists or structuralists argue that poor people may lack access to the basic education and health provision so vital to progressing up the ladder of economic achievement, and will argue for the need for social safety nets to protect the most poor and vulnerable. Within labour markets critics of so-called free markets point to the possibility of discrimination on the basis of gender or ethnicity and the fact that wages might indeed be too low to enable workers to enjoy what might be seen as an 'acceptable' standard of living. Attention is also directed at the need for effective health and safety provision for workforces and the need to regulate the security of employment and amount of hours that workers are required to work.

For critics of market capitalism inequality distorts the whole basis of the economic system. The economic problem becomes circular with the demands of the rich determining what should be produced. A free market system will then reinforce inequality and make it difficult for the less advantaged to either get what they need or make their way in society. We return to these debates in Chapter 12.

Macroeconomic instability

Macroeconomics is the study of markets at the aggregate level and fluctuations in economic activity mean that the processes of economic growth are far from smooth in the way that Smith assumed. We have seen that during the nineteenth century while the long-run growth of the emerging capitalist economies was indeed spectacular, there were periodic booms and slumps. It was in the early twentieth century that it appeared that this macroeconomic instability might be the death knell of the march of free market capitalism. In the interwar period 1919–39, national and global economics in the US and Western Europe were dominated by financial crisis and economies mired in recession. This was all the more marked because, as we will see in Chapter 10, against all expectation Russia had raised the red flag of socialism in 1917 and was attempting to build a new society based on the principles of Marxism-Leninism which directly sought to redistribute income and wealth to peasants and workers. It was in this context that the British economist John Maynard Keynes argued for a 'middle way' between Marxism and neoclassical theories. Keynes argued in his most famous work that there will be occasions when economies can fail at the macroeconomic level to ensure that there are sufficient levels of demand to produce full employment of all the available resources in an economy and that in these cases it was necessary for the government to intervene in the economy. The precise way in which this can be done will be explored in more detail in Chapter 9.

Competing perspectives—social reform and socialism

The history of the twentieth century can be seen as the gradual and, in some cases, painful development of modern political and economic systems with each country working out its own specific ways of combining the state and the market economy. In 1917 the Russian Revolution brought about an attempt to dramatically re-shape the business environment by developing the Soviet model of state planning and what was to become known as 'real existing socialism'. After 1945 many other countries most notably in Eastern Europe, South East Asia, parts of Africa, and of course Cuba and China were to attempt to build socialist economies. In Western Europe and the US capitalism thrived but not as an unregulated free market. This involved a much greater role for the state in providing welfare systems, supporting industry, and overseeing the macroeconomic environment. In Britain this has been called the 'Keynesian welfare consensus' and in Western Europe, the 'social market'. There was a widespread acceptance of the need for governments to intervene both at the macro- and microeconomic levels as well as directly taking responsibility for social transformation in the fields of education, health, and social security. Indeed, particularly in Europe, many key industries were taken into state ownership. For many commentators, the period between 1945 and the mid 1970s in the first world was the 'Golden Era', with an unprecedented period of economic growth. There was a general rise in prosperity, and the big gains in productivity brought about by the increase in mass production techniques and constant technological improvement meant that there were reductions in the prices of household goods. This, coupled with rising wages, meant that people could fill their houses with a range of consumer goods. Three countries performed spectacularly well during this period, namely the two losers of the Second World War, Japan and Germany, and of course the US. In the case of Japan, the key was in the way it had based its development on new technologies as well as changing the nature of the production process itself. In the case of Germany, it was argued that its tripartite partnership of government, business, and trade unions coupled with the strength of its manufacturing *Mittelstand* (small and medium-sized enterprises) was at the heart of its *Wirtschaftswunder* (economic miracle).

In the newly emerging 'postcolonial' countries which gained their independence after 1945 there was an explicit recognition that their development paths needed to be different to the 'first world' paths of the US and Western Europe and the 'second world' paths of the USSR and other socialist countries, Their optimistic belief was the state and markets would work together to deliver a distinctive 'third world' approach to development which emphasized the need to put the needs of the poor first.

These highly modified forms of capitalism at the national level were mirrored at the global level with the establishment of the three key institutions of the World Bank, the International Monetary Fund (IMF), and the General Agreement on Trade and Tariffs. We will explore the development of the global economy and different approaches to economic development in Chapter 10.

However, the optimism of the 1950s and 1960s was knocked by the severe economic crisis that many countries across the world experienced in the 1970s. In the developed countries the type of balances that had been struck between the state in intervening in the economy and the market appeared now not to be working. Increasingly, unemployment levels began to rise, and growth slowed down while many economies also began to experience a rapid rise in inflation rates. Keynesian analysis could not explain how economies could experience both inflation and unemployment at the same time. In addition, the oil price rises of the 1970s imposed great strains on these economies. This sudden and unexpected rise in oil prices was a result of oil producers' willingness, especially in the Middle East, to exert their political and economic power. This brought into stark view the degree to which oil underpins the technologies that create the economic prosperity of the developed world.

Across the range of developed economies government budgets were under severe strain. In the communist world, especially the Soviet Union and Eastern Europe, it was increasingly recognized that the systems were suffering from economic stagnation and that a policy change was needed. In the developing countries, against a backdrop of spiralling debt problems (especially in Latin America) and falls in living standards in Africa, it appeared that their attempts to adopt a different model of development had failed.

This period at the end of the 1970s and into the 1980s saw a change in ideas about the policies that should be adopted across the world at national level, and in the thinking that took place at the supranational level. The right wing of the political spectrum and the neoclassical school of economic thought believed the lesson that needed to be learned was that there is no substitute for the free market at both the national and global level.

It was felt that the role of government had simply become too large and wherever you looked it was this that could explain the economic slowdown across the world. In the developed world excessive spending on welfare benefits had encouraged a 'dependency culture' and the high taxes to provide for such spending was undermining the incentives needed to create an 'entrepreneurial culture'. Too much economic activity had been taken out of the market and, where industries had been nationalized, they now needed to be returned to the private sector through privatization. Excessive government regulations, especially in financial markets, needed to be removed to enable credit to flow more readily both within and between countries. Finally, it was felt that the desire to reduce inequalities in society had resulted in too many social protection measures for workers and, coupled with the rise of organized labour's power, too much of the wealth was going to workers and not enough was being retained as profits.

In this analysis the best way to create an ideal business environment was to go back to the basic economic principles based on free markets. In the US this approach to economic policy was called Reaganomics after the then President Ronald Reagan and, in the UK, Thatcherism after Prime Minister Margaret Thatcher. In many Western European countries too, especially West Germany, there was a move towards more emphasis on the market although there was a view that this should be done with a little more caution than in the Anglo-American vision of the new capitalist model. Meanwhile countries such as Sweden, Denmark, and Norway, which had developed a particular Nordic model of capitalism, were less willing to dismantle their social democratic structures.

However, not all parts of the three worlds were suffering this slowdown. It was clear many of the countries in South East Asia were industrializing very rapidly. These so-called 'Asian Tigers' (e.g. Hong Kong, Taiwan, Singapore, South Korea, and Thailand) were experiencing very rapid growth, and at the same time were exporting a range of manufactured and high technology goods. The lesson appeared obvious from these regions that the path to growth lay down the route of globalization and that this meant rapid trade liberalization. A recent convert to this economic policy was China with a move to 'an open door' policy in the late 1970s.

The adoption of new economic policies based on the liberalization of markets in the developed world spread to the developing world, especially in Latin America and India. In the late 1980s the collapse of the Soviet Union and rapid changes in Eastern Europe saw these countries eager to effect a transition from state planning to market liberalization. These new free market-based economic policies came to be called the 'Washington Consensus'. Here enterprise, competition, free trade, and technological change are key.

By the end of the 1980s people began to talk about the triumph of the market and express the view that all economic success could be reduced to the set of universal economic principles known as 'the Washington Consensus'. At first this restoration of a more market-oriented environment caused economic turmoil but as the 1980s gave way to the 1990s economic growth rates began to pick up in the developed world and, increasingly, in some of the countries of the former Soviet bloc. Coupled with the success of East Asian economies and other developing countries, the world business environment appeared in robust health. Of course, the developing country that was now leading the way was China, but while purporting to be communist it was using unashamedly capitalist methods to open up its economy. China was not alone and in 2001 Jim O'Neill of Goldman Sachs (a major global merchant bank) developed the term 'the BRICS' to highlight the success of Brazil, Russia, India, China, and South Africa.

However, there was one looming problem that began to emerge. It was not only the constant issue of inequality that market reforms seem to lead to, but the sheer rate of the widening of this inequality and the very high incomes being earned by people at the top of global corporations as well as in the increasingly global financial markets. There was reluctance by governments to interfere in these areas. After all, the success of these global companies and the financial sector was fuelling the steady growth rates experienced across the developed world. In particular, the economies of the UK and US were heavily reliant on their financial sectors. Not only were 'the City' and 'Wall Street' responsible for bringing in large amounts of export earnings as they served as the financial centres of the global economy, they provided governments with large taxation revenues from their profits and salaries. Businesses and consumers also benefited as the seemingly never-ending rise of the financial sector allowed large increases in credit which in turn fuelled growth.

However, the experiment in the restoration of free market policies itself has recently come under attack from structuralist and Marxist/socialist critics. The actual experience of implementing these policies appeared not to be so simple. The credit crunch of 2008 and the onset of the second biggest global economic crisis since the Great Depression has called for yet another reappraisal of how we can best create that elusive environment which will ensure growth and prosperity.

The world economic problems caused by the banking crisis have led to a reassessment of the need for greater government involvement, both at the national and global levels, to regulate the banking sector and provide cooperation to ensure a stable global economic environment.

Looking ahead

There now exists a substantial body of research on the conditions needed to produce successful economies. Acemoglu (2012) seeks to review this literature and evaluate the evidence. For Acemoglu, it is not simply markets or entrepreneurs that are the key to innovation and growth but what is crucial is that governments help create the correct mix of institutions that can direct entrepreneurs' energies towards seeking gain from innovation and then developing the markets to realize that gain. He distinguishes between 'inclusive institutions' such as secure property rights, low barriers to entry to ensure competition, equal opportunities, efficient public services and infrastructure, and the existence of democratic states which can maintain effective law and order and 'extractive institutions' which will distort growth. We will explore this further in Chapters 3 and 10.

It is better not to talk of capitalism as such but as a variety of capitalisms across the world, linked together through trade, and with various attempts to regulate this trading system both nationally and internationally. Nationally, capitalism differs from country to country with each system trying to manage the mix between market and state in its own way.

The global economic crisis that began in 2008 has created an ongoing debate about the future of capitalism. This has intensified the debates between those who instinctively feel that the clues to economic success lie in less, not more, state regulation and those who argue that, far from governments being inimical to the creation of a favourable economic environment, they are instrumental in achieving it.

Summary

- The economic environment is created by the existence of scarcity. The study of business from an economic standpoint is the study of the role that businesses play in efficiently resolving the economic problems of allocation, production, and distribution.
- There are a range of competing perspectives as to the best type of economic system to encourage businesses to be economically efficient.
- Markets play a significant role in setting the economic environment of business in modern economies and all economies are involved in trying to better develop these market systems.
- It is clear that markets can often fail both at the microeconomic and macroeconomic levels. So, any examination of the economic environment must involve a close examination of the role of government in correcting these problems.

Case Study: The global financial system: efficient markets or a fatally flawed system?

The financial services sector occupies a vital intermediary position in the business environment. The functions of financial institutions are fourfold:

- they act as a way of channelling the individual savings of businesses and/or households to enable them to pay for the things that they need;
- they match the needs of borrowers and lenders;
- they enable the management of funds across individual lifetimes and across generations; and
- they insure against risk.

In theory, the role of financial markets is to provide a service ensuring the efficient allocation of resources to enable both businesses and individuals to prosper. In practice, however, there can be a conflict of interest between the retailing function of banks and their ability to use assets deposited with them to engage in more speculative activities in the wholesale or investment banking sector to make profits for themselves. At the heart of the banking sector lies the need for savers and depositors to have confidence in their ability to withdraw their money should they wish to do so. Banks have the ability to issue credit based on their initial deposits to many times the value of the original deposits. There is nothing wrong in their doing this, as, on a day-to-day basis, only a fraction of the deposits they receive will ever be withdrawn, and their ability to issue credit is vital if modern economies are to function. However, the potential risk of a loss of confidence in a bank, and an ensuing rush on that bank causing a more general banking crisis, as occurred to such devastating effect in the interwar period of the twentieth century in the US and Western Europe, has meant that countries have developed a whole host of rules and regulations, as well as state intervention in the form of strong central banks that can act as 'lenders of last resort' to prevent banking collapses. In the US, a key regulation was the Glass–Steagall legislation that was brought into force in 1933 and which sought to prevent one bank performing both commercial and investment bank functions.

After 1945, as the global economy has expanded, this need for regulation led to the development of global financial institutions, such as the IMF, to coordinate international financial flows.

During the 1970s and 1980s, it was felt that these regulations had become far too constrictive and driven by the rise of neoliberalism in the developed world it was argued that if the financial system was to flourish then many of them needed to be relaxed. For many critics this was now the era of **financialization** whereby the overwhelming majority of trades in the system are no longer to service the needs of the real economy but are simply to generate profits for the sector itself through extensive speculation. The two key areas of exponential growth were initially the trade of securities, which are loans that can be made based on claims on earnings, income, capital, and profits as well as in foreign exchange markets. However, what came to prove highly problematic for the stability of the system itself and then the wider economy as a whole was the growth in the trade of derivatives which often are bundles of different types of securities associated with different levels of risk.

It was argued that the increase in financialization allowed much more credit and many more loans to flow, releasing the funds vital for investment and allowing banks to both compete globally and fuel economic expansion. It was further argued that with the explosion in the amount of financial information available as a result of rapid innovation in information technologies, prices of financial assets would also reflect underlying values in the market and that financial markets would operate efficiently with minimum regulation.

In 2008, the world economic environment was thrown into turmoil by the crisis that first started in the banking sectors of the US and UK as a result of a growing realization that many loans that had been made were not going to be paid back. It became clear that the root cause of the credit crunch was that bankers, in their desire to earn ever higher annual bonuses, were doing all they could to make more and more trades and were not paying due care and attention to the risk of these loans not being repaid. This was part of a wider risk culture that involved individual brokers in a range of financial markets effectively gambling with the assets of their institutions in order to try to make speculative profits in the knowledge that if their institutions were to get into trouble, the government, in order to retain the stability of the economy, would have to step in and save them. In other words, 'banks were too big to fail'.

Alan Greenspan, who as the former US Federal Reserve Chairman had resisted calls for regulation in financial markets, admitted that he had 'found a flaw' in the free market ideology he had adhered to all his life. He explained, 'I made a mistake in presuming that the self-interests of organizations, specifically banks and others, were such that they were best capable of protecting their own shareholders and their equity in the firms' (Clark and Treanor 2008).

Across the globe, other banks found themselves embroiled in this general panic and they themselves were soon found to have been dealing in highly risky operations. The world financial system was thrown into turmoil and governments found themselves having to 'bail out' or, in other words, take direct or part ownership of many prestigious financial institutions. This global financial crisis meant that credit all but dried up, businesses found themselves suffering large reductions in demand for their goods, and the world was engulfed in recession. In the developed world average real incomes fell on average by 10 per cent and public sector debts rose by 35 per cent. In the developing world, the BRIC countries suffered the effects of falling exports that they had hitherto been targeting to countries in the developed world.

Structuralists/institutionalists have not been slow to expose what they see as the problem of too naive a belief in the ability of financial markets to be left free and Marxist economists like David Harvey (2011) argue that 'financial capital' acts as a mechanism to redistribute income and wealth from the public into the pockets of a tiny elite of private financiers. Joseph Stiglitz argues that it was this free market ideology that led to the 'freefall' of the global financial system from which we saw the deepest falls in economic activity across the developed world since the Wall Street Crash and ensuing depression of the 1930s (Stiglitz 2010).

John Kay argues that in the process the theoretical 'servants of the people' have indeed become the 'masters of the universe' as characterized by Tom Wolfe. For Kay, 'The industry mostly trades with itself, talks to itself and judges itself by reference to performance criteria it itself has generated' (Kay 2016: 5).

At the domestic level, in the US and EU, there has been huge short-term intervention to prevent the financial system from failing which has mostly meant providing the banking system with the funds needed to keep them in business, but even former regulators such as Adair Turner in the UK argue that reforms need to be deeper (Turner 2016). While there is a widespread recognition that more controls over the financial sector need to be considered, fault lines have appeared regarding both the extent of and the urgency with which these changes can be effected. In the US and the UK, the strength and influence of finance is strong and politicians are more reluctant to frame rules to constrain the power of banks.

Questions

1. **Why was it argued that the pursuit of individual remuneration by many people in the investment banking sector created the economic conditions that caused the global recession from 2008 onwards?**
2. **How might governments intervene in financial markets to make them more efficient?**

Review and discussion questions

1. What is meant by the economic problem and its three constituent parts? Why do we need to consider these three parts when assessing the efficiency of business behaviour?
2. How and why might the private goals of a business conflict with the threefold definition of efficiency as outlined in the chapter?
3. How will an economic recession generally impact on businesses, and which businesses will be likely to cope best in such difficult trading times?
4. (a) Identify the opportunity costs of the resources that will be used to enable you to pursue your studies.

   (b) What are the benefits of your studying?

   (c) Who should pay for giving you the opportunity of studying?
5. Why might businesses prefer to operate in markets where the demand is relatively price inelastic, and how can they seek to create such market conditions?
6. What do you feel are the essential legal, social, and political institutions needed to ensure that we minimize the problems markets can cause and maximize the benefits they can bring?

Assignments

1. Write an essay which addresses the following question: Critically examine the extent to which university students should be asked to pay full fees to cover all the tuition and associated living costs of undertaking an undergraduate programme. Is there a case for government support for students, and in what other ways might governments have a legitimate interest in shaping the business environment in which universities operate?
2. Write a report that analyses the causes of the financial crisis that started in 2007/8 and which evaluates the extent to which there is agreement that the financial policy reforms enacted in the US, EU, and UK are going to be successful in preventing a future financial crisis.

Further reading

Chang (2011) *a review of what the author sees as the fundamental myths of the neoliberal view of economics.*

Chang (2014) *an entertaining introduction to the importance of economics and which ends each chapter with a useful guide to (even) further reading.*

CORE (2017) *the CORE team consists of leading teachers of economics who through the CORE project have produced new learning materials for students of economics.*

Gillespie (2013) *an excellent textbook which introduces business students to how economics is used in business.*

Mulhearn and Vane (2015) *a clear and accessible introductory economics text which explicitly relates economics to the business context and is written by one of the authors of Chapter 9.*

Test your understanding of this chapter with online questions and answers, explore the subject further through web exercises, and use the weblinks to provide a quick resource for further research. Visit the online resources at www.oup.com/uk/wetherly_otter4e/

Useful websites

www.project-syndicate.org
Project Syndicate that hosts blogs from the world's leading academics and commentators. You can link here to specific economics and business sections.

www.bbc.co.uk/programmes/p00fvhj7
This is the BBC World Service World Business Report site that profiles the big issues that affect business and the environment.

www.ft.com
The website of the *Financial Times.*

www.mckinsey.com/insights
A website operated by McKinsey & Company, one of the world's leading management consultancy firms, which profiles leading themes and issues that affect global businesses.

www.wsj.com
The website of the *Wall Street Journal.*

References

Acemoglu, D. (2012) 'The world our grandchildren will inherit: the rights revolution and beyond', in Palacios-Huerta, I. (ed.), *Economic Possibilities for Our Grandchildren* (Cambridge, MA: MIT Press)

Clark, A. and Treanor, J. (2008) 'Greenspan: I was wrong about the economy. Sort of' (accessed 21 May 2013) **www.guardian.co.uk/business/2008/oct/24/economics-creditcrunch-federal-reserve-greenspan**

Harvey, D. (2011) *The Enigma of Capitalism and the Crises of Capitalism* (London: Profile)

International Data Corporation (2016) 'Smartphone vendor market share, 2016 Q3' (accessed 12 June 2017) **www.idc.com/promo/smartphone-market-share/vendor**

Kay, J. (2016) *Other People's Money: Masters of the Universe or Servants of the People?* (London: Profile)

Kemp-King, S. (2016) *The Graduate Premium—Manna, Myth or Plain Mis-selling* (London: The Intergenerational Foundation) (accessed June 2017) **www.if.org.uk/wp-content/uploads/2016/07/Graduate_Premium_final.compressed.pdf**

OECD (2016) *Education at a Glance 2016: OECD Indicators* (accessed 20 June 2017) **www.keepeek.com/Digital-Asset-Management/oecd/education/education-at-a-glance-2016_eag-2016-en#.WUeoDvnyvs0#page1**

Smith, A. (1976) [1776] *An Inquiry into the Nature and Causes of the Wealth of Nations* (Chicago: University of Chicago Press)

Stiglitz, J. (2010) *Freefall: America, Free Markets and the Sinking of the World Economy* (London: Penguin)

Sui, L. (2016) 'Strategy Analytics: Apple captures record 91% share of global smartphone profits', Strategy Analytics (accessed 12 June 2017) **www.strategyanalytics.com/strategy-analytics/news/strategy-analytics-press-releases/strategy-analytics-press-release/2016/11/22/strategy-analytics-apple-captures-record-91-percent-share-of-global-smartphone-profits-in-q3-2016#.WUfagdFwbs0**

Turner, A. (2016) *Between Debt and the Devil: Money, Credit and Fixing Global Finance* (New York, NJ: Princeton University Press)

Chapter 3
The technological environment

Dorron Otter

Learning objectives

When you have completed this chapter, you will be able to:

- Explain the meaning of technology and its impact on business.
- Examine the conditions that need to exist for the creation of an effective innovation environment.
- Critically evaluate the role of technology and its impact on business performance, as well its contribution to economic growth.

THEMES

The following themes of the book are especially relevant to this chapter

- INTERNAL/EXTERNAL The focus of this chapter is on the external environments that are conducive to the development and implementation of technological improvement, but we will also explore how this shapes business strategy.
- COMPLEXITY There is a range of political, economic, and social conditions that need to be present in the external environment if technological change is to be supported.
- LOCAL TO GLOBAL Globalization is rapidly combining with new technologies to transform the external business environment.
- DYNAMIC We live in a world where technological change is rapid, and no business can afford to stand still in the face of this change.
- VALUES Technology alters the business environment by providing new opportunities, however, while we are all fascinated by its potential, there are fears that there may also be harmful consequences.

Introduction

In this chapter we will explore the advantages of technological change, not only within individual businesses, but also in relation to its wider impact on the nature of economic growth and on society as a whole, as well as the competing views about both the nature of the technological environment and its impact. Neoclassical economists see the potential for technology to increase productivity, and see the central catalyst for change residing in markets both at the national and global levels. Structuralists argue that in order for an effective technological environment to be created, there needs to be corresponding help from the government in the form of direct state-sponsored research and development (R&D) or, at the very least, direct and indirect incentives and subsidies for private businesses. There is broad agreement that there needs to be rules and regulations to protect intellectual property rights, and that a range of supporting institutions need to be in place ranging from business advisory services to the provision of extensive education and training institutions. Structuralists are cautious about linking technological change to increases in aggregate levels of productivity, and argue that businesses may well be able to develop unfair competitive advantage from establishing technological leads and that technology might not bring about universal developments but may cause rising inequality, unemployment, or an increase in low-paid insecure employment. Marxist and radical critics argue that, ultimately, the aim of technological development in a capitalist economy with primarily private ownership is to increase profits for those at the top of business organizations.

What is technology?

Technology is the application of knowledge to production and this can happen in a variety of ways. **Invention** occurs when completely new ideas about products or ways of producing things arise. However, technological advances are fuelled by the process of innovation, which improves or enhances original inventions (**product innovation**) or develops production processes (**process innovation**) that enable the original inventions to be developed into more marketable and/or more profitable products and services. The technological environment can be seen as encompassing both the creation of new knowledge and its application to improve business efficiency and, in so doing, improve the standards of living and quality of life of us all. **INTERACTION** It is how this technology is used or applied that is important, and that fundamentally depends on the wider political, economic, and sociocultural environment and the way in which people within business seek to exploit its commercial potential.

While individuals can be the source of original inventions or innovations there is rarely a single 'lightbulb' moment of original inspiration. Often a long road is travelled before ideas or prototypes are converted into the finished commodity. The effort, work, and initiative of many other people are involved between the original spark of the inventor and the point when the final product emerges.

The World Wide Web is a good example of this. The Web has allowed the Internet to take off in relation to commercial uses. The basis for this explosion was developed out of the scientific work at the CERN particle lab which is aiming to discover the building blocks of matter. This involves cooperation of scientists across the globe, and in 1989 Tim Berners-Lee, a scientist at CERN, invented the World Wide Web as a means of enabling better communication between these science communities. The Web brings together the developing technologies of personal computers, their ability to be networked, and the new language of hypertext to produce an instant global information system (for more information, see http://info.cern.ch).

It is the way in which businesses and users have sought to use the Internet that has opened opportunities for its commercial exploitation. Without the Internet the world of information and communication technology (ICT) and the 'digital age' would not have been able to have expanded so exponentially. The Internet has had a major influence on shaping the process of globalization as communication across the world has been speeded up so rapidly.

Stop and Think

What were the conditions in the external environment that led to the development of the Internet?

The impact of technology on business and the implications for business strategy

LOCAL TO GLOBAL **INTERACTION** Michael Porter emphasizes the importance of technology in creating the competitive environment at the level of the individual firm. He also emphasizes the danger of seeing technology as a goal in itself. All too often it is easy to assume that any technological change is good and, further, that the more costly and sophisticated the investment in technology, the better it will be. However, technological change does not have to be so costly and complicated. Using the concept of the **value chain**, Porter (1985) shows how every activity of a business in combining inputs into outputs has the potential to use technology to alter the production process and add value. In practice, a firm is a collection of different technologies that can be applied, enhanced, or implemented across all the different activities of the business.

A value chain can be seen as consisting of the following functions and processes:

- *Horizontal* functions or support services of a business in terms of its basic infrastructure (finance, planning, information systems, office technology), human resources (training and development), technology development, and purchasing departments.
- *Vertical* or primary business operations in terms of inbound logistics (transport, handling, storage, information systems), production operations (process, materials, machines, packaging, design, and testing), outbound logistics, marketing and sales, and finally service.

These activities comprise the value chain and each operation involves the use of technology to combine inputs into outputs, so there is the opportunity for technological improvement across the range of activities to improve the profit margins of the business. One technology that occurs across the range of activities is that of ICT. The use of e-mail and other forms of communication devices such as Skype and videoconferencing facilities have enabled communication across all ranges of the business to be vastly improved, meaning that information can be rapidly shared and networks more easily established.

In relation to production, there is now the widespread use of computer-aided manufacturing to improve both the speed and quality of production. In many cases, this has resulted in computer-integrated manufacturing across the production chain, as in the case of the use of robotic technology in car manufacturing. Computer-aided design has radically altered the design process, and this has been given a further boost by the development of 3D design technologies.

Across retailing the development of electronic point of sales (EPOS) and EFTPOS (electronic funds transfer at point of sale) technologies has both reduced the running costs for businesses as well as improving the speed and quality of service. They also allow retail outlets to keep an accurate record of stock levels and indicate what consumers are buying, which in turn can then feed into customer relationship marketing (CRM) techniques such as the use of loyalty cards (See Mini-Case 3.1).

E-commerce (purchasing via a computer) and increasingly m-commerce (purchasing via a mobile device) are increasing at a rapid rate. China leads the world in terms of volume or B2C (business to customer) e-commerce retail sales with the US and then the UK in second and third places. In 2016 e-commerce accounted for 19 per cent of total business turnover in the UK and it had the highest proportion of Internet users in Europe (80 per cent) who engaged in online shopping (statista.com).

The increase in the use of the Internet to search for information and the use of social media has vastly increased the potential for businesses to mine this data to analyse customer

Mini-Case 3.1 The technological revolution of the food business

The modern food sector in the developed world is a complex value chain. At the 'downstream' end we have the primary food producers consisting of farmers, as well as those involved in fisheries, and to a lesser extent, hunting. These producers are supported by what has been termed 'agribusiness', an industry involved in providing essential inputs like machinery, seeds, fertilizers, and pesticides, as well as a range of 'extension services' such as veterinary services and agronomists. As food moves 'upstream' from farm to table, so we move up the food value chain through food processing, packaging, transportation, wholesaling, and retailing.

We saw in Chapter 2 how the division of labour and specialization allowed economic growth to occur, and how the changed focus in agriculture, from self-subsistence to producing for the market, allowed big increases in productivity. This enabled the production of surplus food to contribute towards a growing urban sector, in addition to the movement of labour from rural areas to towns. The development of agribusiness further fuelled the enormous increases to productivity in agriculture. Technology has impacted across the food value chain. The Mason jar invented in 1859 allowed food to be preserved at home, followed by the invention of canning and then the refrigeration techniques pioneered by Clarence Birdseye in the early twentieth century (Gordon 2017). Other developments included refrigerated transport, dehydration, heat processing, and controlled packaging.

In 1870 the proportion of the population employed in agriculture was more than 50 per cent in both the US and the UK. Today, it has decreased to less than 2 per cent in the US, and 1 per cent in the UK despite vast increases in food production. Across the wider food value chain however, employment as a proportion of the total labour force is much greater, and in the US currently stands at 10 per cent with people employed in occupations ranging from serving staff, supermarket cashiers, delivery drivers, food scientists, and marketing executives.

The big increase in agricultural productivity as a result of technological change has enabled the structure of developed economies to be radically altered. Resources shifted from being employed in the primary sector to the manufacturing sector initially, and then continued to shift into the services sector as the twentieth century progressed. Rising levels of food production and better quality of food has led to big increases in nutrition and falling food prices, enabling a much larger proportion of household incomes to be spent on non-food items. Household spending on food has fallen steadily and as a share of disposable income is down to 6.2 per cent in the US and 8.6 per cent in the UK.

The process of innovation is unrelenting. Supermarkets enable vast economies of scale to be produced and new technologies in-store, such as bar coding and EPOS, make shopping a much more efficient process. ICT has brought huge advantages in terms of procurement, supply chain management, knowledge management, and customer relationship management, as well as the increasing use of social media in marketing. Biotechnology and genetic modification are transforming many of the food products that we eat.

Where we eat and cook food has dramatically changed in the last fifty years too, with spending in the 'food at home' (FAH) market, where food is prepared and eaten at home, falling behind that of the 'food away from home' market (FAFH) provided by restaurants and other forms of food outlets. The negative income elasticity of demand for basic food products explains this movement, and also explains why there have been increases in R&D and much product innovation in the food industry and to show the scale of this innovation in 2010 in the US 26,240 new food and product beverages were introduced.

Sources: CED (2017), Gordon (2016), USDA (2016)

Questions

1. **What impact has technology had on the pattern of employment in the US and other developed countries?**
2. **How has technology transformed the working lives of those people employed in the food sector?**
3. **What have been the main technological changes that have affected the horizontal and vertical functions and processes in the food industry?**

behaviour and to use technology to develop CRM across sales, marketing, customer service, and technical support. It is argued that we are just at the start of the 'big data' era. Our individual use of the Internet has generated and will generate at an exponential rate collectively enormous amounts of information about ourselves and our lifestyles. Through analysing this data, which in itself will require the ever more sophisticated data analysis techniques now made possible through ever-increasing computing power, new products will be developed.

In sum, the impact of technology in a business potentially can reduce costs, improve quality and productivity, and enable new products to be developed and/or differentiated. Ultimately, the incentive for firms to develop a technology strategy is to improve their competitiveness and add value to the firm. It is to the strategic implications that we will now turn.

Technology strategy: private or public?

DYNAMIC Technological change can improve the competitiveness of the firm if it either reduces costs or allows a business to differentiate its products or services from that of its rivals. Changes in the external market can create the possibility of untapped economies of scale that in turn call for a technological response to boosting production. Individual businesses are intimately linked to technological changes in other businesses and in other industries. If competitors gain a technological advantage a business needs to respond or else lose out. Changes in the technology of suppliers may impact on the business and, if there are technological advances in related support industries, a business needs to adapt. Furthermore, a technical change in one part of the activities of a business might well call for changes in technologies elsewhere.

Technology cannot be ignored by business and it can either boost a firm's individual position or improve the profitability of the industry in which it operates. Conversely, it can lead to a business declining as its competitors develop a technological advantage, or a technological change boosts alternative industries. If it is likely that a business would be able to maintain the technological advantage over time, then there is an incentive for firms to innovate and/or develop new products. This can be the case where firms are able to assert their intellectual property rights through patents or where the cost of the R&D is so high as to deter competitors. Some firms may try to simply outspend their rivals and hope that the market appeal of such products allows costs to be more than recouped. The rapid pace of technology, though, means there is always the prospect of a rival using alternative cheaper technology.

It is important for a business to adopt a technology strategy that enables it to respond to external changes as well as one which allows it to develop a consistent approach in relation to its goals. A major decision that businesses need to make is whether to be a technology leader or technology follower. In general terms, this requires a balance of risks. Moving first can mean that a business is able to establish a reputation that survives even when alternative competitors enter the market. Being first can mean that a business can develop a strong lead, be in a position to set industry standards, or develop favourable channels of distribution. Conversely, there is a huge risk in going first. Considerable sums of money can be expended and there is the risk that someone else will learn from your mistakes and develop a leaner and fitter product.

In terms of risk, there is the obvious cost of the investment of resources in technological research. Here we can distinguish between two types of research:

Basic or experimental research: research which attempts to discover completely new ideas and knowledge. This is sometimes referred to as 'blue-skies thinking'.

Applied research: research which seeks to find the best ways to develop these ideas into commercial commodities.

There are two key questions that need to be resolved. Should R&D be left to individual businesses or should the government play a role either directly in investing in R&D, or indirectly in providing incentives for private firms to do so—and is there a clear link between investing in R&D and increases in economic growth?

Basic research is ultimately the original 'seed corn' for the developments in knowledge that will act as the catalyst for technological change, but may only have a small chance of being developed into successful products or services and so business might be averse to the risks of failure. There are time horizon problems in that even when research can be translated into future possible revenue earning products these may take a long time to exceed the considerable short-term costs of the investment. Finally, there are plenty of cases where the benefits of the new ideas may well be taken up and adopted by other firms (so called 'spillover effects') but an individual firm would not be selfless in being prepared to shoulder the private cost burden to provide for the much greater benefits to the wider society. In such cases of potential market failure, it is argued that governments should fund such research either directly or indirectly by subsidizing research within companies or by allowing companies a high degree of monopoly power to preserve the future commercial rights of the products they have helped to develop.

There is empirical evidence that not only is investment in basic research too low in absolute terms but also, in relative terms, that governments focus too much on giving incentives for applied research in private business (Akcigit, Hanley, and Serrano-Verlade 2016).

In relation to the link between spending on R&D and rates of growth the empirical evidence is mixed. At the aggregate level there is a positive correlation and higher levels of R&D can be associated with higher rates of growth, but there are exceptions. In 2015 the average proportion of GDP spent on R&D in the OECD countries was 2.4 per cent ranging from Israel with 4.25 per cent to Chile with only 0.38 per cent (OECD 2017), but what seems to be more important is not the quantity of R&D spending but the proportion of spending between basic and applied research as above and the overall quality of that research, which depends in turn on the precise ways in which governments complement the private sector in terms of promoting R&D.

The evolution of technological change and its role in promoting growth and improving living standards

INTERNAL/EXTERNAL Prior to the Industrial Revolution in Europe self-subsistence agriculture was the dominant sector in the economy. In England it has been estimated that it took 1,000 years for agricultural production to boost food yields from 0.5 tonnes per hectare to 2 tonnes, but in the eighteenth century it took only forty years to raise this to 6 tonnes.

It was capitalism and the increase in markets that changed this system of agriculture. Now the landlords saw that they could make more money by directly selling produce themselves in the marketplace. They sought to specialize in the use of their land and sell the products on the market. Peasant farmers were now either forced to specialize in the production of certain marketable foods or products or were evicted from the land to allow an increase in the scale of the production by combining farms and benefiting from economies of scale.

One of the first marketable products was wool. Vast tracts of land were given over to sheep rearing and the wool was then transformed into woven cloth through the process of spinning and weaving. Initially this was achieved through small-scale 'cottage' industries where wool was largely spun at home by 'spinsters' and then woven into cloth in small-scale weaving factories. However, in the eighteenth century, industrialists began to develop the large-scale modern factory systems powered initially by water and then steam. In these modern factory systems, a clear division of labour took place with the introduction of new and vastly more productive machinery such as Hargreaves's spinning jenny, the water frame developed by Richard

Arkwright, often regarded as the person who first developed the modern factory system, and then the combination of these two processes in the form of Crompton's 'mule'. However, these innovations in themselves were not scientifically complex but made use of simple ideas and mechanical devices and yet with spectacular results in terms of output.

Cotton joined wool as the main product in the textile industry. The production of cotton entailed the creation of a global market both in terms of sourcing the raw material and in terms of expanding the world market for this. The British had first learned about the possibility of manufacturing cotton by discovering the quality of Indian textiles. The Empire now ensured cheap and plentiful supplies of cotton especially from the US where slavery meant that cotton was cheap. Techniques developed to produce woollen cloth more cheaply were now used to spur the development of cotton. Developments in steam power to work the textile mills, and then, of course, for transportation of goods via the railways and on steam ships, further served to reduce costs dramatically as well as expand world trade. Finally, the move to transporting goods via roads brought in the development of the container as a way of cutting transport times and costs (see Mini-Case 3.2).

The evolution of the factory system brought about the rise of the industrial world and in turn the rates of growth which enabled living standards to increase. Electricity has literally brought light into the darkness and further fuelled industrial growth. Transport costs have fallen dramatically and with this the expansion of markets both nationally and now globally. However, each technological change has had its fierce critics with people fearful of the impact and being labelled Luddites or technophobes. The term 'Luddite' has come to mean anyone who is opposed to technology. The Luddite movement had its biggest influence in the early nineteenth century and was concentrated in the North Midlands and particularly in Lancashire and West Yorkshire. The Luddites were mostly traditional workers in the textile industry who were suffering from the lower prices of wool and cotton that were made possible by the introduction of the new stocking frames and from the prospect of being made unemployed as capital replaced labour. Their response was to break into factories at night and attempt to smash the new machines. Their resentment of the new technologies was rooted in the fact that for them, the new technology would result simply in a loss of their livelihoods. The containerization case, discussed in Mini-Case 3.2, also showed that technological change has not been a universal benefit. The structural unemployment in the traditional ports of Liverpool and London created long-term economic and social problems that are only now being overcome.

The countries of Europe, North America, and Australasia were able, through rapid industrialization and the production of thousands of new goods, to bring about big improvements in the social welfare of their people in the fields of health and education and poverty reduction. Not only did increases in productivity increase standards of living, in turn they led to the development of new industries and associated processes.

The next most influential change was that brought to production as a result of the developments in the motor car industry with the mass production techniques pioneered by Henry Ford being transferred to the production of a wide array of other goods. Some commentators indeed refer to this external business environment as being one of **Fordism**, which it is argued predated the Second World War but found its greatest expression in providing the technological backdrop for the rapid economic growth in the developed world in the post-Second World War period. Human development is also in turn an important influence on technological development. Higher levels of education mean that people have the skills and are able to develop the knowledge to promote new products and processes. Higher education can produce the skilled personnel to pioneer new developments but a general increase in educational skills allows people at all levels in organizations to adapt to change and master new techniques.

Mini-Case 3.2 Containerization—the steel box that changed the world

Without container ships the expansion of global trade that is at the heart of globalization would not be possible. The container is simply a steel box in which goods can be placed to be transported. The simplicity of the container is that it can be carried on a multi-modal basis, i.e. on a lorry, by rail, by sea, or air. However, it has revolutionized the logistics of transporting goods to such an extent that to all intents and purposes it has reduced transport costs to an almost negligible level.

The reason for this is simple. Economies of scale mean that by doubling the dimensions of a box you expand the storage capacity of this box many more times meaning that more goods can be placed into one container. Previously, loading and unloading goods for freight by sea was highly labour intensive and goods were in individual crates of different sizes and shapes that then had to be manually lifted and stowed in the holds of ships. While the longshoremen involved in this were skilled at packing in the cases, the odd shapes meant that great care had to be paid to how the crates went in and not all available space could be used. There was the real risk that badly loaded cargo would shift when at sea and lead to breakages or even the capsizing of the vessel.

Upon unloading, this cargo had to be sorted and transferred onto vehicles en route to the final destinations. Containerization did many things: first, it made it much easier to stack containers, requiring far fewer workers; second, it made it much easier to load and unload the containers. Each container is simply lifted onto a lorry and then off it goes.

The container ports of today are much more capital and technologically intensive compared to the docklands of old. Marc Levinson (2006) charts the conditions that led to the development and the huge impact the container has had on the world. In making shipping cheap the container also made it possible to have a world economy. Cheap transportation has revolutionized the supply chain for businesses. Firms no longer need to locate near to ports or locate different parts of the supply chain close together but can split it up and locate each production stage where costs are lowest. Firms could thus be truly international and in many ways are forced to go global as competitor firms exploit their global reach.

While containers had been in limited use as one way of transporting goods by sea, it was in the 1950s that the US McLean Trucking Corporation really appreciated the revolutionary potential of containerization and that this, if used widely, would radically transform the whole transportation industry. McLean's first venture into containerization was to avoid the road congestion along the Eastern seaboard interstate highways (his first ship, the *Ideal X*, carried just fifty-eight containers). Trucks would deposit containers onto ships for these then to be sent by sea to destinations along the seaboard and then offloaded onto other trucks to be taken to the final destination. What McClean did was to see the potential in integrating shipping and road transportation and the huge economies of scale that could be derived from converting ships into container ships and the necessary changes that would need to be made to the trucks that would pull them and the way in which docks would operate in the future.

The vast increase in global trade that has occurred since 1945 would not be possible without containerization and it has had a transformative effect on all our lives. Modern container ships are behemoths and every year sees the launch of bigger and bigger ships. In 2017 the biggest container ship was the OOCL (Orient Overseas Container Line) Hong Kong. It is able to carry 21.413 TEU (containers are notionally measured in a '20-foot equivalent' size). This ship was produced at the Daewoo shipbuilding yard in South Korea. Other South Korean shipbuilders are Samsung Heavy Industries and Hyundai Heavy Industries (see Mini-Case 10.3).

Sources: Levinson (2006), www.worldshipping.org/about-the-industry/history-of-containerization

Question

What is containerization and how did the innovative use of containers transform the global distribution of goods?

Throughout the long evolution then of industrial capitalism from the eighteenth century up until the 1970s, with the exception of the turbulent events between 1914 and 1939, generally technological change dramatically increased the quality of life and living standards for all. After 1945 not only did the developed world restore growth and competitiveness but also many developing countries began to follow industrial and technology-based strategies that led to their fast emergence as newly industrialized countries.

So, why weren't the views of the Luddites confirmed, and why hasn't the rise of technology in the form of machines and new production processes replaced the need for labour? Well, in

Mini-Case 3.3 I'll see you on Facebook!

Mark Zuckerberg initially developed Facebook as a site solely for his fellow Harvard University students in 2004. However, it quickly established itself as the leading global social networking site. Social networking sites have been made possible by the widespread penetration of the Internet through faster broadband and the development of IT skills in the wider population as well as the increase in the number of ways of accessing the Internet through handheld smart phones and tablets.

Prior to Facebook there were other social networking sites, such as Bebo and Myspace, but Facebook has quickly come to dominate the global social networking market. In 2010 there were 400 million monthly users which rose to 1 billion in 2013 and passed the 2 billion mark in June 2017.

For a networking site to prosper and grow it needs to establish itself as a large network and ensure that its users stick with it. Sites such as Myspace and Bebo have suffered from users jumping ship. The strength of Facebook's business model lies in its ability to create networks, its ability to use the information that its users give to customize adverts and potentially other applications, as well as its sheer market reach.

While there would appear to be no potential rival to usurp Facebook, it does face some strategic problems. The basic problem for Facebook is that users access it for free, but the Facebook business model is powered by the willingness with which users are prepared to give away their personal data for free which enables Facebook to be a highly lucrative marketing vehicle with its main source of income being from hosting adverts. In 2016 its revenue was £26 billion. While it is clear that Facebook's rise has been rapid, businesses in the IT sector can fall as dramatically as they can rise, and Facebook is keen to develop other revenue streams. As a platform for hosting adverts Facebook faces severe competition from many other rivals. There is always the possibility that a new competitor will appear offering something that Facebook currently does not and so the company is keen to acquire potential rival network platforms. Two key acquisitions have been the photo-sharing company, Instagram, in 2012 and the instant messaging service company, WhatsApp, in 2014 both of which have proved to be very successful.

Questions

1. **Why have social networking sites grown so much in the last decade?**
2. **What are the potential threats to the continued success of Facebook and how might Facebook respond to these?**

one immediate sense the Luddites were correct. Industrial machinery in the textile industry did mean that many skilled artisans were replaced but as well as substituting for labour, technology can complement it. There was still a need for relatively unskilled people to operate the new machines but, while certain occupations did become redundant, the general increase in income that resulted from technological change lowering prices meant that although agricultural jobs were being displaced, as were artisan jobs in traditional occupations, the rise in aggregate income meant that new demands were being created and new industries and services were being created. There was a growing need for manufacturing workers, clerks, administrators, managers, and professional services. Not surprisingly then countries needed to ensure that educational systems developed to provide the need for these higher skills. In the language of the economist there is both a substituting effect of labour for capital as a result of technological change but there is also a complement effect. Technological change, in raising productivity, increases incomes and so enables displaced workers to gain work albeit in different jobs.

Stop and Think

What were the main social, economic, and political changes that created the climate for entrepreneurial activity and the rapid development of technology in the early stages of industrialization?

Stop and Think

If you were a dock worker who had been displaced by containerization what would you need to do if you saw that there were new opportunities in the growing legal and financial services sectors in your area? What problems might you face in securing employment and what help might you need?

Robert Gordon has sought to compress the history of the development of capitalism into three periods. IR1 comprised developments in steam, cotton, and rail. IR2 saw the development of the internal combustion engine, electricity, and highways, but he also includes a range of technologies that enabled a huge reallocation of labour (especially female labour) from the home to the workplace. Chief amongst these was indoor plumbing, running water, and a range of domestic household appliances. We are now in IR3 which is, of course, characterized by the use of the computer and Internet and is characterized as a digital revolution. E-commerce embraces a whole host of activities that we now take for granted, and yet which are relatively new. The first mobile phone was only produced in prototype in 1986, we have seen that Tim Berners-Lee introduced the World Wide Web in 1989 and Facebook only launched in 2004 (see Mini-Case 3.3). Texting, social networking, online banking, online shopping, e-ticketing, and e-mail are all a fundamental part of daily life and yet are all relatively new products.

However, the pace of technological change in ICT in particular has in recent years given rise to the belief that we are now entering a new IR4 age. This fourth industrial revolution builds on the digital revolution by combining this with the physical and biological worlds.

Perspectives on the creation of favourable technological environments

COMPLEXITY INTERNAL/EXTERNAL For Adam Smith it was the development of widespread markets that allowed the conditions for the rapid improvements in productivity that led to the rapid advance of capitalism. The greatest source of technological advance lay not in the sophisticated application of science or complex new technologies. It was the expansion of markets that propelled businesses to reorganize production to meet these new market opportunities in their pursuit of profit. The crucial change in production techniques was in developing production processes that utilized the division of labour and specialization. Taking the example of an industrial product, a 'pin' (or nail) in the *Wealth of Nations* (1976 [1776]), Smith showed how huge gains in productivity could be obtained by a simple change in the organization of the production process to allow a greater division of labour. Smith demonstrated how specialization or the splitting of production into separate tasks allowed great gains in productivity of 'pins' to be gained.

On the back of this increase in the 'wealth of nations' it is clear that from the profits generated new ways of producing could be sought, but these technological advances are independent of the initial growth in markets that made these profits possible. In this sense, technology can be seen as 'exogenous' to the process of growth. In other words, technology can give growth in business profits an added boost, but it is not the primary source of the profits.

This could be seen as a strong endorsement of the neoclassical view of a world in which the role of the private entrepreneur and free markets are pivotal for economic success. An important element in propelling the technological change is the response of the business so we need to look at the entrepreneurial activity within the business (see Chapter 15). How do such entrepreneurs behave and what are the conditions that are most likely to exploit technology?

However, as we have seen, Smith was well aware of the wider structural or institutional factors that would be needed to support the market. It took changes in the political and social structure to allow the expansion of trade and a robust legal system to provide the rules to both protect the rights of businesses as well as the wider society from the possible exploitation by business. While the roles of the entrepreneur and markets are critical, so are these wider institutional and structural ingredients in the external business environment and we will explore these later.

For Karl Marx, technology is indeed seen as being vital for the competitive strategy within a business as the capitalist constantly strives to boost profits. However, as with Smith, it is not the primary source of value, as for Marx, all value comes from the ability of the capitalist to exploit labour. Marx is fulsome in his praise for the extent to which this can potentially transform and improve well-being but for him the problem lies in precisely the disjunction between the potential social benefits of technological change and the private motivation of the capitalist desires to pursue individual profit. The main benefit of technology to the capitalist is that it enables an increase in the productivity of labour, thus enabling more value to be squeezed from the labourer and into the balance sheets of the business. This expansion of technology also has many other consequences including the inevitable 'concentration and centralization' (monopoly control and widening inequality in society) of business and the constant pressure on profit rates as more and more resources are devoted to the 'accumulation of capital' (investment in technology). Ultimately, Marx argued, this process of capitalist accumulation will result in an inevitable crisis in capitalism when the workers, who are the true source of all the wealth, will rise up and transform private ownership into common ownership so that industry is set to work for the social good rather than private profit. However, for Marx the implication is clear, businesses have no choice but to constantly seek to invest in new technology, but, in the process, the share of income going to the workers will fall in relation to that going to the owners of capital.

Writing in the early years of the twentieth century, Joseph Schumpeter was the first person to develop a formal theory of the centrality of innovation to explain the development of capitalism. In other words, for Schumpeter, technology itself is the driver of capitalist growth but technology emerges from within business organizations and the competitive environment. In economic terms, this is an **endogenous** theory of growth, or in other words, stems from the internal processes within businesses themselves. For Schumpeter, the origins of capitalist growth lie in the important function of the entrepreneur but, as business organizations began to develop and grow, it was clear that this entrepreneurial function was moving away from the initial individual pioneers of the early Industrial Revolution to the specialist R&D personnel within businesses. In response to Marx's belief that capitalism as an economic system would fail as a result of crisis, Schumpeter argued that indeed capitalism would constantly renew itself as technologies first rose and then fell through what he saw as a process of '**creative destruction**'. For Schumpeter this theoretical view of change very much tied in with the empirical observations of the Russian economist, Nikolai Kondratiev, who had explained the succession of booms and slumps in the business cycle (see Chapter 9) that occurred in capitalism from the late eighteenth century to the early twentieth century as being explained by waves of successive technological development. It was Schumpeter who coined the term 'Kondratieff waves' in his honour (Schumpeter 1942).

Many people have indeed explained the subsequent development of capitalism in this way. Freeman and Louça (2002) trace the development of the modern world in a series of five

Kondratieff waves from the start of the Industrial Revolution of the late eighteenth to early nineteenth century: 'The Age of Cotton, Iron, and Water Power'; 'The Age of Iron Railways, Steam Power, and Mechanization' from the early nineteenth century to late nineteenth century; 'The Age of Steel, Heavy Engineering, and Electrification' from the early twentieth century to 'The Age of Oil, Automobiles, Motorization, and Mass Production' that formed the main part of the twentieth century. Of course, we are now in the fifth 'Age of Information and Communication Technology'.

After the Second World War and in response to the economic recession that occurred in the developed world between the wars, and the relative state of backwardness of many developing countries, much attention focused on the role of government in actively encouraging growth. To many the Great Depression of the 1920s and 1930s seemed to confirm Marx's predictions of the inevitable decline of capitalism, not least because the slowdown of growth in the West could be contrasted with the spectacular growth rates in the Soviet Union where the government had assumed responsibility for industrial production and capital investment.

As we shall see in Chapter 9, in Western Europe and North America countries adopted the policy proposals of John Maynard Keynes. In the Keynesian framework, governments through spending on capital infrastructure such as roads, schools, and welfare services could both act to boost demand at the macro level and improve the human capital of the people through investment in education and skills and training. If the private sector was reassured that the economy was stable this would give them the confidence to borrow and invest. Public investment in R&D would also ensure that adequate research investment was made and provide the pool of skilled research personnel required. There was an implicit belief that capital growth would lead to economic growth. Despite initial successes in both the developed and developing world, growth rates slowed markedly in the 1970s and many countries found that government borrowing had spiralled out of control.

It was Solow, in 1956, who first argued that while a focus on capital growth and savings were important as economies grew and full employment was achieved the diminishing returns on extra capital investment would mean that growth would slow and eventually reach a 'steady state'. If economies were at this position and yet growth was still occurring, then it must be the result of technological improvement. Economists seek to measure the extent of increases in productivity through the use of total factor productivity. This is the residual increase in total output having allowed for the increase in the inputs of labour and capital. For Solow, technology is the explanation for this additional growth. If technology, then, is the key, what causes this? In his model technology was seen as being exogenous, meaning that it occurs as the independent application of new knowledge in a business area which, if this is free to be adopted both within businesses in a country and then globally should allow rates of growth not only to increase but for growth rates between countries to converge providing that they have similar levels of capital investment.

INTERNAL/EXTERNAL Solow's theory did not explain how technological change occurred but simply assumed that it must be the reason for growth given the diminishing returns for increasing capital alone. Lucas argued that indeed it is the application of knowledge objectified in technological change that is the driver for growth and so there has to be a focus on boosting human capital (Lucas 1988) and from the 1980s **neoclassical endogenous growth theory** was developed to explain how this happens. Technology is the result of individuals or firms seeking profits through research and developing and adapting existing technologies. The expansion of knowledge and these spillover effects mean that knowledge is subject to increasing returns. There is though the potential problem we referred to earlier in that if the creators of knowledge cannot exclude others from simply copying them then they may not be willing to make the necessary investment in R&D. For economists such as Romer (1987) this may well mean that there is a need to allow monopoly control over ideas and then protection of the intellectual property through patents and copyrights as well as the need for subsidies and other support measures such as tax credits to private businesses. This will mean though that governments will need to be mindful of ensuring that there is also a clear competition policy to ensure that monopoly power will not lead to exploitation of consumers. Governments will also have a role in ensuring that there are high-class education systems to ensure that employees bring to businesses high levels of human capital and there may well need to be direct government support for basic research in universities or specialist research bodies.

Also of importance is the openness to trade between countries, with technology flowing across frontiers referred to as technology transfer, as well as across businesses within one country. In this view, technology will itself allow increases in productivity and decreases in costs. Thus, the causes of economic growth can be seen as being the following: trade openness with the addition of diffusion of technology through education, research, and development.

LOCAL TO GLOBAL Writing primarily about the development of the US economy in the 1950s, J. K. Galbraith warned of the dangers of a growing concentration of economic power in the industrial system. It was indeed the case that few sectors of the economy now fitted the neoclassical ideal of competitive markets and instead it is monopoly power that comes to predominate. In standard neoclassical theory the danger of monopoly is that businesses will restrict output and charge higher prices but as Romer indicated there may be offsetting advantages that monopoly profits might fuel R&D and innovation. Galbraith argues that the insidious power of the large corporations goes beyond their role as economic agents. In order to sell the output that they produce firms will be involved in a constant process of trying to ensure that they can sell their ever-growing produce. In competitive markets it should be consumers that dictate to the market their wants but in modern capitalism businesses are engaged in aggressive marketing activities to persuade consumers to keep on buying. One way of doing this is to constantly upgrade product specifications to keep us buying. This innovation is not so much about decreasing costs and increasing productivity but a way of ensuring that demand keeps rising. In *The Affluent Society* (1958) Galbraith offers a fierce critique of the damaging effects of rampant materialism in US society and argues that too many resources are directed into the private sector at the expense of vital public goods. In *The New Industrial State* (1967) he argues that in effect large corporations are now controlled by a 'technostructure' of professional managers and skilled technocrats who disproportionally gain the lion's share of national income. The power of big business is such as to ensure that government regulation will be weak and supportive always of corporate interests.

Galbraith's work is centred in the structuralist critique of the need to consider the institutional framework in which technological developments are occurring. Structuralists warn that if economic growth is to be genuinely inclusive and benefit all then there does need to be careful attention paid to how the rewards of economic growth are shared out.

Marxist economists too sense real dangers in the ability of technological leaders to capture the state and unfairly abuse their privileged positions. One of the first examples of a neo-Marxist conceptualization of modern capitalism is the work of US Marxists Baran and Sweezy (1966). In their analysis the US economy of the 1950s had changed form from its origins as an economy based on competition. However, the motivation for capitalists is still the same and profits depend on the ability to extract surplus value from their workers. The problem for capitalists though is that in order to realize their profits they need to sell, but the sheer productive capacity of monopoly capital means that there is always potentially too much surplus to dispose of. This means that capitalism is always on the cusp of a crisis. One way of dealing with the surplus is to plough resources into military spending or to adopt aggressive exporting strategies. In this way a new form of imperialism based on the economic imperative of disposing of the surplus is created. Another way of dealing with the surplus is through allocating more resources into the financial system but the inevitable problem here would be the danger of speculative instability.

Is the world becoming 'flat'?

INTERACTION We shall see in Chapter 10 that there is a fierce debate about the impact of globalization on poorer less-developed countries and whether the development of trade and investment across country borders will be beneficial to both rich and poor countries alike.

Technology has traditionally flowed from rich countries to poor countries, with multinational corporations (MNCs) seeking to enhance their global competitive advantage. Technology transfer can occur directly through joint ventures or strategic alliances, or through the issuing of licences to domestic firms to operate on behalf of the MNC. Trade itself does allow the possibility for domestic firms in less-developed countries to reverse-engineer products to explore whether they can be improved. For neoclassical economists, this technology transfer is at the heart of the growth of the newly industrializing countries and should lead to convergence between rich and poor countries to everyone's benefit.

The influential US journalist Thomas Friedman places technology firmly at the centre of globalization. For Friedman, the ability of less-developed countries to exploit technology through the use of relatively low-cost but well-educated labour forces will mean that, far from being at a disadvantage compared to the developed world, developing countries will be able to exploit their comparative advantages in lower-cost labour with the emerging new digital and information technologies. Friedman starts his influential book, *The World Is Flat* (2007), in Bangalore, India—the centre of the Indian software industry. For Friedman, what he saw in Bangalore reflects the wider changes that are occurring in economic systems, especially in the developing world, as a result of developments in the new information technologies. These technologies have allowed ICT to be applied across the whole value chain referred to above and have acted as a platform to unleash a whole series of 'flattening' tendencies. Fundamentally, the ability of computers to talk together through common software protocols such as HTML has allowed businesses to go global. This has allowed greater controls over supply chains, so production can be situated where costs are lower or nearer to markets. It has enabled outsourcing of both manufacturing and service activities (e.g. call centres), and countries such as India and China have been at the forefront. Above all, the development of these platforms has enabled the rapid sharing of information and made collaboration online so much easier.

Friedman argues that initially globalization was powered by the expansion of governments and countries and he refers to this as the globalization 1.0 era. In globalization 2.0, multinational companies were the motor force, but now in globalization 3.0, it is the ICT technologies that are driving globalization and allowing the flattening of the world, both in terms of spatial proximity and in terms of living standards, as developing countries quickly converge with the developed ones.

All too often throughout history and still to this day in many parts of the world it is 'extractive institutions' that are the norm. Here narrow elites control the resources available and monopoly power predominates. In such circumstances, while wealth is created it is done through narrow elites of the rich and the powerful exploiting labour forces and natural resources through their economic and political power.

In these environments, while technology undoubtedly leads to impressive increases in quantitative growth, the qualitative nature of this growth is distorted. In particular it is argued that the impact of technology transferring over from the developed world to the developing will exacerbate the tendency for income inequality to widen in the developing countries as profits rise relative to wages (Acemoglu and Robinson 2012).

In this way paradoxically the growth that has occurred in societies founded on rights-based inclusive institutions has allowed growth to increase in countries not characterized by democracy and with extractive institutions which benefit small elites who are able to exploit the labour and natural resources of their countries. This is especially the case in many parts of the developing world where democratic institutions are not well developed. In this case, it is argued that the fruits of economic growth often are underpinned by the development of export industries reliant on imported technology from the developed world. Baran referred to this type of capitalism as being 'comprador capitalism'. His explanation for the lack of development in many 'backward' countries is that the structure of the economies was geared to export production controlled through foreign corporations in cooperation with indigenous elites. This type of extractive growth would lead to widening income inequality both within and between countries as opposed to the type of inclusive growth envisaged by neoclassical theorists.

Sources of technological change

Evolution of ideas and team work

It is perhaps inevitable that when attention is paid to technological change it tends to be personalized and both invention and innovation are associated with the 'genius' of (mostly) great men and some women. However, while this enables stories to be told and helps us in answering pub quiz questions where we can neatly link inventions to people and dates, in reality the process of invention and innovation is more complex. Walter Isaacson (2014) is clear that while we cannot ignore the contributions of genius and dynamic entrepreneurs (who are often not the same people), in reality invention and innovation can be a layered process of ideas evolving over the long run in the minds and experiments of different people over time and in the immediate short term will depend on the work of teams of people and not one celebrated individual. The basic fundamentals of computing were developed by Charles Babbage who is widely credited with the development of the ideas for a machine that could compute numbers and it was Ada Lovelace who collaborated with him that is credited with developing the idea of computer programming based on algorithms. This was in the 1840s! Alan Turing is then seen as the key figure in translating these ideas into the practical reality of a computing machine through his work in the team that was tasked with breaking German secret codes during the Second World War. What must not be lost here is that the background of these key figures was not in private enterprise but what could be seen as basic research funded by government in the form of the University of Cambridge that allowed Babbage and Lovelace to perform their work and in the case of Turing the 'spillover' effects of his work for the War Ministry. The origins of the Internet lie in the military research conducted through university research bodies in the US, and the protocols that govern how the networks operate are developed through collaborative networks of computer scientists so that no one person owns or controls it.

Private enterprise—head or tail?

Of course, it has been the private sector that has then pioneered the commercial uses of computing and the Internet and so it is clear that it is the desire to make private profits in the marketplace that is a key driver of change. While Google's original motto was 'Don't be evil' and in the newly incorporated form of Alphabet this is now expressed as 'Do the right thing' this does not mean that Google is not motivated by profit, which it delivers in abundance. There is a keen debate in the economic literature on technology as to how market forces will best deliver the incentives to translate ideas into products. For critics like Brynjolfsson and McAfee the nature of new technologies is that they will be pioneered by small highly flexible business start-ups who will spring up in a future explosion of dynamic entrepreneurialism creating a flattening in terms of concentration of market power, the long tail of which will wag the dog of capitalism. We can see evidence of such potential in the vast numbers of small firms in places like Silicon Valley in the US, the Cambridge Scientific Park in the UK, or the Digital Media City in Seoul, South Korea where there are over 10,000 small-scale digital, game, and Internet firms (see WEF 2015 for a discussion of the relative merits of such 'clusters'). However, as we have seen, there is a countervailing tendency to this explosion of competition in that it is all too easy for markets to be dominated by a concentration of power in the 'head' global companies who can potentially then simply acquire companies to acquire the future profits or to potentially kill off rivals.

However, there are clear advantages in terms of such control by the 'head'. With large profits comes the ability to take risks and engage in 'blue-sky thinking', e.g. without the large cash reserves built up by Google from its key business in search and Uber's key business in taxi services, both these companies would not be able to risk such large sums on the development of effective and safe driverless cars.

Role of government

There is a clear case for direct government influence on the pace and direction of technological change to address the possible market failure of under-provision of basic research. However, it is when countries are able to establish the best balance between this basic research and then the applied research in the private sector that countries are the most successful in terms of creating strong technological environments. In relation to market economies, governments have a role in promoting the conditions for enterprise and here there are a range of supply side measures that will be important. Perhaps the most important of these is the development of effective education and training schemes not only at the level of higher education to produce the highly skilled technical, engineering, and scientific personnel but also the entrepreneurial knowledge and specialized business expertise in relation to management, finance, human resource management, production, supply management, marketing, sales, and customer relations. There is a need for strong research institutions via public research bodies or universities. It might not be the case that direct public funding of basic research is the most appropriate policy as freed from the restraining need to realize profits public funding may simply become a never-ceasing drain on the public purse. There is then a case for providing subsidies, grants, and tax concessions to the private sector or to help firms in having access to sources of finance and business advice.

Governments clearly have a role in ensuring that the private sector does not indeed lead to market power exploiting consumers or workers, and that polarization of wages and distribution of employment does not undermine social stability (see end of chapter case study). There is nothing wrong per se in market concentration of power if this fuels innovation and growth, but everything wrong if it stifles competition and leads to abuses of market power, so governments need to have effective competition and regulatory policy including striking a careful balance between legitimate protection of property rights and yet open access to new ideas to fuel technology transfer. This will involve international cooperation to both enhance the ability of domestic firms to capitalize on their investments through exports free from the risk of global intellectual piracy of intellectual property while also allowing there to be global cooperation and collaboration of ideas of R&D. For the dreams of a flat world then it is vital that technology is free to transfer across borders subject to fair treatment of property rights, so the creation of an effective global technological environment requires effective and commonly agreed rules to promote competition and collaboration at the global level as well as at the domestic level. If knowledge is free to move across borders accompanied by free movement of capital and goods it is vital too that people are free to move so that collaboration can occur, and innovation can spread across frontiers. It is argued that without the influx of skilled Indian ICT engineers to Silicon Valley in the US it would not have been the powerhouse that it has been, and this would have hindered the mutual transfer of ideas that has enabled India's development of its own technology industries. Steve Jobs was the son of Syrian refugees and the founders of Google are both from immigrant communities into the US.

There are a range of potential supply side interventions that governments can make to the creation of a vibrant entrepreneurial environment, and one which is conducive to encouraging sources of investment will be a stable and growing economy. Above all what is to be avoided is macroeconomic instability, the main sources of which could be rising inflation which causes uncertainty for savers and borrowers so affecting financial flows, unemployment, inequality, and finally levels of aggregate demand. If economies experience instability at the macro level, this is likely to cause uncertainty and a lack of confidence in the business community so reducing the incentive to invest (see Chapter 6).

While neoclassical economists will always lean to the private sector as the main source of dynamism and growth and ask for limited institutional interventions and as 'light touch' a regulatory regime as possible, structuralists will argue that it is vital that there is a wide and deep intervention by states to support markets in delivering innovation and Marxists and radical writers will highlight the dangers of corporate greed and exploitation and therefore the need for strong democratic scrutiny.

The great innovation debate: the effect of technological change on productivity, employment, inequality, and market power

Growth

In recent times sceptical views have been expressed about the simple formulation that technology does indeed lead inevitably to increased growth and productivity at the national level.

This debate has especially been directed at the effects of the digital age and stemmed from the following observation by Solow himself in an article in the *New York Times* in 1987, 'We can see the computers everywhere except in the productivity statistics'. This is the so-called 'IT productivity paradox'.

Gordon charts the way in which productivity and growth has altered in the US across three time periods. The periods 1870–1920 and 1920–70 correspond to his formulation of IR1 and

IR2. In the period 1870–1920 annual average growth was 1.84 per cent and annual average productivity was 1.79 per cent. For the period 1920–70 this was 2.41 and 2.82 and for the period 1970–2014 this was 1.77 and 1.62 respectively. It is clearly the middle period that represents the most successful phase for US growth. Not only is this the highest period for both the rise in growth and productivity but also it was accompanied by a fall in average hours worked as workers took advantage of higher wages to enjoy more leisure time. Since the 1970s though despite the so-called ICT revolution of IR3 growth has fallen and ICT does 'not fundamentally change labour productivity or the standard of living in the way that electric light, motor cars or indoor plumbing changed it' (Gordon 2013). In the more important areas of food, housing, transportation, health, and working conditions, ICT has yet to make a significant contribution. Furthermore, the gains that have been made will encounter future 'headwinds' such as the ageing in developing countries, poor education standards, growing personal and national debt, and rising inequality.

In similar vein, Ha Joon Chang (2011: ch. 4) argues that the invention of the washing machine did more to fundamentally affect economic growth than the computer. He argues that in every age the new inventions are the ones that attract awe and admiration, but that often it is the old technologies that have done most to transform the world. The washing machine was one of a range of household devices that enabled women to enter the workforce transforming not only economic performance in general, but their lives and the lives of their families in particular.

Cowen (2011) seeks to explain the apparent technological plateau that appears to have been reached in the US and other developed nations. He argues that in the US there is now what he terms a 'great stagnation'. Initially, the US was able to exploit the 'low hanging fruit' of extensive discoveries of new natural resources, taking advantage of the influx of waves of new immigrants and also bringing education up to secondary level for all citizens as well as dramatically improving access to higher education for many. However, eventually these productivity gains have begun to diminish. In relation to technology, he too argues that the major innovations of the eighteenth and nineteenth centuries have essentially slowed and that, while we continue to improve and enhance these, there have been no fundamental breakthroughs as before. In relation to ICT, while this has undoubtedly improved people's lives, especially in relation to communication and entertainment, there is little evidence that this has increased productivity.

In terms of the development of new ideas, it has been argued that, given the huge amount of knowledge that there is now to know, it takes even our most potentially innovative people a long time to reach a position where they can attain the scientific or technical knowledge required to be in a position to innovate. This has been referred to as 'the burden of knowledge' (Jones 2012). The implication of this is that over time it becomes increasingly harder to maintain increases in economic growth through technological change.

Reviewing the growth data in the US, Brynjolfsson (1993) and Stressman (1997) initially confirmed that there was indeed this IT paradox, but in recent years Brynjolfsson has come to the view that the reason for the paradox is simply that the future huge potential of the new technologies has yet to be unlocked and while it is true that the link between productivity and traditional innovation inputs has weakened, the surge in ICT investment will lead to an increase in productivity (Brynjolfsson and Hitt 1998).

In 1965 the co-founder of Intel, Gordon E. Moore, predicted that the number of transistors on a chip would double every two years and this has turned out to be an accurate prediction. In particular, it is digitization that will have the biggest effect as it will change the way that innovation itself is done and will enable businesses to escape the 'burden of knowledge'. A concept that is similar to Moore's law is 'the second half of the chessboard'. There is a fable that the inventor of chess was asked by the emperor to name his reward for developing this new game. The inventor asked the emperor to pay him in rice grains starting with one grain on the first square of the chessboard, then doubling the amount on the next, and so on until all the squares were filled. Initially this doubling of the amount of rice on each successive square is quite modest but as we move into the second half of the chessboard the amounts of rice rise exponentially. Kurzweil applied this concept to the world of technology strategy arguing that as we move onto the second half of the chessboard each technological leap will be staggering (Brynjolfsson and McAfee 2012, Kurzweil 2000).

Stop and Think

On a calculator work out how many gains of rice will be on the 64th square of the chessboard if, starting with 1 grain on square 1, you then double the amount on the next one and then keep doubling the amount of grains on each successive square compared to the previous one! (The answer is more grains of rice than the world produces every year!)

Employment and inequality

Technology optimists, such as Brynjolfsson and McAfee (2012), do though warn about the potential problems that can arise in terms of the disruption that technology can cause for employment and the structure and ownership of businesses. They do see as possible a future in which humans are involved in a 'race against the machine', and see evidence that this is indeed happening and argue that the answer will lie in the ability of businesses to create what they term a 'race with the machine strategy'. They argue that digital technologies will enable a large number of new entrepreneurs to come to the fore and that the nature of the technology means that there is a need for innovations in management techniques, business models, work processes, and human resource practices.

In their more recent work (2014) they characterize the new digital age as 'The Second Machine Age' but warn that while this will bring transformational change the computational power of automation and artificial intelligence (AI) brings the real danger that technology will substitute the need for labour for all but the most technically skilled in the economy.

Pessimists warn that there are real dangers facing societies in the future. Paul Krugman (2012) agrees with the view that technology will grow apace with developments in robotics and digitization, but he warns that

> Smart machines may make higher GDP possible but also reduce the demand for people—including smart people. So we could be looking at a society that grows ever richer but in which all the gains in wealth accrue to whoever owns the robots.

Market power

Other critics argue that across the developed world, and in the US in particular, the reason for this lies in the increasing concentration of monopoly power especially in banking, manufacturing, and retail and there is the danger that big business will lack the incentive to innovate but will strangle the competition, often by a strategy of 'innovation through acquisition' (Lynn 2010, Lynn and Longman 2010). For Lynn and Longman, Schumpeter was right to focus on the role of entrepreneurship in the process of 'creative destruction' but he didn't pay sufficient attention to the problems that monopoly power would create.

Krugman (2012) sees that there is indeed a potential problem of big companies coming to dominate the development of technology and seeking to swallow up the more innovative small companies. He warns

> I think our eyes have been averted from the capital/labour dimension of inequality for several reasons. It didn't seem crucial back then in the 1990s and not many people (me included) have looked up to notice that things have changed. It has echoes of old fashioned Marxism—which shouldn't be a reason to ignore facts, but too often is, and it has really uncomfortable implications. But I think we had better start paying attention to those implications.

In 2016 the EU imposed a fine of €13 billion on Apple, as it argued that Apple was using the low corporate tax rates in Ireland to avoid paying taxes on the profits that it was making from selling iPhones across the EU. This was seen as an example of a dominant MNC exploiting its market power. In 2017 Google was accused by the EU of abusing its power on its online shopping service by giving unfair prominence to its digital services compared to rival services and was fined €2.3 billion, and investigations were started into the tax affairs of Amazon and the way in which Facebook was gathering and using personal data.

Other concerns are expressed at the way in which the major corporations are able to use the considerable reserves of money that they have to snap up new and emerging start-ups. Between 2005 and 2016 Facebook acquired over fifty companies including the highly successful Instagram and WhatsApp, but some of these it immediately shut down, prompting fears of stifling the competition. Google was reorganized under the name of the holding company Alphabet in 2015 and at the time of writing had acquired over 200 companies mainly in Silicon Valley in the US.

Stop and Think

Why are the large Silicon Valley tech companies so active in terms of mergers and acquisitions?

Looking ahead

The global economic crisis from 2008 onwards has caused an immediate headwind in relation to innovation. Across both the developed world and the emerging economies growth rates in productivity have fallen and investment in R&D has fallen. In the case of the developed world this slowdown had already occurred before the crisis and in the case of the emerging countries the effect of the downturn in the growth of the global economy has led to a deceleration in their productivity growth rates. In the short term this represents the most significant headwind in the way of fostering the climate for innovation.

However, in the longer term there are other headwinds that need to be addressed as outlined by Gordon. Rising unemployment or rising job insecurity in labour markets, polarization of incomes and rising inequality, the ageing of populations especially in the developing world, the decline in trade, and the rise in fear of globalization and migration in many countries and falls in investment in human capital are all structural problems that need to be addressed at both the domestic and global levels.

VALUES **STAKEHOLDERS** While there is the promise that as yet we are still at the start of what will turn out to be a period of transformational change brought on by the technologies of IR4 there is a need for policymakers to restore stability in the macroeconomy in tandem with policy to the supply side of their economies especially in relation to fostering innovation, addressing inequality, and improving education and training.

Stop and Think

Are you a technological optimist or pessimist?

Summary

- Successful use of technology potentially improves the performance of business both in terms of performance and productivity and so raised general prosperity for all.
- For technological change to be successful it is a combination of entrepreneurial endeavour and institutional factors that are important. For businesses to be successful there are key strategies that need to be pursued at the national level and so public policy is important. Increasingly as business goes global these strategies also need to be coordinated at the supranational level.
- Despite the undoubted benefits to individual business profitability, the aggregate effects of technology to overall economic growth are disputed. Technological optimists are confident that the digital age will truly revolutionize business and society to the benefit of all. However, pessimists question how extensive these changes will really be and argue that the gains from technology will be concentrated in the hands of fewer and fewer people causing job insecurity for many workers unless governments pay sufficient attention to ensuring macroeconomic stability and institutional supply side change.

Case Study: Automation, robots, and AI: is this time different or will it be both 'dazzling and disappointing'?

The transformative potential of technology in production systems is widely recognized, even while the precise configuration and extent of the possible transformation remain unknown. Trends towards higher levels of automation promise greater speed and precision of production as well as reduced exposure to dangerous tasks for employees. New production technologies could help overcome the stagnant productivity of recent decades and make way for more value-added activity. The extent of automation is, however, causing significant anxiety about issues of employment and inequality.

(WEF 2017)

The World Economic Forum (WEF) sees the five key technologies in IR4 as being the Internet of things, AI, 3D printing, advanced robotics, and wearable technologies (including augmented and virtual reality). The concept of 'disruptive technology' or 'disruptive innovation' has been widely used in the literature about the effect of technological change on the structure and strategy of businesses.

The Internet of things has the potential to network all Internet enabled devices to deliver a range of automated services, e.g. in relation to controlling and monitoring domestic appliances, monitoring, and controlling energy use. 3D printing is enabling many manufactured products to be produced much more cheaply. The Industrial Revolution mainly allowed machines to replace human physical processes and the ICT revolution allowed computerization to replace essentially routine human cognitive and manual tasks. Essentially computerization is possible when programmers are able to break down production or processes into a series of steps and then write programs that enable the machines to replicate these steps. However, the development of AI and robotics is enabling a wide range of non-routine tasks to be computerized and in which the machine itself can learn and modify the steps.

IBM's Watson allows companies the potential to develop 'chatbots' and virtual agents to deal with customer enquiries; Google's Deep Mind is being used to deliver medical diagnoses; and Apple's Siri and Amazon's Alexa act as a personal assistant to handle a range of functions. Algorithms enable the rapid analysis and use of big data making way for better decision-making, faster and more customized search options, and a more in-depth analysis of consumer behaviour helping to develop effective digital marketing. Developments in robotics are leading to fast reductions in costs and the combination of robots and AI are allowing for a range of functions, previously only capable of being performed by humans, to be automated. The race is now on to produce driverless automated vehicles (Google and Uber) and for total automation from warehouse logistical functions (e.g. Amazon's Kiva Systems which it bought in 2012) to mining.

For Klaus Schwab (2017), the founder and Executive Chairman of the WEF, the technologies of the fourth industrial revolution are indeed disruptive, and will lower employment while potentially unleashing high rates of growth, but only for those companies that revolutionize their organizational structures. We are already seeing evidence of this in the way high-tech businesses are using shared networks, and in the creation of the 'gig' economy for many workers. Facebook creates a global network which allows people to share data freely, and yet it itself produces little content; Uber owns no vehicles, and yet is now the world's largest taxi company; Airbnb owns no accommodation, and Alibaba is the world's largest online retailer and yet has no inventory. New start-ups such as Lyft, Fiverr, and Task Rabbit which act as an auction market to bring workers and work together, have created new forms of the labour market in which working is for 'piece rates' as opposed to agreed contractual wage rates. Potentially this way of working ensures that labour, rather than being displaced from work, is much more flexible and workers have the opportunity to choose their own hours and rate of pay.

As with the Luddites in the eighteenth century, today there is a high level of 'automation anxiety' in relation to loss of jobs, worsening labour conditions, and rising levels of inequality. It has been estimated that in the US, 47 per cent of jobs are threatened by automation, and those occupations paying the lowest wages and requiring the lowest levels of educational attainment are at most risk (Frey and Osborne 2013). In this scenario there really is a race between humans and machines and this 'Second Machine Age' will be different to the first machines ages of IRs 1, 2, and 3 (Brynjolfsson and McAfee 2014).

Not all critics agree that there will be an inevitable decline in employment opportunities, although they do agree that certain occupations and, more importantly, aspects of some occupations will be replaced by these new technologies. Autor (2015) argues that in the first years of the ICT revolution there was a complementarity between the rise of the computer and labour, but that there was a polarization in labour markets across the developing world and those in the newly industrialized countries. Many former white-collar clerical and administration jobs and blue-collar factory operatives did lose their jobs as a result of automation. However, there are many tasks at both the bottom and the top of the occupational skills ladder that could not be automated. At the top end are jobs that can be referred to as 'abstract', requiring high levels of education and skills of analysis, abstract reasoning, communications ability, and the need for specialized expertise. The supply of these skills is inelastic and so people in these roles attract high wages. At the lower end, while many dirty, routine, and dangerous jobs have been reduced by automation, there is still a need for 'manual' tasks that cannot be automated, e.g. food preparation and serving jobs, caretakers and maintenance, care workers, hairdressers, and cleaning services. Here, the problem is that while the demand for such types of personal services may rise, the elastic supply means that wages will fall. However, while technological change may lead to rising inequality, it does not necessarily lead to loss of overall employment levels. Autor argues that this polarization may now not continue for much longer because while automation may well replace some of the routine tasks performed by middle-level workers it will not be able to replace many of the non-routine tasks. People still have a comparative advantage over machines in relation to interpersonal skills, flexibility, adaptability, problem-solving, and common sense!

For critics like Gordon, this has been an era which has been both 'dazzling and disappointing' (2017a, 2017b). The effects of ICT dazzle us, but only in the relatively narrow fields of entertainment, communication, and collection and processing of information. Peter Thiel, a successful entrepreneur and investor in the US tech sector, once remarked 'We wanted flying cars but we got 140 characters'. As the first outside investor in Facebook, this could simply have been seen as a snide swipe at the rival company, Twitter, but also chimes with the view that while companies like Twitter (and indeed Facebook) have been successful, they have not fundamentally improved living standards.

Other critics take a middle path between being optimistic and pessimistic about the impact of IR4. Furman argues that this time is not fundamentally different, and we are not witnessing a brand-new paradigm shift. Citing research by Graetz and Michaels, he accepts that robotics may have added at most one-tenth to the growth of GDP between 1993 and 2007 in the top seventeen industrial economies. He also argues that it is difficult to assess the precise impact of AI on employment and refers to research conducted across the OECD that concluded 'only' 9 per cent of occupations are threatened because, while many tasks within occupations might be replaced, there remains an overall need for human input into many more; however, such losses of jobs will still be significant. There will also be continuing and significant impacts on income inequality. The Council of Economic Advisers in the US estimated that 83 per cent of jobs making less than $20 an hour would come under pressure from automation, compared to 31 per cent of jobs making between $20 and $40 and only 4 per cent of jobs making more than $40.

Clearly, there will be a need for policymakers to take action to mitigate the effects of both rising unemployment and the continuing polarization of incomes between those at the top of the occupational skills ladder and those at the bottom.

Questions

1. **What areas of the economy will be most affected by the developments of AI and robotics?**
2. **What actions should policymakers take to mitigate the effects of rising unemployment and address the growing inequality between workers?**

Review and discussion questions

1. How does technology potentially increase productivity and allow a business to establish competitive advantage?
2. What are the main conditions in the external national business environment that it is argued are necessary for technological change to increase economic growth?
3. Explain what is meant by the 'productivity paradox' in the context of the impact of technology and critically examine the competing views that seek to explain this.
4. What are the main general disadvantages associated with technological change?
5. What are going to be the main technological advances in the future?

Assignments

1. Research and then outline the main technological changes that have occurred in food systems since the start of the Industrial Revolution. What have been the effects of these changes on the producers and other stakeholders during this time? On balance have the changes in modern food systems been universally beneficial?
2. Prepare a market evaluation report which explains the rise of one of the following global technology companies: Google, Apple, Amazon, or Facebook, and critically examine the way in which the technological environment has impacted on and been influenced by your chosen company.

Further reading

Brynjolfsson and McAfee (2014) *the authors argue that technological progress will accelerate and that this has profound implications for how business and society need to respond.*

Isaacson (2014) *Isaacson is the CEO of the Aspen Institute and profiles the work of key innovators and the reasons for their success.*

Test your understanding of this chapter with online questions and answers, explore the subject further through web exercises, and use the weblinks to provide a quick resource for further research. Visit the online resources at www.oup.com/uk/wetherly_otter4e/

Useful websites

These websites profile the latest debates and trends in technology:
www.bbc.co.uk/technology
www.guardian.co.uk/business/technology
https://techcrunch.com

References

Acemoglu, D. and Robinson, J. A. (2012) *Why Nations Fail: The Origins of Power, Prosperity and Poverty* (New York: Crown)

Akcigit, U., Hanley, D., and Serrano-Verlarde, N. (2016) 'Back to basics: basic research spillovers, innovation policy and growth', NBER Working Paper No. 19473 September 2013, revised March 2017 (accessed 11 July 2017) **www.nber.org/papers/w19473.pdf**

Autor, D. H. (2015) 'Why are there still so many jobs? The history and future of workplace automation', *Journal of Economic Perspectives*, 29(3): 3–30

Baran, Paul A. and Paul M. Sweezy (1966) *Monopoly Capital* (New York: Monthly Review Press)

Brynjolfsson, E. (1993) 'The productivity paradox of IT', *Communications of the ACM*, 36(12): 7–77

Brynjolfsson, E. and Hitt, L. (1998) 'Beyond the productivity paradox', *Communications of the ACM*, 41(8): 49–55

Brynjolfsson, E. and McAfee, A. (2011) *Race Against the Machine: How the Digital Revolution Is Accelerating Innovation, Driving Productivity and Irreversibly Transforming Employment and the Economy* (Lexington, MA: Digital Frontier)

Brynjolfsson, E. and McAfee, A. (2014) *The Second Machine Age: Work, Progress, and Prosperity in a Time of Brilliant Technologies* (New York: Norton)

CED (2017) 'Economic contribution of the food and beverage industry, Arlington, USA: Committee for Economic Development of the Conference Board' (accessed 1 July 2017) **www.ced.org/events/economic-contribution-of-the-food-and-beverage-industry**

Chang, Ha Joon (2011) *23 Myths of Capitalism* (London: Penguin)

Cowen, T. (2011) *The Great Stagnation: How America Ate All the Low-Hanging Fruit of Modern History, Got Sick and Will (Eventually) Feel Better* (New York: Dutton)

Freeman, C. and Louça, F. (2002) *As Time Goes By: From the Industrial Revolutions to the Information Revolution* (Oxford: Oxford University Press)

Frey, C. and Osborne, M. (2013) 'The future of employment: how susceptible are jobs to computerisation?', Oxford Martin School: University of Oxford (accessed 14 July 2017) **www.oxfordmartin.ox.ac.uk/downloads/academic/The_Future_of_Employment.pdf**

Friedman, T. (2007) *The World Is Flat* (London: Penguin)

Galbraith, J. K. (1958) *The Affluent Society* (New York: Houghton Mifflin Harcourt)

Galbraith, J. K. (1967) *The New Industrial State* (New Jersey: Princeton University Press)

Gordon R. J. (2016) 'The End of Economic Growth', *Prospect Magazine*, February 2016 (London: Prospect Magazine)

Gordon R. J. (2017) *The Rise and Fall of American Growth: The US Standard of Living since the Civil War* (New Jersey: Princeton University Press)

Isaacson, W. (2014) *The Innovators: How a Group of Hackers, Geniuses and Geeks Created the Digital Revolution* (New York: Simon & Schuster)

Jones, B. F. (2012) 'The burden of knowledge and the death of renaissance man: is innovation getting harder?', *Review of Economic Studies*, 76(1): 283–317

Krugman, P. (2012) 'Is growth over? The conscience of a liberal', *New York Times*, 26 December (accessed 15 March 2013) **http://krugmanblogs.nytimes.com/2012/12/26/is-growth-over**

Kurzweil, R. (2000) *The Age of Spiritual Machines* (London: Penguin)

Levinson, M. (2006) *The Box—How the Shipping Container Made the World Smaller and the World Economy Bigger* (Oxford: Princeton University Press)

Lucas, R. (1988) 'On the mechanics of economic development', *Journal of Monetary Economics*, 22: 3–42

Lynn, B. C. (2010) *Cornered: The New Monopoly Capitalism and the Economics of Destruction* (New Jersey: Wiley)

Lynn, B. C. and Longman, P. (2010) 'Who broke America's jobs machine?', *Washington Monthly*, March/April (accessed 15 March 2013) **www.washingtonmonthly.com/features/2010/1003.lynn-longman.html**

OECD (2017) 'Gross domestic spending on R&D (indicator)', doi: 10.1787/d8b068b4-en (accessed 12 July 2017)

Porter, M. E. (1985) *Competitive Advantage—Creating and Sustaining Superior Performance* (London: Collier Macmillan)

Romer, P. (1987) 'Growth based on increasing returns due to specialization', *American Economic Review*, 77: 56–63

Schumpeter, J. (1942) *Capitalism, Socialism and Democracy* (New York: Harper Row)

Schwab, K. (2017) *The Fourth Industrial Revolution* (New York: Crown Business)

Smith, A. (1976) [1776] *An Inquiry into the Nature and Causes of the Wealth of Nations* (Chicago: University of Chicago Press)

Solow, A. (1987) 'We'd better watch out', *New York Times Book Review*, 12 July, p. 36

Stressman, P. (1997) *The Squandered Computer* (New Canaan, CT: Information Economics Press)

USDA (2016) *What Is Agriculture's Share of the Economy?* US Department of Agriculture, Economic Research Service, 14 October

WEF (2015) 'Which policies are best at boosting innovation?'

WEF (2017) *Technology and Innovation for the Future of Production: Accelerating Value Creation*, White Paper (Geneva: World Economic Forum)

Chapter 4
The political environment

Paul Wetherly

Learning objectives

When you have completed this chapter, you will be able to:

- Explain the nature of **politics** as concerned with making choices for society as a whole through law and public policy, including decisions and rules concerning the conduct of business.
- Analyse the interdependence of business and government.
- Identify key features of the UK political system as a **liberal democracy**.
- Analyse the variations that exist within liberal democracies, different types of political regime, and disparities in levels of economic development in the modern world.
- Examine the link between democracy and economic success.
- Explain the concept of multilevel governance.

THEMES

The following themes of the book are especially relevant to this chapter

- **DIVERSITY** Within the UK, relationships between business and government are diverse. On a global scale there is diversity of political and economic systems.
- **INTERNAL/EXTERNAL** Politics is an important element of the external business environment, but it also has an internal dimension, e.g. in the form of organization or 'office politics'.
- **COMPLEXITY** The relationship between business and politics is a key aspect of the complex business environment, including social, technological, and other dimensions.
- **LOCAL TO GLOBAL** Politics and governance operate on a number of levels or spatial scales—subnational, national, and supranational.
- **DYNAMIC** The relationship between business and government is subject to a continual process of negotiation and adjustment. In a democracy the policy environment can be uncertain due to changes in government. The role of the state in relation to the market has been characterized by periods of intervention and of disengagement. At a global level, major transformations are occurring in political and economic systems and relations between states.
- **INTERACTION** Business and government are interdependent. Political decisions can be highly consequential for business, but business has a voice in the political process and governments are dependent on business decisions and performance.

- **STAKEHOLDERS** In a liberal democracy the political process is pluralistic, characterized by a range of stakeholder groups with different values and interests. Governments seek to provide favourable conditions for business, but this needs to be balanced with other interests and goals.

- **VALUES** In all societies the need for politics arises from disagreements and conflicts over values and interests. There are different views about the proper role of government and the nature of the 'good society'. A key focus of political controversy concerns the balance between the market and the state.

Introduction

This chapter begins by introducing the nature of politics and explaining its relevance for business, emphasizing that the nature of the economic system is a matter for political deliberation and choice. We will then examine the relationship between politics and business and the forms of interdependence that exist between the two. The UK system of government is usually described as a liberal democracy and this is explained as a combination of 'liberal' and 'democratic' aspects. There is a strong association between capitalism and liberal democracy in the modern world and we will look at the extent to which there is a fit between a capitalist economy and democratic political system. We will see that there is quite a lot of variation between states both in terms of how democratic they are and the models of capitalism that have developed with different roles for the state.

What is politics? What has politics got to do with business?

VALUES Politics can be defined in terms of competing views about the kind of society we want to live in—the '**good society**'—and what this requires in terms of the role of government. It is because there are disagreements about the nature of the 'good society' that politics is necessary as a way of handling these disagreements. For example, the 2016 referendum on the UK's membership of the European Union (EU) brought different visions of the future of the country to the fore. This involved disagreements on key issues such as: whether the UK should be an independent state making its own laws or should be involved in an intergovernmental process of lawmaking as a member of the EU; whether the UK should retain its place within the EU single market and customs union; and whether immigration from other EU states is seen positively or negatively. Immigration was a key issue motivating Leave voters, so many of them were in effect saying that their vision of a good society requires government to restrict immigration in order to limit what they saw as its negative economic and cultural impacts. Immigration was not a big issue for Remain voters, so many of them were in effect saying that their vision of a good society is one which welcomes immigration, values the economic contribution made by immigrants, and embraces diversity (see also Chapter 6).

These issues require collective decisions, or decisions made for society as a whole. The referendum vote in favour of leaving the EU ('Brexit') was a collective decision (though not legally binding) made directly by the UK population. As the UK government stated that it accepted and would implement the referendum result ('Brexit means Brexit'), it formally notified the EU of the UK's intention to leave (Article 50) and entered into negotiations involving a series of collective decisions to determine the terms of the 'divorce' and the future relationship between the UK and the EU. Through these negotiations different visions of the UK's future continued to be in play through attempts to influence and shape the government's negotiating position, with what Brexit means in reality resulting from this process.

Thus, government can be seen as a mechanism for implementing collective decisions. Government is, first, a source of authority, capable of making and enforcing rules or laws that govern how we live together. This is often expressed in ideas of parliamentary and popular sovereignty. Sovereignty means the highest form of authority within a society and this is located in Parliament which makes the law of the land. The related idea of popular sovereignty is that, in a democracy, Parliament is ultimately accountable to the people and should make decisions in the interests of the people or the nation. (Here we can see that Brexit was a demand to 'take back control' from Brussels so that the British people are able to make their own laws through their own Parliament and not be subject to EU law, whereas 'Remainers' had a vision of the peoples of Europe cooperating to make laws in areas of shared interests.) An important aspect of law is the way it can be used to regulate economic activity in the market and shape economic outcomes. But government is not just a source of authority: it is an economic actor in its own right through ownership of resources and its capacity to raise taxes and undertake public spending. (The role of the state as an economic actor is examined in Chapter 14.)

The 'agenda' of government

The fundamental political question concerns what role government should play in society or the 'agenda' of government. For example, the market can be seen as a system of voluntary exchange in which free and self-reliant individuals make decisions for themselves about how they use their own resources, on the basis of their own preferences or interests. What, then, should the role of government be in the economy? Should it leave individuals and businesses to get on with managing their own lives and their own affairs and accept whatever outcomes flow from that? Or should it intervene to influence or shape market outcomes? For example, should governments seek to reduce inequalities generated by markets? Or to minimize harmful environmental effects of economic activity? The answers to these questions clearly depend on the view we take of: (a) what are socially desirable outcomes (our view of the good society); and (b) whether the market left to its own devices can achieve these desired outcomes or government action is necessary.

The way the economy is organized looms large in any conception of the good society because the economy affects our lives in highly consequential ways (see Mini-Case 4.1). In fact, there is, strictly speaking, no such thing as a 'free market', because markets cannot operate without some forms of government action, including the protection of property rights, enforcement of contracts, and maintenance of law and order. Thus, there is an unavoidable relationship between business and government, between the market and the state. The question is what kind of relationship this should be—whether, for example, the aim is to minimize the role of government or to enlarge it, to favour the small state or the big state. The economic role of government is one of the central questions in political debate. The answers to that question involve different proposals for how the economic system should be *designed* in order to achieve desirable outcomes. That process of design and redesign is a political process. In other words, the economic system is based on political decisions that we make as a society about the way we want to organize our economic life and the rules or laws which are necessary to create and sustain this system.

Mini-Case 4.1 Business, the market, and the good society

VALUES When people think about the good society—the kind of society they want to live in and have their children grow up in—some of the most important issues bear directly on the economy and the role of business, as expressed in the following questions:

- What are my prospects for finding a job? Is my job secure? Do I have an opportunity to get on in life?
- Is my job satisfying and rewarding? Do I have any say over how I do my work? Is it monotonous or does it involve exercising skills?
- Does my job pay enough so I can live decently? Is my pay fair compared to what others get? Are people at the top paid too much? Is there a problem of greed in society?
- Do businesses act responsibly in society? Do they care only about profits? Do they pay their taxes as they should? Do they have too much political influence? Are they doing enough to help to tackle social problems like obesity? Do they treat workers in poor countries unfairly by using sweatshops? Can we trust businesses to act responsibly towards the environment?

We might all agree that these are important questions, but the nature of politics is that people do not agree on the answers and, in particular, the proper role for government. For example, some people might argue that obesity is a question of individual choice and responsibility, while others say the food industry is to blame and tougher government regulation is required. This and other issues show how the nature of the market system and business behaviour are at the heart of how we think about the good society and are therefore inherently political. We shouldn't think of business as something that is separate from politics, for one is bound up with the other.

Stop and Think

Some people say that politics should be kept out of business. Would that be desirable, or even possible? What are the key aspects in your view of a good society?

Let's look a little closer at the nature of rules. The workplace is governed by rules which are in part established by the employer as an important mechanism of control of employees and of ensuring organizational goals are achieved. The legitimacy of these rules is based partly on support for the market system based on private property and acceptance of the related notion of a right to manage on the part of employers. However, this right to manage is liable to be contested by employees when they feel that rules designed to secure corporate goals of efficiency, competitiveness, and profitability do not pay sufficient regard to their values and interests. This process of contesting and negotiating rules on the basis of the different values and interests of employers and employees may be described as a form of internal workplace politics. In this sense, politics is a feature of the internal as well as external environment of business and is not concerned exclusively with government. But the right to manage is also, crucially, subject to the exercise of external political constraint, for in creating their own rules businesses have to comply with the law of the land. In fact, many of the rules governing workplaces are laid down in law, including a range of laws designed for the purpose of employee protection, such as laws concerning unfair dismissal, redundancy, paid leave, or health and safety. A key difference between the internal rules of businesses and the laws of the land is that while the former have essentially private aims (i.e. business goals), the latter are public and ostensibly justified with reference to an idea of the public interest. Thus, unfair dismissal laws prevent (some) employers behaving as they would otherwise choose to do in pursuit of business goals but are justified on the grounds that society benefits from providing some measure of job security to employees.

VALUES **STAKEHOLDERS** Politics is necessary because disagreement and conflict over values and interests is a feature of all societies—your idea of the good society might be very different from mine. For example, we can see that although nobody would say they are in favour of treating people unfairly, laws protecting against unfair dismissal, those governing hiring and firing more generally, and other forms of employee protection, are in fact highly controversial. There can be disagreement over what we mean by fairness, and fairness might conflict with other values such as efficiency or competitiveness. Employers and employees may have conflicting interests: employees wanting stronger protection and employers wanting more freedom to make decisions about hiring and firing in the interests of the business. Proponents of **labour market flexibility** argue that regulations governing hiring and firing decisions can be a burden that gets in the way of competitiveness and job creation and look to free up these decisions. For example, if the law makes it difficult to dismiss employees this can hamper a firm's efforts to reduce costs, and so firms may be reluctant to take employees on in the first place. But while one vision of the good society emphasizes businesses being able to respond flexibly to market conditions, an alternative vision puts more emphasis on employees being protected from the vagaries of market forces. In recent years this issue has moved up the political agenda with the growth of 'zero-hours' contracts and other forms of precarious work (see Chapter 12) (see Taylor 2017). Employee protection laws can be seen as trying to balance the interests of employers and employees as stakeholders in business. Also important is the ways in which employees are involved in decision-making processes within business, such as through trade union representation of employees or mechanisms of co-determination through employees being directly represented on boards of directors (see Mini-Case 4.2).

Mini-Case 4.2 Employee representatives on boards of directors

STAKEHOLDERS Corporations are organizations with a range of stakeholders—managers, shareholders, employees, customers, etc.—and these stakeholders may have different interests and therefore different views about corporate strategy and decisions. Therefore, corporations face the basic political problem—how to resolve disagreements between individuals and groups who have different views and interests which involve incompatible allocations of resources. How should decisions be made in business? How should power and influence be shared among stakeholders? How can different interests be reconciled? In other words, politics isn't something that happens only outside of corporations but also inside them. How corporations are run—corporate governance—is a matter of great public interest, and therefore of national political debate.

In a speech during her campaign to become leader of the UK Conservative Party and prime minister in 2016, Theresa May advocated 'changes in the way that big business is governed' and made a commitment that 'we're going to have not just consumers represented on company boards, but employees as well' (May 2016). This proposal for employee representatives on boards of directors can be seen as a step towards industrial or workplace democracy, or co-determination. In May's speech this idea was linked to the aspiration to 'make the economy work for everyone', so the implication is that, in order to make sure that companies work for employees as well as directors and shareholders, those employees need to have a 'voice' on the board. This would ensure that non-executive directors are not simply 'drawn from the same, narrow social and professional circles as the executive team' and would improve 'scrutiny' of the executive team (May 2016). If implemented, this represents an important shift in the relationship between the company and its workforce—employees are no longer seen simply as 'hired hands' but partners in the running of the business. As well as being more democratic, there is a business case for employee representation: 'The historical and international evidence is that workers on the board can be beneficial both to the business and to the wider economy' (Michie 2016).

Of course, May's speech merely stated support for an idea and did not provide detail on implementation. The idea was strongly supported by the TUC (Trades Union Congress), which also argued that 'six in ten (59 per cent) people support the election of worker representatives onto the boards of large companies' (TUC 2016). The TUC (2016) wanted a policy that would meet its three tests:

1. The representatives must be company workers, not anyone else given a remit to speak for workers.
2. The workers who sit on the board must be elected by the workforce, not appointed by anyone else.
3. Worker representation on the board must be a legal requirement for companies over a minimum size.

However, the policy was not supported by business, as represented by the CBI (Confederation of British Industry) which argued for a voluntary approach:

On employee engagement, different approaches will work for different businesses but a starting point is firms being able to outline and explain what approach they are taking—whether that's employees on boards, employee committees, dedicated representatives, or other models that genuinely address the issue. (CBI 2016)

In fact, in a later U-turn, Prime Minister May ruled out a mandatory approach in a speech to the CBI, and in doing so apparently succumbed to concerted campaigning against the proposal from business (Gall 2016).

Question

Should employees have a voice in business by having elected representatives on boards of directors?

The interdependence of business and government

INTERACTION Government involvement in economic life is a feature of all capitalist economies, though its precise nature and scope vary considerably between different societies. Politics and business are not separate but *interdependent*—in some ways business depends on government, and government in some ways depends on business. In all capitalist or market-based economies business is involved in a variety of *relationships* with government (Wilson 2003: 1–8). Government:

- determines the legal framework within which business operates;
- influences or determines the scope of market relationships and the balance or mix between the market and other sectors (public and voluntary/third);
- relates to private sector business as a major customer;
- relates to private sector business as a provider of services and resources;
- relates to private sector business as a tax collector;
- manages the macroeconomic environment; and
- represents business interests overseas, in relation to foreign governments and international organizations.

These relationships are all expressed in terms of what government does, but they can be turned around to make clear the interdependence between business and government. Thus:

- government consults business on law and public policy, and often relies on self-regulation;
- the dynamism of private sector business tends to extend the scope of the market in relation to the other sectors;
- business supplies goods and services to government;
- business is a major user, directly or indirectly, of services provided by the public sector;

- business activity is the principal source of tax revenues, so that economic growth generates expanding tax revenues;
- private sector investment is a key driver of macroeconomic performance—economic growth and prosperity; and
- the strength of the domestic economy is a key ingredient of the influence of governments in world affairs.

Regulation

As we have seen, the basic task of government in all societies is to determine the rules within which people live, including rules governing business behaviour. Although business is often seen to be in favour of less regulation, the law plays an important role in creating markets and enabling them to operate. For example, although markets are based on voluntary agreements and exchanges, the law ensures the enforceability of contracts. Where there may be little basis for trust between buyers and sellers the law gives each side the basis for confidence that the agreement will be honoured, and that redress can be sought if it is not. In modern capitalist economies the law affects all aspects of business activity:

- corporate governance (e.g. legal duties of directors);
- relations with employees (e.g. employee protection);
- relations with customers (e.g. consumer protection);
- competitive behaviours and relationships (e.g. competition policy); and
- impacts on third parties and the environment (e.g. planning law).

Taxation

The development of modern government and the public sector has depended on the capacity to raise revenue through taxation. The overall level of taxation is determined by the level of planned public expenditure and by considerations of macroeconomic policy (Chapter 9). But governments also have to decide what forms of taxation to use (mainly income tax, corporation tax, national insurance, and taxes on spending) and therefore who pays, and these decisions will have consequences for income distribution in society and can influence behaviour. For example, the UK Labour Party made a commitment in the 2017 general election campaign to introduce a 45 per cent rate of income tax on earnings above £80,000 and a 50 per cent rate on earnings above £123,000 on grounds of fairness (that the rich should pay more) and in order to finance increased spending on public services, but this was criticized on the basis that such a high rate would, for example, encourage tax avoidance or induce highly paid individuals to earn their living elsewhere and thus would not raise the revenues projected by Labour (Institute for Fiscal Studies 2017a). Thus, decisions regarding taxation—how much to raise and who should pay it—have always been highly contentious. Although the necessity of taxation is generally recognized, it touches on key political arguments about individual freedom or liberty (expressed in terms of individuals being free to decide for themselves how to spend their own money) and fairness or equity (expressed in terms of what is a fair share of taxation in relation to what others pay, and in relation to services that are provided/value for money). A key question is what contribution to overall tax revenues should be made by business, particularly in the form of corporation tax and national insurance contributions, and by highly paid business leaders (see Case Study).

Public services

STAKEHOLDERS Law or regulation and taxation are key elements of the government–business relationship, with business often being seen as favouring less of each. However, the other relationships are also important. In the developed capitalist economies not all economic or business activity is left to private enterprise and the market. In mixed economies there is substantial public sector involvement in certain areas of business (recall the broad definition of business in Chapter 1). Although public ownership of industry has been largely reversed, in the UK and elsewhere, through privatization, governments continue to have an important role in financing and providing a range of public services such as education, health and social care, and income support (see Chapter 14). In countries such as the UK, citizens rely mainly on the welfare state rather than private sector businesses for provision of these services. We tend to think of welfare states primarily in terms of the benefits they bring to individuals, but it is important to recognize that business also has a stake in these services. That is because the efficiency and competitiveness of business depend on such favourable conditions as a healthy and educated workforce. Beyond what we conventionally think of as the welfare state, business has a stake in other areas of government activity that impact upon business performance, including grants, support for research and development, and the transport infrastructure.

Government as customer

Business has an important stake in these and other areas of government activity not only because businesses are direct or indirect users or beneficiaries but also because private business supplies goods and services to the public sector. Government is the principal customer for some firms and industries, such as pharmaceuticals, armaments, and civil engineering, because government is the main or sole provider of healthcare, defence, and physical infrastructure. Government could, in principle, own pharmaceutical or civil engineering businesses as part of the public sector but chooses to purchase these outputs from the private sector. As Wilson points out, 'government is a customer, but a customer of a very special type, one that can be persuaded to buy a product not only through a combination of the usual commercial skills but also through political pressures' (2003: 1).

Managing the economy

As we will see in more detail in Chapter 9, government plays an important role in maintaining a favourable macroeconomic environment for business. During the period of Keynesian consensus in the 1950s and 1960s managing the economy entailed a range of objectives including economic growth, high or 'full' employment, control of inflation, and a favourable balance of payments. More recently the shift to 'monetarism' and '**neoliberalism**', inaugurated in the 1980s, involved a narrowing of these objectives, with emphasis on the fight against inflation. All businesses have a stake in government macroeconomic policy both because the goal, such as a low inflation climate, may be beneficial for business and the specific policy tools and decisions, such as decisions to raise or lower interest rates, have a direct impact on business. Although low inflation is generally good for business, higher interest rates which may be deemed necessary to realize this goal can be harmful, especially to certain sectors that rely upon borrowing such as construction and consumer durables.

The international dimension

LOCAL TO GLOBAL International trade and foreign investment, associated with the phenomenon of globalization, mean that business operations (exchange and production) span national borders so that business–government relations are not confined to a business' own national government. UK companies exporting to China or establishing production facilities there have to deal with the political institutions, rules, and procedures of that country. In pursuing overseas expansion businesses may look to their own governments for assistance in, for example, negotiating market access and favourable trade rules. 'It is arguable that, in an era of increasing globalization, corporations need the assistance of their own home government more . . . in order to obtain favourable trading arrangements and protection of their property—including intellectual property—overseas' (Wilson 2003: 5).

INTERACTION STAKEHOLDERS These diverse relationships between business and government remind us that businesses never operate in a truly free market, but always in a political environment in which government decisions, to varying degrees, influence the threats and opportunities that business confronts. Second, these relationships are two-way, in the sense that they involve interdependence between business and government and that they have to be continuously negotiated and adjusted between the two sides.

Stop and Think

For each type of relationship between business and government say whether you think this shows government as a friend of business, an enemy of business, or as acting in the public interest as a whole.

Reflect on how easy or difficult it is to make these distinctions.

Liberal democracy

Government exercises a unique form of power—to make and enforce the rules under which we live—and good governance matters to all members of society. Among western capitalist societies some variant of **liberal democracy** has become the predominant framework governing who rules and the lawmaking process. A liberal democracy is a form of government that combines democratic procedures with forms of individual freedom and equality that have been championed in the liberal political tradition, hence 'liberal + democratic'. Liberalism sees **individual freedom** as the most important value and the hallmark of a good society, and holds that ensuring freedom is one of the primary purposes of government. This means protecting people from each other so that they can go about their daily business and live their lives as they choose, for example protecting individuals from theft or violence. But in the liberal view it also means that government has to be kept in check so that it does not interfere in people's lives more than is necessary. This certainly means preventing government using its power in a manner that is oppressive, but some liberals have also argued more generally for government to play a minimal role in economic and social life.

Historically, two of the most important ways of keeping government in check in western societies have been by creating a framework of individual rights, such as freedom of speech, and through the principle of the **rule of law**. The rule of law means that all citizens are equal before the law and have to obey it, but also that the actions of government must be lawful. For this reason, the 'rule of law' is often contrasted with the 'rule of men', since state officials can only act within their lawful powers, and so the rule of law prevents arbitrary government.

A third way of keeping government in check is through democracy. The basic principle of democracy is 'rule by the people' or popular sovereignty, meaning that political power is in the hands of the people as a whole. In liberal democracies the people rule indirectly by electing representatives to act on their behalf (hence the term *representative* democracy). The basic features of a democracy include the following:

- universal suffrage (all adults have the right to vote, thus involving formal political equality);
- regular elections (the UK now has fixed-term parliaments of five years);
- choice of candidates (usually standing for election as members of a political party in a multiparty system, e.g. as a Conservative or Labour candidate); and
- civil liberties or rights (such as freedom of speech), media organizations that are independent from government, and a culture that accepts diversity of lifestyles, values, and beliefs.

Having the right to vote is of little value unless elections are held at regular intervals and voters can choose between candidates offering alternative policies or programmes for government. Thus, political parties campaign on the basis of competing proposals for running the country, with prominence usually given to policies dealing with business and the economy. Civil liberties or rights, such as freedom of speech and association, are important conditions for political participation as they are supposed to enable the free exchange of ideas through media organizations that are independent of government and through expanding 'social media', and allow people to criticize the government (or business) and engage in protest.

In essence, democracy is supposed to ensure good government because the people choose their lawmakers. If the current set of lawmakers are doing a bad job—such as mismanaging the economy—democracy provides a peaceful and orderly mechanism (elections) for replacing them with a different set. Of course, this does not mean that democratic politics always produces especially competent governments with high public approval ratings. On the contrary, opinion surveys often reveal low, or negative, approval ratings for politicians and low levels of satisfaction with the political system in the UK. For example, although a majority of people (73 per cent) agree that Parliament is essential to democracy, only three in ten people (30 per cent) report being at least 'fairly satisfied' with the way Parliament works (Hansard Society 2017). It seems that people are in favour of the idea of democracy but sceptical or even cynical about the actual practice of democratic politics.

Stop and Think

What do you understand by the term 'liberal democracy'?

The 'fit' between liberal democracy and capitalism

Today western societies are characterized by a combination of capitalist economic system and liberal democratic political system, and in some important ways there is a good 'fit' between capitalism and liberal democracy. The liberal commitment to freedom and rights can be seen as embodied in a capitalist economy through property rights which are a foundation of private enterprise, and freedoms to set up a business and to buy and sell. Indeed, supporters of free markets often express their arguments in terms of freedom: a market is portrayed as a system of voluntary exchanges into which each party—buyer and seller—enters freely on the basis of a calculation of their own self-interest. This view is often linked to the argument that government should play a minimal role in markets and leave people free to make decisions for themselves as far as possible. Democracy can be a good fit for capitalism in so far as it is associated with the rule of law and measures against corruption, protection of property rights, political stability, effective government, and peaceful transfers of power between governments through elections, but also because business is able to have an effective political voice (see Chapter 11).

However, operating in a liberal democracy also involves challenges for business because it allows for an ongoing process of competition between rival views and interests and therefore can create uncertainty about the policy environment. Policies introduced by one government can be overturned by the next, creating uncertainty affecting long-term investment decisions, such as in renewable energy. Uncertainty can result from elections that result in a 'hung' Parliament in which no party has a majority and therefore cannot form a stable government able to implement its manifesto, as happened in the 2017 UK general election. This followed the uncertainty about the UK's future relationship with the EU created by the unexpected vote for the UK to leave the EU in the 2016 referendum (Brexit). The uncertainty (and pessimism) caused by Brexit and the 2017 election outcome are shown by the fall in the value of the pound following these events (Cox 2017). Brexit also shows in a dramatic way how democratic decisions can go against business interests: although business opinion was divided, the predominant business view was in favour of continuing membership of the EU.

However, it can be argued that there are deeper tensions between capitalism as an economic system and a democratic political system which make for a fragile partnership (Wolf 2016). Democracy enshrines a principle of political equality ('one person, one vote') but capitalism generates economic inequalities in terms of income and wealth. When these inequalities are allowed to become too great and large sections of the population feel that they are 'left behind' and not benefiting from economic growth, this can undermine the legitimacy of the economic system and lead to political unrest. Therefore, tackling inequality and ensuring 'inclusive growth' can be advocated as necessary to maintain the popular legitimacy of the economic system (Flanders 2016, RSA 2017) and even save capitalism from itself (see Chapter 12). In addition, when extremes of income and wealth are allowed to develop, it can undermine political equality and the democratic ideal of popular sovereignty (rule by the people) because rich individuals and corporations are able to exert great influence within the political system, effectively converting economic resources into political power (see Chapter 11). The election of Donald Trump and the vote for 'Brexit' have been seen as expressions of the rise of right-wing 'populist' political movements and parties that claim to speak on behalf of 'the people' against an out-of-touch and corrupt elite comprising political and business leaders. And 'populist' eruptions have been attributed in part to the anger felt by the 'left behind', and as 'unpleasant political consequences of . . . longstanding economic failure' (Flanders 2016).

DIVERSITY Although today liberal democracy is the norm among the developed capitalist economies, this has not always been the case and there are important differences between them. These differences are important for business because they can affect business confidence and performance, and because businesses that have the option to locate their activities in different countries (MNCs) need to take them into account.

One of the central political issues in capitalist economies, is whether the liberal view of minimal government is desirable or whether government should play a more active or 'interventionist' role in social and economic life. This 'market versus the state' debate provides a key yardstick for measuring variation in the political environment both historically and comparatively. It enables us to identify different 'models' of capitalism.

Models of capitalism

LOCAL TO GLOBAL **VALUES** **INTERACTION** As we have seen, capitalism is not a spontaneous or natural economic order, but should be seen as shaped by processes of design. The designs are formulated and implemented through politics and government. For much of the twentieth century two radically opposed designs confronted each other: the free market view of classical liberalism (revived by neoliberalism) that favours a minimal role for the state, and the Marxist vision of abolishing capitalism and replacing markets with economic planning (Chang 2014: 378). The Marxist vision has limited appeal today, but this does not mean that the neoliberal vision has triumphed. This is because the apparent dichotomy is better understood as a spectrum of designs with different ways of combining the market and the state. The neoliberal vision has been dominant since the 1980s, but it is contested by other views which advocate a more active economic role for the state, involving important elements of state ownership and planning (see also Chapter 14). Three fairly distinct 'models' or designs can be identified (Heywood 2007: 99–102):

- minimal state;
- developmental state; and
- social-democratic (Keynesian welfare) state.

The minimal state is associated with neoliberalism and the attempt to roll back the state, whereas the social-democratic or Keynesian welfare state involves an interventionist role for government, particularly in economic and social policy, within what would remain a largely capitalist economic system (see Chapter 14). The developmental state is like the social-democratic state in that the market and private enterprise remain the principal mechanisms for allocating resources, but the state 'intervenes in economic life with the specific purpose of promoting industrial growth and economic development' (Heywood 2007: 100). Thus, rather than disengaging from economic life and leaving it to the market, as in the minimal state model, there is more of a partnership between business and government involving a form of 'indicative' planning. 'This is planning that involves the government . . . setting some broad targets concerning key economic variables (e.g., investments in strategic industries, infrastructure development, exports) and working with, not against, the private sector to achieve them', for example by providing subsidies (Chang 2011: 204). Such a developmental role for the state through indicative planning has been used successfully in European countries, such as France, and in Japan and other East Asian 'tiger' economies (Chang 2011: 204–5).

In these three models of the role of the state in a capitalist economy we can see a basic distinction between a minimal state and an interventionist role for the state. The minimal state is based on an optimistic view of markets. They are seen as driving efficiency and customer responsiveness through competition and the profit motive and as systems of voluntary exchange that embody individual freedom. Each version of the interventionist state is based on the belief that the market cannot be left to its own devices, but the socially desirable objectives that state intervention is intended to realize are quite different. While the social-democratic state is focused primarily on the question of social justice and sees the market as intrinsically unfair in its outcomes, the developmental state is focused on development and economic growth and sees the market as prone to a suboptimal performance.

In considering these models, it is important to note that there is, as we have seen, no such thing as a free market (in the sense of being entirely free from any kind of government regulation or intervention) in the world today, and such an idea would be impossible to realize. This is because the operation of the market depends on certain forms of law and public policy (e.g. private property rights, law of contract, the regulation of money as a means of exchange, law and order). Thus, even the minimal state involves some irreducible forms of state action to enable markets to work. Furthermore, attempts to implement a neoliberal agenda by rolling back the state, such as in the UK in the 1980s, fell a long way short of creating a minimal state and free market. Despite major changes, such as privatization, we still live in a world of 'big government' in the West.

Which of these models is best for business? The answer to this question depends on the view you take of how markets work and what the interests of business are (see Chapter 1). In the minimal state (free market) approach, the purpose and responsibility of business is principally, or even exclusively, to maximize profit. What business is deemed to want is to be left to get on with it, using its own expertise and knowledge of the market and without government interference, especially in the form of 'burdensome' taxation and regulation. Thus, neoliberalism is often presented as being explicitly on the side of business, and indeed often the aim of business lobbying is to reduce business taxes and regulation. Free market philosophy relies on an assumption that businesses, and other actors, are on the whole rational and know what they are doing in pursuit of their own self-interest (e.g. making a profit). But if this is wrong the minimal state will not be the best political environment for business. The financial crisis of 2008 shows clearly that supposedly rational experts did not really know what they were doing in relation to highly complex financial products, and their mistakes had disastrous consequences, not only for the financial institutions that employed them, but for business as a whole and the wider society through the cost of government 'bailouts' of banks and the subsequent recession. This is an example of minimal government (i.e. deregulation of financial markets) not being best for business. Therefore, 'if we are to avoid similar financial crises in the future, we need to restrict severely freedom of action in the financial market' (Chang 2011: 177). Such regulation would be good for the banks, even though they strongly resist it, and good for business and the economy as a whole. Even when firms do behave rationally in their own interest this may induce them to do things that are bad for business as a whole in the long term (or not do things that would be good for business) and regulation requiring firms not to do what they otherwise would (or to do what they otherwise would not) would be pro-business (even though they might resist it). For example, in competitive markets it may be rational for individual profit-seeking businesses to continue emitting carbon into the atmosphere, but when all businesses behave in this way the result is the threat of catastrophic global warming, making this, as shown by the Stern Review, the greatest example of market failure in history (Stern 2007). Thus, state action (on a global scale) is required to reduce carbon emissions to within safe limits by inducing or requiring firms (and households) not to do what they otherwise would and, in effect, save business (and humanity) from itself.

Since there is no such thing, in the strict sense, as a free market the question is how far the state should intervene. Supporters of the minimal state argue that government should act only where it is necessary to enable markets to function (e.g. to secure property rights and enforce contracts) and to deal with clear cases of market failure (e.g. pollution). The approach is 'markets wherever possible and government only when necessary'. In this view government is regarded with suspicion both in terms of its competence and its motives. Governments cannot know as well as individuals or businesses what their interests are, and the problem of government failure (i.e. government action creating economic problems, such as inflation) may be worse than market failure. So, the fact that the market isn't perfect doesn't justify government intervention. Worse than this, it is feared that government action might not be motivated by doing good for society but by the interests of politicians and officials, such as increasing their own power. For these reasons the preference is to minimize the role of government and maximize the role of markets.

Both the developmental state and social-democratic state models clearly have a more positive view of the motivations and competence of government, and a more pessimistic view of markets. The developmental state model has a positive view of the capacity of government, through 'indicative planning', to help business to achieve a higher rate of growth. Through intervention in specific industries or sectors (industrial policy) governments may be able to perform better than markets in picking winners, that is, industries with the potential for growth and profitability. This approach is critical of the market but business-friendly as it aligns state intervention with business interests, and it also benefits the wider society through growth (see Mini-Case 4.3). However, there can be a conflict between what is good for the national economy and what is in the interests of individual firms, in which case, 'the government picking winners may hurt some business interests but it may produce a better outcome from a social point of view' (Chang 2011: 134).

VALUES **STAKEHOLDERS** The need to balance the interests of business against what is good for the wider society, and for government to adopt anti-market principles and policies, is taken further by the social-democratic state model. Although there is overlap with the developmental state (e.g. through state-owned enterprises or 'nationalized' industries) and the two approaches can be combined (as in some European countries such as France), the principal failing of the market from the social-democratic point of view is not suboptimal growth but the unjust distribution of property, income, and life chances. It thus advocates extensive state intervention in the name of social justice, particularly through the development of the welfare state, and represents a shift from the narrowly economic focus of the minimal state and developmental state models to a broader social focus. The idea that what's good for business is good for society is challenged by the idea that government action in the interests of employees and the poor entails confronting the interests and privileges of business and the wealthy. Most obviously this is through regulation to give employees more protection and power in the workplace, and welfare services in cash and in kind financed through progressive taxation redistributing income from rich to poor. Thus, businesses and high-income individuals are expected to contribute through the tax system (corporation tax and income tax) to financing welfare services that mainly benefit those who are at the lower end of the income scale, thereby reducing poverty and inequality. Many of those who criticized decisions by UK Conservative governments to reduce corporation tax and the top rate of income tax, and attempts by large corporations such as Starbucks and Amazon to minimize their tax liability through lawful avoidance measures, were expressing a social-democratic idea that the self-interest of businesses and wealthy individuals runs counter to what is good for society in terms of fairness. It is, therefore, the job of government to ensure that a sense of obligation on the part of business and the wealthy to the rest of society is enforced—sometimes expressed in the demand that 'the broadest shoulders should bear the greatest burden'. This inevitably involves commitment to big government in terms of levels of taxation and public spending.

The social-democratic state might be characterized as anti-business because it advocates forms of big government—regulation, tax and spend, public ownership, and public provision—that businesses often oppose. Social democrats argue that markets and business interests are not sacrosanct but always have to be weighed in terms of what is good for society, and in their view what is good for society is fairness and this is not compatible with markets left to their own devices and private enterprise and businesses being left just to pursue their own self-interest. It is important to see that this debate comes down to a choice of values: social democrats prize fairness, but others might not share the belief that reducing inequality is a worthwhile goal for government to pursue, or they may prize liberty (and low taxes) more highly.

In any case, the idea that the social-democratic state is anti-business is questionable. First, as already noted, the social-democratic state does not seek to replace markets and private ownership with central planning: in the 'mixed economy' of private and public sectors the former remains dominant. Second, the welfare state provides direct and indirect benefits to the private sector. Because of its public spending commitments in areas such as infrastructure, health, and education, government is a key customer for many firms and industries. Public services such as education and health may benefit business by improvements to 'human capital', such as the health and skills of the workforce. Redundancy payments and unemployment benefits may make labour markets more flexible and the transfer of labour from declining firms and industries to those that are growing easier because the costs for workers of losing their jobs are reduced. Redistribution of income to alleviate poverty and reduce inequality can benefit business because of the higher propensity to spend of those on lower incomes. Minimum wage and 'living wage' policies have the same beneficial effect on demand. It can be argued that measures to promote greater fairness in society can benefit business by reducing social tensions that can foment problems of crime and disorder. Finally, social-democratic states turn out to be the best performing states in terms of economic growth: for example, the US has tended to grow more slowly than European countries such as Sweden, Norway, and Finland with much larger welfare states (Chang 2011: 228–30).

Stop and Think

Which model is best for business? Is what is best for business necessarily best for society as a whole?.

Economic and political differences in a globalizing world

LOCAL TO GLOBAL In the post-war period (i.e. post 1945) in the last century, until the collapse of communism in the Soviet Union and the east European states that were under its control in the 1990s, it was common to divide the global system of states roughly into three 'worlds' with reference primarily to their levels of development, but also their political and economic systems. The poorest countries were referred to collectively as the 'third world', to distinguish them in developmental terms from the 'first world' of rich capitalist economies and the 'second world' of industrialized communist states that were intermediate in terms of economic development. The poorest states were based mainly on agriculture with the vast majority of their populations engaged in subsistence production for direct use rather than for exchange. These countries were also largely characterized by non-democratic authoritarian political systems. The 'second world' comprised industrializing collectivized (centrally planned) economies controlled by authoritarian states, which were unable to match the performance of the rich capitalist nations (which ultimately became a prime reason for their collapse). Looking at this tripartite division in terms of the business environment, the focus would be almost entirely on the 'first world' in the sense that this is where the vast bulk of business activity took place and it was these countries that western companies were primarily interested in: the poor countries were undeveloped as markets and the second world was hostile to private enterprise.

DYNAMIC This tripartite division was always a simplification but is no longer relevant due, in particular, to the collapse of communism (the demise of the second world) and rapid development of some poor countries (internal differentiation of the third world, and some countries moving up), with implications for the business environment. Thus, the global political and economic system is dynamic, with changes occurring within countries and in their positions in the international order. Countries achieving rapid development can move up the international league table in terms of their productiveness and wealth, and play a more important role in the world economy in terms of trade and investment. In other words, such countries become more important places to do business, and so more significant parts of the global business environment. Shifts in the pace and level of development of countries are also then bound up with the process of globalization as they lead to new forms of interrelationship and interdependence among nations. It can be argued that the world is moving closer towards the creation of an integrated global market incorporating all regions.

Rapid growth can be the result of capacity to export primary products, as exemplified by countries whose wealth is based primarily on oil exports, particularly the members of the Organization of the Petroleum Exporting Countries (OPEC: http://www.opec.org/opec_web/en). However, a more sustainable means of achieving growth is through the development of manufacturing capacity, as achieved by the Asian 'tiger' economies (including Japan, South Korea, Singapore, and Hong Kong) and, more recently, China. By 2011 the four tiger economies had joined the high-income group of countries as defined by the World Bank, and China had joined the upper-middle-income group.

In the 'three worlds' classification democracy was associated primarily with the West or 'first world': the second and third worlds were largely non-democratic. However, political changes have also rendered this division out of date as democratic reforms have spread to new countries and regions. The most notable shift, again, was a consequence of the collapse of communism in Europe which initiated a dual process of both market reform and democratic reform. In other words, these countries appeared to be in transition to becoming 'western' in economic and political organization, leading to an interpretation at the time that liberal democracy had triumphed. In recent years support for democratic reform has been apparent in the so-called 'Arab spring' in a number of countries in the Middle East and North Africa, although the initial optimism that these countries might make the transition to western-style liberal democracies has faded, most obviously in the context of the prolonged civil war in Syria.

Democratic change can go in either direction, of advance or regression, within individual countries or, in aggregate, on a global scale. For example, in a recent survey the number of 'full democracies' had declined from twenty-five in 2011 to nineteen in 2016. The US was among the six states to have regressed (in 2015) to a 'flawed democracy'. As a result of this shrinkage in the number of full democracies the proportion of the global population living in a full democracy reduced from 11.3 per cent to just 4.5 per cent, or less than one in twenty people (Economist Intelligence Unit 2016).

As this distinction shows, the simple dichotomy between democratic and non-democratic regimes is rough and ready, for countries can be more or less democratic. For this reason, it is better to think of political systems in terms of a spectrum ranging from full democracies that closely approximate the democratic ideal to authoritarian regimes in which few or no democratic procedures are present, including rule by a dictator and/or the military. There is no agreed method of measuring democracy or classifying political regimes, but an approach along these lines has identified four types of regime based on five criteria or categories:

- electoral process and pluralism;
- civil liberties;
- the functioning of government;
- political participation; and
- political culture (Economist Intelligence Unit 2016).

In between 'full democracies' and 'authoritarian regimes' are 'flawed democracies' and 'hybrid regimes', as shown in Table 4.1. According to this analysis, nearly half of the world's population (49.3 per cent) live in a democracy but less than one in ten of these people enjoy the benefits of a full democracy. In terms of countries, only one in four of the seventy-six democracies are fully democratic.

Table 4.1 Types of regime—the spectrum of democracy

Type of regime	Authoritarian	Hybrid	Flawed democracy	Full democracy
Number of countries	51	40	57	19
% of the world's population	32.7	18.0	44.8	4.5

Source: Adapted from Economist Intelligence Unit 2016.

Mini-Case 4.3 Is democracy linked to economic success?

It continues to be the case that the global business environment is characterized by striking disparities between nations in terms of income level and democratic governance. The World Bank classifies countries into four income groups as shown in Table 4.2.

Table 4.2 shows that just less than one-sixth of the world's population live in the just over one-third of countries defined by the World Bank as high income. In other words, it is still the case that a relatively small number of countries constitute the environment in which business activity is concentrated. At the other end of the scale about one in twelve of the world's population live in low-income countries. In terms of the global business environment these countries are marginal. The income gap is very striking, with average income per head in the high-income countries being nearly seventy times the average in the low-income group. Looked at another way, the one in twelve who live in low-income countries receive 0.5 per cent of world income, while the one in six who live in high-income countries receive 64 per cent of income. This comparison understates the gap because the income per head average for each group conceals inequalities between countries. For example, in the high-income group the average income per head in Norway is US$93,530 which is nearly 240 times the average income of US$390 at the other end of the spectrum in Niger. Even this understates the global gap between the richest and poorest people in the world because these data do not tell us the distribution of income within countries. The richest individuals in the world do not live in Norway because although it has the highest per capita or average income level it is a more egalitarian country than the US or UK. Similarly, though the richest people by and large live in the richest countries, inequality within some low-income countries means that a few people are very rich while most are very poor. In terms of wealth, it has been estimated that 'just eight men own the

Table 4.2 Average GNI (gross national income) per head 2015 in current US$, with countries grouped by income level

Income group	Per capita income thresholds (2015 GNI US$)	2015 GNI per capita US$—average in each income group	Number of countries (2016)	Population (billion & %) (2015)	
High income	12,476 or more	41,932	79	1.187	16.16
Middle income	1,026–12,475	4,959	107	5.521	75.16
(Upper middle)	4,036–12,475	8,263	(55)	(2.594)	(35.31)
(Lower middle)	1,026–4,035	2,029	(52)	(2.927)	(39.84)
Low income	1,025 or less	619	31	0.638	8.68

Source: World Bank (**data.worldbank.org**). See World Bank Country and Lending Groups at **https://datahelpdesk.worldbank.org/knowledgebase/articles/906519**

same wealth as the poorest half of the world', headed by Bill Gates (Oxfam 2017).

A small number of countries are rich, and a small number of countries are democracies; and there is a notable overlap between these two categories.

Table 4.3 shows that:

- 88% of high-income countries are democracies;
- 97% of low-income countries are non-democratic;
- 95% of full democracies are high income; and
- 88% of authoritarian regimes are low- (33%) and middle- (55%) income countries.

Thus, rich states are normally democracies, and poor states are largely non-democratic. These data show a suggestive correlation between democracy and national income and, since the high-income countries are mainly capitalist, between capitalism and democracy. But they do not tell us about the direction of causation, or what factors might strengthen or weaken this connection. It can be argued that the development of capitalism promoted democratic change in Europe as the rising middle class of industrialists demanded a share of political power, followed by economically weaker groups campaigning for an extension of the franchise to give workers a voice in Parliament. 'Historically, the rise of

Table 4.3 Relationship between democratic status and income level

	Full democracy	%	Flawed democracy	%	Hybrid	%	Authoritarian	%	Total
High income	18	38	24	50	0	0	6	13	48
Middle income	1	1	32	36	28	32	28	32	89
Low income	0	0	1	3	12	40	17	57	30
Total	19	11	57	34	40	24	51	31	167

Sources: Economist Intelligence Unit 2016, World Bank.

capitalism and the pressure for an ever broader suffrage went together' (Wolf 2016). In turn democracy can be seen as providing a favourable environment for businesses to flourish, as suggested earlier.

But the idea that capitalism and democracy are mutually supportive or reinforcing may hide a more fragile relationship. The optimistic view may be a product of the relatively recent experience of the second half of the twentieth century. The first half of the century was characterized by the disappearance of democracy and the rise of authoritarian regimes through most of Europe. It can be argued that the combination of capitalism and democracy has endured in the post-war period because democracy was able to tame capitalism through reform, ensuring 'inclusive growth' in which the benefits of prosperity were widely shared. Thus, capitalist democracy can be at risk today from the failure to sustain inclusive growth—growth faltering or its benefits not being shared widely. Thus

if the legitimacy of our democratic political systems is to be maintained, economic policy must be orientated towards promoting the interests of the many not the few. . . . If we fail to do this, the basis of our political order seems likely to founder. . . . The marriage of liberal democracy with capitalism needs some nurturing. It must not be taken for granted. (Wolf 2016)

Question

Is democracy the best political environment for business?

Multilevel governance

LOCAL TO GLOBAL In a globalizing world the largest businesses operate across national borders, may have production facilities in many countries, and create global brands. Such companies have to operate management structures and implement business strategies that are transnational, meaning that they span national borders. In contrast, government largely still operates within national borders—the nation state still provides the primary context for democratic political decisions. There is thus an apparent tension between the spatial scale of governance (within borders) and business (across borders), or between democracy and the global nature of contemporary capitalism. This has tended to strengthen the hand of business in dealing with government since multinational corporations (MNCs) have some capacity to pick and choose between countries when making investment decisions, while governments find it more difficult to regulate business and manage the economy, and feel that they are in a global competition with other countries to attract investment. However, the political environment of business does not consist just of a series of national environments, for governments have found ways to cooperate and act collectively to deal with common problems that cannot be handled effectively at a national level. In this way governance also operates at an international scale—across borders. Multilevel governance is an aspect of the globalizing world and an increasingly important dimension of the business environment.

The idea of **multilevel governance** points to the way political decisions are made at a variety of levels or spatial scales, 'above' and 'below' the nation state:

- subnational, i.e. a level of political authority below or within the nation state (e.g. local government);
- national, i.e. the nation state; and
- supranational or intergovernmental, i.e. a level of political authority above the nation state, of which the EU is the most important example.

In all democratic states the division of political power between national and subnational (local and regional) tiers is an important question, and important aspects of business and economic development policy can be decided at the subnational level, reflecting local needs and priorities. The UK is distinctive in its tradition of highly centralized government and relatively weak local government. However, there have been important departures from that tradition in recent decades through processes of devolution, handing power down from Westminster along two tracks:

- devolving power to the constituent nations of the UK through a Scottish Parliament, Welsh Assembly, and Northern Ireland Assembly; and

- devolving power to 'city regions' through 'devolution deals' inspired by the vision of a 'Northern Powerhouse'.

A major revision to the UK's centralized system of government has been the creation of a Scottish Parliament and Welsh Assembly with limited legislative powers, and the achievement of devolved government in Northern Ireland. This can be seen as moving away from the UK's centralized 'unitary' state in which power is concentrated in London (Westminster) towards a 'quasi-federal' state in which power is dispersed to subnational tiers of governance. A common driver of both tracks is resentment against London dominance and, at the same time, the feeling that Westminster is too remote to govern the regions and nations of the UK effectively. Thus, devolution is about making decisions closer to the people who are affected by them. The first track responds to the long-established sense of distinct national identities and desire for some degree of self-government. The second track is driven by an agenda of 'rebalancing' the economy, fostering economic development to reduce the North–South divide by devolving limited economic powers to city regions (BBC 2016, Centre for Cities 2016).

Scotland: in or out of the UK?

Devolution to Scotland was largely seen as a way of satisfying the desire of people in Scotland for self-government short of independence from the UK. However, the rise of the Scottish National Party (SNP) with its key demand of independence persuaded the Coalition government to hold a referendum in 2014 which resulted in a fairly close vote in favour of remaining part of the UK (55 per cent to 45 per cent) (*The Guardian* 2014). Scottish independence would constitute a significant change in the business environment, raising questions about the prospects for the Scottish economy and management of economic policy. However, as members of the EU, Scotland and the diminished UK would both have remained members of the single market. This has been thrown into uncertainty by the 2016 UK referendum vote in favour of leaving the EU (Brexit). Part of the complexity of this situation is that a majority in Scotland voted in favour of remaining in the EU. This led to calls for a second referendum on Scottish independence to prevent Scotland being 'dragged out' of the EU against its will. Assuming that Brexit goes ahead by 2019, including leaving the single market, this would imply a choice for Scotland between continuing to be a member of a single market with the rest of the UK by giving up on independence, or continuing to be a member of a single market with the rest of the EU by becoming independent from the UK. The loss of seats by the SNP in the 2017 UK general election seemed to indicate diminished support for a second Scottish independence referendum, at least for the time being.

Supranational governance—the EU

The most important example of supranational governance is the EU. Membership of the EU represents a substantial revision of parliamentary sovereignty, for EU law takes precedence over national law. In other words, EU law can be seen as the supreme law of the UK (and all other member states).

> The Community constitutes a new legal order for whose benefit the states have limited their sovereign rights, albeit within limited fields, and the subjects of which comprise not only the member states, but also their nationals.
>
> (ruling of the European Court, 1963, in Dearlove and Saunders 2000: 717)

The 'limited fields' are those governed by EU treaty—in other areas member states retain their ability to make their own laws (their 'sovereign rights'). Some commentators see this legal order as involving a straightforward loss of sovereignty, but others see it as a pooling or sharing of sovereignty because the EU is a form of intergovernmentalism through which each member participates in developing laws by which all are bound (see Chapter 13).

From reluctant Europeans to Leavers?

STAKEHOLDERS The UK's membership of the EU has also been a matter of political division and controversy, both between and within the major political parties, and the UK has generally been seen as a 'reluctant European', joining late (1973) and often resisting closer integration (e.g. not joining the single currency). In 2016, as a consequence of the (again highly divisive) referendum vote on EU membership, the UK moved on from being a reluctant member to a Leaver of the EU ('Brexit', or British exit).

British debate on EU membership had always been marked by a strong strain of Euroscepticism. This scepticism often reflected economic concerns—to maintain our own (felt to be superior) 'model of capitalism' and to fit economic policies to the requirements of the national economy (e.g. monetary policy). Yet the development of the EU was driven largely by economic considerations, and the UK's entry reflected a desire to share the economic benefits. Chief among these are the gains in efficiency, competitiveness, and growth that flow from the creation of a single market. The rationale is that, by removing barriers to cross-border investment, trade in goods and services, and migration (the 'four freedoms' of the single market), businesses can shift activities to the most advantageous locations and have unfettered access to a vastly expanded market on a 'level playing field', and competitive pressures drive up efficiency. For this reason, the EU can be viewed as pro-market, but some commentators have also seen in the EU the opportunity for more effective regulation of business in order to afford stronger protections to other stakeholders such as employees, consumers, and the environment (see Chapter 13).

Antipathy to the EU became a major element in UK politics with the rise of the UK Independence Party (UKIP) with its principal purpose of campaigning for UK withdrawal from the EU. Although only ever achieving one seat in the House of Commons through a by-election victory, UKIP won the EU election in 2014 with the largest share of the vote and was perceived by the Conservative Party as an electoral threat. In this context the Conservative Prime Minister, David Cameron, pledged to renegotiate the terms of the UK's membership of the EU and hold an in–out referendum on the basis of the new settlement if the Conservatives were to win the general election in 2015, hoping that this would see off the UKIP challenge.

It didn't. The vote in favour of leaving the EU was a political shock because at the start of the campaign there was confidence that the Remain side would secure victory. The result was a shock to business which had, in the main, supported UK membership on economic grounds, as expressed by the CBI: 'It's essential we stay at the table to bang the drum for businesses and defend our national interest.' Rejecting the argument for withdrawal the CBI stated: 'Businesses don't want the baby thrown out with the bathwater—not with 50 per cent of our exports heading to Europe.' As well as the benefits of trade inside the EU single market, the CBI argued that EU membership also offered the best prospect of securing trade deals with non-EU states such as the US: 'we pack a bigger punch in securing trade deals inside the EU than outside. The US wants the big prize—access to a market of 500 million customers across the EU, not just 60 million on our own shores. So, the best way of getting the right deal for the UK is on an EU-wide basis. The EU must be the launch pad for UK business to trade with the rest of the world, carving out a new global role for ourselves' (CBI 2012).

Against this the Leave campaign argued that the UK could prosper outside of the EU by being free to strike its own trade deals. However, whereas Remain voters tended to cite economic considerations as most important, Leave voters tended to place less emphasis on the economy and emphasized instead the desire to 'take back control' of our laws and to be able to control (i.e. restrict) immigration.

The outcome of the referendum, followed by the commencement of a two-year period of negotiation after the formal notification of the UK's intention to withdraw from the EU (triggering Article 50) in March 2017, has created a very high level of uncertainty for business. Although the Conservative Prime Minister affirmed that 'Brexit means Brexit' there was continuing lack of clarity about the future relationship with the EU that the government was seeking to achieve (characterized in terms of 'hard' versus 'soft' Brexit). In June 2017 uncertainty about the approach to the negotiations was intensified by the UK general election which resulted in a 'hung' Parliament, with no party having a majority of seats in the House of Commons.

Stop and Think

What is multilevel governance? What are the implications for business?

Looking ahead

- Recent political shocks (Brexit, Trump, and the 2017 UK general election) reaffirm that politics is highly unpredictable.
- For the foreseeable future two issues will dominate political debate and the political environment in the UK: austerity and 'Brexit'.
- UK politics and the economy are still dealing with the aftermath of the financial crisis, 'austerity', the slow recovery, and the squeeze on living standards (see Chapter 9). Although the government remains committed to austerity—essentially, to reduce public spending and cut the budget deficit—the target to eliminate the deficit by 2020 has been abandoned, implying that austerity will go on for longer than envisaged.
- The UK vote to leave the EU (Brexit) means that the two years to 29 March 2019 (when the UK is scheduled to leave) will be dominated by the negotiations over the terms of the 'divorce' and the future relationship between the UK and EU. These negotiations create a high level of uncertainty for business.
- The UK general election in 2017, at which the Conservative Party lost its majority, has thrown both Brexit and austerity up in the air. This is because the election was called specifically to increase the Conservatives' parliamentary majority and strengthen Theresa May's negotiating hand to achieve her vision of Brexit. The election result was interpreted as a rejection of a 'hard' Brexit associated with May, and the 'hung' Parliament means it will be hard for the government to win parliamentary votes on Brexit Bills. Therefore, the outcome of negotiations has become more uncertain, with a 'soft' Brexit more possible (or even the UK not leaving the EU).
- The election result was also interpreted as an expression of dissatisfaction with austerity. The gains made by the Labour Party on the basis of an anti-austerity manifesto suggest support for a return to a more social-democratic model of capitalism.

- The general election has also transformed the political environment in relation to the other great constitutional issue: the future of the union with Scotland. Losses incurred by the SNP seem to make a second referendum on Scottish independence unlikely in the foreseeable future.
- At a global level, the business environment is changing as a result of democratic and market reforms and rapid economic growth in some countries and regions, notably the BRIC nations. The western model of a capitalist economy and democratic government is becoming more prevalent, a new global balance of economic power is emerging, and a new pattern of interdependence between nations through trade and investment is developing.
- Because the world is divided into nation states, the global political environment will continue to be characterized by the opposing pulls of seeking cooperation to deal with common problems such as climate change and the pull of national self-interest in a 'global race'. 'Brexit' and the election of Donald Trump in the US have been interpreted as 'populist' revolts against political and business elites and their support for globalization, stimulating commitments to ensure that the benefits of globalization are shared more widely. The Trump victory has created uncertainty about the US' engagement with other states in areas such as trade agreements and efforts to tackle climate change due to the 'America first' stance.

Summary

- Politics is concerned with decisions and choices that affect the whole society: determining the rules under which we live together and creating a '**good society**'.
- Politics is a key element of the business environment. There is interdependence between business and government. One of the key questions in political debate concerns the nature and responsibilities of business and the type of capitalist economy we want to live in. In other words, business is politically controversial.
- The UK political system is a liberal democracy based on the principle of rule by the people. Government exercises a unique form of power in society—to make and enforce rules. However, rule is no longer the main function of modern states—they have become responsible for a range of public services and steering social and economic development.
- The UK has a combination of a democratic political system with a market or capitalist economy. On a global scale these economic and political forms have become more prevalent in recent decades. However, the world is characterized by great disparities in economic development and democratization. There is a close relationship between level of development and democracy: all of the large high-income OECD countries are democracies (either 'full' or 'flawed'), and almost all full democracies are high-income OECD countries.
- Politics is not conducted just at a national level but is characterized by multilevel governance. The EU is the most important example of supranational politics in the modern world.

Case Study: Taxing questions for business

VALUES Taxation is a highly contentious and divisive political issue. It is usually seen as a clear left-right issue, with 'big state' political parties on the left committed to higher tax rates to finance higher levels of public spending and 'small state' parties on the right favouring lower spending and taxes. Thus, UK Prime Minister Theresa May was essentially correct in her 2017 general election campaign to say that voters faced 'a choice between a Conservative Party that has always been a low-tax party . . . and a Labour party that is about raising taxes' (May, quoted in Nutall and Cousins 2017). Certainly, it is true that the aspiration to reduce taxes has been a central aspect of the neoliberal agenda of the Conservative Party since the 1980s. The rationale was set out by George Osborne (then Shadow Chancellor of the Exchequer) in 2006.

I want lower taxes. Because lower taxes would help Britain to compete. I think we're crazy as a country to be raising our taxes when most of our competitors are cutting theirs. . . . I believe that lower taxes extend the space of freedom in our society. I believe they help people to take greater social responsibility over their own lives, and the lives of others.

In this speech the support for lower taxes is stated clearly, and involves three elements:

1. Individual freedom—people should be free to decide for themselves how to spend their own money.
2. Competitiveness—reducing the 'burden' on business.
3. Self-reliance—individuals should do more to help themselves and rely less on the state.

The opposing case, for higher taxation, rests on the following ideas:

1. Public spending financed by taxation often expands individual freedom by providing opportunities and resources that individuals might not be able to pay for in the market, e.g. health and education.
2. Public services often meet the needs of business (e.g. for an educated workforce or efficient transport) and therefore enhance competitiveness.
3. Spending on public services reflects an ethic of solidarity or community whereby we look after each other in society. We all pay taxes according to our income, and benefit (e.g. from healthcare) in time of need. Further, the system of taxation and public spending should be used to redistribute income from richer to poorer households in the name of a fairer society or social justice.

Note that in this debate both sides accept the need for taxes—government is necessary and has to be paid for—but they contest the level of taxation and the size of government, and who pays the necessary taxes. The competitiveness argument mainly concerns the rate of corporation tax (tax on profits). The corporation tax rate has been steadily lowered in the UK since the 1980s. In 2010 Osborne, who then became Chancellor of the Exchequer in a Conservative-Liberal Democrat coalition government, inherited a corporation tax rate of 28 per cent and made reducing it a key element of economic policy for the sake of improving competitiveness. By the general election of 2017 the rate had been reduced to 19 per cent, and the Conservative Party were committed to a further reduction to 17 per cent. In sharp contrast, the Labour Party planned to increase the rate of corporation tax to 26 per cent by 2020/21, although this would still be lower than in 2010. How do we assess these alternative proposals? The basic case for raising the rate of corporation tax is that corporations should make a contribution to raising the revenue that government needs, and that the amount business pays has to rise in order to finance necessary increases in public spending. Labour argued that corporations (together with high-income individuals) should pay a bit more tax in order to pay for increased education spending and other commitments. The choice looks like this: if corporations and the rich do not pay more tax, then either: (a) the improvement in education will have to be foregone; or (b) the tax will have to be raised in some other way, e.g. by increasing the rate of income tax for middle- and low-income earners. There is some evidence that increasing corporation tax has public support. In a poll conducted in March 2017 60 per cent of respondents supported 'Increasing corporation tax . . . from the current rate of 20 per cent to 25 per cent' while 26 per cent opposed the suggestion (Cowburn 2017). Thus, Labour could claim that its proposal to increase corporation tax was necessary (to finance spending), fair (business must make a contribution), and legitimate (has public support).

Opponents of increased corporation tax must argue either that the spending is not necessary or, if it is necessary, that the taxes should be raised in another way. It is fair to say that business is generally in favour of lower corporation tax, seeing it as a cost to be reduced if possible, through 'tax management' (avoidance) or by lobbying government to lower the rate (see Chapter 11). This can be seen as a question of rational self-interest (just as we might infer that the 60 per cent of the public who support an increase are also expressing their own self-interest—they want more spent on education, but want others to pay for it). However, business does not always clamour for lower taxes—in a survey of businesses by PwC in 2016 'The majority of businesses (71 per cent) said

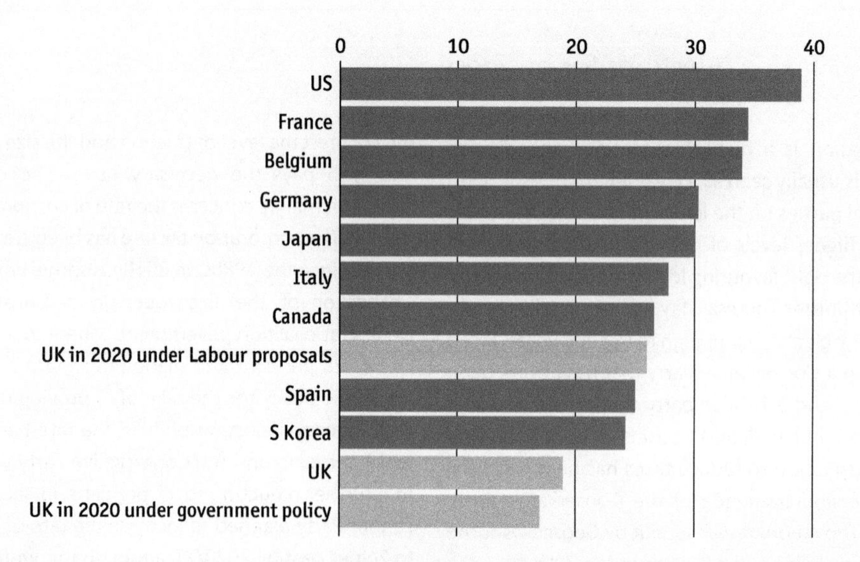

Figure 4.1 UK corporate tax rate compared with selected countries (2017) (combined local and central government taxes)
Source: Organisation for Economic Co-operation and Development Tax Database.

corporation tax should either stay at 20 per cent or not go below the 17 per cent cut pencilled in [by the Conservative government] for April 2020' (Stone 2016). Businesses might take this view as corporate citizens on a moral basis that business should pay its 'fair share'. But it might also reflect a self-interested awareness of the need to maintain the 'licence to operate' in the form of public support. In the PwC survey the view was expressed that reducing the corporation tax rate could 'risk alienating the public' (Stone 2016). This recognizes that there has been considerable public concern over large corporations seeking to minimize their tax liabilities (see Chapter 6).

The case for lowering corporation tax is often made in terms of showing that a country is 'open for business' or provides a business-friendly environment that will attract foreign investment. In effect governments engage in 'tax competition'—competing with each other to be the best place to do business by lowering the tax on profits. Advocates of this policy argue that reducing the tax *rate* can even increase the tax *take* by encouraging increased investment and business activity, and conversely that increasing the rate might reduce revenue by deterring investment. However, these effects, in both directions, are highly uncertain making it difficult to forecast tax revenues, especially in the medium-to-long term.

Nevertheless, according to the Institute for Fiscal Studies, 'Cuts to corporation tax rates announced between 2010 and 2016 are estimated to reduce revenues by at least £16.5 billion a year in the short to medium run' though probably less in the long run (IFS 2017b). And Labour's planned increase 'could raise around £19 billion in the near term, but substantially less in the medium to long run because companies would respond by investing less in the UK' (IFS 2017c).

One of the problems with the policy of reducing corporation taxes is that it involves a relentless 'race to the bottom' that not everyone can win, and in the process governments may erode their own tax base. Arguably governments would benefit by cooperating over corporate tax in order to avoid this competition. Critics also point out that the rate of corporation tax is only one factor among many that companies take into account in making investment decisions. Countries may be attractive places for businesses to invest in partly because of the public services that support business activity and that corporation taxes help to pay for.

According to the *Financial Times* (Figure 4.1), in 2017 the UK had the lowest corporation tax rate among G7 countries plus Belgium, Spain, and South Korea, and under Labour's proposal to increase the rate to 26 per cent by 2020 it would still be lower than all other G7 countries. Of course, this assumes that they do not lower their rates. Emmanuel Macron, elected President of France in 2017, pledged to reduce corporation tax from 33 per cent to 25 per cent (Atkinson 2017), and Donald Trump proposed cutting US corporation tax to 15 per cent from 39.6 per cent (Jacobs et al. 2017, Reich 2017)—the race to the bottom continues.

Question

Should the UK corporation tax rate be lowered to 17 per cent or raised to 26 per cent?

Review and discussion questions

1. Explain the nature of politics, and consider whether it is possible or desirable to keep politics out of business.
2. With reference to the UK political system, explain what is meant by the term liberal democracy.
3. Explain the differences between the minimal, developmental, and social-democratic models of the role of government. Where does the UK fit in this classification?
4. What evidence is there to support the argument that democracy is the best political environment for business?
5. With reference to the UK political system, explain the concept of multilevel governance.

Assignments

1. Prepare a briefing paper for the TUC outlining the arguments in favour of employee representatives on company boards, to inform discussions with the Secretary of State for Business, Energy & Industrial Strategy

   or

   Prepare a briefing paper for the CBI outlining the arguments against employee representatives on company boards, to inform discussions with the Secretary of State for Business, Energy & Industrial Strategy.
2. Examine *The Global Competitiveness Report 2016–2017* produced by the World Economic Forum (WEF). Identify the twelve 'pillars of competitiveness' described in the report, consider how these pillars bear on the political environment, and examine how far these pillars exist in the UK (**http://www3.weforum.org/docs/GCR2016-2017/05FullReport/TheGlobalCompetitivenessReport2016-2017_FINAL.pdf**).

Further reading

Coen et al. (2010) *a comprehensive edited collection of articles dealing with all aspects of government-business relations.*

For very useful analyses of the relationship between business and politics, see:

Moran (2009) and Wilson (2003)

RSA (2017) *an interesting and important report with recommendations for the role of government in fostering inclusive growth—making the economy work for everyone.*

Test your understanding of this chapter with online questions and answers, explore the subject further through web exercises, and use the weblinks to provide a quick resource for further research. Visit the online resources at www.oup.com/uk/wetherly_otter4e/

Useful websites

http://news.bbc.co.uk
The BBC website is a useful source for reports on contemporary politics and current affairs.

www.parliament.uk
Parliament website

www.number-10.gov.uk
10 Downing Street

http://www.oecd.org
Organisation for Economic Co-operation and Development (OECD)

http://www.worldbank.org
World Bank

http://www.cbi.org.uk
Confederation of British Industry (CBI)

http://www.ifs.org.uk
Institute for Fiscal Studies (IFS)

http://www.weforum.org
World Economic Forum (WEF)

References

Atkinson, S. (2017) 'Macronomy: what are Emmanuel Macron's economic plans?', BBC, 8 May **http://www.bbc.co.uk/news/business-39841164**

BBC (2016) 'A guide to devolution in the UK' **http://www.bbc.co.uk/news/uk-politics-35559447**

CBI (2012) 'UK must carve out a new trading role in the world for 2013, urges CBI director-general', 31 December **http://www.cbi.org.uk/media-centre/press-releases/2012/12/uk-must-carve-out-a-new-trading-role-in-the-world-for-2013-cbi**

CBI (2016) 'Our response to Prime Minister Theresa May's speech at #CBI2016.' **http://www.cbi.org.uk/news/our-response-to-prime-minister-theresa-may-s-speech-at-cbi2016**

Centre for Cities (2016) 'Everything you need to know about metro mayors: an FAQ' **http://www.centreforcities.org/publication/everything-need-know-metro-mayors**

Chang, H.-J. (2011) *23 Things They Don't Tell You About Capitalism* (Harmondsworth: Penguin)

Chang, H.-J. (2014) *Economics: The User's Guide* (Harmondsworth: Penguin)

Coen, D., Grant, Wyn, and Wilson, Graham (eds.) (2010) *The Oxford Handbook of Business and Government* (Oxford: Oxford University Press)

Cowburn, A. (2017) 'Brits in favour of higher income tax on country's wealthiest, poll finds', *The Independent*, 18 March **http://www.independent.co.uk/news/uk/home-news/income-tax-raise-backed-brits-poll-a7636846.html**

Cox, J. (2017) 'Pound sterling slips again after slumping in aftermath of UK election', *The Independent*, 12 May **http://www.independent.co.uk/news/business/news/pound-sterling-latest-updates-uk-election-2017-result-hung-parliament-currency-exchange-rate-a7785301.html**

Dearlove, J. and Saunders, P. (2000) *Introduction to British Politics* (Cambridge: Polity Press)

Economist Intelligence Unit (2016) *Democracy Index 2016: Revenge of the 'Deplorables'* **http://www.eiu.com/topic/democracy-index**

Flanders, S. (2016) 'Growing together', *RSA Journal*, issue 3.

Gall, G. (2016) 'May's backtrack on workers on boards shows the old guard is still in business', *The Conversation*, 22 November **https://theconversation.com/mays-backtrack-on-workers-on-boards-shows-the-old-guard-is-still-in-business-69235**

Guardian, The (2014) 'Scottish independence referendum: final results in full', 18 September **https://www.theguardian.com/politics/ng-interactive/2014/sep/18/-sp-scottish-independence-referendum-results-in-full**

Hansard Society (2017) *Audit of Political Engagement 14: The 2017 Report* **https://assets.contentful.com/xkbace0jm9pp/1vNBTsOEiYciKEAqWAmEKi/c9cc36b98f60328c0327e313ab37ae0c/Audit_of_political_Engagement_14__2017_.pdf**

Heywood, A. (2007) *Politics* (Basingstoke: Palgrave Macmillan)

Institute for Fiscal Studies (2017a) 'Labour's income tax rise would hit 1.3 million high income individuals', 16 May **https://www.ifs.org.uk/publications/9230**

Institute for Fiscal Studies (2017b) 'What's been happening to corporation tax?', Briefing Note (BN206) **https://www.ifs.org.uk/publications/9207**

Institute for Fiscal Studies (2017c) 'Labour's reversal of corporate tax cuts would raise substantial sums but comes with important trade-offs' **https://www.ifs.org.uk/publications/9206**

Jacobs, B. et al. (2017) 'Trump to unveil proposal for slashing corporate tax rate to 15%', *The Guardian*, 26 April **https://www.theguardian.com/us-news/2017/apr/26/trump-tax-proposal-corporate-tax-rate-15-percent**

Jones, B. et al. (2007) *Politics UK* (Harlow: Pearson)

May, T. (2016) 'We can make Britain a country that works for everyone', 11 July (speech) **http://press.conservatives.com/post/147947450370/we-can-make-britain-a-country-that-works-for**

Michie, J. (2016) 'How Britain could benefit by bringing workers into the boardroom', *The Conversation*, 12 October **https://theconversation.com/how-britain-could-benefit-by-bringing-workers-into-the-boardroom-66693**

Moran, M. (2009) *Business, Politics and Society: an Anglo-American Comparison* (Oxford: Oxford University Press)

Nutall, J. and Cousins, K. (2017) 'Fact check: have the Conservatives always been the low tax party?', *The Conversation*, 22 May **https://theconversation.com/fact-check-have-the-conservatives-always-been-the-low-tax-party-77742**

Oxfam (2017) 'An Economy for the 99%', Briefing Paper, January **https://www.oxfam.org/sites/www.oxfam.org/files/file_attachments/bp-economy-for-99-percent-160117-en.pdf**

Reich, R. (2017) 'Robert Reich: 5 reasons why Trump's corporate tax cut is appallingly dumb', Salon, 28 April **http://www.salon.com/2017/04/28/5-reasons-why-trumps-corporate-tax-cut-is-appallingly-dumb_partner**

RSA (2017) *Making our Economy Work for Everyone: Final Report of the Inclusive Growth Commission* **https://www.thersa.org/discover/publications-and-articles/reports/final-report-of-the-inclusive-growth-commission**

Stern, N. H. (2007) *The Economics of Climate Change: The Stern Review* (Cambridge: Cambridge University Press)

Stone, J. (2016) 'Corporation tax is low enough already, don't cut it again, businesses say', *The Independent*, 7 November **http://www.independent.co.uk/news/uk/politics/corporation-tax-rate-uk-17-20-pwc-business-survey-a7402766.html**

Taylor, M. (2017) *Good Work: The Taylor Review of Modern Working Practices*, Royal Society for the Encouragement of Arts, Manufactures and Commerce (RSA) **https://www.thersa.org/globalassets/pdfs/reports/good-work-taylor-review-into-modern-working-practices.pdf**

TUC (2016) '6 in 10 people support elected workers on large company boards, new TUC poll reveals' **https://www.tuc.org.uk/economic-issues/corporate-governance/6-10-people-support-elected-workers-large-company-boards-new**

Wilson, G. K. (2003) *Business and Politics* (Basingstoke: Palgrave)

Wolf, M. (2016) 'Capitalism and democracy: the strain is showing', *Financial Times*, 30 August

Chapter 5
The legal environment

David Amos

Learning objectives

When you have completed this chapter, you will be able to:

- Outline the different sources of law.
- Understand the relevance and working of European Union law as an example of international law.
- Appreciate the complex nature of international law and its relationship with international politics.
- Identify the different legal structures that businesses can adopt, and understand how that can have an effect on their development and decision-making.
- Identify and appreciate the different competing interests that will influence the law.
- Explore the different arguments for and against legal intervention in business.

THEMES

The following themes of the book are especially relevant to this chapter

- **DIVERSITY** The different legal structures businesses can adopt vary according to the size, nature, and history of the business, and can change as it develops. The legal structure a business adopts can affect its decision-making.
- **COMPLEXITY** The law is shaped by a number of factors—social, economic, and political. To fully understand the law and the direction it is taking, it is necessary to understand the broader context within which it is made. The legal environment therefore encapsulates many of the major themes within this book.
- **LOCAL TO GLOBAL** Legal systems operate within geographical boundaries or jurisdictions, and the law in different nation states varies. However, the legal environment is an area where the impact of globalization has been felt strongly with law increasingly being made at an international level. Law that is made outside of a national legal system can be central to the law within it, and international agreements known as treaties form one of the sources of law. To illustrate the working of international law we will look at the European Union, some legal aspects of Brexit, and the systems for adjudicating on international investment disputes.
- **DYNAMIC** The law changes on a daily basis, and adds to the complexity of the business environment. At the same time, this reflects the different influences that there are on the law. The law isn't changed for the sake of it but is altered in line with broader changes in society.
- **INTERACTION** The law is a balance between different competing interests of which business is just one. Business has an active role to play in influencing government policy (and therefore the law) so that it is sensitive to its needs. The legal environment determines the parameters

within which businesses can operate, and the success of a business can be determined by how it manages the legal requirements imposed upon it.

- **STAKEHOLDERS** In this chapter we will consider how competing interests can influence what the law is, and how the law regulates the relationships between stakeholders connected to business organizations.
- **VALUES** Neither values, nor the law, exist in a vacuum but represent the views of important social groups. In this chapter we will look at the impact these groups, and the ideologies they espouse have on the law.

Introduction

This chapter will consider the role of law in society and in particular the way that the law impacts on business activity. It will consider the effect that the law has on businesses in shaping both their internal workings and the external environment in which they operate.[1]

We will start with the basic question of what is the law and go on to look at various aspects of the infrastructure of the law such as the court system and the different sources from which the law is derived. It is clear that the structure of the law has been affected by changes in the political environment and globalization. We will therefore look at the changing nature of international law. In particular we consider the role of the European Union (EU) as an example of a developed trading bloc with its own legal infrastructure. We will also look at international trading agreements and their interaction with broader political considerations.

Having sketched out the overall legal framework, we will then consider issues that are more specific to businesses. In particular, we will look at the different legal structures that businesses can adopt and how those structures can affect and even determine how businesses operate.

It will be apparent from this discussion that the law is not a static entity and its direction may be altered by broader changes in society and any one of many competing interests. We will look more closely in Chapter 11 at the way in which businesses can exert their influence on politics and the law.

We will conclude this chapter by weighing up the arguments for and against legal intervention and indeed regulation in its wider forms, considering the competing interests that need to be balanced and the tension between business freedom and regulation. This discussion will reflect the ideological divides that are dealt with elsewhere in this book (see Chapters 2 and 4).

What is the law?

Our starting point has to be to think about what law is. This is not a straightforward question and there are many different views on this. At a superficial level, law is simply what both judges and governments decide. However, that does not tell us why some situations are covered by the law and others are not.

If we think a little more deeply, we can see that laws are made to help govern the numerous relationships that we have with other individuals and organizations. The assumption behind this is that people will adjust their behaviour to comply with the law. It is clear that this does

[1] The law in this chapter is as at 1 January 2017.

not always happen—otherwise prisons would be empty. Sometimes, breaking the law may simply be a result of ignorance, but more often it reflects the fact that people's behaviour is governed by other considerations than the law. Indeed, many of the rules which determine how we act are not part of the law at all.

VALUES Some of these rules arise from our moral beliefs or accepted standards of behaviour rather than being determined by any law. It is perhaps more accurate to call these norms rather than rules as they prescribe how situations should be and how things should happen.

The issue of what is legal but generally socially unacceptable is not always clear-cut. It is legal in England to have sex with whoever you wish even if they are married to someone else or are the same gender as you, provided they consent and are old enough. However, this may not be socially acceptable to all in a society characterized by diversity of values and beliefs.

On the other hand, in other countries which have different belief systems sexual behaviour is more regulated. Thus, under Islamic law adultery is considered a crime while homosexuality is illegal in over seventy countries and punishable by death in some. This helps to illustrate the relationship that there is between society more generally and the law. Marxists such as Cohen (1978) argue that the form that law takes is determined by the economic basis of society. A capitalist society would therefore have different legal relationships and forms of government than those that operate under feudalism.

Although the Marxist view is not widely accepted, it does help answer the question of why some situations are dealt with legally. Law is one of the mechanisms used to preserve order within society and will be shaped by the interests of those in power. The law will also reflect broader movements within society and the interests of influential sectors such as business.

Law is therefore formed as the result of the interaction between a whole series of different factors. These can be economic, political, social, and ethical. Often there are quite important material interests involved and those who make laws have to balance the needs of these different interests.

Stop and Think

Are there any laws that you would like to change?

If so, explain why this is. For example, do the laws concerned offend your moral beliefs, infringe your personal freedoms, or affect you economically?

At the same time, are there any laws that you would like to pass? Explain why you would like such laws put into place.

Sources of the law

In this section we will concentrate on the sources from which the law derives in England and Wales, although the picture we describe here is similar to most other jurisdictions. Until recently these have been twofold:

- case law/precedent; and
- legislation.

However, the passing of the Human Rights Act has had a huge influence on these main sources.

The role of international law has also now become central and will remain so even when the UK leaves the EU.

International law is founded on treaties. These are agreements between states on particular issues, and constitute the highest form of international law.

As we shall see, in certain circumstances citizens and businesses can use the provisions of a treaty in court action. This has been a source of some controversy as such mechanisms can be used to influence or indeed overturn the policies of democratically elected governments.

Case law/precedent

England and Wales operate under what is known as a common law system. This means that the law can be developed by the courts through the system of **precedent**. Under this system a court must follow the decision made by an earlier court. On the face of it, this would lend itself to a great deal of certainty, as to find out the law all you have to do is to refer to an earlier similar case.

However, there are various qualifications to this basic rule and indeed the Supreme Court does have the option to overturn one of its previous decisions. The system of precedent is therefore not entirely satisfactory as it leaves many grey areas.

Codes

It should be noted that most of continental Europe, and indeed Central and South America, operate under a completely different system known as codified or civil law. Here the basic law is contained in a series of detailed codes which judges must simply apply to the situation that faces them. There is therefore no system of binding precedent. The law of the EU borrows heavily from such systems.

Legislation

This is now the primary source of law in the UK and is divided between Acts of Parliament and what is known as delegated legislation. Acts of Parliament go through a detailed system of scrutiny within Parliament before they are passed. Once they are approved, however, they are the highest form of law.

Until the UK voted to leave the EU, Acts of Parliament could have been overridden by EU law. This is still the case for the legislation of the existing member states but will no longer be the case for the UK when it leaves.

No less important is delegated legislation, so called as the power to make the law is often delegated to the relevant ministers or authority. This is usually published in the form of what are known as statutory instruments.

This legislation is also subject to scrutiny, but such monitoring is limited. There are normally in excess of 3,000 statutory instruments a year as against around thirty Acts. Most legislation is therefore passed with little comment. Despite this lack of monitoring, important areas of the law are passed in this way as, for example, with the Companies (Model Articles) Regulations 2008 which set out a standard set of articles for a company which effectively act as its internal rule book.

It is the case that there is a vestige of judicial control over legislation, in so far as a court can issue what is known as a **declaration of incompatibility** if the legislation does not comply with the Human Rights Act 1998. The courts can also interpret legislation if there are ambiguities within it. However, technically Parliament is supreme and thus the courts should simply apply the legislation that it has enacted.

One by-product of the supremacy of Parliament is that legislation is subject to influence that can be exerted on government and MPs by pressure groups and lobbyists (see Chapter 11).

Indeed, many MPs have relationships, paid or otherwise, with outside bodies. There is therefore a strong connection between this branch of lawmaking and the political environment that businesses operate in.

For more information on the process of lawmaking in Parliament, go to www.parliament.uk (see the section on how Parliament works).

Constitution

The doctrine of parliamentary supremacy derives from the constitution. A constitution can serve a number of purposes; in particular, it can outline the structure of the state and its powers, set out the principles on which the state is based, and confer rights on citizens.

In Britain there is no core document which forms the constitution. However, in other countries, most notably the US, the constitution is contained in either one or a small number of core documents. Typically, such constitutions are drawn up following a change in power such as the American and French revolutions. With the change in power comes a change in values which is reflected in the constitution. While these are legal documents their content is therefore determined by political considerations, again illustrating the interaction between the legal and political environment.

> *Stop and Think*
>
> In this section we noted that legislation is the primary source of law and that Parliament is supreme.
>
> What is meant by this?
>
> Why do you think that this is an important principle?

Structure of the courts

We mentioned earlier how the system of binding precedent was one of the two main sources of domestic law in England and Wales. In order to fully understand how this operates, we need to look at the structure of the courts. To help you understand this section, you should look at Figure 5.1.

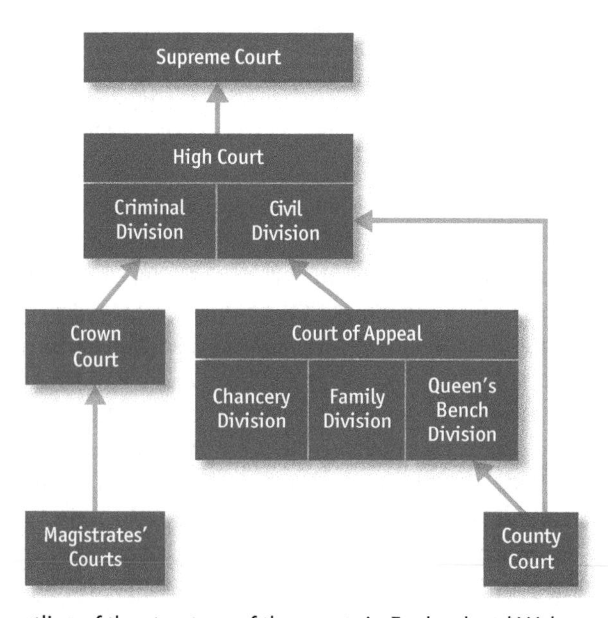

Figure 5.1 Simple outline of the structure of the courts in England and Wales

The court that a case is heard in is largely determined by the type of issue that is being dealt with. The primary split in the UK in this regard is between civil and criminal courts. However, there has been the advent recently of more specialist courts such as those dealing with technology and construction cases and commercial disputes.

Criminal cases

Criminal cases will always start in the magistrates' court. Less serious matters, such as most driving offences, will stay in that court with more serious cases being referred to the Crown Court.

If a party is unhappy with the decision made by the magistrates' court, they can appeal and have the matter reconsidered in either the Crown Court or the High Court depending on the nature of the appeal. In turn, if a party is dissatisfied with the decision in the Crown Court they would generally appeal to the Criminal Division of the Court of Appeal.

Any appeal from the Court of Appeal would be to the Supreme Court. For the purposes of considering precedent, the Supreme Court is the highest authority. Any decision made there would therefore bind the Court of Appeal, and so on down the line.

Although businesses might be involved in criminal cases less frequently than civil matters nevertheless they can still be prosecuted, for example when they breach health and safety legislation.

Civil claims

As for civil disputes, such as an argument over a contract or a personal injury compensation claim, where the case starts can vary according to the value and complexity of the claim. Traditionally the lower value and less complex claims would start in the County Court.

The High Court has three divisions which deal with different types of case. These are Family, Chancery, and Queen's Bench. For businesses, the latter two are the most important as they contain within them a separate Business and Property Court.

As with criminal matters, parties can appeal to the Court of Appeal—in this case the Civil Division. Again, from there the final recourse domestically is to the Supreme Court with this being the highest authority for the purposes of precedent.

The European Court of Justice

In line with developments in the political and economic sphere, the role of the EU in the structure of the courts in England and Wales will change as a result of Brexit. The UK Prime Minister Theresa May has, however, made clear the UK 'will take back control of our laws and bring an end to the jurisdiction of the European Court of Justice in Britain' (May 2017).

For existing member states, national courts still have a responsibility to protect and apply EU law and the European Court of Justice (ECJ) is the highest court when there is a European dimension to a case.

Tribunals and alternative dispute resolution

Aside from the system outlined above there are less formal fora for resolving disputes. An example of these which is important for businesses is the Employment Tribunal (ET) which can be used to deal with breakdowns in the employment relationship. Despite their less formal approach, there is still a right of appeal from such tribunals to the Court of Appeal and subsequently to the Supreme Court.

There has also been a rise in what is known as alternative dispute resolution (ADR). This takes different forms, but the basic principle is that parties to a dispute should try to resolve it in their own way without the formalities, costs, and delays inherent within the court system. Indeed, such an approach is suggested in the rules governing the Civil Courts which have been reinforced by a number of important court decisions.

For more about judges and the way courts work, go to https://www.judiciary.gov.uk

Comparison of court systems

While the system described above is specific to England and Wales, the core features of this system are common to most jurisdictions. In France, for example, the primary divide in the court system is between administrative and judicial courts which in turn reflect the division between public and private law in that country. However, within these courts there are specialist courts for criminal, civil, and other matters. Similarly, there is a hierarchy of courts which allows for review and appeal of decisions.

In the US, the court system reflects the constitutional divide between the federal/national government and the state governments. The courts therefore have jurisdiction over the matters that the government they are linked to has power over. Again, however, there are specialist courts and the core hierarchy of first instance court, intermediate appellate court, and highest court remains the same.

> *Stop and Think*
>
> In this section we have looked at the different courts that cases can be heard in. Why do you think that in all systems there are courts that parties can appeal to?

The European Union

LOCAL TO GLOBAL So far we have concentrated on national legal systems but there are a number of worldwide bodies and agreements which have an influence on international business, such as the United Nations, World Trade Organization (WTO), International Monetary Fund (IMF), and World Bank. A good example of a 'supranational' legal order can be seen in the development of the EU (see Chapters 4 and 13).

The first thing to appreciate about the EU is that although it is a union it is, in fact, still a collection of sovereign independent states. At the same time, each member state has to surrender elements of its sovereignty. In particular, EU law becomes an integral part of that country's domestic law. This was, of course, a central theme of the referendum campaign in Britain. It is essential to have some knowledge of EU law as it has a tremendous impact on how and where businesses can operate within the EU.

Sources of European law

Primary sources

The primary sources of European Law are the Treaty on European Union (TEU) and the Treaty on the Functioning of the European Union (TFEU) the current consolidated versions of which were published in 2016. The clauses in these treaties are called articles and, as we shall see, these can confer rights on individuals as well as institutions.

Secondary sources

Article 288 of the TFEU sets out the five types of secondary European Community law:

- Regulations;
- Directives;
- Decisions;
- Recommendations;
- Opinions.

Regulations have general application and therefore bind all of the member states. They do not need to be put in force by national legislation and are intended to achieve uniformity of law across the union. An example of this is Regulation 2679/98 on the functioning of the internal market.

Directives are addressed to specific member states and are not directly applicable. Instead they will direct that members enact appropriate national legislation to achieve a set aim by a set date. They are therefore aimed at achieving harmonization rather than uniformity of the law so that while all member states will be expected to achieve the same result they have flexibility as to the means by which they do so. Prominent directives include Directive 2004/48 on the enforcement of intellectual property rights.

Decisions represent a sort of hybrid of the above two. Like directives these are addressed to specific bodies although these can be institutions and individuals as well as member states. However, like regulations they are directly applicable and therefore do not require legislation at a national level. They are frequently used by the European Commission to grant companies import or export licences, and to notify member states of their Common Agricultural Policy and Structural Funds allocations.

Recommendations and opinions are not legally binding, but should be taken into account by national courts. These are sometimes known as soft law—a term which covers other items such as codes of conduct issued by Community institutions. It is still necessary to be aware of these as while they may not have direct legal force they still constitute part of the regulatory regime that companies operate under.

As in the UK, legislation is supplemented by the work of the courts, in this instance the ECJ. This court is made up of one judge per member state.

In terms of secondary sources, the influence of the court has been twofold. First, it has set out a number of general principles of Community law to assist in considering Community legislation. The principles are necessarily widely drawn and include equality, fundamental human rights, and legal certainty.

More specifically, the case law of the court has helped develop understanding of European law. Probably the most striking example of this came with the development of the principles of 'direct effect' and supremacy which we will consider later.

Who makes European law?

Having seen what the different sources of the law are in the EU it is instructive to briefly consider who makes the law in the EU, particularly as the system is different to that which operates in the UK and is therefore subject to influence in a different way.

Essentially there are three separate entities which have an input into the legislative process:

1. the Commission, the representative organ of the general interests of the Community;

2. the Council of the European Union (or the Council of Ministers as it is popularly known), the representative institution of the member state governments; and
3. the European Parliament, the representative body of citizens of the member states.

In terms of the composition of these bodies, there are twenty-eight commissioners—one from each member state. They are led by the Commission President, currently Jean-Claude Juncker, who decides who is responsible for each policy area. Once appointed, a commissioner's responsibility is to the EU as a whole. They therefore have to be approved by the European Parliament and take an oath to act in the interests of the EU rather than their national government.

The Council meanwhile is made up of one representative from each member state who is authorized to bind the government of that state. The personnel of the Council will change depending on the subject being discussed, so for example if the issue at hand is farming, then the agriculture minister will attend.

As with the UK Parliament, the European Parliament consists of directly elected representatives.

It is beyond the scope of this chapter to consider exactly how EU legislation is made. However, there is an opportunity for the Parliament, Council, and Commission to each have an input into the process. Essentially it is the Commission which initiates legislation, but it is the Parliament and Council which adopt it. The Commission and the member states will then implement the measures that have been adopted.

For more information on the process of making law in the EU, go to https://europa.eu/european-union/about-eu/institutions-bodies_en#law-making

In addition to the above bodies, in 2009 the European Council became one of the EU's official institutions. This body is made up of the Heads of State and the President of the Commission. The Council has its own President, currently Donald Tusk, and a High Representative for Foreign Affairs and Security Policy. Its role is more strategic in that it does not pass laws but sets out the general political direction and development of the EU.

Who enforces European law?

There are two main institutions which play a role here: the ECJ and the Commission. The Court has two functions. First, it decides whether the Commission, Council, or national governments are operating in a way that is compatible with Treaty obligations. Such actions can be brought before it by any EU institution, national government, individual, or organization. Second, national courts can request authoritative rulings on points of EU law.

As for the Commission its role is essentially twofold. First, it can bring before the ECJ a member state which is not fulfilling its obligations. Second, it ensures that the Community rules on competition, which are of direct relevance to businesses, are adhered to.

It is important to note that EU laws do allow rights for individual citizens which can be enforced through their own national courts. It does this through the concept of 'direct effect'. This principle was first elucidated by the ECJ in the *Van Gend en Loos* case 26/62 (1963) ECR 1, as illustrated in Mini-Case 5.1.

EU law is therefore a central component of the legal environment in its member states. Indeed, the EU plays a fundamental role in determining the parameters within which a company can operate. In particular, in order to achieve its aim of a single market the EU has established rights for the free movement of:

- goods (established in Article 34 TFEU and the *Cassis de Dijon* (120/78) case);
- persons (found in Article 45 TFEU); and
- services (laid down in Article 56 TFEU).

Mini-Case 5.1 Van Gend en Loos and direct effect

In September 1960 Van Gend en Loos imported a chemical product called unreformaldehyde from Germany into the Netherlands. They were charged a duty of 8 per cent. This was 5 per cent higher than the duty which operated when the 1957 EC Treaty came into force.

Van Gend en Loos sought to recover the difference between the two rates. They therefore took the matter to the Tariefcommisie—the administrative tribunal having jurisdiction over customs duties in the Netherlands. In turn, the Tariefcommisie referred the matter to the ECJ.

The case was based on Article 12 of the Treaty of Rome which dealt with fiscal barriers to trade. (This is now Article 30 TFEU.) The imposition of the additional tariff was argued to be in breach of this article.

In order to be successful in their case, Van Gend en Loos had to show first of all that Article 12 had 'direct effect'. This means that it gave them individual rights that they could rely on in the court in the Netherlands.

In considering this issue the court argued that the Treaty didn't only create obligations between nations but covered individuals as well. Indeed, they pointed out that the preamble to the treaty 'refers not only to governments but to peoples'.

As a result, the court concluded

the Community constitutes a new legal order of international law for the benefit of which the states have limited their sovereign rights . . . and the subjects of which comprise not only Member States but also their nationals . . . Community law, therefore, not only imposes obligations on individuals but is also intended to confer upon them rights.

The rights and obligations of EC law could therefore be enforced by individual parties in national courts. This, along with the concept of the supremacy of EU law established in the Costa (6/64) case, has worked to ensure the uniform application of EU law across all of the member states. It has therefore been central to ensuring the effectiveness of the European legal system and the attainment of the aims of European integration.

There are certain criteria to be fulfilled for direct effect to apply and therefore it does not cover all EU legislation. There have also been various refinements to the general principle. However, it does show the importance that the EU has in the legal environment.

Questions

1. **In this Mini-Case, we have looked at how, under the principle of direct effect, individuals have been given rights to enforce certain elements of EU law in their own national courts.**
2. **Why do you think that this principle is important?**

Allied to these is the right to freedom of establishment (Article 49 TFEU) which allows individuals and companies to set up businesses in other member states under the same conditions as citizens/companies of the host state. These positive rights are supplemented by measures to control anti-competitive practices such as agreements between companies to share markets or price fixing (see Articles 101 and 102 TFEU).

The extensive powers of the Commission can be seen in the size of the fines they are able to levy on companies that infringe these articles. In 2016 four truck manufacturers—Volvo, Daimler, Iveco, and DAF—were fined a combined total of over €2.9 billion for coordinating prices and colluding over the manner in which they dealt with emission technologies (European Commission 2016). The fine would have been higher had a fifth company, MAN, not revealed the cartel and thus received immunity from any fine.

The Commission had previously imposed a fine of over €1.4 billion on a number of companies, including Phillips, LG, and Panasonic, for price fixing and dividing markets between them in relation to components for TVs and computers (Chee 2012). This fine was upheld on appeal (European Commission 2015). One notable feature of this case was that it involved companies who weren't primarily based in the EU. It therefore illustrates that companies which trade internationally have to take account of the legal position in the jurisdiction they are working in.

Business organizations

DIVERSITY INTERNAL/EXTERNAL So far we have looked purely at the external legal environment. Businesses clearly have to be aware of this, as it can have a huge impact on the decisions they make. However, in order to understand fully how businesses operate and make decisions, we have to look internally, particularly at the different legal structures that businesses can adopt:

- sole traders;
- partnerships;
- limited liability partnerships; and
- companies.

In this section we will focus by way of illustration on the law in England and Wales. The core features of the different types of business organization are largely the same throughout the world. However, as we illustrate in Mini-Case 5.2, the precise form may vary according to the context within which the company operates.

Sole traders

Here an individual is the sole proprietor of the business. They therefore have sole control over the business and can take all the profit from it. However, at law they also have unlimited personal liability. What this means is that they are responsible for any debts and losses.

In terms of setting up the business, as the sole owner they have to finance it themselves, although of course they can take out a loan to do so. Legally there are virtually no formalities involved in starting such a business, although they do have to keep the necessary financial records for tax purposes.

This freedom from regulatory constraint may be an incentive for an individual to set up such a business although becoming a sole trader may not always be a positive choice. In some industries it may benefit larger companies to classify people who are in effect employees as self-employed. This is because it may allow them to avoid certain elements of the legislation governing employment.

Indeed, this is a key feature of the so-called 'gig economy' where individuals work on a job-by-job basis for companies such as Uber or Deliveroo. The status of those who work in such roles is a subject of some controversy. Most notably in October 2016 the GMB Union brought a successful test case against Uber arguing that at law the drivers concerned were workers. This meant that they enjoyed rights such as paid annual leave, maximum hours, and a minimum level of pay. Such rights are not available to those who are classified as self-employed. While Uber have appealed the decision, a similar case was won by a bicycle courier against CitySprint (see O'Connor 2017).

Partnership

Partnerships are also characterized by a relatively light regulatory touch. They are governed by the Partnership Act 1890 which defines the relationship as one 'which subsists between persons carrying on business in common with a view to profit' (s. 1(1)). Usually when a partnership is formed the partners will draw up a document called a deed which is in effect a constitution for the partnership. This will deal with issues such as who provides the capital for the organization, the management structure, and the allocation of the profits.

Mini-Case 5.2 Company structures and their environment

While looking at the legal issues surrounding the different business forms it may help to briefly consider the history of two major companies to see how their structure was influenced by their development and the context they operated within.

A company that adopted the main different legal structures described in this section was the chocolate manufacturers, Cadbury. The company started in 1824 with John Cadbury setting up on his own in a shop in Birmingham. His business was sufficiently successful for him to rent a small factory in 1831. In 1847, John Cadbury went into partnership with his brother Benjamin and rented a larger factory in the centre of Birmingham. The company continued to grow, expanding its range of products and the size of its manufacturing base so that by 1899 Cadbury Brothers incorporated as a limited company.

Cadbury listed on the London Stock Exchange in 1969 in the same year as it merged with Schweppes who had a similar organizational history. However, although the company enjoyed success—becoming the world leader in sugar and functional confectionery—it demerged with Schweppes in 2008. In 2010, Cadbury was taken over by Kraft after a high-profile hostile bid which was reported to be in the region of £12 billion (see, for example, Sibun 2010).

At the time this takeover was a controversial step and Unite, the union which represents Cadbury employees, called for a Cadbury law. Under such a law, hostile takeovers of British companies would be banned (Inman 2010). However, while a committee of MPs who investigated the matter welcomed moves to consider a review of the rules and legislation concerning takeovers in the UK, they did not feel any changes should be directed specifically against foreign companies (House of Commons Business, Innovation and Skills Committee 2010). Nonetheless, the ramifications of the takeover are still being felt. The UK Prime Minister, Theresa May, has used the example of the Kraft takeover to propose measures to control foreign investment in a similar manner to the Foreign Investment committees that operate in the US and Australia (Walker 2016).

Some governments take a more interventionist view as we shall see in the case of LG, who are one of the world's largest electrical companies. LG is one of the chaebols, a group of largely family-owned conglomerates based in South Korea. The company was formed as Goldstar in 1958 by Koo In-Hwoi to produce the first domestically produced radio in Korea.

While not an immediate success, the company benefited from various changes in Korean government policy. Initially, they were able to expand as a result of the government's move to supply radios to rural areas. More fundamentally, in the 1960s a series of plans were announced by the government to grow Korean industry with Goldstar expanding alongside the implementation of the electrical industry development plan. Under these plans the government supported export-led industrialization and gave various forms of financial support to companies engaged in that process (see Powers 2010).

Goldstar grew to such an extent that in 1969 it was able to set up a series of subsidiary divisions. This use of subsidiary companies aided its development internationally and by the mid 1990s a new vehicle was adopted to oversee this development as Goldstar became LG. Nevertheless, the structure of the ownership of the firm meant that there was a complicated system of shareholding which helped to maintain the position of the Koo family who founded the firm.

Like many countries in Asia, Korea's economy was adversely affected by the currency crisis of 1997 and 1998. Under pressure from the IMF, the government pursued a policy of reforming the governance of the chaebols. As part of this process, LG became a holding company in 2001, as the group sought to ensure that its model of governance met the diverse needs of its numerous subsidiaries throughout the world. The LG companies also appointed more outside board members (Hiraga 2010). However, there is still a strong interrelationship between the different companies and the Koo family remain at the heart of the organization.

Question

Explain what factors you think might influence businesses such as Cadbury and LG to adopt different legal structures over time.

However, it is not essential to have such a document, as the Partnership Act will govern the relationship in the absence of the necessary provisions. Under the Act there is an assumption of equality between the partners. Thus, in the absence of any agreement to the contrary, partners are deemed to have equal rights to manage the business. In addition, they will be entitled to an equal share of the profits but will contribute in equal share to any losses.

As with sole traders, most partnerships have unlimited liability. However, as there is more than one person involved the liability is joint and several. This means that while each partner is jointly responsible for all of the debts a debtor can choose to recover the money from only one partner. If that did happen, the partner who paid the debt could recover the money they had paid out from the other partners.

The necessary corollary of this is that any partner can bind the firm. They can therefore enter into contracts on behalf of the firm, sign cheques, hire employees, and other such matters. A partnership can remove this power but has to notify people outside the partnership that it has done so. The partnership relationship does therefore involve an element of trust as the individual's business identity is not separate but bound up in their membership of the partnership.

The finance for partnerships comes from the partners themselves. While they can take out loans this means that there is a limit to the amount of capital they will have access to and therefore the size of undertakings that they can pursue.

The other factor which can inhibit the size of partnerships is the problems associated with unlimited liability. The bigger the partnership, the greater the risk is for the individual partners. This problem has recently been addressed with the advent of limited liability partnerships.

Limited liability partnerships

Limited liability partnerships (LLPs) are a relatively new innovation being allowed for under the Limited Liability Partnerships Act 2000. They are something of a hybrid. While they are still technically partnerships they share many of the central features of companies, so, for example, the owners are called members rather than partners.

As their name suggests the main advantage of such an organization is that a member's liability will be limited. This means that their responsibility for any debts of the LLP would be restricted to the amount that they invested. At the same time, they have a **separate legal personality**. We shall discuss this in more detail in relation to companies but essentially this means that any legal action will be taken against the organization rather than the individual partners.

On the downside, LLPs are regulated more closely than a traditional partnership, as they have to abide by many of the rules which cover companies.

Companies

INTERNAL/EXTERNAL Despite its merits, the LLP does not solve the other issue that tends to inhibit the size of undertaking that a partnership can contemplate: access to large amounts of capital. Companies, of whatever type, have managed to resolve this problem by allowing unlimited numbers of people to invest capital in the business. The number and size of the investments are controlled by the company itself which can issue what are known as shares to the value of the capital that they require.

Having large numbers of investors does pose problems over who runs the company. Clearly it would cause difficulties if thousands of investors wanted to have a say on every minute aspect of the company's operation. This issue has been resolved by separating the people who own the business (shareholders) from those who run it on a day-to-day basis (directors and company secretary).

The reality for many small companies is that this separation may be illusory as the shareholders will also be directors (see Chapter 15). For larger and thus economically more important companies this separation is often central to their existence.

Public versus private companies

To some extent the size and method of operation of a company is reflected in the regulatory regime that governs it. Smaller companies will typically be classified as private companies, while larger companies tend to be public limited companies (PLCs) with shares that are traded on either the London Stock Exchange or the Alternative Investment Market.

Under the Companies Act 2006 there are more relaxed requirements on private companies in relation to auditing, the holding of meetings, and the requirements for a company secretary. The running of larger public companies also tends to come under greater scrutiny.

The distinction between such companies has become more important with the rise of private equity companies. These companies will invest in other companies where they see a prospect for growth and therefore a high return for their investment. Such investments have included high-profile companies such as RJR Nabisco and Alliance Boots (now Walgreens Boots Alliance).

There have however been criticisms of the way that such firms operate. First, they often use high levels of debt to fund their transactions, although the capital can come from other investors. Second, it is felt that in order to achieve high returns they are quick to cut staff costs and 'asset strip' firms they have taken over. Third, there has been concern about the secrecy of such firms. This last point led to a high-profile report being prepared by Sir David Walker, a prominent British banker. This resulted in a series of voluntary guidelines on transparency and disclosure in the private equity industry which are overseen by the Private Equity Reporting Group (**http://privateequityreportinggroup.co.uk**).

Whatever the size or designation of a company, there are still common components to it even in businesses with complicated structures such as LG. To understand how these work in practice we need to look at the different individuals involved in such organizations and what their roles are. You should consider Figure 5.2, showing the structure of a company, to help you grasp the interrelationship between the different bodies and individuals concerned.

Separate legal personality

COMPLEXITY The starting point for considering a company's structure is the idea that the company itself has a *separate legal personality* as this provides the context within which to place the various elements of a company's organization.

The notion that a company should be a separate legal entity was first established in the case of *Salomon* v. *Salomon* (1897) AC 22 (see Mini-Case 5.3).

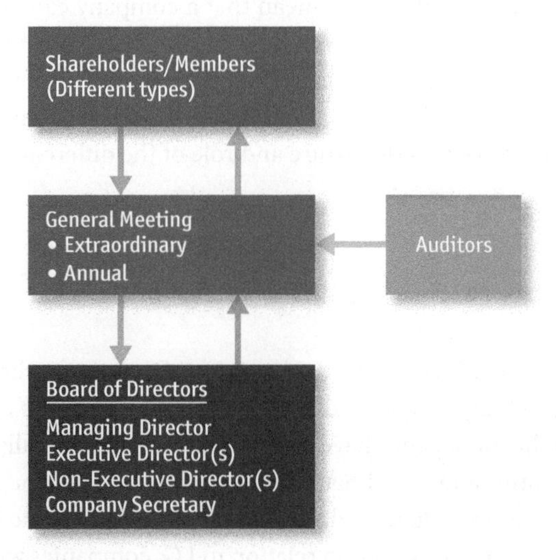

Figure 5.2 Company structure

Mini-Case 5.3 *Salomon v. Salomon* and separate legal personality

For many years Aron Salomon had successfully traded on his own as a leather merchant and bootmaker. It was a family business and four of his sons worked with him. His sons pressed him to give them a share of his business, and in 1892 Mr Salomon set up a company to carry their wishes into effect.

The shareholders of the company were Mr Salomon, his wife, and his four sons. The company bought the business from Mr Salomon for £40,000; £10,000 of this was financed by a loan given by Mr Salomon to the company which was secured on the company's assets (this is known as a debenture). Despite the sale, Mr Salomon retained a majority interest in the company and was one of its directors—the other two directors being his sons.

Unfortunately, the company hit hard times as a result of both a downturn in the footwear trade and a series of strikes. Mr Salomon obtained a loan for the company from a Mr Broderip by using his debenture as a security. However, the interest payments on this loan were not met and Mr Broderip wound up the company. The company's assets were sold which paid off Mr Broderip and left some money available for other creditors.

Mr Salomon sought to recover this money to pay off the debenture/loan that he had secured over the company's assets. The other (unsecured) creditors objected to this on various grounds but argued in particular that the company never in reality had an independent existence. It was in effect Mr Salomon under another name and he could not owe money to himself.

The House of Lords (now the Supreme Court) roundly rejected this argument. The company had complied with the necessary legal formalities to be properly incorporated. It therefore had an entirely separate legal identity and so could be in debt to Mr Salomon. As his loan was secured he therefore took precedence over the creditors.

Questions

1. **When you look at the facts of this case can it really be said that the company was separate from Mr Salomon?**
2. **Do you think the court's decision was a fair one for the unsecured creditors?**
3. **Assume your answer was no to one or both of these questions: how do you think you could justify this decision?**

Effect of separate legal personality

As we saw with LLPs, separate legal personality means that individuals within a company are largely protected from legal action which has to be taken against the company rather than individuals within it. The concept does also mean that a company can enter into contractual relationships with its shareholders/members. Most obviously, a shareholder can be an employee of the company and can take action against it if the contract of employment is breached. STAKEHOLDERS INTERNAL/EXTERNAL The designation of the company as a separate legal entity also has an impact on the nature and role of the different individuals within it.

Shareholders/members

These are the people who provide one of the two sources of finance for the company, the other being loans. They are essentially people who make an investment in the company in the hope of making some gain on the money they have put into it. They are generally a mix of large institutions such as pension funds and individuals although this does depend on the size and type of the company. As noted above, when we discussed private equity, some firms largely exist to invest in other companies while, as we saw in relation to LG, companies within the same group can invest in each other.

Although technically these investors are known as members, they are commonly referred to as shareholders. This is because the capital of the company is divided into shares with those who have invested in the company being given certificates recording the amount of capital that they have. The liability that a member will have for any debts of the company is limited to the extent of the shareholding that they possess.

The shares provide the potential profit that a member can make on their investment. First, the share itself is a form of property and can thus be bought or sold as with any other form of property. For many larger companies the price of their shares is quoted on a stock exchange. Second, if the company is doing well it can give its shareholders a sum of money called a dividend. This will be calculated according to the size of holding that a member possesses.

The shareholders are the owners of the company and although they may not run it on a day-to-day basis they do have some control over what happens within it. This control can be exercised internally at a general meeting or externally through court action. The most notable example of this in recent times came with the so-called 'shareholder spring' in 2012. Disputes over directors' pay and corporate performance led to investors voting against remuneration packages for senior executives with prominent individuals across large companies stepping down.

Directors

The people who do have hands-on control of the company are the directors. They are collectively known as the board and are given the opportunity to discuss the operation of the company at board meetings. Their role has been subject to much scrutiny with a series of reports including Cadbury (1992), Greenbury (1995), Hampel (1998), Higgs (2003), and Smith (2003) being prepared.

These reports looked at various aspects of the running of companies and led to the evolution of a code of best practice known as the UK Corporate Governance Code with similar codes operating in countries other than the UK. Among other things, the Code covers the make-up and operation of the board, directors' pay, accountability and auditing, and relationships with shareholders.

One important area that the Code looks at is the different types of directors. These will have more or less involvement with the running of the company and indeed some directors may not be members of the board. We need to look in particular at:

- the managing director;
- executive directors; and
- non-executive directors.

The managing director (sometimes called the chief executive) is central to the running of the company, providing a link between the board and the senior executives within the company who will implement the board's decisions. The Code clearly sets out that there should be a division between the running of the board and the running of the company. This is to avoid any one individual becoming too powerful and not subject to sufficient checks on their actions.

Executive directors are working directors who are employees of the company. They will generally have responsibility for a particular function within the company such as production or marketing.

Non-executive directors are less engaged with the running of the company on an ongoing basis but are no less important. They may well be part-time and will often be appointed for their expertise outside of the company. The reason for this is bound up with the role that they play. First, they can act as monitors of the performance of the company. Second, on a more long-term basis they can have an input into the strategic direction of the company.

Non-executive directors therefore have an important supervisory role to play which is recognized in the Code. It suggests that except in smaller companies at least half the board should be non-executive directors while in smaller companies there should be at least two directors of this type (Financial Reporting Council 2016: section B.1.2, p. 11). The Code also places store on the independence of non-executive directors from the firm. Independence here is considered largely in financial terms (see section B.1 of the Code for the full list of criteria)—although of course non-executive directors will still be paid by the firm.

Directors' legal duties

As can be seen from the above, the directors hold a powerful position within the company. It is they who act on its behalf, concluding contracts, taking out loans, and other such matters. Given that they are in effect dealing with other people's money there are some protections built into the system.

Specifically, Part 10 of the Companies Act 2006 provides the legislative framework within which directors work and sets out their central duties. These duties are a mixture of the general and the specific. A director must therefore manage the company with reasonable diligence, care, and skill and exercise independent judgement. As a result, they should avoid conflicts of interest and not accept benefits from third parties.

As noted above, directors are powerful individuals and to help limit that power the Act specifically requires them to act in accordance with their company's constitution. Whatever they do, s. 172 of the Act makes it clear that they must promote the success of the company. What is success for the company may be a matter of debate (see Chapter 1) but it is clear that the company's best interests must be central to what a director does. This statutory requirement is reinforced by the Code. It should be noted that if the directors breach their statutory duties legal action can be taken against them.

For more detailed information on directors, see the website of the Institute of Directors (IOD) (https://www.iod.com). The IOD publish a series of factsheets about directors and their role.

Company secretary/auditor

The other two main elements within the organization are the company secretary and the auditors. Since the 2006 Act private companies are not obliged to have a company secretary but most of them will do so. Those companies that do have a secretary can decide whether or not they are a director and have flexibility in determining their precise role. However, normally this will largely be administrative and will involve issues such as convening meetings, keeping company records, and accounts.

The auditors have a more important role in monitoring the company's activities in relation to financial matters. The Companies Act 2006 requires both private and public companies to appoint professionally qualified and independent auditors who will review and approve the company's accounts. They will then report to the members on the accounts. This process is subject to some discretion on behalf of the directors and again there is a lighter regulatory touch for small private companies.

In theory, the auditors can act as an important check on any financial abuses. However, several high-profile cases in the US have exposed weaknesses in the system with the auditors,

Arthur Andersen, being implicated in the scandals surrounding Enron and WorldCom. In both of these cases the companies concerned grossly misrepresented their financial position.

There was widespread concern after these scandals broke that they represented a deeper systemic problem with the auditing of companies (see, for example, the documentary *Bigger than Enron* https://www.youtube.com/watch?v=TCpZUDIquQw). As a result, legislation was passed in both the US and UK which imposed stricter controls on auditors.

However, it is not clear how effective this has been, as is illustrated by the collapse in 2008 of Lehman Brothers—an event which helped bring about a worldwide financial crisis. In a report[2] prepared in March 2010 as part of the court proceedings arising out of the collapse it was alleged that the company removed $50 billion from its balance sheet by use of an accounting device known as Repo 105. It was also alleged that the company's auditors were aware of the use of this device but did nothing to question its use or the failure to disclose it. It should be noted that the auditors for the company defended their position and no prosecutions arose out of the report. However, as Anton Valukas, who compiled the report, commented: 'If there's anything I've learned, being both in the government as a prosecutor and on the civil side as a defense attorney, is that it's effective regulation that prevents it from happening in the first place, which is the critical part of the process' (Harris 2012).

Stop and Think

In this section we have looked at the different parties involved in the structure of a company and have highlighted the role played by non-executive directors and auditors.

Why do you think it is important to have independent scrutiny of what a company is doing?

General meetings and written resolutions

STAKEHOLDERS INTERNAL/EXTERNAL Having looked at the different entities and the roles that they play we now need to consider the arenas where the different entities come together and the owners of the company (the shareholders) can exercise some vestige of control. This is one area where, at least in law, there is quite a big difference between private and public companies.

Private companies can dispense with the need for meetings altogether and instead can conduct their business by means of written resolutions. These resolutions perform the same function as the equivalent resolutions at a general meeting.

Most companies do still hold general meetings and public companies are required to hold an annual general meeting (AGM). A key issue at the AGM is likely to be finances, as this meeting gives the shareholders the chance to see the annual accounts. The meeting may also present an opportunity for members to remove a director and indeed challenge the board more generally over pay and performance as happened in the 'shareholder spring'.

There may be issues that need to be decided between the AGMs, and the directors have a general power to call such a meeting. Members also have the right to call such a meeting but only if together they hold more than 10 per cent of the company's shareholding. They might do this, for example, to allow consideration of a resolution to remove a director. Finally, both members and directors can apply for the court to exercise its power to call a meeting.

[2] The full text of the report is available at https://jenner.com/lehman

Legal action by shareholders

COMPLEXITY INTERNAL/EXTERNAL The limited internal control which can be exercised by shareholders is supplemented to some extent by the legal action they can take. Shareholders' rights in this regard have been extended dramatically by the 2006 Act. Any member can now bring an action where there has been negligence, breach of duty, or breach of trust by a director. However, any member wishing to bring an action in this way must first obtain permission from the court.

Stop and Think

So far in this section we have looked at the different types of business organizations and the law surrounding them. Imagine you were starting up a new business with a group of friends which involved making high-quality chocolates.

Which form of business organization would you adopt?

Explain the reasons for your decision.

Would your answer differ if you were merely seeking to open a small shop with your spouse to sell such chocolates?

In answering these questions, you can, if you wish, refer back to your answer to the question posed about Cadbury and LG.

What is the company for?

Having considered the company's structure, we need now to consider the purpose of a company and in whose interests it is run. The answer to this question is fundamental to our understanding of the way that a company might act in any given situation.

STAKEHOLDERS There is a whole series of individuals and organizations who might have an influence on the decisions that a company makes, referred to as stakeholders. How does a company balance all of those interests before deciding what to do?

Some guidance is given in s. 172 of the Companies Act 2006. It is instructive to read this in full.

1. A director of a company must act in the way he considers, in good faith, would be most likely to promote the success of the company for the benefit of its members as a whole, and in doing so have regard (among other matters) to—
   a. the likely consequences of any decision in the long term,
   b. the interests of the company's employees,
   c. the need to foster the company's business relationships with suppliers, customers and others,
   d. the impact of the company's operations on the community and the environment,
   e. the desirability of the company maintaining a reputation for high standards of business conduct, and
   f. the need to act fairly as between members of the company.

When the section was framed it was said to embody the notion of 'enlightened shareholder value'. This notion recognizes that while the core duty of directors is to ensure the success of the company, for the benefit of its members, they have to take into account a series of other factors. However, there has been some scepticism expressed as to the effectiveness of this provision given that it doesn't confer a right to legal action on those stakeholders mentioned in the section (see Lynch 2012).

Where the courts have considered the section, they have reached the view that it restates the existing law and that where companies take broader considerations into account they should only do so to the extent that this preserves the value of the company—see *R. (People & Planet) v. HM Treasury* (2009). At the same time, most commentators have seen this section as ensuring that directors put the interests of the shareholders first (see, for example, Alcock 2009) albeit that they have to take cognizance of broader factors.

The practical importance of this is the impact it has on the way that companies act on a day-to-day basis. Shareholders are investors and so their main motivation is in a suitable return on their investment. As Lord Goldsmith, then Attorney General, said when discussing s. 172 before a parliamentary committee: 'for a commercial company, success will normally mean long-term increase in value . . . For most people who invest in companies, there is no doubt about it—money, that is what they want' (*Lords Grand Committee* 6 February 2006, col. GC256).

Indeed, some institutional investors have by law to secure a good return. Thus, in *Cowan* v. *Scargill*, Megarry VC made it clear that in a pension fund 'a power of investment . . . must be exercised so as to yield the best return for the beneficiaries' and that trustees (the people who run pension funds) 'must put to one side their own personal interest and views' (1985 Ch. 270, p. 287). If we consider that the OECD (2017) estimated that pension funds in the UK alone accounted for over £1.8 trillion of assets in 2016 we can see how important this decision was.

In order to satisfy the shareholders, a company must therefore have the maximization of profit at the core of its activities. However, as s. 172 suggests the profit motive does not necessarily mean that it is in the best interests of the company to act unethically or not be alive to social issues.

As we have pointed out in other chapters, such behaviour can result in damaging consumer boycotts as, for example, with the campaigns against companies who traded in South Africa during the apartheid era. More recently, there have been campaigns in Britain against Starbucks and other companies who were paying little or no corporation tax. Indeed, some campaigning bodies, such as the Campaign Against the Arms Trade, seek to persuade investors to sell their holdings in companies who they believe are guilty of unethical behaviour.

However, given that the core purpose of companies is to maximize the return for investors there is a limit on the level of social responsibility that a company can exercise. Indeed, some have argued that the law governing companies, in placing primacy on shareholders' interests, acts to prohibit ethical behaviour.

In his critique of the corporation Bakan points to the 'best interests of the corporation' principle. The principle was most notably outlined in the US case of *Dodge* v. *Ford*, although s. 172 of the Companies Act 2006 is a variant of it. The principle determines that 'managers and directors have a legal duty to put shareholders' interests above all others and no legal authority to serve any other interests' (Bakan 2005: 36). According to Bakan this means that corporate social responsibility is illegal unless in some way it benefits the company.

If this is the case then is the answer simply to change the legal structure of companies and to regulate them in a way that forces them to pursue social rather than economic goals?

This approach was suggested by Wilkinson and Pickett (2010) who argued that 'democratic employee-ownership' which involved participative management methods would have a number of advantages over the external share ownership model. They argued that dividends to shareholders were a drain on a company and could be better used to improve performance by investment in technology and equipment.

More fundamentally, they felt in reality that a company is composed of the skills, knowledge, and abilities of its employees. With a move from shareholder ownership which saw business as property to a community-focused model based on employees, the skills of the workforce could be harnessed more effectively. In particular, the company would work in a more ethical way which was more in harmony with the communities in which it operated.

Stop and Think

In this section we have considered the legal structure of a company and how that might impact on its behaviour.

What issues and personalities do you think a company should take into account when making decisions? Should the wording of s. 172 be amended to put other interests on an equal footing with those of shareholders? Should employees be the focus of the company?

How far should the law intervene—regulation vs. deregulation

Deregulation?

VALUES **INTERACTION** Deregulation involves reducing or removing the 'burden' that regulation places on business. It is based on the view that businesses should have more freedom to run their own affairs and to compete freely in the market.

Freer competition can encourage efficiency. A negative example of this comes with the EU's Common Agricultural Policy (see Chapter 13). Under this policy, the EU pays subsidies to farmers to both stabilize their income and assist them 'if normal market forces fail' (European Commission 2017). This is backed up by tariffs which help block imports of goods from outside the EU. As a result, not only is there no incentive for farmers to increase their productivity but prices for consumers are set at an artificially high level.

It is also argued that deregulation, particularly of labour laws, encourages flexibility and therefore can act to reduce costs. These costs can be substantial. Thus in 2010 the IOD estimated that regulation costs UK businesses £80 billion per year (Gammell 2010). Attempts have been made to address these costs. In Britain, the Small Business, Enterprise and Employment Act 2015 imposed a requirement on the government to publish a target in respect of the economic impact of regulation on businesses. The first of these 'Business Impact Targets' aimed to reduce the cost of regulation by £10 billion between 2015 and 2020. The implementation of this Target has not been without controversy. The National Audit Office (2016) indicated that the Target was subject to manipulation and that the government did not have accurate figures for the cost to business of regulation.

Despite the difficulties in measurement, this issue is still central to any argument in favour of a lighter regulatory touch as reducing costs means increased competitiveness. This does not only mean competitiveness for individual companies but nation states as well, who can encourage inward investment by promoting the business-friendly environment that they offer.

The World Bank in their annual *Doing Business* reports provides indices of these sorts of policies (see www.doingbusiness.org). Countries are ranked according to a variety of measures relating to regulation. Clearly in a globalized and increasingly competitive world economy this imposes pressures on countries to offer the most 'competitive' and business-friendly conditions. Indeed the 2017 *Doing Business* report indicated that 'better business regulation' was associated with greater amounts of foreign direct investment (International Bank for Reconstruction and Development/World Bank 2017: 21–2; for a more nuanced discussion of this point, see Corcoran and Gillanders (2015) and Jayasuriya (2011); see also Chapter 11). The report also indicated that countries throughout the world were pursuing regulatory reform that was informed by the indicators in the *Doing Business* reports. The benefits of deregulation can arise in a more indirect fashion. In its Annual Report for 2006, the Better Regulation Commission argued 'Tying people up in red tape makes innovative thinking all but impossible' (p. 10). However, it did not use that as a justification for complete deregulation but rather regulating in a different way.

The arguments for relaxing the burdens of regulation are therefore primarily economic. Those in favour of regulation are more multifaceted although they still have an economic dimension.

Regulation?

The case for regulation was summed up rather neatly by Brendan Barber when he was General Secretary of the British Trade Union Congress who pointed out that

> everyone is protected by regulations every day. At work we are protected from exploitation. When shopping we are protected from shoddy deals. And as citizens we are protected from toxic pollution, fire-trap buildings and dangerous vehicles. Law, including regulation, is the difference between anarchy and civilization.
>
> (TUC 2006)

There are therefore different strands to the arguments advanced by those in favour of regulation. Primarily these are defensive, being largely concerned with protection of employees, consumers, and the environment. However, they are underpinned by a positive ideological argument that emphasizes the social benefits of regulation.

The argument in favour of protecting employees can take various different forms. From a strictly economic point of view a workforce that feels vulnerable is likely to plan its spending accordingly. Workers who feel that they could lose their jobs tomorrow are less likely to make long-term or expensive purchases such as houses, cars, or holidays.

The strictly economic argument can intersect with those of a more social nature as can be seen if we look at the issue of health and safety at work. The Health and Safety Executive has estimated that workplace accidents and work-related ill health costs the British economy as much as £14.1 billion a year (Health and Safety Executive 2016: 2). Coupled with that, economic cost is the social cost in terms of pain, grief, and suffering. A stark example of this comes when we look at the effect of exposure to asbestos (see Mini-Case 5.4).

Alongside the economic and social arguments there may be political reasons for intervention. In recent years, awareness of the need to protect the environment has increased resulting in legislation such as the Pollution Prevention and Control Act 1999 which implemented an EU directive on pollution control. The Act provides for a system of permits underpinned by a number of offences which are designed to regulate the activities of potentially polluting companies.

While such legislation could be said to inhibit business freedom it does fit neatly with the ideas of democracy and social solidarity which underpin the case in favour of regulation. This is that if a company's behaviour is detrimental to the lives of a country's citizens and communities the electorate should have the power, through their representatives, to control that company (Bakan 2005). The Bhopal disaster which took place in India in 1984 provides an instructive example.

Mini-Case 5.4 Asbestos

Asbestos is a mineral which was used widely in the UK until the 1980s because of its heat-resistant qualities. There are three main types of asbestos: blue, brown, and white.

As a result of the potentially fatal consequences of exposure to asbestos the use of blue and brown asbestos in Britain was banned in 1985. A similar ban was placed on the use of white asbestos in 1999. Despite the ban in Britain asbestos is still used in many countries throughout the world.

Inhalation of asbestos fibres can cause a number of diseases, particularly lung cancer, asbestosis, mesothelioma, or pleural plaques. The most serious of these conditions is mesothelioma which accounted for 2,542 deaths in 2015 alone (Health and Safety Executive 2017a). It was estimated by the Health and Safety Executive that in the UK the number of deaths from mesothelioma will continue at the same level for the rest of the decade before the number of deaths starts to decline (Health and Safety Executive 2017b).

The reasons why the figures are continuing at such a level despite the ban are twofold. First, there is a time lag between exposure to asbestos and the onset of symptoms. This can be anything between fifteen and sixty years. Second, there is still a large amount of asbestos that was fitted in buildings that has yet to be removed.

Not surprisingly there has been extensive litigation relating to exposure to asbestos. In England, one of the more important recent cases related to pleural plaques, which is a form of scarring to the lungs. The case went up to the House of Lords, which at the time (2007) was the highest court in England. The Law Lords rejected the claim for compensation. The importance of this decision can be seen when we look at the financial consequences of asbestos litigation. In 2009, the Institute and Faculty of Actuaries UK Asbestos Working Party estimated that the undiscounted cost of such claims could amount to £10 billion between 2009 and 2050 (Institute and Faculty of Actuaries UK Asbestos Working Party 2009 GIRO update: 4). However, as has already been suggested the economic argument may not be the most fundamental in deciding when and how far the law should intervene. In the case concerning pleural plaques the victims obtained judgment in their favour in the High Court. After this decision, one of their lawyers, Ian McFall, commented 'This is good law, which puts people before profits' (Dyer and Jones 2005), suggesting a deeper moral and philosophical argument for intervention.

Since the case was heard, the government has announced a scheme to compensate those who had started claims related to pleural plaques before the Law Lords' decision. They did not, as they could have done, overturn the court's decision and allow such claims in the future. This did provoke some criticism (see, for example, Lazenby 2010) and bills were presented which would have taken such a step. Indeed, the Scottish Parliament enacted legislation allowing compensation for sufferers of pleural plaques. The Act was challenged in the courts by UK insurance companies, but the challenge was rejected.

Questions

1. **Do you agree that law which puts people before profits is good law?**
2. **Assume that you do agree; should this be the criterion for deciding what the law is in every situation?**

In this incident there was a chemical leak from the factory of US corporation, Union Carbide. The leak resulted in the death of more than 20,000 people and the injury of many thousands more. After several years the company reached a multimillion-dollar settlement of the lawsuit that arose out of the disaster.

However, controversy still surrounds the incident and led to the resignation of Meredith Alexander from the Commission for a Sustainable London in the lead-up to the 2012 Olympics. Her resignation arose out of sponsorship of the games by Dow Chemicals who took over the assets and liabilities of Union Carbide. Dow deny any responsibility and argue that Union Carbide's assets and liabilities in India were taken over by a third party. Nonetheless, there are still ongoing proceedings relating to the case with the *Times of India* reporting in January 2017 that a summons had been issued against Dow Chemicals by the Court of Chief Judicial Magistrate.

There are, therefore, a number of political and economic arguments in favour of intervention. Indeed, greater regulation is not necessarily inimical to business success. As we have seen, the political and moral argument that economic gains should be enjoyed by all potentially has the economic benefit of greater consumption.

In fact, the argument that there should be some level of regulation is not as controversial as it may seem. The EU regulates how companies compete with each other, and even the WTO, which has free trade philosophy at its core, supervises the Agreement on Trade Related Aspects of Intellectual Property (TRIPS).

The agreement was entered into as manufacturers, particularly from developed countries, were increasingly concerned by the billion-dollar trade in pirated products which was affecting their profitability. The regulations oblige WTO members to grant and enforce rights to property which is the product of intellectual activity such as new inventions.

There is therefore not a completely free market. The state has to intervene in order to correct the distortions that can arise from the market and create the conditions in which businesses can flourish. As the Better Regulation Commission (2006: 12) say: 'We would all be rather disappointed if basic protections such as a clean environment . . . and a good education for our children were not fulfilled.' The issue therefore is not regulation versus deregulation but rather what level and what type of regulation is acceptable.

Alternatives to regulation?

It is important to recognize that the process of regulation is not simply carried out by the state through legislation. Indeed, in their document 'Reducing Regulation Made Simple' (2010) the Better Regulation Executive set out a number of alternatives to what they called 'command and control' regulation. These included self-regulation and co-regulation and broader mechanisms such as economic instruments, information, and education. Indeed, businesses may sometimes judge it better to regulate themselves through their own codes of conduct and trade associations or other similar measures as a way of fending off more stringent regulation by government.

However, it may not always be possible and desirable to use one of the alternatives to regulation. In such situations the law will intervene. The process of lawmaking is a balancing act between different competing interests and value systems. The level and type of legal intervention is therefore very much a result of the political process.

INTERACTION Businesses do have a role to play in this as, while they do not have votes, they can still influence legislators both directly and indirectly (see Chapter 11). This influence can be used in both a positive and a negative way. Businesses may therefore press for laws to be removed as well as passed in order to protect their position. As we will see in our final case study, businesses can also use court action or even just the threat of such action to influence the behaviour of governments. Such actions have excited a lot of controversy as arguments of democracy and national sovereignty have been used to counter measures allowing businesses to trade as they wish.

Looking ahead

As with the other elements of the business environment the future direction of the law will be affected by developments in politics. This is exemplified by the impact of Brexit on the UK. This political decision has raised fundamental questions about the law in the UK. Most notably, what should be retained of EU law, what role should the ECJ have, and how does the UK see itself as a legal centre?

Looking first at the retention of EU law, the simple answer is that in the short term there may be surprisingly little change. The government has presented a European Union (Withdrawal) Bill (sometimes referred to as the Great Reform Bill) to Parliament. This makes it clear that legislation and rights which have emanated from the EU—the *acquis*—will continue to be part of domestic law after what is called 'exit day'. There are good practical reasons for the government to adopt such a position given that around 13 per cent of UK law originated in the EU (Simson Caird 2017). If this were all repealed instantly large areas would become unregulated.

After exit day, however, the bill states that the principle of supremacy of EU law will no longer apply. In addition, courts will not be bound by principles of EU law and will not be able to refer any matter to the ECJ. The UK will also withdraw from the Charter of Fundamental Rights. This Charter protects basic rights such as freedom of expression, equality before the law, and the right to property.

At the time of writing, the bill is at its early stages, but it has already attracted some criticism. This has focused on the mechanisms that the government has used to control what elements of the acquis will remain in force. The bill will give the government the power to remove elements of the acquis without a vote in Parliament. This has been seen as an undemocratic move with Sam Fowles from Another Europe is Possible commenting that 'This is the most wide ranging power grab by an executive in Britain's peacetime history' (Another Europe is Possible 2017).

Allied to this question is the jurisdiction of the ECJ. British Prime Minister, Theresa May, made it clear at the Conservative Party conference in October 2016 that withdrawal from the Court was one of her 'red lines'. However, as negotiations have started on the UK's withdrawal from the EU the difficulties presented by such a position have become clear. This is because of the ECJ's role in a whole series of areas such as aviation and security where the UK wishes to maintain cooperation with the EU. In any event, as can be seen in our final case study, if Britain is to enter into trade agreements it will most likely have to accept the oversight of some form of international court.

The final case study also points out the importance of a stable legal superstructure to a country's trading position. This has been recognized by senior members of the judiciary such as the President of the Supreme Court, Lord Neuberger, and the Lord Chief Justice, Lord Thomas of Cwmgiedd, who have stressed the strength and competitiveness of the English legal system particularly when deciding on commercial disputes (Thomas 2017, Neuberger 2017). Lord Thomas (2017) in particular has emphasized the need for the government to 'work with the EU to ensure that there is a simple and flexible regime for the mutual recognition of enforcement of judgments for the future'.

The reasons for such pronouncements are clear as legal services are a large contributor to the UK economy. A report by TheCityUK in 2016 indicated that the contribution of UK legal services to the economy amounted to £25.7 billion with a trade surplus of £3.4 billion. The UK will have to reach some accommodation with the EU to help preserve such a healthy position.

The final area that will have an impact on the development of the law and the manner in which it is administered is the use of artificial intelligence (AI). There isn't sufficient space to discuss the full ramifications of the use of AI in the law. It is worth noting though that technology has developed which can predict court decisions to a high level of accuracy (see for example the work of Aletras et al. (2016) at University College London). At the same time, there is a move to much greater use of online dispute resolution. These developments do raise important questions about role of the judiciary and legal reasoning. In the short term, however, they are unlikely to replace the role that judges perform in assessing the credibility of evidence or exercising their discretion when deciding between opposing views.

Summary

- The law is not a monolithic entity. It is therefore formed in different ways. This is not surprising given the range of activities that are covered by the law.
- The law cannot be seen in isolation and in particular is closely linked to the political environment. The law has therefore been influenced by the process of globalization which is considered elsewhere in this book. Law is therefore increasingly made at an international level rather than within the nation state. A good example of this is the EU whose actions and decisions are a central part of the legal environment of business.
- The law also determines the different structures a business can adopt. For companies in particular their structure does much to determine their decision-making process. Some commentators argue that as a result a company's underlying dynamic is the mere pursuit of profit to the exclusion of social responsibility.
- The law does not exist in a vacuum and therefore is strongly influenced by the prevailing values within society. These values reflect different competing interests. This diversity of views and interests is partly played out in arguments over how much legal intervention there should be, particularly in areas which affect business activity. However, there is always a level of regulation and on occasions that may be helpful to business.

Case Study: Investor-state dispute systems (ISDS) and the Transatlantic Trade and Investment Partnership (TTIP)

One of the major themes of this book is the importance of globalization. A key element to this phenomenon is foreign direct investment. As we noted above, when discussing the World Bank's *Doing Business* reports, investors will look to place their money in countries which have the most favourable conditions. In a legal context, this means that their investments will be protected, or they will be able to take action if these investments are interfered with.

The necessary legal mechanisms that investors can take advantage of are contained in treaties called international investment agreements (IIAs). Unsurprisingly the number of such agreements have grown dramatically in recent years with over 3,324 in place by the end of 2016 (UNCTAD 2017)—see Figure 5.3.

Typically, an IIA will contain a series of measures to protect foreign investors. These include requirements for fair and equal treatment by the host nation and full protection and security for the investment, most notably against 'expropriation'. This latter term can include not just physical seizure of assets but also measures affecting ownership and profitability.

These protections can be enforced directly by investors through investor-state dispute settlement (ISDS) mechanisms which are provided for in the IIA. These ISDS have attracted a lot of criticism for the manner in which they operate, as they often allow foreign investors to bypass local courts and so give greater rights to foreign rather than domestic investors. They are also seen as undemocratic as their proceedings are often held in private and can overturn the decisions of elected governments.

We can perhaps see the reasons for the suspicion that ISDS attract if we look at two cases that have been brought before the International Centre for the Settlement of International Disputes (ICSID) by the Swedish energy company, Vattenfall.

ICSID is one of the key ISDS and was set up by the World Bank in 1966 to help encourage investment in developing countries. It was felt that a neutral dispute settlement process would make such countries more attractive to foreign firms who would not have to contend with the difficulties attendant on suing a host nation in its own courts.

ICSID tribunals are composed of a single or more likely an uneven number of arbitrators who are appointed by the parties. Criticisms have been made of the composition of such panels which are drawn from a small pool of individuals. Meetings of the tribunal tend to take place in private and remain confidential with the decisions only being published with the consent of the parties. Once a decision is made there is no right of appeal, although a decision can be annulled and thus invalidated; applications for annulment are rare (Collins 2017).

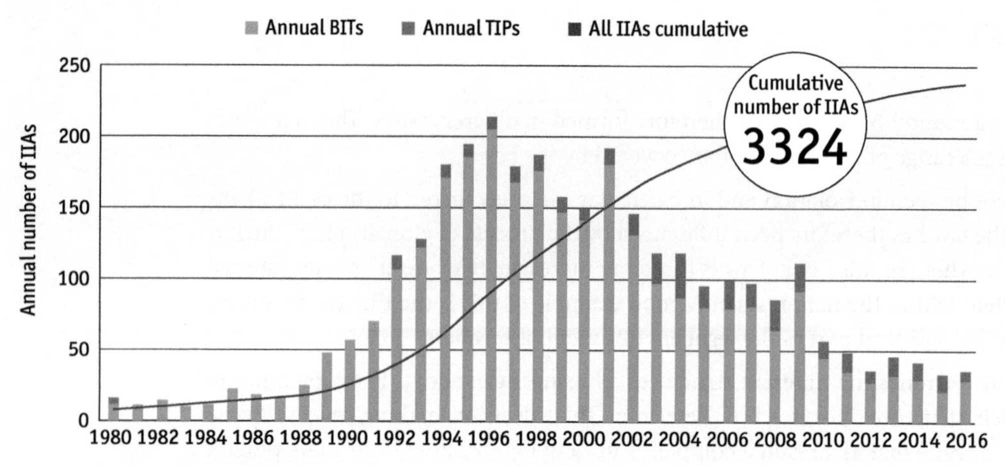

Figure 5.3 There has been a huge growth in the number of IIAs since 1980

Source: UNCTAD, World Investment Report 2017.

The cases brought to ICSID by Vattenfall both involved the environmental policies of the German government. In the first case, Vattenfall sued the German government for €1.4 billion under the Energy Charter Treaty. The case settled after Germany agreed to weaken environmental standards. Vattenfall then took a second action to ICSID after the German government changed its policy on nuclear energy. The compensation claimed was reportedly €4.7 billion plus interest with legal costs in excess of €3 billion (Bernasconi-Osterwalder and Brauch 2014). At the time of writing this case is still being considered.

Such cases have brought ISDS into the public eye and have provoked a lot of opposition to the system. Much of this has revolved around the power that the ISDS system has given to companies over government policy with a group of leading US lawyers and economists arguing 'ISDS . . . risks undermining democratic norms because laws . . . enacted by democratically elected officials are put at risk in a process insulated from democratic input' (Resnik et al. 2015). Indeed, even the threat of referral to ISDS can have a chilling effect on government policy. One former Canadian government official commented 'I've seen the letters from . . . law firms coming up to the Canadian government on virtually every new environmental regulation and proposition in the last five years . . . Virtually all of the new initiatives were targeted and most of them never saw the light of day' (Greider 2001).

The level of public concern this has excited is exemplified by the debates that have taken place concerning the TTIP. This is a proposed trade deal between the EU and the US. The core aim of the deal is the liberalization of trade by removing barriers to market access (see the Council of the EU's negotiating mandate for the talks–Council of the European Union (2013)). It is hoped that such an approach will reap economic benefits with John Healey MP, Leader of the British All Party Group on TTIP, arguing that it would result in 'a much needed boost to UK GDP of £4–10 billion a year, thousands of new jobs and wage gains for workers' (Healey 2014).

Despite the potential economic benefits to the treaty there is a high level of opposition to it. The campaigning alliance, Stop TTIP, managed to collect over 3 million signatures on a European Citizens' Initiative (ECI) calling on the EU to suspend the negotiating mandate for TTIP. An ECI allows citizens within the EU to influence policy by calling on the European Commission to make a legislative proposal. It requires the support of over one million voters across the EU and has to be registered (for more information on ECIs, go to http://ec.europa.eu/citizens-initiative/public/basic-facts).

In the case of Stop TTIP the initiative was only registered after a ruling by the ECJ but the public opposition to the treaty still had an impact on EU policy. This was particularly the case for the ISDS that was to be part of the treaty and played a large part in the antipathy to TTIP. The EU launched a public consultation into this area of the treaty which received around 150,000 replies. Of these 97 per cent expressed a negative view of the investment protection systems (European Commission 2015a).

EU Trade Commissioner, Cecilia Malmström, commenting on the consultation noted that 'it clearly shows that there is a huge scepticism against the ISDS instrument' (European Commission 2015a). She therefore set about to reform it with a new system called the Investment Court System. The key elements of this new system included publicly appointed judges, a system of appeals, and greater transparency. Alongside this a government's right to regulate was to be enshrined in any future investment agreements (European Commission 2015b).

While these measures were designed to tackle the concerns expressed during the consultation they did not meet with approval from campaigners with one famously describing them as being 'little more than putting lipstick on a particularly unpopular pig' (Global Justice Now 2015). Certainly, most campaigners felt that the proposals contained many of the features of the existing system including lack of judicial independence with a bias towards investors, privileges for investors, and the possibility of government policy being influenced by actual or threatened lawsuits (see for example Eberhardt 2016).

Negotiations on TTIP stalled after President Trump was elected and pulled the US out of a similar proposed treaty, the Trans-Pacific Partnership (TPP). However, both the US and Germany have indicated their willingness to resurrect the talks. Whatever happens, the debate about the balance to be struck between investment protection and the rights of governments, which reflects some of the key themes of this chapter, will continue.

Questions

1. **Discuss whether the EU's proposed Investment Court System is a successful reform of the ISDS system.**
2. **What factors should be taken into account when deciding how to balance the needs of investors against a government's right to regulate.**
3. **It has been argued that the process of negotiation of TTIP and the response to it has had a positive effect on the EU in that it is more responsive and transparent (Fahey 2016). Should international trade agreements take such factors into account?**
4. **Discuss whether legal action is the best way to protect investors' interests.**

Review and discussion questions

1. Outline the different sources of the law in the UK. In what areas can business have an influence on what the law is?
2. How does the law of the EU affect businesses? Do you think its impact has been positive or negative?
3. Describe the different legal structures that a business can adopt. What are the advantages and disadvantages of the different structures?
4. How far should decisions made about legislation be influenced by ideological considerations?
5. Summarize the arguments for and against legal intervention. Could the different viewpoints be reconciled through greater degrees of self-regulation?

Assignments

1. Consider again the chapters which have looked at the different belief systems which might potentially have an impact on lawmaking. Outline the influence that these belief systems, both religious and ideological, should have on the law.
2. Commenting on the takeover of Cadbury by Kraft, David Cumming, Head of UK equities at Standard Life—one of Cadbury's shareholders—said: 'It's sad that Cadbury is gone, but business is business.'[3] Using the Cadbury takeover as an example comment on whether business should just be business, or whether companies can and should take into account broader concerns.
3. Is regulation that prevents events from happening in the first place the best way to change how businesses operate, or do the alternatives to regulation offer better mechanisms for doing this?

Further reading

The law is forever changing and therefore care should be taken when reading any book on the law as its contents may be out of date. It is also the case that law books can prove to be something of a struggle even for lawyers as they are necessarily very technical. With this in mind, the books recommended below are geared towards those who are not experts in the law and give you an overview of the relevant areas.

[3] www.news.bbc.co.uk/1/hi/8467007.stm

Oxford Dictionary of the Law 8th edn (2015) *law, like many other subjects, has its own language. You may well find in your reading that you come across a term you are unfamiliar with. If so, this is the book for you.*

Holland and Webb (2016) *this book provides a good starting point for studying and applying the law. If nothing else, you should read chapter 1 which gives a good overview of the basic structure and sources of the law.*

Davies (2013) *European law can be very difficult to grasp. This book provides a simple and helpful overview of the main issues.*

Riches and Keenan (2013) *this covers all the central elements of business law. It therefore looks at the different types of business organization as well as broader legal issues affecting businesses such as the formation of contracts and employing labour.*

Collins (2017) *a very readable introduction to a complex and increasingly important area of the law. As well as an overview of the main agreements and their development, there is an explanation of the protections afforded to investors and methods of dispute settlement.*

Griffiths (1997) *a seminal text on the role of the judiciary. While not specifically related to business, it does give an insight into a central element of the legal system.*

Bakan (2005) *(see also the film of the same name). A critique of the company as an institution written by a Canadian law professor. Bakan argues that the legal structure of a company makes it act in a way that puts profit before social considerations.*

Test your understanding of this chapter with online questions and answers, explore the subject further through web exercises, and use the weblinks to provide a quick resource for further research. Visit the online resources at www.oup.com/uk/wetherly_otter4e/

Useful websites

www.companieshouse.gov.uk
Companies House incorporates companies and collects and stores all the information they are expected to file on incorporation and annually.

www.legislation.gov.uk
Has the full text of all UK legislation since 1987.

www.europa.eu
The EU website which gives plenty of information on the institutions and working of the EU.

www.cbi.org.uk
Confederation of British Industry.

www.britishchambers.org.uk
British Chambers of Commerce.

www.iccwbo.org
International Chambers of Commerce. The site has a number of useful resources for business including a section on dispute resolution.

https://www.gov.uk/government/organisations/department-for-business-energy-and-industrial-strategy
Department of Business, Energy and Industrial Strategy, which contains a wealth of information that is helpful to businesses.

www.tuc.org.uk
The website for the main employee organization in the UK. Has a wealth of material relating to all aspects of employment and regulation.

www.unctad.org
United Nations Conference on Trade and Development. It contains a lot of useful information about international trade generally with a specific section on investment.

https://www.judiciary.gov.uk
Information about judges and the way courts work.

https://europa.eu/european-union/about-eu/institutions-bodies_en#law-making
Information on the process of making law in the EU.

https://www.iod.com
Institute of Directors (IOD). The IOD publish a series of factsheets about directors and their role.

References

Alcock, A. (2009) 'An accidental change to directors' duties?', *Company Lawyer*, 30(12): 362–8

Aletras, N., Tsarapatsanis, D., Preotiuc-Pietro, D., and V. Lampos, V. (2016) 'Predicting judicial decisions of the European Court of Human Rights: a natural language processing perspective', *PeerJ Computer Science*, 2(e93) (accessed 27 July 2017) **https://peerj.com/articles/cs-93**

Another Europe is Possible (2017) 'Revealed: the great Tory powergrab' (accessed 26 July 2017) **http://www.anothereurope.org/revealed-the-great-tory-power-grab**

Bakan, J. (2005) *The Corporation* (London: Constable)

Bernasconi-Osterwalder, N. and Brauch, M. D. (2014) 'The state of play in *Vattenfall v Germany II*: keeping the German public in the dark', International Institute for Sustainable Development (Manitoba) (accessed 16 November 2017) **http://www.iisd.org/sites/default/files/publications/state-of-play-vattenfall-vs-germany-II-leaving-german-public-dark-en.pdf**

Better Regulation Commission (2006) *Annual Report for 2006* (accessed 12 April 2007) **www.brc.gov.uk/downloads/07/2006_annual_report.pdf**

Better Regulation Executive (2010) 'Reducing regulation made simple' (accessed 25 March 2013) **https://www.gov.uk/government/uploads/system/uploads/attachment_data/file/31626/10-1155-reducing-regulation-made-simple.pdf**

Chee, F. Y. (2012) 'EU imposes record $1.9 billion cartel fine on Philips, five others', *Reuters*, 5 December (accessed 1 March 2013) **http://uk.reuters.com/article/2012/12/05/us-eu-cartel-crt-idUSBRE8B40EK20121205**

Cohen, G. A. (1978) *Karl Marx's Theory of History: A Defence* (Oxford: Clarendon Press)

Collins, D. (2017) *An Introduction to International Investment Law* (Cambridge: Cambridge University Press)

Corcoran, A. and Gillanders, R. (2015) 'Foreign direct investment and the ease of doing business', *Review of World Economics*, 151(1): 103–26

Council of the European Union (2013) 'Directives for the negotiation on the Transatlantic Trade and Investment Partnership between the European Union and the United States of America' (accessed 27 July 2017) **http://data.consilium.europa.eu/doc/document/ST-11103-2013-DCL-1/en/pdf**

Davies, K. (2013) *Understanding European Union Law* (6th edn, Abingdon: Routledge)

Dyer, C. and Jones, R. (2005) 'Workers win test case in asbestos claim', *Guardian*, 16 February (accessed 12 April 2007) **http://business.guardian.co.uk/story/0,,1415567,00.html**

Eberhardt, P. (2016) *The Zombie ISDS* (Corporate Europe Observatory) (accessed 26 July 2017) **https://corporateeurope.org/international-trade/2016/02/zombie-isds**

European Commission (2015) 'Commission welcomes General Court rulings upholding TV and computer monitor tubes cartel', fact sheet, 9 September (accessed 23 January 2017) **http://europa.eu/rapid/press-release_MEMO-15-5616_en.htm**

European Commission (2015a) 'Report presented today: Consultation on investment protection in EU-US trade talks', press release, 13 January (accessed 26 July 2017) **http://europa.eu/rapid/press-release_IP-15-3201_en.htm**

European Commission (2015b) 'Commission proposes new Investment Court System for TTIP and other EU trade and investment negotiations', press release, 16 September (accessed 26 July 2017) **http://europa.eu/rapid/press-release_IP-15-5651_en.htm**

European Commission (2016) 'Antitrust: Commission fines truck producers 2.93 billion euros for participating in a cartel', press release, 19 July (accessed 23 January 2017) **http://europa.eu/rapid/press-release_IP-16-2582_en.htm**

European Commission (2017) 'Agriculture and rural development—CAP at a glance' (accessed 17 February 2017) **http://ec.europa.eu/agriculture/cap-overview_en**

Fahey, E. (2016) 'On the benefits of the Transatlantic Trade and Investment Partnership (TTIP) negotiations for the EU legal order: a legal perspective', *Legal Issues of Economic Integration*, 43(4): 327–40 **http://openaccess.city.ac.uk/15785**

Financial Reporting Council (2016) *The UK Corporate Governance Code* (London) (accessed 27 July 2017) **https://www.frc.org.uk/Our-Work/Publications/Corporate-Governance/UK-Corporate-Governance-Code-April-2016.pdf**

Gammell, K. (2010) 'Regulation costs UK businesses £80bn a year', *The Telegraph*, 19 April (accessed 27 July 2017) **http://www.telegraph.co.uk/finance/yourbusiness/7604755/Regulation-costs-UK-businesses-80bn-a-year.html**

Global Justice Now (2015) 'New ISDS is "little more than putting lipstick on a particularly unpopular pig"', 12 November (accessed 22 January 2017) **http://www.globaljustice.org.uk/news/2015/nov/12/new-isds-little-more-putting-lipstick-particularly-unpopular-pig**

Greider, W. (2001) 'The right and US trade law: invalidating the 20th century', *The Nation*, 17 November (accessed 26 July 2017) **https://www.thenation.com/article/right-and-us-trade-law-invalidating-20th-century**

Griffiths, J. A. G. (1997) *The Politics of the Judiciary* (5th edn, London: Fontana)

Harris, M. (2012) 'Chicago confidential: Lehman Brothers bankruptcy examiner believes lessons not heeded', *Chicago Tribune*, 28 October (accessed 3 April 2013) **http://articles.chicagotribune.com/2012-10-28/business/ct-biz-1028-confidential-valukas-20121028_1_anton-valukas-lehman-brothers-balance-sheet/2#sthash.HiZS3M0o.dpuf**

Healey, J. (2014) 'There's a progressive case for an EU–US trade deal—let's start making it', *Huffington Post*, 27 February (accessed 25 July 2017) **http://www.huffingtonpost.co.uk/john-healey/eu-us-trade_b_4865271.html**

Health and Safety Executive (2016) 'Costs to Britain of workplace fatalities and self-reported injuries and ill health, 2014/15 update', p. 2 (accessed 27 July 2017) **http://www.hse.gov.uk/statistics/pdf/cost-to-britain.pdf?pdf=cost-to-britain**

Health and Safety Executive (2017a) 'Asbestos related disease' (accessed 21 February 2017) **http://www.hse.gov.uk/statistics/causdis/asbestos.htm**

Health and Safety Executive (2017b) Mesothelioma in Great Britain (accessed 16 November 2017) **http://www.hse.gov.uk/statistics/causdis/mesothelioma/mesothelioma.pdf**

Hiraga, T. (2010) 'Developments in corporate governance in Asia—the case of Korea's LG Group published by NLI research' (accessed 24 January 2017) **http://www.nli-research.co.jp/en/report/detail/id=51222**

HM Treasury (2001) *Institutional Investment in the UK: A Review* (accessed 12 April 2007) **www.hm-treasury.gov.uk/media/2F9/02/31.pdf**

HM Treasury (2006) *Budget Report 2006* (accessed 12 April 2007) **www.hm-treasury.gov.uk./media/20E/EA/bud06_ch3_192.pdf**

Holland, J. and Webb, J. (2016) *Learning Legal Rules: A Students' Guide to Legal Method and Reasoning* (9th edn, Oxford: Oxford University Press)

House of Commons Business, Innovation and Skills Committee (2010) *Mergers, Acquisition and Takeovers: The Takeover of Cadbury by Kraft*, HC 234 (accessed 10 May 2010) **http://www.publications.parliament.uk/pa/cm/cmbis.htm**

Inman, P. (2010) 'Unions call for "Cadbury law" to protect British industry', *Guardian*, 6 April (accessed 8 April 2010) **http://www.guardian.co.uk/business/2010/apr/06/unions-cadbury-law-kraft-takeover**

Institute and Faculty of Actuaries (2009) *UK Asbestos Working Party 2009 GIRO update* (accessed 21 February 2017) **https://www.actuaries.org.uk/search/site/asbestos%20working%20party**

International Bank for Reconstruction and Development/World Bank (2017) *Doing Business 2017: Equal Opportunity for All* (Washington, DC: IBRD/World Bank) (accessed 27 July 2017) **http://www.doingbusiness.org/~/media/WBG/DoingBusiness/Documents/Annual-Reports/English/DB17-Chapters/DB17-Mini-Book.pdf?la=en**

Jayasuriya, D. (2011) 'Improvements in the World Bank's ease of doing business rankings: do they translate into greater foreign direct investment inflows?', Policy Research Working Paper 5787 (Washington, DC: World Bank)

Lazenby, P. (2010) 'Asbestos: Straw upholds an injustice', *Guardian*, 1 March (accessed 9 April 2010) **http://www.guardian.co.uk/commentisfree/2010/mar/01/jack-straw-asbestos-ruling**

Lords Grand Committee (2006) 6 February, col. GC256 (accessed 16 March 2013) **http://www.publications.parliament.uk/pa/ld200506/ldhansrd/vo060206/text/60206-29.htm**

Lynch, E. (2012) 'Legislative comment section 172: a ground-breaking reform of director's duties, or the emperor's new clothes?', *Company Lawyer*, 33(7): 196–203

May, T. (2017) 'The government's negotiating objectives for exiting the EU: PM speech' (accessed 27 July 2017) **https://www.gov.uk/government/speeches/the-governments-negotiating-objectives-for-exiting-the-eu-pm-speech**

National Audit Office (2016) *The Business Impact Target: Cutting the Cost of Regulation* (accessed 17 February 2107) **https://www.nao.org.uk/report/the-business-impact-target-cutting-the-cost-of-regulation)**

Neuberger, L. J. (2017) 'Access to Justice: welcome address to the Australian Bar Association Biennial Conference' (accessed 26 July 2017) **https://www.supremecourt.uk/docs/speech-170703.pdf**

O'Connor, S. (2017) 'London bike courier wins "gig economy" legal battle', *Financial Times*, 6 January (accessed 27 July 2017) **https://www.ft.com/content/fff3a320-d43b-11e6-b06b-680c49b4b4c0**

OECD (2017) *Pension Funds in Figures* (accessed 27 July 2017) **https://www.oecd.org/daf/fin/private-pensions/Pension-Funds-in-Figures-2017.pdf**

Office for National Statistics (2009) *United Kingdom Balance of Payments: The Pink Book* (accessed 8 May2010) **www.statistics.gov.uk/downloads/theme_economy/PB09.pdf**

Office for National Statistics (2012) *Annual Survey of Hours and Earnings 2012 Provisional Results* (accessed 27 March 2013) **http://www.ons.gov.uk/ons/dcp171778_286243.pdf**

Oxford Dictionary of the Law (2015) (8th edn, Oxford: Oxford University Press)

Powers, C. M. (2010) 'The changing role of chaebol', *Stanford Journal of East Asian Affairs*, 10(2): 105–16

Resnik, J., Reynoso, C., Sarokin, H. L., Stiglitz, J. E., Tribe, L. H. (2015) 'Letter to congressional leaders' (accessed 26 July 2017) **https://www.afj.org/wp-content/uploads/2015/05/5-Luminaries-Oppose-ISDS-Letter.pdf**

Riches, S. and Allen, V. (2013) *Keenan & Riches' Business Law* (2013) (11th edn, Harlow: Pearson Education)

Sibun, J. (2010) 'Cadbury takeover: a crafty bit of business or an overpriced confection?', *Daily Telegraph*, 20 January (accessed 10 May 2010) **http://www.telegraph.co.uk/finance/newsbysector/retailandconsumer/7031633/Cadbury-takeover-a-crafty-bit-of-business-or-an-overpriced-confection.html**

Simson Caird (2017) 'Legislating for Brexit: the Great Repeal Bill', House of Commons Briefing Paper 7793 (accessed 26 July 2017) **http://researchbriefings.parliament.uk/ResearchBriefing/Summary/CBP-7793#fullreport**

TheCityUK (2016) *UK Legal Services Report 2016* (London) (accessed 27 July 2017) **https://www.thecityuk.com/assets/2016/Reports-PDF/UK-Legal-services-2016.pdf**

Thomas of Cwmgiedd, LCJ (2017) 'Speech by the Lord Chief Justice at the dinner for Her Majesty's judges at Mansion House' (accessed 26 July 2017) **https://www.judiciary.gov.uk/wp-content/uploads/2017/07/lcj-mansion-house-speech-july-2017.pdf**

Thompson, J. (2010) 'Kraft to close Cadbury factory near Bristol', *The Independent*, 10 February (accessed 10 May 2010) **http://www.independent.co.uk/news/business/news/kraft-to close-cadbury-factory-near-bristol-1894520.html**

Times of India (2017) 'Chief judicial magistrate orders summons to be served on Dow via email' (accessed 21 February 2017) **http://timesofindia.indiatimes.com/city/bhopal/chief-judicial-magistrate-orders-summons-be-served-on-dow-via-e-mail/articleshow/56530272.cms**

TUC (2006) 'TUC comment on red tape review', press release, 11 December (accessed 12 April 2007) **www.tuc.org.uk/law/tuc-12771-f0.cfm**

UNCTAD (2017) *World Investment Report 2017* (Geneva: United Nations) (accessed 26 July 2017) **http://unctad.org/en/PublicationsLibrary/wir2017_en.pdf**

Walker, J. (2016) 'What are Theresa May's policies?', *Birmingham Mail*, 12 July (accessed 23 January 2017) **http://www.birminghammail.co.uk/news/midlands-news/what-are-theresa-mays-policies-11600184**

Wilkinson, R. and Pickett, K. (2010) *The Spirit Level: Why Equality Is Better for Everyone* (London: Penguin)

Case law

Cowan v. *Scargill and Others* (1985) Ch. 270

Dodge v. *Ford Motor Company* 204 Mich. 459 (1919)

NV AlgemeneTransportenExpeditieOnderneming van Gend en Loos v. *NederlandseAdministratie der Belastingen* Case 26/62 [1963] ECR 1

R. (People & Planet) v. *HM Treasury* [2009] EWHC 3020 (Admin.)

Salomon v. *Salomon* (1897) AC 22

Chapter 6
The social and cultural environment

Paul Wetherly

Learning objectives

When you have completed this chapter, you will be able to:

- Explain the nature of the social and cultural environments, and their importance for business.
- Analyse demographic trends and the implications of an ageing population for business.
- Examine the impact of immigration on business and society.
- Evaluate class differences in Britain, and relate these issues to business responsibility.

THEMES

The following themes of the book are especially relevant to this chapter

- **DIVERSITY** This chapter deals with aspects of diversity in British society, e.g. age, ethnicity, and social class. We also examine how far this diversity is reflected in business and find evidence of an 'ethnic penalty' in the labour market.
- **INTERNAL/EXTERNAL** The issues examined in this chapter have an important internal dimension in respect of organization culture and business decisions. For example, class differences are associated with differences in the nature of employee relations.
- **COMPLEXITY** This chapter demonstrates the complexity of the business environment by showing that it is not just economic but also has important social and cultural dimensions.
- **LOCAL TO GLOBAL** This chapter focuses mainly on the UK, but aspects of social life and social trends are influenced by the growing interconnectedness of societies as a result of globalization, e.g. migration.
- **DYNAMIC** This chapter identifies key social trends, showing how many aspects of social and cultural life are different today than in the past.
- **INTERACTION** Business not only has to respond to changes in the social and cultural environment, it also shapes social change, e.g. migration responds to labour market conditions.
- **STAKEHOLDERS** Analysing the social environment also involves identifying a range of stakeholder groups with differing interests in relation to business, e.g. sections of the population defined by social class, ethnicity, and age.
- **VALUES** Modern societies are pluralistic or 'cosmopolitan', characterized by diversity of lifestyles and values.

Introduction: what is the social and cultural environment?

INTERACTION **DYNAMIC** In this chapter we will examine some key aspects of society and culture in order to understand how these interact with business—business activity is influenced by the social and cultural setting in which it takes place, but also shapes that setting. Here 'social' is used to mean the social structure in terms of age, ethnicity, and class, and 'culture' refers to habits and lifestyles. British society has a growing and ageing population, with a particular racial and ethnic (multicultural) mix that continues to be shaped by immigration, and has a distinctive class structure. In analysing the social and cultural environment of business, it is important to recognize that society and culture are not homogeneous or fixed. Rather, social and cultural change is a hallmark of modern societies and, again, business can be seen as both driving these changes and having to respond to them.

Demographic trends—a growing and ageing population

In this section and the subsequent one we will focus on the following dimensions of the UK population and demographic change:

- population size; and
- population structure (by age, sex, and ethnicity).

The UK population is growing, and the rate of increase has been rising. According to the 2011 census estimate it reached 63.2 million—its highest ever level, and an increase of 4.1 million (nearly 7 per cent) over the decade since 2001. This was much higher than the increase in the previous decade to 2001 (2.9 per cent), and was the highest decennial increase of the century from 1911. Over the course of that century the UK population increased by 50 per cent (Office for National Statistics 2012). By mid 2016, the population of the UK had increased further to an estimated 65.6 million, an increase of 538,000 (0.8 per cent) over the year from mid 2015 (Office for National Statistics 2017).

Population change (growth or decline) is determined by the combined effects of:

- natural change resulting from birth and **death rates** (i.e. the number of births/deaths per 1,000 of the population); and
- net migration (i.e. the difference between inward and outward migration flows).

Figure 6.1 shows that both natural change and net migration have contributed to population growth between 1992 and 2013. Until the late 1990s, natural change was the main driver of population increase, but with net migration exceeding natural growth between 1999 and 2011. In 2004–5 net migration contributed 69 per cent of the population growth. The annual population change has tended to rise, increasing year on year in fourteen of the twenty-one years.

What will happen to the UK population in the future depends on changes in these components, and therefore population projections are fraught with uncertainty, especially over the long term. The UK population is projected to go on rising during the coming decades, increasing to 74.3 million in 2039 with natural increase and net migration contributing fairly

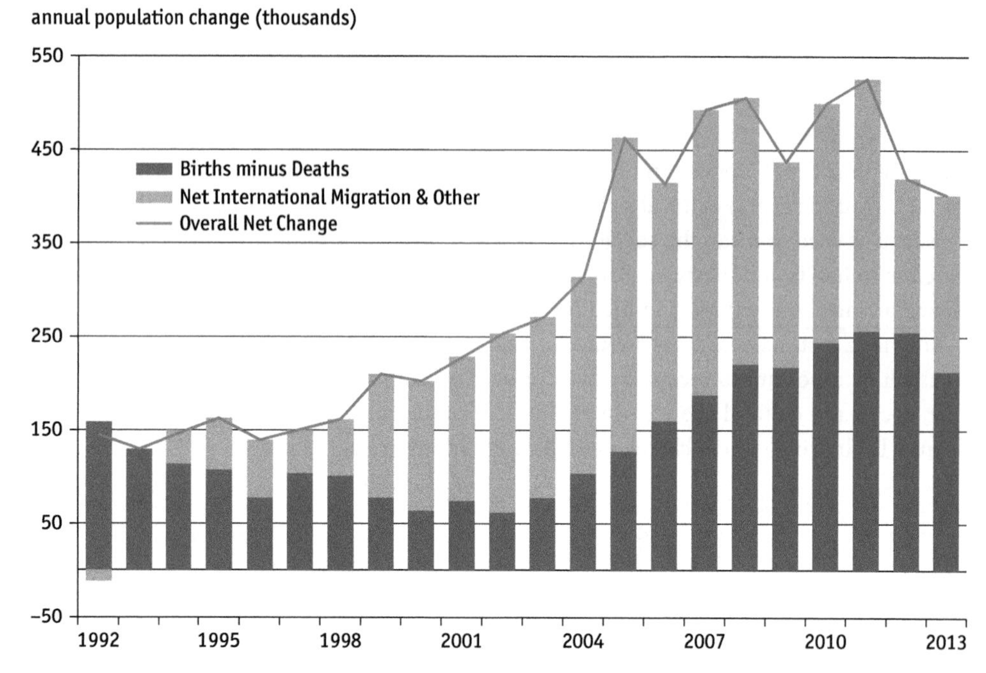

Figure 6.1 Main drivers of population change mid 1992 onwards (mid-year estimates)
Source: Office for National Statistics 2014: figure 2.

equally to this rise. This constitutes a 15 per cent increase over twenty-five years from 2014, at an average annual rate of 0.6 per cent (Office for National Statistics 2015).

> *Stop and Think*
>
> Take time to review the data on UK population change shown in Figure 6.1, and describe them in your own words.

LOCAL TO GLOBAL The projected rate of population growth for the UK is one of the highest among EU member states. According to Eurostat projections (which differ slightly from the ONS), the UK population will increase by 14 per cent between 2014 and 2039 compared to 3 per cent on average for the EU-28 as a whole. The UK population is projected to grow more quickly than all other member states except Luxembourg, Belgium, and Sweden. According to Eurostat projections, thirteen of the EU-28 countries will experience population decline between 2014 and 2039, with Germany's population projected to fall by 3 per cent. In consequence, the UK will move from being the third most populous EU state in 2014, behind Germany and France, to having the largest population by 2047 (Office for National Statistics 2015).

The implications of ongoing population growth on this scale are contested. Some argue that the UK is a crowded island and population increase will cause a strain on resources, such as water, housing, the transport infrastructure, and public services. Others argue population growth through increased births and net migration can contribute to economic dynamism.

Figure 6.2 shows UK population growth in a global context. Although the global population is projected to increase throughout the century, the rate of increase is slowing. The UK and Europe as a whole have a lower rate of population growth than the world as a whole, but the

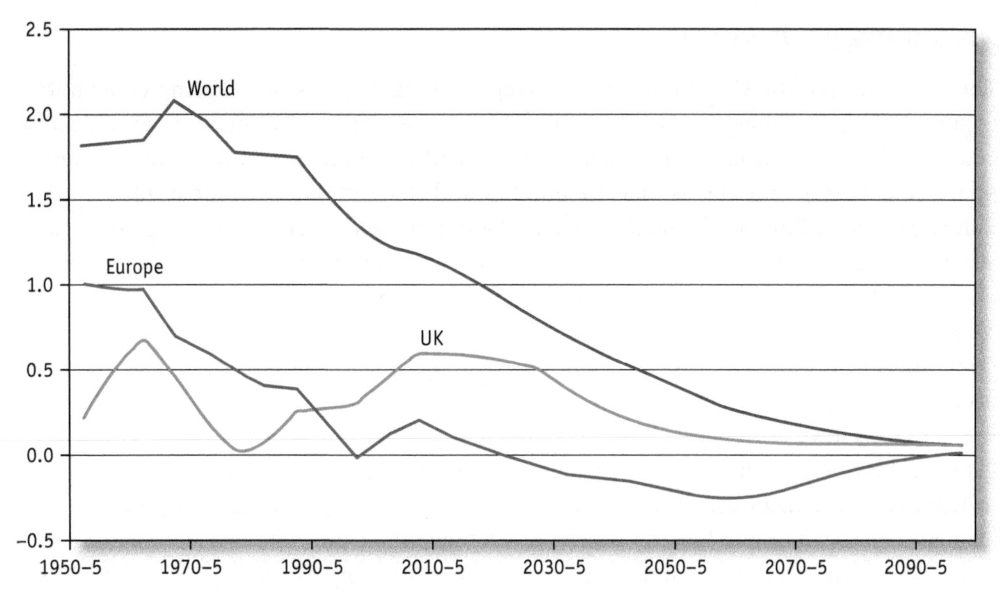

Figure 6.2 Average percentage population growth rate: UK, Europe, and the world

Source: Office for National Statistics 2012a: p. 3, figure 1.

UK has a higher rate than Europe. The projection shows the population of Europe as a whole declining (negative growth) from 2020 to the last decade of the century. Europe is the only region of the world that is expected to experience population decline over the course of this century. World population is projected by the United Nations to increase from around 6.8 billion in 2010 to over 9 billion by the middle of the century and over 10 billion by its end (Office for National Statistics 2012a).

Table 6.1 shows that most of the projected growth of world population in the first half of this century will occur in less developed regions, with the fastest rate of growth occurring in the very poorest (least developed) countries, particularly in Africa. On this basis the share of world population living in regions defined as less developed in 2000 will increase from 68 per cent in 1950 to 86 per cent in 2050. Figure 6.2 shows that the annual rate of growth of world population peaked at over 2 per cent in the 1960s, and is on a downward trajectory, meaning that world population is rising at a decreasing rate. Figure 6.2 also shows world population stabilizing towards the end of the century, although such long-term projections are highly uncertain.

Table 6.1 World Population 1950–2050 (billions)

	1950	2000	2050	% change, 2000–50
World	2.53	6.12	9.15	+50
More developed regions	0.81	1.19	1.28	+8
Europe	0.547	0.727	0.691	-5
Less developed regions	1.72	4.92	7.87	+60
Least developed countries	0.200	0.677	1.672	+147

Source: United Nations https://esa.un.org/unpd/wpp

An ageing population

The population of the UK is not only growing—it is also ageing, and ageing contributes to growth. Increased longevity (or life expectancy) shows up in a falling number of deaths and mortality rate (because at each age fewer die and more survive than would have done in previous years), and means that the number and share of older people in the population rises, also pulling up the median age of the population. Changes in the age structure also reflect trends in birth rates (or fertility rates) and net migration. An ageing population in the UK is the effect both of people living longer and an increase in the number of older people as the cohort of post-war 'baby boomers' move up through the age structure. Declining fertility rates also contribute to ageing by causing the proportion of younger people to decrease.

Figure 6.3 shows the remarkable increase in life expectancy in the UK from 1841 to 2011. Between those years, average life expectancy at birth has nearly doubled, increasing from 42.2 to 82.8 years for females and from 40.2 to 79 years for males. Figure 6.3 also suggests that the main reasons for increased life expectancy were falling infant and child mortality in the early part of the twentieth century and health improvements among the elderly since the 1950s. Before the second half of the last century a relatively high child mortality rate significantly lowered the average life expectancy at birth.

Reflecting the contribution to increased life expectancy of the fall in the rate of child mortality in the first phase, Table 6.2 shows that in 1841 average life expectancy for males was over 14 years lower at birth than at 5 years. In contrast by 2011 the rate of child mortality was so low that it made very little difference to average life expectancy at ages 1 year and 5 years.

The ageing of the population can be seen in a growing number and proportion of people at the top end of the age structure, particularly those who are above retirement

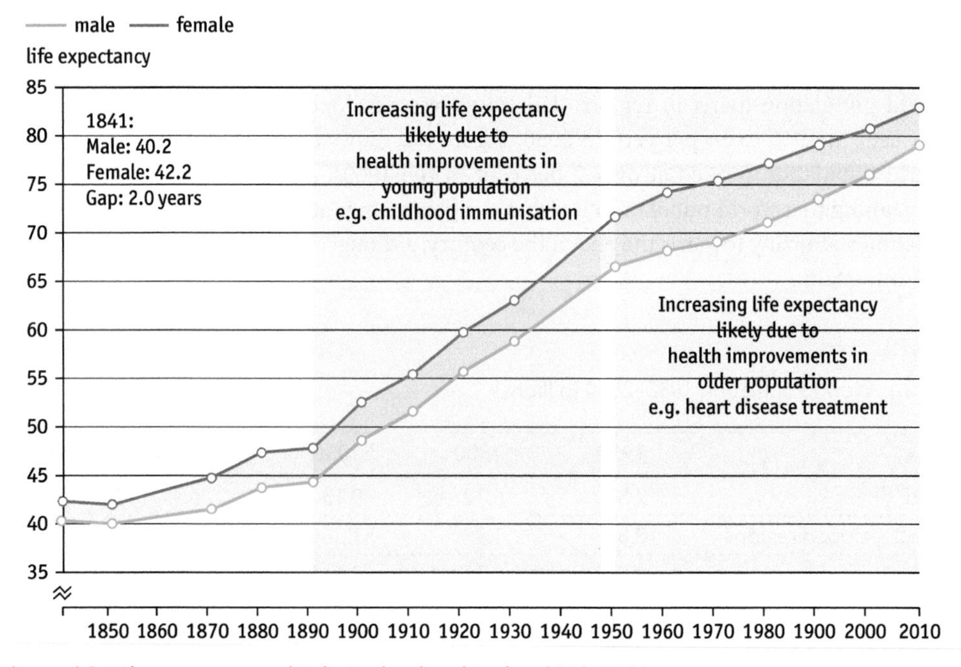

Figure 6.3 Life expectancy at birth, England and Wales, 1841–2011

Source: Office for National Statistics 2015a.

Table 6.2 Average male life expectancy at birth and at 5 years, 1841 and 2011, UK

	Average life expectancy at birth	Average life expectancy at 1 year	Average life expectancy at 5 years
1841	40.2	47.7	54.6
2011	79.0	79.3	79.4

Source: Office for National Statistics 2015a.

age. Table 6.3 shows that this is a long-term trend: the proportion of the UK population aged 65 years and over ('retirement age') is projected to increase from just under 1 in 7 (14.1 per cent) in 1975 to nearly 1 in 4 (24.6 per cent) in 2045, or from about 7.9 to 18.7 million. Conversely, the proportion of the population of 'working age' (16–64 years) is declining, being projected to fall from 64.7 per cent in 2005 to 57.8 per cent in 2045. The combined effect is that the ratio of people of 'working age' to those of 'retirement age' is projected to fall from 4:1 to 2.3:1—there are fewer 'workers' to support each 'retiree'. This can also be expressed the other way around, as an increase in the 'old-age dependency ratio': the ratio of 'retirees' to 'workers' was less than one in four in 2005, and this is projected to increase to 1.7 to 4 in 2045. Table 6.3 also shows that, over the period from 1975 to 2045, the proportion of elderly (65 years +) catches up with and then, after 2015, overtakes the proportion of young people (0–15 years), so that the old will outnumber the young in 2045 to roughly the same extent that the young outnumbered the old in 1975. Hidden in the table is the fact that the increase in the number of people aged 85 and over (the 'oldest old') is particularly notable—by 2026 it is projected that there will be nearly five times as many people in this age group compared to 1971 (compared to a near doubling of the number aged 65 and over). Ageing of the population is also manifested as a rise in the median age (the age that divides the population with 50 per cent being younger and 50 per cent older), which increased from 33.9 to 40 years in the UK between 1974 and 2014 (Office for National Statistics 2015b).

The number of deaths registered in the UK in 2015 was 602,800, an overall reduction of 9 per cent from the total number of deaths (662,500) registered 40 years ago (ONS 2017a). The mortality rate (deaths per 100,000 population) in the UK has also declined, in a growing

Table 6.3 Age distribution of the UK population, 1975 to 2045 (projected)

Year	UK population	0-15 years (%)	16-64 years (%)	65 years and over (%)
1975	56,226,000	24.9	61.0	14.1
1985	56,554,000	20.7	64.1	15.2
1995	58,025,000	20.7	63.4	15.8
2005	60,413,000	19.3	64.7	15.9
2015	65,110,000	18.8	63.3	17.8
2025	69,444,000	18.9	60.9	20.2
2035	73,044,000	18.1	58.3	23.6
2045	76,055,000	17.7	57.8	24.6

Source: Office for National Statistics 2017a: p. 4, Table 1.

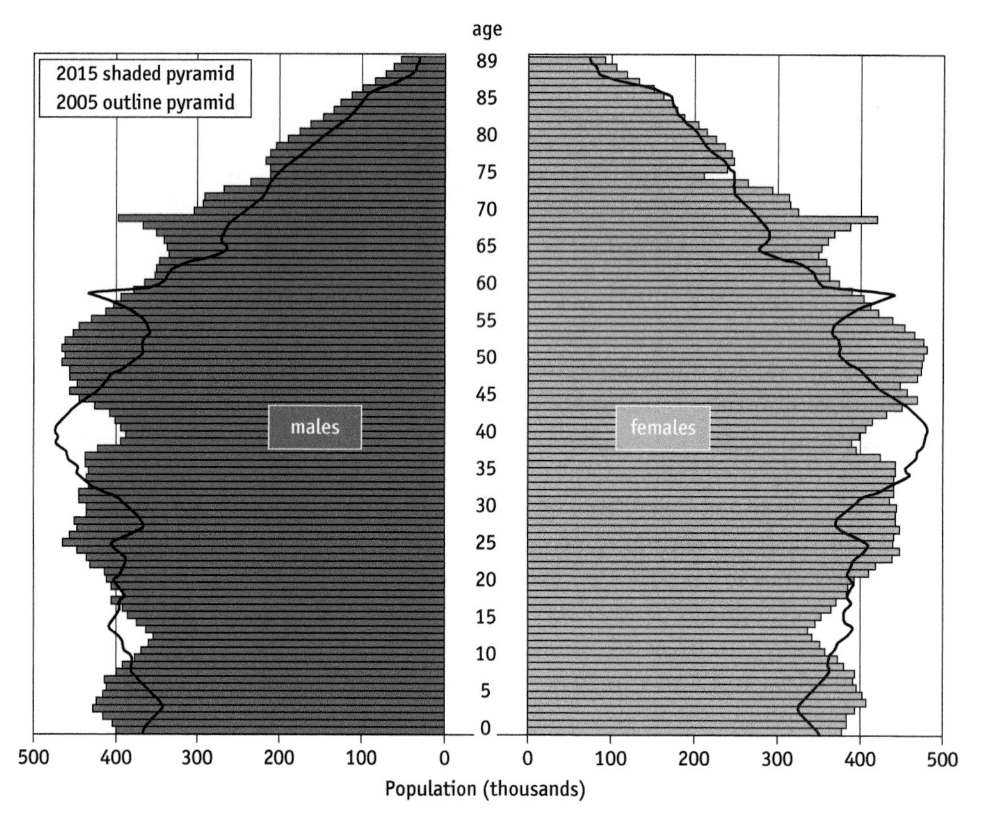

Figure 6.4 Population pyramid for the UK, 2005 and 2015
Source: Office for National Statistics 2017a: p. 4, figure 2.

population, from 2,158 (males) and 1,357 (females) in 1983 to 1,183 deaths per 100,000 males and 865 deaths per 100,000 females in 2013.

Figure 6.4 shows 'snapshots' of the age structure of the UK population in 2005 and 2015, and reveals demographic change by comparing the 2005 outline with the 2015 pyramid. Increased life expectancy can be seen by the shift outwards of the pyramid at all ages above 65 years between 2005 and 2015. Figure 6.4 also shows the effects of peaks in the birth rate in the late 1940s and again in the late 1950s and early 1960s as these cohorts move up the age structure and begin to enter old age. Thus, the peak in the number of births in 1947 and 1964 can be seen in the bulges at ages 58 and 41 in the 2005 outline, and at ages 68 and 51 in the 2015 pyramid (Office for National Statistics 2015c).

It is not certain whether this trend will continue in the future as it depends on the balance between factors that have a positive or adverse effect on life expectancy. It has been projected that the number of 100-year-olds will increase by more than nine times, from 6,000 in 2017 to 56,000 by 2050 (Cumbo 2017). However, high rates of child obesity and the implications for health later in life have raised fears that today's children may have a shorter life expectancy than their parents. In 2017 it was calculated that the rate of increase in life expectancy in England for males and females had nearly halved since 2010 compared to the previous decade, possibly as a result of 'austerity' (BBC 2017). (See Mini-Case 6.1.)

Mini-Case 6.1 Ageing in international context

LOCAL TO GLOBAL Figures 6.5 and 6.6 compare the UK with other EU member states and show that population ageing is an international phenomenon. Although the percentage of the population aged 65 and over in the UK is projected to rise from 17 per cent to 23 per cent between 2010 and 2035, other countries are projected to experience a greater rise, with the effect that the UK will become one of the least aged societies among current EU members by 2035. Whereas in 2010 twelve countries were less aged than the UK, by 2035 there will be just four. Germany is shown as the most aged society in both years, with the proportion aged 65 and over projected to increase to 31 per cent in 2035 (Office for National Statistics 2012b).

Population ageing is also a global phenomenon, not confined to the rich countries such as the EU but affecting nearly every country, and happening fastest in poor countries. 'In 2012, people aged 60 or over represent almost 11.5 per cent of our total global population of 7 billion. By 2050, the proportion is projected to nearly double to 22 per cent' (United Nations Population Fund 2012).

Question

Summarize the data shown in Figures 6.5 and 6.6 in your own words.

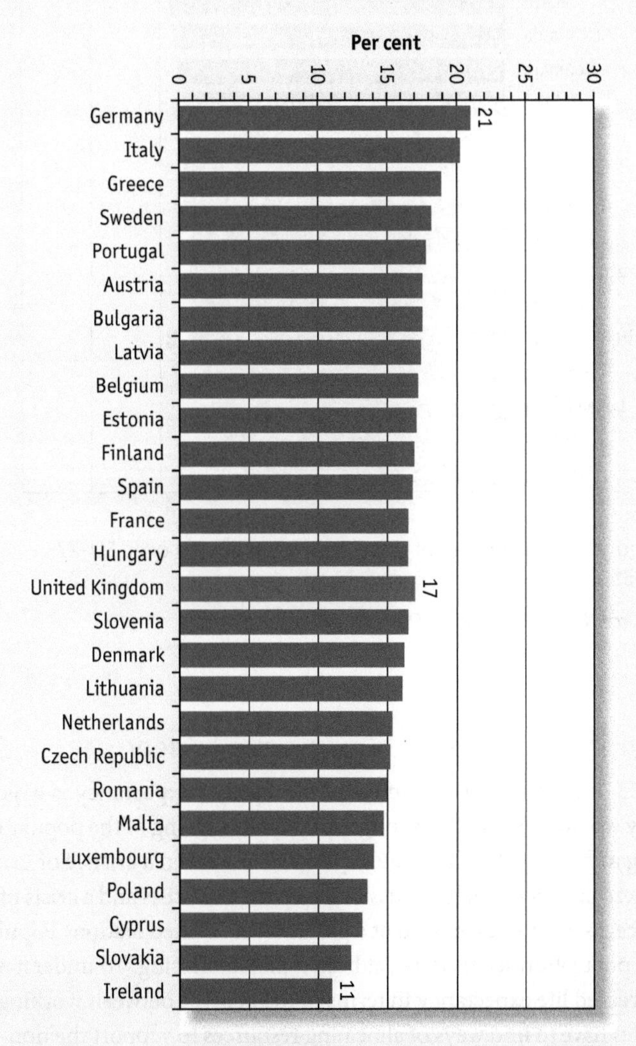

Figure 6.5 Percentage of persons aged 65 and over, EU-27, 2010

Source: Office for National Statistics 2012b.

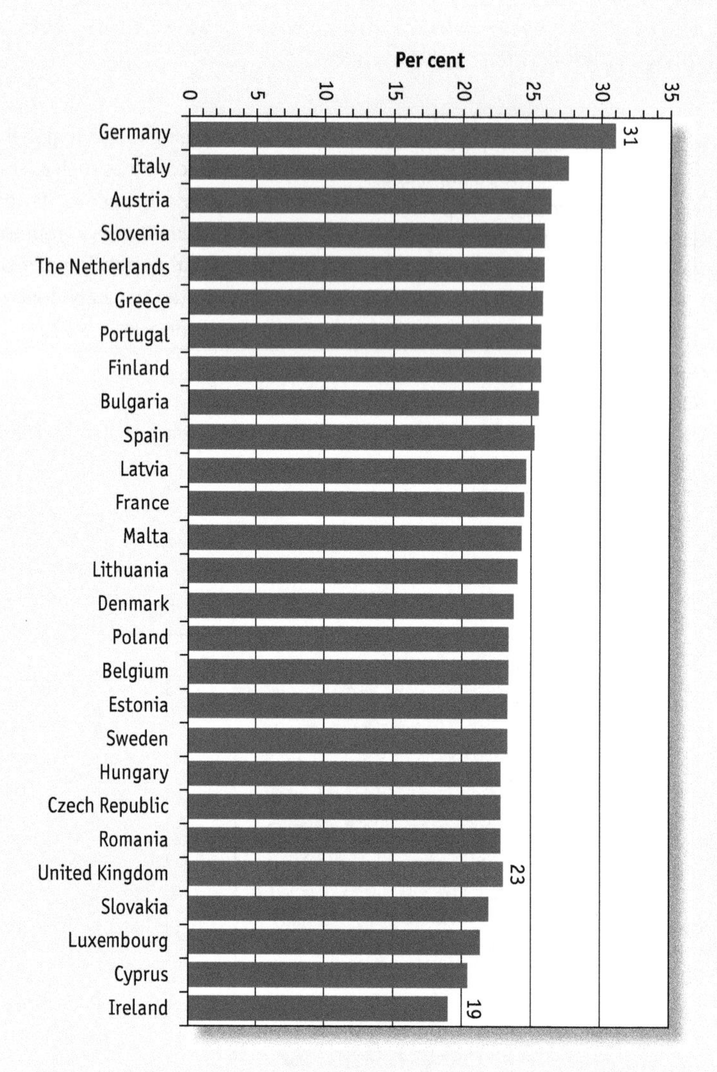

Figure 6.6 Percentage of population aged 65 and over, EU-27, 2035

Source: Office for National Statistics 2012b.

Implications of ageing for business and society

VALUES It is obvious that increased average life expectancy is a 'good thing', since almost everybody would prefer to live a longer life. Yet the ageing of the population is often portrayed as presenting a challenge for the economy and society, even a crisis. For example, in recent years in the UK there has been much discussion of a pensions crisis and a crisis of care for the elderly, and these concerns are also expressed at a global level (United Nations Population Fund 2012). Ageing of the population seems to be, at best, a mixed blessing. To understand this, it helps to think about increased life expectancy in terms of the balance between working life and 'non-work life'. All societies have to find ways of allocating resources to support the non-working population (or the periods in individuals' lives when they are not working, including old age) from the output produced by the working population. Increased life expectancy presents a challenge to society because it increases the *number* of elderly and the *ratio* of elderly to those of working age. This implies that more resources for each employed person have to be used to fund pensions and health and social care services needed to support people who have retired. However, the implications of an ageing population depend on a number of factors and assumptions, including the age at which people retire and move from the working to the non-working part of the population, and whether increased life expectancy translates into more years of ill health and inability to live independently. There are two broad issues here:

- At what age is it reasonable for individuals to expect to be able to retire from employment? Is it possible, as people live longer, for society to support more years in retirement? (See the case study at the end of the chapter.)
- How should the incomes of the retired population (pensions) and the health and social care services required by the elderly be funded, and who should be responsible for this funding?

The three logical options for dealing with the pensions crisis (i.e. to avoid the 'fourth option' of inadequate retirement incomes) were set out in the first report of the Pensions Commission (the *Turner Report* after its chair, Adair Turner) as follows:

> - increased taxes and/or National Insurance contributions devoted to pensions
> - higher savings for retirement
> - later retirement.
>
> (Pensions Commission 2004)

STAKEHOLDERS **VALUES** In other words, the increased liability may fall on current taxpayers (i.e. largely the working population) through increased taxation to fund public spending, people may be encouraged or required to save more during their working lives for retirement (but this might involve a double burden on the current workforce: saving more for their own retirement at the same time as paying higher taxes to support the currently retired), or people may be required to work longer so that the balance between work and non-work life remains more or less stable as people live longer. These adjustments (singly or in combination) are difficult to make because people prefer to retire sooner rather than later, and are reluctant to save more for their own retirement or pay higher taxes to support the currently retired. Governments are faced with making unpopular decisions. But there are also important issues for business as a stakeholder, particularly:

- how far businesses should be responsible for ensuring decent pensions for their own employees through occupational schemes, balancing affordability for the business and adequate pension benefits for employees;
- the extent to which the burden of increased taxation or NI contributions to finance state pensions should fall on business; and
- the willingness of business to tackle age discrimination and afford opportunities for people to extend their working lives on a full- or part-time basis and retire later.

In the UK, government has responded to the looming pensions crisis in part through phased increases in the state pension age (SPA) so that people must work longer before becoming entitled to the state pension (see the case study at end of chapter). Later retirement has the effect of reducing the old-age dependency ratio—the number of people of SPA and over for every 1,000 people of working age—thus mitigating the effect of population ageing. In other words, governments have acted to ease the projected fiscal burden (the burden on public spending and taxation) of an ageing population.

> *Stop and Think*
>
> What is the pensions crisis?
>
> Why is it thought that neither the state nor the market can alone ensure an adequate pensions system?

It is one thing to require employees to work longer before they reach SPA, but later retirement also requires that there are opportunities in the labour market for older workers. However, a report for government has found that 'Age discrimination and unconscious bias remain widespread problems in the UK labour market' and urges employers to adopt 'age-friendly' policies. The report advocates three principles to guide employment practices, the 3 'R's:

- Retain—keeping older workers and their skills in the workplace through, for example, flexible working;
- Retrain—ongoing workplace training irrespective of age, and opportunities for mid-life career reviews; and
- Recruit—stamp out age discrimination from the recruitment process (Altmann 2015).

Changes in the age structure of the population affect business not only in terms of workforce participation but also through their impact on the pattern of consumer spending. In this regard what matters is not just the size of each age cohort but income level and tastes. In the 1950s and 1960s business responded to the new phenomena of 'youth culture' and a growing youth market resulting from the coming together of the post-war baby boom and affluence. As these same 'baby-boomers' reach retirement they are now contributing to the ageing population and the novel phenomenon of a growing market of older consumers. Old age and retirement has traditionally been a period of relative poverty but, while this is still true for many, in recent decades there has been increasing affluence among the elderly due, in part, to the growth of occupational pension schemes in the second half of the last century and an increase in employment among pensioner households, as well as increases in the state pension. Indeed, by 2017, typical pensioner household incomes in the UK had overtaken those of working-age households for the first time (Corlett 2017). Increased numbers and increased wealth has meant important new markets for business. The pattern of spending by the elderly has also shifted, due to a change in the 'meaning' of old age, as people want to maintain more active lifestyles than was typical of earlier generations. This is reflected, for example, in the growth of leisure and tourism marketed specifically for older people.

> *Stop and Think*
>
> Why is an ageing population seen as a challenge for society as well as a good thing?

Immigration and cultural diversity

STAKEHOLDERS We have seen that migration affects the size and age structure of the population. Net migration contributes to population growth (see Figure 6.1), and mitigates ageing and the old-age dependency ratio because migrants are younger on average. It also brings economic and cultural effects. A prime motivation for migration is economic—in search of improved job opportunities and living standards—so immigration increases the size of the workforce and alters its composition in terms of skills. Immigration also affects the ethnic composition of the population and the cultural make-up of the society in terms of life-styles, religion, first language, and so on. The pattern of immigration to the UK has created a 'multicultural' society, characterized by the coexistence of many cultures rather than a single homogeneous culture (though it would be misleading to claim that there ever existed a homogeneous culture prior to the impact of immigration—rather, immigration has added to existing diversity). A sense of this diversity in Britain can be gained from Table 6.4, which shows the composition of the population in terms of self-defined ethnic group at the last census in 2011.

Although Britain has experienced immigration throughout its history, the creation of a **multicultural society** is largely the product of immigration in the period after the Second World War—from the Caribbean in the 1950s and 1960s, and from India, Pakistan, and Bangladesh in the 1960s and 1970s. In the post-war boom years of full employment, immigration was encouraged as a way of meeting labour shortages. More recently immigration from other EU member states under free movement rules has been important, particularly since the expansion of the EU in 2004.

Table 6.4 shows that all non-white ethnic groups make up 14 per cent of the population of England and Wales, nearly one in seven people, with 86 per cent defined as white. Of the

Table 6.4 Population by ethnic group, England and Wales, 2011 (all usual residents)

Ethnic group		Number (thousands)	Per cent
Other ethnic group	Arab	231	0.4
	Any other ethnic group	333	0.6
Mixed/multiple ethnic groups	White and Black African	166	0.3
	Other mixed	290	0.5
	White and Asian	342	0.6
	White and Black Caribbean	427	0.8
Black/African/Caribbean/ Black British	Other Black	280	0.5
	Caribbean	595	1.1
	African	990	1.8
Asian/Asian British	Chinese	393	0.7
	Bangladeshi	447	0.8
	Other Asian	836	1.5
	Pakistani	1,125	2.0
	Indian	1,413	2.5
White	All White ethnic groups	48,209	86.0
White	Gypsy or Irish Traveller	58	0.1
	Irish	531	0.9
	Other White	2,486	4.4
	English/Welsh/Scottish/Northern Irish/British	45,135	80.5

Source: Office for National Statistics 2012c.

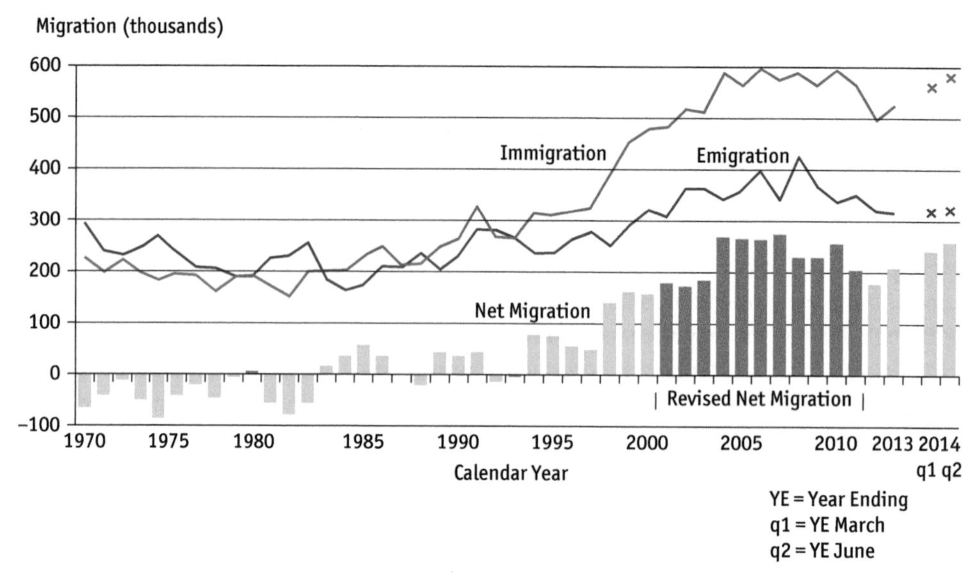

Figure 6.7 Long-term international migration, 1970–2014

Source: Office for National Statistics 2014b, Fig.1.1.

non-white ethnic groups, just over half are defined as Asian/Asian British, predominantly from India and Pakistan. Black people make up about one-quarter of the non-white ethnic population, and just over one in seven of the non-white population are of mixed ethnicity. Overall, the table shows the non-white population to be ethnically diverse. 'Black' and 'Asian' residents are not, of course, all immigrants as many are second or third generation descendants of immigrants who came to Britain in the post-war decades, and together constitute what may be termed 'immigrant-origin' communities.

More recently the UK has experienced significant immigration from other EU states, particularly the Eastern European 'A8' former communist 'accession countries' that joined the EU in 2004. Such migrants are included in the 'other' white category which makes up around 5 per cent of the population of England and Wales. Thus 'white' is no more a homogeneous category than 'non-white'.

A map of multicultural Britain shows that ethnic minority communities are not evenly spread. Major cities, especially London, have higher proportions of ethnic minorities and are more cosmopolitan, meaning that their populations comprise a wide range of ethnic groups. But small towns can also become highly diverse: the 2011 census revealed Slough to be the most ethnically diverse local authority outside London, in which no single ethnic group makes up more than half of the population.

Figure 6.7 shows long-term immigration, emigration, and net migration since 1970. In the 1970s net migration was negative (emigration exceeded immigration), and it was not until the early 1990s that net migration became consistently positive, with immigration nearly doubling from around 300,000 to nearly 600,000 in the 2000s. Annual immigration peaked at 650,000 in June 2016, with net migration of 335,000. This was followed by a slight reduction by year-end December 2016, with immigration at 588,000 and net migration of 248,000 (Office for National Statistics 2017b).

Figure 6.8 shows the composition of net migration since 1975, broken down into EU, non-EU, and British, and Table 6.5 shows the same breakdown of net migration for the year ending June 2016 together with the underlying data for immigration and emigration.

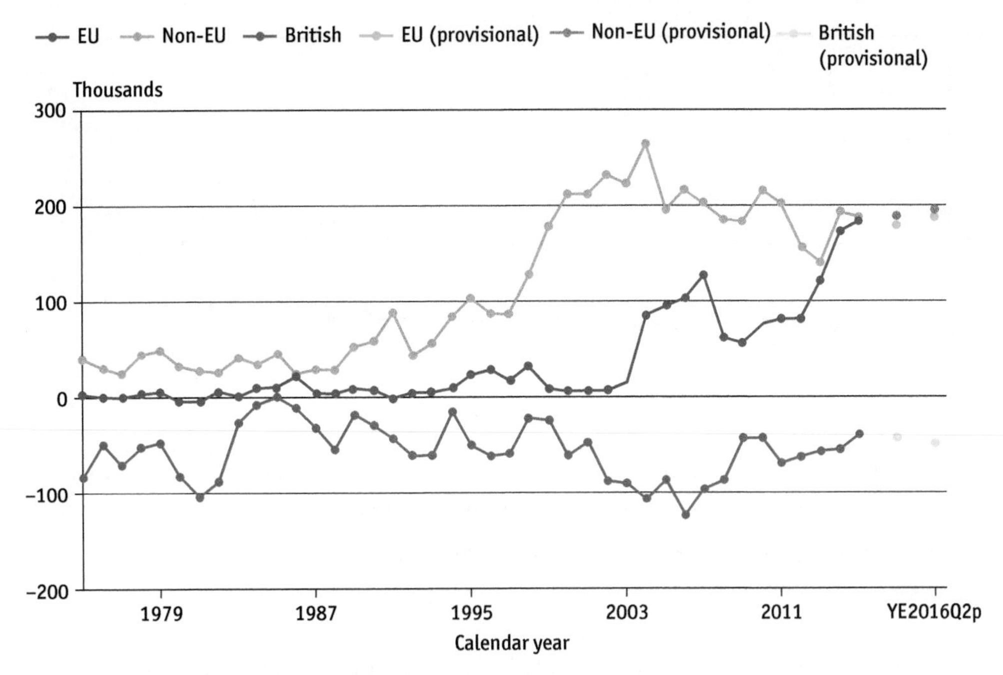

Figure 6.8 Net long-term international migration by citizenship, UK, 1975–2016 (year ending June 2016)

Source: Office for National Statistics 2016.

In year ending June 2016 immigration and emigration flows were nearly equal from EU and non-EU countries, so they contributed roughly equally to net migration (Table 6.5). However, this equalization is the result of a recent convergence. In the thirty years since the mid 1980s, net migration from non-EU countries has been higher than from EU countries. Since 2004, with immigration from the new A8 Eastern European member states, net migration from the EU has increased while net migration from non-EU countries has declined (Figure 6.8). Figure 6.8 and Table 6.5 also show how net migration is affected by movements of British citizens. British net migration has been negative in nearly every year since the 1970s, meaning that more British people leave than enter the UK.

Large scale immigration from the EU over this period has increased the stock of EU-born residents in the UK. By 2016 (Q1) there were 3.5 million EU-born residents in the UK. Figure 6.9 shows that almost all of the increase of EU-born residents in the UK since 2004 has come from the A8 countries, starting from a low base. By 2015 UK residents from A8 countries exceeded the number from EU14 countries.

Table 6.5 Immigration, emigration, and net migration by citizenship, UK, year ending June 2016

	Immigration 000s (%)	Emigration 000s (%)	Net migration (000s)
EU	284 (43.7)	95 (30.2)	189
Non-EU	289 (44.5)	93 (29.5)	196
British	77 (11.8)	127 (40.3)	-49
Total	650 (100)	315 (100)	335

Source: Office for National Statistics 2016.

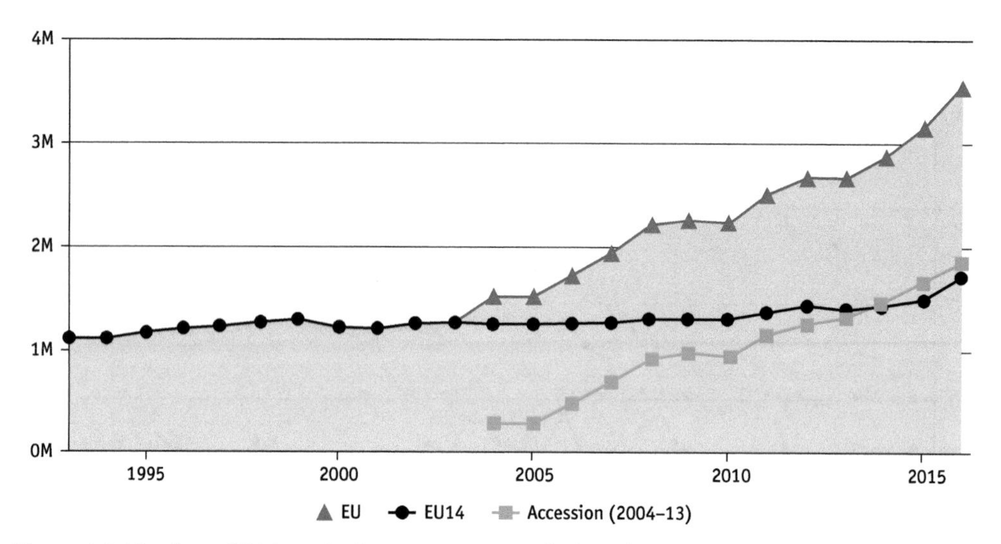

Figure 6.9 Number of EU-born in the UK, 1993–2016 (millions)
Source: Vargas-Silva and Markaki 2016.

The main reasons for immigration into the UK are for work or study, and this is true for both EU and non-EU immigrants. The third main reason is to join or accompany family members. In 2016, 69 per cent of EU immigrants came to the UK for work (45 per cent to take up a definite job and 24 per cent to look for work) and a further 14 per cent came for study (Figure 6.10).

LOCAL TO GLOBAL Immigration from EU countries has been enabled by freedom of movement within the EU. This is an important right for EU citizens but arguably brings wider economic benefits through the creation of an EU-wide labour market in which labour can move across borders in response to demand in different countries. Thus, Polish workers have come to the UK primarily motivated by better job opportunities, and it can be argued that in doing so they have benefited UK employers and the economy as a whole by meeting the demand for labour.

However, large-scale immigration from A8 countries since 2004 shows that migration can be difficult to predict, both in terms of the number of immigrants and whether migrants would settle in the UK or only stay temporarily (the UK government at the time of Poland's accession to the EU expected far lower numbers to come to the UK and settle). It is to be expected that the number coming to the UK and returning will be sensitive to the success of economic

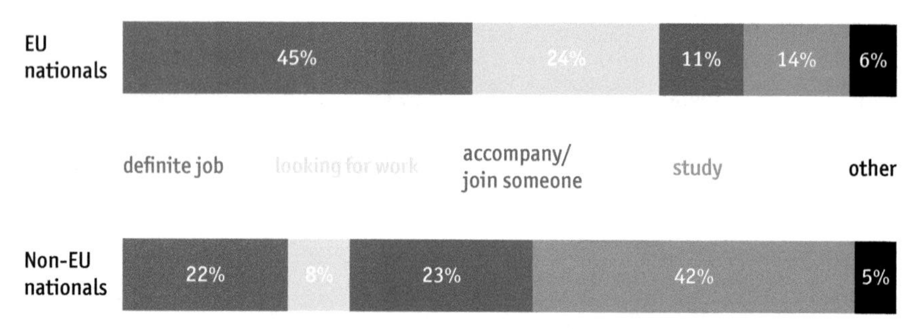

Figure 6.10 Reasons given for immigrating to the UK. Immigration of EU and non-EU nationals by main reason stated for migrating, 2016

Source: FullFact 2017.

development in Poland and the other accession states in increasing job opportunities and raising living standards, and the performance of the UK economy, as appears to be shown by reduced immigration following the onset of the financial crisis. A decline in EU immigration since the referendum on EU membership in June 2016 might be due to uncertainty about the implications of 'Brexit' for the rights of EU-born residents in the UK, and perhaps a feeling that the vote signals that the UK is less welcoming.

The Brexit vote seems to be a clear indication that large-scale immigration can give rise to anxiety among some sections of the population in relation to both economic and cultural impacts: there may be concern that immigration may lower wages in certain sectors of the economy, increase pressures on public services, and alter the 'feel' of areas of settlement and bring unwelcome change in terms of culture and identity. These anxieties, whether justified or not, create difficult dilemmas for politicians (though some politicians actively promote public concern about immigration), such as trying to gain the economic benefits of continued immigration while responding to public demand for a reduction in the level of immigration. Public concern about the level and impact of immigration has flared in many EU states, and mainstream political parties have had to deal with challenges from 'outsider' anti-immigration parties and movements. In the UK immigration has consistently been at or near the top of the most important issues as seen by the public, and there has been long-standing majority support for a reduction in the level of immigration. The UK Independence Party (UKIP) was able to increase its popular support on the basis of its primary objective of securing UK withdrawal from the EU, with a strong focus on the issue of controlling immigration. The vote to leave the EU in the UK referendum in June 2016 ('Brexit') revealed deep divisions over attitudes to immigration. Among Leave voters concern over immigration was one of the main motivations, together with the aspiration to 'take back control' of laws from the EU. Thus the implications of immigration for business and society have to be understood not just in terms of 'real' economic effects, such as on labour supply, wages, or the fiscal impact, but also in terms of how people 'feel' about these effects.

Implications of immigration for business and society

VALUES Immigration and the creation of a multicultural society in the UK has never been free from controversy. Hostile and racist attitudes towards non-white ethnic groups are less prevalent than in the 1960s and 1970s but have not gone away. Aside from these reactions, the terms of engagement between immigrants and their descendants and the 'indigenous' population have been debated continually. Should this involve support for a multicultural society in which immigrant communities preserve their own cultures? Should a new hybrid culture—a new shared sense of Britishness—emerge from a process of mixing and two-way influence? Or should minority immigrant communities assimilate by basically adopting the culture of the majority indigenous population? A key aspect of integration concerns the extent to which members of ethnic minorities participate in all aspects of social, political, and economic life on equal terms with the majority population. First generation immigrants tended to find employment in less skilled and lower paid occupations. However, the principle of **equal opportunity**, established in law for nearly forty years since the 1976 Race Relations Act, means that ethnic minorities should have the same opportunities to realize their aspirations through educational attainment and access to occupations and careers as members of other groups. Support for the principle of equal opportunity has become more widespread, but there is evidence that ethnic minorities continue to experience various forms of prejudice and disadvantage in modern British society and business (see Mini-Case 6.2).

Mini-Case 6.2 Ethnic penalties in the UK labour market

The first black chief executive of a leading UK company was appointed in 2009. At the time there was only one other black director of a FTSE 100 company. This is an instance of a more general pattern of disadvantages experienced by non-white ethnic minorities in the labour market, or 'ethnic penalties'. Research for the Department for Work and Pensions (DWP) showed that:

a number of ethnic minority groups, notably Pakistani, Bangladeshi, Black Caribbean and Black African men continue to experience higher unemployment rates, greater concentrations in routine and semi-routine work and lower hourly earnings.

(Heath and Cheung 2006)

There is a clear pattern of occupational segregation in the private sector—just as ethnic minorities are overrepresented in routine and semi-routine occupations they are underrepresented in professional and managerial occupations. In contrast, ethnic penalties tend to be 'markedly lower' in the public sector. These differentials could not be explained in terms of educational attainment or other factors, and therefore:

unequal treatment on grounds of race or colour is likely to be a major factor underlying the pattern of ethnic penalties.

(Heath and Cheung 2006)

To test the claim that unequal treatment, i.e. discrimination, is a major cause of observed ethnic penalties a method sometimes described as the 'CV test' has been used. Research for the DWP involved submitting three applications (CVs) which were alike except for the ethnic identity of the applicant (indicated by the use of distinctive English, Asian, or African names) to each of 987 job vacancies in a variety of occupational categories. In each of the 987 cases there was one application with a white name and two with ethnic minority names. Differential success in securing an invitation to interview provides a measure of discrimination on ethnic grounds.

One or more of the three applicants received a positive response in 155 of the 987 cases. Among these the success rate for ethnic minority applications was 39 per cent compared to 68 per cent for white applicants. 'So, the net discrimination in favour of white names over equivalent applications from ethnic minority candidates was 29 per cent' (Wood et al. 2009).

Comparing the overall success rates for the 987 applications with a white name and the 1,974 applications with an ethnic minority name, the research showed that:

16 applications from ethnic minority applicants had to be sent for a successful outcome . . . compared with nine white. That is, 74 per cent more applications from ethnic minority candidates needed to be sent for the same level of success.

(Wood et al. 2009)

Question

What can business do to reduce or eliminate ethnic penalties in the labour market?

In recent years there has been renewed debate over whether the UK's 'experiment' in multiculturalism has been successful, and the costs and benefits of continued immigration, particularly from the A8 countries, are contested. The arguments are broadly cultural and economic in character.

- In cultural terms there is a division between those who emphasize the enrichment of British society as a result of immigration and those who see multiculturalism undermining social cohesion or as a threat to our 'traditional' culture and way of life. In the first view, interaction with people from other cultures enriches our lives because it introduces us to new ideas and experiences, such as new styles of cuisine or music. In the second view, multiculturalism can be seen as having emphasized difference at the expense of a shared sense of Britishness, encouraging separateness rather than social cohesion and integration. Some argue that multiculturalism brings with it the danger of ethnic tensions because, it is believed, people generally prefer to live among their 'own kind'. However, such views can be criticized for actually fuelling the intolerance and ethnic tensions of which they claim to be warning.
- In economic terms, the benefits of immigration are seen in terms of augmenting the supply of labour, bringing important skills and talents into the economy, mitigating ageing of

the population, and creating business start-ups. For example, immigration in the 1950s and 1960s was encouraged to meet labour shortages, particularly in relation to low-skilled and low-paid occupations. More recently, EU-born immigrants, who are more highly skilled on average than the indigenous population and are more likely to be in work than UK nationals (FullFact 2017), make an important economic contribution in many sectors and make a net fiscal contribution (i.e. pay more in taxes than they consume in benefits and public services). For these reasons, a 'hard Brexit' that prioritized control, and reduction, of immigration, as signalled by Theresa May in the aftermath of the referendum, would be economically damaging. The economic downside of immigration, as argued by Leave campaigners and voters, is seen in terms of pressure on public services in particular areas (such as housing, schools, and family doctors), and competition for jobs resulting in downward pressure on wages in some sectors. However, evidence of the economic impact of immigration from EU countries goes against these concerns. It finds that

> the areas of the UK with large increases in EU immigration did not suffer greater falls in the jobs and pay of UK-born workers. The big falls in wages after 2008 are due to the global financial crisis and a weak economic recovery, not to immigration. There is also little effect of EU immigration on inequality through reducing the pay and jobs of less skilled UK workers.
>
> (Wadsworth et al. 2017)

The political debate on immigration continues. The Coalition government that came into office following the 2010 UK general election was committed to a controversial Conservative Party policy of reducing annual net migration to fewer than 100,000, a commitment that was renewed at the 2017 general election. Following the UK referendum decision to leave the EU the new Prime Minister Theresa May (a Remain supporter during the referendum campaign) made the commitment that 'Brexit means Brexit' and signalled that priority in the negotiations would be given to what she saw as the public demand to be able to control (and reduce) immigration. However, following the Conservatives' failure to achieve a majority after calling a general election in 2017 specifically to strengthen May's hand in the negotiations with the EU, the UK's stance became a more open question and a shift towards a 'soft' Brexit which prioritized single market access became possible.

Stop and Think

Is immigration good for Britain?

Class structure

The meaning of class

VALUES An important way of thinking about the structure of modern societies is in terms of social (or socio-economic) classes. The idea of a 'class structure' highlights a key, though contested, principle of organization of society and social life: the members of society are classified into more or less distinct groups (classes) with the dual implication that members of the same class share a common position in society in some sense and, by the same token, that there are differences between classes. Class simultaneously identifies what people have in common and what separates them. To be a member of, say, the 'working class' means that there is a likeness with other members of the class and that you are separated from the 'middle class'. In addition, a class structure is normally conceived as a hierarchical arrangement: some people are in higher positions in society and some in lower positions. Some people are 'better off' (enjoy a higher standard of living) than others, or simply 'better' (enjoy a higher social status). For this reason, class may give rise to a sense of shared identity as people see others who are similarly situated, have similar lifestyles, and face the same problems as sharing the same interests. Thus, class differences may be a key source of social division and conflict. (This hierarchical conception of class is emphasized to comic effect in the famous 'I know my place' sketch, available at http://www.bbc.co.uk/programmes/p00hhrwl.)

In British society people are familiar with the language of class, and most, when asked, can easily define their own class position. Indeed, Britain is often seen as a society in which there is a peculiarly heightened awareness of and sensitivity to class differences. The most familiar terms are 'working', 'middle', and 'upper' class, though finer distinctions are often made such as 'lower-middle' and 'upper-middle' (but see BBC 2013 for a revised approach). But class remains a contested concept and many questions are still debated: how is class defined? How has the class structure changed? How far do people's 'subjective' understandings of class correspond with social researchers' 'objective' definitions? Are class distinctions and differences still as important as they perhaps once were? Is it possible for individuals to move from one class into another? What are the implications of class structure for business? (See Mini-Case 6.3.)

Mini-Case 6.3 Class identification and awareness in modern Britain

Who is working class today? And who is middle class? Dominant ideas about class differences and boundaries have been based on occupation—the kind of job you do determines whether you are working class or middle class. Traditionally, the working class was conceived in terms of manual work, and so the decline of this type of occupation since the early twentieth century has been interpreted as a decline of the working class (discussed later). Using an alternative classification of occupations, the working class has also been defined in terms of semi-routine and routine occupations. On this definition, too, the working class has been shrinking. Today it accounts for less than one-quarter of the workforce (see Table 6.7).

These are 'objective' definitions of class used by social scientists and statisticians to map the class structure and chart processes of change. They are objective in the sense that they do not depend on what people think about their class position. Yet what people think about their class position—their 'subjective' understanding of class—does matter because it has implications for attitudes and behaviour. Indeed, the whole point of objective definitions might be that, by highlighting that groups share a common position in society with common experiences, they might be predictive of the way people respond to that common position in terms of shared interests, attitudes, and behaviour. For example, historically the working class was strongly associated with the creation of organizations such as trade unions and political parties to represent their interests.

However, recent research shows a marked discrepancy between objective and subjective class. Whereas only about 25 per cent of the population are 'objectively' working class, 60 per cent identify as members of this class when asked, the remaining 40 per cent identifying as middle class. While most working-class people (about eight in ten) identify this as their class, quite a lot of middle-class people (47 per cent of those in professional and managerial occupations) think of themselves as working class as well (Evans and Mellon 2016). Further, people who identify as working class also tend to be more 'class aware', being more likely to see class as a barrier, and to think that class differences are wide and increasing.

One reason why middle-class people might identify with the working class is if this identification reflects the occupations of their parents and therefore their family backgrounds rather than their own occupations—having a working-class background 'goes a long way to explaining the continuing sense of being working class among many people in middle class jobs' (Evans and Mellon 2016: 9). Educational attainment is also a factor—middle-class people with degrees are less likely to identify as working class. But there is also evidence that class identification also depends on how people visualize the structure of society. In recent years there has been a lot of debate about growing inequality, sometimes expressed in terms of a division between an elite 1 per cent of high-income, wealthy individuals, and the rest, the 99 per cent (see Chapter 12). This conception does not identify a distinct middle class as it is incorporated in the 99 per cent. So 'People who see themselves as at the bottom of a structure in which there are a few super rich and then everyone else might well think of themselves as "working class" relatively speaking even if they do hold a middle class job' (Evans and Mellon 2016: 10).

Questions

1. **Do you think of yourself as working class? Or middle class?**
2. **What are the reasons for your class identification?**
3. **Do you feel that your class identity has a significant effect on your life, or not?**

It is common to see class distinctions in terms of aspects of behaviour, for example, accent, manners, lifestyle, beliefs, and attitudes. It can be argued that British people are highly sensitive to these behavioural markers of class, such as whether a person speaks with a 'posh' or 'common' accent. However, these behavioural differences may be seen as outward expressions of more basic determinants of class, relating especially to economic factors such as income and economic role. Income seems to provide a straightforward way of defining class: on the whole the middle class is better off than the working class, and the upper class is at the top of the income scale. Income is correlated with behavioural differences to some extent, partly due to the obvious point that higher incomes afford more expensive lifestyles.

STAKEHOLDERS Income is closely related to economic position and role, because income is generated primarily by business activity and each person's share is determined by the role they play in business. There are two ways of relating class differences to the business system: the first sees the basic class distinction in capitalist economies as between employers and employees, and the second defines class position in terms of a person's occupation.

Capitalism and class

Capitalism is based on private ownership of business, and the vast majority of people depend for their livelihood on the wage or salary they earn as employees through selling their labour or ability to work to an employer in the labour market. Some have seen this employer–employee relationship as a basic form of class division that is characteristic of capitalist economies. This conception of class is found in the socialist tradition, and particularly Marxism. Employers make up a **business class (capitalist class)**, while the very large group of employees constitute the working class. In this view the economic role that defines class position is ownership and control (or not) of business. This is also a distinction in terms of income: profit (business class) versus wage/salary (working class). The importance of this class division is that it may be seen as a perpetual source of tension and conflict because the interests of the two classes are opposed: the profit motive of the business class leads to pressure to hold down wage costs and increase effort and productivity, and members of the working class will resist this pressure. Thus, industrial relations are inherently prone to conflict. This two-class model has plausibility due to its focus on the central relationship—between employers and employees—of a capitalist economic system. However, it can be argued that this view is too simplistic as a way of understanding class differences today, for a number of reasons:

STAKEHOLDERS

- Some critics claim that employers and employees, far from being in conflict, share a basic interest as stakeholders in the success of the business, that they are members of the same team instead of opposed teams. Employees have a stake in competitiveness and profitability to ensure their own job security. These two views can be reconciled by arguing that employees' interests do tend to bring them into conflict with employers, but that this conflict is played out within limits imposed by the need to secure the survival of the business. Further, the stakeholder conception can be understood as a business model that can be made a reality by the (re)design of the corporation, especially through employee representation on the board, or co-determination, and committed long-term ownership (e.g. see Hutton 2015—see also Chapter 11).

- Identifying the business class in terms of ownership is not straightforward, not least due to the separation of 'ownership' and 'control' or management in modern economies dominated by public limited companies (PLCs). While ownership is in the hands of shareholders, control is in the hands of chief executives and boards. Whether owners and managers constitute a single business class with unified interests has been questioned. In the past it has been argued that while shareholders are interested in profit, professional managers who are not share-owners may have various non-profit objectives, and this may alter the employer–employee relationship. However, against this, it can be argued that the overriding objective of business in a capitalist economy must be profitability which is critical to the firm's survival. Nevertheless, ownership does matter. In relation to capitalism in the US and UK Hutton is critical of the 'disengaged', 'uncommitted', and 'short-termist' nature of share ownership which drives the search for short-term profit maximization by businesses at the expense of long-term investment. In addition, executives are tied in to delivering share-price performance by the way they are rewarded through bonuses and incentive plans. And this has implications for the employment relationship: 'One of the fastest ways of boosting profits . . . is to downgrade employees' terms of employment and working conditions, and reduce wages' (Hutton 2015: 99). In other words, to exacerbate the conflictual nature of the employment relationship.
- Although earning a wage or salary is something that all employees share in common, to refer to them all as 'working class' seems to overlook differences between occupations in terms of skill, status, and income. It can be argued that it makes more sense to see employees as constituting different classes—such as 'working' and 'middle'—according to occupation.

The occupational order

The occupational order provides a snapshot of the character of the economy at a particular time, a framework for identifying processes of change, and also provides a way of thinking about class. Occupation is the common currency of class—we tend to define a person's class in terms of the type of job they do. Social classes (or 'socio-economic' or 'occupational' classes) are identified by grouping occupations together in broad categories. Although there are a very large number of individual job titles, the logic of this approach is that broad groups of occupations are alike in some way and distinct from other groups.

DYNAMIC The occupational order is dynamic. During the last century the UK experienced a transformation of the occupational order, so that the types of jobs that people are engaged in today, the skills that they are required to exercise, and the distribution of people between those jobs, are very different from early in the twentieth century. As we will see, these changes have been interpreted by some as involving a transformation of the class structure—a decline of the working class and expansion of the middle class.

Table 6.6 shows the changing occupational class structure during the last century. Here occupations are divided into eight broad categories or occupational classes, including employers and proprietors. The class of manual occupations is further divided into three subgroups on the basis of level of skill. A major transformation was the decline by half in the share of manual (or 'blue collar') workers within the workforce, from approximately three in four in 1911 to three in eight in 1991. You can see that this decline accelerated in the second half of the

Table 6.6 Occupational class in Great Britain, 1911–91 (%)

	1911	1931	1951	1971	1991
Higher professions	1.0	1.1	1.9	3.3	5.3
Lower professions	3.1	3.5	4.7	7.8	13.9
Employers & proprietors	6.7	6.7	5.0	4.2	3.3
Managers & administrators	3.4	3.7	5.5	6.8	15.1
Clerical workers	4.5	6.7	10.4	13.9	15.4
Foremen, supervisors	1.3	1.5	2.6	3.9	3.8
Sales	5.4	6.5	5.7	5.5	5.6
Manual workers	74.6	70.3	64.2	54.7	37.7
Skilled manual	30.6	26.7	24.9	21.6	14.4
Semi-skilled manual	34.4	28.8	27.2	20.6	17.6
Unskilled manual	9.6	14.8	12.0	12.5	5.7
Total in employment (000s)	18,347	21,029	22,514	25,021	24,746

Source: Adapted from Gallie 2000: p. 288, Table 8.4.

century. Early in the last century manual workers constituted the vast bulk of the workforce, but by its close had become a minority. At the same time there was expansion of all other (non-manual or 'white collar') occupations (except employers and proprietors). The shares of the professions, managers and administrators, and clerical workers increased by factors of between 3.4 (clerical) and 5.3 (higher professions). The actual numbers, within an expanding workforce, have increased by larger factors. For example, the number of people employed in the higher professions increased by a factor of 7.14, from 184,000 to 1,314,000 (1911–91). 'In short, there was a change from an occupational structure heavily dominated by manual work to one where there was a fairly even division between three broad categories: professional/managerial work, intermediary occupations and manual work' (Gallie 2000: 289). This occupational shift can also be understood in terms of:

- The shift of the industrial structure from *manufacturing* to *services*. The dominance of manual work in the first half of the century reflected the importance of manufacturing and primary industries (e.g. mining) within the economy (although manual jobs are not confined to manufacturing, and the manufacturing sector also contains non-manual occupations). The declining share (and number) of manual workers in the second half mirrored the process of manufacturing decline. Conversely, the growing non-manual occupations were predominantly in (though not confined to) the expanding service sector.
- The growth of non-manual jobs (particularly professional occupations) is explained partly by the growth of the welfare state in the period after the Second World War (post 1945) (see Chapter14).
- There is a *gendered* dimension to occupational change. The expansion of non-manual service occupations has been a major source of increased female participation in the workforce. This is particularly marked in the feminization of clerical occupations. In fact, clerical occupations switched from being male-dominated at the start of the century to being female-dominated at its end. It is interesting to note that as clerical work has become more feminized there has been a decline of its relative pay and status. It

can be argued that this reflects the undervaluation of 'women's work' in our society (see Chapter 12).

- In general, the shift in the occupational structure is associated with a process of **upskilling** of the workforce, meaning a rise in the average level of skill required. Although this average conceals ups and downs, with some occupations experiencing deskilling, upskilling is the predominant trend. Gallie reports that in 1992, 63 per cent of all employees reported that the level of skill required to do their job had increased during the last five years.
- The transformation of the occupational order during the twentieth century has commonly been interpreted as an overhaul of the **class structure** of British society, involving a decline of the working class and expansion of the middle class. This interpretation stems from a definition of the working class as comprising all those in manual occupations and the middle class as being made up of non-manual workers. In this view, Britain's social structure has changed from one that was overwhelmingly working class to one in which the middle class predominates.

Since 2001 official statistics have been published using the National Statistics Socio-economic Classification (NS-SEC), based on the Standard Occupational Classification 2000 (SOC 2000) (Hall 2006). This classification differs from that used in Table 6.6, particularly in not distinguishing manual and non-manual occupations. Table 6.7 shows the occupational structure for the period 2001–17 based on NS-SEC. The table shows continued expansion of managerial and professional occupations (classes 1 and 2), accounting for 44.6 per cent of employment by 2017. At the same time there has been decline in the share (and number) of people employed in occupations at the bottom end (classes 5, 6, and 7). Routine occupations (class 7) now make up less than 10 per cent of the total. This is consistent with the trend of upskilling observed in the last century.

Table 6.7 also shows the class structure in 2017 made up of three classes based on NS-SEC occupational groupings. The working class, defined in terms of semi-routine and routine occupations, accounts for less than one in four employees and is only just over half the size of the middle class, defined in terms of higher and lower managerial and professional occupations. Since 2001 the long-run trend of a diminishing working class and expanding middle class has continued.

Table 6.7 All in employment by socio-economic classification (NS-SEC) (%)

	2001 (Q2)	2017 (Q1)	Class structure (2017)
1. Higher managerial & professional	13.2	16.6	Middle class
2. Lower managerial & professional	26.4	28.0	44.6
3. Intermediate occupations	13.1	13.7	Intermediate class
4. Small employers & own account workers	9.2	11.3	32.9
5. Lower supervisory & technical	11.3	7.9	
6. Semi-routine occupations	15.4	13.2	Working class
7. Routine occupations	11.6	9.4	22.6

Sources: Office for National Statistics 2017c: Table 19: All in employment by socio-economic classification (NS-SEC); EMP11: All in employment by socio-economic classification (17 May) https://www.ons.gov.uk/employmentandlabourmarket/peopleinwork/employmentandemployeetypes/datasets/employmentbysocioeconomicclassificationemp11

Relevance of the class structure to business

DYNAMIC **VALUES**

- The changing class structure (whether understood in terms of ownership or the occupational order) is driven largely by the dynamic operation of the business system, influenced by state intervention.

INTERNAL/EXTERNAL

- Class distinctions are closely bound up with the nature of the employment relationship and managerial strategies. 'Working-class' occupations tend to be characterized by a 'labour contract' whereas 'middle-class' occupations tend to be characterized by a 'service relationship' (ONS 2012d). Managerial and professional occupations (in particular class 1) are characterized by a 'service relationship' in which employees enjoy not only higher salaries in return for a 'service' rendered to the employer, but also a high level of discretion and control in their work based on trust, job security, and opportunities for career advancement (Table 6.7). At the other end of the scale, class 7 (routine occupations) is characterized by a 'labour contract' in which a wage is paid on the basis of hours worked or level of output. In a labour contract, employees perform routine tasks with little discretion, are subject to managerial authority rather than controlling their own work, and have less job security and little opportunity for advancement. These features are typical to a lesser degree of occupations in classes 5 and 6. Thus, the workforce tends towards a dichotomy between these two types of employment relationship, with intermediate forms characterizing class 3. The nature of the employment relationship involves managerial choice. This will be guided by efficiency considerations, but it also raises questions about how employees should be treated.
- The degree of social mobility (e.g. the chances of someone born into a working-class household 'moving up' into a middle-class occupation) has implications for competitiveness and economic performance. A low level of social mobility not only means that individuals from working-class backgrounds may not have the opportunity to realize their talents and improve their standard of living but also suggests that business is missing out on a pool of untapped talent (see Chapter 12).

INTERNAL/EXTERNAL

- Class is a useful concept for understanding attitudes to work and conflict in the employment relationship. Working-class occupations and a labour contract type of employment relationship have been associated with conflictual 'us and them' attitudes and the development of trade unions to represent employees' interests in the workplace (though there is a trend towards increased middle-class trade unionism, particularly among professional occupations in the public sector—see Chapter 11).
- Class is a useful concept for understanding the behaviour of consumers because of the link between class, income, and lifestyle. In this way class can be used as a way of analysing different market segments.

Stop and Think

What is the meaning of the term 'social class'? How would you define your own class position? What criteria do you use to define your own class position?

Looking ahead

As we have seen, population growth is projected to continue in the future at a faster rate in the UK than in the rest of Europe. However, projections are not predictions and there is uncertainty concerning all dimensions of population increase—the birth rate, life expectancy, and net migration.

Ageing of the population is a long-term and largely predictable trend that will continue to influence political and business agendas. However, health concerns, particularly around obesity, have led to some predictions of falling life expectancy.

Immigration can be quite volatile and therefore difficult to predict. In the last decade immigration from the A8 countries far exceeded initial expectations and has been added to since 2014 by immigration from Bulgaria and Romania. However, more recently the flow of migrants from these countries has reduced. Immigration has become a source of political controversy, and the outcome of the Brexit negotiations will determine immigration rules and numbers after the UK leaves the EU in 2019. The Coalition government set reducing immigration as a key policy objective.

Britain is still learning how to operate successfully as a multicultural society. Sensitivities relating to different values and lifestyles, such as the wearing of religious symbols, will continue to pose challenges for politics and business.

The occupational order and class structure will continue to alter, as a result of economic change. In particular, globalization will continue to make it difficult to sustain low-skill jobs in manufacturing in the UK.

Summary

- Business activity takes place within a social and cultural context, which it both shapes and has to respond to.
- The UK population is increasing, and growth is expected to continue to the middle of the century. In recent years, immigration, notably from Eastern Europe, was the principal driver of population increase, but natural increase has again become the main factor.
- The UK has an ageing population—an increased number and proportion of elderly people in the population. A key aspect of this is the increasing old-age dependency ratio.
- Immigration to the UK, particularly during the last fifty years, has created a multicultural or cosmopolitan society. Immigration is a politically controversial issue and was a main cause of the UK vote to withdraw from the EU. However, evidence suggests that, overall, immigration has a positive economic impact.
- Class is an important feature of British society. There are different ways of conceptualizing the class structure—a common approach is to define class in terms of occupation. Changes in the class structure are driven by economic change. In the twentieth century, the major transformation involved the decline of manual occupations. This experience has stimulated a debate about the decline of the working class.

Case Study: Does living longer mean we should retire later?

The notion of retirement and a definite retirement age has become deeply rooted in the cultures of western societies like the UK, linked to the development of welfare states in which the provision of income in retirement is seen as a key responsibility of government and as a citizenship right. In the UK, old-age pensions were first introduced in the 1908 Old Age Pensions Act (with a retirement age of 70). A fixed retirement age is seen by many as a right so that proposals that people should work longer are often resented and resisted.

This notion of retirement is consistent with a 'threefold life course model' (Guillemard 2001: 241) involving three successive stages (or 'ages'): education, work, and non-work (retirement). However, this model is actually a fairly modern innovation, associated with the rise of industrial societies: 'retirement' is not a natural part of life but a social convention. It is open to question whether the concept of retirement that we have got used to is the best arrangement for individuals, business, or society as a whole. Indeed, Guillemard argues that this model is in fact breaking down and being replaced by a more flexible model in which these ages overlap. Education as a prelude to entry into the labour market might be replaced by life-long learning, and an abrupt shift from employment to retirement might be replaced by a gradual transition involving working for more years and starting to draw on a pension while working fewer hours.

Until 2010, the state pension age (SPA), at which the state pension is paid, was 65 for men and 60 for women. However, recent changes have introduced equalization between men and women (at 65 years by 2018), and a subsequent phased increase of SPA for males and females in order to ease the 'fiscal burden' of an ageing population. By postponing the payment of state pensions, public spending will be reduced, and tax revenues will increase as people continue earning. The Turner Commission had proposed that the SPA should rise by one year per decade to 68 by 2050. However, the 2007 Pensions Act set out a timetable under which the SPA would rise in phases to 68 for both men and women by 2046. Further changes are likely, phasing in retirement at 68 more quickly and possibly further raising the SPA. In 2017 the Cridland review proposed that retirement at 68 be phased in by 2039, bringing the date forward by seven years and therefore extending the work life for more of the current workforce (Cumbo 2017). In line with the Cridland report the government announced in July 2017 that the increase of SPA to 68 would be phased in between 2037 and 2039 (gov.uk **https://www.gov.uk/government/news/proposed-new-timetable-for-state-pension-age-increases**). The World Economic Forum (WEF) has also argued that the retirement age needs to rise to 70 by the middle of the century in Britain and other rich countries to avert a pension crisis, characterized as 'the financial equivalent of climate change' (World Economic Forum 2017).

In 2013 the then Chancellor, George Osborne, stated that people should be able to spend a certain proportion of their adult life drawing a state pension. This principle could be used to adjust the SPA as life expectancy increases. Assuming adult life is calculated from 20 years and that the proportion spent drawing a state pension should be 32 per cent, a report by the Government Actuary's Department in 2017 suggested that retirement at 68 should be introduced as early as 2028 with two further extensions to SPA, to 69 by 2040 and 70 by 2054 (Government Actuary's Department 2017). This would return the SPA to the same age as when the state retirement pension was first introduced in 1908.

These changes and proposals are intended to make the state pension more 'affordable'. Their premise is that the state pension is unsustainable. Another way in which this debate has been conducted is in terms of setting the value of the state pension. In the 2017 UK general election campaign the Conservative Party proposed to remove the 'triple lock' which had, since 2011, guaranteed that the basic state pension would rise each year by the highest of three rates: inflation, the increase of average earnings, or 2.5 per cent. According to the Institute for Fiscal Studies, the policy significantly increased the pension relative to earnings:

Between April 2010 and April 2016 the value of the state pension has been increased by 22.2%, compared to growth in earnings of 7.6% and growth in prices of 12.3% over the same period. This has pushed the value of the basic state pension up to its highest share of average earnings since April 1988. (Institute for Fiscal Studies 2017)

Under the Conservative proposals, the triple lock would be replaced by a double lock, linking the pension to either earnings or inflation, meaning that the pension would always keep pace with earnings or better. So, the gap between the pension and earnings would still narrow but more slowly than it might under the triple lock if inflation and earnings growth remain below 2.5 per cent. Again, this change, opposed by the other main parties, was proposed on grounds of affordability. The Cridland review had also proposed ending the triple lock mechanism. Another way to reduce the 'burden' of the state pension in terms of public spending would be to make it selective by withdrawing it from high earners who, it could be argued, do not need it.

However, critics of these changes and proposals argue that the state pension needs to increase to tackle pensioner poverty, and that increasing the SPA is unfair because people from poorer backgrounds have lower life expectancy. The UK state pension is not generous in international terms, being among the least generous within the OECD group of rich economies (Monaghan 2017). Although pensioner poverty has decreased, in 2016 one in seven pensioners (1.6 million or 14 per cent of pensioners in the UK) lived in poverty, according to the charity Age UK (http://www.ageuk.org.uk/professional-resources-home/policy/money-matters/poverty-and-inequality).

Although a uniform SPA appears to treat everyone equally, in fact it means significant differences in the proportion of adult life spent in retirement due to persistent differences in average life expectancy between people from different social classes, or living in poor or well-off areas. Increasing the retirement age to 70 would significantly reduce the years in retirement for the poorest. The difference in life expectancy between males in the most deprived areas of England and those in least deprived areas is over nine years: on average males can expect to live into their early seventies in the former and into their early eighties in the latter (Office for National Statistics 2014a). In the US a study has found a life expectancy gap of over twenty years between the most affluent and poorest counties (Luscombe 2017).

In terms of social class, it has been found that males in the highest class category (higher managerial and professional) have a life expectancy at 65 years of 85.3, whereas males in the lowest social class (routine occupations) have a life expectancy of just 81.4 at 65 years, a difference of nearly four years (Office for National Statistics 2015d).

The SPA determines eligibility for receipt of the state pension, but it does not involve a requirement to retire at that age, and employees can continue working beyond 65 if they wish to. Under UK law introduced in 2006, 65 was set as a default retirement age (DRA), which means that private and public sector employers were able to set this as a mandatory age at which employees must give up their jobs. Such a rule is convenient for employers as it enables them to manage the size of their workforces through 'natural wastage', avoiding the need to follow costly redundancy procedures, and may afford the opportunity to replace older workers at the top of their pay scales with younger employees on lower pay. The DRA was set at 65 to prevent employers imposing a lower compulsory retirement age, and so can be seen as a form of employee protection. However, campaigners against this rule argued that it was a form of unfair discrimination against older workers, and that performance in a job should be the criterion for determining whether a person can continue working rather than an arbitrary age restriction. It is also argued that age discrimination reflects a more general prejudice, or 'ageism', in which negative stereotypes are held of older people. For example, older workers might be stereotyped as less flexible than younger workers. Finally, the DRA was criticized as being at odds with the recognition, expressed in the report of the Turner Commission and reflected in the rise in SPA, that people need to work longer in line with increased life expectancy. There is a growing number of healthy and active older people—the so-called 'wellderly'—who are capable of making a contribution to economic life. In line with these arguments and considerations the DRA was abolished in 2011, meaning that employees cannot be forced to retire unless there is an objective justification.

Questions

1. **What should the retirement age be?**
2. **Is the idea of a retirement age anachronistic in Britain today?**

Review and discussion questions

1. What are the implications of population ageing for business?
2. Is immigration good for Britain's economy and society? You should identify the implications for different stakeholders.
3. 'Class is still a key feature of British society and has important implications for business.' Discuss this statement.
4. In terms of class structure and demographic profile (age structure, ethnic composition), British society has changed fundamentally since the 1970s. Outline these changes and consider their implications.

Assignments

1. Prepare a briefing paper for the TUC outlining the main arguments against increases in the SPA.
2. Produce a report on the economic impact of immigration to the UK from the EU from 2004 to 2016. On the basis of your findings, make recommendations for immigration policy after the UK leaves the EU.

Further reading

On ageing, see:

Office for National Statistics (2017a)

World Economic Forum (2017)

On the impact of immigration, see:

Wadsworth et al. (2017)

Ruhs and Vargas-Silva (2015)

McGuinness and Hawkins (2016)

OECD (2014)

On the nature and significance of class differences, see:

Evans and Mellon (2016)

Savage (2015)

Test your understanding of this chapter with online questions and answers, explore the subject further through web exercises, and use the weblinks to provide a quick resource for further research. Visit the online resources at www.oup.com/uk/wetherly_otter4e/

Useful websites

www.statistics.gov.uk
Office for National Statistics

http://www.ifs.org.uk
Institute for Fiscal Studies (IFS)

http://www.dwp.gov.uk
Department for Work and Pensions

http://www.equalityhumanrights.com
Equality and Human Rights Commission (EHRC)

http://www.migrationobservatory.ox.ac.uk
Migration Observatory

References

Altmann, R. (2015) *A New Vision for Older Workers: Retain, Retrain, Recruit* (London: Department for Work & Pensions) **https://www.gov.uk/government/publications/a-new-vision-for-older-workers-retain-retrain-recruit**

BBC (2013) 'Huge survey reveals seven social classes in UK' **http://www.bbc.co.uk/news/uk-22007058**

BBC (2017) 'Life expectancy rises "grinding to halt" in England' **http://www.bbc.co.uk/news/health-40608256**

Corlett, A. (2017) *As Time Goes By: Shifting Incomes and Inequality between and within Generations*, Resolution Foundation **http://www.resolutionfoundation.org/publications/as-time-goes-by-shifting-incomes-and-inequality-between-and-within-generations**

Cumbo, J. (2017) 'Pensions review recommends later retirement age', *Financial Times*, 23 March **https://www.ft.com/content/c73181de-0eff-11e7-a88c-50ba212dce4d?mhq5j=e1**

Evans, G. and Mellon, J. (2016) 'Social class: identity, awareness and political attitudes: why are we still working class?', British Social Attitudes 33, National Centre for Social Research (NatCen) **http://www.bsa.natcen.ac.uk/media/39094/bsa33_social-class_v5.pdf**

FullFact (2017) *EU Immigration to the UK* **https://fullfact.org/immigration/eu-migration-and-uk**

Gallie, D. (2000) 'The labour force', in A. H. Halsey (ed.), *Twentieth Century British Social Trends* (Basingstoke: Palgrave)

Government Actuary's Department (2017) *Periodic Review of Rules about State Pension Age* **https://www.gov.uk/government/uploads/system/uploads/attachment_data/file/603136/periodic-review-of-rules-about-state-pension-age-gad-report.pdf**

Guillemard, A.-M. (2001) 'Work or retirement at career's end?', in A. Giddens (ed.), *The Global Third Way Debate* (Cambridge: Polity)

Hall, C. (2006) *A Picture of the United Kingdom using the National Statistics Socio-economic Classification* (London: Office for National Statistics)

Heath, A. and Cheung, S. Y. (2006) *Ethnic Penalties in the Labour Market: Employers and Discrimination*, Research Report No. 341 (London: Department for Work & Pensions)

Hutton, W. (2015) *How Good We Can Be: Ending the Mercenary Society and Building a Great Country* (London: Little, Brown)

Institute for Fiscal Studies (2017) *Would You Rather? Further Increases in The State Pension Age v Abandoning the Triple Lock* **https://www.ifs.org.uk/publications/8942**

Luscombe, R. (2017) 'Life expectancy gap between rich and poor US regions is "more than 20 years"', *Guardian*, 8 May **https://www.theguardian.com/inequality/2017/may/08/life-expectancy-gap-rich-poor-us-regions-more-than-20-years**

McGuinness, F. and Hawkins, O. (2016) *Impacts of Immigration on Population and the Economy*, House of Commons Library Briefing Paper Number 7659 **http://researchbriefings.parliament.uk/ResearchBriefing/Summary/CBP-7659**

Monaghan, A. (2017) 'UK should axe state pension for rich people, says OECD', *Guardian*, 27 April **https://www.theguardian.com/business/2017/apr/27/uk-state-pension-rich-oecd**

OECD (2014) 'Is migration good for the economy?', *Migration Policy Debates* **https://www.oecd.org/migration/OECD%20Migration%20Policy%20Debates%20Numero%202.pdf**

Office for National Statistics (2012) 2011 *Census: Population Estimates for the United Kingdom, 27 March 2011* **http://www.ons.gov.uk/ons/rel/census/2011-census/population-and-household-estimates-for-the-united-kingdom/stb-2011-census--population-estimates-for-the-united-kingdom.html**

Office for National Statistics (2012a) *Measuring National Well-being, Social Trends 42—Population*, **http://www.ons.gov.uk/ons/rel/social-trends-rd/social-trends/social-trends-42---population/art-social-trends-42---population.html**

Office for National Statistics (2012b) *Population Ageing in the United Kingdom, its Constituent Countries and the European Union* **http://www.ons.gov.uk/ons/rel/mortality-ageing/focus-on-older-people/population-ageing-in-the-united-kingdom-and-europe/rpt-age-uk-eu.html**

Office for National Statistics (2012c) *2011 Census: Key Statistics for England and Wales, March 2011* **http://www.ons.gov.uk/ons/dcp171778_290685.pdf**

Office for National Statistics (2012d) *Patterns of Social Mobility by NS-SEC: England and Wales 1981–2001* **http://www.ons.gov.uk/ons/search/index.html?newquery=Patterns+of+Social+Mobility+by+NS-SEC%3A+England+and+Wales+1981-2001**

Office for National Statistics (2014) *Changes in UK Population over the Last 50 Years* **http://webarchive.nationalarchives.gov.uk/20160105160709/http://www.ons.gov.uk/ons/rel/pop-estimate/population-estimates-for-uk--england-and-wales--scotland-and-northern-ireland/2013/sty-population-changes.html**

Office for National Statistics (2014a) *Inequality in Healthy Life Expectancy at Birth by National Deciles of Area Deprivation: England, 2009–11* **http://webarchive.nationalarchives.gov.uk/20160107064053/http://www.ons.gov.uk/ons/rel/disability-and-health-measurement/inequality-in-healthy-life-expectancy-at-birth-by-national-deciles-of-area-deprivation--england/2009-11/stb---inequality-in-hle.html**

Office for National Statistics (2014b) Migration Statistics Quarterly Report: November 2014 **https://www.ons.gov.uk/peoplepopulationandcommunity/populationandmigration/internationalmigration/bulletins/migrationstatisticsquarterlyreport/2015-06-30**

Office for National Statistics (2015) *National Population Projections: 2014-based Statistical Bulletin* **https://www.ons.gov.uk/peoplepopulationandcommunity/populationandmigration/populationprojections/bulletins/nationalpopulationprojections/2015-10-29#tab-Main-points**

Office for National Statistics (2015a) *How Has Life Expectancy Changed over Time?* **http://visual.ons.gov.uk/how-has-life-expectancy-changed-over-time**

Office for National Statistics (2015b) *Overview of the UK Population* **https://www.ons.gov.uk/peoplepopulationandcommunity/populationandmigration/populationestimates/articles/overviewoftheukpopulation/2015-11-05**

Office for National Statistics (2015c) *Trends in Births and Deaths over the Last Century* **http://visual.ons.gov.uk/birthsanddeaths**

Office for National Statistics (2015d) *Trend in Life Expectancy at Birth and at Age 65 By Socio-economic Position Based on the National Statistics Socio-economic Classification, England and Wales: 1982–1986 to 2007–2011* **https://www.ons.gov.uk/peoplepopulationandcommunity/birthsdeathsandmarriages/lifeexpectancies/bulletins/trendinlifeexpectancyatbirthandatage65bysocioeconomicpositionbasedonthenationalstatisticssocioeconomicclassificationenglandandwales/2015-10-21**

Office for National Statistics (2016) *Migration Statistics Quarterly Report: December 2016* **https://www.ons.gov.uk/peoplepopulationandcommunity/populationandmigration/internationalmigration/bulletins/migrationstatisticsquarterlyreport/dec2016**

Office for National Statistics (2017) *Statistical Bulletin: Population Estimates for UK, England and Wales, Scotland and Northern Ireland: Mid-2016* **https://www.ons.gov.uk/peoplepopulationandcommunity/populationandmigration/populationestimates/bulletins/annualmidyearpopulationestimates/latest**

Office for National Statistics (2017a) *Overview of the UK Population: March 2017* **https://www.ons.gov.uk/peoplepopulationandcommunity/populationandmigration/populationestimates/articles/overviewoftheukpopulation/mar2017**

Office for National Statistics (2017b) *Migration Statistics Quarterly Report: May 2017* **https://www.ons.gov.uk/peoplepopulationandcommunity/populationandmigration/internationalmigration/bulletins/migrationstatisticsquarterlyreport/may2017**

Office for National Statistics (2017c) 'Table 19: All in employment by socio-economic classification (NS-SEC)' and EMP11: All in employment by socio-economic classification (17 May) **https://www.ons.gov.uk/employmentandlabourmarket/peopleinwork/employmentandemployeetypes/datasets/employmentbysocioeconomicclassificationemp11**

Pensions Commission (2004) *Pensions: Challenges and Choices*. First Report of the Pensions Commission **www.pensionscommission.org.uk**

Ruhs, M. and Vargas-Silva, C. (2015) *Briefing: The Labour Market Effects of Immigration*, the Migration Observatory **http://www.migrationobservatory.ox.ac.uk/wp-content/uploads/2016/04/Briefing-Labour_Market_Effects_of_Immigration.pdf**

Savage, M. (2015) *Social Class in the 21st Century* (London: Pelican)

United Nations Population Fund (2012) *Ageing in the Twenty-First Century: A Celebration and A Challenge* **http://www.helpage.org/resources/ageing-in-the-21st-century-a-celebration-and-a-challenge**

Vargas-Silva, C. and Markaki, Y. (2016) *Briefing: EU Migration to and from the UK*. Migration Observatory **http://www.migrationobservatory.ox.ac.uk/wp-content/uploads/2016/04/Briefing-EU_Migration_UK.pdf**

Wadsworth, J. et. al. (2017) *Brexit and the Impact of Immigration on the UK*, Centre for Economic Performance/London School of Economics and Political Science **http://cep.lse.ac.uk/pubs/download/brexit05.pdf**

Wood, M. et al. (2009) *A Test for Racial Discrimination in Recruitment Practice in British Cities*. Research Report No. 607 (London: Department for Work & Pensions)

World Economic Forum (2017) *We'll Live to 100—How Can We Afford It?* **http://www3.weforum.org/docs/WEF_White_Paper_We_Will_Live_to_100.pdf**

Chapter 7
The ethical environment: corporate responsibility

Simon Robinson

Learning objectives

When you have completed this chapter, you will be able to:

- Define **corporate responsibility (CR)**, **corporate citizenship**, and **business ethics**.
- Examine and assess the free market views of the market and CR, and how these relate to ethics.
- Examine and assess the stakeholder view of business and bring out the implications for CR practice.
- Make a case for CR in business.
- Develop and use a framework for corporate social responsibility (CSR) that connects to the practicalities of business.

THEMES

The following themes of the book are especially relevant to this chapter

- **DIVERSITY** CR applies across the wide diversity of business, from small and medium enterprises to global corporations.
- **COMPLEXITY** The case study on Caterpillar at the end of this chapter shows the complexity of the business environment. This is the context in which CR has to be worked out. It shows that responses to CR cannot be simplistic and demand the development of an effective CR decision-making process. This process is not about asserting or prescribing predetermined views of CR but about finding appropriate responses through planning.
- **LOCAL TO GLOBAL** The business environment operates internally, locally, regionally, nationally, and at the global level. The operation of CR will be examined in this context.
- **DYNAMIC** The constantly changing environment leads to new CR challenges. Effective CR policy looks to respond to that dynamic environment by ensuring that business managers reflect on their operational practices, including regular reporting on how the business responds to that environment.
- **INTERACTION** This chapter shows the rise of corporate citizenship, in which business sees itself as part of a wider community, with mutual and shared responsibilities. In this model, business not only shares responsibilities for the wider social and physical environment but also contributes to the development of ethical meaning in that environment.

- **STAKEHOLDERS** Awareness of stakeholders, their needs and responsibilities, forms the basis of how CSR is determined. This chapter focuses on the need to negotiate responsibility with stakeholders.
- **VALUES** Any business embodies values and purpose. These form the basis of any CR policy. Regular audits reflect on how these values are embodied in practice.

Introduction

Chapter 2 introduced us to the debates about the ability of the free market to produce economic efficiency, and this was further explored in Chapter 4 when we considered the ideological divide between left and right. It is clear that attitudes to business depend on where people are located along this ideological spectrum. Put simply, for those on the right, business makes the world go round. It is business (and especially the private sector) that creates the wealth on which all of society depends. For those on the left, businesses (private) are simply out for themselves and will put profits before people, ignoring their wider responsibilities. Any notion of CR is a contradiction in terms. Corporations only recognize their economic self-interest.

Advocates of the free market argue that in acting out of self-interest businesses are able to realize the common good provided that there is competition and freedom. Critics argue that, in fact, the free market allows business to acquire the power to restrict competition and to exploit consumers and employees. They argue that this will require close government supervision, regulation, or direct control and that there is a need for a vibrant 'third sector' of voluntary groups and non-governmental organizations (NGOs).

There has been a growth in social activism from this sector, highlighting what is seen as corporate irresponsibility and there have been many examples of this indeed. The explosion of a chemical plant run by the US-owned Union Carbide in Bhopal, India, in 1984, caused a huge loss of life and a continuing genetic legacy of birth defects. It is argued that the company did not face up to its responsibilities (see www.bhopal.org/whathappened.html for an example of this view and www.bhopal.com for the company's defence of its actions).

The environmental movement has been particularly vocal in its condemnation of what it sees as the cavalier approach taken by corporations to the environment. For example:

- Shell's record, highlighted by the Brent Spar case (Entine 2002), is still under intense scrutiny by a range of environmental groups.
- Another oil company, Exxon, has been attacked as trying to deny that global warming is a problem by funding 'climate change denial' scientists and using its money to influence politicians not to pass legislation to curb oil consumption.
- In 2007, BP, which had managed to brand itself as a green company, suffered a blow to its image when it was accused of ignoring health and safety legislation in the North Sea (http://www.guardian.co.uk/business/2007/may/08/oilandpetrol.frontpagenews). This reputational damage was severely increased by the Deepwater Horizon oil rig blowout in 2010 in the Gulf of Mexico just off the US coast. Eleven people lost their lives in the initial explosion that caused the blowout and the resultant oil spill was the largest accidental oil spill in history (Otter 2011).

Recent years have seen some spectacular examples of major company malpractice, resulting in the collapse of companies such as WorldCom and Enron. This chapter explores competing perspectives about the degree to which businesses operate in a responsible manner and how CR can best be promoted.

> *Stop and Think*
>
> Before you proceed further with this discussion of CR, pause to reflect on the purpose of business. Do you agree that it is just to make profit? Or are there other benefits that business should deliver for society?

The emergence of the CR agenda

CR is not new. Rowntree of York, now owned by Nestlé and makers of confectionery and cakes since 1725, for example, had a long history of care for employees and the wider community (see Mini-Case 7.1).

However, during the twentieth century old conceptions of CR weakened:

- Government took increasing responsibility for the fulfilment of individual and community needs, from education to health and pensions.
- There was an increase in cultural and religious diversity within society. This led to many different perspectives about the nature of responsibility in society.
- Communities became more fragmented and short term. There was a breakdown in patterns of behaviour and institutions such as marriage and the family, caused partly by greater wealth and increased mobility.
- With the economic boom and practices such as the division of labour, Bauman (1985) suggests there was an increasing fragmentation of responsibility. He argued that the division of labour had the effect of creating distance between the individual and the larger group, thus decreasing any sense of overall responsibility, the scale of which was exacerbated by transnational corporations.

With such changes, the idea of CR that seemed to occur naturally for companies such as Rowntree now had to be explicitly articulated and justified. Moeller and Erdal note several elements in the experience of business that have led to the increased concern to do just that (2003: 3–4):

- Globalization. This has seen the growth of multinational business such that it is estimated that over half of the largest 'economic units' in the world are corporations. Where such companies could act at one time with little apparent concern for CR, their effect on the social and physical environment has led to calls for improved accountability. The increase in NGOs, such as Oxfam, Christian Aid, and Amnesty International, has further encouraged multinational corporations to reflect on their responsibilities at every stage of the production process.
- Information and communications technology (ICT). This has led to increased global transparency, with instant access to immediate information and judgements from many different sources. The result is that companies find it less and less easy to hide what might be controversial aspects of their business.
- Fiscal pressure. Growing fiscal pressure has forced companies to pull out of previous philanthropic ventures. At the same time, this has led to greater discussion about the different roles of government and business.

Mini-Case 7.1 Timeline of Rowntree in the twentieth century

1904	The company appoint a dentist and a doctor
1904	A model village for the workers is developed
1906	A pension scheme is made available to all employees
1909	Yearsley swimming baths are given by the company to the City of York
1913	Dining facilities for 3,000 employees are built
1916	One of the first widows' benefits funds is established
1916–18	Works councils are created, developing democracy at work; profit sharing is introduced at about the same time
1921	An unemployment scheme is introduced

Throughout this time, community involvement with schools, the local mental hospital, and other local institutions is seen as a key part of the company's role. Three things marked out the experience of Rowntree:

1. A strong sense of, and pride in, the company's identity as part of the local community. For instance, they wanted local school children to understand the role, purpose, and values of the business and how they related to the community.
2. The capacity to reflect on, and respond to, needs in the workforce and community such that their view of responsibility was developed over time.
3. Responsibility was played out in relevant practice. There was no division between ethical ideas and their practice.

Part of this emerged from the Quaker tradition of social activism (**www.quaker.org.uk**), exemplified in concern for prison reform and the abolition of slavery. Part was also about a simple and immediate awareness of the local community and the company's part in that community. Any responsibility was not extra to the role of business, but was developed in that context. Hence, they felt no need to justify their concern for the community. This was also a time when:

(a) There was limited government social care, leaving many very obvious social needs unmet, and thus a strong sense of shared responsibility.

(b) There were strong local communities which stayed together over time and had a practical sense of interdependence.

Question

Why do you think that Rowntree developed such responsible practices?

- In the 1960s and 1970s business came under increased scrutiny in the areas of equal opportunities and health and safety at work. This led to the establishment of legal standards, which have been a continuing feature of CR.
- The growing importance of intangible or 'post-material' values. This has involved recognition that in the new economic environment there are an increasing number of values shared by significant parts of society on which depend the continued success of the corporation. This is partly about increased awareness in society of key issues such as the sustainability of the environment (Jonas 1984).
- As indicated at the start of the chapter, there have been a number of well-documented business disasters, such as Enron, which have brought into question the role and trustworthiness of business.

Stop and Think

How far do you agree that responsibility (e.g. for community or environmental concerns) should be the preserve of government or the state rather than corporations? What are the reasons for your conclusion?

Key terms in the discussion of CR

VALUES COMPLEXITY In order to understand the debate on the ethical responsibilities of business, we need to look more closely at three related terms:

- CR;
- corporate citizenship; and
- business ethics.

Corporate responsibility

A simple definition of the term CR is 'companies integrating social and environmental concerns in their daily business operations and in their interactions with their stakeholders on a daily basis' (European Commission 2001: 366). The term began as CSR, as the focus then was largely the responsibility of business to society. The concept, developed in the 1960s and 1970s as work practice (especially in the areas of health and safety and equal opportunities), was increasingly questioned, leading to legislation. Since then the definition of the concept has continued to develop. The Institute of Public Relations, for instance, sees this responsibility as involving philanthropy, enlightened self-interest, and straightforward self-interest (Gregory and Tafra 2004).

The first of these involves donations of some kind to the local community. The second is about the generation of positive publicity for the company through sponsoring worthy organizations or causes. Such positive images can be useful also in times of crisis. Prior to the most recent campaigns against Shell, it had been involved in a court case about the environment. The court found against the company, but the judge implied that he would have fined them more, had Shell's record on environmental work sponsorship not been so excellent. This is partly why Shell is so keen to promote itself as a socially responsible company (see www.shell.com). Self-interest refers to investments that would directly benefit the organization, such as involvement in economic regeneration projects or staff training developments.

Gregory and Tafra (2004) note that expectations of the business community are becoming greater all the time. Three themes increasingly stand out:

- the environment;
- corporate governance and related business standards; and
- human rights.

In all these areas mere compliance with codes or standards is seen as no longer adequate. Respect for human rights, for instance, may involve active empowerment of some stakeholders. Increasingly then responsibility in business is referred to as CR not CSR. The responsibility of business is now seen as more holistic, something involving all the relationships, inside and outside the corporation. Hence, this chapter will use the term CR, noting that many corporations continue to use the term CSR most often meaning the same thing.

Corporate citizenship

Andriof and McIntosh (2001) define this as 'understanding and managing a company's wider influences on society for the benefit of the company and society as a whole'. Zadek (2001) employs the useful term 'footprints', the visible effect of the company on the social and physical environment.

Viewing the corporation as a citizen is to set down legal and moral expectations. As citizens we have legal rights and duties, but also a wider role in supporting and enabling the well-being of society. Is it possible to see a corporation as having this role?

Views differ on the relationship between CR and corporate citizenship. Some see the two as synonymous, while others see corporate citizenship as focused in community relations. Increasingly, the more holistic view of CR seeks to integrate corporate citizenship. In effect, it is the civic responsibility of the corporation.

Business ethics

VALUES Ethics is the systematic study of how to behave in the right way and how we judge what is right. Business ethics includes exploration of:

- the underlying ethical values of business, including those of any particular professions in business, such as accountants or managers;
- how any ethical values might be embodied in the corporation (including the development of codes of ethics);
- particular ethical policies in areas such as corporate governance or workplace relationships; and
- underlying ethical theories.

There are three main theories or approaches to ethical reasoning. One view of ethics is that they should be based on core general principles. A good example of this is the Ten Commandments, which see actions such as killing or stealing as wrong in themselves. In philosophy, this is referred to as the **deontological** tradition. We have a duty (or *deon* in ancient Greek) to behave in this prescribed manner.

Another philosophical tradition is **utilitarian** theory (utility in this sense means happiness or benefit) which questions whether principles are always right and suggests that we discover what is right by looking at consequences. The action that maximizes the best consequences for the most people or groups is seen to be good.

Both these theories have their problems. In the first, there can be no absolute principles, principles that do not have an exception. The second theory is not so much a theory as a means of calculation. It does not say anything about what the good is that should be maximized. Increasingly, then, business ethics has focused on a third theory, 'virtue ethics'. Building on the ethics of Aristotle, this argues that ethics is not so much about determining what is right or wrong, but rather about building a good character. The character is informed and sustained by the stories of the community, which embody the virtues (moral strengths or dispositions) (MacIntyre 1981, Moore 2012). The virtues are learned through practice, and good character will enable good ethical decision-making. This does not preclude elements of the first two theories. On the contrary, a virtue such as integrity (Robinson 2016, Scherkoske 2013) helps one to identify what principles are important. Practical wisdom (the capacity to reflect on core purpose, MacIntyre 1981) helps one to identify principles and consequences. The key characteristic of virtues is that they are of the 'mean', between extremes. Courage, for instance, stands between cowardice and foolhardiness. Hence, virtues enable the person to handle more effectively the stresses of decision-making in business, increasing awareness and appreciation of the self, the organization and of the surrounding social environment, and of responsibility to each of these. CR is then a critical aspect of business ethics, focusing on how the moral responsibility of business is worked out in relation to internal and external stakeholders.

Ethical values can be distinguished from other values, such as intellectual values or social values. Ethical values are often summed up in terms of principles such as justice, respect, non-maleficence (do no harm), or beneficence (seek the good) (Beauchamp and Childress 2013). However, as Aristotle (cf. MacIntyre 1981) argues, different kinds of values need to work together in order to make good decisions. Hence, ethical decisions need to make rational sense. Practical wisdom is characterized as an intellectual virtue.

Stop and Think

Consider the following dilemma that illustrates the three approaches to ethical thinking.

A valued and long-serving employee has been recorded on camera stealing food from a vending machine late at night. The code of conduct states that anyone found guilty of theft should be dismissed, regardless of the value of the goods stolen. A simple deontological approach would apply the rule, partly because it is wrong to steal, and partly because not to dismiss the employee would lead to lack of clarity about the code. A simple utilitarian approach would look to the consequences. For instance, how might dismissal affect the reputation of the firm if the press found out? A virtue ethics approach would take account of both theories but spend more time in dialogue with the employee and relevant colleagues to ascertain context and motives, and how the identity, purpose, and vision of the firm relates to this.

Justifying CR

In this section we will examine two alternative perspectives on CR: free market theory and stakeholder theory. We will reflect on these perspectives with the help of a scenario involving a computer game (Mini-Case 7.2). In this case there is a fundamental question about whether the computer game company should have any sense of responsibility beyond signing the contract and ensuring work for the ninety employees.

VALUES There are two broad perspectives that seek an answer to this question and we deal with these in the following two sections.

Mini-Case 7.2 Computer games

Following the success of a computer game based upon a scenario set in the frozen north the computer software development company was commissioned by the client company to develop a second game. This time the client wanted increased shock value, the inclusion of the death of young children. As an added incentive, if the computer company agreed to this there would be rapid release of monies outstanding from the first game. The manager of the software firm and his engineering staff were uneasy about this request—though initially a little unsure why they felt this unease. They felt there may be wider issues about how such games affect players and about how their firm might be perceived.

As a result of discussions with his staff, the manager decided that it was important to clarify the situation. He wrote to his client's legal department and asked if they would confirm in writing that the company wished him to develop a second game and that it was their intention that this should involve increased horror and the death of children. No such confirmation was received—and the money owed to the software development company was rapidly released.

Questions

1. **Why do you think the legal department responded in this way?**
2. **There were two businesses involved in this case. Does the responsibility of each of them differ, and if so why?**
3. **Who are the important people in this case that might be affected by the decisions of these two companies?**

The free market view of CR

Milton Friedman is often seen as one of the foremost modern advocates of the free market. In relation to the debate about CR his argument is simple (Friedman 1983). The role of business is the creation of wealth and thus the prime responsibility of business is to make a profit for its owners, usually the shareholders. In this, the executive director acts as an agent serving the interests of 'his principal', i.e. the owners. The interest of the principal is profit maximization, and involvement in any activities in the community outside this sphere would be a violation of trust and thus morally wrong. Friedman does not argue against the social involvement of the company as such, rather simply that the company, and the owners especially, can decide to do what they think is fit. There is no moral or legal obligation on the company to be more socially involved, and the company can follow its own ends, so long as they are legal.

If the company executive does decide to get involved in a community project Friedman argues that this is not an obligation but rather a means of achieving the company aims, such as improving the image and reputation of the company and thus contributing to improving profits.

For Friedman, pursuing such responsibility would involve costs that would have to be passed on to the customer, possibly to the shareholder in reduced dividends, and to the employee in reduced wages. Not only is this unfair, it also constitutes a form of taxation without representation and is therefore undemocratic. Moreover, it is both unwise, because it invests too much power in the company executives, and futile, because it is likely that the costs imposed by this approach will lead to a reduction in economic efficiency.

Finally, he argues that the executive is not the best person to be involved in making decisions about social involvement. S/he is neither qualified, nor mandated, to pursue social goals. It is social administrators that understand the needs of the local area and who can determine local priorities. Such a task is better suited to local government and social concern groups, whose roles and accountability are directly related to these tasks. For business to enter this field would lead to a confusion of roles and a raising of false expectations.

According to the free market argument, the social responsibility of the computing firm in Mini-Case 7.2 should have been to take the new contract. To take it would be within the law, and it would fulfil the interests of the owner and the employees. The law would have been responsible for placing an over-18 restriction on any major horror content. In turn, it would then be the responsibility of the individual who buys the game to deal with any negative effects, or the responsibility of parents to monitor what their under-18 children are doing. The computer firm could also say that it had no wider responsibility, and that such responsibility to wider society lay with the commissioning company.

> *Stop and Think*
>
> Is there one core purpose of business? If so, how does that relate to any other role of business?
>
> Is there one purpose generic to all business or do different businesses have different purposes?
>
> Make a list of all the possible purposes of your business or university. How might a public organization, such as a university, differ from a business?

There are a number of criticisms of this free market view. First, seeing profit maximization as the exclusive purpose of business is simplistic. Managers may have several different purposes each of equal importance: care for shareholders, clients, the physical environment, and so on. Shareholders may want profits, but they could be concerned for the environment or for the community in which they live. Our different value worlds are connected. This can only be tested in dialogue with each group of shareholders, and in light of the nature of the business and its effects on society.

Second, there is an assumption that the ethical worlds of social concern and business are quite separate. The initial response of the computer firm's employees shows that this is not the case. They were all very concerned about being involved in such a project. Much of that worry related to their personal sense of responsibility and, also, the firm's reputation.

Third, it is difficult to predetermine what the responsibility of the business person or the business should be, any more than it is possible to be precise about the responsibility of, for instance, local or national government. In practice, there are broad responsibilities, but these are continuously being debated and negotiated.

Stakeholder theory and CR

DIVERSITY **DYNAMIC** **STAKEHOLDERS** The computer firm case was, of course, deceptively complex. First, there were two companies involved each of whom was a stakeholder in the other's business. For the commissioning company this was a minor, but potentially lucrative, relationship. For the computer firm this was a potentially critical deal that would help to keep them alive. Second, each company had some very different stakeholders, with different and sometimes conflicting values. The commissioning company, for instance, had a strong line in family entertainment. The game, however, was targeted at late adolescents. This could potentially spoil the company's family image. We do not know precisely why the legal department responded in the way they did, but it can be assumed that they did not want to affect the reputation of the commissioning company. In recent times, there has been also an increase in customers from different cultures, including the Muslim world, with a strong family ethic. Again, this would seem to be an important argument against involving gratuitous horror.

Up to this point, responsibility to any possible customers would seem to coincide with self-interest. There is little point in trying to sell to one group in a way that would actually affect the company's reputation with other potential customers. It may, of course, be that there are wider responsibilities to children and families. What is the effect of violent games on younger people? Research is inconclusive about this. The precautionary principle might well apply here then. If you are not sure what negative effect your project might have on children or wider society, or how that might reinforce other negative social changes, the precautionary principle suggests that the firm exercise precaution and not become involved in gratuitous horror. Alternatively, it might be possible for such a company to be involved in developing further research around this area. At the very least, there are questions about what the responsibility of the company might be.

For the computer games company these questions are a little different. There are responsibilities to the owner and the employees. However, as computer engineers, many employees were part of a wider professional body of engineers. That profession is itself a stakeholder in the sense that any decision made by a computer firm might affect the standing of computer engineers in wider society. Recent work on the responsibility of engineers stresses the importance of maintaining the integrity of the profession. The profession itself has a real concern about the effects of any computer games on the wider society.

Reflecting on the different stakeholders reveals the complex and dynamic nature of any situation, and it is often not possible to simplistically divide the interests of the shareholders and the wider stakeholders. Does stakeholder theory then act as the basis for determining CR?

A stakeholder was initially defined in terms of those groups which were critical to the survival of the business, including employees, customers, lenders, and suppliers (Sternberg 2000: 49).

This has been further developed to 'any individual or group who can affect or is affected by the actions, decisions, policies, practices or goals of the organization' (Carroll and Buchholtz 2000). This widens stakeholders to government, the community, and beyond. For multinational corporations this becomes even more complex.

It is possible to identify different versions of stakeholder theory (SHT), as argued by Heath and Norman (2004). They include:

- strategic SHT: a theory that attention to the needs of stakeholders will lead to better outcomes for the business;
- SHT of governance: a theory about how stakeholder groups should be involved in oversight of management, e.g. placing stakeholders on the board; and
- deontic SHT: a theory that analyses the legitimate rights and needs of the different stakeholders and uses this data to develop company policies.

It is possible, however, to see all these theories as simply aspects of the larger stakeholder view.

Sternberg (2000: 49ff.) argues against basing CR on SHT on the following grounds:

- to be responsible to someone, we have to be accountable to them, but it is not at all clear to which stakeholders a company is accountable; and
- it is likely that the interests of stakeholders conflict—how does the firm resolve this?

However, stakeholder theorists argue that it is perfectly possible to be accountable to shareholders and also recognize a shared responsibility for wider stakeholders, including the environment that has to be worked out in practice. It is not a question of a polarized model of stakeholders versus shareholders but one of identifying shared interests and finding ways of responding to them.

Carroll suggests a way of getting over that polarized approach which involves four areas: economic, ethical, legal, and philanthropic (1991: 41). He argues that these different responsibilities are set in consecutive layers within a company, with CR involving addressing all four layers one after another.

Corporations have an economic responsibility towards their shareholders to be profitable and provide reasonable returns on shareholders' investments. Economic and financial gain is the primary objective of a corporation in a business sense and is the foundation upon which all the other responsibilities rest (see Chapter 1).

However, at the same time businesses are expected to comply with the laws and regulations as the ground rules and legal framework under which they must operate. A company's legal responsibilities are seen as coexisting with economic responsibilities as fundamental precepts of the free enterprise system (see Chapters 5 and 11).

Ethical responsibilities within a corporation ensure that the organization performs in a manner consistent with expectations of ethics in society. Good corporate citizenship is defined as doing what is expected ethically, and it is important to recognize and respect new or evolving ethical trends adopted by society. It must be noted that the corporate integrity and ethical behaviour of a company go beyond mere compliance with laws and regulations and entail the obligation to do what is right and fair, and to avoid harm.

Finally, Carroll suggests that philanthropic responsibilities include corporate actions that are in response to society's expectation that businesses be good corporate citizens, involved in activities or programmes to promote human welfare or goodwill. Philanthropy, 'love of fellow humans', is highly desired by society, however it is not ultimately necessary (Carroll 1991: 44).

Carroll's view is comprehensive and usefully brings together different views of CR. However, we are still left with some difficult questions. First, while the primary aim of a business may not be promoting human welfare, if there is evidence that parts of the business are abusing the human rights of its workers, then this is most directly the concern of the business. A good example is modern slavery. The ILO (International Labour Organization) estimates that modern slavery in business leads to over $150 billion profits annually (ILO 2016). Second, if businesses are operating in social and political contexts where corruption or repression exist should the business simply go along with this? It could be argued that businesses should at the least not collude with corruption (Transparency International 2013) or actively promote democracy in, for example, areas of economic and political transition. Such considerations bring together concern for the 'common good', based in business ethics, and the focus on the triple bottom line (Elkington 1997). The triple bottom line places social and environmental needs alongside financial, and seeks to develop adequate ways of reporting on all three aspects of the firm's practice (see below on audit, and further in Chapter 8).

This takes the complexity of the business environment even further, and leads to more developments in CR. Business is itself a stakeholder in wider society and, thus, is more accountable in terms of corporate citizenship. Underlying this are arguments that business is a quasi-social entity, which is part of the interdependent local and global community, whose value in society is tied to social and economic well-being, and a broad professional purpose which is beyond simple profit (Nohria and Khurana 2008).

The sense of shared responsibility is further stressed by Heath and Norman (2004). Learning lessons from disasters such as the Enron case, they argue that the real problems emerge from managers who keep their actions secret from the shareholders. Hence, the shareholders are not able to be part of a conversation about values, purposes, and ways in which a business is run. They argue that when business is not transparent, responsibility is easily lost at all levels. Responsibility is worked out through dialogue between all stakeholders and shareholders. Only such dialogue can determine a creative and feasible response, and what the possibilities and limits of any CR might be. This would mean that CR has to work hard at developing a culture of critical dialogue within and beyond the company.

How does this view help the computer games company? It takes them beyond simple stakeholder models, and into the practice of effective dialogue. In their case the dialogue began by trying to clarify just what the commissioning company meant. If the dialogue had continued it might have led the games company to explore whether the use of horror, or the death of children, in a computing game was necessarily wrong. It is possible to see these as being used in the context of a game with a moral framework where those who kill the children, or allow that to happen, can be brought to book. Hence, it might be possible to take the contract and develop a game based in a broader ethical context, thus contributing to a wider social responsibility. Either way the effect of dialogue was to ask the commissioning company to give an account of what it intended, and thus caused the leadership to take responsibility for their actions and how they related to values and stakeholders. Hence, dialogue becomes central to the practice of responsibility.

Stop and Think

In the light of the discussion on CR, how would you have responded to the request of the commissioning company?

Imagine that you are on the board of the computer games firm. Because of this problem you have been asked to draw up a CR policy. What would be the main things you would include?

The nature of responsibility and motivations for pursuing a CR policy

VALUES DIVERSITY COMPLEXITY DYNAMIC Reflection on the computer games case also helps to reveal the nature of responsibility. Robinson (2009) outlines a three-fold view of responsibility made up of:

- agency;
- accountability; and
- liability.

The first of these is about taking responsibility for values and purpose, and how these relate to practice. The computer games company took time to work through what it believed about its responsibility and what effect any actions might have inside and outside the business. This demands critical thinking about what values and ideas are held by the corporation and awareness of effects on the physical and social environment.

The second is about accounting to particular groups. These are most often defined in terms of contractual relationships or roles within and outside the firm. However, developments in SHT suggest a broader view of accountability which is plural and mutual.

The third goes beyond contract to a sense of proactive moral responsibility for wider projects, including care for the environment and the community. This places the firm as one among many other groups in society, sharing responsibility for the social and physical environments now and in the future (Jonas 1984). This involves working through how responsibility might be effectively shared in any situation.

The three elements are interconnected, and go towards establishing the identity of the firm. The so-called 'credit crunch' was characterized precisely by a lack of responsibility in each of these areas. First, there was often a lack of clarity and even understanding about the nature of the financial instruments used to generate profits. In the period leading up to the credit crunch this was exemplified by the sale of Green Tree Finance to Conseco (Robinson 2010). Green Tree had increased their profits through subprime mortgages on mobile homes. Conseco focused on insurance and had little experience or understanding of the mortgage market. Nonetheless, the firm increased this new side of their business, leading directly to bankruptcy. Typically, the dynamic of the credit crunch businesses was to avoid any critical dialogue about the nature of the products and their effects.

Second, the firms involved had little sense of their accountability to any of the stakeholders. In the subprime mortgage firms, for instance, there was no accountability to the clients, leading in some cases to thirty-year mortgages being taken out on properties that did not have that life expectancy. Even accountability to the shareholders was questionable. Shareholders were simply told that the sale of mortgage debts was risk-free, something that had not been effectively assessed.

Third, there was a lack of awareness of any responsibility for the wider community. The thinking of leaders was insulated. Merrill Lynch and WaMu, for instance, built large portfolios of mortgage-related securities that were based on the assumption that housing markets were localized, and thus that failure in one area would not affect other areas. The credit crunch showed that markets were interconnected, linking Kansas to Shanghai, and thus that leaders need to take responsibility for being aware of the possible effects of any practice. Most strikingly, the banks and finance companies did not evince any responsibility for the finance industry as a whole, and thus the industry they brought to its knees (Tett 2009).

In the light of all this, it can be seen that motivations for fulfilling CR in practice can reasonably be mixed, including:

- self-interest;
- mutual interest; and
- shared interest (cf. Palazzo and Richter 2005).

Self-interest

In the computer games case it is clear that both companies saw that it was not in their interest to be associated with a request for more violence. It could easily have affected their reputation in other areas of the market, leading to loss of trust by customers and in the market as a whole. In the long term, this also helps in avoiding stringent regulative legislation.

Mutual interest

While the software firm did not address the immediate worries about the effect of horror games on the players, it is clear that they felt it was in everyone's interest to be aware of this issue. Business has a moral obligation to solve social problems that it has caused or perpetuated. It also has great power that it can use to solve problems. It has even greater power if it works in partnership.

Shared responsibility

This involves a shared sense of obligation, such that the good of the whole is of concern for all. The business sees itself as part of that whole and, thus, has a commitment to work out social responsibility in context. This moves CR into the perspective of corporate citizenship. In the computer game case this stage was not reached, largely because there was no full debate or dialogue within the game firm about values or responsibility, and not at all between them and the client. Shared responsibility demands a framework of dialogue and partnership that will lead to the most effective CR response. CR then becomes an interactive and learning process, based in core values, working to develop a response in each context through partnership and dialogue.

It is possible to argue that the business which develops CR because it has to, or because of self-interest, is not 'genuinely' ethical. The term 'greenwashing' is often used for companies who develop environmental policies in an effort to be seen as trustworthy (see http://greenwashingindex.com/about-greenwashing). However, self-interest is not per se wrong, any more than altruism (concern for the other) is the exclusive focus of ethics. Corporate sustainability has to be held together with social and environmental sustainability.

To deny the interest of the corporation would be to deny the interest of a key part of the local or global community.

Sethi and Post (1989) characterize this debate in terms of responsibility rather than interest, involving:

- social obligation;
- social responsibility; and
- social responsiveness.

The meaning and practice of each of these emerges through dialogue.

An overview of CR policy and process using Unilever as a case study

A good example of CR in practice is that of Unilever, which for fifteen out of the last sixteen years has led the Food, Beverage and Tobacco industry group of the Dow Jones Sustainability Index (DJSI) (http://www.sustainability-indices.com).
Unilever's approach involves:

INTERNAL/EXTERNAL STAKEHOLDERS

- A holistic approach that sees CR as engaging all stakeholders, internal and external.
- The inclusion of stakeholders in dialogue and planning—Unilever is concerned to enable staff and external stakeholders to develop as global citizens.
- A transparent framework that includes monitoring and regular reporting.
- Staff development that seeks to communicate core standards across the group, particularly important in light of the transnational nature of the group.
- Finally, a CR policy that is grounded in reflection on purpose, values, and in standards of conduct, including a concern for staff development, integration, reporting, record keeping, and effective monitoring and auditing.

In all of this CR is not separate from governance, human resources, marketing, and so on but is developed as central to the culture and decision-making of the organization.

The process and practice of CR

COMPLEXITY STAKEHOLDERS VALUES As noted above, CR is not something that can be determined beforehand and simply applied to any situation. The appropriate CR response can only be worked out in the particular situation. Hence, the company needs to have a process or method for working out CR in complex and dynamic situations. (See Mini-Case 7.3.)

Robinson et al. (2007) have suggested a fourfold approach to this involving:

- data gathering, ensuring the development of awareness of the situation in which the firm operates and the effects of the firm on the social and physical environment;
- value clarification and management;
- responsibility negotiation and planning; and
- monitoring and auditing such that profit can be balanced with concern for the social and physical environment.

Data gathering

DIVERSITY COMPLEXITY DYNAMIC INTERACTION STAKEHOLDERS

This involves developing an awareness and appreciation of all issues and stakeholders in any situation. Often this requires the perspectives of more than one group, because any situation might be very complex, and any one group will have a partial perception of the situation. When this is not done, major controversies can be sparked about what the actual data is, with

Mini-Case 7.3 Unilever's CR policy

The title of Unilever's policy is the Sustainable Living Plan. It is important to note that the term sustainability (often used in terms of responsibility for the ecosystem, cf. Jonas 1984) is increasingly being used with reference to the social responsibility, and is seen by some as a term which brings together the cognate concepts of CR, business ethics, and corporate governance. Hence, the Unilever plan covers the social and physical environments under three headings: improving health and well-being, reducing environmental impact, and enhancing livelihoods.

Improving health and well-being

- Health and hygiene. Recognizing that lack of health and hygiene lead to millions of preventable deaths worldwide, especially for children, Unilever have identified ways in which some of their products can address this issue. They also target ways of changing behaviour to sustain healthy lifestyles.
- Improving nutrition. Unilever aim to reduce salt, saturated fat, sugar, and calories across their brands, to ensure that foods are sustainably sourced and made with ingredients that are recognized and trusted.

Reducing environmental impact

- Greenhouse gases (GHGs). Unilever aims to lower its GHGs impact from sourcing, manufacturing, and innovation, and is working towards eliminating deforestation from its supply chains.
- Water use. In the context of growing water scarcity globally, Unilever are working to meet the domestic water needs of its consumers in water-scarce countries, and to reduce water use from suppliers and in its own factories.
- Waste and packaging. Given an annual purchase of more than 2 million tonnes across Unilever's brands, it is committed to finding ways to reduce waste.
- Sustainable sourcing. Unilever aims to use its scale and advocacy to contribute to sustainable agriculture and create inclusive supply chains for smallholder farmers, who produce around 70 per cent of the world's food.

Enhancing livelihoods

- Fairness in the workplace. This is linked both to the human rights agenda and the principles of justice and respect.
- Opportunities for women. This focuses on women's rights and workplace inclusion. Unilever also note the 'ripple effect' on the well-being of families and communities through greater inclusion.
- Inclusive business. Unilever recognizes the importance of working with suppliers in this inclusive way, promoting 'strong, healthy communities that work to respect rights'.

(https://www.unilever.co.uk/sustainable-living)

Question

How effective a CR policy do you think this is? How would you improve it?

polarized thinking and judgement based on negative perceptions of the other stakeholders. A good example of this is a report from War on Want in 2007 into the operations of transnational mining corporations (see Mini-Case 7.4). How might an effective CR policy in this instance have avoided what then happened? Both War on Want and mining corporations such as Anglo American have a concern for social responsibility. However, neither the NGOs nor the transnationals took into account the fact that data is rarely value-free, and is often heavily affected by the perceptions of the values and motives of the different groups, leading to lack of clarity about what the data involves.

Many major global industries now have as part of their CR policy a commitment to dialogue with relevant NGOs (Entine 2002). Hence, Unilever work closely with Oxfam, recognizing that this NGO has a unique contribution to data gathering. This underlines the importance of identifying and working with stakeholders at the earliest stage. Complex situations demand an awareness of how the company relates not simply to the immediate situation but to broader aspects, such as the supply chain, and how subsidiaries do business. A good example of that is British American Tobacco's (BAT) involvement in Malawi (see Mini-Case 7.5).

The very fact of the global controversy surrounding BAT shows the importance of developing a proactive awareness of all aspects of the supply chain. In a global context this can be very

Mini-Case 7.4 War on Want: Anglo American the alternative report

In August 2007 the respected NGO War on Want published a report (http://www.waronwant.org/component/content/article/14777) which alleged that Anglo American, among other transnational corporations, were involved in a number of activities that went against stated CR policies. The report noted 'devastating effects' on the host communities, including collusion with governments to evict families and tribes to make room for mining operations.

Ten days later Anglo American published a response (13 August 2007, http://www.angloamerican.com/media/releases/2007pr/2007-08-09), in which it asserted that the accusation about its involvement in the various cases was groundless. They provided specific refutations, including clarification about the exact relationship of Anglo American to various companies and governments. In particular, they argued that none of the allegations had been checked with the company itself, leading to a corruption of the data. One example of that was the allegation that in 2004 paramilitaries had violently subdued a village whose people were protesting against the proposed building of a railway. In fact, the railway had been built over a decade earlier.

The result of this exchange was two very different views of the truth, and an increasing lack of trust. Neither side necessarily disputed that some wrong things had happened, but the exact narrative was not clear.

Question

As CR director of Anglo American how would you have handled this report?

difficult to achieve—hence, the need to work with all relevant stakeholders. Analysing just what the responsibility of business might be, and developing an effective response that balances all the interests and needs, can be complex. The complexities surrounding child labour, for instance, are spelled out in a UK Department for International Development report entitled, *Helping Not Hurting Children* (DFID 1999, see http://www.bridge.ids.ac.uk/sites/bridge.ids.ac.uk/files/docs_gem/index_policy/helping_children.pdf). Central to the awareness of the situation is a clear grasp of accountability, to whom is the company accountable; and liability, where the company shares responsibility for a proactive and creative response to key issues. Both issues in this section fall more under liability than accountability.

Mini-Case 7.5 Tobacco poison surrounds child workers

15 November 2009 *Sunday Times*
Dan McDougall

A *Sunday Times* investigation in the southern African state of Malawi has uncovered an environmental travesty that is being inflicted by the tobacco industry on some of the continent's poorest people.

Downstream from the tobacco processing plants that dominate the outskirts of Lilongwe, the Malawian capital, rivers run yellow and green from industrial outflow–water used for bathing by villagers who have no other option.

Even more alarming, however, is that in a community already plagued by Aids, cholera, malnutrition, and one of the highest infant mortality rates in the world, toxic tobacco waste is being dumped by contractors in open landfill sites where hundreds of children are picking through the remnants.

This article cited a recent report by a UK-based charity, Plan International, which estimated that close to 2.5m women and children are working in conditions of semi-slavery in the tobacco industry and being paid as little as £160 a year. The report claimed that children forced to work as tobacco pickers in Malawi are exposed to nicotine levels equivalent to smoking fifty cigarettes a day. Child labourers as young as 5, it alleged, were suffering severe health problems from a daily absorption of up to 54 milligrams of nicotine through their skin.

This case raises questions about awareness of the environmental effect of products, the supply-and-effect chain, the employment of adults and children, and even the role of governments and how the corporation should respond.
(http://www.thesundaytimes.co.uk/sto/news/world_news/article190548.ece)

Question

As CR director of British American Tobacco how would you respond?

Stop and Think

Whose responsibility is it to deal with human rights violations?

Value clarification and management

VALUES **DIVERSITY** This is the second element in the fourfold approach to CR in practice. A company must begin with clarity about its own values and core purposes, such that they can be held to account for them. This means being able to defend them in critical debate.

A striking example of such a statement is Unilever. The context of this is a call to action in which the CEO, Paul Polman, argues the importance of an awareness of the complex global business environment, characterized by growing social inequality, low trust in business and institutions, and the increasing effects of climate change (https://www.unilever.co.uk/sustainable-living/a-call-to-action).

The following is part of the strategy for sustainable business:

> Our strategy for sustainable business
>
> Unilever has, from its origins, been a purpose-driven company. Today our purpose is simple but clear—to make sustainable living commonplace.
>
> We are living in a world where temperatures are rising, water shortages are more frequent, food supplies are increasingly scarce and the gap between rich and poor increasing. Populations are growing fast, making basic hygiene and sanitation even more of a challenge. At Unilever we can see how people the world over are already affected by these changes. And the changes will pose new challenges for us too, as commodity costs fluctuate, markets become unstable and raw materials harder to source.
>
> We believe that business must be part of the solution. But to be so, business will have to change; there is not 'business as usual anymore'. Sustainable, equitable growth is the only acceptable business model. Our strategic vision is to double the size of our business while reducing our environmental footprint, and increasing our positive social impact.
>
> In 2010 we launched the Unilever Sustainable Living Plan, which is our blueprint for sustainable business. We will achieve our vision through our Plan, which is helping us to decouple our growth from our environmental impact while increasing our positive social impact, driving profitable growth for our brands, saving costs and fuelling innovation.
>
> (https://www.unilever.co.uk/sustainable-living/our-strategy/index.html)

Unilever has carefully thought through its position. It wants a sustainable business, in the sense of one that will make profits and survive. This also communicates a strong sense of shared responsibility, hence, a strong desire that stakeholders share responsibility for stewardship of the environment. The idea of stewardship accepts that the social and physical environment as a whole is owned by no one, and hence all share responsibility. Far from being a marginal position, this connects strongly universal values held across different cultures, including Judaeo-Christian and Islamic (cf. Robinson 2017).

A statement such as that of Unilever is central to the development of the ethical identity of a corporation. It involves both attitudes and values. It is aspirational, recognizing that CR cannot be summed up completely in prescriptive codes, involving as it does continued interaction with society. It embodies the transformative nature of CR, enabling stakeholders to become part of the vision. Customer behaviour and values are transformed through involvement in sustainability. The focus of purpose establishes the value or worth of the organization and from that ethical values emerge, not least, for Unilever, integrity (cf. Fort 2010 and Robinson 2016).

The Globally Responsible Leadership Initiative (GRLI) (2005), based in the United Nations Global Compact, suggests that the underlying values of CR include:

- fairness;
- freedom;
- honesty;
- humanity;
- responsibility and solidarity;
- sustainable development;
- tolerance; and
- transparency.

Managing values, however, involves more than stating the core values of the corporation and enabling others to share and embody them. The business environment includes many different values and raises questions about how they are handled.

- Within the corporation are the values of the different staff and professions, and the shareholders. We have seen that shareholders may not simply want profits, and there is a need to learn what the values of shareholders and staff actually are. This may involve dialogue about the development of value statements with the internal stakeholders.
- Any business may have a number of conflicting values that have to be held together. The public business of higher education is a good example of this, holding together both excellence, in terms of education, and equality, in terms of widening participation.
- There may be occasions where complex and different values lead to conflict and a demand that the company or someone within the company make a stand. A classic example of this is the *Challenger* case (Mini-Case 7.6).

Mini-Case 7.6 The *Challenger* 51-L

On 28 January 1986 it took only 73 seconds for the *Challenger* space shuttle to explode in one of the most high-profile disasters of the last century. Never before had there been such a programme of space flight, setting out hugely ambitious targets that would have political, social, and scientific implications. Many different firms and government agencies worked together. At the same time, there was increasing competition, not least from the European Space Agency. With that came concern about the danger of losing contracts, and attendant financial constraints, raising questions about the purpose of the project.

The engineers employed by Morton-Thiokol Industries identified major structural problems in the *Challenger*, and struggled between 1985 and 1986 to communicate the implications to the management, to NASA, and to other client organizations. Up to the launch itself, the questions asked by the engineers were about the values of safety, responsibility, and the awareness of the risks involved. Such values clashed with managerial values (survival of the firm, keeping the client, maintaining a high political profile). The managerial values triumphed.

Ultimately, of course, the explosion adversely affected all the key stakeholders and focused on the ethics of 'whistleblowing' (the practice of an employee within a business informing someone outside of the organization about any potential malpractices they have come across). This underlined that an effective whistleblowing system was in the interest of all stakeholders and thus should be a key part of any CR policy.

Question

What are the problems with whistleblowing?

Even within the *Challenger* case there is a diversity of business: engineering firms, government organizations such as NASA, and many different subcontractors. The diversity meant that there were different values that were fuelling any view of CR. For the engineers, CR meant the values of safety and proper risk assessment. For NASA and other groups, it meant enabling creative partnerships and keeping the US ahead in this particular race. The diversity of business and their related values was made even more complex because of the engineering firm's perspective that there seemed to be several different 'clients', companies and government organizations. The subsequent Presidential Commission noted how, among other things, this led to a sense in which responsibility was not fully shared by the different companies.

Responsibility negotiation and planning

STAKEHOLDERS **LOCAL TO GLOBAL** **INTERACTION** Responsibility negotiation is the third element in deciding what a particular CR response might be. First, this involves identifying the stakeholders in any situation. Second, there is an analysis of the stakeholders in terms of power and responsibility. This enables a full appreciation of constraints and resources in the situation, and leads to an awareness of creative possibilities. Third, responsibility can be negotiated. This does not simply look to the development of goods for all stakeholders, but accepts the need for mutual responsibility and enables its embodiment. Hence, it facilitates a maximization of resources for social responsibility through collaboration.

In this process, several things can be achieved:

- the further development of the ethical identity of the company;
- the development of trust and of a sense of shared values with the stakeholders;
- reflection on appropriate levels of responsibility; and
- reflection on how the power of the company can both respond to the effects that they have on the physical and social environment and how they might enable other stakeholders who have little power to fulfil their responsibility.

A good example of this is Taylors of Harrogate (Mini-Case 7.7).

Similar questions emerge with the issue of human rights. Nike, for instance, were faced with human rights abuses by contractors in developing countries who made their running shoes (http://www.nytimes.com/1998/05/13/business/international-business-nike-pledges-to-end-child-labor-and-apply-us-rules-abroad.html). Their response was to set out a code of practice for all involved in that industry, partly to ensure that CR was not seen as the responsibility of one company. The question remains of how a company might respond to a culture that relies on the income from questionable labour or a country that consciously abuses human rights. The answer to the first might be to maintain relations with these groups and to seek to influence the workplace conditions. The answer to the second should involve negotiation with the governments, and, where necessary, reserving the right to stand out against governments who abuse human rights in relation to the company's work.

Stop and Think

How does your company or university negotiate responsibility in terms of CR?

Mini-Case 7.7 Taylors of Harrogate: ethical sourcing and fair trade

Taylors is a small to medium size company which aims to trade fairly and sustainably, and enable members of its supply chain to develop similar responsible practice.

Their ethical trading policy has two overarching priorities:

1. the welfare of workers in their supply chain; and
2. to ensure a sustainable environmental impact.

(http://www.taylorsofharrogate.co.uk/TradingFairlyHome.asp)

To achieve this, they align themselves with organizations such as the ILO, making use of certification schemes such as Fairtade, Rainforest Alliance, and Utz Certified. This certification is extended to the suppliers. Taylors then assist suppliers in gaining certification, meeting the social and environmental criteria set out in the scheme. In cases where investment is required to improve social and/or environmental standards, suppliers may apply to Taylors for seed funding. Over time, producers that demonstrate commitment to continuous improvements in such standards become preferred suppliers.

Question

Does the company have a responsibility or obligation to act in this way?

Audit

DIVERSITY COMPLEXITY INTERACTION STAKEHOLDERS If the development of CR policy and practice is a learning experience, then a core part of that has to be reporting. This is clearly set out in the first human rights report of any business by Unilever in 2015. It notes the aims of the report as:

- to highlight our efforts in embedding the respect and promotion of human rights into the fabric of our business;
- to outline the salient issues we face;
- to report on our progress publicly and share our challenges candidly;
- to outline our priorities for the future;
- to seek feedback and guidance from our stakeholders.

We share these in the spirit of continuous improvement, in the knowledge that the remaining challenges are considerable and in the hope that other businesses may benefit from the lessons we've learned so far.

(https://www.unilever.com/Images/slp-unilever-human-rights-report-2015_tcm244-437226_en.pdf)

This responds to the call to action which recognizes that respect for human rights is a critical part of the social environment. The human rights report, additional to the sustainable plan report, is aligned with the International Bill of Human Rights, and the principles set out in the International Labour Organization's Declaration on Fundamental Principles and Rights at Work, and the OECD Guidelines for Multinational Enterprises. The underlying principles of this report are: transparency; stakeholder consultation, dialogue, and action: collective responsibility; collaboration and inclusion in public–private partnerships; innovation, including developing new business models, capacity building, and effective remedy.

Reporting of this nature serves to establish benchmarks for performance, but also seeks to engage the imaginations of the different stakeholders through narrative. It also acts to increase awareness of the immediacy of human rights in the context of business, thus increasing identification with these issues. Hence, Unilever focus on rights in the context of discrimination, fair wages, forced labour, freedom of association, harassment, health and safety, land rights, and working hours.

Broader sustainability reporting includes information on:

- total material use;
- direct energy use;
- indirect energy use;
- total water use;
- impacts on biodiversity;
- GHG emissions;
- ozone-depleting emissions;
- total amount of waste; and
- environmental impact of products (https://www.globalreporting.org/Pages/default.aspx).

More detail of sustainability reporting is found in Chapter 8.

Another approach to auditing is the Business in the Community (BiTC) Corporate Responsibility Index. Companies involved in this, such as Shaftsbury plc, complete an extensive index questionnaire and the results are published in the BiTC index. It provides a way to assess and compare progress across companies.

Looking ahead—beyond the triple bottom line

The rise of CR has had a patchy development over the past two decades. Disasters still occur, partly because industries do not take responsibility for thinking through what is involved. Banking and the finance industry ushered in the credit crunch of 2008/9 (Tett 2009). In the search for a risk-free industry, business practices developed that allowed the sale of mortgages to customers who could not sustain payment. The debt was then sold on, leading to the loss of a massive number of homes and the near collapse of the banking and finance industries. There was no evidence of a sense of responsibility for the customer, the industry or profession, the global market, or the global economic environment. In addition to these failures to be either accountable to key stakeholders or be morally liable for wider environments there was also the failure of the industry to even understand what some of the products were, and therefore what effect they might have. This provides a reminder that CR is more than simply the development of codes and policies, and more than the monitoring of the triple bottom line. The failure of the credit crunch was as much a failure to take responsibility for critical thinking about ideas, purpose, and practice, as it was a failure of awareness. That provides corporate responsibility with a fourth bottom line, regular reflection on the identity, purpose, and meaning of the corporation. This demands careful attention to the ethos and integrity of the organization (Brown 2005). Integrity in this sense is not simply about standing up for principles. It also involves awareness of the possibilities and how it can make a difference in a complex social environment. Werhane (1999, cf. Lederach 2005) suggests that this involves the practice of the 'moral imagination', focused in creativity. Fort (2007) describes this as total integrity management.

This explores way in which business can contribute even to the alleviation of poverty and peacebuilding. The Portland Trust (2013) reports cases in Cyprus, Northern Ireland, South Africa, and South Caucasus where businesses have been significantly involved in reconciliation and security as well as economic development in post-conflict areas.

At another level there is increasing focus on developing the sense and practice of responsibility in the members of the corporation, enabling them to critically engage values and practice, thus owning both. This relates CR directly to corporate governance. The King reports on governance from South Africa bring this together. They provide a view of governance between the US approach (focused in legal regulation) and the UK (focused in self-regulation). King IV stresses:

- Integrated thinking. Recognizing that moral, intellectual, practical, and social values are interconnected, and that values and practice have to be subject to critical reflection.
- Underlying worldview. In this case the concept of *ubuntu* (pan-African idea of interdependence) is suggested as key to the African continent. Worldviews literally determine how you view the world, and in the case of the credit crisis who you exclude from that perception.
- Key principles of leadership, sustainability, and citizenship. Leadership involves sharing responsibility. This reaches ultimate expression in companies such as John Lewis, where employees are genuine members of the Partnership (Robinson 2002). They share responsibility and power for values, practice, and relationships with community and the environment, expressed in genuine workplace democracy.
- The development of ethical culture as well as codes of ethics. This demands the development of a culture of dialogue enabling all to practice virtues (Moore 2012). Unilever have systematically developed such a culture: developing internal champions for their sustainability plan, ensuring effective non-executive directors (NEDs) on the board, setting up effective oversight through the board CR committee (made of NEDs) and providing external perspectives through the Sustainable Living Plan Council (made up of international experts in the area). The tone is less about 'compliance' and more about the practice of the moral imagination.
- Stakeholder regulation. King III and IV suggest that the most effective regulation is focused in dialogue with stakeholders, developing a sense of mutual accountability.
- Integrated reporting. Bringing all elements together through narrative and metrics.

This philosophy extends to stakeholders developing and practising their own responsibility. This will see the development of more CR partnerships, not least between NGOs and transnational corporations. In a global context the pressure from NGOs and the modern media will force global business to keep reflecting on values and responsibility in practice. This will become ever more complex as business relates to cultures such as China where there is a very different view of the role of business and of responsibility. Together this will take CR increasingly into corporate global citizenship.

All of this goes to the heart of CR that is based less on following rules and more on organizational and personal engagement. Responsibility, in other words, cannot be summed up in terms of tools to solve discrete ethical problems. On the contrary, these 'problems', arising from factors such as personal gain, competition, conflicts of interest and values (with underlying polarization of values), and scarcity of resources, are an ongoing part of any business, requiring the ongoing practice of responsibility.

Summary

This chapter has suggested that CR has moved on from a limited model, largely to do with philanthropy, to one that takes into account the stakeholder network of the business environment. Business still has to make a profit, but can see itself as a corporate citizen, sharing responsibilities with other groups in society. These responsibilities have to be carefully negotiated to achieve the best result for stakeholders and the business itself. In all this it is argued that in the global context companies have moved beyond a threshold, accepting 'the fact that, beyond profits there is a political, social and environmental dimension to their activities that cannot be ignored. They have moved beyond compliance' (GRLI 2005: 20). This involves:

- An increasing sense of the company as corporate citizen. Faced by environmental and social issues that are greater than any particular interest, there is a position of shared responsibility from which CR begins.
- An awareness and appreciation of the complex and dynamic business environment, including values, issues, and stakeholders connected to the company's business.
- Business being responsive to a social and physical environment that is constantly dynamic. This means that CR can only be worked out interactively, negotiating responsibility with the different stakeholders. This includes awareness of and responsiveness to human rights in all aspects of the value chain, from suppliers to consumers. This makes CR developmental and transformative.
- Codes of practice and mission statements that will help the core values of CR to be embedded. However, the ongoing learning process also requires that outcomes be audited.

Case Study: Caterpillar

According to the UN, a total of 4,170 Palestinian homes were destroyed by the Israeli army between September 2000 and December 2004 (War on Want 2004: 4). Other sources suggest the effect of such demolition since 1967 has been to make 70,000 people homeless (2004: 5). The Caterpillar D9 was the main bulldozer used by the Israeli army to demolish homes and destroy farm land in the Palestinian territories. This sustained action was justified by the Israeli government as punitive action against the family homes of Palestinians engaged, or suspected of engagement, in armed activities against Israel. The claim was that this involved hiding terrorists in the homes. War on Want (2004: 6) questioned the evidence for this claim. Regardless of that issue, the practice breaches Article 53 of the Fourth Geneva Convention (to which Israel is a party): any destruction by the Occupying Power of real or personal property belonging individually or collectively to private persons, or to the state, or to other public authorities, or to social or cooperative organizations, is prohibited, except where such destruction is rendered absolutely necessary by military operations (http://www.icrc.org/ihl.nsf/385ec082b509e76c41256739003e636d/6756482d86146898c125641e004aa3c5).

The worst example of such actions was the Battle of Jenin in April 2002. Jenin was a densely populated refugee camp of over 14,000 people. Eyewitness accounts claim that house demolitions continued after the end of the action (War on Want 2004: 13), leading to the flattening of an entire district including the camp. People were unable to escape from houses because of the crossfire and many were buried alive, including ill and disabled people. Following the death of the activist Rachel Corrie at one of the Palestinian sites being cleared (rachelcorriefoundation.org) the argument has increasingly focused on legal issues, with lawsuits filed by the Corrie family in the US and Israel. The thrust of the lawsuits is to hold the different parties accountable for their actions. US companies that aid and profit from violations of human rights can be held responsible under US law (www.guardian.co.uk/world/2010/mar/10/rachel-corrie-civil-case-israel).

Whose responsibility?

Can Caterpillar be held to be responsible in some way for the use to which the Israeli government puts its product?

Con

One argument suggests that no company can be held responsible for how a government uses its product. Think of the analogy of the sale of a kitchen knife. No company or individual who sells kitchen knives can be held responsible for customers using these to kill someone. A second argument used by Caterpillar is that the product itself was designed for earth removal not as an instrument of war. The latter would have to be licensed by the home government. Modifications to the D9 occurred after the sale. Hence, the responsibility for the destruction of the Palestinian homes lies purely with the Israeli government (parallel to Friedman's argument noted in section, 'The free market view of CR', above).

Supporting this is a pragmatic argument that if Caterpillar accepted responsibility for these acts they would be open to legal liability, with associated financial loss. This would endanger the sustainability of the firm and the profits of shareholders.

Pro

The argument by analogy above is only partial. While it is true that the knife seller cannot be held responsible for what a person does with the knife, a different sense of responsibility emerges if the buyer has made it clear that he or she intends to use the product for an unethical or illegal purpose, or if there has been a record of this happening. If the seller knows what negative use the product is being put to, even if this was not the intention of the design or sale of the product, then he or she shares responsibility for the eventual end, and thus responsibility for refusing to sell.

The argument that the killer would have got a knife from someone else does not diminish the shared and proactive responsibility.

STAKEHOLDERS The argument so far might be seen as too simplistic, and the customer might want to redefine the end to which the product was put. Hence, the Israeli government might argue that this was not a violation of human rights, or an act of murder, but justified in the light of the defence of the Israeli people, to whom it is responsible. Here moral responsibility moves to the terrorists who have intentionally involved families and their houses.

Exercising critical agency, the responsibility to test arguments, the firm could test their customer's assertion. But can it actually make a judgement about justice and human rights, and should it? For a disinterested judgement, the firm might involve an appropriate international agency, such as the United Nations, to determine the exact nature of the actions in question. The UN has a strong record in enabling multinational corporations to engage governments in human rights issues, providing judgement on the nature of any abuses and positive ways of influencing behaviour (see e.g. http://198.170.85.29/Ruggie-protect-respect-remedy-framework.pdf).

> ***Excerpts from the Caterpillar Global Code of Practice***
>
> **Commitment**
>
> The Power of Responsibility
>
> **We Protect the Health and Safety of Others and Ourselves** As a company, we strive to contribute toward a global environment in which all people can work safely and live healthy, productive lives, now and in the future ...
>
> We actively promote safe practices throughout our value chain—from suppliers to end users. We are committed to providing our customers with products and services that are safe and reliable in the marketplace.
>
> **We Are Pro-Active Members of Our Communities** As individuals and as a company, we contribute significant time and resources to promoting the health, welfare and economic stability of our communities around the world ...
>
> We believe that our success should also contribute to the quality of life in, and the prosperity and sustainability of, communities where we work and live. *As a company and as individuals, we hold ourselves to the highest standard of integrity and ethical behaviour . . . If we do any less, we put Caterpillar's name and our reputation for integrity at risk.*

Other stakeholders with concerns include the shareholders (see http://www.ekklesia.co.uk/node/8595), the wider industry, and members of the firm itself. This would also involve critical reflection on the vision and values of the firm and any code (see www.cat.com/Code-of-Conduct, see box).

Far from simple 'stakeholder management' this draws all stakeholders into creative dialogue about ethical meaning and responsible practice, involving shared responsibility.

Questions

As the head of CR, you have to give a report to the board to frame Caterpillar's response.

1. **What options would you place before them?**
2. **How would you assess the risks of each of these options?**
3. **How would your recommended choice of option be informed by the Global Code above?**
4. **Compare that Code with the UN guidelines on business and human rights noted above. What are the differences in the two approaches to responsibility?**
5. **What response would you recommend to the board in relation to the attacks from NGOs?**

(See http://electronicintifada.net/content/photostory-israeli-bulldozer-driver-murders-american-peace-activist/4449 for some material about Rachel Corrie the activist.)

Review and discussion questions

1. How would you define the nature and limits of CR?
2. What are the arguments for and against CR?
3. What part do NGOs play in the development of CR?
4. How far do the models of CR noted above apply to small and medium size businesses?
5. Is it possible for an industry that causes harm, such as the tobacco industry, to have a policy of CR?

Assignments

1. If you are in work, find out if your employer has a CR policy. What are the differences and similarities with Unilever's policy?

   OR

   If you are a full-time student, find out what the CR policy of your educational institution is and compare it with the Unilever policy.

2. Write a new CR policy for your educational institution or place of work, including:
   - the vision, ethos, and values of the institution;
   - the different areas within the institution that need policies;
   - suggestions about how to motivate the staff, and develop ethos and transparency; and
   - suggestions about how to monitor practice.

3. Imagine that you are starting up a small business. How would you build concerns about CR into that process? See the BiTC small business page (http://www.bitc.org.uk/sites/default/files/res_bus_checkup_small_bus_fact_sheet_260213.pdf).

Further reading

To pursue CR and the global and developmental agenda read:

Crane and Matten (2016)

Hopkins (2016)

To pursue underlying ethical ideas and cases read:

Robinson (2016)

Test your understanding of this chapter with online questions and answers, explore the subject further through web exercises, and use the weblinks to provide a quick resource for further research. Visit the online resources at www.oup.com/uk/wetherly_otter4e/

Useful websites

Business in the Community
www.bitc.org.uk

Codes of ethics for different professions (Centre for Study of Ethics in the Professions, Illinois Institute of Technology)
http://ethics.iit.edu/research/codes-ethics-collection

Computing Professionals for Social Responsibility
www.cpsr.org

Corporate responsibility
www.corporate-responsibility.org

Corporate Watch
www.corporatewatch.org.uk/?lid=2670

Enterprise and CSR
http://ec.europa.eu/enterprise/policies/sustainable-business/corporate-social-responsibility/index_en.htm#content

Global footprints
www.globalfootprints.org

Green Globe 21 (sustainability for travel and tourism)
www.greenglobe21.com

Institute for Global Ethics
www.globalethics.org

International Business Ethics Institute (IBEI)
www.business-ethics.org

Scientists for Global Responsibility—Ethical Careers Guide
http://www.sgr.org.uk/projects/ethical-careers

Institute of Science in Society—Science, Society, Sustainability
www.i-sis.org.uk

References

Andriof, J. and McIntosh, M. (eds.) (2001) *Perspectives on Corporate Citizenship* (London: Greenleaf Publishing)

Bauman, Z. (1985) *Modernity and the Holocaust* (London: Polity)

Beauchamp, T. and Childress, J. (2013) *The Principles of Bio-Medical Ethics* (Oxford: Oxford University Press)

Brown, M. (2005) *Corporate Integrity* (Cambridge: Cambridge University Press)

Carroll, A. B. (1991) 'The pyramid of corporate social responsibility: towards the moral management of organizational stakeholders', *Business Horizons*, July–Aug., 39–48, 40

Carroll, A. B. and Buchholtz, A. K. (2000) *Business and Society—Ethics and Stakeholder Management* (London: Thompson)

Crane, A. and Matten, D. (2016) *Business Ethics: Managing Corporate Citizenship and Sustainability in the Age of Globalization* (Oxford: Oxford University Press)

Elkington, J. (1997) *Cannibals with Forks: Triple Bottom Line of 21st Century Business* (London: Capstone)

Entine, J. (2002) 'Shell, Greenpeace and Brent Spar: the politics of dialogue', in C. Megone and S. Robinson (eds.), *Case Histories in Business Ethics* (London: Routledge), 59–95

European Commission (2001) *Green Paper: Promoting a European Framework for Corporate Social Responsibility*, Brussels, 18 July, Com(2001) 366 final **http://eur-lex.europa.eu/LexUriServ/site/en/com/2001/com2001_0366en01.pdf**

Fort, T. (2007) *Business, Integrity and Peace: Beyond Geopolitical and Disciplinary Boundaries* (Cambridge: Cambridge University Press)

Fort, T. (2010) 'Peace through commerce: a multisectorial approach', *Journal of Business Ethics*, 89: 347–50

Friedman, M. (1983) 'The social responsibility of business is to increase its profits', in T. Donaldson and P. Werhane (eds.), *Ethical Issues in Business* (New York: Prentice-Hall), 239–43

Gregory, A. and Tafra, M. (2004) 'Corporate social responsibility: new context, new approaches, new applications: a comparative study of CSR in a Croatian and a UK company', paper given at International Public Relations Research Symposium, Bled, 2004 **www.bledcom**

GRLI (2005) *Call for Engagement* **http://www.grli.org/index.php/component/docman/cat_view/13-source-documents**

Heath, J. and Norman, W. (2004) 'Stakeholder theory, corporate governance and public management: what can the history of state-run enterprises teach us in the post-Enron era?', *Journal of Business Ethics*, 53(3): 247–65

Hopkins, M. (2016) *CSR and Sustainability: From the Margins to the Mainstream. A Textbook* (Sheffield: Greenleaf)

ILO (2016) *Forced Labour, Human Trafficking and Slavery* **http://www.ilo.org/global/topics/forced-labour/lang--en/index.htm Accessed 7/12/2016**

Jonas, H. (1984) *The Imperative of Responsibility* (Chicago: Chicago University Press)

Lederach, J. P. (2005) *The Moral Imagination* (Oxford: Oxford University Press)

MacIntyre, A. (1981) *After Virtue* (Notre Dame: University of Notre Dame Press)

Moeller, K. and Erdal, T. (2003) *Corporate Responsibility Towards Society: A Local Perspective* (Brussels: European Foundation for the Improvement of Living and Working Conditions) **http://edz.bib.uni-mannheim.de/www-edz/pdf/ef/03/ef0327en.pdf**

Moore, G. (2012) 'The virtue of governance, governance of virtue', *Business Ethics Quarterly*, 22(2): 293–318

Nohria, N. and Khurana, R. (2008) 'It's time to make management a true profession', *Harvard Business Review*, 86(10): 70–7

Otter, D. (2011) 'The ecological environment', in L. Hamilton and P. Webster (eds.), *The International Business Environment* (Oxford: Oxford University Press)

Palazzo, G. and Richter, U. (2005) 'CSR business as usual? The case of the tobacco industry', *Journal of Business Ethics*, 6(4): 387–401

Portland Trust (2013) *The Role of Business in Peacemaking* (London: Portland Trust)

Robinson, S. (2002) 'John Lewis Partnership', in C. Megone and S. Robinson (eds.), *Case Histories in Business Ethics* (London: Routledge), 131–40

Robinson, S. (2009) 'The nature of responsibility in a professional setting', *Journal of Business Ethics*, 88: 11–19

Robinson, S. (2010) *Leadership Ethics* (Oxford: Peter Lang)

Robinson, S. (2016) *The Practice of Integrity in Business* (London: Palgrave)

Robinson, S. (2017) *The Spirituality of Responsibility* (London: Continuum)

Robinson, S., Dixon, R., and Moodley, K. (2007) *Engineering, Business and Professional Ethics* (London: Heinemann-Butterworth)

Scherkoske, G. (2013) *Integrity and the Virtues of Reason* (Cambridge: Cambridge University Press)

Sethi, S. and Post, J. (1989) 'Public consequences of private actions: the marketing of infant formula in less developed countries', in P. Iannone (ed.), *Contemporary Moral Controversy in Business* (Oxford: Oxford University Press), 474–87

Sternberg, E. (2000) *Just Business* (Oxford: Oxford University Press)

Tett, G. (2009) *Fool's Gold* (London: Little Brown)

Transparency International (2013) *Business Principles for Countering Bribery* (London: Transparency International)

Werhane, P. (1999) *Moral Imagination and Management Decision Making* (Oxford: Oxford University Press)

Zadek, S. (2001) *The Civil Corporation: The New Economy of Corporate Citizenship* (London: Earthscan)

Chapter 8
The natural environment: global warming, pollution, resource depletion, and sustainable development

Eamonn Judge

Learning objectives

When you have completed this chapter, you will be able to:

- Articulate the importance of current key issues in the natural environment as they impact on business, especially global warming, pollution, and resource depletion.
- Define the meaning of sustainable development (SD) in relation to business.
- Identify the influences leading to changes in the significance of SD.
- Evaluate alternative views about SD as it relates to business.
- Examine links between the external environment of a business in relation to SD and the internal strategic response of business.

THEMES

The following themes of the book are especially relevant to this chapter

- **INTERNAL/EXTERNAL** It is clear that business activity imposes external costs on the natural environment and this will require firms to change their internal production processes.
- **COMPLEXITY** Businesses are asked to take responsibility for their activities which are allegedly having a serious effect on the global natural environment, yet our knowledge of these effects is the outcome of very complex research and most people struggle to understand the science behind this research. Furthermore, not all observers are equally agreed about their causes.
- **LOCAL TO GLOBAL** Environmental impacts range from the global to local levels and are crucial to our understanding of issues associated with SD.
- **INTERACTION** Business in its myriad activities has a major impact on the natural environment, but this impact can strike back at business.

- **STAKEHOLDERS** A wide range of stakeholders can be directly and indirectly affected by a firm's impact on the environment. These may be local sufferers, or sufferers in another country. Firms are not islands, but parts of complex supply chains, and other firms forwards or backwards in the supply chain may be part of an environmental problem with which a firm is directly, if often unknowingly, involved.
- **VALUES** Sustainable development raises complex ethical issues precisely because the main contributors to the problems of environment and resources are not necessarily those who suffer from them. Environmental damage today can store up problems for the future and so firms are forced to consider directly their ethical stance in relation to present day equity issues as well as the future impact on equity of decisions taken today.

Introduction: the natural environment of business

The natural environment of business is a term which covers a series of fairly obvious categories such as climate and weather conditions, natural resources, and topography. These may affect a firm on a purely local level, or there may be global implications.

Historical context

Up to about 1800 human influence on the global environment was limited: the globe was sparsely populated and still largely in its natural state, and no matter what disasters happened in one particular local area, civilizations prospered elsewhere.

COMPLEXITY Chapter 3 discussed the changes that occurred from about 1800 in the UK with the Industrial Revolution. Rapid population growth, urbanization, and industrialization, along with colonization and empire building created both spectacular wealth and poverty. Despite massive changes, with a growing world economy interrupted by world wars and depressions up to 1945, there was still a perception until the 1970s that the undesirable 'side effects' of such rapid economic development were 'local'. Since then, the global environmental impact of business (and other actors) has been a major concern.

LOCAL TO GLOBAL This was highlighted by environmental disasters in the 1980s: the Union Carbide disaster (1984) at Bhopal, India, the world's worst ever industrial accident (see Chapters 7 and 10); the Chernobyl (Ukraine) disaster (1986); and the Exxon Valdez oil spill off Alaska (1989). One could regard these disasters' effects as localized, yet they were generated by globalized processes of economic development. However, a more pervasive phenomenon from the 1980s onwards was argued to be the melting of the polar ice caps, with effects on sea levels and climatic patterns, while hurricanes were argued by some to be more frequent.

Moving from history to the present day

Studies in the 1980s by the United Nations culminated in the Brundtland Report (WCED 1987). This advocated long-term strategies to counter the threat posed by these trends. It used, but did not invent, the term **sustainable development** (this was coined by the World Conservation Union in 1980, but it did not define it). It advocated the exploration of the complex relationships between people, resources, environment, and development as being essential to the development of sound strategies of cooperation and mutual trust within the world community.

The Brundtland Report projected the most well-known definition of SD:

> development which meets the needs of the present without compromising the ability of future generations to meet their own needs.

This definition was apt, but it was a 'lowest common denominator' definition which everyone could agree with. More practical steps were needed, and this happened with the UN Conference on Environment and Development at Rio de Janeiro in 1992, the 'Rio Summit' or 'Earth Summit'. Before we consider this, let us outline the nature of the problems in more detail, to see how business helps generate them, but also suffers from them.

The current global environmental problem and business, and the international response

Global warming

Global warming is not the only issue, but possibly the most discussed. Global warming describes the effect of greenhouse gases (GHGs). These gases (mainly carbon dioxide (CO_2), but consisting also of methane, and other gases) are generated by burning fossil fuels (coal, oil, natural gas, etc.) for space heating, electricity, industrial processes, and transport. But natural processes also generate GHGs; waste from farm animals produces much methane. Work by the World Resources Institute (www.wri.org) indicates that CO_2 is 77 per cent of the total and methane is 15 per cent. But methane is 43 times worse in global warming terms than CO_2, and is not mentioned nearly as much. Figure 8.1 illustrates the rapid growth of CO_2 emissions since 1900.

COMPLEXITY They are called GHGs because of their action. They collect in the upper atmosphere and prevent solar heat being reflected back into space. This heat collects, so it is like a greenhouse. The immediate effect, over many years (see Figure 8.2) but only recently noticeable, is argued to be the melting of the polar ice caps which will cause rising sea levels to flood low lying coastal regions, e.g. Bangladesh. The possible consequences for business and the economy if these predictions come to pass are obvious. But climate change is also serious: warm areas may get cold, wet areas may become dry, and agriculture may suffer, especially in poorer countries. Unpredictable and disastrous weather phenomena, it is suggested, will emerge.

These changes, if they occur, will produce enormous economic costs. Disasters are costly, but the threat of disaster increases insurance costs. The UK insurance industry estimates that a four degree increase in global temperature could result in the cost of extreme inland floods rising by 30 per cent to £5.4 billion. Threats to business are paralleled by political instability. Water resources can become scarce, and the possibility of conflict between countries which share river systems increases. Though we talk of sea levels rising, in fact usable water is scarce, and various types of business activities accentuate the problem (see Mini-Case 8.1).

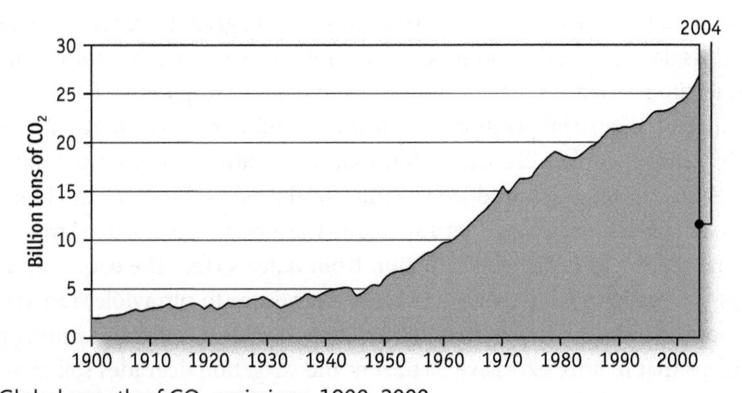

Figure 8.1 Global growth of CO_2 emissions, 1900–2000

Source: World Resources Institute, www.wri.org

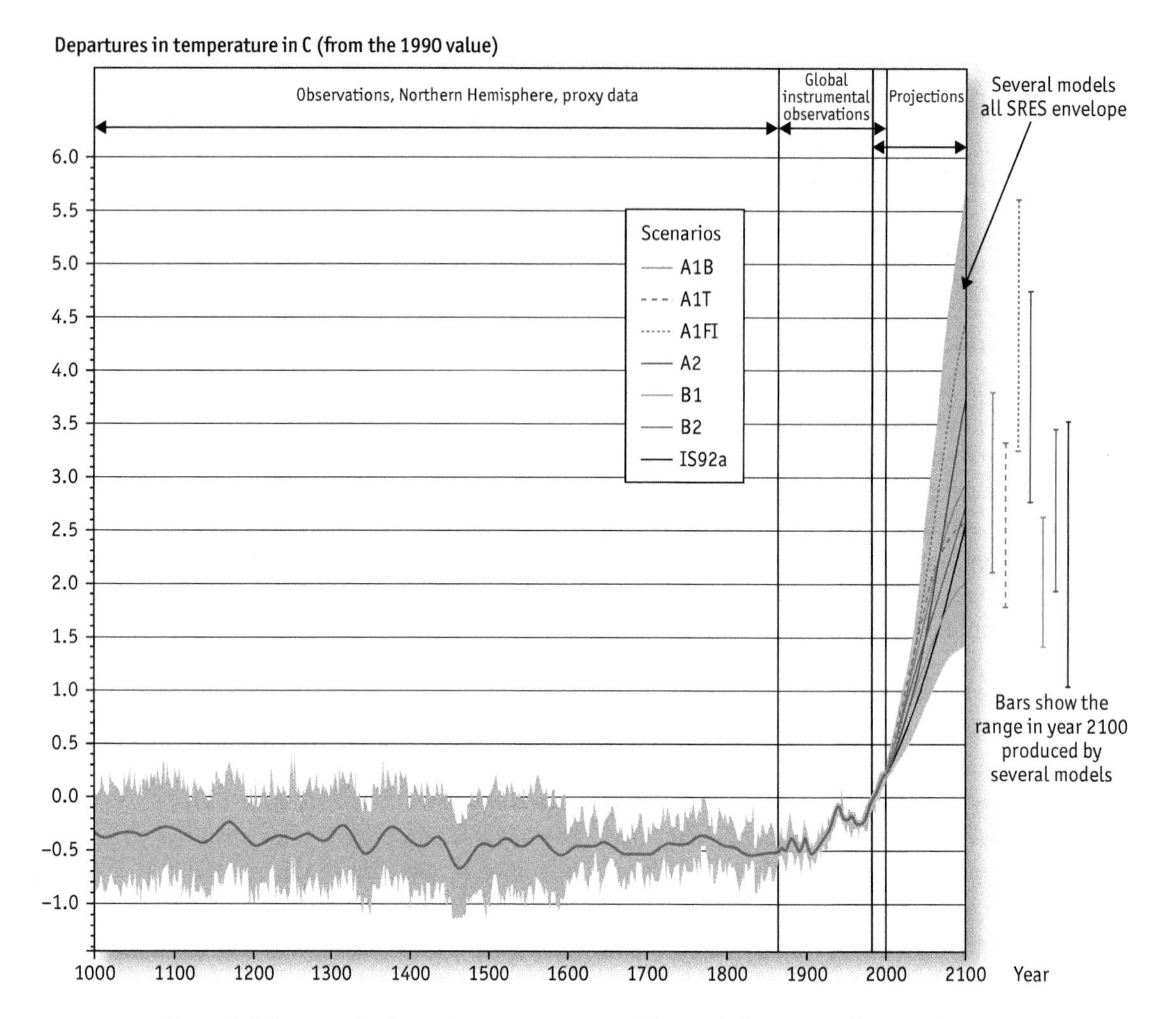

Figure 8.2 Increase in the surface temperature of the Earth from AD 1000 to AD 2100

Source: Intergovernmental Panel on Climate Change (IPCC), www.ipcc.ch

Pollution and resource depletion

INTERACTION Burning fossil fuels produces acid rain. Sulphur dioxide in the smoke from coal burning power stations combines with atmospheric moisture, making sulphuric acid. This falls as rain, maybe far away, and destroys forest and agricultural areas because the soil is too acidic. This damages both food production and tourism. Equally, motor exhausts cause photochemical smog which is a health hazard. People die of respiratory failure, and in cities such as Los Angeles, industrial plants close down if pollution rises too high. (As Vidal (2016) pointed out: 'Far more people will die from filthy air in our cities than from any warming of the atmosphere'.) Also, certain gases produced by industrial processes (especially chlorofluorocarbons or CFCs) accumulate at a height of 15–50km. This destroys the ozone layer in the upper atmosphere, and allows in ultraviolet radiation from outer space. The ozone layer above the polar ice caps is already much depleted. Excessive exposure to ultraviolet radiation leads to increased blindness and skin cancer. In addition, it aggravates the global warming process.

Growing crops that require excessive fertilizers and irrigation degrades soil quality and exhausts water supplies. Industrial production generates waste products polluting air, water, and land, and ultimately degrading the agricultural resource base. Rivers run to the sea, and liquid

Mini-Case 8.1 Water, water everywhere, and not a drop to drink?

VALUES Most water is sea (97.5 per cent), and, of the remaining 2.5 per cent, 70 per cent is in the polar ice caps, and only 30 per cent (or only 0.7 per cent of global water) is usable from rivers, lakes, underground water, etc. (Climate Institute 2009). This is unequally available. Minimum daily personal requirements for consumption and sanitary needs are 50 litres. Where water is scarce, much less than that might be available. Consumption in the European Union is 200 litres, and in the US 500 litres. The real problem, however, is not personal consumption, but the water to grow products. Water to grow a kilogram of potatoes is 1,000 litres. A kilogram of beef requires 42,500 litres. And it takes twenty-five bathtubs to produce 250 grams of cotton for a shirt. This might not seem problematic until one appreciates where some products are grown. Thus, for example, US farmers are subsidized to grow cotton in areas requiring irrigation (see Chapter 10). This cotton is sold on world markets below production cost, bankrupting cotton producers in developing countries.

Many major rivers are declining, not just because climate change reduces rainfall, but because of water abstraction for irrigation (Pacific Institute 2009). The Rio Grande between the US and Mexico has declined over the years to almost a dribble, and the gushing river of cowboy films is just a memory. Where this occurs in politically dangerous areas in Africa, the Middle East, and Asia, there is a war risk (WEF 2010). As population and production increase the problem gets worse. Countries like the US are in fact exporting water (embodied in products as 'virtual water') from areas where it is scarce, while common sense suggests that products should be grown where the natural conditions are optimal without needing scarce water.

Even a bunch of flowers from your local supermarket is problematic. Flower companies in areas like Kenya which export to the UK are accused of stealing water illegally at night from rivers, and hence endangering the livelihoods of local farmers who have inadequate water for their crops.

It is an indication of the complexity of analytical issues in the global environment that some revision of the accepted views (IPCC 2007) on climate change and drought has been necessary. Recent research (Sheffield et al. 2012) shows that with the use of superior drought modelling methods it can be concluded that worldwide drought has actually changed very little since 1950. However, the authors stress they are not arguing that climate change is not happening. But climate change is not the only issue of SD. Water availability remains a problem because it is overall scarce, vis-à-vis increasing population globally combined with unwise usage practices across wide areas. Two good current examples are India and China. Mallet (2016) reports, in an aptly titled article, the dire water situation in India, made worse by mismanagement, while Leavenworth (2016) reports that the Chinese capital Beijing is sinking at a rate of 11cm per year because of abstraction of groundwater for its burgeoning population, while Buckley and Piao (2016) report that 'More than 80 per cent of the water from underground wells used by farms, factories and households across heavily populated plains of China is unfit for drinking or bathing because of contamination from industry and farming.'

Question

Why does the relative scarcity of water mean we need to carefully consider the equity issues surrounding its distribution?

run off from land fertilizers and other chemicals concentrates pollutants in the food chain, as they are absorbed by marine life and then eaten by humans, with consequent health problems. Equally, fish stocks decline not only through overfishing but because the sea is polluted. This problem is aggravated by direct waste dumping at sea.

VALUES The ecology of regions is delicately balanced. Habitat destruction may eliminate species (for instance, logging in rain forests of Amazonia or Southeast Asia which feeds raw materials to the furniture industries) which may have unpredictable effects. Equally, the long-term migration of species as climate changes brings new flora and fauna which can destroy native species. Even more unpredictable is its effects on genetic diversity, by the introduction of genetically modified organisms (GMOs) and plants. These are often associated not just with attempts to design disease-free and improved plant varieties, but are feared by some to represent attempts by multinational companies to take patents on seed varieties on which they have a monopoly. At the same time, Ridley (2016) reports the results of recent research by the

American National Academies of Sciences, Engineering and Medicine, saying it 'leaves no room for doubt that genetically engineered crops are as safe or safer, and are certainly better for the environment than conventionally bred crops'.

Apart from water, oil is a major problem, but emerging nations, like China and India, exacerbate the problem. Their high populations have rapidly increasing car ownership: in 2008 China produced about 7 million cars, and 21 million in 2015, and is now the world's largest producer (www.statista.com). It was predicted that by 2030 China alone will consume 99 million barrels of oil daily, but current world production is only 96 million barrels (2016 estimate by International Energy Agency at: www.ies.org). There has been much debate about when peak oil production will be reached. The widely accepted forecast from the International Energy Agency was that the peak would occur after 2030, but the UK Energy Research Council predicted in late 2009 that the peak would occur as early as 2020, which would cause soaring oil prices and recourse to more polluting fuels. (This was of course before the surge from shale oil discussed below.)

Mini-Case 8.2 Beyond muscle power: the basis of modern economies and issues of SD

Economic growth scarcely existed before 1750. Up to that time economies were in a relatively steady state, and the ability to produce anything depended largely on muscle power, human or animal, and on natural energy sources such as wind and water power. Prior to 1750, most populations lived on the edge of existence. Gordon (2012) suggests that, for the 400 years prior to 1700, there was no growth in GDP per capita in the UK.

After 1750 the Industrial Revolution produced unprecedented increases in output, spreading around the globe. A key element of this was the steam engine, using unlimited energy from coal. The ability to transcend the limits of muscle power, and other crude forms of energy, was a substantial part of the basis for the modern global economy. After coal and steam power came electricity, and then the internal combustion engine, using oil. These cheap energy sources all allowed quantum leaps in our productivity, plus rapid change in the location of industry and population. Finally, we have the revolution of high-speed communications and computing.

Perhaps the world then became a victim of its own success. First, we had worries from the 1920s about oil supplies, which came and went regularly up to the present day. And then we had the issue of global warming, which was argued to be caused by the carbon dioxide generated by combustion of coal, oil, and gas. The need to reduce carbon dioxide emissions arguably provided an impetus for us to economize on oil and gas, the reserves of which were going to run out if we did not economize, and switch to renewable energy sources (wind turbines, wave power, hydroelectricity, etc.). The way to economize was to increase the price by various taxes, though the price was leaping anyway. Alternative energy sources, such as wind turbines, needed to be subsidized until they became economically viable, and energy companies in the UK had to charge customers more to pay for the subsidies. The result, controversially, has been rapid increases in household energy bills, though a basic component of this is actually the increase in the cost of energy rather than the taxes and subsidies. More broadly, critics suggested that the direction of energy policy was likely to drive our economies back to the Stone Ages and muscle power by making energy so expensive.

The elephant in the room in the middle of this debate was shale oil and gas. It was true that easily accessible oil/gas was a diminishing resource, and the threats that reserves might be exhausted in the foreseeable future seemed unarguable. But we have been aware for many years that in many regions there were geological strata permeated with vast deposits of oil and gas. The problem was that there was no practicable method of extracting the energy from the earth. However, the fairly recently developed technique of 'fracking', which involved pumping water at very high pressure into these strata and pushing the oil/gas deposits to the surface where they could be gathered, was widely introduced in the US.

This technique was criticized by environmental groups who said that the fracking technique caused earthquakes and polluted groundwater. But development of shale oil and gas has thrust ahead in the US and totally transformed its energy position, being almost self-sufficient in gas and oil, and also its general manufacturing position (American Chemistry Council 2011). The cost of gas has halved in the US, and the cost of vital inputs to chemical processes has dropped by up to 70 per cent. Manufacturing in the US is becoming competitive with China, and the US has a cost advantage over countries such as Germany, France, and UK. Manufacturing is pulling back from these and other countries to the US, 're-shoring' as it is called (Boston Consulting Group 2012).

A strange aspect of this transformation of the US energy position, apart from the economic benefits, is that it has been accompanied by significant falls in US CO_2 emissions. Gas emits less CO_2 than coal, and so although the US is only latterly coming round to participation in Kyoto Treaty targets, its CO_2 emissions are falling while those of the UK and similar countries are falling only marginally or are still increasing. Also, while countries like the UK have scarcely less rich shale gas/oil reserves than the US, many objections are raised against their exploitation. But, nevertheless the UK government in January 2013 gave the go ahead for the resumption of exploratory drilling in the shale strata around Blackpool, though the application by Cuadrilla was turned down by Lancashire County Council in 2015. However, the government is now proposing to fast-track the planning process, and the Oil and Gas Authority has announced twenty-seven more sites in England where licences to frack for shale oil and gas will be offered (Edgar 2015).

This discussion illustrates both the fundamental significance of energy availability for sustaining the basis of the economy, while presenting an environmental sustainability threat, and the way in which forecasts about energy availability can be overtaken by events and completely change the perspective of the future.

Question

Critics say the transformation of the US energy situation may be exaggerated because once the most isolated oil/gas reserves in a large country are exhausted, the exploitation of reserves nearer to population centres will run up against the same constraints which are pointed out in this country, in terms of potential geological shocks and pollution of water resources. Assess the view that hopes of a transformed energy future for the UK are premature, due to these constraints.

One problem with these predictions is the unpredictable. The worry that oil will become scarce is not new.

We examine this in Mini-Case 8.2.

Thus, while global warming captures most attention, there is a range of other linked effects which relate to issues of SD. Our discussions of water and oil shortages lead quickly to food shortages, which are also related to global population growth. Again, nothing is simple: half the food produced globally, about two billion tons, is simply wasted through various types of mismanagement plus the desire of supermarkets for cosmetically perfect vegetables (Fox 2013). We may now consider the international responses to these issues.

International responses: the 'Earth Summit' and after

The UN Conference on Environment and Development at Rio de Janeiro in 1992, the 'Earth Summit', changed the international legal framework for environmental issues. It created an 'Earth Charter', or an environmental bill of rights which set out the principles for economic and environmental behaviour of peoples and nations. Several agreements emanated from the Conference, in particular:

- the Rio Declaration;
- Agenda 21; and
- UN Framework Convention on Climate Change.

The Rio Declaration

This covered many issues relating to the mutual environmental behaviour of nations. Overall, it aimed to establish:

> a new and equitable global partnership through the creation of new levels of cooperation among States, key sectors of society, and people.
>
> (Ison et al. 2002: 109)

However, the declaration could be described as 'soft law', that is, it lacked an enforcement or compliance system.

Agenda 21–Global programme of action on sustainable development

Agenda 21 is:

> a comprehensive plan of action to be taken globally, nationally and locally by organizations of the United Nations System, Governments and Major Groups in every area in which humans impact on the environment.
>
> (http://sustainabledevelopment.un.org/content/documents/Agenda21.pdf)

Again, it had no legal sanctions, but lots of commitment:

> Perhaps the most important impact of Agenda 21 has been at the local level where Agenda 21 officers have been able to try out practical ideas which seek to implement sustainable development on the ground.
>
> (Ison et al. 2002: 111)

UN Framework Convention on Climate Change

COMPLEXITY VALUES This convention was directly concerned with the problem of global warming, and led to the 1997 Kyoto Protocol. Here the developed countries committed to reducing 1990 emission levels of six GHGs by 5 per cent by 2012. It introduced emissions trading, whereby countries which were having difficulty meeting their emissions reduction targets could buy emissions allowances from other countries with spare capacity. The Kyoto Protocol was a significant initiative. But the US, producing 25 per cent of global GHGs, refused to sign the protocol, and still refused up to the election of President Obama in 2008, after which US attitudes started to change in the lead-up to the December 2009 Copenhagen Conference. Thus, global warming is generated by few countries, but many, mainly the poorest, suffer from it (see Figure 8.3). This is an enormous injustice.

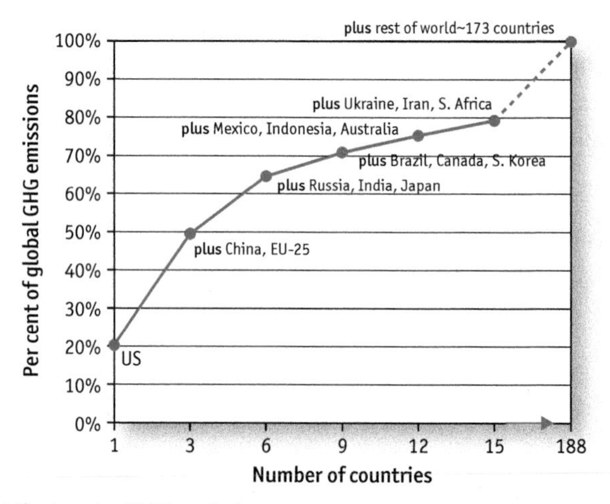

Figure 8.3 The main contributors to GHG emission

Source: World Resources Institute, www.wri.org

A related issue is lack of universal agreement on global warming. While it is argued that most scientific opinion suggests global warming is fact, evidenced in tornadoes, glaciers melting, and so on, other key experts disagree with this view. But even if you are of the majority opinion, suggestions of what to do are not simple. If you look at Mini-Case 8.2, you can see the difficulty.

It is true that the research underpinning conclusions about global warming is at the frontiers of science, but the weight of 'officially accepted' scientific opinion seems to be on the side of its current reality and future imminence. We must now consider how these arguments have been taken forward up to the present day.

From Rio 1992 to Doha 2012

LOCAL TO GLOBAL The two decades after Rio 1992 were punctuated by a series of conferences which sought to cement a binding climate change agreement. What was hoped to be the 'clincher' took place in Doha (Qatar) in 2012. This was preceded by conferences in Johannesburg (2002), Bali (2007), and Copenhagen (2009). The conferences basically focused on replacing the Kyoto Protocol, and their themes were: the target limit on global warming (2°C agreed at Copenhagen); how to finance measures to achieve this in developing countries; and how to get the main CO_2 emitters (the US, Russia, China, and India) to agree to sign up to it. But the 2°C target is based on one specific view of the underlying science. How sure can we be? This issue is explored further in Mini-Case 8.3.

Mini-Case 8.3 Even when we think we know, what do we do?

The dominant scientific opinion on many issues has very often run counter to what subsequently turned out to be the case.

Critics of those who argue climate change is generated by human activity say that a similar failure of the conventional wisdom (the 'scientific consensus') is occurring (Booker 2009). However, the fact remains that the consensus seems to be that anthropogenic global warming is the most probable possibility (Hulme 2009). But, it is important to remember that scientific hypotheses are not tested by majority voting: all hypotheses are provisional; and can be, and frequently are, displaced by a better one (Popper 1963). What matters is not what most scientists think, but whether the hypothesis stands up to empirical testing. Thus, when in 1931 a book attacking Einstein's special theory of relativity was published ('A Hundred Authors Against Einstein', in German), Einstein commented: 'Why 100 authors? If I were wrong, then one would have been enough.' His theory was verified observationally in 1959.

Despite the doubts expressed in some quarters, some analysts have said that the forecasts on which views about global warming are based are substantially correct (e.g. Frame and Stone 2012). Silver (2012) in his general study of issues in forecasting was also of this view, but qualified his conclusions by saying that we were still not very far into the 100-year period covered by the IPCC forecasts, and much could happen to stop the forecasts coming to fruition (a few major volcanic eruptions occasionally could have a significant cooling effect).

While one might agree with this view, there can still be much argument about many of the responses to it. Some scientists say that focusing on single issues like CO_2 reduction will not necessarily produce the desired results, because the complexity of the physical systems is too great to make reliable predictions. (Thus, the idea that once the global atmosphere warms up by 2°C, runaway uncontrollable warming will occur is a prediction of the forecasting models being used. But critics say that this is because the models are based on positive feedback mechanisms, whereas in nature it is more usual to observe negative feedback, or a damping down of oscillations.) This problem of predictions becomes even worse when issues become politicized (Giddens 2009). Then global warming becomes one of a range of issues that influence the seesaw movement of international relations. Reducing US GHG emissions involves great economic costs, while stopping the growth of Chinese and Indian emissions will reduce their economic growth. Who will give way? (As we saw in Mini-Case 8.2 solutions, at least for the US, may suddenly appear!) Behind this is power politics, with nations jockeying for position across a range of issues, only one of which is SD. Another root of the issue is corruption: some poor nations which need international funding for their participation in carbon dioxide reduction strategies are, alas, also among the most corrupt governments in the world. The unspoken fear is that money provided would simply disappear.

The issues around global warming are prodigiously difficult and controversial, and they present policymakers with major issues on how to respond directly, and also how to balance them with other policy areas. But there can be little doubt about the existence of shorter term climatic variations which are argued to produce major problems alongside issues of resource shortages of water, food, oil, and so on, and pollution and environmental degradation.

Question

Look back at Figure 8.2. This well-known graph is referred to as the 'hockey stick'. This is meant to reflect about 900 years of broadly stable world surface temperatures, followed by the Industrial Revolution, leading to rocketing temperatures from now onwards if we do not control them. This graph is controversial. Do an Internet search for 'hockey stick graph' and explore sites which seem to argue in favour of the validity of the graph and, also, those that criticize it. What are your impressions about this debate?

After Copenhagen there was Cancun (2010), then Durban (2011). All these conferences were marked by failure to agree on most of the main issues, though from 2009 the US started to become involved. The Doha Climate Change Conference (November–December 2012) was billed as a last chance to come up with an agreement to rescue the Kyoto Treaty from oblivion. It failed to come up with such an agreement, except to keep talking and to come back in 2015 for another attempt. But the Doha Conference marked more than twenty years since the Rio Conference in June 1992. What had actually been achieved after such a long period? The view of some critics is that the whole process has been a failure of epic proportions (Fleming and Jones 2013: 2).

At Doha it was resolved to meet again in Paris in December 2015. The Conference was attended by 30,372 people, and finished on 12 December 2015; 196 official parties were in attendance from 195 countries plus the EU. Agreement from the Conference commits countries to try to keep global temperature rises 'well below' 2°C (the level which is likely to signal the worst effects of climate change), and 'well below' is interpreted as 1.5°C. The agreement requires countries to set increasingly ambitious targets ('pledges') for cutting national emissions, and to report on their progress. But it leaves the actual targets for cutting emissions (which are also not legally binding) to individual countries to decide for themselves. It requires developed nations to continue to provide funding to help poorer countries cut their carbon emissions, and to adapt to climate change. But it does not set a legally binding level of money for this. Financing as ever is the stumbling block: developing countries want legally binding agreements, but the US will not agree. The agreement asks countries to come back before 2020 to revisit their pledges, and make new, more ambitious pledges every five years thereafter. As usual, sceptics say the conference was a failure.

A further conference of the parties to the Paris Conference took place at Marrakech, Morocco, 7–18 November 2016. The website of the UN Framework Convention on Climate Change reported that: 'The Conference successfully demonstrated to the world that the implementation of the Paris Agreement is under way and the constructive spirit of multilateral cooperation on climate change continues.' However, climate campaigners expressed themselves disappointed with the outcome, expecting practical follow-up to the Paris Conference, especially in financial terms. There was also worry about the impact of the election of Donald Trump as US President: he is a well-known sceptic of climate change.

More generally, Helm (2012) notes that use of coal over the period 1992–2012 has risen from 25 per cent to 30 per cent of energy use, significantly because of new generating capacity in the booming Chinese economy. The UK and European countries congratulate themselves on reducing emissions, but are focusing, says Helm, on the wrong variable, namely carbon production, rather than carbon consumption. That is, the shift of production to China means that carbon is being produced there in the process of producing goods which are consumed here (and which, formerly, were produced here). And, the emissions reductions obtained from current renewable energy policies, such as subsidized wind turbines, involve the most expensive ways of reducing emissions known to man.

He concludes, therefore, that we must focus on carbon consumption, and tax imports of it. And we should move from coal to gas in a transition which is now possible with the availability of lower carbon shale gas reserves.

The application of SD frameworks to environmental issues

Conventional frameworks for dealing with environmental issues

VALUES INTERNAL/EXTERNAL Before the idea of SD evolved, conventional, or classical, economics saw pollution and environmental problems as 'side effects' of the production/consumption process. The approach of conventional economics was not to ignore environmental costs, but to keep them in balance with the societal costs and benefits of economic activity. Hence, such side effects were called 'externalities' and were considered to be 'divergences between private and social costs' (these were explored in Chapter 2). Externalities can be positive or negative, but in the cases we are considering they are usually negative. That is, social costs are greater than private costs, and social costs can be reduced to acceptable levels by instituting taxes to equate social marginal cost with social marginal benefit. A classic example of this is the use of road pricing to reduce traffic congestion. Economists refer to this as 'internalizing the externality' and it is popularly referred to as 'making the polluter pay'. Such ideas have existed for many years, and have been implemented on a small scale in UK cities, like Cambridge and Durham, and on a larger scale in cities like Singapore. The successful introduction of the London congestion charge in February 2003 is probably the largest example to date.

Road congestion is an easy example of the use of the conventional economic approach to controlling an environmental problem. Despite the practical implementation, the situation is simpler in that most of the problem consists of road users imposing costs on other road users. But other types of environmental goods can be more difficult. Unlike road traffic, the perpetrators are most often not sufferers. It may also be difficult to identify who actually are the perpetrators and sufferers. Also, you can only impose charges if it is possible to establish ownership of, or property rights in, the thing that is being charged for (such as road space). The problem is that many environmental goods have badly defined property rights. Who owns the atmosphere? Who owns the oceans? But even if we can establish ownership, it may still be hard to quantify the environmental costs that have to be charged for, and then establish practical charging systems. Nevertheless, as we have indicated already, it is not impossible, and the Kyoto Protocol has already instituted the idea of 'emissions trading' (see Mini-Case 8.4).

Mini-Case 8.4 Carbon trading or 'funny money'?

The principle of **emissions trading** is simple. It keeps the level of a pollutant (in this case CO_2) at a target level by putting a price on it. Producers get permits which allow them to emit a certain amount of carbon, and they use these permits to cover their own emissions, or else invest in clean technologies which allow them to sell some of the permits to another company which has exceeded its permit quota. This creates a market in the permits. The problem is that once you set the overall total and allocate permits you are merely keeping within that total, shifting the total around between those who are buying and those who are selling permits. Thus, the total does not decrease by definition, though it could in principle be organized to do so over a period, and this would be the intention of Kyoto (Hulme 2009).

After the establishment of the Kyoto Protocol, the European Union instituted an Emissions Trading Scheme (ETS) (European Commission 2009). Each member state set a cap on the carbon emissions that would be allowed and issued permits accordingly. The first round of the scheme during 2005–7 had mixed results. The caps were set too high in some countries (but not high enough in Britain), and several countries produced much lower emissions than they estimated. Hence, prices collapsed. But there is inevitably a learning process, and it was hoped that the 2008–12 round could be run with tighter limits. However, the ETS suffered a setback at the end of 2009 after the European Court overturned European Commission caps on the amount of carbon Poland and Estonia are permitted to emit between 2008 and 2012 (causing the price of carbon to dip 2.5 per cent) because they appealed against the financial burdens entailed. This could mean similar rulings being made on other countries' emissions caps with adverse consequences for the cap-and-trade scheme.

Potentially, the effect of ETS on companies is remarkable. Their possible liabilities for purchase of permits have to be indicated on their balance sheets, and investors are very keen to know what a company's emissions position is. The Stern Review, a major government report about the threats facing us from climate change, raised the possibility that emissions may be taxed in the UK and this could have a very significant effect on the stock market. Climate change, it argues, may cost us 20 per cent of world GDP if it is not checked, and taxing emissions is just one specific aspect of the general message of the Stern Review: the polluter must pay (HM Treasury 2006). This view was reflected in the passing of the Climate Change Act on 26 November 2008. But at a European level, some uncertainty was introduced by the 2009 court decision. Other difficulties have accumulated. In late November 2012 the US Congress passed a law forbidding US airlines from paying any carbon dioxide emission charges for flights to/from the EU, as the EU was seeking to extend the ETS to airline emissions.

A more general worry as emissions trading becomes more widespread is how, in the light of the financial crisis, to avoid the scheme becoming the basis of another scandal (Giddens 2009). The downturn in the world economy, with low gas and coal prices, has meant that the permits issued are too numerous to sustain a reasonable trading price. On 30 November 2012—in the middle of the Doha conference—it was reported that the price of carbon had dropped to €5.89 per tonne, when many analysts consider a minimum price of at least €20 is necessary to convince industry and utilities to adopt cleaner forms of energy over coal and gas (Chestney 2012).

Question

What are the problems of attempting to levy taxes on polluters?

The concept of sustainable development (SD)

Definitions of SD

As well as the Brundtland definition already discussed, there are over seventy other definitions of SD. The Brundtland definition is intuitively graspable and we can point to two key ideas:

- **Intergenerational equity** (IRGE): that is, fairness between generations, or, being as fair to our grandchildren as we are to ourselves.
- **Intragenerational equity** (IAGE): that is, fairness between different interest groups in the same generation.

It is common to talk about the two ideas from the point of view of what is called 'weak' and 'strong' sustainability:

- Weak sustainability (WS): to achieve IRGE we should aim to pass on to future generations a constant 'aggregate capital stock' (AGS), though its composition may change; to achieve IAGE we should aim to compensate the poor and disadvantaged by support programmes.
- Strong sustainability (SS): to achieve IRGE, the idea of AGS does not apply: losses of environmental capital must be replaced; to achieve IAGE, we still compensate, but we also emphasize the collective value of ecosystems and environment.

But whether we go for strong or weak definitions, we need to consider how we measure them.

Development of SD initiatives

VALUES The key issue here is how to value environmental goods. There are problems which are well known in using conventional GDP measures with environmental goods. An increase in GDP can be consistent with an increase in environmental degradation.

Expenditures to reduce degradation are regarded in economic accounting terms as an increase in welfare because they increase GDP, rather than being a cost which actually reduces welfare. Hence, alternative measures which reflect this have been devised, for instance, the Index of Sustainable Economic Welfare (ISEW) devised by the Stockholm Environmental Institute in 1994. Thus:

$$\begin{aligned}\text{ISEW} = {} & \text{Personal consumption} + \text{non-defensive public expenditure} \\ & - \text{defensive private expenditures} + \text{capital formation} \\ & - \text{costs of environmental degradation} \\ & + \text{services from domestic labour} - \text{depreciation of natural capital}\end{aligned}$$

In a conventional GDP measure, the first two negative quantities would be positive, while the last two items, one negative and one positive, would not appear in the equation at all. Thus, in the UK since the 1970s GDP has increased annually, but ISEW has declined.

> ***Stop and Think***
>
> Think of two concrete examples each for (a) and (b) which probably:
>
> (a) increase GDP but reduce ISEW; and
>
> (b) reduce GDP but increase ISEW.

From here the development of environmental indicators is a key step. The UK government published its first set of indicators of SD in 1996, and these have been updated since, and form the basis for evaluating the progress being made towards both national and international sustainability targets. The current version is from 2013 (DEFRA 2013). This relates to the 2005 UK Government Sustainable Development Strategy (DEFRA 2005), updated in 2011 (DEFRA 2011). This indicator set is formed of twelve headline and twenty-three supplementary indicators, comprising twenty-five and forty-one measures respectively. The indicators cover the areas of sustainable consumption and production, climate change and energy, protection of natural resources and environmental enhancement, and the creation of sustainable communities and a fairer world. The indicators include GHG emissions, resource use, waste generation, bird populations, fish stocks, ecological impacts of air pollution, and river quality.

Once we can quantify the main things that need to be influenced, the next step is to consider how we influence them.

Types of approaches for dealing with environmental problems

As suggested already, while we talk about the global dimension of environmental problems, many of the responses to them are implemented at a local level. So, we often hear the phrase: 'Think globally, act locally'. It is common to classify policy responses into either 'market based' or 'non-market based'.

'Market based' policy measures

VALUES A first approach is by processes of bargaining and negotiation. If property rights in the environmental goods—air, water, or whatever—can be assigned to some party, this is possible. The question, of course, is who will they be assigned to? Equity and ethics suggest that 'the polluter pays'. But if there are too many polluters or sufferers, bargaining is difficult, and it may be impossible to set up any scheme. In this case, the alternative may be a tax.

With environmental taxes, the polluter pays a tax related to the environmental damage. This creates an incentive to reduce the damage, for instance as in the case of a carbon tax. The problem here is that it may be hard to estimate the correct tax level, so that if it is set too high, society loses out because the polluter cuts back production too much, whereas if it is set too low, there is insufficient reduction in the environmental damage.

'Non-market based' policy measures

Here government establishes standards for things like air quality, water quality, chemical processes, waste incineration, and so on. The polluter then decides how to meet standards, adopting the least costly approach. A regulatory body may be appointed to monitor compliance and to take action for breaches of standards. Regulatory systems can be rather blunt instruments. Different firms may be more easily placed to achieve the targets, and might be encouraged to overachieve if some form of trading solution were possible, whereas if the target is easy to achieve, the company can sit back and do little. Equally, if the targets are set too stringently, firms may incur unnecessary costs to meet them.

We may also include, under non-market based measures, the use of public exhortation, persuasion, and education in environmental matters. This may include direct measures which encourage people to do more by giving them a little encouragement to make a start, especially if regulation is going to eventually make things a requirement. A good example here is the campaign to encourage people to start using energy-saving light bulbs. There is a lot to do in informing both the public and business about the nature of environmental problems, to facilitate the introduction of appropriate policy measures.

Policy frameworks

LOCAL TO GLOBAL This section considers what has actually been done in policy terms for the UK and the European Union. Up to the 1970s environmental regulation in the UK was piecemeal, with several inspectorates working independently in relation to land, air, water, and nuclear power. From the 1970s there were attempts to unify the various areas of environmental regulation and, from the 1980s, in the light of developments outlined at the start of the chapter, environmental policy ceased being a national concern and took on progressively a European and then global dimension. The attempts to unify or integrate the various areas of environmental regulation led in 1990 to the Environmental Protection Act which gave legislative backing to the idea of integrated pollution control (IPC), looking to control pollution across media (land, water, air, etc.). This embodied in environmental regulation the principle of requiring the implementation of the Best Available Technique Not Entailing Excessive Cost (BATNEEC), whatever the process. This gave explicit recognition to the economic dimension in what had, up to then, been the principle of the best practicable means (BPM). Following the Environment Act 1996, all the functions of the different environmental agencies were incorporated for the first time into the Environment Agency.

In the 1970s, changes at the UK level took place in parallel to Europe-wide and subsequently international initiatives, as the cross-boundary dimensions of environmental processes expanded with growth in the European and global economy. One might think that after the European referendum vote of 23 June 2016 on whether or not to leave the European Union, there could be change in store, but the interlocking of the EU with international agreements will likely mean that any change may be slow and, in any case, unnecessary.

SD and business

VALUES Business is one of the significant contributors to environmental problems, yet, simultaneously, it provides us with our livelihoods. The need to focus environmental measures so as not to impose excessive economic costs on society as compared with the reduction in environmental costs has also emerged in discussion. Overall, we need to maintain high/stable economic growth within acceptable environmental limits. Thus, this section considers SD issues within the context of the internal operations of a business. It will become quickly apparent that this presents not only challenges to a business in terms of how it can reduce its environmental impact, but also opportunities, in terms of the way in which these challenges collectively also present business opportunities in helping businesses to meet the challenges facing them. It also raises the issue of the responsibilities of businesses in terms of considering their activities in ethical terms, which is explored in detail in Chapter 7.

Defining sustainability in relation to business

The following definition of sustainable business conveniently places it in parallel with the Brundtland definition:

> Sustainable business . . . means taking the goal of sustainability, living and working in such a way that human society will be possible for generations to come, and translating that into the changes required of an individual organization—changes which maintain the organizations capacity for producing human benefits, including the profitability needed for survival, while optimizing the environmental balance of its operations.
>
> (Crosbie and Knight 1995: 15)

Another way of expressing this idea of sustainable business is the **'triple bottom line'**. While an enterprise is normally judged by its profit and loss account, or 'bottom line', the 'triple bottom line' adds in social and environmental criteria, shortened into 'people, planet, profit'. The idea was set out by Elkington (1997).

LOCAL TO GLOBAL There is almost no aspect of the operations of the average business which does not have an impact on the natural environment. We can usefully employ here the format of Hutchinson and Hutchinson (1997) in terms of looking at four aspects of a business: its site history; the production processes it employs; its product and the communications processes surrounding it; and the external environment of the business. These fit into the well-established framework of what is generally called **environmental and ecological auditing**, and the processes developed from about the mid 1980s in the US. This was further boosted after the 1992 'Earth Summit', and not long after in 1995 the European Union devised an Environmental Management and Auditing System (EMAS). In the same year the International Standardization Organization (ISO) set up a committee to develop an environmental management system for global application. It established ISO 14001. While EMAS applies to the EU, and is especially prevalent in German-speaking countries, ISO 14001 is applied worldwide. The EU has adapted its system so that those firms which have ISO 14001 can achieve EMAS by a series of modifications to ISO 14001.

The audit is a broad way of looking at the operations of a company or organization to sketch out how sustainability issues reach into every part of its operations. Each of the four aspects mentioned above can be broken down into several sub-aspects, and many of them are whole areas of research by themselves. But once we have considered each of the four aspects, we shall look at a difficult issue. What do these issues actually mean to a business and government in practice?

Site history

All sorts of dangers may lie hidden in a site, and once a company buys it, it buys all the associated risks. Insurance companies may refuse to insure if they suspect hidden risks. There may, perhaps, be concealed noxious substances which could be disturbed and released into the atmosphere during construction or production. An environmental impact assessment (EIA) would be necessary, which is one aspect of an eco-audit. An EIA involves gathering all the information that exists on the site, and developing an assessment of the environmental issues and risks pertaining to past activity on the site, and the relationship of this to any proposed expansion of existing activities, or initiation of completely new activities.

The production process

This concerns the actual production process, particularly energy use and waste generation, plus the product life cycle. Companies waste about 30 per cent of their energy (mainly in buildings). Thus:

> Electricity and gas metering in business appears to be chaotic. Many businesses have estimated metering, and most are unable to be really sure what energy they actually use, unless they have an energy saving programme in place. This situation is untenable.
>
> (Sustainable Development Commission 2005: 31)

It has been calculated that a 20 per cent reduction in energy costs is equivalent to a 5 per cent increase in sales. So, helping the environment can be good business.

Reducing total energy use is only one aspect. The sources of energy can also be examined to encourage recycling of energy and the use of renewable energy (e.g. wind and solar power). This can also represent business opportunities in terms of developing new ideas and techniques. The whole area of micro-power generation has started to mushroom as new designs of small wind-powered turbines which can be attached to buildings come on the market (but note that wind power can be variable and back-up is needed).

Apart from wasting energy, firms may produce substantial waste in the production process. Dealing with waste after generation to minimize impact (for instance, ensuring that companies hired to take waste away do not dump it illegally) is an obvious first requirement, but even more useful are efforts at minimizing the waste generated in the first place.

INTERNAL/EXTERNAL Looking at energy use and waste generation leads to the whole product in terms of a **life cycle assessment** (LCA). An LCA examines all environmental impacts associated with the life of a product from raw material extraction, to pre-production processes, to actual production, and through to distribution and final disposal of the used product. This is easily said, but for many products each of these stages involves quite significant environmental impacts, apart from the production process itself. For instance, furniture industries need to ensure that scarce timbers illegally gathered from threatened tropical forests are not being used by them. Equally, so many harmless-looking products wear out and have to be disposed of, and they often contain poisonous components which leak into the atmosphere, the earth, or water systems: fridge mountains, PC mountains, old cars, and so on. So, there are regular calls to put a tax on such items to pay for their eventual disposal.

Product and communications

The environmental features of a company's production activities can be exploited for its own wider advantage. This may be in terms of protecting itself from the wider public consequences of unforeseen environmental crises, promoting its products, or promoting the image of the company in terms of not only its financial reporting, but also its environmental reporting.

STAKEHOLDERS In terms of crisis management and risk assessment we have already referred to environmental disasters, but these can also be public relations disasters which damage the wider image of the company by affecting adversely its product brands and stock market standing. Environmental disasters are nearly always unexpected, yet require immediate company responses to restore confidence and minimize damage to its reputation. When disasters occur, there may be attempts to conceal information. However, openness and transparency is the best policy, and companies should prepare for unlikely but possible eventualities, by carrying out risk assessments of what could happen, and making reaction plans ready in case something does go wrong. But PR disasters can be self-inflicted as we have seen with the VW debacle, out of which very few parties emerged with reputations intact. In September 2015 the US Environmental Protection Agency, working with clean air advocacy organizations, was able to show that VW had, by fitting devices to the engines of their diesel vehicles, massively and deliberately corrupted testing procedures which allowed its vehicles to be shown as meeting the legal limits on emissions of nitrogen oxide, a highly poisonous air pollutant. This affected 600,000 US vehicles, and up to 11 million European ones. The damage to the reputation of VW was enormous, its share price dropped catastrophically, and VW had to set aside enormous sums to cover fines and damages. Many other companies are involved, and the case will rumble on for years, but an astonishing feature of the case is that, despite its responsibility for, and advocacy of environmental protection, the European Union knew what was happening, and did nothing about it (Gillingham 2016: 177–80).

VALUES Disasters apart, the daily operations of the company may be an asset to be exploited. Companies which have ensured that they source their inputs from other companies which have employed environmentally desirable methods, have produced their products to the highest environmental standards, and have ensured that waste products can be disposed of in the most environmentally efficient way, have a story to tell, or sell, in their marketing activities. This is called **green marketing**, and it is a story to tell not only to consumers and customers, but also to staff, shareholders, investors, the media, and regulatory authorities. However, it has to be a believable and honest story. Consumers and the media soon spot exaggerated or false claims which are intended to boost sales or public image. Such claims are often called **greenwash** (see Mini-Case 8.5).

Product design, packaging, and eco-labelling also present opportunities for environmental gains. Materials can be saved in production and packaging. Packaging can be used not only to provide useful environmental guidance on the product, but also information on safe disposal of the used product and packaging (eco-labelling). Clearly, some of these features will have an obvious benefit to the company, in terms of saving raw materials and the use of energy. But others will have benefits further down the line reducing transport costs, and landfill or incineration costs. Moreover, the opportunity exists, by doing this, to portray the company in the best possible light. Finally, there is environmental reporting. Companies are required to produce annual reports setting out their accounts and financial position. While there is not the same legal requirement for a corporate environmental report (CER), the environmental threats which companies now face both at home and abroad mean that a CER can be almost as important to judging the health of a company, and whether it is a safe investment prospect, as its annual financial statement. Hence a transparent annual CER is produced by major companies. These set out the environmental policies and targets of the company, the systems in place to achieve them, and progress towards achievement.

Stop and Think

Think of three examples where a company uses claims about the environmental dimension of its products or activities in a genuine way, and three examples where false or exaggerated claims are made.

The external environment

Here we consider two aspects of the external environment of the company which are important to the theme of this chapter, but which seem to get little coverage in the many textbooks that now exist on 'corporate environmental management'. The external environment will here refer to the links which a company maintains with other firms, customers, and organizations to produce its goods and services. The first aspect of these links we call the supply chain, and the second aspect will be the environmental management of the transport demands generated by the activities of the firm or organization.

We highlighted the nature of supply chains in Chapter 3. Regarding its environmental management, any company or organization is only one link in the long process which leads to someone somewhere getting a product or service they need. A tree felled in a forest in Scandinavia leads by a long intervening set of operations—raw materials processing, transport, warehousing and storage, further intermediate manufacturing, further transport and storage, final processing, transfer to retail distributors—to a box of matches purchased from a corner shop. A company examining its environmental profile will need to look at not only its own internal operations and processes, but at the supply chain as a whole, to see where changes can be made which will improve the overall environmental performance of the chain.

DYNAMIC In relation to environmental transport strategies, transport is one of the most important factors in the whole global environmental problem, yet it is one of the most intractable, and getting worse. It is forecast that by 2020, 'transport is likely to account for more than half of global oil demand and roughly one fourth of global energy-related CO_2 emissions' (International Energy Agency 2001).

The demand for cars and commercial vehicles is growing much faster than technological improvements in engines can reduce CO_2 emissions, especially in central and Eastern Europe, and developing countries like China and India. The demand for air transport is growing rapidly too. Also, it is not just a growth in numbers: road transport (and air transport to a lesser extent) is a very flexible form of transport which reduces the constraints on location, and leads to not only more journeys but longer journeys.

Reducing the environmental footprint of the transport activities of a business raises conflicts to the extent that critics argue it may raise costs and reduce economic growth. It is often argued that investment in transport infrastructure boosts the rate of economic growth generally, and that it is crucial for improving the economic prospects of declining or peripheral regions. However, if the forecasts of the effects of unrestricted growth in GHGs are borne out, and to which transport is a major contributor, it can be argued that the effects on economic growth of global warming will be much more disastrous than the effects of cutting back transport growth in the first place. This was the basic message of the Stern Review (HM Treasury 2006).

Thus, a company or organization seeking to reduce the demands it places on transport systems and energy-related requirements will need to consider a range of factors and devote considerable effort to developing 'company travel plans', or 'green transport strategies', which look at several or all of these factors, and for which much government advice has been published (DfT 2005). Let us examine these factors:

- *Choice of mode*: in many cases the choices available in the mode of transport a company uses to receive and forward goods may be restricted by site characteristics, the type and value of the goods, and the urgency of receipt and dispatch. But it is clear that different modes have different environmental characteristics regarding energy use and emissions, and companies may be able to adjust their practices accordingly.
- *Storage and packaging for transport*: for large companies the demand for warehousing and storage facilities, and for facilities to pack up and dispatch goods, can be massive. Inventories are dead money, and companies try to minimize them. One way is to have **just in time** production methods, so that component suppliers are organized in the supply chain to bring in deliveries just before they are needed. Thus, transport substitutes for storage. This is accentuated in the activities of companies like large supermarket chains, such as Tesco and ASDA. These companies need to keep their stores supplied around the clock. Cash tills connect directly to the computerized inventory systems to indicate instantly the demand around the country for any product. Economies of scale combined with an efficient motorway system encourage the concentration of warehousing and distribution systems into large logistics centres serving the whole country from a few major bases. This substitution of transport for storage facilities generates energy use. And it also leads to situations where goods which could be obtained locally are shipped from the other end of the country.
- *Input sources and product destinations*: this means that companies seeking to minimize their environmental footprint in transport terms need to consider where they get their inputs from, and where they send them to. As just indicated, it is surprising how many resources are spent shifting goods around the country to places where they already are, and generating GHGs in the process.
- *Employee travel patterns and alternatives to travel*: journeys to work, school, or college constitute a major proportion of daily travel. Growing car use and declining public transport are key features of this phenomenon. The drive to reverse the use of the car and to encourage us to use more environmentally friendly modes like public transport, cycling, or walking has been going on for many years as a way of reducing the peak hour problem. But growing recognition of the GHG problem has sharpened this drive. Companies also need to ask if travel is necessary in the first place. This applies especially to travel on company business. Is it always necessary to drive? Can public transport be used? Can an employee work at home and not travel to work? Can telephone/videoconferencing be used to avoid travel?

INTERNAL/EXTERNAL

- *Other factors—site access, health and safety, noise, and so on*: increased car ownership means more workers drive to work. Insufficient parking space may be available. Larger delivery vehicles may have difficulty approaching and manoeuvring around within the site. Problems of noise, inhalation of toxic fumes, visual intrusion, etc. become an on-site as well as off-site problem. Dealing with these problems can be considered an internal issue, not related to sustainability issues, but they do relate back. Take parking. If employees drive to work and you have the land, why not pave it over? But land is expensive, and there may be more productive uses for it. Moreover, paving land has a significant impact on water resource problems, as it reduces the area into which water can soak to build up groundwater reserves, and the rain runs into drains and to the sea.

STAKEHOLDERS

- *Company travel plans*: unlike the local transport plans which UK local authorities produce, these plans (also called **green transport plans**) are for a company or organization. But they do relate to local transport plans, and are usually developed in close consultation with the local authority and public transport operators, and also with other employers facing the same issues. Studies show that even limited travel plans can achieve 3–5 per cent reductions in the number of employees travelling to work alone by car, and more ambitious plans which include such measures as public transport discounts and parking restrictions on site can achieve 15–30 per cent reductions, or even more, within two to four years. Environmental sense is good economic sense. Research shows that it typically costs a firm £300–£500 per year to maintain a car parking space, but to operate a travel plan costs only £47 a year per full-time employee.

> ***Stop and Think***
>
> Think of as many examples as you can of situations where goods which are available locally are shipped in from a distance. Can you think of reasons why this might have occurred in each instance?

The significance of SD for business

VALUES The previous sections have indicated how a business may review its operations and interpret them in an SD context. But would they all want to? Would it not reduce their profits?

Critics accuse some companies of being against SD measures. The oil company EXXON has been accused of funding pressure groups that cast doubt on the scientific basis of predictions of global warming. Other companies are accused of using their SD or 'green' initiatives as a way of advertising but without any serious basis to them, while others are accused of using them to cover up other undesirable aspects of their business ('greenwash'). For instance, Tesco has been accused of doing this to cover up the hold it has developed on the food and convenience goods business, driving many small operators out who might have sourced goods from the local market area, and been actually much more sustainable than Tesco in their operations.

Equally, the suggestion is made that many companies may see SD initiatives as expensive frills which interfere with making profits, and they only engage in them to the extent that it generates good publicity and promotes the image of their products generally. No doubt this may be so in some cases. A much stronger and more recent version of this view, in the more general context of **corporate social responsibility** (CSR), is that the logic of corporate capitalism in terms of profit seeking means that the 'win, win' idea of pursuing the triple bottom line in sustainable business is inherently delusory and simply serves as a means of deflecting criticism away from the more questionable practices of large corporate organizations (Fleming and Jones 2013). We explore this in Mini-Case 8.5.

It is, of course, easy to pick out individual companies like Starbucks and point to inconsistencies between what they do in one area of their operations, and what they do in another. It then makes it easy for critics to say that sustainable business is all 'greenwash' to cover up a massive rip-off of the taxpayer. But the techniques of transfer pricing which allow companies to switch revenues from a high tax to a low tax jurisdiction have been known about and debated for decades. It is not illegal, though most would say it is unethical. But companies only have to obey the law. Tax evasion is illegal, but tax avoidance is not (Shaxson 2012). But tax avoidance is conspicuously absent from discussions of CSR. Why?

A more difficult issue for writers like Fleming and Jones (2013) to show is that on balance most companies behave like Starbucks. This would be almost impossible to show, as we simply do not have the internal evidence to assess the true scale of 'greenwash'. But unless one is a believer in global conspiracies, there is mounting substantial evidence that companies are taking more and more notice of SD issues, both because of straight issues of survival, and because they realize it makes good business sense and presents business opportunities. And, the fact that they do it because they see it is advantageous does not devalue their activities or motivations. The whole basis of the market economy is self-interest, where individual actions for one's own benefit redound to the common good. Sustainable business may be seen as being driven not only by enlightened self-interest, but also by the realization that companies should be doing this anyway in the light of an overall evaluation of their activities.

Mini-Case 8.5 Putting your money where your mouth is: Starbucks, SD, and taxes

Large corporations stress their responsibilities in the area of CSR, of which sustainable business is but one aspect. Starbucks is an international corporation with chains of coffee shops around the world (24,464 outlets in 2016). Its UK turnover was nearly £405.6 million in 2015. On the home page of its website http://www.starbucks.com/ as of May 2013 there were a number of key headings, of which one was 'Responsibility'. If you were to have clicked on the six subheadings that then appeared, you would have noted that they told a great story about Starbucks running a sustainable business. Here are some of the quotes:

Our commitment to diversity reaches beyond us to the suppliers we work with.

We are working to shrink our environmental footprint and meet the expectations of our customers by reducing the waste associated with our business, increasing recycling and promoting reusable cups.

Our commitment to communities extends beyond our stores to include the regions that supply our coffee, tea and cocoa, and other agricultural products.

These searches would clearly have generated signals in the mind of the reader. The same site contained their *Global Responsibility Report*. The current report is from 2015. It tells an impressive tale of sustainable business, community involvement, and ethical sourcing in every imaginable aspect of the business.

A controversial issue which emerged in 2012 was the fact that, despite its great turnover in the UK, Starbucks had paid no tax to HM Revenue & Customs for five years. In December 2012 it was taken to task by the Parliamentary Public Accounts Committee, and the outcome was that it volunteered to pay £20 million in tax for the next two years. Starbucks was not doing anything illegal. It has good accountants, and, like all international corporations, it has clever arrangements in place to shift funds around the world so that it only pays minimal, if not actually minute, levels of tax. It is legal, but is it ethical? Is Starbucks really running a sustainable business if it is sucking funds out of the UK which could make a major contribution to the country's own sustainability efforts? Are the global responsibility reports all 'greenwash' as Fleming and Jones (2013) no doubt would claim?

Question

Google and Amazon were also taken to task by the Public Accounts Committee about their tax payments. Study their websites and assess the extent to which they make similar promises regarding their responsibility to sustainability.

LOCAL TO GLOBAL Companies with global operations, such as the banks, HSBC and Standard Chartered, are highly conscious of the risks that global warming presents. Apart from increased insurance premiums, they face the risk that many of their global operations may simply be submerged by rising sea levels. Equally, looking at current operations from a sustainability point of view actually starts to indicate that there may be a lot of money to save. And the business opportunities which are possible by responding to global warming have been estimated to be about £500 billion, so there is much for the enterprising company to go for.

Many companies have determined to become carbon neutral in their operations. BSkyB was the first company in the FTSE 100 to become carbon neutral in 2006. By 2011 there were six companies in the FTSE who were carbon neutral (Carbon Retirement 2011). This may not appear a large number, but one has to consider how long it takes to become carbon neutral. Thus, Marks & Spencer (Smithers 2012) reported in June 2012 that it was the first major UK retailer to meet its sustainability targets, becoming carbon neutral after a five-year effort.

We may also look dispassionately at what government is doing. One would get the impression from the foregoing discussion that government at all levels is working hard to promote SD. The UK government and the European Union have numerous measures to promote it, and there are many international agreements. However, we should consider many aspects of the discussion in a wider perspective that merges into considerations addressed in other chapters of this book. Many environmental objectives and measures conflict with measures and objectives in other parts of the economy. It is said that politics is the art of the possible, and governments try to stay in power by seeming to satisfy as many as possible of the conflicting objectives of as many pressure groups and stakeholders in society as possible. Thus, the best possible gloss will be put on every aspect of government activity. A sharp observer needs to watch out for 'greenwash' not only from companies, but from government too.

The difficult part

While one can list all the aspects of a company's operations that may be focused on to improve its sustainability characteristics, the difficult part is to actually bring about a holistic change where the company as a whole works in this direction, rather than sustainability managers located outside operational functions trying to bring about change, or enthusiasts in different parts of the company working in isolation simply doing the best they can. Thus, sustainable businesses trying to operate a 'triple bottom line' are run by people, people who have to learn to work together to achieve sustainable working across the company. How does this happen?

- It might be suggested that this is where the ideas of Senge (Senge et al. 1994) and the **learning organization** could be applied. A learning organization is said to be a company that facilitates the learning of its members and continuously transforms itself. The idea has been widely promoted and discussed as a theoretical concept in general business circles, but as Smith (2001) noted: 'while there has been a lot of talk about learning organizations it is very difficult to identify real-life examples', while Caldwell (2011) refers to its 'failures to deliver a practical guide to organizational learning', adding in 2012: 'Unfortunately, Senge's learning organisation never really matched up to these theoretical and practical challenges, and we must now countenance its final abandonment as a vision of organisational change and human agency' (Caldwell 2012: 17). It is hard in fact to find any example of the application of this approach in integrating sustainability initiatives into the fabric of business organizations, though it has been explored in a higher education context (e.g. Albrecht et al. 2007, Atkinson-Palombo and Gebremichael 2012, Glantz and Kelman 2010, Naude 2012). To be honest, most articles seem highly generalized. It is interesting to see so many appear after Grieves (2008: 472) wrote: 'The ideal of the learning organization, to which organizations could aspire, is an impracticable and unobtainable myth . . . I believe we should now abandon the idea of the learning organization.' It is even more interesting that in 2001 Senge was classified as a management guru and the learning organization as a management fashion (Jackson 2001), though as Senge has sold one million books, he may not be too worried. But we still see, even more recently, a study on the application of learning organizations to sustainable hotels (Brazdaukas and Galgalaite 2015), though again highly generalized.

- Another approach which might initially seem promising is what one might call the 'checklist' approach. These are 'how to do it' manuals written for practising managers, and go through all aspects of the operations of a company to indicate how the company may 'green' its operations (e.g. Epstein and Buhovac 2014, Olson 2009, Weybricht 2010). In fact, they follow very closely, though in much greater detail, the necessarily brief outline in the sections above on sustainable business, though adding the treatment of issues in leadership, training, and internal cultural change. What is interesting is that, though these sources refer to examples from particular companies on particular aspects, they are devoid of complete examples of the application of the guides as a whole to individual companies, and evaluations thereof. In fact, the most detailed and recent of these (Epstein and Buhovac 2014) says:

> Rather than searching for one best company example to model, those companies and managers that want to improve their sustainability performance should instead look to adapt and adopt the various best practices of individual sustainability elements illustrated in this book. Through the detailed model, measures, and guidance to implementation presented here and the extensive best practice company examples from around the world, companies can select those practices that can be used to better implement sustainability in their own organizations to simultaneously improve corporate social, environmental, economic, *and* financial performance.

This approach may be OK for a manager in a large company, but it is not OK for teaching purposes, to show a student what might happen in an individual company or organization. And, to be somewhat critical, it is a rather partial approach, and not holistic, looking at the bits, rather than how they fit together. Maybe we want not a 'one best company example', but a 'one company example' with all the bits there. So a third approach is what we may call a pragmatic approach, but we see it going on all around us in most universities around the country, and with a substantial involvement of students. Let us look first at the broad principles of a pragmatic approach, making a summary of some key points from Epstein and Buhovac (2014). Then let us look at a real case study based on a UK university.

'Pragmatic' is the opposite of 'idealistic' (which might be applied to Senge's ideas). It describes a philosophy of 'doing what works best'. It is derived from the Greek 'pragma' or 'deed', and the word pragmatic has historically described philosophers and politicians who were concerned more with real-world application of ideas than with abstract notions. We want to get across to you what is involved in practice in developing sustainability principles in a company or organization in a way that you can grasp easily.

In their book, Epstein and Buhovac (2014: 204–5) describe a well-known tool to apply in this situation: the PDCA cycle (plan, do, check, and act). They say: 'PDCA is a valuable tool for learning and promoting change in organizations and provides a valuable framework for continuous improvement' (2014: 204). And it really is quite straightforward. The PDCA cycle consists of four phases, each involving key activities:

1. Plan
   - Conduct initial sustainability reviews
   - Define sustainability strategy
   - Design sustainability programs
   - Set objectives and targets
2. Do
   - Develop structure
   - Provide training
   - Introduce programs
3. Check
   - Conduct internal audit
   - Monitor and measure performance
4. Act
   - Management review

(Epstein and Buhovac 2014: 204)

In the case study to follow at the end of the chapter, we shall take Leeds Beckett University as an example. The PDCA cycle will not be referred to as such, but you will see a quite recognizable similarity. Why take this university? Is it the best in terms of its approach to sustainability issues? How would we know? In fact, there is a very active student organization which carries out annual sustainability rankings of UK universities. Leeds Beckett is quite good, but there are quite a few ranked higher. Given that previous editions of this book have taken the university as a case study of sustainable transport, it seems sensible to carry on the connection.

Stop and Think

Bearing in mind the discussion in this section, can you think of ways in which a company could embed sustainable thinking across the whole of its workforce, rather than just make piecemeal progress in limited aspects of its operations?

Looking ahead

The global environmental crisis makes progress with SD policies an immediate priority, yet progress seems to be slow. Many still disagree with arguments about global warming, though few disagree with the existence of other issues in SD such as pollution and resource scarcity. But even where people agree on the existence of all issues, including global warming, they may feel that policies suggested in response are wrong, or even disastrous. Where will we be in another five or ten years? Much depends on a variety of imponderable factors. Clearly, if we carry on as we are the future looks gloomy. Climate change (man induced or not), along with environmental degradation and exhaustion of key resources, especially oil, may suggest periods of future global instability.

On the other hand, some changes have taken place which promise to improve the prospects for achieving SD. The change of policy direction in the US, which produces about a quarter of global warming emissions, was one such positive aspect, and the US, via the shale oil/gas revolution, has done more to reduce, almost by accident, its CO_2 emissions than the UK or EU, where they are constant or have actually increased slightly. This change in the US position was reinforced at the December 2015 Paris Conference. However, the election of Donald Trump as US president on 8 November 2016 created an air of uncertainty. On 20 January 2017 he was inaugurated as the forty-fifth president. While he was an outspoken critic of environmental regulation during the presidential campaign, since becoming president his rhetoric has become more mixed, such that by midsummer 2017 as this book goes to press it is still very difficult to predict exactly what his future environmental path will be. Even at the G20 Summit in Hamburg on 7–8 July 2017 he declined to commit to joining with the other world leaders present on furthering the plans emanating from the December 2015 Paris Conference. In contrast, the continuing growth of China and India threatened to wipe out any gains from expected change in the US prior to the election, unless all can be persuaded to sign up to international agreements. But even here, attitudes in China and India concerning the environmental challenges facing the world seem to be changing. There is much debate about air pollution in China, and the need to reduce coal use and increase renewables. However, developing nations generally will only come on board to work towards implementation of the Paris Accords if compensated by developed ones, but, in a post-credit crunch period, can it be afforded? Here, progress after the December 2012 Doha Conference and the 2015 Paris Conference will be important. The twenty years post-Rio 1992 have been declared a massive failure. How long can we go on having conference after conference? The reactions from the November 2016 Marrakech Conference do not seem too promising. We seem to be on the threshold of both technical change, which may produce rapid change in many areas such as the evolution of cheaper non-polluting power sources (such as shale oil/gas); and of political change, where public attitudes are changing cumulatively, making many environmental measures more publicly acceptable in some countries but less so in others. And above all this, the world security situation has taken a gloomy turn. We have, of course, to hope that it is an optimistic scenario which actually occurs.

Summary

- Until the last two hundred years humankind made very little impact on this planet. But since about 1800 cumulative processes have led to a situation where in the last thirty to forty years we see ourselves faced with a variety of disasters induced by climate change, and threats to economic, social, and political stability, through to resource shortages and environmental pollution.
- The idea and strategy of SD is put forward as a way of ensuring that we collectively live within the constraints of our resources, and the capacity of the environment to absorb the effects of our presence on the planet.
- SD involves cooperative action at global, national, and local levels. Governments at all levels may set frameworks of laws and regulations involving a variety of market and non-market tools to keep the impact of our activities on the environment within acceptable limits.
- Business in all its forms is a central part of this process; being a major source of the problems in the first place but also a major contributor to solving them; and, as well, a major beneficiary in many ways from having them solved.

In conclusion:

- Business activity is a major contributor to global environmental problems (though not everyone agrees with this).
- And global environmental problems are a major threat to business activity.
- But global environmental problems are also a potential opportunity for business.
- Concepts of SD provide a framework for global thinking and local action.
- Most areas of business activity can be reframed in the light of these concepts to make a contribution to SD, while at the same time in most cases actually improving its economic efficiency.

Case Study: SD strategies in a large business: the case of Leeds Beckett University

There were 2,266,075 students in UK higher education in 2014/15 (www.hesa.ac.uk). A high percentage live away from home, or come from abroad, and they are heavy consumers of transport. There were 198,335 full-time and part-time academic staff (2014/15), plus many administrative and support staff. Higher education is a large foreign currency earner. It is big business. But some universities are massive, and equate with very large corporations both in their financial turnover and in the environmental footprint generated by their great range of activities. Thus, you the reader, and every student in the UK, are directly and intimately connected with this chapter's theme and you have your part to play.

Leeds Beckett University is a good example, being one of the largest universities in the country, with 19,827 full-time equivalent students in 2014, and about 3,200 staff (http://www.leedsbeckett.ac.uk/about/facts-and-figures.htm). Its turnover is about £215 million per annum (according to financial statement for year ending 31 July 2015), and it contributes about £520 million per annum to the regional economy (as per above website on 26 November 2016). Its economic impact is far larger than its turnover, as the student body, drawn from 144 countries, is a significant proportion of the total population of the city, and they are all consumers and spenders. The university has two major campuses. One of the campuses is on the edge of the city centre, while the Headingley campus is 4.4 miles north from the city centre on an outstanding parkland site, plus there is an intermediate small campus at Headingley Stadium (see Figure 8.4).

By any standards, the university is a big business, generating lots of activity and movement, consuming lots of resources, generating lots of waste, and, generally, having a very large environmental footprint. Like all universities of this scale, it is very conscious of its impact in all dimensions, especially sustainability, and this case study describes how the university began grappling with this issue, and its progress up to the present day. It will be compared with other universities in the process, and the contribution of the student body will be stressed.

The process to be described, which can be likened easily to the PDCA cycle outlined above, began in 1992 with an 'Initial Environmental Audit'. This followed the report of a government committee (the Toyne Committee 1993) which said: 'Every FHE institution, after consultation with its staff and students, should formally adopt and publicise, by the beginning of the academic year 1994/5, a comprehensive environmental policy statement together with an action plan for its implementation.' The final version of the university's Initial Environmental Audit, published in September 1993, did the following:

1. it assessed the current situation within the university with regard to the ground level of environmental awareness and management provision;
2. it examined in detail a number of aspects and sectors of university activity which had particular significance; and
3. it offered a number of initial conclusions and recommendations.

The Initial Environmental Audit covered the following areas: environmental awareness and management in the university; purchasing; paper; water; waste; litter; buildings; and energy.

The report noted that 'priorities will have to be isolated in order to provide a number of demonstration projects which illustrate the benefits to be obtained from improved environmental awareness and performance'. That is, not everything could be done at once. Using the information gathered in the audit was to be the basis for consulting and involving all staff and students, and establishing priorities for action. It is interesting that on several of the headings, the university lacked basic information. It illustrates that the triple bottom line often makes organizations do what they should be doing anyway.

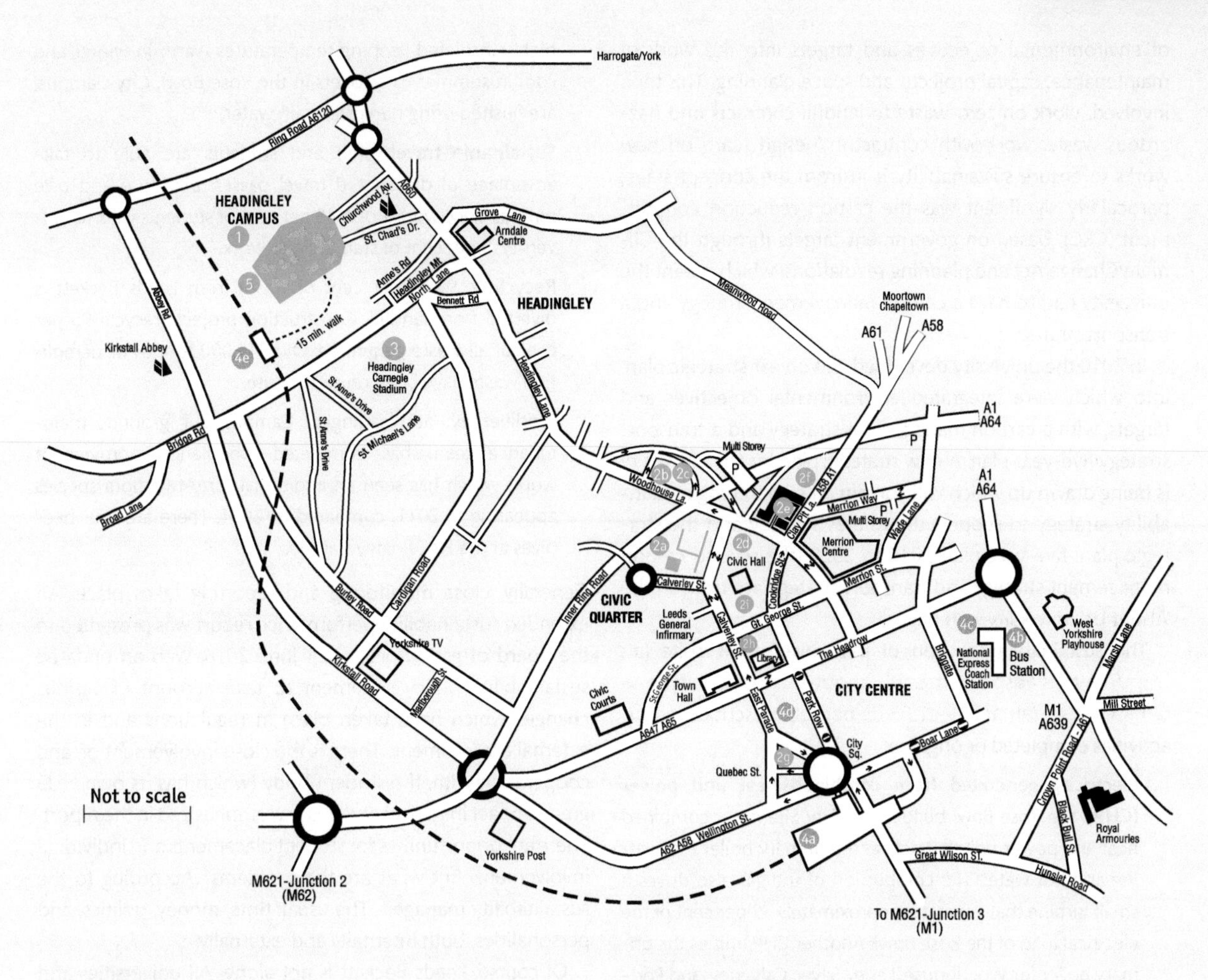

1 Headingley Campus
2 Civic Quarter
2a Calverley Street
2b Broadcasting Place – Humanities Building
2c Broadcasting Place – Arts Building
2c The Rose Bowl
2d Queen Square
The Northern Terrace
Queen Square Court
2e Hepworth Point
2f Cloth Hall Court
2g Old School Board
2h Electric Press Building
3 Headingley Carnegie Stadium & The Carnegie Stand
4 Travel
4a Leeds City Train Station
4b Leeds City Bus Station
4c National Express
Coach Station
4d Infirmary Street bus stop
4e Headingley Train Station
5 Carnegie Village

Figure 8.4 Location of main university facilities in Leeds

Note: Central area 'Civic Quarter' sites are 1a to 1h; suburban site or Headingley campus is 2; and student residences are 3a to 3j.

Source: www.leedsbeckett.ac.uk

An Environmental Steering Group was then established. Work then progressed to deal with some of the issues. A part-time environment manager was appointed in 2000. Then a full-time sustainability manager was appointed in 2002, initially based 50/50 between procurement and facilities management (i.e. land and buildings, later called estates services). In 2007 it was concluded that the most significant direct environmental impacts were in the estate, so the sustainability manager was based there full-time. Certification to ISO 14001 (referred to earlier in this chapter) was obtained in 2003 to recognize work done from 1992 to 2000. Various other standards were also used.

From the development of a sustainability strategy work progressed to implementation. This involved the integration of environmental objectives and targets into the work of maintenance, capital projects, and space planning. This then involved: work on zero waste to landfill contracts and hazardous waste; work with contractors/design team on new works to ensure sustainability is in from the concept stage; particularly significant was the carbon reduction commitment (CRC), based on government targets through the Climate Change Act and planning regulations, which meant the university had to have a carbon management strategy and a transport strategy.

In 2010 the university developed a five-year strategic plan, into which were integrated environmental objectives and targets, with a carbon management strategy and a transport strategy five-year plan. A new strategic plan for the university is being drawn up which will contain an overarching sustainability strategy to support the estates strategy and the strategic plan: five-year plan 2016 to 2021 (the revised carbon management strategy and transport strategy are now on the 'About Us' university web pages).

The sustainability section of the university website (at: http://www.leedsbeckett.ac.uk/about-our-university/sustainability/sustainability-at-leeds-beckett) describes various activities completed or ongoing:

(a) **Electricity generated from combined heat and power (CHP):** the Rose Bowl building on City Site has a combined heat and power unit that acts as the primary boiler for heating and hot water. The combustion of the gas also drives a small turbine that generates approximately 19 per cent of the electrical load of the Rose Bowl. Another CHP unit as the primary boiler for Woodhouse, Lesley Silver, Calverley, and Portland buildings has been installed. This is expected to reduce the carbon emissions for those buildings by 20 per cent. The unit was commissioned in January 2016.

(b) **Electricity generated from solar power:** there is a photovoltaic array on the Blue Gymnasium and Tennis Centre at the Headingley Campus, which generates 120,000 kWh per annum. This was commissioned in July 2014 and benefits from the feed-in-tariff at 10.8 pence per kWh. So, this saves on the electricity bill and generates an income.

(c) **Environmental management system:** the university is certified to the international environmental management standard ISO 14001. This is easily said, but as the Sustainability Manager points out: '14001 is based on a process of continual improvement (aka learning by doing) and I believe it is a good approach. The downside is it takes time and you need a dedicated team to do it.'

(d) **Carbon reduction:** in 2005 carbon emissions were 17,675 tonnes. Since then the university has reduced emissions to 13,779 tonnes, a total reduction of 22 per cent.

(e) **Sustainable construction:** Leeds Beckett is one of the first universities in the world to get Passivhaus status for Carnegie Village Halls of Residence. Passivhaus buildings are highly insulated keeping temperatures warm in winter and cool in summer. The toilets in the Rose Bowl, City Campus, are flushed using harvested rain water.

(f) **Sustainable travel:** staff and students are able to take advantage of discounted travel passes, bike hire and bike maintenance workshops; 48 per cent of students walk to university; 9 per cent of staff cycle to work.

(g) **Recycling:** 99.44 per cent of waste from Leeds Beckett is diverted from landfill. Construction projects recycle 95 per cent of all waste generated. Over 10,000 tonnes of demolition waste have been reused on-site.

(h) **Biodiversity:** at Headingley Campus our grounds maintenance team has completed woodland improvement works which has seen an additional forty-two flora species appearing in 2011, compared to 2004. There are four beehives at the Headingley Campus.

Generally, close monitoring and reporting takes place. An extended sustainability performance report was presented to the board of governors on 24 June 2016, with an updated sustainability policy statement to take account of various changes which have taken place in regulations and in the external environment. There is the close involvement of, and cooperation with, the student body (which has its own NUS green impact initiative) and this was emphasized in the report. There are opportunities for student placements and individual involvement. But what are the problems? According to the sustainability manager: 'The usual: time, money, politics, and personalities, both internally and externally.'

Of course, Leeds Beckett is not alone. All universities and institutes of higher education in the UK will be doing something of a similar nature to Leeds Beckett, depending on enthusiasm and circumstances to a higher or lower level: Leeds Beckett is just an example, and university websites around the country will have diverse stories to tell. From this point of view there is a very useful student-led initiative called People and Planet (at: https://peopleandplanet.org) which ranks the activity of 150 universities on a very wide range of criteria in the area of social justice and the environment. Clearly, its ambit is rather wider than the sphere of sustainability, and would encroach onto other chapters in this book. But it is still possible to pick out a range of criteria that you are interested in and compare universities. Plymouth University was top in 2015, but for 2016 Keele University was top. In 2015, Leeds Beckett was 45th out of 150, but in 2016 it had slipped to 46. This of course may be nothing to do with its sustainability performance, but relate to performance on social justice criteria (but it's still in the 2:1 class!) But we may hold back from further comment now, because the questions at the end of the case study will ask you to do some examination of your own university compared to another one: you may choose Keele, but clearly the circumstances of different universities vary, so you need to be making a relevant comparison. This is of course not an easy thing to do. Some universities have withdrawn from People and Planets, because of changing criteria and scoring mechanisms over the years. This does raise the question of how you can equitably compare sustainable performance across diverse institutions. Hence the need to make comparisons between comparable institutions.

So, to conclude, universities provide good pragmatic examples which are good for teaching purposes based on real, very large and complex businesses. Students can relate to them, and also think of making a contribution to sustainability issues. We have looked, perhaps arbitrarily, but with some reason, at Leeds Beckett, and this can be compared with many others on the People and Planet website.

Questions

1. **Compare the case study above to the PDCA cycle described earlier in the chapter. Does what happened at Leeds Beckett seem to follow the cycle? Compare with your own university. Basically, is it a simple, useful guide, in your opinion?**
2. **From a perusal of the Leeds Beckett website (sustainability section), do you feel there are any areas where you might have expected to see a greater emphasis, which does not appear to be addressed. Can you think of any reasons why this might be so?**
3. **Choose a university to compare with Leeds Beckett. This need not be your own university. Universities vary significantly in terms of size, location, age, and structure of the estate. Choose a similar one. Consider what you think are the most significant aspects of the Leeds Beckett situation where you could make useful comparisons with your chosen university (you will not be able to consider everything). If you choose a university above Leeds Beckett in the league table, assess in what ways it is supposed to be better than Leeds Becket, and say if you agree with this judgement by the compilers of the table. Equally, if you choose a university below Leeds Beckett in the league table, assess in what ways it is supposed to be worse than Leeds Beckett, and say if you agree with this judgement by the compilers of the table.**
4. **Then choose a university which may be your own, and compare it with another similar university in the league table. Repeat the process. Are any contrasts emerging?**

Review and discussion questions

1. It is sometimes argued that climate change has positive aspects for business, e.g. melting polar ice caps reduces transport distances for some sea voyages. Consider what other positive aspects of climate change there might be for business, and how they compare to the costs of climate change.
2. How would you respond to someone who argued that business had no real interest in becoming more environmentally responsible and that only compulsion by government would bring about change in business practices?
3. There are still groups who argue that the changes associated with what is described as 'global warming' fall within the range of natural variation, and policies to change business practices to counter its effects will impose needless costs on the economy and yet not make any difference to what is happening. What would you say in response to such arguments?
4. 'Market' approaches to environmental regulation are increasingly preferred to 'non-market' approaches and are gaining more public acceptability in areas like paying for road use. But do you feel that the public will accept the idea of paying for the amount of rubbish each household produces? What problems do you foresee in implementing such a policy?
5. What would you say if you heard someone express the view that global environmental problems are too complex and too far away for individuals and businesses to have any influence on them?

Assignments

1. Look at the environmental policies of your own university or college, or one near you. Does the institution you have chosen seem to be addressing the issues raised in this chapter?
2. This is the fourth edition of this chapter. The previous three editions are available to inspect in the online resources. Knowledge changes quickly in the three/four years between each edition. Compare this edition with the previous three editions, and assess what the main changes have been.
3. Visit the website of a FTSE 100 company of your choice and study critically its environmental profile. Choose a company and type its name into Google, Yahoo, or an other search engine. Each company has a lot of environment-related information on its site. Does it convince you?

Further reading

Blair and Hitchcock (2001) *provides a useful contextualization of environmental issues in business, and will allow many aspects of this chapter to be explored in greater depth.*

Epstein and Buhovac (2014) *a strongly practice-oriented text on implementing sustainability measures in a business.*

Ison, Peake, and Wall (2002) *a rigorous but readable background to many of the technical, theoretical, and policy issues discussed in this chapter.*

Olson (2009) *emphasis on strategic overview of incorporating the environmental dimension into business practices.*

Weybrecht (2010) *strong focus on translating ideas of sustainability into everyday business practices.*

Test your understanding of this chapter with online questions and answers, explore the subject further through web exercises, and use the weblinks to provide a quick resource for further research. Visit the online resources at www.oup.com/uk/wetherly_otter4e/

Useful websites

The following suggestions are a tiny proportion of even the most useful sites. Generally, surf with care, and consider whether promoters of a site have an axe to grind.

The quality daily newspapers:
www.guardian.co.uk
www.thetimes.co.uk
www.telegraph.co.uk
www.independent.co.uk

Government departments and related organizations:
www.defra.gov.uk
DEFRA (Department of Environment, Food and Rural Affairs)

www.gov.uk
Department for Transport

www.parliament.uk/commons
House of Commons Environment, Transport and Regional Affairs Committee

UK local authority sites all have the same address format, e.g. Leeds City Council is www.leeds.gov.uk

European sites:
www.europa.eu
European Union general site

www.eea.europa.eu
European Environment Agency

www.ec.europa.en/dgs/environment
European Union Environment Directorate

Various United Nations sites:
www.oneworld.org/uned-uk
UN Commission on Environment and Development

https://sustainabledevelopment.un.org
UN Commission on Sustainable Development

http://unep.frw.uva.nl
UN Environment Programme (UNEP)

Environmental pressure groups, e.g.:
www.foe.org.uk
Friends of the Earth

www.greenpeace.org.uk
Greenpeace

Other environmental websites:
www.wri.org
World Resources Institute

www.ieep.org.uk
Institute for European Environmental Policy

References

Albrecht, P., Burandt, S., and Schaltegger, S. (2007) 'Do sustainability projects stimulate organisational learning in universities?', *International Journal of Sustainability in Higher Education*, 8(4): 403–15

American Chemistry Council (2011) *Shale Gas and New Petrochemicals Investment: Benefits for the Economy, Jobs, and US Manufacturing* (accessed November 2017) **http://americanchemistry.com/ACC-Shale-Report**

Atkinson-Palombo, C. and Gebremichael, M. (2012) 'Creating a learning organization to promote sustainable water resources management in Ethiopia', *Journal of Sustainability Education*, 19 March (accessed November 2017) **http://www.jsedimensions.org/wordpress/content/creating-a-learning-organization-to-promote-sustainable-water-resources-management-in-ethiopia_2012_03**

Blair, A. and Hitchcock, D. (2001) *Environment and Business* (London: Routledge)

Booker, C. (2009) *The Real Global Warming Disaster: Is the Obsession with 'Climate Change' Turning out to Be the Most Costly Scientific Blunder in History?* (London: Continuum)

Boston Consulting Group (2012) 'Rising U.S. exports—plus reshoring—could help create up to 5 million jobs by 2020', 21 September (accessed November 2017) **http://www.bcg.com/media/PressReleaseDetails.aspx?id=tcm:12-116389**

Brazdaukas, M. and Gaigalaite, L. (2015) 'Sustainable hotels as learning organisations: innovative approaches towards employee training', *Journal of Creativity and Business Innovation*, 1 (accessed November 2017) **http://www.journalcbi.com/uploads/3/1/8/7/31878681/sustainable_hotels_as_learning_organisations_innovative_approaches_towards_employee_training..pdf**

Buckley, C. and Piao, V. (2016) 'Tainted wells across plains of China add to anxieties', *International New York Times*, 12 April, p. 7

Caldwell, R. (2011) 'Leadership and learning: a critical reexamination of Senge's learning organization', *Systemic Practice and Action Research*, 18(4)

Caldwell, R. (2012) 'Leadership and learning: a critical reexamination of Senge's learning organization', *Systemic Practice and Action Research*, 25(1): 39–55

Carbon Retirement (2011) *The State of Voluntary Carbon Offsetting in the FTSE100*, 17 April (accessed November 2017) **http://www.carbonretirement.com/sites/default/files/The%20State%20of%20Voluntary%20Carbon%20Offsetting%20in%20the%20FTSE%20100.pdf**

Chestney, N. (2012) 'EU climate fight hit by new record low carbon price', Reuters, 30 November (accessed November 2017) **http://uk.reuters.com/article/2012/11/30/us-carbon-price-idUKBRE8AT0U020121130**

Climate Institute (2009) 'Water and climate change' **http://www.climate.org/topics/water.html**

Crosbie, L. and Knight, K. (1995) *Strategy for Sustainable Business: Environmental Opportunity and Strategic Choice* (Maidenhead: McGraw-Hill)

DEFRA (2005) *Securing the Future: UK Government Sustainable Development Strategy* (accessed November 2017) **https://www.gov.uk/government/publications/securing-the-future-delivering-uk-sustainable-development-strategy**

DEFRA (2011) 'Mainstreaming sustainable development—the government's vision and what this means in practice', February (accessed November 2017) **http://www.environmental-mainstreaming.org/documents/UK%20Govt%20mainstreaming-sustainable-development%20(2011).pdf**

DEFRA (2013) *Sustainable Development Indicators July 2013* (accessed November 2017) **https://www.gov.uk/government/organisations/department-for-environment-food-rural-affairs/series/sustainable-development-indicators**

DfT (2005) *Making Travel Plans Work: Lessons from UK Case Studies*, Department for Transport (accessed November 2017) **http://www.dft.gov.uk/pgr/sustainable/travelplans/work**

Edgar, L. (2015) '"Fast track fracking" stirs up debate', *The Planner*, September, p. 6

Elkington, J. (1997) *Cannibals with Forks: The Triple Bottom Line of 21st Century Business* (Oxford: Capstone)

Epstein, M. J. and Buhovac, A. R. (2014) *Making Sustainability Work: Best Practices in Managing and Measuring Corporate Social, Environmental, and Economic Impacts* (2nd edn, Sheffield: Greenleaf Publishing)

European Commission (2009) *EU Action against Climate Change: The EU Emissions Trading Scheme* (accessed November 2017) **http://ec.europa.eu/environment/climat/pdf/brochures/ets_en.pdf**

Fleming, P. and Jones, M. T. (2013) *The End of Corporate Social Responsibility: Crisis and Critique* (London: Sage)

Fox, T. (2013) *Global Food: Waste Not, Want Not*, Institute of Mechanical Engineers, January (accessed November 2017) **www.imeche.org**

Frame, D. J. and Stone, D. A. (2012) 'Assessment of the first consensus prediction on climate change', *Nature Climate Change*, 9 December (accessed November 2017) **http://www.nature.com/nclimate/archive/issue.html?year=2012&month=12**

Giddens, A. (2009) *Politics of Climate Change* (London: Polity Press)

Gillingham, J. R. (2016) *The EU: An Obituary* (London: Verso)

Glantz, M. H. and Kelman, I. (2010) 'Universities as learning organisations for sustainability? The task of climate protection', in W. L. Filho (ed.), *Universities and Climate Change: Introducing Climate Change to University Programmes* (Heidelberg: Springer), 179–92

Gordon, R. J. (2012) 'Is US economic growth over? Faltering innovation confronts the six headwinds', Policy Insight No. 63, September, Centre for Economic Policy Research (accessed November 2017) **http://www.cepr.org/active/publications/policy_insights/viewpi.php?pino=63**

Grieves, J. (2008) 'Why we should abandon the idea of the learning organization', *Learning Organization*, 15(6): 463–73

Helm, D. (2012) *The Carbon Crunch: How We're Getting Climate Change Wrong—And How to Fix It* (Newhaven and London: Yale University Press)

HM Treasury (2006) *The Economics of Climate Change: The Stern Review* (accessed November 2017) **www.hm-treasury.gov.uk**

Hulme, M. (2009) *Why We Disagree about Climate Change: Understanding Controversy, Inaction, and Opportunity* (Cambridge: Cambridge University Press)

Hutchinson, A. and Hutchinson, F. (1997) *Environmental Business Management: Sustainable Development in the New Millennium* (Maidenhead: McGraw-Hill)

International Energy Agency (2001) *Towards a Sustainable Energy Future* (Paris: OECD)

IPCC (2007) *Climate Change 2007: Synthesis Report* (Fourth Assessment Report of the Intergovernmental Panel on Climate Change), ed. R. K. Pachauri and A. Reisinger (Geneva: IPCC)

Ison, S., Peake, S., and Wall, S. (2002) *Environmental Issues and Policies* (London: Prentice Hall)

Jackson, B. (2001) *Management Gurus and Management Fashions* (London: Routledge)

Leavenworth, S. (2016) 'Thirst for water means Beijing is sinking', *Guardian*, 25 June, p. 33

Mallet, V. (2016) 'Water wars', *Financial Times*, 14 April, p. 7

Naude, M. (2012) 'Sustainable development and organisational learning: mutually supportive', *International Journal of Business and Management Studies*, 1(1): 523-40

Olson, E. G. (2009) *Better Green Business: Handbook for Environmentally Responsible and Profitable Business Practices* (Pennsylvania, PA: Wharton School Publishing/Pearson)

Pacific Institute (2009) *Water Scarcity and Climate Change: Growing Risks for Businesses & Investors* (accessed November 2017) **http://www.pacinst.org/reports/business_water_climate/full_report.pdf**

Popper, K. (1963) *Conjectures and Refutations: The Growth of Scientific Knowledge* (London: Routledge)

Ridley, M. (2016) 'Time to embrace GM crops . . . and reap the rewards', *The Times*, 18 May, p. 4

Senge, P. M., Kleiner, A., Roberts, C., Ross, R. B., and Smith, B. J. (1994) *The Fifth Discipline Fieldbook* (New York: Currency Doubleday)

Shaxson, N. (2012) *Treasure Islands: Tax Havens and the Men Who Stole the World* (London: Vintage)

Sheffield, S., Wood, E. F., and Roderick, M. L. (2012) 'Little change in global drought over the past 60 years', *Nature*, 15 November, 491: 435–8

Silver, N. (2012) *The Signal and the Noise: The Art and Science of Prediction* (London: Allen Lane/Penguin)

Smith, M. K. (2001, 2007) 'The learning organization: principles, theory and practice', *Encyclopedia of Informal Education* (accessed November 2017) **http://www.infed.org/biblio/learning-organization.htm**

Smithers, R. (2012) 'M&S becomes "carbon neutral"', *The Guardian*, 7 June

Sustainable Development Commission (2005) *Climate Change Programme Review: The Submission of the Sustainable Development Commission to HM Government*

Toyne Committee (1993) *Environmental Responsibility: An Agenda for Further and Higher Education: Report of a Committee on Environmental Education in Further and Higher Education Appointed by the Department for Education and the Welsh Office* (London: HMSO)

Vidal, J. (2016) 'The politics of climate change is blinding us to dirty air', *Guardian*, 20 February, p. 29

WCED (1987) *Our Common Future, UN World Commission on Environment and Development* (Oxford: Oxford University Press)

WEF (2010) *Global Risks 2010: A Global Risk Network Report*, World Economic Forum, January (accessed November 2017) **http://www.weforum.org/pdf/globalrisk/globalrisks2010.pdf**

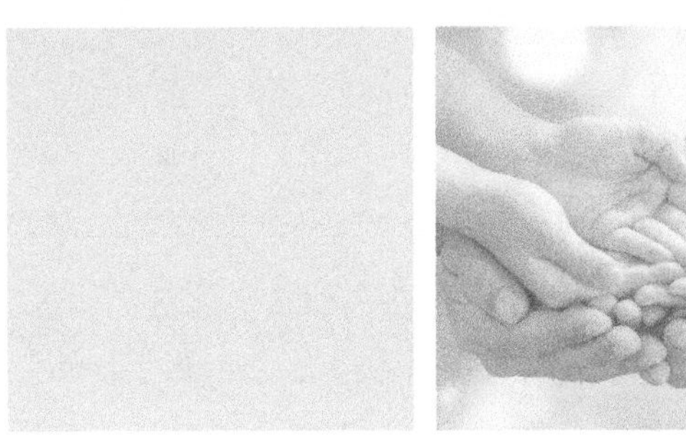

PART TWO
ISSUES

Chapter 9

How has macroeconomic policy changed in an era of uncertainty?

Chris Mulhearn and Mike Franco

Learning objectives

When you have completed this chapter, you will be able to:

- Define the terms macroeconomics and macroeconomic policy.
- Describe the three main objectives of macroeconomic policy and explain their importance.
- Articulate the importance of macroeconomic stability.
- Appraise the two sides of the stabilization policy debate.
- Explain how the UK's macroeconomic policy framework has been informed by the continuing debate over stabilization policy.
- Identify some of the possible implications of **Brexit** for the UK economy.

THEMES

The following themes of the book are especially relevant to this chapter

- COMPLEXITY Economies are complex entities—they are the product of millions of decisions taken every day by businesses, governments, and individuals. Macroeconomics is an attempt to render this complexity more manageable.
- DYNAMIC This chapter will show that macroeconomic thinking is itself an evolving phenomenon. Macroeconomic priorities change over time and therefore so too do the policies that governments pursue at the macroeconomic level.

Introduction: the economy, macroeconomic policy, and globalization

LOCAL TO GLOBAL In Chapter 2 we saw that it is convenient to think of the business environment as operating at microeconomic and macroeconomic levels. **Microeconomics** focuses on issues at the level of the individual—the individual consumer, the individual firm or public sector organization, the individual market, and so on. Typical questions here ask:

- What motivates consumer decisions to buy or not buy goods and services in a market?
- What steps should a firm take to ensure profit maximization?
- What factors explain the presence of many or few firms or even one firm in a particular industry?

In the present chapter our interest is in macroeconomics. Macroeconomics is concerned with the behaviour and performance of the economy as a whole. Here, rather than looking at individual consumers, business organizations, and markets, we focus simultaneously on *all* consumers, firms, and organizations in *all* the markets that together compose a national economy such as the UK. What are the principal features of interest in the macro economy? To an extent, these are simply the aggregations of the things we find relevant at the microeconomic level. For example, the micro issue of the output of goods and services of an individual firm or industry becomes, at the macro level, the output of all firms and industries. Similarly, an interest in the rate of change of the price of a particular product becomes an interpretation of the rate of change of all prices taken together—something conceptualized as the macroeconomic phenomenon of inflation.

Macroeconomic policy is concerned with the attempts of policymakers to influence broad economic conditions in order to improve the performance of the whole economy. All governments practise macroeconomic policymaking; however, the extent and form in which they do so are controversial. There are continuing debates about whether governments actually need to do very much at the macroeconomic level and, indeed, about whether they are actually capable of engineering the positive economic outcomes they desire.

Before reviewing some of these debates, we first need to establish what exactly it is that governments, business, workers, and other economic agents actually want from the economy. There is some degree of consensus here and we can in fact identify a number of macroeconomic policy objectives. Broadly, when these are *consistently* attained it is safe to say that we have a well-functioning business environment.

The objectives of macroeconomic policy

COMPLEXITY It is possible to identify three main macroeconomic policy objectives. These are:

- a stable and satisfactory rate of economic growth;
- a high and stable level of employment, and a consistently low level of unemployment;
- a low and stable rate of inflation.

Before discussing each of these objectives in some detail it is worth noting a common theme across all three—the notion of macroeconomic *stability*. This is particularly important in a business context. It should be intuitively evident that increased uncertainty in the economy makes business, organizational, and, indeed, personal decision-making more difficult processes. In the corporate world, decisions regarding output levels, recruitment, investment, diversification, acquisitions, and so on, carry more risk when decision-makers have less reliable information about general economic prospects. It would, for example, be more questionable for a firm to embark on a major investment project when the medium-term prospects for the economy are unclear than it would when economic growth, growth in consumer demand and inflation are settled at satisfactory rates for the foreseeable future. The implication is that uncertainty in the business environment tends to inhibit business activity—firms become hesitant about investment and expansion—and this in turn may provoke a vicious circle of deepening macroeconomic malaise. Overall then, while it is important to achieve specific macroeconomic policy objectives per se, it is just as important that this happens in a general climate of economic stability.

Macroeconomic objective 1: a stable and satisfactory rate of economic growth

Economic growth, introduced in Chapter 1, is the most basic measure of a country's economic performance. It measures the percentage rate of increase, year on year, in the value of the output of goods and services of countries like China, the UK, Vietnam, Zambia, or any other. We use value or price because this reflects the estimate of worth people freely put on the goods and services they buy. The total value of all goods and services produced by an economy each year is known as its **gross domestic product**, or **GDP**.

Table 9.1 shows that from 2005 to 2007 the UK's GDP growth rate hovered between 2.5 per cent and 3.0 per cent. This means that on average in each of these three years the UK produced 2.7 per cent more goods and services than it did in the previous year—more houses, cappuccinos, medical and educational services, music downloads, cinema attendances, and so on. Note that over the same period the UK's performance was actually bettered by each of China, Vietnam, and Zambia, where growth respectively averaged 12.7 per cent, 7.2 per cent, and 7.8 per cent per year. During the financial crisis that began in 2008 and subsequent recession, UK growth turned negative with an initial annual rate of –0.6 per cent before turning sharply negative in 2009 at –4.3 per cent. In 2008 and 2009 the UK was actually producing *fewer* goods and services than it had in the previous years—recording its worst growth performance since the **Great Depression** of the 1930s. In 2008/9 Chinese and Vietnamese growth slowed but continued to remain well above UK levels. Zambia appears to have weathered the crisis altogether though its recent growth record is a cause for concern, as too is China's. The UK's recovery has been sluggish with only 2014's growth rate surpassing the noted 2005–7 average. (See Mini-Case 9.1.)

But these comparisons are only half the story. Table 9.2 shows that, in per capita terms, the UK is a long way ahead of the other three economies. Per capita GDP is simply total GDP divided by the population among which it is 'shared'. In fact, expressed in dollars (to make comparisons easy), GDP or national income per person in the UK crept up from $41,567 in 2005 to $49,974 by 2007, before falling back to around $38,000 in the recession that started in 2008. It recovered unevenly thereafter and stood at $40,412 in 2016. In China in 2016 per

Table 9.1 Real percentage GDP growth for selected countries, 2005-16

	2005	2006	2007	2008	2009	2010	2011	2012	2013	2014	2015	2016
China[a]	11.3	12.7	14.2	9.6	9.2	10.6	9.5	7.9	7.8	7.3	6.9	6.6
UK[a]	3.0	2.5	2.6	-0.6	-4.3	1.9	1.5	1.3	1.9	3.1	2.2	1.8
Vietnam[a]	7.5	7.0	7.1	5.7	5.4	6.4	6.2	5.2	5.4	6.0	6.7	6.1
Zambia[b]	7.2	7.9	8.4	7.8	9.2	10.3	5.6	7.6	5.1	5.0	3.0	3.0

Source: International Monetary Fund.

Notes: [a] estimates after 2015; [b] estimates after 2014.

Mini-Case 9.1 Macroeconomic stability and its relevance to students at university

We can see that until the financial crisis in 2008 the British economy had grown at a relatively stable and satisfactory rate, especially when compared to its performance during the 1970s and 1980s. This was a positive thing for people—such as students and school leavers—who were about to enter the labour market. When the economy slumped the job prospects of new entrants to the labour market were dimmed as employers—depressed by a climate of uncertainty—shelved recruitment plans. Student readers of this book will be aware that the decision to stay in education carries some notable opportunity costs. Students must contribute significantly to their education in terms of tuition fees, living costs, and earnings foregone while at university. Such costs are worth incurring when set against potentially higher earnings in the future. But in the presence of economic instability, self-investment on this scale may appear a riskier proposition than when the economy is growing steadily and producing new jobs. So, economic stability is good for students: it makes the future a little more certain and helps them make more informed and better choices. However, even in a recession, it still makes sense to invest in one's own skills.

Question

Why, despite the economic downturn, was there a surge in applications to UK universities in 2009?

capita GDP was $8,261; in Vietnam $2,164; and in Zambia $1,231. This means that although the UK has been growing more slowly than the other economies and even had to cope with a period of sharp contraction, this relatively modest growth performance still translates each year into a lot more goods and services produced per person.

These data provide an important clue as to why we are interested in economic growth. Simply, the maintenance of a satisfactory growth rate over a sustained period means that a country is generating the potential to significantly raise its standard of living. And this—ultimately—is what a society wants: to generate high material living standards for its inhabitants. The UK enjoys a comparatively high standard of living because it is one of the world's biggest producers of goods and services and it has a relatively modest population size: it produces, and earns, a lot per head. (The UK's population is 61 million, compared to China's 1.3 billion; Vietnam's 87 million; and Zambia's 12 million.)

Can economies that are poorer than the UK catch up? At its recent growth rate, it would take Vietnam more than fifty years to surpass the UK's *present* level of overall output, and because of its larger population, even then its per capita income would not match that presently achieved by the UK. And the UK will itself continue to grow in the future meaning that the prospects for Vietnam to close on European-style prosperity levels must reside in the very distant future. Comparisons with China are equally interesting.

Table 9.2 GDP per capita expressed in US dollars, selected countries, 2005–16

	2005	2006	2007	2008	2009	2010	2011	2012	2013	2014	2015	2016
China[a]	1,766	2,111	2,703	3,467	3,838	4,524	5,583	6,329	7,081	7,719	8,141	8,261
UK[a]	41,567	44,096	49,974	46,890	38,181	38,738	41,260	41,684	42,453	46,479	43,902	40,412
Vietnam[b]	700	797	920	1,154	1,181	1,297	1,532	1,753	1,902	2,049	2,088	2,164
Zambia[c]	692	1,030	1,103	1,366	1,135	1,456	1,636	1,725	1,840	1,726	1,352	1,231

Source: International Monetary Fund.

Notes: [a] estimates after 2015; [b] estimates after 2014; [c] estimates after 2010.

China is now the world's second largest economy behind the US. Its GDP in absolute terms is about 20 per cent larger than the UK's: that is, it produces about 20 per cent more in goods and services than the UK. On the other hand, its population is about *twenty* times bigger which accounts for the UK's much higher per capita GDP—the UK produces nearly as much but with far fewer people. Again, if it can achieve consistent double-digit growth rates, China may eventually close the GDP per capita 'gap' between itself and countries such as the UK but it will take a long time to do so (which means that China's single-digit growth so far this decade is a worry). Why exactly is the UK so far ahead? One crucial factor among many others is that the UK's modern growth period began around 1750—so the UK has been engaged in the industrialized growth process for much longer than any of the comparator economies discussed here. We will return to the factors that influence long-term growth shortly.

Although GDP is relatively straightforward to understand as the sum total of the value of goods and services an economy produces, there are two additional points to make about it at this stage. First, to avoid the problem of double counting, we refer here only to **final or finished goods and services**. Think about the physical components of the book you are reading: essentially paper, glue, and ink. If we included the price of the book as a GDP item and then also included the price paid by the publisher for each of the paper, glue, and ink, we would be counting all these components twice—once on their own as raw materials and then again in the final good—the book itself. To avoid artificially inflating the GDP total in this way, we count only *final* goods and services.

Second, consider what would happen to GDP if most prices in the economy were rising rapidly. The market price of books would also be rising and so would their 'contribution' to GDP—we would end up with a bigger total; note this would be the case even if the output quantity of books in the economy remained the same. For this reason, we are interested in **real GDP**. You will notice that in Table 9.1 the GDP figures are given in real terms. This means that the figures have been adjusted to strip out the effects of continually rising prices or inflation. Increases in real GDP tell us that output is definitely rising—we have *more* goods and services. Increases in GDP solely generated by higher prices for a given quantity of goods and services—what is known as **money GDP**—do not indicate that there has been any improvement in economic performance as we don't have more output.

Stop and Think

When you work are you interested in whether any increase in your earnings is a real or money increase? You should be able to see that money increases may not leave you better off and could even leave you worse off. Real increases always leave you better off. If prices on average are rising by 3 per cent and your money wages also rise but only by 2 per cent, your real wages—meaning what you can afford to buy—have fallen by 1 per cent. You earn more money, but you can't buy as much as you did before. On the other hand, a real increase, above 3 per cent, leaves you unambiguously better off. The lesson here is that it's not the amount of money we have that counts but the quantity of goods and services into which money can be turned.

Long-term growth

Before we discuss in more detail economic growth as an objective of macroeconomic policy, let us briefly review the growth performance of the UK economy. Figure 9.1 depicts the long-term growth in real GDP since 1955. One thing is immediately clear—over this long period the UK has indeed tended to produce more and more output, to the extent that

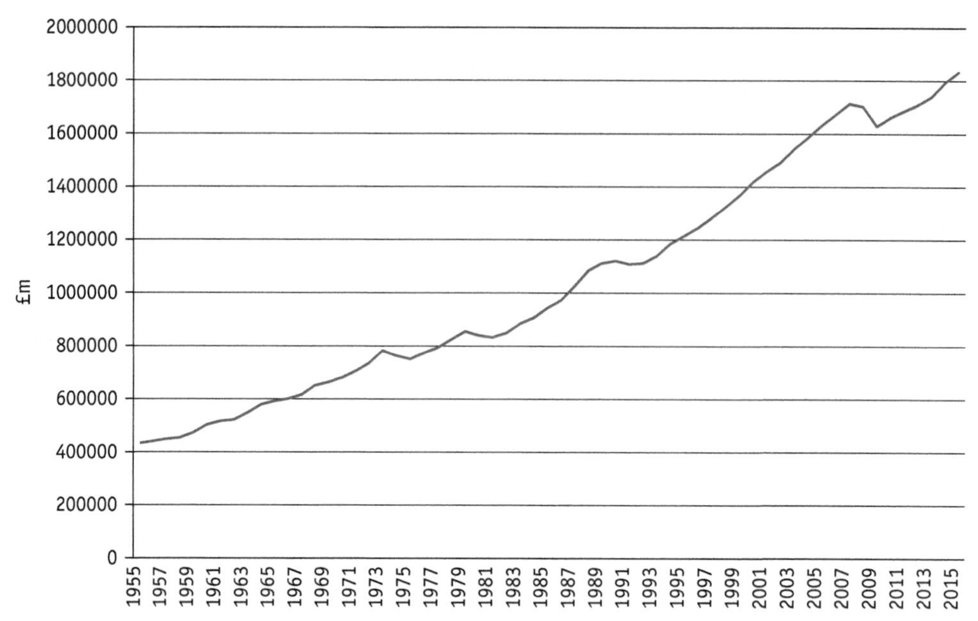

Figure 9.1 UK real GDP 1955–2015, £m

Source: ONS 2015.

it is now a trillion (a thousand billion) pound income economy, a milestone of prosperity reached in the mid 1990s; the two trillion mark should be reached in the next few years. Is the broad upward trajectory of GDP a testament to the competence of macroeconomic policy as practised by governments over the past sixty-odd years? Unfortunately, the answer to this question is no. In the longer term, capitalist economies tend to grow because of certain innate properties that have relatively little to do with the characteristically shorter-term time horizons of many governments. Long-term growth in these economies is predicated on rising **productivity** as discussed in Chapter 3. This chapter highlighted the combination of factors that are necessary if productivity growth is to be maintained.

Productivity refers to the quantity of goods and services that people produce in a given time period. Referring back to our country comparisons, it is clear that the UK is much more productive than China, Vietnam, or Zambia: it has a per capita GDP much higher than any of these countries. So, what explains the UK's relatively high productivity?

There are five main factors determining a country's capacity to efficiently produce:

- its investment in physical capital;
- its investment in human capital;
- its application of new technologies;
- its endowments of natural resources; and
- its level of institutional sophistication and institutional reliability.

Physical capital is the tools and equipment used in factories, offices, shops, hospitals, schools, transport systems, and so on. Physical capital makes the people who use it more productive. It follows that the more we invest in advanced machinery or computing systems or intelligently designed buildings, the more productive our economy becomes.

Human capital is the skill and knowledge accumulated by people that can be deployed in an economic setting. As you progress through the course you are presently studying you are investing in your own human capital. This is personally beneficial because, in the future, it increases your earning potential. Human capital increases the range of tasks of which we are all capable. So, employers pay highly qualified people more because they are likely to be more productive than the less qualified.

The application of new technologies entails taking advances in human knowledge and using them in an economic setting. A good modern example is the diffusion of information and communication technologies—most obviously mobile phones and the Internet—throughout very many aspects of economic life. These devices have revolutionized the quantity and quality of opportunities for human interaction and information gathering, creating wholly new kinds of activity and forms of business on a worldwide scale. Note that new technology is not precisely the same thing as physical or human capital. Presently, genetic engineering holds out the possibility that it may transform the productive potential of activities such as agriculture, animal farming, and medicine. Only if the potential of this new technology is fulfilled will we then see investment spilling out into related forms of physical and human capital.

Fourth, some countries enjoy prosperity and satisfactory rates of economic growth because they are able to produce particular goods or services in large quantities given their natural resource endowments. The obvious example here is oil, which has transformed the economic trajectories of many of the economies that possess it. In a similar manner, the possession of a good climate and attractive landscape enables countries to efficiently produce tourist services.

Finally, the institutional frameworks of economies are important: the stability of their political systems and legal and financial frameworks, for example. These provide the necessary setting within which economies develop and grow. The importance of reliable institutions was amply demonstrated during the financial crisis. There is little doubt that the world's banking system was in serious trouble with customers losing confidence in the banks and the banks losing confidence in one other. Had matters deteriorated further the threat to the integrity of whole economies would have quickly become evident. We rather take our financial systems for granted, but think what might happen if ATMs froze and banks simply closed their doors because they lacked money to meet their obligations: how could what we think of as normal life carry on?

So, the UK is a high-productivity economy in comparison to China, Vietnam, and Zambia because it scores highly on most, in fact probably all, of the above characteristics and has done so for a very long time. The UK is fortunate enough to be able to invest heavily and consistently in physical and human capital, it is a technologically sophisticated society, it also possesses a valuable natural resource in North Sea oil, and, finally, despite recent travails, its institutional framework is sophisticated and usually reliable. It is this combination that explains the long-term pattern of growth depicted in Figure 9.1.

Stop and Think* *From long-term to short-term growth

Look again carefully for a moment at Figure 9.1. Notice that the GDP curve is not very smooth in places. When is it bumpiest? Answer: roughly between 1974 and 1993, and then again, dramatically, since 2008. During the 1974–93 period, the curve both rises above its long-term trend and falls below it, exhibiting *variations in short-term growth rates* around the long-term trend. Now, while governments cannot really claim much credit for long-term growth, they can significantly influence the pattern of growth in the short term. This is what many governments were trying desperately to do as a result of the anticipated impact of the financial crisis. Whether or not they should attempt to do this is a highly controversial matter in macroeconomics and one we explore in some detail below.

Short-term growth

DYNAMIC Figure 9.2 depicts recent short-term UK GDP performance. The bars indicate growth each quarter. The recession immediately after the financial crisis is clearly evident, with five consecutive quarters of negative growth in 2008–9. Recession is defined as two successive quarters of negative growth. The recent plight of the UK economy may be contrasted with the long period up to 2007 when the economy enjoyed a reasonably steady rate of growth. Indeed, for the period 1993–2007 UK growth averaged almost 3 per cent per annum—the most sustained run since records began (glance back to Figure 9.1 to see this performance in a longer-term setting).

So, if an objective of macroeconomic policy is that economic growth should be stable and satisfactory, then this objective was being attained up until the financial crisis. But while growth at around 3 per cent for more than a decade is certainly stable, why exactly is it satisfactory? If China, Vietnam, and Zambia can enjoy the kind of rates indicated in Table 9.1, why cannot the UK do the same? After all, if growth is the key to living standards, higher growth would mean still higher living standards for UK citizens. The point here is that the trend line in Figure 9.1 approximates **potential GDP**, that is, the real GDP associated with the full employment of all the economy's resources. Look carefully again at Figure 9.1. Notice the steepness of the curve in the late 1980s. Here the UK expanded beyond this long-run potential with a growth rate between 1985 and 1988 of 4.3 per cent; in other words, it used its resources very intensively for a short time but found this impossible to sustain.

One last issue here—if the UK's potential GDP growth rate is somewhere around 3 per cent, how do poorer countries often manage to sustain much higher and, as in China's case, sometimes double-digit rates? The answer is that their relatively low levels of development mean they have both under-utilized resources and much greater scope for catch-up in productivity improvements.

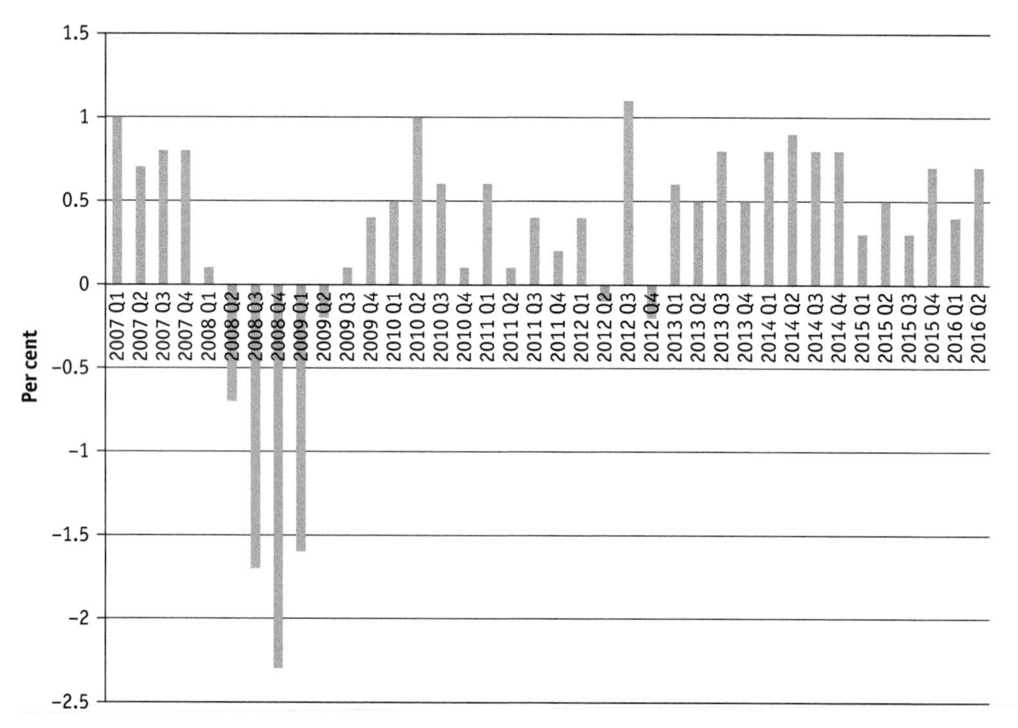

Figure 9.2 UK real quarterly GDP, 2007–16

Source: ONS 2016.

Macroeconomic objective 2: a high and stable level of employment, and a consistently low level of unemployment

There are strong connections between economic growth, employment, and unemployment. When the economy grows consistently near potential GDP its resources—including labour—are close to being fully utilized; there is, in other words, near-full employment. Conversely, in periods of slow growth or outright recession resources are under-utilized and higher levels of unemployment emerge as a policy problem.

Before we consider the actual path of employment and unemployment in the UK, let us reflect on the structure of the UK's labour force. The UK government divides the working-age population into two main categories:

- the economically active = the employed + those unemployed people actively seeking work; and
- the economically inactive: those of working age, not seeking work and therefore excluded from the unemployment figures.

Members of this last group would include, for example, people engaged in full-time care of their own children, early retirees, and lottery winners who've walked away from their jobs.

We are now in a position to define the unemployment and employment rates. The unemployment rate is the proportion of economically active people (i.e. those in employment or actively seeking work) without work. The unemployment rate is calculated as follows:

$$\text{unemployment rate} = (\text{number of unemployed/number economically active}) \times 100.$$

The employment rate is the proportion of the working-age population that is in employment. It is calculated as follows:

$$\text{employment rate} = (\text{number of people employed/working-age population}) \times 100.$$

Figures 9.3 and 9.4, when read in conjunction with Figure 9.2, illustrate the dynamic relationship between economic growth and the labour market. As growth starts its precipitous fall early in 2008 (see the quarterly data in Figure 9.2) unemployment rapidly increases from a little over 5 per cent to a peak of 8.4 per cent in the last quarter of 2011 (see Figure 9.3). Over roughly the same period the employment rate departs from its pre-crisis peak of 73 per cent and falls to a little over 70 per cent (see Figure 9.4). The most recent data show the employment rate to be approaching 75 per cent.

But why do we desire high rates of employment? We know that economic growth is desirable as it is an effective means of securing rising living standards. The same reasoning applies in the case of employment. The greater the proportion of the economically active population that is able to secure employment, the greater the number of goods and services that can be produced and the better off the UK plc becomes.

The issue of unemployment is slightly more complex as here there are social as well as economic difficulties. We will deal with the economic difficulties first. Any introductory economics textbook tells us that economics explores the choices that all societies have to make in matching the scarce resources they possess to the limitless wants of their populations. No matter how materially wealthy it becomes, no society can escape difficult decisions about which wants to meet and which to leave unfulfilled. What is left understood here is that societies try to use all the resources they have; waste is not really on anyone's agenda. Yet this is actually what unemployment amounts to—a waste of what is arguably society's most precious resource: its economically active people. And it gets worse. It costs nothing to leave coal or oil

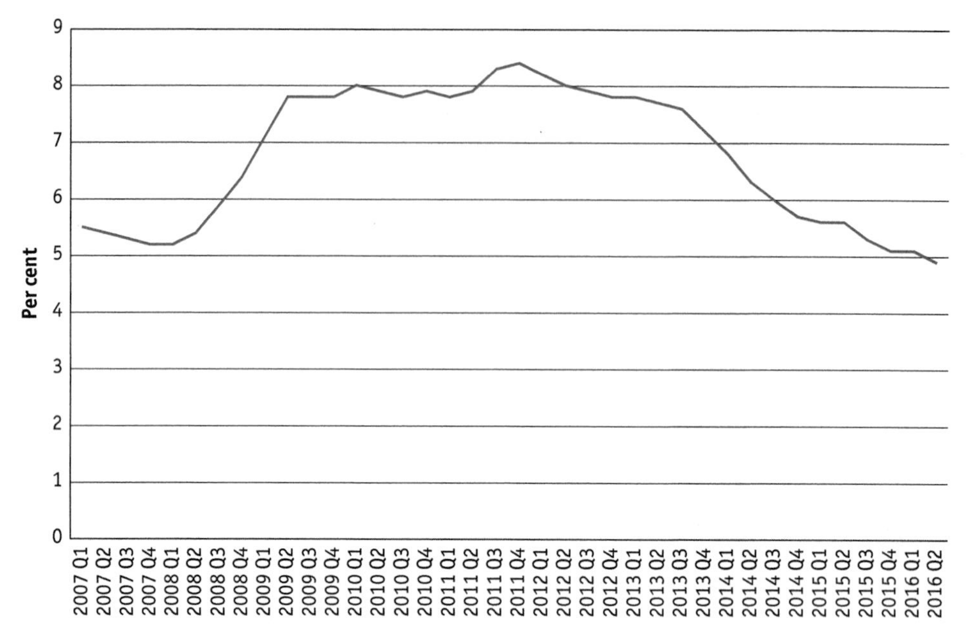

Figure 9.3 UK unemployment rate, 2007–16
Source: ONS 2016.

reserves in the ground; nor do these reserves decay or disappear if we neglect them. The same cannot be said for labour. In a modern, civilized society unemployed people are supported through the tax and benefits system. Those in work pay tax and a proportion of this money is transferred to the unemployed—thus it actually costs society as a whole to waste resources in this way. Also lost are the direct taxes (i.e. income tax and national insurance contributions) the unemployed themselves would have contributed were they in jobs, as well as lost indirect taxes (i.e. VAT) associated with a fall in expenditure by the unemployed. Moreover, the longer

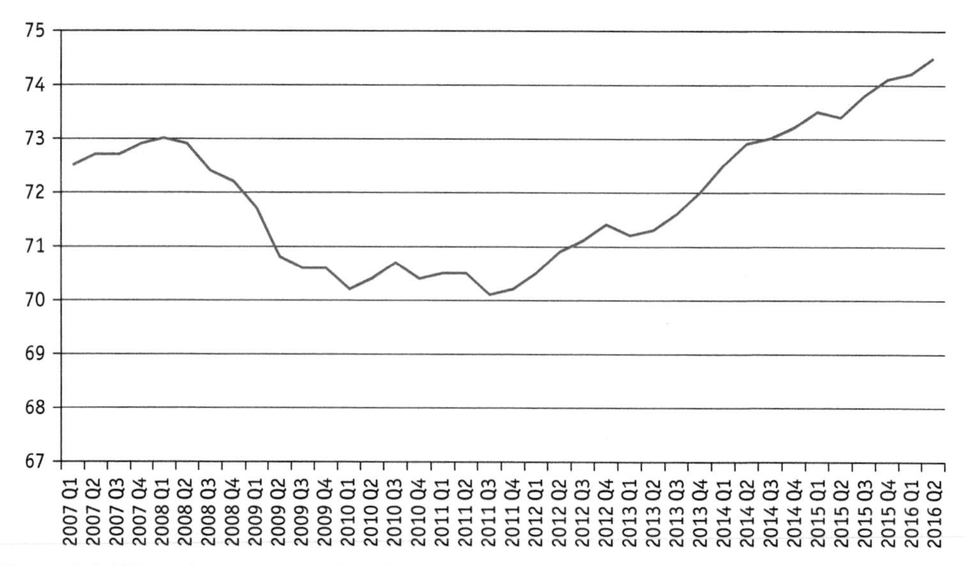

Figure 9.4 UK employment rate, 2007–16
Source: ONS 2016.

people are unemployed the more likely it is that they will find their skills outdated and their human capital eroded, even to the point at which they may become so disillusioned as to stop seeking work entirely, thus joining the economically inactive.

STAKEHOLDERS **VALUES** The social difficulties that unemployment brings are of two kinds. First, those experienced by the unemployed themselves and their families. Despite the social security systems in the advanced economies, unemployment is associated with low incomes and poverty. Lack of money leads to other problems: for example, unemployed people and their families tend to suffer poor health and lower than average levels of educational attainment. More generally, the effect of unemployment—especially if it is prolonged—is to economically disenfranchise sections of the population. Such social exclusion may carry a range of wider consequences: political and ethnic tensions and rising crime have all been associated with high levels of unemployment.

DYNAMIC **COMPLEXITY** Finally, let us think about policy objectives in the area of employment and unemployment. It would be simple to assume that the government's preference would be for everyone who is economically active to be in work—in other words, the unemployment rate would be zero. This is a nice idea, but impossible in a practical sense. Why? Consider Figure 9.5. This illustrates the dynamism and complexity of the macroeconomic labour market, with unemployment conceptualized as a pool of unemployed labour. The rate of unemployment will reflect the depth of the pool and the force of the flows into and out of it.

Taking inflows first, the pool deepens as new entrants join the labour market from school or college but do not immediately find work. Similarly, re-entrants to the labour market who have been economically inactive but now want to work again will deepen the pool if they do not go straight into a job. People who leave employment involuntarily through redundancy and those

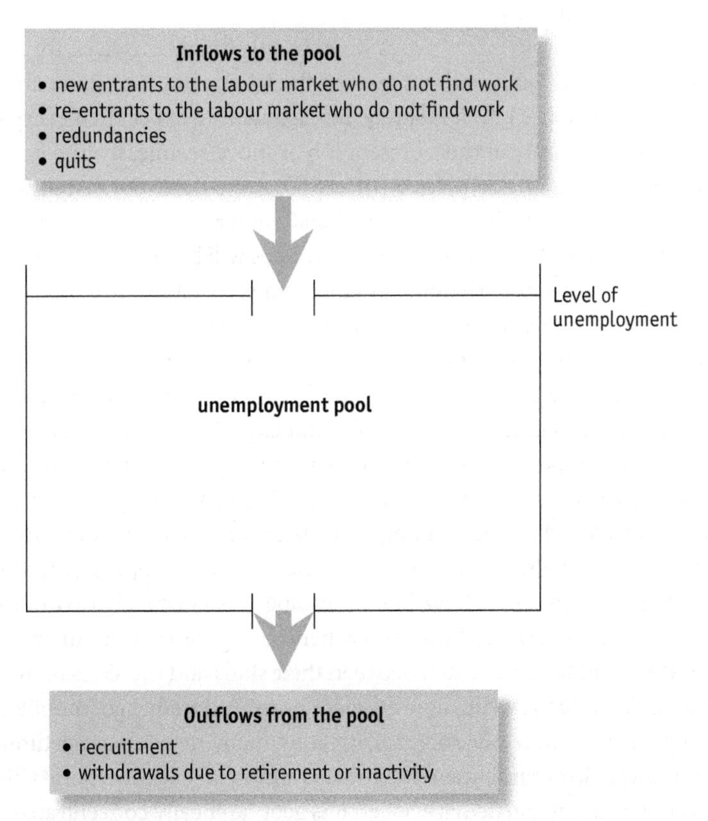

Figure 9.5 The unemployment pool

who choose to leave their jobs will also cause the pool to deepen. In both cases we assume that there is a determination to stay in the labour market and find new work.

Now outflows. Unemployed people who find work will cause the pool to become shallower, as will those who decide to end a period of unemployment by ceasing to look for work (they become economically inactive), or permanently retire.

Think for a moment about what will happen to the pool in a period of decelerating economic growth or recession. The forces generating inflows gather momentum. Fewer new entrants and re-entrants to the labour market will immediately find work; more firms are likely to be making workers redundant, and people who voluntarily quit jobs are less likely to quickly find new ones. On the other hand, recession minimizes recruitment and stems outflows—overall then, the pool deepens and the unemployment rate climbs.

Stop and Think

What happens to the unemployment pool's inflows and outflows and the unemployment rate when growth is stable and satisfactory?

Your answer to this question may have been that inflows should dwindle and that outflows should increase, perhaps to the point at which the pool is drained completely and unemployment is indeed zero. But in truth, zero can never happen. Figure 9.5 suggests that the labour market is a fairly complex entity but there is still a little more to say about it. We can in fact identify two categories of unemployment that in a modern and innovative economy can never be entirely eliminated. These are frictional (or search) and structural (or mismatch) unemployment.

Frictional or search unemployment arises when people find themselves, for any number of reasons, temporarily between jobs without leaving the labour market. There are now around 29 million people in work in the UK. It is surely unreasonable to expect that every single one of these people will either continue in their present job or move seamlessly into another without experiencing a single period of unemployment. At the same time, the fortunes of individual business organizations will vary. Some will lay off staff, others will be recruiting new employees; some organizations will close entirely, while new ones will be created. In this environment of change and displacement some frictional unemployment is naturally to be expected.

Structural or mismatch unemployment is also a consequence of economic evolution and results from a mismatch between the skills or location of existing job vacancies and the present skills or location of the unemployed. It reflects the fact that over time whole industries decay and disappear, casting the people who have skills and experience attuned to those industries economically adrift. These people are said to be structurally unemployed in as much as the entire industry in which they worked has disappeared. Not too long ago, Britain had large numbers of people employed in coal mining. Now there are relatively few miners as we rely more on imported coal and alternative sources of energy. The scrapping of the coal industry was a serious problem for people whose human capital was effectively tied to that industry. Redundant miners cannot overnight become teachers or engineers. Until unemployed people can be retrained there will be a mismatch between their skills and the skills required to fill job vacancies. But as some industries die, new ones are born. A decade ago, mobile phones were relatively rare, now they saturate our societies, creating many new job opportunities, perhaps for retrained ex-miners. Structural unemployment is simply a reflection of this kind of industrial change. It is not pleasant, particularly when it is geographically concentrated in particular places as mining was, but in a market economy it is to some extent inevitable.

Given these complications, what is the employment/unemployment macroeconomic policy objective? Reflecting the complexity and dynamism of the labour market, there is often no particular target for the unemployment rate. Rather, for many governments, there is an ambition to ensure that those economically active people looking for work are able to find it.

Macroeconomic objective 3: a low and stable rate of inflation

Inflation is a process of continually rising prices. The inflation rate is the average rate of change of the prices of goods and services in the economy over a given period. For example, in July 2017 the inflation rate in the UK was 2.6 per cent. This means that the prices in the UK were on average then rising by 2.6 per cent per year. Inflation in the UK is measured by the consumer prices index (CPI) which reveals changes in the cost of a representative basket of goods and services—a range of items that most people buy.

A low and stable rate of inflation is desirable for a number of reasons. For the most part these have to do with the fact that we live in economies that rely heavily on markets to allocate resources. In Chapter 2 we saw how markets are coordinated by price signals. The movements of prices provide incentives to producers and consumers to behave in particular ways. For example, higher prices may signal the possibility of greater profit to producers and encourage them to expand output. On the other hand, consumers may respond to higher prices by contracting demand. But what defines a good signal? One important property is stability. Think what would happen to traffic flows if traffic signals were to have their timings randomly set. You pull up at a stop light and you're unsure if you're going to be stuck there for one minute, three minutes, or even ten. The same is true for all other drivers. Our guess is that this would soon result in gridlock and accidents as people jumped traffic lights and made bad driving decisions. Traffic signals do a good job when they're predictable and people feel they can rely on them. In markets, price signals are also better if they're reliable and people feel they can use them to make informed choices—this happens when inflation is low and stable.

INTERACTION We can in fact identify a number of specific costs of inflation. The first of these—in keeping with our example above—has to do with uncertainty. Consumers and producers make decisions in markets by taking account of **relative prices**, that is the price of one good or service compared to another. When inflation is low and stable, relative prices are easy to read and consumers can make informed choices about whether to buy this or that good, taking price into account. Similarly, producers have good indicators of which markets offer better prospects for investment, and which are best left alone. In the presence of high and, therefore, increasingly variable inflation, such clarity is lost. The general process of inflation across all goods and services masks relative price movements between particular goods and services, leading to poorer decision-making. Thus, in a low-inflation environment, if the price of outdoor-wear clothing starts to rise, this is a signal for firms like Timberland to invest more. But in a high-inflation environment poor old Timberland just can't tell if this is a definite signal from the rugged outdoor types populating this market that they want more kit, or just part of the background noise of general inflation. Replicate Timberland's uncertainty across the whole economy and an inflation-induced recipe for some very poorly informed decision-making begins to emerge.

VALUES Inflation can also arbitrarily redistribute income and wealth between different groups in society, abstracting from what might be deserved or socially desired. For example, in a low-inflation environment, borrowers find the real values of their debts are largely maintained and they must pay them off as expected. But in the presence of high inflation the real values of debts are quickly eroded as prices and money wages surge upwards—an unlooked

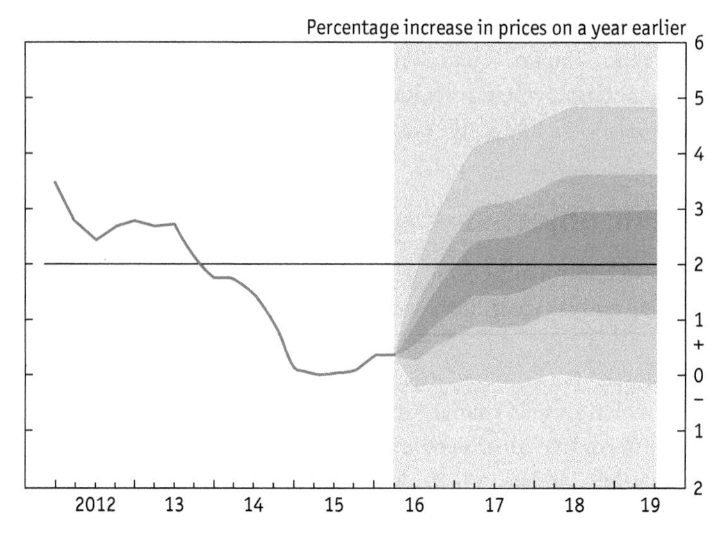

Figure 9.6 UK CPI inflation rate and projection
Source: Bank of England *Inflation Report* August 2016.

for but hardly merited bonus for borrowers. Savers find themselves in the opposite position. A pensioner may have saved over a working life to provide for his or her retirement but a sudden surge in inflation could rapidly reduce the real value of what has been saved, with no further opportunity to start again. These arbitrary changes are unhelpful in a market economy where it is expected that reward should bear at least some relation to effort or sacrifice.

The British government has established an annual target of 2 per cent for UK inflation. Figure 9.6 depicts recent UK inflation performance, and the evidence is that the actual inflation performance for the moment is close to but slightly above target. The shaded area of the figure contains an inflation projection in which the intensity of the shading reflects variation in the probability of outcome.

The case for stabilizing the economy

VALUES One of the big unresolved questions in macroeconomics is whether or not policymakers should try to stabilize the levels of output and employment in the economy. There really is no agreement here and we introduced the broad competing perspectives regarding this question in Chapter 2. Some economists—following the tradition established in the 1930s by the famous British economist John Maynard Keynes—suppose that capitalist economies often behave erratically. If they are caught up in some unforeseen circumstances—an economic shock—they can move into devastating recessions from which it may take some time to recover. The implication these economists draw is that, because economies tend not to recover spontaneously or quickly, it is up to governments to help them get back into shape using particular macroeconomic tools in fairly expansive ways. This could mean decisive stabilization policy measures such as those used to counteract the sharp deceleration in growth in 2008–9.

However, a second set of economists, broadly in the neoclassical school and including the late American economist Milton Friedman, is deeply suspicious of this argument. People like Friedman argue that capitalist economies, while they can slide into recession, have well-developed and relatively fast-acting powers of recovery. This means that there is no need for governments to excessively meddle in the economy—it can take care of itself. Moreover, in this view, while government intervention does little or nothing for output and employment in the long run, it does have the very dangerous side effect of increasing the money supply and hence potentially fuelling inflation. For this reason, this group of economists is referred to as 'monetarists'. The implication of their argument is that, if the economy is mostly but not exclusively left to itself, one should expect a GDP growth path similar to that in Figure 9.1, but without any substantial or lengthy deviations away from potential GDP.

To fully understand the basis of the differences between these two groups it is necessary to consider their contrasting views about what can be reasonably done with the two major tools of macroeconomic policy: **fiscal policy** and **monetary policy**. We also need to review a little economic history to see how these tools have been used—with mixed results—in the more distant and recent past. We will begin with brief definitions of fiscal and monetary policy.

Fiscal policy involves government expenditure and taxation. As taxation is government income, fiscal policy is the balance between government income and expenditure. For example, expansionary fiscal policy involves governments spending more than they raise in taxation.

Monetary policy is implemented chiefly through the setting of interest rates, which, in the UK, are controlled by the Monetary Policy Committee of the Bank of England. More recently it has also encompassed what for some economists is the highly controversial process of *quantitative easing*—a rather benign phrase for the (electronic) printing of money by the authorities.

LOCAL TO GLOBAL The story of modern macroeconomics really begins with the work of Keynes and, in particular, with his 1936 book, *The General Theory of Employment, Interest and Money*. In this volume, and elsewhere, Keynes provided the first comprehensive explanation of how recessions can occur, how they can persist, and what governments can do to help economies recover from them. Keynes's work was developed first in the 1920s in response to extremely sluggish British growth throughout this decade; however, it gained a new relevance from 1929 when not just one economy but the whole world slid into a depression of unprecedented proportions. This became known as the Great Depression.

Keynes's explanation of the Great Depression and, indeed, of recessions generally was relatively simple. He argued that the level of activity in an economy was determined by the prevailing level of **aggregate demand**, that is, the total level of demand for all goods and services. In Keynes's view it was relatively easy for aggregate demand to fall, and once it did there was nothing in the economy which would prompt its early recovery: an economy in recession would very likely stay in recession. Take an economy that is enjoying steady growth with low unemployment. If, for some reason, businesses become generally pessimistic about the future, they will tend to reduce investment—cutting their own spending until a time when economic prospects have improved. But, because *many* businesses act in this way, the results for the economy and everyone in it are catastrophic. As investment falls, firms are doing two things. First, they are reducing the business that they do with each other—cancelling or not renewing orders for materials and equipment. Second, they are shelving recruitment plans, and some will be laying off employees. You will agree that things do not look good, but potentially this is just the start. The process becomes a reciprocally confirming one. Business confidence was low and businesses reacted as they thought appropriate. But now, as orders dry up and unemployment begins to rise, it's clear they were right—things *are* bad. Demand in the economy now falls even further—firms buy less and less from each other and rising unemployment means that consumer demand is weakening considerably. At some point, this downward spiral will slow but it may be very a long time before any recovery happens. In the US during the Great Depression, for example, real GDP fell by 28 per cent and unemployment increased to 25 per cent. For a time there, it looked like **capitalism** itself was collapsing.

COMPLEXITY **STAKEHOLDERS** In Keynes's view, the correct way to understand what was going on in such circumstances was to appreciate the importance of aggregate demand. It is the fall in demand which triggers and feeds economic decline. Eventually the process will come to a halt but, critically, there is no natural recovery mechanism. If aggregate demand eventually falls by, say, a quarter, firms will have no incentive to produce more output than can be bought by this lower level of demand, and they will require many fewer workers than before as they are now producing much less. We illustrate the process in Figure 9.7. In panel (a) of the figure, the economy is operating at potential GDP (1) and the output of goods and services (2) is bought by consumers and firms (3), meaning that the current level of aggregate demand (4) is sufficient to maintain the economy at potential GDP. However, in panel (b) of Figure 9.7,

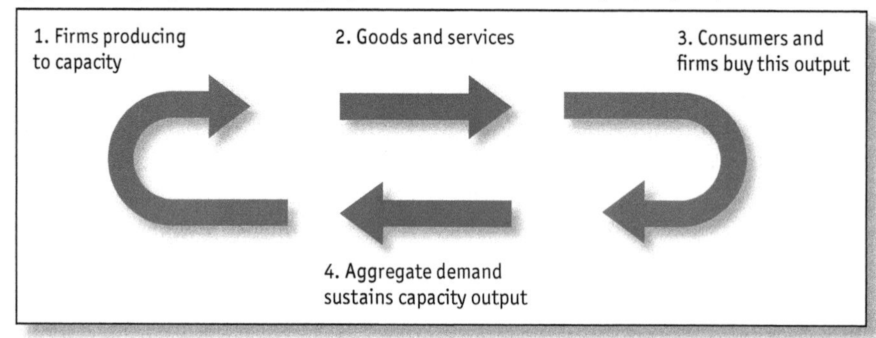

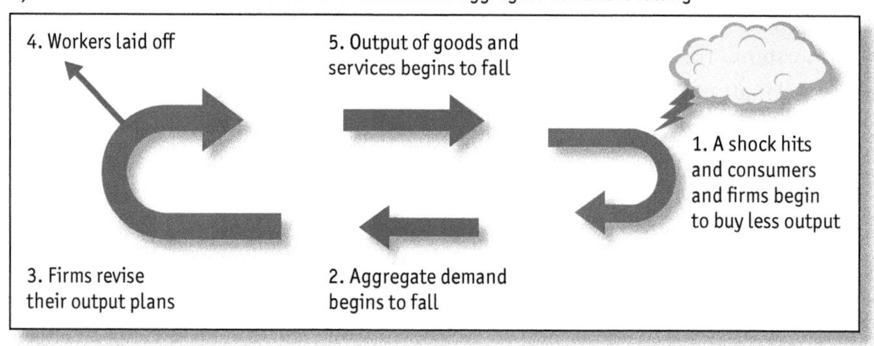

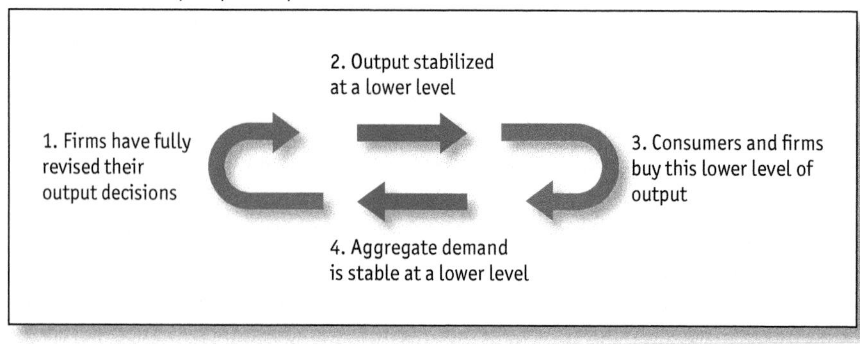

Figure 9.7 A demand-driven economic collapse

an adverse shock hits the economy and consumers and firms begin to buy less output (1). This means that aggregate demand is falling (2). Accordingly, firms begin to revise their output plans (3), and lay off workers (4). Output in the economy begins to fall (5). Finally, in panel (c) it is evident that the process has spiralled down to a sustainable level. Here, firms have fully revised their output decisions (1), and output has stabilized at a lower level (2). We know that this position is stable and sustainable because consumers and firms buy all this output (3), which means that aggregate demand is once again sufficient to maintain GDP (4), but now at a level below its potential. The economy is mired in recession: GDP has fallen and unemployment has risen and, most important, there is nothing on the horizon that will change things anytime soon.

From a Keynesian perspective, then, economies are fragile things, prone to crises of confidence. Aggregate demand is the key to improving matters, but how can demand be revived given, in Keynes's phrase, 'the haltering, wavering mood' of business? His solution was relatively simple. If there was no natural force in the economy capable of generating a recovery in aggregate demand and business confidence, one would have to be created. Keynes proposed that governments should themselves step in and raise demand using expansionary fiscal and monetary policy. Over time this would rejuvenate business confidence and reverse the depressive processes outlined in Figure 9.7, bringing the economy back close to potential GDP and full employment.

As noted, one form of expansionary fiscal policy involves the government spending more than it receives in taxes, financed by borrowing. The new spending might be on, for example, new schools, roads, or hospitals. In many ways its actual form is less important than the fact that it is happening. Once the process has started business takes heart and begins to plan once again for expansion. Of course, some firms benefit quickly and directly—those building the schools, roads, and hospitals. But others will also respond as employment and consumer demand begins to revive. In effect the government needs only to initiate economic revival—it is not required to make good the entire aggregate-demand 'gap' on its own. Moreover, as either a supplement or alternative to spending more itself, the government can decide to cut taxes leaving businesses and individual tax payers with more disposable income. This is also a means of prompting an increase in aggregate demand.

Expansionary monetary policy might also be used as a tool of recovery. Were the government to engineer a reduction in interest rates, firms and consumers may respond to the availability of cheaper finance by investing and spending more freely. However, Keynes was less sure that this approach would work as quickly and directly when compared to fiscal expansion. Lower interest rates would, in all likelihood, prompt business and individuals to spend more, but if the government increased its spending there was no possible doubt that aggregate demand would rise.

As noted, in response to the 2008–9 recession, the UK authorities engaged in so-called quantitative easing, a euphemism for the printing of money. This unprecedented step was taken because UK interest rates had already been pushed down to the historically low level of 0.5 per cent and as interest rates cannot be less than zero there was little room to reduce them further (although at the time of writing they have fallen by a further 0.25 per cent). The authorities have since implemented a programme designed to inject £445 billion into the British economy, principally by buying government and other bonds held by private sector firms; the intention is to encourage these institutions to add to demand in the economy by increasing their own spending.

Stop and Think Spending and interest rates

Why might business organizations and individuals choose to increase spending as interest rates come down? The answer is that interest rates indicate the cost of borrowing. With lower interest rates all forms of borrowing become cheaper and therefore economic agents are encouraged to both borrow and spend more. Why might the stimulant effect of lower interest rates be reduced as they approach zero?

Table 9.3 GDP growth rates for the G7, 1870–2016 (%)

Country	1870–1913	1913–50	1950–73	1973–98	1998–2016[a]
France	1.63	1.15	5.05	2.10	1.53
Germany	2.83	0.30	5.68	1.76	1.36
Italy	1.94	1.49	5.64	2.28	0.39
UK	1.90	1.19	2.93	2.00	2.01
US	3.94	2.84	3.93	2.99	2.20
Canada	4.02	2.94	4.98	2.80	2.35
Japan	2.44	2.21	9.29	2.97	0.62

Sources: Snowdon and Vane (2005), adapted from Maddison (2001); IMF.

Note: [a] data for 2016 are estimated.

According to the late Nobel Prize-winning economist Franco Modigliani, what Keynes had outlined in the *General Theory of Employment, Interest and Money* was the following 'need/can/should' case for stabilizing the levels of output and employment:

- governments *need* to stabilize the economy—capitalist economies have a tendency to slip easily into recession; they are inherently unstable;
- governments *can* stabilize the economy—they have the requisite fiscal and monetary tools; and
- governments *should* therefore stabilize the economy—there is no case for them not to do so.

Following the end of the Second World War in 1945 **Keynesianism** came to dominate macroeconomic policymaking in the capitalist economies and stabilization policy was widely practised, to apparently good effect. The period from 1945 until the early 1970s became known as the post-war boom during which, in practically all of the western industrial economies, GDP expanded at unprecedented and sustained rates and, as a corollary, employment rates increased, and unemployment remained low and stable. Table 9.3 shows average annual growth rates for the so-called G7—the world's leading industrial nations—since 1870. The subperiod from 1950–73 clearly stands in a class by itself in terms of the growth rates collectively achieved by these economies, with particularly strong performances in continental Europe and Japan.

Questioning the need to stabilize output and employment

DYNAMIC Unfortunately, the post-war boom petered out in the early 1970s and the effectiveness of stabilization policy began to be disputed. This was not just because, as Table 9.3 indicates, growth was much slower in the period 1973–98 for all of the G7, but also because of

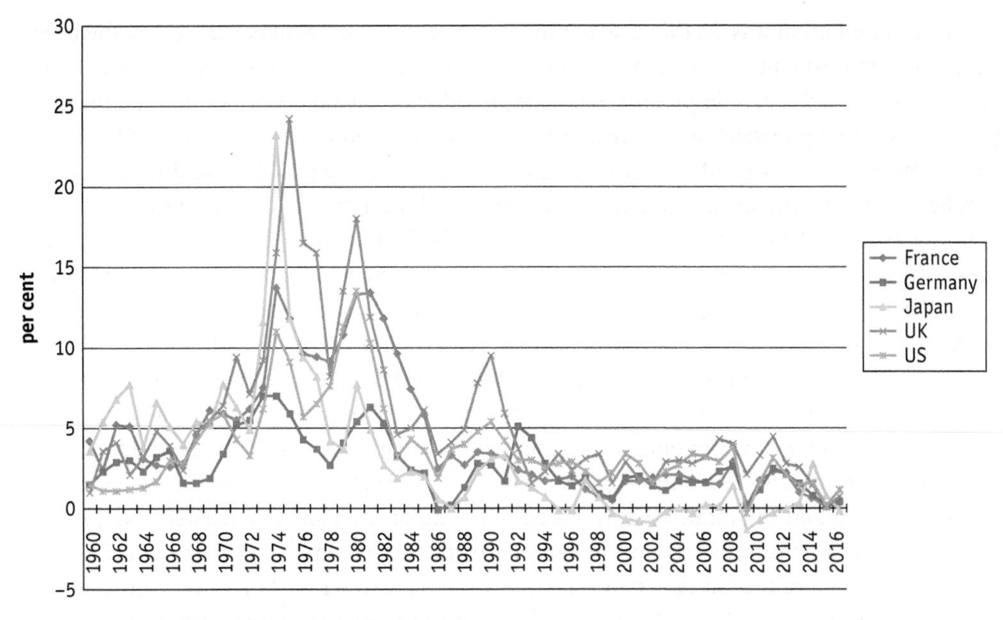

Figure 9.8 G5 Inflation 1960–2016 (2016 est.)

Source: Data from IMF.

the appearance of a new macroeconomic problem—inflation. This had never really been much of a cause for concern during the post-war boom when policymakers' minds were quite firmly focused on the need to avoid anything like another Great Depression. However, from the beginning of the 1970s inflation became a worldwide phenomenon. It caused serious difficulties both for economies generally and for Keynesian economics in particular. Figure 9.8 illustrates the acceleration of inflation in the G5 economies. Particularly noteworthy are rates close to 25 per cent in Japan and the UK in the mid 1970s. On Japan, see Mini-Case 9.2.

Mini-Case 9.2 Japan: from boom to bust

After the Second World War, against all expectations, the Japanese economy enjoyed an 'economic miracle' so much so that by the 1980s it had become the second largest economy in the world and many businesses sought to copy Japanese techniques of production.

So, when in the early 1990s the Japanese economy plunged into a recession that was to linger for more than ten years there was universal surprise. The years 2004 and 2005 began to see a gradual, if tentative recovery, unfortunately ended by the world recession of 2008–9.

The reason for the so-called 'lost decade' of the 1990s was the end of a speculative 'bubble' that had seen land prices surging and stock market prices booming. When this bubble burst, the banks, which had incautiously issued large numbers of loans, were owed vast sums that could not be repaid. The resultant economic shock meant that unemployment began to rise and prices fall. This further cut aggregate demand as consumers stopped spending in the anticipation that prices would *continue* to fall.

Faced with these mounting problems the government embarked on a Keynesian expansion programme by hugely increasing government spending (at one point government debt rose to 130 per cent of GDP), and by reducing interest rates to nearly zero.

Questions

1. **What was the Japanese government trying to achieve by this combination of expansionary fiscal and monetary policy?**
2. **Given the extent of this stabilization programme would you have expected Japan to have recovered from the recession sooner than it did?**

The surge in inflation was, in the view of monetarist economists, actually caused by the over-ambitious employment targets of Keynesian stabilization measures. Furthermore, the monetarists also argued that—despite the evidence provided by the post-war boom—stabilization policy was actually ineffective as a means to maintain economies at potential GDP and full employment. The work of Milton Friedman was extremely influential here and we now need to reflect on the Friedman-led monetarist counter-revolution in macroeconomics.

In the 1950s and 1960s Keynes's ideas had been highly influential in policy terms because they seemed to provide a policy solution to the devastating problem of depression. Similarly, in the 1970s, Friedman's arguments gained currency because they too addressed a burning economic issue, albeit a different one. Friedman revived and restated an old quantity theory of money tradition in economics. Broadly, this held that inflation is 'always and everywhere a monetary phenomenon in the sense that it can be produced only by a more rapid increase in the quantity of money than in output'. In other words, inflation is caused by too much money chasing too few goods. Two things followed from the relationship between the quantity of money supplied and inflation. First, to reduce the rate of inflation to a desired level, it was necessary to commensurately reduce the rate of growth of the money supply (measured for example by the Bank of England's definition of *narrow money* which includes notes and coins in circulation and reserve balances held by commercial banks and building societies at the Bank of England). Second, because government controlled the money supply, the rate of inflation an economy experienced was both its choice and responsibility.

Stop and Think

Most of us as children have heard an exasperated response from parents: '*money doesn't grow on trees you know, so you can't have a new bike/pony/PlayStation*'. But what if, magically, it did—would we all be better off? Would you get your PlayStation? Well, no, all that would happen is that money would be rapidly devalued because of its abundance and this would happen via high and rising inflation. Too much money would be chasing too few goods. PlayStations would cost thousands, then millions, then billions; but probably somewhere along the way we'd all lose faith in increasingly worthless notes.

To understand Friedman's interpretation of what governments could and could not do in the economy we need to introduce a concept known as the Phillips curve, named after its originator, A. W. Phillips, whose pioneering study was published in 1958. The Phillips curve describes the nature of the statistical relationship between the rate of change of money wages and unemployment in the UK for the period 1861–1957. Remarkably, the relationship appeared to be a stable one. This allowed economists to infer a similar relationship between price inflation and unemployment as depicted by the curve in Figure 9.9. Keynesians supposed that the Phillips curve provided a choice for policymakers—they could select from a menu of possible combinations of inflation and unemployment. Most Keynesians at the time viewed inflation as a **demand-pull** phenomenon, in that inflation is caused by an excess demand for goods and services when the economy is at or above full employment. We can now understand the policymakers' choice as provided by the Phillips curve. Policymakers could—using aggregate demand management—squeeze inflation out of the economy entirely if demand was sufficiently suppressed but at the cost of some higher level of unemployment. In Figure 9.9 this possibility is illustrated by a combination of zero inflation and 2.5 per cent unemployment. On the other hand, lower levels of unemployment are obtainable through expansionary fiscal and monetary

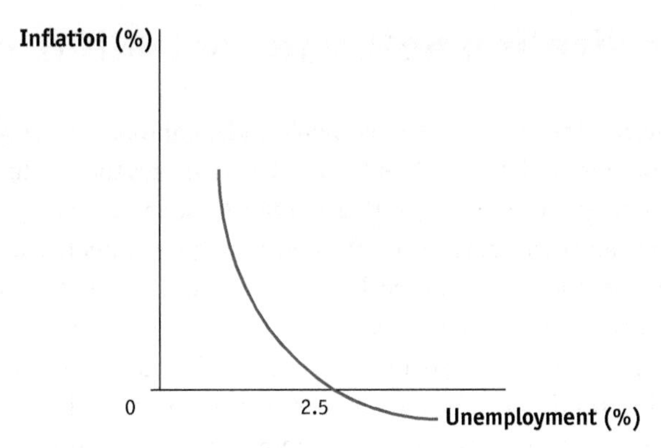

Figure 9.9 The Phillips curve

policy but at the cost of higher inflation. Thus, in Figure 9.9, as unemployment falls below 2.5 per cent the rate of inflation increases.

For a time, it appeared that the Phillips curve fitted snugly into the Keynesian orthodoxy and people like Friedman, with alternative views of how the economy worked, struggled to be heard. However, all that began to change from the early 1970s when two things happened. One was the surge in worldwide inflation seen in Figure 9.8; the second was the re-emergence of unemployment in many economies, as depicted for the G5 in Figure 9.10. Together these became known as **stagflation**—a combination of economic **stagnation** and **inflation.** Stagflation was a real problem for Keynesian economics and its 'either inflation or unemployment, but not both' Phillips curve view of the world. This is where Friedman was able to seize his opportunity. He had to hand an explanation of stagflation and a set of policy measures to deal with it.

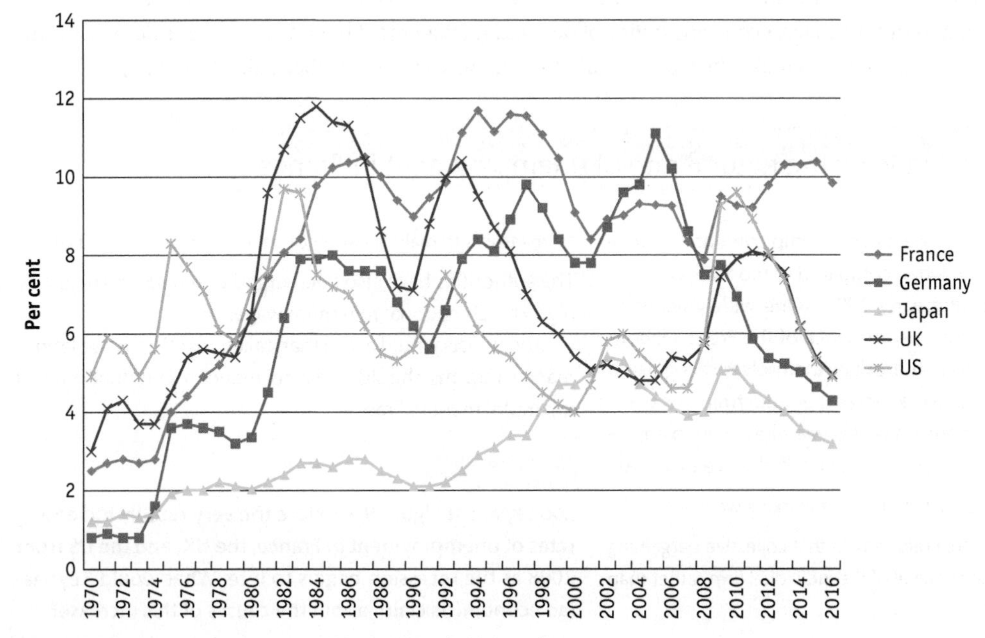

Figure 9.10 G5 Unemployment 1970–2016 (2016 est.)

Source: Data from IMF.

From stabilization policy to controlling inflation

We have already covered the essence of Friedman's understanding of the worldwide inflation shock of the 1970s. Because inflation in Friedman's view is always the product of an overexpansion of an economy's supply of money (so that *too much money is chasing too few goods*), the inflation rate, good or not so good, is always the choice of government. The very high inflation of the 1970s was therefore the fault of the world's governments that had for too long followed the traditional Keynesian policy prescription of spending their way out of any threatened downturn.

Friedman's interpretation of the stagnation (high unemployment) element of the 1970s stagflation revived another tradition in economics. Friedman considered unemployment to be a *microeconomic* rather than a macroeconomic phenomenon. What counted was not the level of aggregate demand in an economy but the way in which the labour market functioned. If the labour market was competitive it would, like any other market, tend towards a market-clearing equilibrium at which the demand for labour and its supply were closely aligned. But if the labour market was uncompetitive, then unemployment could easily result. For example, if wages were set permanently above the market-clearing equilibrium because of the monopoly power of trade unions there would be a greater supply of labour than demand for it: in other words, there would be some persistent unemployment. Wages might also be pushed above their market-clearing equilibrium by forms of government intervention in the labour market such as the setting of minimum wages or the generosity of the government itself as a major employer. Alternatively, the government could also adversely affect labour market conditions by, for example, paying unemployment-related benefits at a level that discouraged workers from taking jobs.

Friedman summarized the outcomes of these and other dimensions of poor labour market competitiveness in a new concept: *the natural rate of unemployment*. The natural rate of unemployment was not natural in the common-sense meaning of the word in that it implied unemployment was permanent or immutable, rather the natural rate in an economy was commensurate with the level of competitiveness in the economy's labour market in any particular period. Better competitiveness would mean falling unemployment and vice versa. Note too that the solution to unemployment is not the macroeconomic policy of demand management but a spectrum of microeconomic polices designed to make the labour market work more efficiently. (See Mini-Case 9.3.)

Mini-Case 9.3 Reducing the natural rate of unemployment in France

Figure 9.10 indicates that the rate of unemployment in France has been relatively high when compared to most other members of the G5 since the early 1990s. One widely acknowledged reason is the poor performance of the French labour market which the French authorities themselves recognize is beset with a number of weaknesses that undermine its competitiveness. Their response in recent years has been to implement a series of labour market reforms which have included:

- measures to extend the length of the working week;
- the reform of industrial relations so that collective bargaining takes place more at the level of the individual firm rather than nationally;
- reform of the benefits system to make payments to the unemployed dependent on active job hunting; and
- measures to make it easier for small firms to fire workers.

The authorities have also been urged to reduce the relatively high French national minimum wage.

Monetarists would argue that, taken together, these labour market reforms should begin to reduce the natural rate of unemployment in France.

Question

Look again at Figure 9.10. Note the very rapidly increasing rates of unemployment in France, the UK, and the US from 2008 as the recession begins to bite. What would Keynesian economists claim about the causes of this increase?

Let us now return to Modigliani's 'need/can/should' framework for the interpretation of government policy to stabilize the levels of output and employment in the economy. How does Friedman's work fit in here? The Keynesian view suggested that governments need to intervene, they can intervene, and therefore they should. Friedman's conclusion about stabilization policy is precisely the opposite:

- Governments *don't need* to stabilize the economy—capitalist economies are inherently stable—all governments should do in macro terms is control inflation.
- Governments *cannot* stabilize the economy—macroeconomic policy is ineffective in tackling unemployment and stimulating output in the long run; reducing the natural rate of unemployment is a task for microeconomic policy.
- Governments *should not* therefore try to stabilize the economy—there is no case for them to do so.

So, the big question is who's right: should governments try to stabilize the economy or not? Notwithstanding the theoretical debate, the practical answer seems to be *it depends*. It depends on how much trouble economies are in; how *unstable* they are. As the hurricane of the global financial crisis hit country after country in 2008 and 2009, followed by deep and lasting recessions, many governments around the world decided that waiting for the system to fix itself posed too great a risk. They collectively dusted off the central message of Keynesian theory and intervened like hell: with expansionary fiscal policy, borrowing heavily to spend more themselves and cutting taxes to encourage their citizens and firms to consume and invest; and with expansionary monetary policy, at first cutting interest rates and then resorting to the highly unconventional policy of quantitative easing—printing money and pushing it out into the economy by the boatload.

For example, in the UK, the government's budget deficit (the balance between its annual income and spending) required it to borrow almost £150bn in 2010–11. That's about 10 per cent of GDP, an unprecedented debt in peacetime. The UK authorities also cut VAT. On the monetary side, they reduced interest rates to a record low of 0.5 per cent (reduced still further to 0.25 per cent in 2016) and printed some £445bn.

But it would be wrong to conclude that all this means that Keynesian ideas about stabilization policy have made a decisive comeback. In the UK the picture is complicated by two things:

- The introduction of a programme of **austerity** as the central element of government macroeconomic policy.
- The fallout from the UK's Brexit referendum decision to leave the EU after more than forty years of membership for entirely unchartered waters.

Elsewhere, in Europe the appetite and capacity for Keynesian stabilization policy is constrained by a further issue:

- For a large group of European countries, macroeconomic policy freedoms are limited by membership of the euro area.

In what follows we address each of these points in turn.

Macroeconomic policy in the UK: six years of austerity

DYNAMIC The concept of austerity dominated UK macroeconomic policy between 2010 and 2016. Austerity requires contractionary fiscal policy adjustments—cuts in public expenditure or tax increases but usually with a strong emphasis on the former—to try to ensure that government lives within its means. In essence, government must restrict expenditures to match income, most of which comes from taxes. The ambition of successive UK governments under the stewardship of the then Chancellor of the Exchequer, George Osborne, was to achieve a budget surplus by the end of 2020 at the latest. That the central theme of macroeconomic policy should be the rapid elimination of a budget deficit incurred largely to stabilize the economy in the face of the global financial crisis was controversial. A Keynesian reading of such a strategy suggests that it would dampen domestic demand and induce, at best, sluggish growth. In the event, this is what happened as the UK economy endured the longest ever recession in its history. GDP remained below its 2007 peak until 2013.

A more sympathetic interpretation of the UK's poor performance might point to weaknesses in Europe—the UK's largest market—as a drag on economic growth, as well as highlighting the plight of heavily indebted governments in Greece and elsewhere that could no longer borrow to finance their spending and were, literally, bankrupt. As chancellor, Osborne specifically held up the Greek catastrophe as justification for his insistence on the elimination of the budget deficit.

Whatever construction is put on the wisdom of UK austerity, the policy was abruptly abandoned in the autumn of 2016 in the aftermath of the referendum on continued UK membership of the EU. Osborne himself had conceded that a 'no' vote might sufficiently derail UK growth prospects to the extent that his ultimate ambitions for a budget surplus could not be realized. After the referendum this position was formalized by his successor as chancellor, Philip Hammond, who announced a 'fiscal reset' to provide what was termed *some necessary flexibility* in the conduct of fiscal policy. The potential economic shock from Brexit might then be tempered by a less restrictive fiscal stance.

Looking ahead—Brexit: a shock to the system

INTERACTION Let's start here with a nice story. When asked in the early 1970s about his thoughts on the French Revolution of 1789, repeat 1789, Chinese leader Zhou Enlai replied that it was *too early to say*. The implications of Brexit may be equally hard to fathom (also see Chapter 13).

Brexit means the UK leaving the EU, a process that in all likelihood won't be completed until around 2020. What is the UK leaving? In economic terms the most important element is the European single market, a unique economic space in which goods and services from almost all European countries are freely traded and between which people and firms may move unhindered. This means that, for example, for a British citizen or firm there is, in effect, no difference between London, Berlin, Milan, and Budapest. Europeans can live, work, and invest anywhere in the single market, of which there are twenty-seven members along with the UK, with a number of candidates for membership in the pipeline. It is the world's richest market. Being part of this market conveys great opportunities: to export, invest, pursue personal ambitions, and so on. Almost half of UK goods exports are sold in the single market. It is also true that when economies isolate themselves from one another their economic prospects are dimmed. One of the key drivers of the Great Depression was the division of the world economy into rival blocks between which international trade and investment became highly restricted.

So why is the UK leaving? The rationale for doing so is not something we have the room to fully explain here, but one of the central economic issues in UK politics for some time has been immigration (see also Chapter 6). One of the founding principles of the single market is the free movement of people which allows UK citizens to move to other EU countries and EU citizens the opportunity to move to the UK. In the run-up to the Brexit referendum there was a focus on the tendency of the UK to be a net importer of people. This was often portrayed as a negative thing in the sense that new arrivals could take jobs that existing residents might otherwise get, or that more competition in the labour market might drive down wages. Less well rehearsed during the referendum was the counterargument that improving a country's labour supply is a dynamic way to raise GDP and improve living standards.

What then are the possible economic implications of Brexit? Again, we have space only for a few reflections here.

Economists from both sides of the referendum debate agree that there will be a negative shock to the UK economy from Brexit. In the short term it is expected that UK growth will slow, given increased political and economic uncertainty following the vote to leave. Domestic shocks damage business confidence at home, hitting demand and domestic investment, and may prompt foreign investors to rethink their relationships with a country heading out of the single market. The weaker pound—driven down chiefly by the same evaporating confidence in the UK economy—has the effect of pushing up import prices and inflation, and may hit the business plans of firms that use imports in the production process. In general, all this appears a rather alarming scenario but one that may be tempered by the nature of the terms agreed for Brexit. A so-called *hard* Brexit, in which access to the single market is lost, poses the greatest threat. A *soft* Brexit, which retains access to the single market after the UK has left the EU, would have an extremely positive effect on confidence in the UK economy. Norway, for example, though not an EU member is a full participant in the single market. The longer-term implications of Brexit are likely to turn on the outcome of the exit negotiations.

Stop and Think

Is a weaker pound wholly bad news? In the aftermath of the referendum result, the value of the pound fell by around 20 per cent against the world's major currencies such as the US dollar, the euro, and the Japanese yen. The negative impacts include higher inflation as the prices of imported goods rise. This means that consumers will pay more but it also pushes up the costs that businesses incur when they buy raw materials, production goods, and technologies that are priced in other currencies. As noted, these things may dent consumer demand and business investment. But the plummeting pound has a positive side too. Because foreign residents and businesses in the US and elsewhere get 20 per cent more for every unit of their own currency they swap for pounds, UK goods and services become suddenly very cheap and so more attractive than they were before. If the UK is able to increase exports on the back of a weaker pound, there may be a boost to economic growth. This may be amplified by a switch in the consumption habits of UK residents away from more expensive imports to relatively cheaper domestic goods.

What of the effect of Brexit on the labour market? Around 12 per cent of final demand for UK goods and services comes from other EU countries and directly underpins around 3.3 million jobs (Begg and Mushövel 2016). If the UK fails to secure either access to the single market, or the next best alternative of laborious industry-by-industry trade agreements, it is likely that some sectors will shed jobs. Such direct effects may of course be magnified by any poorer performance of the UK economy as a whole. On the other hand, they may be tempered by new trade agreements the UK is able to reach with non-EU countries. You may now be beginning to appreciate the wisdom of Zhou Enlai's remark!

In response to the expected short-term shock from the Brexit result, the Bank of England's Monetary Policy Committee (MPC) reduced UK interest rates to a new record low of 0.25 per cent. Mark Carney, the Bank's governor explained why:

> the economic outlook has changed markedly, with the largest revision to our GDP forecast since the MPC was formed almost two decades ago . . . by acting early and comprehensively, the MPC can reduce uncertainty, bolster confidence and blunt the slowdown.

Brexit is an unfolding story. The UK is likely to remain a member of the EU until near the end of the decade and, for the moment, free and open relationships with its European partners continue. Confidence in the UK economy may have been shaken by the referendum result but until the UK actually leaves the EU, and the terms under which it leaves become clear, the true impact cannot really begin to be fully assessed.

Summary

- Macroeconomic stability is a desirable thing but there has been a lengthy and continuing debate in economics about how to best secure it.
- The main aims of macroeconomic policy are to produce an environment that promotes stable and satisfactory growth, high and stable employment and low unemployment, and a stable and low rate of inflation.
- Economists once urged governments to actively and consistently employ the Keynesian tools of fiscal and monetary policy to keep economic growth and employment on track. This approach has enjoyed a pronounced comeback as a result of the recent crisis.
- The inflationary experiences of the 1970s and 1980s suggested a different, less hands-on approach was needed. It was argued that government intervention to reduce unemployment could only work in the short run and was the cause of the inflation.
- Recently, in many of the world's economies, a somewhat eclectic approach to the economy—one that draws on both interventionist and non-interventionist traditions—has given way to Keynesian-inspired strategies to deal with the fallout from the 2008–9 crisis.
- In the UK a six-year-long programme of austerity that sought to unwind this Keynesian emphasis was abandoned in favour of a more pragmatic approach following the referendum decision to leave the EU.

Case Study: Austerity in and out of the euro area: a necessity or a choice?

Many of the world's governments reacted to the recession that followed the financial crisis by increasing spending. They briefly forgot—or conveniently put aside—the strictures of economists like Milton Friedman and embraced old-style Keynesian fiscal measures that supported aggregate demand in their economies. Simply, they spent their way out of recession. More recently, some of these governments—the UK is a prime example—once again changed their policy emphasis in favour of austerity with priority given to reducing the level of government debt that Keynesian policies necessarily ran up.

As we've characterized it here, this era of austerity—in the sense that morally strict governments try to live within their means by tightly controlling expenditure—is an *optional* path: one that has been chosen. While this might be true for governments such as the UK's, it is not true for others that have, in effect, become *predisposed* to austerity. And it is not just governments; whole societies have fallen into this position.

How? Why? The answer is that they are all members of the euro area.

There is a strong economic case for the euro. Because the nineteen members of the euro area all use the same currency they are likely in the future to trade more intensively with one another. As more trade generates additional demand for goods and services and allows participant economies to realize economies of scale across the whole continent, there should be a fillip to euro area growth. In addition, because there are no longer any nominal exchange rates inside the euro area there is no longer any risk posed by the tendency for exchange rates to shift in a dramatic and potentially destabilizing way. The euro in France is the same as the euro in Germany. The French franc can never again slide or climb against the German mark. Both have gone, forever. The absence of an internal exchange rate risk makes trade, investment, and decisions about where to work much easier and, again, the payoff comes in the shape of more of these transactions in the euro area and consequently more growth and prosperity.

But the case against the euro area may also appear compelling, especially to those on whom it has the greatest impact: the citizens of countries such as Greece, Portugal, and Spain. The dimensions of the continuing crisis in these places are simply staggering. Figure 9.11 depicts economic growth in these countries since the launch of the euro in 1999 (Greece joined the euro area in 2001). Notice that for these countries, with the exception perhaps of Portugal, growth was relatively stable and satisfactory prior to 2008. Since 2008 it has been neither. Greece is still presently mired in recession; and Portugal is barely growing. On the other hand, the Spanish economy appears to have entered a period of recovery. Figure 9.12 shows the consequences for unemployment of these performances. Unemployment is falling but in Greece and Spain roughly one in every four to five people is jobless. Economic stagnation of such proportions has raised important political questions in all these countries, prompting government instability, mass demonstrations, riots, and even deaths.

The urgent question is what to do about these worrying economic performances. Unfortunately, euro area membership means there can be only one answer: austerity. The principal cost of euro area membership is the permanent surrender of monetary sovereignty. This means that interest rates are no longer set by individual economies in their own interests but by the European Central Bank (ECB) on behalf of all euro member states. The key problem here is what happens when particular countries get into economic difficulties that are not shared by other euro area economies. Macroeconomic stagnation usually prompts a macroeconomic policy response. On the monetary side this may involve lowering interest rates, attempting to lower the exchange rate, or some other more exotic measure such as quantitative easing (the printing of money). But none of these measures is available to members of the euro area as monetary policy is the sole preserve of the ECB. On the fiscal side too there are constraints. Euro area membership carries with it the obligation to keep government expenditure within certain limits and, in any case, the heavily indebted Greek, Portuguese, and Spanish governments have no room for manoeuvre here.

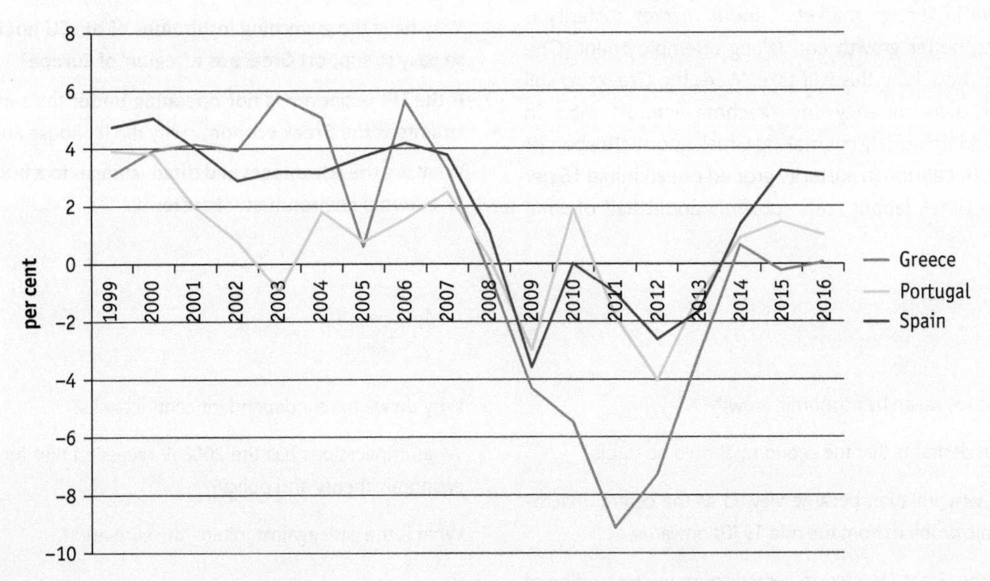

Figure 9.11 Economic growth in selected euro area economies 1999–2016 (2016 est.)

Source: Data from IMF.

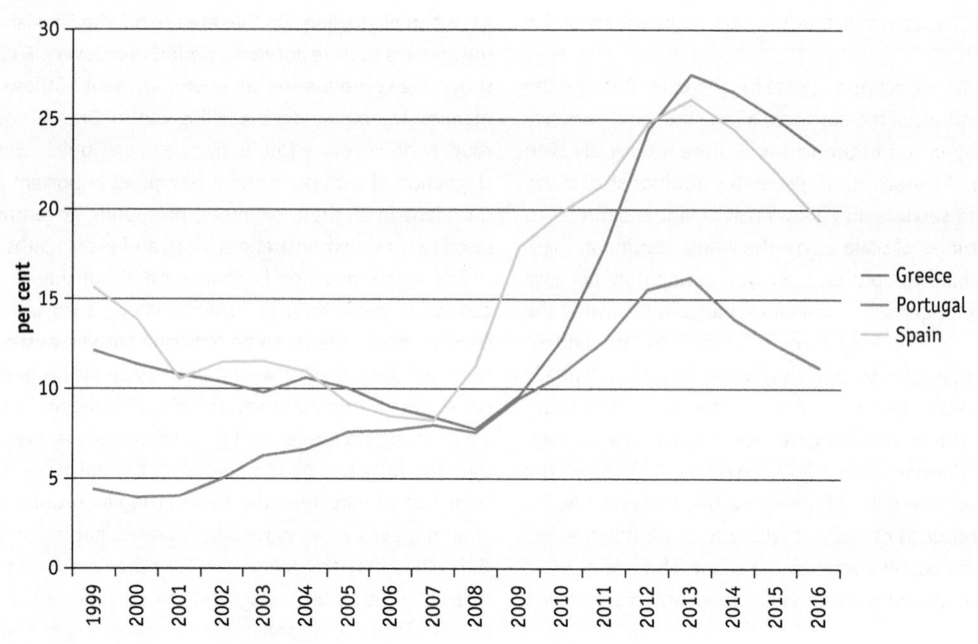

Figure 9.12 Unemployment in selected euro area countries 1999–2016 (2016 est.)
Source: Data from IMF.

INTERACTION What then is the way forward? The unavailability of the tools of macroeconomic policy means that *microeconomic* measures must take the strain. Greece (and others) must become more internationally competitive. They have to find ways to sell more goods and services to their principal trading partners in the rest of Europe. The only way this can happen is through their labour markets. Greek citizens must be prepared to accept lower wages and work longer hours to make the things they produce more competitive in foreign markets. Labour market austerity is the path to better growth and falling unemployment. One key issue is how long this will take. Were the Greeks to still have their own currency—the drachma—interest rates in Greece could be quickly cut making Greek goods cheaper for foreigners. But although austerity ground out an initial 15 per cent fall in Greek labour costs—possibly about half of what is necessary—costs began once again to rise from 2013. This leaves two uncomfortable questions: to what extent has the Greek crisis really been resolved, and for how long can Greece cope with further rounds of poverty-inducing austerity?

Questions

1. **Within a single country such as the US, how is the government able to react to a decline in the competitiveness of one of its own regions?**
2. **Why have the governing institutions of the EU not found it so easy to support Greece as a 'region' of Europe?**
3. **If the UK economy is not operating under the same constraints as the Greek economy why did it choose austerity?**
4. **What are the advantages and disadvantages to a business of an external environment of austerity?**

Review and discussion questions

1. What do we mean by economic growth?
2. Why is it desirable that the economy should be stable?
3. Explain why inflation became viewed as the central macroeconomic problem from the mid 1970s onwards.
4. Why is the Great Depression central to an understanding of the development of macroeconomic thinking and policy?
5. Why do we have independent central banks?
6. What implications has the 2008–9 recession had for macroeconomic theory and policy?
7. What is the case against joining the euro area?

Assignments

1. Take a recent interest rate decision by the Bank of England (summaries available from the Bank of England website). Explain the primary macroeconomic policy concern behind the decision—is it that inflationary pressures in the economy need to be addressed, or is there a more important concern about the prospects for economic growth on the Bank's agenda?
2. Compare growth rates, unemployment rates, and inflation rates for the US, Japan, China, and Germany over the past decade (figures from the IMF—see list of useful websites below). Which countries are doing particularly well and particularly badly? Look at one or two OECD country reports to find out a little about the macroeconomic policies of these economies.
3. Look at the annual reports of some major UK firms. What do these reports suggest about the importance of the UK macroeconomic climate to the performance of firms?

Further reading

Mulhearn and Vane (2015) *an introduction to economics for business by one of the authors of the present chapter.*

Test your understanding of this chapter with online questions and answers, explore the subject further through web exercises, and use the weblinks to provide a quick resource for further research. Visit the online resources at www.oup.com/uk/wetherly_otter4e/

Useful websites

www.hm-treasury.gov.uk
This is a key website which contains a wealth of information about the UK economy and its economic policy.

www.bankofengland.co.uk
Useful for researching the UK economy, especially monetary policy.

www.imf.org
The International Monetary Fund is a vast source of economic information on individual countries. It offers a particularly good interactive free data set.

www.worldbank.org
Although its primary focus is on developing countries, this site also allows you to access economic data and analysis for many economies.

References

Begg, I. and Mushövel, F. (2016) *The Economic Impact of Brexit: Jobs, Growth and the Public Finances* (London: European Institute, London School of Economics and Political Science)

Maddison, A. (2001) *The World Economy in Millennial Perspective* (Paris: OECD)

Mulhearn, C. and Vane, H. R. (2015) *Economics for Business* (3rd edn, Basingstoke: Palgrave Macmillan)

Snowdon, B. and Vane, H. R. (2005) *Modern Macroeconomics* (Cheltenham: Edward Elgar)

Sources

Data from National Statistics website: www.statistics.gov.uk. Crown copyright material is reproduced with permission of the Controller Office of Public Sector Information (OPSI).

National Statistics website: www.statistics.gov.uk. Crown copyright material is reproduced with permission of the Controller Office of Public Sector Information (OPSI).

Data from IMF International Financial Statistics ('consumer prices, per cent change over previous year, calculated from indices').

HM Treasury website www.hm-treasury.gov.uk. Crown copyright material is reproduced with permission of the Controller Office of Public Sector Information (OPSI).

Chapter 10
Globalization of business: good or bad?

Dorron Otter

Learning objectives

When you have completed this chapter, you will be able to:

- Explain the meaning of globalization.
- Outline the sources that are leading to changes in the scope of globalization.
- Identify the range of competing views as to the nature of globalization.
- Explore the ethical dilemmas that arise out of global business activity.

THEMES

The following themes of the book are especially relevant to this chapter

- INTERNAL/EXTERNAL While globalization can be seen as a force that happens 'out there' it is business that both drives this process forward and which in turn has to adopt its internal strategic response to it.
- LOCAL TO GLOBAL Globalization adds the supranational level to the focus on business activity. This is the defining characteristic of globalization, emphasizing the interlinkages across the spatial levels from local through to global.
- DYNAMIC The nature of the global environment has changed over time and is now rapidly being shaped by a combination of the need for the developed countries of the world to emerge from the problems caused by the financial crisis from 2008 onwards and the rapid growth in the emerging markets of the world.
- VALUES Put simply, 'is globalization good or bad'? It is important to recognize the range of views that are expressed when seeking to investigate the impact of the transformations brought about by the shift in the spatial level of globalization.

There is an increasing interest in the role of global ethics to address issues associated with globalization. While operating across national boundaries presents businesses with huge opportunities, what are their responsibilities to the countries in which they operate, especially when operating across cultures with differing ethical norms?

Introduction: the impact of globalization on the business environment

Globalization raises a series of questions that need to be explored: what is globalization? When did it start? Is it increasing and in what way? Is globalization good or bad? Who and what does globalization affect? What are the challenges that globalization poses? In relation to business, though, we need to consider the strategic response of businesses to the 'challenge of globalization'.

VALUES There are two central questions that dominate the debate about globalization. While it is clear that globalization can potentially give rise to an increase in prosperity, there are severe doubts as to whether this process will be fair to all, both in the present and to those in the future. We will see that there are a variety of perspectives about the impact of globalization and that the role of ethics in relation to globalization needs to be explored.

LOCAL TO GLOBAL Second, we have seen in Chapter 2 that for markets to work they need to both be supported by and regulated by states. Since globalization occurs across national boundaries this means that we need to consider the global system of rules and regulations that may be needed. Even before the global recession that started in 2008, there were many people who were arguing that the world lacks robust global governance arrangements to ensure that globalization is a smooth process which will bring greater prosperity for all people and all countries.

Mini-Case 10.1 A 'big ocean that you cannot escape from' or a 'swamp' that needs to be drained?

Two countries with historically different approaches to globalization are China and the US. In the period after the end of the Second World War, it is generally acknowledged that the US took a leading role in promoting not only capitalism on a national level, but also in being a champion for its growth across the developed and developing world. China after the communist revolution led by Mao in 1949 was the first developing country to turn its back on the so-called free market capitalism of the West and opted for its own socialist inward-looking development policy. China's approach to international trade and other forms of globalization was to change with the accession of Deng Xiaoping and, from the 1980s onwards, as the country became a major global economy, China rapidly developed a new 'open door' policy.

At the beginning of 2017, two significant events occurred that changed the relative positions of both the US and China and which may have major implications for the future development of the global business economy. The election of President Donald Trump means that, for the first time since 1945, the US is led by a fierce critic of globalization. At a pre-election campaign speech in a former steel town in Pennsylvania he claimed

Globalization has made the financial elite who donate to politicians very, very wealthy . . . but it has left millions of our workers with nothing but poverty and heartache.

(Jackson 2016)

During the election campaign, Trump targeted what he thought to be the 'bad' trade deals negotiated by America (such as NAFTA), or were about to be negotiated (such as the TPP) (see Chapter 13). In particular, he argued that China was the main reason for the loss of jobs in the US economy since the financial crash of 2008. In Trump's view, it was not only foreign competitors that were benefiting from globalization at the expense of American workers, but also the politicians and rich financiers who lived in the 'swamp' of Washington, DC.

In January 2017, China's leader Xi Jinping gave a speech at the World Economic Forum in Davos, an annual meeting that champions the cause of global capitalism and is often referred to as the most elite gathering of global business and political leaders. In this speech, President Xi placed great emphasis on the benefits of globalization for developing and developed countries alike. While in the past he acknowledged that China had had its doubts, Xi commented that now

To grow its economy, China must have the courage to swim in the vast ocean of the global market. If one is always afraid of bracing the storm and exploring the new world, he will sooner or later get drowned in the ocean.

(Xi Jinping 2017)

Xi's wider speech was not only interpreted by many as being a robust defence of globalization, and China's key role in being a key and responsible global player, but also as a criticism of President Trump's threat to adopt protectionist measures against China.

Questions

1. **How and in what ways did the US take on such a powerful role in shaping globalization after 1945?**
2. **What are the fears that President Trump now has in relation to the impact that globalization has had on US business?**
3. **What are the 'protectionist' measures that the US could consider in relation to China?**

What is globalization?

There are six main aspects of globalization.

International trade and the creation of the global marketplace

DYNAMIC **LOCAL TO GLOBAL** Globalization at its simplest can be seen as the increase over time of international trade (referred to as *merchandise trade*) and services, and often this is how it is described. With trade comes an increase in the amount of markets across national borders.

Trade itself is a vital feature of economic activity within countries or regions. Without trade, businesses would not be able to benefit from the ability to specialize and the associated benefits of an efficient division of labour. With international trade we are moving trade to a different spatial level. The central question then is, does moving trade to the international level change its nature? It is clear that earlier civilizations across the globe were involved in widespread trading within regions. However, what is different about the modern era is that trade was expanding rapidly as capitalism was fuelling the Industrial Revolutions in Europe and North America and thus any understanding of globalization must encompass an understanding of the nature of capitalism on a world scale.

Globally organized production and investment flows

Businesses have recognized the advantages of organizing production across national boundaries to take advantage of lower costs and the specialist benefits of different geographical locations. This can involve placing production facilities abroad, or splitting the stages of production or other functions of the business, to take advantage of lower costs or be nearer to foreign markets.

Allied to this is the increase in the amount and nature of investment that takes place across borders. This can be in the form of **foreign direct investment** (FDI) as well as through financial flows of money and **portfolio investment**.

After 1945 there was widespread talk of a **new international division of labour**. This meant that with the freeing up of financial markets businesses in the developed nations would begin to set up production in new markets where resources were cheapest. In particular, this would help the developing world.

Much attention in the literature is paid to the rise of the multinational corporation. Often the term **transnational corporation** is used to convey the fact that such corporations work across national boundaries.

There has been a big increase in these investment flows, especially in the 1990s. From 1980 to 2002 the world flow of inward investment increased from less than $50 billion a year to $1.2 trillion in 2000. Despite a drop, from 2000–3, inward FDI recovered sharply reaching $2 trillion. The global financial crisis saw this drop and in 2016 the total stood at $1.75 trillion which was still below the 2007 peak (UNCTAD 2017).

As well as flows in FDI the recent explosion in investment has come from the rise of stocks and shares flowing across national boundaries. The international financial system has seen unprecedented growth in the last quarter of a century. In particular, the role of the International Monetary Fund (IMF) and the need for stronger global governance of financial markets has come under intense scrutiny as individual nations have suffered severe financial instability and debt burdens, and where the very integration of these financial markets has meant that such crises can spread quickly to other countries.

Migration

A major feature of the development of trade and investment has been the movements of people across both internal national and international borders. Such movements have had profound effects both on the countries and regions the migrants leave from as well as those they go to.

Often attention is focused on the problems of immigration without an appreciation of the global forces which shape migration and the enormous contributions that migration makes to the growth of business activity both in the private and public sector. An important aspect of the industrialization process within all countries is that, as the towns grow people will move away from rural areas into the urban ones. Globalization offers people in less developed areas the possibility of moving across national frontiers to developed countries.

Communication flows

Globalization has been greatly influenced by the speed with which communications have improved in the world, both in terms of transport and telecommunications.

Cultural flows

VALUES This intermingling of people, and the accompanying rise in communication networks, has brought into focus the question of how cultures combine. It is clear that globalization has brought together people with different cultural beliefs. The challenge for business is how to deal with this and, also, to recognize the potential ethical problems that intercultural interactions can create.

Rapid technological change

DYNAMIC We saw in Chapter 3 how technological change has helped fuel the rapid rise in global economic activity, especially in relation to communication and transport. Transport costs have fallen and worldwide travel has increased exponentially. The rise of the Internet and the global telecommunications revolution, in general, has created a new environment which encourages global business activity.

The growth of globalization

DYNAMIC The World Bank profiles research that depicts three waves of globalization (World Bank 2004). The first wave was in the late nineteenth century with the rapid increase in the industrialization of the main 'western' nations (mainly Western Europe, the US, and Canada). There was a big expansion in the growth of world trade as measured by the ratio of merchandise exports (trade in physical goods) to world GDP. This expansion was propelled by the development of what Eric Hobsbawm (1987) refers to as 'The Age of Empire'. Colonial powers imported commodities in the form of primary resources from their colonies and then manufactured these into commodities for sale in their home markets as well as for export back into their overseas possessions. Allied to this was an outflow of investment to the poorer countries and there were mass migrations. However, there were tensions between the main industrial powers with domestic firms keen to exploit the opportunities within their own 'empires' but hostile to competition from outside. This competitive rivalry between the countries in Western Europe provided the conditions that precipitated the First World War.

The period between the First and Second World Wars was marked by a high degree of instability for the industrial countries with many experiencing severe economic problems. One response to these national problems was pressure by domestic firms to keep out foreign competition by continuing to erect barriers to prevent international trade. In response to the decision by the US to erect tariffs, its trading partners followed suit. This represented a 'retreat' from globalization. There was a fall in the proportion of trade to world income from 22 per cent in 1913 to 9 per cent during the 1930s with a marked slowdown in the growth of the world economy.

The third wave of globalization occurred in certain parts of the world after 1945 and picked up universal speed from the late 1970s onwards (see Chapter 2). This was driven by the belief that trade liberalization (the opening of countries' borders to trade and investment by removal of trade barriers) was 'the engine' for the growth of economies. However, as we have seen in the opening case study, since the global recession that started in 2008 doubts have been expressed about the universal benefits of globalization, showing that the process of increasing globalization is far from inevitable or smooth.

Perspectives on globalization

VALUES Globalization and its effects provoke intense disagreement. The arguments about globalization have been around ever since scholars began to examine the worldwide expansion of markets. Not surprisingly, the different perspectives that we outlined in Chapter 2, when applied to the growth of international economic activity, came up with different conclusions. For neoclassical/neoliberal critics globalization will be a universally good thing as it will deliver the benefits of free market capitalism to all across the globe. For Marxist and socialist writers, given the huge social, economic, and political differences between countries and groups within countries, it is unlikely that globalization will benefit all but, rather, only the rich elites and businesses. Structuralist and institutionalist commentators focus on the need to ensure that the right institutional frameworks are put in place so that the potential of globalization can be achieved and its dangers minimized.

What unites all three perspectives is that globalization has occurred through the expansion of capitalism on a world scale. What divides them are their views as to the nature of this spatial change and its effects.

Neoclassical/neoliberal views

Chapters 2 and 3 show how Adam Smith highlighted the benefits to an economy of market liberalization and trade, and the intimate relationship between trade, development, and growth. If trade was so important in expanding markets, and therefore allowing greater specialization and increased productivity at the domestic level, it was easy for Smith to show why international trade would be so beneficial.

1. It provides a source of external funding that boosts the amount of money available to fuel trade internally.
2. It enables further room for the expansion of markets on an international scale.

To give a simple illustration of Smith's argument in favour of trade, imagine two countries, A and B; and two goods, wool and wine. For this, Smith uses the concept of **absolute advantage**.

If country A has an absolute advantage in producing wool and country B an absolute advantage in producing wine, then it makes sense for country A to specialize in wool and country B in wine. Overall production of both wine and wool will rise as each country is able to benefit from the advantages of specialization and, provided that these gains from trade are shared equitably, both countries will gain.

By the nineteenth century the sheer success of the first wave of industrialized countries was astonishing and across a whole range of commodities these countries experienced huge rises in productivity. Neither was this confined to industrial goods, but the industrialization of agriculture began to see big efficiency gains here. This economic success enabled such countries to both expand and, in the process, benefit from a huge economic expansion into overseas markets both to obtain cheap resources and to find new markets to fully exploit economies of scale.

This then posed a problem for trade theorists. If, for example, Britain was better than India at producing a whole host of commodities, what benefit would the less productive areas of the world get from opening their borders to trade? Wouldn't trade simply benefit the advanced countries at the expense of the growth and development of the less advanced ones?

Ricardo and comparative advantage

David Ricardo, writing in the nineteenth century, refined Smith's theory by arguing that, even if country A is better than country B at producing both commodities, it still makes sense for A to specialize in one and B the other. If A specializes in the commodity in which it has the greater **comparative advantage** and B in the one in which it has the smallest comparative disadvantage, then there will still be overall gains in production. Ricardo still used units of input in relation to output produced as his measure of advantage.

In the world of the nineteenth century it was easy to argue that the industrialized nations should specialize in manufactures (secondary commodities) and the colonies in raw materials and natural resources (primary commodities). It is still the case today that many countries are heavily reliant for much of their export earnings on only one or two primary commodities.

In the twentieth century this theory was refined further by two economists, Hecksher and Ohlin, who argued that advantage was related to the cost of a unit of input in relation to output and that the 'factor endowments' of countries could differ. In countries where resources of a certain type were abundant, then the costs of those resources would be low. On a world scale developing countries were abundant in labour, especially in the rural areas, and so it made sense for them to specialize in primary commodities; while in the advanced industrial countries the shortage of labour but abundance of capital meant they should specialize in secondary goods. Thus was born the idea of 'an international division of labour'.

This belief in the combination of free markets and free trade dominates classical thinking and its modern day neoclassical writers. Given the theory of comparative advantage, there is every reason for specialization and trade to occur on a world scale. Moreover, as well as these static gains from specialization there are also further dynamic gains that can be achieved.

Trade not only potentially increases the amount of goods that can be produced but also encourages increases in productivity through economies of scale. Trade openness forces domestic companies to become more efficient because of the competitive threat and provides great opportunities to seek new markets. Flows of inward investment bring in much needed technical know-how and can also reduce costs. Outward flows of FDI enable firms to take advantage of market opportunities and cheaper resources and provide invaluable technical improvements to the host countries. There is clear evidence that countries which experience high growth rates are also those which are open to trade and investment.

The World Trade Organization offers a summary of the case for open trade (see www.wto.org/english/thewto_e/whatis_e/tif_e/fact3_e.htm).

Stop and Think

What are the benefits of trade and FDI to an economy?

However, as we saw in Chapter 2, after 1945 both developed and developing countries chose to intervene in markets and to engage in trade protection policies. The crisis years of the 1970s provided the ideal conditions for the 'rediscovery' of neoclassical thinking. This was given expression in the political system with the coming to power of governments advocating these free market policies, especially in the US with Ronald Reagan and in the UK with Margaret Thatcher, and the securing of positions by neoclassical policymakers within the two key supranational organizations of the World Bank and the IMF. From the late 1970s there was a discernible shift in the ideas coming from a range of national and supranational bodies, and perhaps this was encapsulated in 1995 with the World Trade Organization replacing GATT.

The 1989 *World Development Report* commented that:

> global integration in the flow of goods, services, capital and labor also brings enormous benefits. It promotes competition and efficiency, and it gives poor countries access to basic knowledge in medicine, science and engineering.
>
> (World Bank 1989)

John Williamson sought to encapsulate neoclassical views in what could be seen as a menu for globalization and he coined the term the **Washington Consensus** to capture this (Williamson 2000). The World Bank in the report above characterized this approach as 'the market friendly approach'. For many it is these views that embody the term globalization.

The Washington Consensus can be seen as a 'wish list' of free market policies that Williamson argued would create the ideal environment in which countries would prosper and grow. The actual policies that comprised the Washington Consensus were summarized in Chapter 9. Where governments had directly controlled industries, the call was for these not to be privatized and government activity should be directed at providing minimum social security safety nets and supporting education and health provision. Governments should aim to reduce spending so that they no longer run long-term budget deficits. In order to create the climate for entrepreneurship, tax breaks should be directed at those on high earnings and there should be deregulation especially in relation to finance markets.

While these policies were primarily aimed at establishing a free market domestically, equally important was the need for countries to achieve closer integration with the global economy. This would be achieved through allowing exchange rates to find their market levels, through encouraging an increase in both inward and outward flows of FDI, and, of course, through rapid trade liberalization.

A significant feature of this consensus was the belief that, not only were such policies appropriate for developed countries, but they were equally possible for the developing world. There was strong support for these policies as being the base on which the fast-growing South East Asian Tiger economies has been built (discussed later in this chapter) and, when many Latin American countries began to suffer economic problems in the late 1980s and needed IMF support, this was granted only on condition that they adopt these policies through what was termed 'structural adjustment policies'.

The dramatic collapse of the Soviet Union and its former satellite Eastern European countries from 1989 only reinforced the view that there was only one way to progress and that was the 'road to the market'.

Socialist/Marxist views: globalization is bad—the dependency tradition

We saw in Chapter 2 that the person most associated with radical views of capitalism was Karl Marx. For Marx, nineteenth-century capitalism posed what he saw as a central 'contradiction'. He was in total agreement with Smith that capitalism led to unprecedented growth, but he argued that there was a fatal flaw. The social system of capitalism is very unequal, and access to resources and political power is concentrated in the hands of the few. Owners of capital are able to exploit their advantage. The source of this growth was the ability of capitalists to exploit their labourers and as growth and wealth increased the conditions of the workers would deteriorate. This is a central Marxist idea: that growth, rather than being combined and even, can be combined and uneven, providing the conditions for a socialist revolution where the workers would seize control of the economy and run things in the interests of the whole of society, not for the rich elites. However, such a revolution would only occur after a long period of capitalist expansion which would have succeeded in industrializing the economy.

Later on in his life he began to argue that world capitalism might lead to even greater problems for the workers in the less advanced areas because of their even weaker position as subjects of an imperial master. It was this central idea that began to provide the background for later radical writers to argue that capitalism on a world scale works differently in different parts of the global economy. This they referred to as **imperialism**. A world system had been developed that linked together the spatial levels of the economy and society in such a way as to lead to big divisions in the levels of income and wealth.

Imperial rivalry between nations had moved on from competitive rivalry between firms within the same nations. In order to obtain global competitive advantage, individual nations sought to protect their own large monopoly firms by imposing tariffs in home markets, but aggressively supporting their expansion in existing colonies and in newly acquired colonies with military support as required. It was inevitable then that war between the imperial powers would break out, as happened with the outbreak of the First World War in 1914.

We have seen in Chapter 2 and again in Chapter 9 that the interwar period was one of unprecedented problems for the world economy, and throughout the world Marxist views about the instability of capitalism and its tendency to increase poverty amongst the many appeared to be true. It is certainly the case that the colonial powers were increasingly finding the strains of controlling their empires difficult.

After the Second World War a period of political decolonization occurred, but for many writers, primarily associated with the **dependency** tradition, the economic, political, and social structures that the postcolonial societies have inherited from the colonial past are so entrenched, that exposure to the world system will lead to their continuing to suffer exploitation.

One line of analysis points to the vastly unequal societies that exist in many Third World contexts. In many of these societies tiny elites control much of the business activities of the country and run these in their own interest often in collusion with foreign multinationals or foreign commercial interests. The legacy of **colonialism** left many economies with an economy that was geared to exporting primary commodities to the world market, and where the huge profits that were gained simply lined the pockets of the rich elites who owned these industries. In the dependency school this class of owners is referred to as being '**comprador capitalists**'. A lot of this money was then invested abroad so stunting the widening of the industrial base of these countries.

Another strand of the dependency tradition points out that the system of world trade is anything other than free and often the trade rules are clearly discriminatory. The power of the leading countries is such that they dominate the supranational governing bodies and frame the rules in their own favour.

Structuralist writers—globalization could be good if . . .

After the Second World War a new discipline of 'development economics' was born out of the belief that indeed the situation of the former colonies, or less developed countries (LDCs), as they now came to be called, was different, and that they could not pursue exactly the same path as the developed countries. Amartya Sen, Nobel Prize winner for Economics in 1998, characterized the nature of the task for these countries not as 'industrialization' but as '**late industrialization**'. LDCs faced an already developed capitalist world and so in order to be fully integrated might need time to catch up and a different set of policies to do so. In other words, the structure of the world economy meant that there wasn't a 'level playing field' between the developed and developing world, to use a more recent phrase. Furthermore, it was argued that the institutions and structures that are needed for the development of a market system were not yet present in many developing countries. These would need to be constructed before the integration of these economies into the world system. This led many countries to develop a set of distinctive non-market policies in order to rapidly industrialize their economies.

At the heart of this process was the government which sought to control and direct agriculture so that agricultural revenues could be used as a source of investment in industry. Many countries looked to the government to either own or at least have a substantial role in developing the industrial base and often this base revolved around key industries such as steel, iron, and transport. Rather than engaging in export-led expansion, import substituting industrialization (ISI) policies were implemented whereby domestic industries could be built up protected by a range of tariff and non-tariff barriers. Where countries allowed private enterprise to develop this was still controlled by the use of industrial licences provided by the government. To raise additional revenue for investment and to enable the buying in of foreign technology, countries used their natural resource commodities to raise foreign exchange but, in order to maximize the revenue streams, exchange rates were often overvalued and strict controls were kept on capital accounts to prevent money leaving the country.

The relative advantages and disadvantages of these models are still debated today but what is clear is that they were developed in response to genuine structural weaknesses in developing countries. Countries reliant on primary commodities tend to suffer from short-term volatility in prices as well as a long-run tendency of falling commodity prices. We explored the importance of price elasticity and income elasticity in Chapter 2. In the 1950s the **Prebisch–Singer hypothesis** was developed to explain the problem faced by primary goods exporters. Many developing countries do have a strength in terms of their economic base in that they can specialize in producing primary commodities such as cotton, coffee, fish, and bananas; precious minerals such as diamonds; and rare earth metals increasingly in demand for use in a range of IT devices. As supply of these increases, given the nature of the highly inelastic demands for these goods, ironically, prices for the commodities can tumble putting pressure on the revenues of the producers.

This structural weakness means that there is a tendency for the growth of monopoly power in the industries which are producing the most valuable commodities as powerful players emerge through takeovers and mergers (or other means more or less lawful) so that they can exert control over the supply of the goods and hence control prices. These monopolies tend to be dominated by small groups of powerful nationals, closely connected with multinational corporate interests.

As well as this in terms of more basic primary foodstuffs as global incomes increase, the proportion of income spent on these declines as people spend proportionately more on manufactured goods and services. It is precisely to protect their own farmers from these harsh market forces that countries in the developed world intervene in agricultural markets so heavily through price support mechanisms, subsidies, and tariffs to keep out foreign imports. This makes it impossible for small-scale food producers in the developing world to export and thus use trade as an engine of growth.

In relation to farmers, they may lack the necessary access to credit or information that enables them to take advantage of free markets. Joseph Stiglitz, Nobel Laureate for Economics in 2001, was awarded this prize for his work on market imperfections. People in markets have 'asymmetric' information; they do not each have access to all the information needed to make the best choice for them. In agricultural markets buyers can often control the market price by restricting supply and they have power to drive harder bargains because of their buying power. There may also be 'missing' markets. Farmers might not have access to credit or distribution facilities that would enable them to sell direct to markets but need to use intermediaries (see end of chapter case study).

While structuralist critics today would not necessarily agree with the precise way in which the problems above were addressed and that undoubted policy mistakes were made, they still argue that if the business environment is to be constructed in such a way as to allow globalization to bring about an inclusive growth and development then these structural weaknesses did need to be tackled.

Globalization and the newly industrialized countries

In the 1970s, the South East Asian economies of South Korea, Thailand, Malaysia, the Philippines, Hong Kong, Taiwan, and others experienced remarkable rates of economic growth (see Mini-Case 10.3 on South Korea). Characterized as the **newly industrialized countries**

(NICs), their success has provoked intense debates as to why they have grown so fast. In recent years attention has been focused on the rise of the BRICS countries, as discussed in Chapter 2.

For neoclassical economists, the NICs and BRICS have shown the success of market liberalization and the triumph of their view of the world. Far from turning their backs on the global economy, these countries have embraced extensive opening up to world trade. In these countries trade truly has been the engine of growth.

However, for structuralists, while it is the case that the NICs have used trade, this was not the only thing that they did and we need to consider the structural changes that they made *before* they felt able to benefit from trade openness. For Sen, it was important for these countries to have the social infrastructure in place before external openness. For Stiglitz, the road to the market has to be a gradual one and in particular cannot begin until the state has taken action to reduce poverty. For Rodrik, the role of the state in controlling which industries to build up was crucial as was the order in which market reforms are made. It is also important that the state puts in place the necessary institutions to control the possibility of fraud and corruption. Rodrik (2011) argues that there is a 'globalization paradox' in that if globalization is to deliver for all then there need to be international rules and national economies need to be able to retain controls over their capital accounts and exchange rates and determine their own social conditions.

Dependency writers and activists have always been concerned about the nature of the type of development that has occurred in developing countries that have increasingly been exposed to globalization. Even in the supposed successful newly industrialized countries it is argued that they have been characterized as being examples of 'crony capitalism' with small elites dominating businesses and government. Corruption has been rife and there has been a widening in income gaps which has helped fuel ethnic and religious tension. In response to this, repressive governments have sought to control their people through denial of human rights. Another major highlight of the development in all these areas has been the environmental damage that has been created. (See Mini-Case 10.2.)

Mini-Case 10.2 Cotton

Wool (and later cotton) sourced from what we now call the 'developing world', but manufactured in British textile mills, played a hugely significant role in providing the profits that fuelled the Industrial Revolution; so, couldn't the same be the case for those countries with a competitive advantage in producing cotton, the most common raw material for the world textile industry today?

Around 15 million people in West Africa are dependent on cotton for their livelihoods. Cotton producers face fierce competition from across the world. The power of global markets does ensure that only the most competitive cotton farmers will survive and in turn guarantees cheap prices for consumers.

However, is this market fair? Cotton farmers face the collective buying power of very large multinational retailers who can afford to shop around for the cheapest supplies, as well as the high levels of subsidy given to the cotton sectors in many developed countries, including that given by the US government to its 2,000 cotton farmers (Fairtrade Foundation 2010). It has been estimated that up to 5 million cotton farmers had gone out of business as a result of these subsidies. In 2003 the 'Cotton Four' (Benin, Chad, Mali, and Burkina Faso, which are among the world's poor countries) requested that the Doha Trade round eliminate such subsidies, and in 2004, the WTO declared that US cotton subsidies were indeed illegal, but despite this no agreement has yet been made to remove these.

The Doha Trade round began in November 2001 and was meant to be the latest round of global trade talks to address, in particular, the problems faced by developing countries in relation to trade in general. However, in December 2015, the Doha Trade round effectively collapsed at a meeting held in Nairobi, Kenya, resulting from differences between the US, the EU, and developing countries in relation to agriculture, industrial tariffs and non-tariff barriers, services, and trade remedies. Developing countries have sought to pressure the US and the EU to remove agricultural subsidies and lower tariffs on the manufactured goods that they produce, while the US and the EU have refused to budge on the issue of the support that they give to their farmers, and have tried to gain access to the industrial and service sectors of the developing countries.

One notable success that came out of the Nairobi meeting was a commitment for countries to begin to phase out agricultural export subsidies. However, for the Cotton Four, it is domestic subsidies in the developed and the richer developing countries to support their own cotton farmers that is the problem. At WTO meetings in 2016, the Cotton Four, and other LDC cotton producers, reinforced their plea for urgent action on the removal of all forms of subsidy, especially in the light of increasing costs and falling prices.

(*Sources:* Fairtrade Foundation (2010), Lester (2016), WTO (2016).

Question

What structures might prevent cotton producers in the developing world from achieving a high profit on their sales?

Structuralist writers argue that globalization can be made to work provided that the right economic and political structures are put in place. Here the challenge for policymakers is to build the right type of internal and external environment in which businesses both at the national and international levels can grow. For writers such as Stiglitz and Rodrik, the world described by the Washington Consensus is not realistic in the context of developing countries. First, such a list does not consider the speed and order (or sequencing) with which countries should try to achieve these goals and, second, and of crucial importance, the structures that might be needed to support these policy reforms are not there. In terms of speed and sequencing, this will very much depend on the unique circumstances of individual national business environments and it is not possible to have a 'one size fits all' approach.

Even before the 2008 global financial crisis there was a growing belief that, while the original Washington Consensus might describe where policymakers would like the economic environments to end up, there was a need to recognize that in order to achieve this a raft of supporting structures needed to be put in place first, and that the precise routes taken in designing an appropriate economic environment for each country will be different.

Mini-Case 10.3 South Korean economic development—the case of Samsung

There are over seventy-eight affiliate companies that comprise the South Korean conglomerate, Samsung, which is now a global business success story. Samsung began life in 1938 as a small exporting company of primary products (dried fish, vegetables, and fruit). Samsung's companies are involved in a huge range of products including textiles, heavy industry, ships, construction, pleasure parks, and, of course, electronic products including mobile phones. Its construction company, Samsung C&T is notable for its role in building the Burj Khalifa in Dubai, the world's highest skyscraper, as well as the Petronas Towers in Kuala Lumpur. In 2017, its Samsung Electronics division alone was the world's fifteenth largest business with a market capitalization of $254.3 billion.

Samsung's business success is indicative of the rapid economic growth of South Korea itself. In 1938, South Korea was an extremely poor country under Japanese occupation, but today it is the world's eleventh largest economy and is one of the widely discussed Asian 'Tiger' or 'Dragon' economies.

As these tigers and dragons roared ahead from the 1980s onwards, neoclassical economists such as Lal and Krueger argued that the success of South Korea was based on the development of a successful domestic free market economy, and a determined drive to exploit exports. South Korea's business environment of private enterprise and integration into the global economy stands in stark contrast with the rigidly state-controlled socialist economy of North Korea (Lal 1983, Krueger 1980). However, structuralist economists have argued that while South Korea does indeed show how globalization can play a vital role in the growth of developing countries, this has only been because of the way in which governments have been able to support the development of the economies with a range of institutional supporting policies.

Samsung is one of a handful of 'chaebol' businesses (others being Hyundai and LG), which are large family-controlled conglomerates that were actively encouraged by South Korea's army general turned President, Park Ching Hee. General

Park, who came to power as a result of a coup in 1961, was determined to develop an economic strategy that promoted rapid growth and a key point of this policy was to enable the chaebols to grow. Control of the Samsung group has stayed within the Lee family, with the original founder, Lee Byung-Chull, handing control to his son, Lee Kun-Hee, who is the current chairman of the group alongside his son, Lee Jae-yong, who is the vice-chair.

The chaebols were given preferential treatment by the government in terms of access to investment funds and were afforded high levels of protection from foreign competition. As well as tight controls to limit FDI, the government preferred to give subsidies and cheap loans to Korean firms. Ha Joon Chang highlights the determination of the government to highlight 'priority sectors' in heavy industry and export promotion, and the belief that to benefit from economies of scale there was a determination to actively encourage large protected monopoly firms to avoid the type of 'destructive competition' that was described in Chapter 2. The period up to 1980 saw Samsung diversify and grow into these sectors. Even after the restoration of democracy, Ha Joon Chang argues that the political economy of South Korea has still been heavily influenced by this state interventionist policy and he highlights the range of such measures that the government used (Chang 1993: 143).

Socialist critics have argued that the growth of South Korea masks a high level of inequity in terms of income distribution, and that the structure of the economy has been distorted by the preferential treatment given to the chaebols and the large income and wealth that have been accrued by the controlling interests in these companies (see, for example, Park and Doucette 2016). Other critics go further and argue that such rewards are even greater than what might be seen as legitimate rewards of economic success, and are indicative of high levels of corruption and the illegitimate exercise of power bought by business from elected politicians. As South Korea has grown, so have the number of legal challenges and allegations of corruption brought regarding the interrelationship between the chaebols and the government. Kun Hee-Lee was twice pardoned for alleged cases of financial misconduct relating to bribery and tax evasion. In 2017, Lee Jae-yong was arrested under suspicion of illegally channelling funds into a political fund used to support the President Park Geun-hye. Park is the daughter of General Park and, one month after Lee Jae-yong's arrest, she became the first President in South Korean history to be removed from office and have her immunity from prosecution removed (Tejada 2017) (see also Todaro and Smith 2011).

Question

What are the relative advantages and disadvantages of the corporate power that companies such as Samsung have for the South Korean economy and its global consumers?

The 2008 global crisis and the end of the Washington Consensus

In practice, up until 2008 it had been difficult to resolve the arguments about the impact of globalization as all views can select data to 'prove' their case.

Average global income levels had been rising across the world largely as a result of the rise of the South East Asian economies and the BRICS. Even in parts of Africa, which for so long has lagged far behind the rest of the world, economic growth has begun to rise. However, relative income inequality has been rising both within countries and between countries and for many critics this growing inequality represents a real challenge for the continuing growth of economies, not least because of the danger of social unrest. Such unrest can be seen in the protests of many terrorist groups across the world that feel a keen sense of injustice.

Paradoxically, as living standards on average across the world have been rising there is still the persistence of crushing absolute poverty. Collier has referred to this as being the 'Bottom Billion' (Collier 2007). It was to address this that the United Nations developed the Millennium Development Goals (MDGs) as a framework to monitor global progress on eliminating poverty and which were to be reviewed in 2015. Others point to the global problems of climate change, the global Aids pandemic and other pandemics, and mass migrations. Free trade, it is argued, is not Fair Trade, with primary goods producers vulnerable and with the rigged rules caused by the power of the western dominated IMF, World Bank, WTO, and MNCs. In many parts of the world corruption is rife and serves only to line the pockets of the few.

Throughout the 1990s and into the new millennium there were many voices that expressed 'discontent' with a globalization based on neoliberal/neoclassical policies (Stiglitz 2003). Where countries moved too rapidly to adopt these policies (so-called 'shock therapy') output collapsed and many people fell through poorly provided social nets and ended up facing severe problems. In the rush to privatize and deregulate there was evidence of poor procedures for corporate governance and in too many cases outright corruption.

In relation to the impact of globalization it was argued that too many countries attempted to liberalize their financial markets too quickly and by allowing exchange rates to float freely exposed fragile economies to severe exchange rate fluctuations.

The model countries that neoliberal critics saw as proving that the path for poor developing countries was an economy based on neoclassical principles were the Asian Tiger or Dragon economies but in 1997 the Asian financial crisis appeared to provide evidence for this structuralist view as did the internal political upheavals in many of the countries of the former Soviet Union as well as Russia itself.

Prior to 1997, the Thai government on the back of years of sustained economic growth as a result of trade-oriented policies sought to attract global capital investment by liberalizing its external capital accounts. This now meant that capital was free to move both in and out of Thailand without restrictions. The booming Thai economy attracted huge inflows of '**hot money**' which are flows of money driven by the speculative hopes that there are big returns to be made by investing in that country. The demand for the Thai currency, the baht, thus rose and so therefore did its exchange rate. This now meant that the price of Thai exports, which of course was the base of the underlying strength of the Thai economy, now rose such that the demand for Thai goods began to fall. The Thai government had been hoping to use the inflows of capital investment to boost the long-term growth of the economy but in response to the short-term falls in the profits of Thai exporters, short-term confidence in the Thai economy faltered and this then caused a dramatic outflow of capital, leading to a sudden depreciation in the value of the baht which caused widespread recession. This recession in Thailand had widespread effects across the region given the interlinked nature of the South East Asian economies.

In the former Soviet Union, the 'shock therapy' of rapid market liberalization led to an unprecedented 40 per cent fall in output in the early 1990s provoking political upheaval and a deterioration in health and well-being. Of particular concern in Russia was the privatization programme which resulted in the ownership of immensely valuable natural resource industries becoming very concentrated in the hands of a very small oligarchy. In the Middle East the 'Arab Spring' has been the result of a feeling by many that they have been left behind by economic progress.

In Latin America, despite some evidence of success, dissatisfaction began to emerge and resulted in the development of a 'Santiago Consensus' which argued for greater attention to be paid to inequality and social justice as well as access to education and, importantly, action to be taken to protect countries from global instability.

As we saw in Chapters 2 and 9, these twin problems were brought together when the excessive risk taking of the banking sector, in part fuelled by the desire to earn more from higher and higher bonuses, precipitated the financial crisis that first occurred in the US in 2007 and which then led to the global recession from 2008 onwards.

Writing in *The Nation*, Stiglitz commented

> This is not only the worst global economic downturn of the post-World War II era; it is the first serious downturn of the modern era of globalization.
>
> (2009)

For Stiglitz, the greatest challenge at the global level was to address the weakness of the international financial regulatory system that would leave countries exposed to external shocks. It was also clear that both within and between countries there was a great increase in the gap between those at the top of the earnings ladder and the vast majority of other people. His argument is not that globalization is harmful but that if it is based on a narrow view of the ability of free markets to deliver then there will be problems. In 2010 the UN-sponsored *Stiglitz Report* sought to identify the best way of reforming the global economic system (Stiglitz 2010a).

Rodrik argued that as well as the free market policies as outlined in the original Washington Consensus, what is needed is an 'augmented Washington Consensus' to show the need for greater attention to be paid to the supporting structures. In order to ensure that businesses behave responsibly, especially in countries where perhaps democratic structures and media scrutiny are less developed, then it is important to have robust and transparent corporate governance procedures in place and measures to root out corruption. Even before the financial crisis of 2008, Rodrik and Stiglitz were arguing for the need for stricter adherence to financial codes and standards underpinned by strong central banks freed from political interference. There was a recognition of the need for countries to regulate their capital accounts and exchange rates to avoid short-term instability. At the social level it was argued that the benefits of growth would need to be more equitably shared through the provision of social safety nets and targeted poverty reduction policies (Rodrik 2004).

Sen argued for the need for countries to invest heavily in the social and physical infrastructure in such things as education, health, transport, food supply, and sanitation provision.

> The overall achievements of the market are deeply contingent on political and social arrangements.
>
> (1999: 142)

Stiglitz, in particular, has highlighted the problems that can occur if there is insufficient financial regulation and too liberal a policy regarding the movements of capital across borders and we will explore this further below.

Rodrik, however, takes his critique of globalization much further by raising some central questions. He argues that the gains of globalization that do exist are not inclusively shared across the society but indeed do go to a privileged global elite leading to widening inequality both within countries and between rich and poor countries. His empirical research shows that in many cases globalization may indeed have gone too far in the sense that as more and more trade occurs, and more and more capital flows across borders, the gains in terms of growth are outweighed by the disruption to domestic production and employment that might occur. For those that remain in work there are associated costs in terms of falling wages and employers and governments find it increasingly difficult to fund pension schemes. This results in a paradox. For globalization to work, as Stiglitz argues and indeed as many in the international organizations now recognize, there would need to be a global set of institutional rules by which all countries need to abide, but it would appear there is intense national opposition to this. It is also a paradox that the countries that have benefited most from globalization have not been those that have abandoned government controls and regulations but have been those that have devised strong institutional arrangements which work with the market rather than allowing the market to replace these (Rodrik 2011).

This latter theme is picked up by Acemoglu and Robinson (whose work on economic growth we highlighted in Chapter 3): it is precisely the institutional nature of many poor countries that explains their poverty, but to explain why a country develops the particular institutions that it has we need to explore the nature of the political environment. While the rich countries of the world have been able to develop 'inclusive' institutions that have enabled growth to occur and to be more broadly spread across the population, poor countries have developed 'extractive' institutions through which wealth is accrued by powerful controlling elites who enrich themselves and ensure that the business environment is run in their own interest. For Acemoglu and Robinson

> while economic institutions are critical for determining whether a country is poor or prosperous, it is politics and political institutions that determine what economic institutions a country has.
>
> (2013)

Without political change, the fruits of globalization can simply be extracted by small controlling elites and lead to high degrees of inequality and corruption.

As we saw in the Samsung and South Korea case, Ha Joon Chang shows how Korea was able to develop so quickly but within a carefully controlled set of state-led policies. While Korea has boomed, critics argue that one persistent problem has been the tendency for too close a relationship to develop between the state and business and it is this weakness that South Korea needs to address.

Regarding the development of the actual global institutions since 1945, both Ha Joon Chang and Rodrik have sought to expose what could be seen as the hypocrisy of the West led by the US. The developed countries never did develop by simply having unregulated free trade and open capital markets in the way outlined in Williamson's Washington Consensus. Having gained such a dominant global economic position by the 1980s, they could at best be accused of suffering from a form of historical amnesia and at worst pursuing a cynical global strategy of urging (or for more radical critics, forcing) neoliberal trade policies on the poorer developing countries. For Ha Joon Chang this is tantamount to the rich countries 'kicking away the ladder' that they themselves had climbed from under the feet of the poorer countries (see Mini-Case 10.4 on China). For Rodrik this form of 'hyper-globalization' exposes the 'trilemma of globalization'. In an ideal world there would be growth, unregulated free trade—and yet countries would be able to have the policy space to have their own sovereign domestic rules and regulations. In reality, it is impossible to have all three. Countries that try to go for rapid growth through free market (hyper) globalization may at first grow quickly but this will come at the cost of high levels of inequality, eventual slowing of growth, and being forced to a 'straitjacket' of Washington Consensus type policies without the structural safeguards of inclusive institutions and the ability of countries to have their own independent economic policies (Chang 2003, Rodrik 2007).

Such views have now moved to the centre of global economic policymaking. Meeting in London in 2009, the G20 was unanimous in its agreement that, if globalization was to deliver its benefits, there would need to be greater attention paid to supporting structures and the need for policy coordination.

> The old Washington consensus is over. Today we have reached a new consensus that we take global action together to deal with the problems we face, that we will do what is necessary to restore growth and jobs, that we will take essential action to rebuild confidence and trust in our financial system and to prevent a crisis such as this ever happening again.
>
> (Gordon Brown 2009)

Mini-Case 10.4 The Chinese dream

Despite recent falls in annual growth, China is still one of the fastest growing economies in the world and is yet a prime example of how its particular road to the market has been carefully managed by the state. The Chinese themselves refer to their system as 'socialism but with Chinese characteristics', and when coming to power in 2013, Xi Jinping laid out his future vision for the country in the form of what he called the 'Chinese Dream' of socialist economic development led by the state, as opposed to the 'American Dream' of free market capitalism.

The opening speech to the WEF in 2017 was the first time a Chinese leader had ever attended this annual meeting. As we saw in Mini-Case 10.1, Xi Jinping's speech saw him move into the leadership role as champion for globalization; a role that had formerly been held by the US president, prior to Donald Trump's election. In Xi's speech he credited globalization as the reason why China had been able to grow so quickly, and outlined what he deemed to be the main tasks needed to bring about a globalization that works for all.

We have seen that this hasn't always been the case. After the declaration of the Chinese Republic in 1949, China attempted to build its economy based on a system of state planning, rapid industrialization, and collectivization of agriculture. The failure of the 'Great Leap Forward' between 1958 and 1961 showed the problems of relying on state planning and suppressing markets, and for a time, Mao Zedong, China's leader, came under criticism from fellow party members, one of whom was Deng Xiaoping. There were calls for the introduction of market reforms, and, in order to defeat what he saw as being 'revisionist' forces, Mao launched the Cultural Revolution which lasted from 1966 to 1976. Essentially this was intended to achieve a wholesale cultural transformation of society to instil in people a respect for working for the common good, rather than for achieving individual success. It also allowed for a widespread purge of all those people who Mao believed posed a threat to his position. One of those who suffered from these purges was, again, Deng Xiaoping.

On Mao's death in 1976, a party struggle broke out between those who defended the Cultural Revolution and those who criticized the economic decline that it had produced. By 1979 the latter group had won power under the leadership of Deng Xiaoping. Since 1979, China has embarked on an opening up and liberalization of its economy. China's strategy has been to allow the development of private enterprises geared towards producing light industrial goods and consumer goods for export, utilizing its skilled and well-educated but cheap labour force. The ensuing transformation in its business environment has brought about a dramatic change in Chinese economic performance and allowed it to reach unprecedented rates of economic growth. According to World Bank figures, just under 800 million people have been lifted out of poverty in the period 1980 to 2015 and there is now a large and growing middle class of urban professionals.

China's success could be seen as a vindication of the neoclassical view that free markets and openness to trade are the essential ingredients for success but, for structuralists, China shows the importance of paying attention to the institutional framework in which market reforms can be embedded. There is still a high degree of state control of the financial system, capital controls, and the Chinese currency (the RMB) is not convertible—the exchange rate is controlled by the government causing President Trump to accuse China of being a 'currency manipulator'. Land in China remains in the ownership of the state, although farmers are able to sell surpluses above that produced for the state in the marketplace. The Communist Party retains a tight grip on all national, regional, and local governance structures and there remain tight social controls and the 'hukou' system of controlling internal migration. However, such rapid economic progress has come at the cost of rapidly rising levels of inequality, overheating of the economy especially in relation to housing costs in urban areas, problems of lack of development in the rural areas, rising pollution levels, and corrupt relationships between business and state officials.

Xi's Chinese Dream is his vision to 'rejuvenate' the particular Chinese road to development which is often referred to as the 'Beijing Consensus'. For Xi, there has to be a recognition that different countries have different paths to development. At home there has been a shift in policy away from a reliance on an export strategy directed at western economies in the wake of the recessions that hit these countries after 2008, to a recognition of the need to build a strong domestic economy and target the home needs of growing affluent Chinese consumers. Globally Xi argues that it is not globalization that has failed, but that it is the western-centric system of global governance that needs to be reformed and China through the development of the BRICS bank, the Asian Infrastructure Bank, and its ambitious One Belt One Road policy is trying to x itself in the centre (see Mini-Case 16.1)

Source: *China Daily* (2013).

Questions

1. **What is meant by the term 'socialism with Chinese characteristics'?**
2. **Is China justified in seeking to control the value of its currency?**

That this was a G20 as opposed to a G8 summit was in itself significant as it heralded a shift in the balance of power between the rich developed and the now fast-growing developing countries. In September 2010 at Pittsburg the G20 was officially recognized as the premier forum for international economic cooperation and at every G20 since there have been calls to develop fairer and more equitable forms of governance.

In order to build an inclusive world economy, it is now recognized in the main global institutions such as the WTO, the World Bank, and the IMF that, important as markets are, they need to be supported by effective global institutions to regulate trade and finance, and this requires international cooperation. In 2015 the United Nations replaced the MDGs with their focus on poverty with the much more ambitious 2030 Agenda for Sustainable Development and its seventeen development goals with a wider focus on poverty, the ecological environment, and the desire to see 'prosperity for all' which on the surface would appear to have been heavily influenced by structuralist views (see http://www.un.org/sustainabledevelopment/sustainable-development-goals). Since 2014, the IMF, for example, has been championing the need for 'inclusive growth' (see e.g. Loungani 2017).

However, the need to rebalance domestic economies in the aftermath of the global crisis of 2008 has meant that little progress has been made on putting these aspirations into practice and the attacks on globalization from President Trump as well as the decision of the UK to leave the EU have indeed highlighted the tension between global consensus and domestic sovereignty.

Global ethics for the global business?

VALUES Any discussion of the impact of globalization must also encompass an analysis of the way in which global business activity itself impacts on the global environment and this must involve a discussion of ethics. For many, the impact of globalization calls for a new way of thinking about business ethics that requires us to develop a framework to especially look at global ethics.

There is no argument that globalization can be seen as an increase in international activity of business, but the question is whether this is simply an increase in quantity of these activities or that globalization represents a qualitative change. In other words, to what extent does globalization transform the nature of the impact of business activity and behaviour? Some commentators have chosen to argue that the use of the term globalization in relation to business as opposed to internationalization is an acceptance that indeed there has been a transformation in the qualitative nature of business activity across national frontiers.

> Implicit in the term 'globalization' rather than the term 'internationalization' is the idea that we are moving beyond the era of growing ties between nations and are beginning to contemplate something beyond the existing conception of the nation-state. But this change needs to be reflected in all levels of our thought.
>
> (Singer 2002)

Singer argues that globalization raises a new set of ethical questions that need to be considered once business operates across national boundaries. According to Singer, attitudes to justice are formed in relation to what people feel a fair society would be within their own national boundaries. In other words, that if people were to consider how to make the worst off richer it is only the worst off in their own societies that they may consider. Given the huge inequalities across societies, Singer argues that a just system defined within a national context can simply ignore the reality of injustices across national frontiers.

Stop and Think

If you were a global manager seeking to locate abroad and considering employment conditions:

Should you pay the local wage even if it is very low and workers complain it is barely enough for them and their families to live a decent life?

What if local health and safety standards are below the minimum standard in your home market but comply with local laws?

What is your responsibility if you use subcontractors who are employing child labour?

Employment practices

To what extent is it ethical for global firms to operate different employment practices across national boundaries? There will be differences in labour market conditions across nations but when does this become 'exploitation'?

While there are clear international laws forbidding the use of child labour, what if a western buyer purchases such goods from local manufacturers? Is this firm being unethical? If the people were not employed, what would they do? What responsibilities should businesses have to try to help these appalling social conditions?

Neither is this simply seen as a problem of the rich world exploiting the Third World. In the former, great disquiet has been expressed about the **outsourcing** of many activities and the effects on the domestic economy.

Many manufacturing, and increasingly service, activities are being outsourced to take advantage of lower costs. This has brought accusations of greed and exploitation, and yet outsourcing brings jobs and investment to developing countries. It is clear that far from resisting such outsourcing moves, developing countries positively welcome them, not least for providing the opportunity for local entrepreneurs to innovate and, in time, develop home-grown enterprises.

While it is the case that wages are lower, compared to local wage rates they are much higher. Not only does this allow the incomes of the workers involved to rise but it provides a much needed boost to local markets through increased purchasing power.

For advocates of outsourcing this is a clear example of the principle of comparative advantage—taking advantage of the different skill levels in workforces around the world—but which will lead, in time, to a convergence of incomes, as higher incomes will help provide the taxes to boost the education systems in the developing world.

Human rights

Many countries do not have full protection of human rights and this presents dilemmas for companies. Is it acceptable for companies to operate in such countries even if they try to treat their employees fairly without trying to pressure the governments for change? What is 'fair' within a national context might not seem so in a global sense. How certain are companies that they are not lowering costs by taking advantage of poor human rights or even by their own actions undermining these?

Environment

LOCAL TO GLOBAL We can here look at two spatial levels. Many countries do not have high levels of environmental legislation, and so it is possible for businesses to benefit from not having to worry about costly environmental compliance. There are numerous examples of the effects of global business on local environments. One particularly devastating example was the explosion of the Union Carbide factory in Bhopal that was discussed in Chapter 7.

Global business itself is a major contributor to possible climate change through the impact of transport systems. Air travel is now the fastest rising contributor to carbon emissions, but shipping also is a major ingredient and all aspects of international trade have severe environmental effects. At the top of all this is the global energy industry which is responsible for the majority of greenhouse gases.

Last but not least there is the worry that growth might be achieved in the poorer countries of the world, not through the development of inclusive institutions that enable prosperity to be achieved by sustainable development but through the extractive institutions that simply exploit the natural resource environment and the majority of the people. Collier has warned of the dangers of a prosperity based on a 'plundered planet' (Collier 2010) and there are many cases of the so-called 'resource curse' whereby the potential for countries to harness resource wealth and use this for development ends in exploitation and enrichment by and for elites, corruption, and in many cases internal civil war (see, for example, Stevens 2015). In response to this challenge many global primary resource extraction businesses have signed up to the Ethical Industries Transparency Initiative (EITI) (see https://eiti.org).

Abuse of market power

What responsibilities do companies have when selling their products in global markets? Tobacco companies have moved sales to the developing world as health concerns and litigation increase in the developed world. Pharmaceutical companies are accused of profiteering from selling drugs at high prices in the developing world and denying desperate people access to the medicines they need by abusive use of copyright.

Attitudes to graft and corruption

Global business will be exposed to environments where corruption and graft might be prevalent. Operating across national legal systems can exacerbate the degree to which corruption and graft are possible and harder to police or detect.

International migration

While a large proportion of migration across national borders is due to war and environmental changes, there are also large flows of economic migrants seeking to improve their living standards by securing better paid employment in countries with better economic conditions. For businesses that receive such sources of labour, there is a responsibility not to exploit migrant workers and in the process undermine pre-existing wage rates.

Global responses to these ethical challenges

The United Nations invites businesses across the world to sign up to its global compact so that businesses can develop strategies of corporate responsibility in relation to the challenges above (see https://www.unglobalcompact.org). There are also a number of other initiatives that seek to encourage ethical behaviour. The Ethical Trading Initiative is an alliance of business, trade unions, and voluntary groups that attempts to address these issues (see http://www.ethicaltrade.org/about-eti).

Looking ahead

While the first decade of the twenty-first century started with a great sense of optimism about the prospects of growth across the global economy, it ended with the gloom and despondency of the global recession. There is now widespread recognition of the structural weaknesses both at the global level and at the national level in many developing countries. It would appear that there is general agreement about the need to take concerted global action to create the necessary international and financial architecture required, and talks now focus on the need to build an inclusive world economy. However, in response to the crisis, individual countries are primarily seeking to address their own problems in their own way, and while there now appears to be a new consensus on the need to address inequality and power imbalances, so far little concrete progress has been made at the global level. There is widespread reluctance in the financial sector toward regulations and curbs on bonuses, and without global cooperation it is easy for the international financial system to avoid any particular national system of regulation. The failure of the Doha Trade round has left the global trading system in an uncertain position. In response to this, the BRIC countries led by China are seeking to assume the leading role on behalf of all LDCs in general. The Asian Infrastructure Bank led by China has also now established itself as a major rival to the World Bank, and its One Belt One Road initiative is seeking to reshape global trading links placing Asia at its heart.

The two countries that did most to shape the twentieth-century trade institutions, the UK and the US, are in a seemingly paradoxical situation. With President Trump in the US, and with Brexit in the UK, these two global powers are reluctant to further multilateral trading agreements, viewing these as a threat to sovereignty, and are instead attempting to negotiate their trading futures through a host of bilateral trade agreements. We will explore this further in Chapter 13 and in the final 'Looking Ahead' chapter.

The history of globalization shows that there is nothing inevitable about its growth, and there can be contradictory tendencies.

Summary

- Globalization links together all the spatial levels of business activity. It has grown as a result of the expansion of capitalism on a worldwide scale, but since 2008 there have been a range of challenges facing the global economic environment.
- There are competing views as to the effects of this expansion. For neoclassical/neoliberal writers, globalization is good in that it will enable worldwide prosperity to grow and the gap between developed and undeveloped countries to decrease. For radical writers, globalization is bad in that it will actually increase inequality both within and between countries and this will lead to instability and conflict. For structuralist writers, globalization can be a force for the good if policymakers put in place the institutions both at national and supranational levels to correct market imperfections and ensure good governance.
- Linking the strategic response of firms to globalization and its impact are the ethical dimensions of global activity. Analysis of the impact of globalization does involve the application of global ethics across the range of global issues.

Case Study: Is trade the engine of growth?

Many of the poorest countries in the world are endowed with a range of natural mineral and agricultural resources which are potentially very valuable on global markets. However, all too often their exports are very dependent on a very narrow range of these commodities and there is a range of problems that they face when seeking to exploit the potential of these commodities. It is argued that all too often the 'blessing' of the resource endowment can then become a 'resource curse'.

For all such basic commodities ranging from coal, oil, copper, raw earth metals, and foodstuffs (such as coffee, tea, bananas, and peanuts) we can distinguish between the 'downstream' business of production where producers struggle to gain adequate incomes and the 'upstream' commercial activities where profits are high (see Figure 10.1).

In the case of coffee, coffee producers have to face fluctuations in prices which makes planning for the future and decisions about investing difficult. On top of this is the constant uncertainty posed by climatic factors and the threat of plant disease.

The upstream end of the coffee market is dominated by four coffee roasters: Kraft, Nestlé, Procter & Gamble, and Sara Lee, each having coffee brands worth US$1 billion or more in annual sales. If we add in the German company, Tchibo, they buy almost half the world's coffee beans each year. The coffee processors and retailers add value to their products by processing and constantly seeking to establish strong brands through ever more sophisticated marketing and product development. This modern form of food production is often referred to as 'agribusiness'. Agribusiness involves a food chain whereby the food producers or farmers are often in fierce competition. On the other hand, upstream food is processed and branded by a relatively few food companies. These companies spend huge sums in developing new types of food products which are then vigorously marketed. These products are then sold, and the structure of the food retailing industry is dominated by a few very large supermarket chains. In the last twenty years there has been a big increase in the demand for coffee in the developed world as incomes have risen and tastes have changed. There has also been the rise of the large global coffee shops such as Starbucks, Costa Coffee, and Café Nero although as markets become mature the rate of growth has been slowing. However, this is now being compensated for by the fast rise in the growth of coffee shops in countries such as China and India.

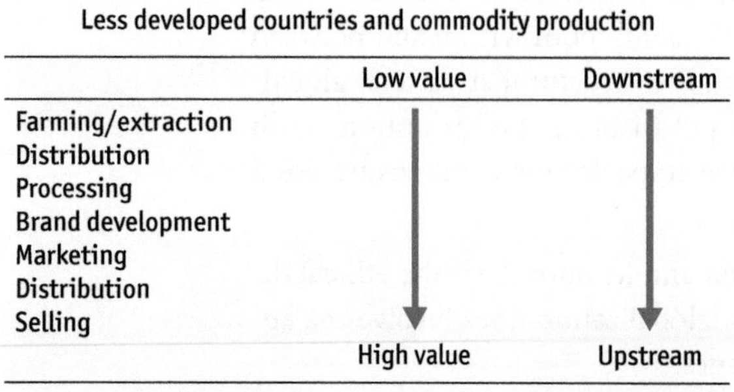

Less developed countries and commodity production

	Low value	Downstream
Farming/extraction Distribution Processing Brand development Marketing Distribution Selling	↓	↓
	High value	Upstream

Figure 10.1 The value chain in commodity production

While potentially profits on the selling of coffee at the upstream end of the process are very high, the incomes of many coffee farmers are very low and in many cases farmers struggle to stay in business. This same problem can be seen in a wide range of natural commodity markets and has provoked a lively debate as to how LDCs with a dependence on a narrow range of resource commodities can best capture the value from these and at the same time restructure and diversify their economies to avoid an over-reliant dependence on these commodities.

The structuralist approach requires a look at the structural problems at the downstream end of the value chain. There may be a lack of basic infrastructure such as roads or transport to local markets, or support to develop technology. Lack of credit or information about prices leaves farmers open to possible exploitation by moneylenders or the ability of buyers to drive down prices. At the global level the market failure is also a manifestation of the problems of the simple belief in the principle of comparative advantage. The concentration of economic activity in a narrow range of commodities has not been natural, but has been as a result of the creation of the historical imprint of colonization or in more recent times the encouragement by the international institutions to specialize in such agricultural products. In some cases, this has led to oversupply as a result of global competition. The logic of the market would be for such farmers to diversify into something else, but this will require support from the government in terms of education and training or in terms of ensuring the availability of credit. What is needed then is for countries to seek ways of capturing the value of their commodities as well as seeking ways to diversify their economies and this will require a range of domestic and global structural reforms.

Coffee initiatives such as Fair Trade have allowed farmers to retain more of the value of their produce. Indeed, some upstream producers have successfully applied for Fair Trade status to be applied to their brands. At the global level the ICO seeks to maintain cooperation between producers to stabilize prices and raise incomes. Many MNCs are keen to be seen to be operating ethically and according to global ethical codes.

Radical writers argue that all too often the export sectors are controlled either by multinational interests or 'comprador capitalists' so that even where profits are generated they do not get redistributed to the wider population. In recent years attention has been focused on the rising tendency for foreign interests in the form of MNCs, hedge funds, and even countries to acquire valuable agricultural land in the poorest places of the world. This could be justified as a way of bringing in much needed investment but for radical critics it is simply a 'land grab' (Pearce 2012).

It is clear, then, that in order for globalization to work for LDCs there is more that needs to be done than to simply seek to exploit their comparative advantages from trade and in some cases an over-reliance on trade can be detrimental to the development of these countries. In order for trade to deliver, it is vital to pay attention to the broader domestic and global conditions in which trade takes place and to ensure that global trade policy is aligned with the overall domestic economic strategy of a country.

Questions

1. **Why is it argued that the 'free market' in coffee is not fair?**
2. **Why do the coffee roasters have different market power than the farmers?**
3. **What are the 'structural' weaknesses that affect coffee farmers?**
4. **Describe the steps involved in the conversion of coffee from bean to finished product.**
5. **Why are countries which have a dependence on a narrow range of export commodities in a vulnerable position?**
6. **What types of structural reform are needed if such countries are to be able to benefit from globalization?**

Review and discussion questions

1. What are the strengths, weaknesses, opportunities, and threats presented to an individual country by globalization? How might such a SWOT analysis differ between a developed and a developing country?
2. What are the key ingredients of the Washington Consensus?
3. What are main institutions and structures that critics of the Washington Consensus argue need to be in place to ensure 'inclusive globalization'?
4. What are the consequences for the business environment of international migration?

Assignments

1. Provide a summary report of the main conclusions of the following global institutions regarding the current challenges facing the global economy:

   International Monetary Fund (see its most recent World Economic Outlook Reports available at **http://www.imf.org/en/Publications/WEO**)

   World Bank (see its regular Global Economic Prospects Reports available at **http://www.worldbank.org/en/publication/global-economic-prospects**)

   World Trade Organization (see its annual World Trade Reports available at **https://www.wto.org/english/res_e/reser_e/wtr_e.htm**)

   United Nations Commission on Trade and Development (see its annual reports available at **http://unctad.org/en/Pages/Publications/TradeandDevelopmentReport.aspx**)

   World Economic Forum (see its reports prepared for its annual meetings at Davos available at **https://www.weforum.org/reports**)

2. Visit the website of the G20 and summarize the main findings and predictions about the current state of the global environment and the prospects for global economic growth.
3. Choose three NICs and compare and contrast the way in which they have taken advantage of globalization.

Further reading

Acemoglu and Robinson (2013) *an accessible and highly readable book which argues that in order to understand how nations grow (or don't grow) depends crucially on developing the most appropriate set of institutions.*

Bhagwati (2007) *a passionate rebuttal of the arguments of the critics of globalization who argue that it works against the interests of the poor.*

Rodrik (2011) *this book explores the potential paradox of globalization and outlines the type of national and global policy responses that are needed so that globalization can ensure inclusive growth.*

Stiglitz (2003) *in theory, globalization should improve living standards for all, but the way in which globalization is managed, especially at the global level, needs to be reformed and he is particularly critical of the role of the IMF and World Bank in promoting free markets without putting in place the rules and regulations to ensure fairness.*

Stiglitz (2010b) *an analysis of the current global economic crisis from an ex-chief economist of the World Bank. He argues that this has been the result of too much faith being invested in free markets and that the balance between state and markets should be restored.*

Friedman (2006) *this book came to be seen as the classic exposition of how businesses can benefit from a globalized world.*

Test your understanding of this chapter with online questions and answers, explore the subject further through web exercises, and use the weblinks to provide a quick resource for further research. Visit the online resources at www.oup.com/uk/wetherly_otter4e/

Useful websites

The following websites contain a host of information presenting the view from the official supranational organizations and a wealth of statistical data:

www.worldbank.org
www.imf.org
www.unctad.org
www.wto.org

This site publishes postings from some of the most prominent global commentators:

www.project-syndicate.org

The following websites offer a critical view of the challenges of globalization:

www.globalisationanddevelopment.com
www.globalwitness.org
www.globalwatch.org
www.eiti.org
www.ethicaltrade.org
www.globalethics.org
www.oxfam.org
www.worldwatch.org

References

Acemoglu, D. and Robinson, J. A. (2013) *Why Nations Fail—The Origins of Power, Prosperity and Poverty* (London: Profile Books)

Bhagwati, J. (2007) *In Defense of Globalization* (Oxford: Oxford University Press)

Brown, G. (2009) Closing speech at the London G20 Summit in April 2009, this speech can be accessed via Ebsco Host Connection **http://connection.ebscohost.com/c/speeches/45565733/g20-summit-london**

Chang, H. J. (1993) 'Political economy of industrial policy in Korea', *Cambridge Journal of Economics*, 17: 131–57

Chang, H. J. (2003) *Kicking away the Ladder—Development Strategy in Historical Perspective* (London: Anthem Press)

China Daily (2013) '"Chinese dream" is Xi's vision', 18 March

Collier, P. (2007) *The Bottom Billion* (Oxford: Oxford University Press)

Collier, P. (2010) *The Plundered Planet* (Oxford: Oxford University Press)

Friedman, T. (2006) *The World Is Flat* (London: Penguin)

Hobsbawm, E. (1987) *The Age of Empire* (London: Abacus)

Jackson, D. (2016) 'Donald Trump targets globalization and free trade as job killers', *USA Today*, 28 June (accessed 23 May 2017) **https://www.usatoday.com/story/news/politics/elections/2016/06/28/donald-trump-globalization-trade-pennsylvania-ohio/86431376**

Krueger, A. (1980) 'Trade policy as an input to development', American Economic Review, Papers and Proceedings

Lal, D. (1983) *The Poverty of Development Economics* (London: Institute of Economic Affairs)

Lester, S. (2016) 'Is the Doha Round over? The WTO's negotiating agenda for 2016 and beyond', *Free Trade Bulletin*, 46, July, Cato Institute (accessed 5 July 2017) **https://www.cato.org/publications/free-trade-bulletin/doha-round-over-wtos-negotiating-agenda-2016-beyond**

Loungani, P. (2017) 'Inclusive growth and the IMF', *IMF Blog*, 24 January (accessed 4 July 2017) **https://blogs.imf.org/2017/01/24/inclusive-growth-and-the-imf**

Park, H. J. and Doucette, J. (2016) 'Financialization or capitalization? Debating capitalist power in South Korea in the context of neoliberal globalization', *Capital & Class*, 40(3): 533–54

Pearce, F. (2012) *The Land Grabbers: The New Fight over Who Owns the Earth* (London: Transworld)

Rodrik, D. (2004) 'Growth strategies', Department of Economics, Johannes Kepler University of Linz (accessed 5 May 2013) **www.econ.jku.at/papers/2003/wp0317.pdf**

Rodrik, D. (2007) 'The inescapable trilemma of the world economy', *Dani Rodrik's Weblog*, 27 June (accessed 4 July 2017) **http://rodrik.typepad.com/dani_rodriks_weblog/2007/06/the-inescapable.html**

Rodrik, D. (2011) *The Globalization Paradox: Democracy and the Future of the World Economy* (New York: Norton)

Sen, A. (1999) *Development as Freedom* (Oxford: Oxford University Press)

Singer, P. (2002) *One World—The Ethics of Globalization* (New Haven: Yale University Press)

Stevens, P. (2015) *The Resource Curse Revisited Appendix: A Literature Review*, August, Chatham House, Royal Institute of International Affairs (accessed 4 July 2017) **https://www.chathamhouse.org/sites/files/chathamhouse/field/field_document/20150804ResourceCurseRevisitedStevensLahnKooroshyAppendix.pdf**

Stiglitz, J. (2003) *Globalization and its Discontents* (London: Penguin)

Stiglitz, J. (2009) 'A global recovery for a global recession', *The Nation*, 24 June

Stiglitz, J. (2010a) *The Stiglitz Report: Reforming the International Financial and Monetary Systems in the Wake of the Recent Global Crisis* (New York: New Press)

Stiglitz, J. (2010b) *Freefall and the Sinking of the Global Economy* (London: Allen Lane)

Tejada, Carlos. (2017) 'Money, power and family: inside the chaebol of South Korea', *New York Times*, 18 February, p. B2(L), *Infotrac Newsstand* (accessed 2 July 2017) **go.galegroup.com/ps/i.do?p=STND&sw=w&u=lmu_web&v=2.1&id=GALE%7CA481620062&it=r&asid=41a3db1cce9d58c16206a512d0e49f37**

Todaro, M. P. and Smith, S. C. (2011) *Economic Development* (Harlow: Pearson), ch. 1, case study 1

UNCTAD (2017) *World Investment Report 2017 Investment and the Digital Economy* (Geneva: United Nations)

Williamson, J. (2000) 'What Washington means by policy reform', in J. Williamson (ed.), *Latin American Adjustment: How Much Has Happened?* (Peterson Institute for International Economics) (accessed 5 July 2017) **www.iie.com/publications/papers/paper.cfm?researchid=486**

World Bank (1989) *Annual Development Report* (Washington DC: World Bank)

World Bank (2004) 'Globalization, international trade, and migration', in World Bank Group (ed.), *Beyond Economic Growth: An Introduction to Sustainable Development*, ch. 12 (accessed 12 May 2013) **https://www.gfdrr.org/sites/default/files/publication/Beyond%20Economic%20Growth_0.pdf**

WTO (2016) 'Cotton-producing countries call for further steps to curb domestic subsidies for cotton', WTO 2016 News Items (accessed 2 July 2017) **https://www.wto.org/english/news_e/news16_e/cdac_23nov16_e.htm**

Xi Jinping (2017) 'Jointly shoulder responsibility of our times, promote global growth', XinHua News Agency (accessed 23 May 2017) **http://news.xinhuanet.com/english/2017-01/18/c_135991184.htm**

Chapter 11
Does business have too much power?

Paul Wetherly

Learning objectives

When you have completed this chapter, you will be able to:

- Understand the concept of power and how it relates to business and the market.
- Understand the reasons for the participation of business as an actor in the political arena.
- Understand the political process as a play of interests and power involving interaction between business, government, labour, and **civil society organizations**.
- Recognize and assess the effectiveness of methods used by business and other groups to influence government decisions.
- Evaluate evidence from case studies and examples relating to the political influence of business.

THEMES

The following themes of the book are especially relevant to this chapter

- **DIVERSITY** Business participates in the political process through companies representing their own interests and/or through associations representing collective business interests. There may be important differences of political values and interests within the business community.
- **COMPLEXITY** Corporate power needs to be understood not just in relation to the political process but in the economy and society as well.
- **LOCAL TO GLOBAL** Globalization has altered the relationship between business and government, arguably enhancing the power of the former.
- **DYNAMIC** Business influence in the political process is not constant but varies over time—it has ups and downs.
- **INTERACTION** Business is involved in a relationship with a range of stakeholders that seek to influence decisions. A particularly important relationship is with government. Because it is affected by government decisions, business has an interest in influencing these decisions to its own advantage.
- **STAKEHOLDERS** The range of actors in the political process with which business has to contend can be understood as stakeholders.
- **VALUES** The values and interests of business have to compete with those of other groups in society.

Introduction

This chapter will examine a key aspect of business behaviour and performance—the exercise of power by business, or corporate power. This involves looking at the market or capitalism not simply through the familiar economic lens as a system of voluntary exchange (buying and selling) but also in terms of relationships of power. We will be concerned with two aspects of power and the connection between them—economic power and political power. These are, roughly, control over economic resources, and the capacity to influence or control political decisions. To what extent does the former lead to the latter? In Wilks's view, it is obvious that 'large business corporations possess political power . . . and anyone who maintains otherwise is peculiarly blinkered' (Wilks 2013: 259). If so, we need to understand how political power is possessed by corporations, and to ask: does business have too much power (or too little)?

Corporate power is certainly an issue of public interest. According to the survey organization Gallup (2016), 'Americans have long been suspicious of the power of big corporations'. Gallup found that 63 per cent of Americans are dissatisfied with 'the size and influence of major corporations', and more than three-quarters of those who say they are dissatisfied want corporations to have less influence.

What is power? What's it got to do with business?

When we think about who has power in modern Britain we might think first of government and the political process (Chapter 4)—political power. UK governments exercise power through their capacity, within the parliamentary system, to make and enforce rules or laws that can affect all aspects of our lives and the future of the country, including laws governing business and economic life. Although national governments remain the key locus of political power in this form, they operate within a framework of multilevel governance. For UK governments the most important aspect of this has been, prior to Brexit, membership of the EU with its lawmaking capacity. A conventional view is that power is in the hands of elected politicians such as members of national legislatures (e.g. UK MPs) or of the European Parliament (MEPs), prime ministers and presidents, or officials such as senior civil servants and members of the European Commission. However, power is more complicated than this view suggests.

This view suggests that political power is exercised in a top-down manner, by the governors over the governed. Governments make and enforce laws and we have to obey them. Governments levy taxes and we have to pay them. However, in a democracy, power and sovereignty are supposed to be in the hands of 'the people' and politicians are elected by us to serve our interests. Through elections we get to choose who is 'in power' and we can get rid of them if we don't think they are doing a good job (Chapter 4). This suggests a bottom-up view of political power. And democracy isn't just about elections, but involves a constant flow of pressures or demands upon government as individuals, groups, and organizations in society compete to influence or control political decisions to achieve outcomes that they favour and prevent those that they oppose. For example, although the UK prime minister declared that 'Brexit means Brexit' following the 2016 UK referendum on membership of the EU, in reality the shape of Brexit depended not just on negotiations with the EU but also a continuing debate in the UK about the country's future relationship with the EU based on different interests and views. Thus, political decisions are continually negotiated in an interaction between the top-down capacity of government to make and implement policies and the bottom-up capacities of groups in society to exert pressure and make demands using resources such as public support, financial resources, expertise, connections with public officials, and organizational capacity. Business is one among many groups in this interaction competing to get its voice heard and its interests advanced. (See Mini-Case 11.1.)

Mini-Case 11.1 The world's most powerful people

LOCAL TO GLOBAL Who do you think are the most powerful people in the world today? How would you rank business leaders in relation to leaders of governments?

Forbes magazine produces a regular list of the world's most powerful people. Its 2016 list contains just seventy-four names from an estimated global population of 7.4 billion (i.e. a tiny elite comprising one very powerful person for every 100 million people on the planet, 'whose actions mean the most'). Of course, there are very many other people who exercise power in some form which seems inconsequential on a global scale, but which can impinge on our daily lives. Russia's President Vladimir Putin might be the most powerful person in the world, making decisions that have national and global consequences, but if you work as a barrista in a Starbucks outlet you might feel that your manager exercises more immediate power in your day-to-day life.

The top 20 from *Forbes* list are shown in Table 11.1. Of these, twelve are politicians and officials from the government sector as might be expected, but six of the twenty most powerful people are from the corporate sector. Within the complete list just over half are from the corporate sector, including many familiar global brands such as Walmart, Google, Exxon Mobil, News Corp, Amazon, Apple, Goldman Sachs, Toyota, and Microsoft.

Table 11.1 The most powerful people in the world, according to *Forbes*

Rank	Name/title	Organization/state
1	Vladimir Putin/President	Russia
2	Donald Trump/President	US
3	Angela Merkel/Chancellor	Germany
4	Xi Jinping/General Secretary	Communist Party, China
5	Pope Francis/Pope	Roman Catholic Church
6	Janet Yellen/Chairman	US Federal Reserve
7	Bill Gates/Co-Chair	Bill & Melinda Gates Foundation
8	Larry Page	Alphabet
9	Narendra Modi/Prime Minister	India
10	Mark Zuckerberg	Facebook
11	Mario Draghi/President	European Central Bank
12	Li Keqiang/Vice Premier	China
13	Theresa May/Prime Minister	United Kingdom
14	Jeff Bezos	Amazon.com
15	Warren Buffett/CEO	Berkshire Hathaway
16	Abdullah bin Abdul Aziz al Saud/King	Saudi Arabia
17	Carlos Slim Helu	América Móvil
18	Ali Hoseini-Khamenei	Iran
19	Jamie Dimon	JPMorgan Chase
20	Benjamin Netanyahu	Israel

Source: Forbes 2016.

The list is not definitive, and the method used may be open to question, but the table amply makes the point that power is in the hands of business as well as government, and therefore that the relationship between business and government is one that involves power.

Power can be understood in terms of being able to make decisions that affect what happens. These decisions will usually involve being able to command the actions of other people carrying out these decisions, and the consequences of the decisions may affect many people. The *Forbes* study uses a four-dimensional concept of power, as follows:

1. *power over lots of people* e.g. Wal-Mart Stores employs 2.3 million people around the world;
2. *financial resources* e.g. GDP (government sector), a company's assets and revenues (corporate sector);
3. *power exercised in multiple spheres* e.g. 'Elon Musk has power in the auto business through Tesla Motors, in the aerospace industry through SpaceX, because he's a billionaire, and because he's a highly respected tech visionary'; and
4. *active exercise of power* i.e. not just having the capacity to exercise power but actually doing so (Ewalt 2016).

This view of power emphasizes wealth as the key resource that can be translated into power, and also highlights being able to command other people's actions (power over people). Thus, wealthy individuals tend to be powerful compared to those without wealth, as shown by the presence near the top of the list of Bill Gates. But although personal wealth can be a source of power, the list shows that the most powerful people exercise power not in their personal capacity but through the positions they occupy within institutions. In other words, it is institutions in the government and corporate sectors that are powerful. Putin, Trump, and Merkel are the most powerful people only during their terms of office, after which they might depart the political scene and drop out of the list (though Trump will remain powerful because of his position in the corporate sector).

The list shows that corporations are intrinsically powerful entities, meaning that they exercise power as part and parcel of their normal commercial activities. For example, Walmart exercises power over people as an employer of over 2 million workers. Of course, Doug McMillon does not directly tell people stacking shelves in Asda stores in the UK what to do on a daily basis, but he is at the peak of a managerial hierarchy which connects him with managers in those stores. Corporations might also be able to exercise power over other stakeholders such as suppliers and consumers through contractual relationships. In all of these cases an important aspect of power exercised by corporations is bargaining power. But bargaining power is two-way, and sometimes corporations have to respond to power exercised by their stakeholders.

Power is an intrinsic aspect of normal corporate behaviour, but corporations can also seek to exercise power in other spheres, particularly in relation to government.

Question

How is wealth translated into power? Does this alter the idea that power is exercised by voters through democratic elections?

Corporate power

The market can be understood not just as a system of production and exchange, as it is often portrayed in orthodox economics, but also as a framework of economic power. Because the market is based on private ownership it places power in the hands of businesses which are able to make decisions about the use of resources. The exercise of power by business is certainly an important matter of public interest and concern because its consequences are far-reaching, affecting individuals, communities, and whole societies. Due to its consequential nature, Luger likens corporate power to a form of 'private government', suggesting that business decisions have an impact on society that rivals that of government. Luger defines 'corporate power' as multifaceted, encompassing a range of decisions:

> the power over what is produced, how these products are distributed, how work is organized, which skills workers need to develop, which advertising images are used to shape consumer consciousness, what kind of technology is developed, and what kinds of pollutants are created. Corporate power shapes the distribution of income, the conditions and location of employment, and thus the future of communities and nations.
>
> (2000: 3)

Luger's definition incorporates two distinct but related aspects of power. 'Power to' refers to the capacity of an individual or organization to perform certain actions and achieve certain outcomes, such as the power to make decisions about investment, what is produced and where. 'Power over' refers to the capacity to exercise power over the decisions and behaviour of others, so that they conform with the wishes of the individual or organization exercising power. This aspect of power can be seen in relation to employees and consumers. The employment relationship is one of authority in which the employer's 'right to manage' is utilized in order to ensure labour productivity and business profitability, including 'how work is organized' and the skills exercised by employees. In relation to consumers, Luger suggests that a type of power exercised by business is the capacity to influence or shape consumer preferences through persuasive advertising. Of course this does not mean that the exercise of power is always successful: 'power to' may be limited by resource constraints, and 'power over' may be limited by resistance or non-compliance.

Political power and corporate power

➤ INTERACTION ➤ STAKEHOLDERS In a modern society like Britain we can conceive two related frameworks for distributing power: the political system (democracy) and the economic system (the market). Political power, exercised by government, involves centralized collective decisions made on behalf of the whole society and ostensibly in the public interest. The government can, subject to parliamentary approval, and with the indirect support of voters expressed through elections, make and enforce laws that are binding on all members of society ('power over'), but it can also make decisions about the allocation of resources by public sector organizations and through decisions about taxation and public spending ('power to').

Corporate power, by contrast, involves decentralized private decisions in the interests of specific businesses and their owners. These decisions are decentralized in that, although corporate power 'shapes the location of employment' and individual corporations can make decisions that affect thousands of employees, the overall spatial pattern of employment within the economy is the outcome of separate decisions by a large number of firms. Thus, a contrast between government power and corporate power is that in the former it is relatively easy to pinpoint who is in charge of government. We can say that responsibility for political decisions in the UK rests with the prime minister and members of the cabinet. In the world of business, on the other hand, although we can easily identify large and powerful corporations and CEOs (such as Doug McMillon and Walmart), no one is in overall charge (Kay 2004). Not even the largest companies are able to control what happens in particular markets since decisions are made in conditions of uncertainty in which competition determines which experiments are successful or unsuccessful—a process described by Kay as 'disciplined pluralism'. For example, it is impossible to predict the future of the car and what type of fuel system will replace the internal combustion engine. No single company, however large, is able to control this. However, Luger emphasizes that the whole framework of corporate power has consequences for society that are as important as those of government decisions.

Another important contrast concerns the accountability of government power and corporate power. Whereas, in a democracy, political power is in the hands of 'the people' through elections, we do not get to choose who is 'in power' in business and, unlike politicians, if we don't think business leaders are doing a good job we cannot kick them out. If democracy is such a good thing, why isn't it extended to the world of business? Traditionally, this lack of accountability has been an important basis of criticism of the capitalist system. Public ownership or government regulation of the private sector have been advocated as ways of effecting some degree of public democratic input to business decisions.

However, two responses can be made to this critique. First, the electorates of capitalist economies like Britain have not supported left-wing schemes of large-scale public ownership and economic planning. Indeed, since the 1980s there has been a reversal, through privatization, of the limited measures of public ownership that had established the 'mixed economy' in the decades after the Second World War. Thus, it can be argued that, although business leaders are not democratically elected and accountable, as a society we have, through the democratic process, chosen an economic system based on private ownership. In other words, if we didn't think business leaders were doing a good job we could take action to change their behaviour through the democratic process. Indeed, public support for renationalization of the rail companies in the UK, as promised in the Labour Party's manifesto for the 2017 general election, shows the potential for this to occur at least on a limited scale. This takes us to the second point, that arguably what matters to us most is how business performs in terms of efficiency and providing customers with what they want. Thus, Kay argues that business has won legitimacy for the exercise of economic power through success. 'We accept, even welcome, the authority of Sainsbury and Tesco in delivering our groceries because of the manifest effectiveness with which they have done this in the past. In ensuring food safety, consumers now have more trust in supermarkets, which are competing to retain their reputation, than they have in government' (2004: 40).

Kay's argument that the economic power of business is legitimized by success means that it is conditional on performance and therefore can be precarious and open to challenge. This is illustrated by the financial crisis and ensuing economic recession stemming from the manifest ineffectiveness of the banking system to serve the needs of the economy. The financial sector, concentrated in London, plays an important role in the UK economy and, in recent decades, was encouraged as a key driver of economic growth and prosperity. Its competitive success was seen as vital to the future of the UK as a nation, and it won legitimacy through this apparent success. However, the financial crisis from 2008 precipitated a reappraisal and the emergence of the view that the banks had become too big and too powerful. It turned out that the future they led us into involved the deepest and most prolonged economic recession since the 1930s. In contrast to the supermarkets, the banks have *lost* legitimacy for the exercise of economic power through *failure*. Because of this, government power was used to intervene in the banking system, including measures of (temporary) public ownership, and proposals for reform and more effective regulation of the banks moved up the political agenda.

A shift in public attitudes to business in the aftermath of the financial crisis and the long recession was reflected in Theresa May's speech launching her bid to become leader of the UK Conservative Party in 2016. In a section of the speech headed 'Getting tough on corporate irresponsibility' May referred to the need to tackle rising executive pay and growing inequality, abuse of market power by utility firms and retail banks, and individual and corporate tax avoidance and evasion (May 2016).

Stop and Think

What do you understand by the terms 'political power' and 'corporate power'? In what ways are they different or similar?

According to Kay, that Tesco is a powerful company and its chief executive is a powerful businessman are matters that we are sensible not to worry about so long as we are happy with Tesco's effectiveness in delivering our groceries (and a wide range of non-food products and services). Yet the success of the supermarkets is not as clear-cut as Kay suggests. For example, in 2013 supermarkets in the UK were caught up in a scandal caused by horsemeat being found in products labelled as containing beef that damaged public trust (Levitt 2016). This involved a failure on the part of supermarkets to properly monitor their supply chains. More generally, the benefits to consumers are not straightforward, and in any case this is a rather limited criterion for judging success as there is a wider set of issues in terms of which the way supermarkets wield their economic power may be questioned (Simms 2007).

Stakeholders and the 'play of power'

STAKEHOLDERS From Mini-Case 11.2 we can see that the power exercised by supermarkets involves relationships with a range of stakeholders, defined as individuals, groups, and organizations that are affected by and therefore have a 'stake' in business decisions and behaviour.

Mini-Case 11.2 Should we welcome or worry about the power of supermarkets?

VALUES Yes, they are good at delivering our groceries, but ... many questions have been raised about the power and impact of supermarkets in modern society, including the following:

1. The supermarket sector in the UK is dominated by just four very large companies: Tesco, Sainsbury's, Asda, and Morrisons together account for nearly 70 per cent of grocery sales (Kantar Worldpanel https://www.kantarworldpanel.com/en/grocery-market-share/great-britain/snapshot/18.06.17).

   In oligopolistic markets consumers have fewer options to 'shop around' and this usually means that competitive pressure is reduced, and the market power of sellers is increased, though the 'big four' have had to respond to competitive challenges from the budget supermarkets Aldi and Lidl.
2. Although supermarkets do engage in price competition, their claims can be misleading, and it is difficult for consumers to make price comparisons, especially in relation to the whole shopping basket.
3. The low prices offered to consumers may be achieved by the capacity of supermarkets to exercise market power in relation to suppliers, forcing down prices paid to farmers in the UK and imposing stringent quality standards.
4. The low prices offered to consumers may be achieved by sourcing products overseas where farmers may be paid very low prices or people have to work for very low wages, sometimes in sweatshop conditions.
5. The growth and diversification of the supermarkets has been at the cost of closure or decline of specialist retailers, such as bookshops, and contributed to the reduction of the diversity and distinctive character of local high streets.
6. Supermarkets use their political and legal clout to win planning battles against local opposition to the opening of new stores.
7. Supermarkets are part of the problem of the marketing and sale of products with adverse social and health impacts, such as cheap alcohol and foods high in sugar, salt, and fat.
8. Supermarkets have damaging environmental impacts through the 'air miles' involved in sourcing food and other products from overseas, and store locations that require most shoppers to travel by car.
9. Some supermarket jobs, such as checkout operators, are among the lowest paid occupations in the UK economy.

Question

Do you agree that consumers get a good deal from supermarkets? Do you agree with Kay that the economic power exercised by supermarkets is legitimated or justified by the good deal that customers get?

Because business decisions can have far-reaching economic and social consequences the number and range of stakeholders can be very large, including:

- shareholders;
- managers;
- employees;
- suppliers;
- customers;
- competitors;
- local community/wider society; and
- government.

The idea of a 'play of power' is used to indicate that power is not exercised in a one-way direction, and that the outcome depends on the resources and actions of the stakeholders involved. In this chapter we will look at corporate power using this stakeholder framework in terms of:

COMPLEXITY

- Relations between direct stakeholders, both internal (shareholders, directors/managers, employees) and external (customers, suppliers). These relations involve both organizational hierarchy and authority, and market relations of exchange involving bargaining power.
- Relations with indirect stakeholders in the form of civil society organizations (CSOs) or 'pressure groups' that seek to influence business decisions in relation to their own interests or some wider public good as they see it.
- Relations with government through the participation of business as an actor in the political arena.

Bargaining power

In markets economic actors—individuals and organizations—attempt to realize their interests through exchange relationships. These relationships of voluntary exchange involve the direct or primary stakeholders in business—customers, suppliers, and employees—and, according to orthodox economic theory, yield mutual benefit on the basis of a price that is acceptable to both buyer and seller. In principle each party is better off after the exchange. However, this idea of voluntarism tends to mask the extent to which an exchange relationship intrinsically involves some degree of bargaining power. Bargaining power refers to the ability of buyer or seller to alter the terms of exchange in their own favour—to bid the price up or down, or to get more or give less. Bargaining power depends largely on the number of buyers and sellers (market structure)—your bargaining power is maximized if you are the only seller (monopolist) or buyer (monopsonist). It is in this sense that conventional economics does recognize power as an aspect of different types of market structure.

Consumer sovereignty?

In competitive markets it is the ability and willingness of consumers to 'shop around' that disciplines firms so that they have to produce what consumers are willing to buy and cannot sell above a market price that is determined by the downward pressure of competition. 'Consumer sovereignty' is secured through 'exit' power, as consumers punish firms that attempt to raise their prices by going elsewhere. Conversely, in oligopolistic markets dominated by a small number of large firms the possibility arises of firms refraining from competition and engaging in unfair practices: price-fixing, bid-rigging, and discussing tenders, and dividing up and sharing markets. The power of government, in the form of competition law, provides a mechanism to deter, investigate, and punish such collusion and to ensure that consumers and other businesses benefit from fair competition on a 'level playing field' (Competition and Markets Authority 2014, 2015). In other words, regulation is used to prevent abuse of power by business and protect consumers. For example, in 2013 the Office of Fair Trading (OFT) imposed fines on the vehicle manufacturer Mercedes-Benz and three commercial vehicle dealers for market rigging, in other words, refraining from competition through market sharing and price coordination (Office of Fair Trading 2013). In 2016 the Competition & Markets Authority (CMA) launched an investigation into possible breaches of consumer law by ticket resale websites including Viagogo (Treanor and Davies 2016).

In a market bargaining power can also be based on differences in information or knowledge. Consumers are generally at a disadvantage because they have limited information about goods or services and rely on what businesses tell them. This creates the risk of consumers being taken advantage of through mis-selling, where they are persuaded by the seller to buy products that the seller knows are not appropriate to their needs.

The Consumer Rights Act 2015 gives consumers rights when they buy goods from a business and provides protection against firms taking advantage of their lack of knowledge or information. Under the Act any contract involves 'implied terms' that the goods are of satisfactory quality, fit for purpose, and as described (Department for Business, Energy & Industrial Strategy [no date]).

INTERACTION Large companies also use advertising and branding strategies to influence consumer preferences and build up customer loyalty or, as Luger puts it, 'to shape consumer consciousness'. The claim here is that advertising is a form of corporate power through which business is able to instil in consumers wants that they would not otherwise have. This is an important form of corporate power since it brings into question the idea of consumer sovereignty—that consumers are ultimately in charge in markets. The claim that businesses respond to independently formed consumer preferences is opposed by the claim that consumer preferences are shaped by businesses. Rather than consumers stimulating supply to satisfy their demand, firms stimulate demand to satisfy their supply. Instead of businesses serving consumers, consumers serve businesses. In reality, each of these views is probably too simplistic: consumers are not mere dupes of corporate advertising, but neither are they unaffected by it.

Advertising is principally intended to persuade us to buy a particular product or brand—to buy a Samsung rather than an Apple iPhone or Corona rather than San Miguel—but it may have a larger social and economic significance. It can be argued that advertising plays a key role in creating and sustaining a **consumerist** or materialist culture in which success and well-being are associated with increased consumption. By continually stimulating new wants, advertising provides business with ever-expanding markets—making more and more money by selling more and more products. This can be seen as a good thing, just as a way of describing the dynamism of the market that has produced prosperity in the rich economies and is now lifting millions of people out of poverty in developing countries. And greater material prosperity may be seen as a basic human desire or preference rather than something that is created by business. But the pursuit of happiness through increased consumption might be self-defeating, particularly in societies that are already rich, since always wanting more is a recipe for dissatisfaction and means happiness is always out of reach. It has also been argued that GDP per head (i.e. average income and material standard of living) is a poor measure of happiness or well-being, and that the pursuit of ever more economic growth is ecologically unsustainable.

Advertising primarily targets consumers in terms of purchasing decisions intended to fulfil our wants or desires. In so far as it is successful in shaping those wants and desires it leads us to question how far consumers are really in charge of markets. But apart from this contested idea of 'consumer sovereignty' which operates through millions of independent purchasing decisions, consumers may exercise power in markets in a more deliberate and organized way through ethical consumerism or consumer activism. This involves consumers seeking to use the power that their purchasing decisions give them to influence business behaviour in order to achieve ethical outcomes. Whereas the conventional idea of consumer sovereignty is essentially concerned with the responsiveness of markets to the self-interest of consumers, consumer activism is concerned with using purchasing power for a wider group or public interest. For example, Nescafé might use advertising to persuade consumers of the superior taste of its coffee, but consumers might be more interested in supporting the Fairtrade movement to ensure a decent price is paid to producers. We will examine ethical consumerism later in the chapter—see Mini-Case 11.3 on advertising and corporate power and Mini-Case 11.4 on ethical consumerism.

Industrial relations

It can be argued that market competition does generally provide a good deal for consumers, but that this is achieved by bargaining power being exerted back along the supply chain (buyer power) in relation to suppliers and employees (Reich 2008). The primary relationship between business and labour (or employers and employees) can be seen as a market relationship of

Mini-Case 11.3 Is advertising a form of corporate power?

Tobacco companies produce products that kill their users, and tobacco companies are powerful organizations, in economic and political terms. They use their power to protect their businesses and increase their sales. According to the World Health Organization (WHO), 'The tobacco epidemic is one of the biggest public health threats the world has ever faced'. There are more than 1 billion smokers worldwide, and 80 per cent of them are in low- and middle-income countries. 'Tobacco kills up to half of its users . . . more than 7 million people each year' (WHO 2017a).

Governments in the UK have moved to restrict advertising of cigarettes as part of public health campaigns to reduce smoking. For example, tobacco advertising and promotion is generally prohibited, the display of cigarettes in supermarkets is prohibited, and cigarettes must be sold in standardized (plain) packaging bearing health warnings. These moves are based on the belief that such advertising has a persuasive purpose and effect in encouraging people to take up smoking (especially young people) or increase their consumption. In other words, advertising is seen as a form of corporate power through which corporations can shape consumer preferences and behaviour. In response to this tobacco companies have asserted that consumers make up their own minds whether and how much to smoke and that the purpose and effect of advertising is to persuade consumers to switch brands. In this view, advertising does not grow the market and has no negative public health effects. People smoke because they want to and not because tobacco companies persuade them to.

Tobacco companies also use their political power to oppose restrictions on advertising and other regulations, including lobbying and mounting legal challenges. In other words, they use their political power to defend their economic power. Much of this effort is now focused on low- and middle-income countries which constitute the largest markets for tobacco, for example in Africa. According to WHO 'the tobacco industry continues to hamper government efforts to fully implement life- and cost-saving interventions' and 'Tobacco industry interference in government policy-making represents a deadly barrier to advancing health and development in many countries' (WHO 2017b).

Question

Who do you think is right in this debate about advertising as a form of corporate power?

contract or exchange—buying and selling—in which a wage or salary is the price paid in exchange for the employee's ability to perform a certain role or range of duties. However, unlike many other acts of exchange, that between employer and employee involves an ongoing relationship—the performance of the business depends on how effectively the two sides work together or collaborate. The relationship can be characterized as a 'wage–effort bargain', meaning how much pay employees receive in return for how much effort they have to put in. This bargain is critical for both parties as it determines the livelihoods of employees and the profitability of business. Each party will try to strike the best bargain that it can, and the outcome will depend on their relative bargaining strengths.

COMPLEXITY This varies between different labour markets, and over time according to shifts in the economic environment and the legislative framework governing industrial relations. Employees have greater bargaining power when they command skills that are in relatively short supply, whereas unskilled workers have weak bargaining power with employers because they are much easier to replace. Historically, the principal motivation for the development of trade unions was the desire to enhance what was perceived as the generally weak bargaining position of employees in relation to employers by bargaining as a group, i.e. on a collective basis. And the development of trade unions was quickly followed by the attempt to gain political representation so as to influence labour law, especially through the foundation of workers' or socialist political parties such as the UK Labour Party, established in 1906 largely at the instigation of trade unions. The rationale for such parties is the need to supplement collective bargaining in the workplace in order to advance workers' interests. For example, collective bargaining requires a supportive legal framework to enable trade unions to operate, to be recognized by employers, and to take forms of collective action such as strikes. Workers' parties also campaigned for expansion of the welfare state to address social problems particularly affecting the working class and poor (Beveridge's 'five giant evils'—see Chapter 14). In addition, trade unions have acted as pressure groups seeking to influence political decisions, for example through the Trades Union Congress (TUC). Among its other purposes the TUC exists to 'make representations to government and represent British workers on European Union and international bodies' (https://www.tuc.org.uk/about-tuc/about_role.cfm). In general, the trade union movement can be seen as a form of countervailing or balancing power in relation to employers both within the workplace and in the political process.

DYNAMIC In the post-war decades (post-1945) high employment, economic growth, and a favourable political environment combined to enhance the bargaining power of trade unions in the UK economy. However, trade union power has undoubtedly declined in the UK since the 1970s due to a number of interrelated factors, including:

- Economic change, particularly deindustrialization involving loss of jobs in highly unionized industries, and the increase of self-employment, part-time, and precarious work.
- Political change involving an ideological shift towards support for 'free markets' and the 'right to manage', expressed in legislative changes designed to weaken trade unions. The idea that trade union power had to be weakened as a condition of improved economic performance was a central plank of the approach of the Conservative governments in the UK in the 1980s.
- Increasing competition in global markets leading to a squeeze on employees (Reich 2008).

Trade union membership increased during the post-war period to a peak of over 13 million in 1979, but has since fallen by more than half to 6.2 million in 2016 (Department for Business,

Energy and Industrial Strategy 2017). As a proportion of employees in the UK trade union membership has fallen from nearly one-third (32.4 per cent) in 1995 to less than one-quarter (23.5 per cent) in 2016.

Most trade union members (3.6 million) are employed in the public sector where they represent over half of all employees (52.7 per cent). In contrast there are only 2.6 million trade unionists in the private sector where they account for just over 1 in 8 employees (13.4 per cent). Although we might think of union membership mainly in terms of lower paid jobs, it is actually highest in professional occupations, especially in the public sector. 'Employees in the professional occupations account for 38.4 per cent of union members, but only 21.2 per cent of employees in the UK worked in these occupations' (Department for Business, Energy and Industrial Strategy 2017). And, in contrast with the traditional male image of trade unions, today women are slightly more likely than men to be members of trade unions. Although trade unionism has declined since the 1970s, trade unions remain important features of the economic and political landscape in modern Britain.

There is no agreement about what the balance of power *should* be in relations between employers and trade unions, and it has been claimed at various times in relation to one side or the other that it has too much power. Conservative governments under Prime Minister Thatcher thought the unions had too much power in the 1970s, but critics argue the pendulum has swung too far the other way (Hutton 2015: 40). Business organizations such as the Confederation of British Industry (CBI) and Institute of Directors (IoD) will naturally take a different view of this matter than the representative body for the trade unions, the TUC. This simply reflects the conflicting interests in the wage–effort bargain. But it is also a debate about different models of a capitalist economy and the meaning of business success.

We can broadly distinguish between two models and ideas of business success by asking whether power ought to be exercised by managers in an essentially top-down fashion over the workforce, or employees ought to be seen as partners in the business. These two approaches are exemplified by the US and Germany, with the UK being identified closely with the US model (Bronk 2000). The top-down approach is expressed in the idea of the 'right to manage': in this view decision-making is the prerogative of managers and employees are essentially hired to carry out instructions in what can be seen as a 'transactional' model of the employment relationship. This can also be expressed in an 'us and them' style of employee relations that emphasizes the conflicting interests of employers and employees and is characterized by low trust. The idea here is that managers represent the interests of owners to whom they are properly responsible, and that business success relies on their talented stewardship. In contrast, the German model sees employers and employees as 'social partners' and corporate governance involves 'co-determination' or power-sharing, in the form of a system of works councils and employee participation on boards. This involves a more collaborative and 'relational' style of employee relations that emphasizes the shared interests of employers and employees and is characterized by high trust.

For Hutton, the weakening of trade unions in the UK since the 1980s has been a major factor in increasing inequality involving 'the organisation of employment at the bottom as forms of subjugation [through precarious work such as zero hours contracts], and at the top as the opportunity for gothic levels of greed [rocketing executive pay]' (2015: 40). Hutton (1996, 2015) advocates reform of the company and British capitalism to create a 'stakeholder' model embedding the voice of employees akin to the German variant. In this view a 'partnership' model would require a willingness by business to cede managerial autonomy and accept constraints on the right to manage, but would also require trade unions to embrace a new role and move away from a 'confrontational' approach to industrial relations.

Buyer power in the supply chain

Bargaining power between businesses operates in the supply chain as the power of buyers or sellers. In this case power is an aspect of relations between businesses. For example, critics argue that supermarkets are able to offer low prices to consumers by 'squeezing' suppliers, who in turn pass these pressures on to their own employees as low wages (e.g. see Tescopoly Alliance http://www.tescopoly.org). The suppliers have to comply with the demands of supermarkets because of their 'buyer power': farmers might be dependent on their contract with a supermarket, but the supermarket can fairly easily switch suppliers. For example, the National Farmers' Union (NFU) has claimed that some British agricultural produce is being 'endangered' by price promotions which are passed on to suppliers as supermarkets are determined to retain their profit margins. This can mean that prices paid to producers do not cover production costs. Supermarkets are also criticized for fining producers when customers complain, even if it is not the farmer's fault (Insley 2013). In order to tackle these and other practices and protect suppliers, the Competition Commission introduced a Groceries Supplies Code of Practice (GSCOP) which came into force in 2010. The provisions of the code had to be incorporated into contracts between supermarkets and their suppliers, and it encompassed all retailers with annual groceries sales exceeding £1 billion (i.e. including all the major supermarkets). The aim of the code was 'to ensure that suppliers do not have costs imposed on them unexpectedly or unfairly by retailers' (Competition Commission 2009). In 2013 the UK government created the position of Groceries Code Adjudicator (GCA) with the role of overseeing the relationship between supermarkets and their suppliers and enforcing the Groceries Code (Seely 2015). In 2016 the GCA ruled that Tesco was in breach of the code, finding that 'Tesco knowingly delayed paying money to suppliers in order to improve its own financial position' and thus 'prioritised its own finances over treating suppliers fairly' (GCA 2016).

Engagement with CSOs

INTERACTION Business also has to engage with a range of indirect stakeholders in the community and wider society which may seek to influence business decisions and behaviour. There is a large number and diverse range of groups and organizations in society (sometimes referred to as 'civil society organizations' or CSOs). They are non-market and non-governmental, representing different interests and causes—including charities, voluntary organizations, professional associations, campaigning groups, and think tanks—which from time to time engage with business in pursuit of their aims.

These aims might be tied to the interests of their members, such as trade unions or professional associations, or local campaign groups. But the aims of CSOs can also be related to a wider public interest, such as environmental or public health concerns, or large businesses seen as acting immorally by avoiding corporation tax. For example, there has been widespread opposition, involving local and national campaigns, to proposals for 'fracking' to extract shale gas by companies such as Quadrilla (Wheatley 2017). UK Uncut is a grassroots movement or pressure group which has campaigned against corporate tax avoidance, targeting multinational corporations including Starbucks and Vodafone, and often engaging in acts of civil disobedience or direct action. The group makes the case that corporations paying their taxes would enable funding of essential public services. A protest in 2014 aimed 'to transform dozens of Vodafone branches into "living rooms, shelters, refuges, bedrooms and hostels" . . .to focus on how tax dodging is "crippling the UK's social housing sector"' (Houlder 2014).

Mini-Case 11.4 Ethical consumerism

VALUES Ethical consumerism can be defined as:

personal allocation of funds, including consumption and investment, where choice has been informed by a particular issue—be it human rights, social justice, the environment or animal welfare.

(Cooperative Bank 2008)

Thus, whereas consumer behaviour might normally be understood in terms of personal wants and self-interest, ethical (or political) consumerism or consumer activism seeks to harness the purchasing power of consumers to make a difference in relation to an issue of ethical concern. This does not mean ignoring self-interest, but trying to balance it with the interests of others, and may involve being willing to pay a higher price. For example, when people decide to purchase Fairtrade products, such as bananas or coffee, they do so out of regard for the interests of the farmers who produce these crops in developing countries—the whole point being to improve their incomes and help them to escape poverty. In choosing Fairtrade products there is an implied criticism of big business for giving farmers a raw deal. In other words, consumers may be motivated by a desire to do something *for* the world's poor and, at the same time, to take action *against* big business.

Ethical consumerism can be essentially an individual act, but it is often linked to a wider campaign or movement the point of which is to mobilize a large number of consumers in a process of collective action so as to bring effective pressure on business to alter its behaviour, such as through an organized consumer boycott, or to provide custom for businesses which are seen as ethical. Campaigning organizations have been important in raising awareness of specific ethical issues or products, and the idea of ethical consumerism more generally. For example, the Fairtrade Foundation was established in 1992 by a range of existing CSOs including Christian Aid, Oxfam, and the World Development Movement. The Foundation licenses use of the FAIRTRADE Mark as a consumer guarantee on products, works to raise public awareness, and 'through demonstration of alternatives to conventional trade and other forms of advocacy . . . empowers citizens to campaign for an international trade system based on justice and fairness' (http://www.fairtrade.org.uk/).

Ethical consumerism appears to be a growing phenomenon in the UK. It has been claimed that the value of ethical purchases in 2015 was £38 billion, an increase of 8.5 per cent on 2014 and the thirteenth consecutive year of growth. The same report states that more than half of respondents had participated in some level of boycott of products and/or services during the year, the main motivations being animal rights, unethical corporate practices, and environmental concerns (Ethical Consumer 2016). A survey by YouGov shows that over one-fifth of consumers have boycotted a product following a scandal or negative publicity, the principal motivations being tax avoidance/evasion, workers being treated unfairly either in the company or in the supply chain, and cover ups. The survey also shows that a high proportion of boycotters do not go back to the product they have boycotted (Harmston 2017).

Questions

1. **Ethical consumerism—do you do it? Does it work?**
2. **Have you ever made decisions about spending based on ethical grounds? Were your decisions part of an organized campaign, such as a consumer boycott?**
3. **Do you feel that ethical consumerism, such as on environmental grounds, is an effective way of putting pressure on companies and bringing about change? Or are consumers likely to be conned by corporate 'greenwash'?**
4. **What do your thoughts on these questions say about corporate power?**

Business in the political arena

INTERACTION **COMPLEXITY** In a democracy it is legitimate for business to engage in the political process in order to influence decisions to its own advantage. However, a range of other groups compete to influence government in pursuit of their own interests and values, for example campaigning against road building or airport expansion, or to introduce new regulations on business to protect the environment. We can understand this competition to exert influence or control over political decisions by identifying three principal groups or interests: business, labour, and CSOs, as depicted in Figure 11.1.

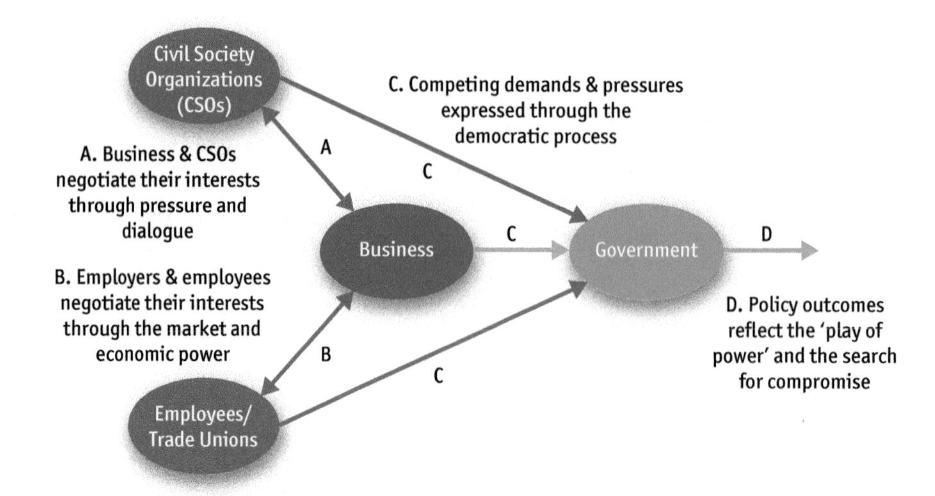

Figure 11.1 The interactions between business, labour, CSOs, and government

Thus, as we have seen, employers and employees negotiate their interests through the market and bargaining power (interaction B in Figure 11.1). However, this economic relationship is governed by law and public policy. For example, labour law determines the individual and collective rights of employees. This means that each party has an interest in trying to shape political decisions so as to alter the economic relationship to its own advantage. For example, trade unions will bargain with employers to try to win higher wages for their members, but they might supplement this with a political campaign to secure a statutory minimum wage (national living wage) as in the UK (see Chapter 1). In other words, we can see how the economic interests of business and labour in the market find expression in political action. Similarly, CSOs, such as environmental pressure groups, which target businesses directly through methods such as public relations campaigns or consumer boycotts (interaction A in Figure 11.1) may put pressure on government to introduce laws or policies that will induce or compel a change in business behaviour.

Thus, competing demands and pressures expressed through the democratic process (C in Figure 11.1) can be related largely to interests generated in, or affected by, the operations of business and markets. Government can be used to alter the distribution of resources and income, and more generally of costs and benefits, that would otherwise result from the operation of the market. Business is an actor in the political arena, and participates in a play of power involving government, trade unions, and a range of CSOs.

> *Stop and Think*
>
> To what extent are political debates and conflicts based on economic interests and values?

Does business enjoy a 'privileged' position in the political process?

It can be argued that in liberal democracies, that ostensibly enshrine the principles of political equality and 'rule by the people', governments in fact come under the influence of business interests to such an extent that democratic ideals are undermined. Thus, Beetham claims that 'corporate and financial elites have inserted themselves into the heart of government over successive administrations, and . . . exercise a predominant influence over it' (2011: 2), and Wilks asserts that 'the overriding purpose of the state is increasingly to serve corporate interests' (2013: 261).

In this view there is a tension between democracy and what Beetham calls an 'unelected oligarchy' (i.e. rule by the few), between the idea that the future of the country is decided through elections in which all citizens may participate and the idea that decision-making is dominated by corporate and financial elites. Wilks argues that 'Until recently the power of the corporation was held in balance [by the power of the vote]. Since the late 1980s that balance has been overturned . . . [and the] imbalance has become clearer and more worrying' (2013: 251).

Not all businesses are political actors and they are certainly not all equally powerful. In general, it makes sense to think of large companies, particularly multinationals, as powerful political actors. In addition, certain sectors or industries may be more powerful than others due to their vital contribution to economic performance in terms of innovation, employment, and growth. For example, in Britain, the financial sector, concentrated in London, has a strategic economic importance that arguably confers unmatched political influence. Other examples might include key sectors of manufacturing such as the car industry (see Mini-Case 11.5). How do corporate and financial elites wield political influence? The claim that democratic politics is characterized by business dominance is based on two ideas:

- the advantages that business enjoys in the electoral process and the representation of group interests—*business as a political actor*; and
- the crucial importance of business decisions for society as a whole—*control without trying* (Lindblom 1980).

Viewing business as a political actor means looking at the various ways in which business, individually or collectively, can decide to participate in the political process at various levels in order to try to influence decisions in its favour. In contrast, 'control without trying' refers to a tendency for government to implement policies that benefit business even in the absence of political involvement by business.

Beetham (2011) analyses corporate influence by making a similar distinction between 'systemic constraints' which emanate from the social and economic context in which government operates, and the ways businesses operate as political actors through two 'modes of corporate influence'. The systemic constraints are:

- the prevailing ideology (neoliberalism or 'market fundamentalism') which frames the range of acceptable policies;
- economic constraints particularly connected with globalization and the dominance of the financial sector;
- corporate tax avoidance eroding the tax base; and
- reliance on private sector expertise and organizational capacity.

In addition there are two modes of corporate influence which echo Luger's analysis:

- buying informal influence (including financing political parties, financing think tanks, and lobbying); and
- 'revolving doors'.

Mini-Case 11.5 Political power of US car makers

Luger has studied the long-term political influence of the US car industry in the twentieth century (between 1916 and 1996). He argues that, although political influence has fluctuated, the US car industry's political influence is evident throughout the whole period and, overall, it is able to exert an 'inordinate impact on public policy' (Luger 2000: 1). How has this influence been exerted? The mechanisms of influence identified by Luger include the following:

- Lobbying—through in-house lobbyists based at the heart of government in Washington, contact between top managers and senior officials in government, and the hiring of specialist lobbyists and PR firms (Luger 2000: 183) (see case study at end of chapter).
- As well as acting on their own behalf firms also rely on business groups and associations to represent their (shared) interests at industry level (e.g. trade associations) and in relation to the business community as a whole (e.g. Chambers of Commerce), and professional lobbyists (Luger 2000: 183).
- Industry is able to finance technical research to back up its political positions and arguments (Luger 2000: 183), e.g. through sympathetic foundations and 'think tanks'.
- Businesses make donations to political parties, particularly in the form of election campaign contributions (Luger 2000: 184). The point is to help parties and/or candidates that are perceived to be sympathetic to business interests to get elected.
- Businesses hire former politicians or government officials to gain inside knowledge of the political process and access to decision-makers (Luger 2000: 184). There is also movement in the other direction—from industry into government ('revolving doors').
- In addition to these efforts by business to influence politics, Luger also refers to 'the industry's privileged economic position'. This means that business may not have to do anything to get government to take heed of its interests 'because economic growth and political stability can hinge on a healthy auto industry' (Luger 2000: 184–5).
- Large corporations and industries may also derive political influence from activities that are ostensibly non-political and commercial, notably advertising. The marketing of cars in ways that connect with core cultural values—as essential to personal freedom and as expressions of identity and status—has, as well as selling cars, 'provided the auto makers with a reservoir of latent public support' (Luger 2000: 182).

Questions

1. **Review your understanding of how the automobile industry is able to exercise political influence.**
2. **Are there any specific characteristics of the car industry that help to enhance its political influence?**
3. **What other groups or interests in society might oppose the car industry and counteract its influence?**

Control without trying?

STAKEHOLDERS Lindblom argued that business occupies a 'privileged' position in policymaking, one that is unmatched by any other group or interest including organized labour. This privileged position arises from the fact that private business makes decisions about the allocation of resources on which the well-being of all individuals in society depends (see the definition of corporate power earlier in the chapter).

INTERACTION Lindblom notes that these decisions 'matter to all members of society . . . [and] loom as momentous as the decisions of most government officials . . . No one can say that . . . [they] . . . are too inconsequential to be labelled public policy' (1980: 72). No other group in society makes decisions that matter to everybody in the same way. Lindblom's argument is that government is dependent on these decisions taken by private business to ensure a healthy economy which voters expect government to deliver. The problem for governments is that they 'cannot positively command business managers to perform their functions' and therefore must 'develop and maintain business profitability through supporting policies'. Thus, dependence by government on decisions taken in the private sector translates into a consistent bias in policymaking in favour of business interests. Governments must pursue policies that maintain business confidence to ensure that business continues to invest, create jobs, and generate growth, so as to ensure voter satisfaction. Lindblom refers to this as 'control without trying' since it does not rely on businesses actually doing anything to influence government (1980: 72–4).

For example, there was no 'bankers' party' contesting UK general elections. However, 'control without trying' can be illustrated in two ways in relation to financial markets and institutions. First, the bank 'bailouts' required to prevent them going bankrupt during the financial crisis were justified by the argument that banks were 'too big to fail'. In other words, governments felt compelled to rescue the banks because of the key role they play in the functioning of the economy and the catastrophic consequences of allowing large interconnected banks to go out of business. The bailouts contributed to the mushrooming of government debt, and dealing with the debt became a key preoccupation of government economic policy leading to the era of austerity. The UK government justified its tough austerity programme of public spending cuts and tax rises on the grounds of the need to maintain the confidence of financial markets, particularly as expressed by the AAA rating conferred by credit rating agencies. If this confidence were to weaken, it was argued, the government would only be able to borrow at higher interest rates with damaging economic consequences. In both cases the interests of financial institutions and markets can be seen as automatically influencing government, thus representing a form of control over policy by financial interests 'without trying'.

Stop and Think

Does the fact that 'many of the functions performed by business . . . are essential to society' justify its privileged position in policymaking?

The consequences of globalization

LOCAL TO GLOBAL Lindblom's analysis of the privileged position of business in policymaking was made in the 1970s. Since that time an ideological shift in politics in the UK and elsewhere towards neoliberal 'market fundamentalism' has arguably reinforced this position. At the same time, it can be argued that economic globalization has made it even more necessary for governments to give businesses what they need.

COMPLEXITY Globalization is a complex phenomenon with many dimensions—political, social, and cultural as well as economic. In broad terms it refers to the increasing tendency of economic and other relationships to become 'stretched' across borders so that the nations and regions of the world become more interconnected and interdependent. Globalization has been facilitated by technological changes—particularly in the fields of transport and communication—that have made, for example, the movement of people between countries both cheaper and quicker (see Chapter 10). Economic globalization itself has a number of dimensions, among the most important of which are:

- the growth and spread of international trade;
- the growth of MNCs that own or control production facilities in more than one country; and
- the increasing integration of global financial markets.

It has been argued that one important consequence of economic globalization is to increase the power of corporations in relation to governments—what Hertz has referred to as a 'power shift' (Hertz 2001). It has done so by increasing the 'exit options' available to business. This means that MNCs can search the world for the most favourable locations for their production activities. To the extent that **locational advantage** is connected with political decisions, governments are under increased pressure to ensure that decisions are favourable to business in order to attract inward investment by MNCs and prevent production and jobs moving elsewhere. For example, MNCs might be expected to favour deregulated (or 'flexible') labour markets where unions are relatively weak, taxation rates are low, and policies are in place to benefit business such as the provision of training and infrastructure. In other words, globalization accentuates what Lindblom refers to as the privileged position of business in policymaking. For example:

> Automobile manufacturers can switch the production of new models of cars relatively easily between different countries . . . and naturally consider which country will give the highest tax concessions, lowest taxes, least cumbersome regulations and most disciplined workforce in making decisions on car production. The automobiles produced in any one of . . . [the EU member states] can be shipped without restriction or tariffs to any other member country; under WTO rules, the automobiles can also be shipped worldwide with only minimal duty being levied.
>
> (Wilson 2003: 17)

It has been argued that globalization tends to produce a '**race to the bottom**' as governments reduce taxes on business and avoid or remove regulations that are perceived as onerous for business. For example, governments may feel that making it easier to hire and fire workers will help to attract inward investment.

Stop and Think

What is meant by a 'race to the bottom'? Why is this sometimes seen as a consequence of globalization?

The ups and downs of business influence over policymaking

DYNAMIC The extent of the 'power shift' from government to business as a result of globalization is disputed. Although MNCs do have increased 'exit options', as shown by the car industry, business is not 'footloose' in the sense of being able to go easily wherever it pleases. The dependence of business on government to provide key inputs such as skills and infrastructure can lock businesses in to particular countries to some extent and give governments some leverage over their activities. More generally, economic globalization is itself not just an outcome of technological drivers but also of government decisions, such as to liberalize trade and capital flows. This means that governments remain, to some extent, in control of the process of globalization.

INTERACTION LOCAL TO GLOBAL It can be argued that economic globalization has increased the power of business in relation to trade unions and CSOs or pressure groups. Trade unions have been left behind by globalization because they don't operate effectively on an international scale. However, globalization has brought with it the rise of effective global pressure groups and protest movements. In particular, the Internet has enabled groups to mobilize international campaigns against business. Well-known examples of successful campaigns are those against Nike (sweatshops) and Shell (pollution), both of which mobilized consumer boycotts.

Business influence—'nothing special' or 'unique'?

To argue that business influence is 'nothing special' is to claim that power is fragmented and dispersed and that many other groups, such as trade unions and pressure groups, are equally well placed to influence government. Against this, the view that business influence is 'unique' points to the many advantages enjoyed by business in the competition for influence, including resources, contacts, and the dependence of government on business decisions. However, these two views might not be as polarized as appears at first sight. The first approach does not say that business never exercises a decisive influence over government policy. Rather, it says that business involvement in political battles is more a case of 'win some, lose some'. On the other hand, the business dominance approach does not say that business wins all political battles. Indeed, it recognizes that 'the precise extent of business control appears to wax and wane' (Lindblom 1980: 82). But the business dominance approach does argue that business influence is special in that, on the whole, it is unmatched by any other group or interest in society.

> *Stop and Think*
>
> Do you agree that the political influence of business is 'nothing special', or that it is unique?
> Does it matter if there is a bias in favour of business interests in the policymaking process? Does this mean that democracy isn't working properly? Or is it healthy for government to attach so much weight to maintaining business confidence?

Is business influence in the political process a good thing?

VALUES You can see that the answer to the question of how much political influence is enjoyed by business is disputed. There is also disagreement over whether business *should* have a dominant voice in the political process. How you answer this question will depend on whether you think that the private interests of business corporations and the business community in general are aligned with the wider public interest, or that there are unavoidable conflicts. It will also depend on whether you believe that business is solely motivated by profit or can be relied on to balance this with concern for the common good.

In the 1950s the president of General Motors famously claimed that 'what was good for the country was good for General Motors and vice versa', a statement that is often translated as 'What's good for General Motors is good for the country'. In this vein it can be argued that we all have a stake in successful business and therefore business should be the most powerful influence on government. Government needs to manage the economy successfully and, in order to do so, needs to take heed of business interests and views. This is the essence of Lindblom's 'control without trying'.

On the other hand, Luger argues that business does have 'inordinate' influence and that this influence is undesirable. In this view business interests may often conflict with the common good. An example in Luger's analysis is the resistance of the car makers to tighter regulation of vehicle emissions. Therefore, business influence in policymaking needs to be checked so that corporate interests can be balanced with, and sometimes subordinated to, those of other groups.

This is not to say that there are no cases in which businesses use their political influence to press for policy change in the wider public interest. For example, some leading UK businesses have publicly called on government to introduce tighter restrictions on CO_2 emissions from industry, and some business leaders have expressed concerns about excessive boardroom pay.

Looking ahead

As we have seen, the power of business is subject to change—it has 'ups' and 'downs'—and this makes it difficult to predict. However, we have also seen that corporate power is structural in the sense that it is built into the operation of a market system—a market is both a framework of exchange and of power. This means that we can say that the interaction of corporate power and political power will remain a fundamental issue. If we follow the arguments of Lindblom and Luger, we can predict that business will continue to exercise power that is not matched by other groups or interests.

We can expect that in five or ten years' time the *Forbes* list of the world's most powerful people will look very much the same. It will continue to be dominated by business and political elites, though the specific names may change as companies and states rise and fall.

It has been argued that economic globalization has resulted in a power shift from government to business in recent decades. As globalization is an ongoing process that is transforming modern societies, this will continue to pose challenges for governments in regulating business behaviour and managing their economies. It also seems likely that the broad pro-business consensus in western societies will continue. In the last century socialist political parties presented a challenge to the power of business, but in the absence of a revival of such parties there is little likelihood of government power in Europe being used to counter the position of business significantly.

However, some factors point in the other direction. We have seen evidence of the political influence of the financial sector in the UK, but the financial crisis has led to an emphasis on the need to 'rebalance' the economy away from financial activities and interests.

Business will continue to operate in the context of a more sceptical public, meaning that it has to work hard to retain public trust, particularly in relation to ethical issues such as climate change. Business will continue to face demands for greater corporate social responsibility and have to engage with CSOs, which may become more active. As we saw at the start of this chapter, there is evidence of dissatisfaction with the influence of business and a desire to see this reduced. We have also seen (Chapter 1) that the political shocks of Brexit and the election of Donald Trump have been interpreted as a revolt by the 'left behind' that has stimulated commitments on the part of political leaders to stand up to corporate interests and demand changes in corporate behaviour. Corporate power is not inevitable and can be challenged. Wilks argued that the power of the corporation was held in balance by the power of the vote before the 1980s. Depending on public attitudes and political will, it is possible, looking ahead, that we could go forward to the past.

Summary

- The market system can be understood as a framework for distributing power as well as a system of exchange.
- Corporate power is based on ownership of economic resources. Business decisions are highly consequential for the rest of society.
- Corporate power is exercised as bargaining power in relation to direct stakeholders, through engagement with CSOs, and in the political arena.
- Large corporations are powerful political actors, and it can be argued that corporate political power has increased.
- Corporate political power has two forms—corporations as 'political actors' and 'control without trying'.
- The effectiveness of business in the political arena matters to business but it also matters to the rest of society. The question here is whether business interests are aligned with the common good. Is what is good for General Motors good for the country?

Case Study: Under the influence? Lobbying and 'cabs for hire'

What is lobbying?

As defined on the UK Parliament website 'Lobbying is when an individual or a group tries to persuade someone in Parliament to support a particular policy or campaign. Lobbying can be done in person, by sending letters and emails, or via social media' (**http://www.parliament.uk/get-involved/contact-an-mp-or-lord/lobbying-parliament**). Along similar lines, Transparency International define it as 'any direct or indirect communication with a public official that is made, managed or directed with the purpose of influencing public decision-making' (Transparency International 2015b). These definitions refer to 'someone in Parliament' and 'a public official' as the person being lobbied—lobbying can involve a range of target audiences including backbench MPs or members of the House of Lords, members of the government including junior ministers and cabinet members, senior civil servants, and special advisers.

There is general agreement that lobbying is an essential part of democracy, enabling individuals and organizations to have a voice in policymaking and allowing policymakers to gauge opinion and gather evidence on policies from those who will be affected or have a stake. Those who engage in lobbying can include individual voters/constituents, firms and business associations, professional associations, trade unions, and CSOs or pressure groups (Goodrich 2015). It is rational and legitimate for business to engage in lobbying as a normal part of corporate strategy, seeking to minimize threats and maximize opportunities emanating from the political environment. For example, in the context of uncertainty created by the UK vote to leave the EU, businesses actively engaged in trying to influence the Brexit negotiations

Brexit

Businesses—individual firms and associations—have sought to have a voice and influence government strategy in relation to the Brexit negotiations—calling for a particular approach (a 'hard' or 'soft' Brexit), or simply seeking clarity and to minimize uncertainty. For example, following the UK general election on 8 June 2017 resulting in a hung Parliament, the BBC reported lobbying in relation to Brexit by a range of business associations: Federation of Small Businesses (FSB), IoD, Engineering Employers' Federation (EEF), CBI, as well as the car maker Aston Martin. The EEF demanded that business have a voice in the negotiations: 'Industry should be at the table, alongside whatever administration is formed, to help ensure we have the right negotiating position, which is something that's been sadly lacking until now' (BBC 2017).

At the same time 'specialist "Brexit" units in lobbying firms have sprung up to capitalize on the uncertainty surrounding the next steps for Britain . . . showing businesses the best way to get what they want out of the negotiations'. Five firms operating in this area are Interel, Hanover, Portland, Quiller Consultants, and Teneo. These firms often employ ex-special advisers and/or ministers, showing the connection between lobbying and 'revolving doors'. For example, three members of the government employ ex-Hanover lobbyists as special advisers, and Teneo employs former Foreign Secretary William Hague as a lobbyist (Unlock Democracy 2016a).

A scandal waiting to happen?

Although an intrinsic part of democracy, lobbying has also been seen as a manifestation of a democracy that is not working well, as a problem to be fixed in many liberal democracies, including the UK, the US, and the EU. This view was expressed by David Cameron as leader of the UK Conservative Party in 2010. He argued that although lobbying can be 'perfectly reasonable' when it is 'open and transparent', it constitutes

the next big scandal waiting to happen. It's an issue that . . . exposes the far-too-cosy relationship between politics, government, business and money. . . . [W]e all know how it works. The lunches, the hospitality, the quiet word in your ear, the ex-ministers and ex-advisors for hire, helping big business find the right way to get its way. . . . I believe that it is increasingly clear that lobbying in this country is getting out of control.

We don't know who is meeting whom. We don't know whether any favours are being exchanged. We don't know which outside interests are wielding unhealthy influence. This isn't a minor issue with minor consequences. Commercial interests–not to mention government contracts–worth hundreds of billions of pounds are potentially at stake.

I believe that secret corporate lobbying . . . goes to the heart of why people are so fed up with politics. It arouses people's worst fears and suspicions about how our political system works, with money buying power, power fishing for money and a cosy club at the top making decisions in their own interest.

(Cameron 2010)

Cameron identifies four aspects of the problem:

- Lobbying involves a potentially corrupt relationship between the lobbyists and the lobbied, with the possibility of 'favours being exchanged' and 'money buying power'.
- Much lobbying is not transparent but secret or 'behind closed doors' so it is impossible to know the basis of decisions or who is wielding influence.
- There is not a 'level playing field': Cameron especially highlights the role of business and money, i.e. corporations and wealthy individuals.
- Lobbying has undermined confidence and trust in the political system and big business.

Corporate dominance

The predominance of business interests in the UK is shown by the finding that '8/10 of the most frequent lobbyists are from FTSE 100 companies–lobbying is dominated by the corporate world' (Transparency International UK 2015a).

The picture is similar in the EU where 'Analysis of the 4,318 lobby meetings declared by the top tier of European Commission officials between December 2014 and June 2015 shows that more than 75% were with corporate lobbyists. . . . Google, General Electric and Airbus are some of the most active lobbyists at this level, with 25 to 29 meetings each. Google and General Electric are also some of the biggest spenders in Brussels, each declaring EU lobby budgets of around €3.5 million per year' (Transparency International 2015c).

Cabs for hire

The potential for corrupt relationships to develop has been shown in a number of lobbying scandals. For example, in 2010 three former ministers were suspended by the Labour Party after 'boasting that they had changed government policy and secured preferential access to ministers for private companies' to journalists posing as representatives of a US lobbying firm. 'The MPs offered their services for up to £5,000 a day', with one of them, Stephen Byers, saying that he was like a 'cab for hire'. Byers was found guilty of bringing Parliament into disrepute by the House of Commons Standards and Privileges Committee and barred from Parliament for two years (Prince 2010, Winnett 2010).

The Lobbying Act

The 2014 Lobbying Act (Transparency of Lobbying, Non-Party Campaigning and Trade Union Administration Act) was meant to make good on Cameron's pledge to fix the problem of lobbying, largely by creating a register of lobbyists to bring transparency to the activity. However, the register was criticized as ineffective because: it uses a narrow definition of 'lobbyist' that only includes hired lobbyists (i.e. lobbying firms) and excludes the majority of lobbyists who are in-house (i.e. employees of the corporation they are lobbying for), and requires lobbyists to register only if they have contact with ministers or senior civil servants and thus excludes the majority of lobbying that occurs at a lower level. For these reasons, only a minority of lobbyists are covered by the requirement to register. An analysis by Transparency International showed that less than one in twenty lobbying firms appeared on the register. In addition, the register provides very little information as lobbyists are not required to record who they are lobbying or in relation to what policy (Pegg 2015, Unlock Democracy 2016b).

Proposals for reform of lobbying

The inadequacy of the existing register has led to proposals for reform. The point of reform is not to deter lobbying but to address the problems that Cameron identified. The Lobbying (Transparency) Bill, supported by Unlock Democracy and Spinwatch, proposed that the register must be universal, applying to everyone who is paid to undertake this activity and therefore including in-house lobbyists. And it must contain adequate information including 'who is lobbying and for whom; which agency of government is being lobbied; and broadly what they are seeking to influence' (Unlock Democracy 2016b).

Transparency International argue that reform should incorporate the principles of

- transparency (i.e. open to scrutiny through a detailed register);
- integrity (i.e. standards of conduct for public officials and lobbyists including, for public officials, pre- and post-employment restrictions to deal with revolving doors concerns); and
- participation (i.e. equal opportunity for participation for various interest groups and the public at large, or a level playing field), backed up by effective sanctions (Transparency International 2015b).

Questions

1. **Why is lobbying an important aspect of democracy?**
2. **Is lobbying out of control?**

Review and discussion questions

1. Examine the nature of corporate power and how it is exercised within a stakeholder framework.
2. Analyse the claim that business occupies a privileged position in policymaking, and that this has been enhanced as a consequence of globalization.
3. Explain how CSOs can bring pressure to bear on business to change its behaviour.
4. Does corporate political influence enhance or undermine democracy?

Assignments

1. You are required to produce a briefing paper as the basis for evidence to be given to a parliamentary enquiry into lobbying. Your briefing should be written for EITHER

   The Association of Professional Political Consultants (APPC) **https://www.appc.org.uk**

   OR

   Transparency International **https://www.transparency.org**

2. Produce a report on the funding of political parties/candidates in the UK or the US, with a focus on the US 2016 presidential election or the 2017 UK general election. Your report should:

   - present data on political funding, with a focus on corporate donations;
   - summarize the rules on donations; and
   - make recommendations for reform.

   Useful sources:

   Federal Election Commission (FEC) **http://classic.fec.gov/index.shtml**

   Electoral Commission **https://www.electoralcommission.org.uk**

3. Compile a brief report on ethical consumerism. Your report should include the following elements:

   - the meaning of ethical consumerism;
   - an analysis of trends and projections in ethical consumerism;

- an outline of the methods used to promote ethical consumerism by campaigning organizations; and
- an analysis of the response to ethical consumerism by a large supermarket or retailer.

Further reading

Coen, Wyn Grant, and Wilson (eds.) (2010) *this comprehensive collection provides an indispensable resource on the relationship between business and government. See especially Part 2: Firm and State.*

Wilson (2003) *is an introduction to business and politics. It uses a comparative approach and considers the implications of globalization for the relationship between business and government. Also see Grant (1993).*

Moran (2009) *analyses the relationship between business and government, comparing the UK and USA.*

Bakan (2005), Hertz (2001), Beetham (2011), and Wilks (2013) *all provide critical perspectives on the power of the modern corporation.*

Reich (2008) *examines the relationship between the market and democracy, and argues that as capitalism has triumphed democracy has weakened.*

Test your understanding of this chapter with online questions and answers, explore the subject further through web exercises, and use the weblinks to provide a quick resource for further research. Visit the online resources at www.oup.com/uk/wetherly_otter4e/

Useful websites

Democratic Audit UK http://www.democraticaudit.com

Find out about the role of business associations by going to the websites for:

www.cbi.org.uk
Confederation of British Industry

www.chamberonline.co.uk
Chambers of Commerce

http://www.iod.com
Institute of Directors

For campaigning and investigative organizations try out:

Center for Public Integrity
www.publicintegrity.org

Transparency International
www.transparency.org

Bureau of Investigative Journalism
http://www.thebureauinvestigates.com

References

Bakan, J. (2005) *The Corporation: The Pathological Pursuit of Profit and Power* (London: Free Press)

BBC (2017) 'Business leaders demand answers over Brexit strategy', 9 June (last accessed 20 July 2017) **http://www.bbc.co.uk/news/business-40216650**

Beetham, D. (2011) *Unelected Oligarchy: Corporate and Financial Dominance in Britain's Democracy*, Democratic Audit (last accessed 20 July 2017) **https://democraticaudituk.files.wordpress.com/2013/06/oligarchy.pdf**

Bronk, R. (2000) 'Which model of capitalism?', *OECD Observer*, 221/222 (last accessed 20 July 2017) **http://www.oecdobserver.org/news/archivestory.php/aid/345/Which_model_of_capitalism_.html**

Cameron, D. (2010) Speech: 'Rebuilding trust in politics', available at Spinwatch (last accessed 20 July 2017) **http://www.spinwatch.org/index.php/issues/lobbying/item/5579-the-next-big-scandal-cameron-s-lobbying-speech**

Coen, D., Grant, W., and Wilson, G. (eds.) (2010) *The Oxford Handbook of Business and Government* (Oxford: Oxford University Press)

Competition Commission (2009) 'News release: CC publishes code of practice and ombudsman recommendation', 4 August (last accessed 20 July 2017) **http://www.competition-commission.org.uk/assets/competitioncommission/docs/pdf/non-inquiry/press_rel/2009/aug/pdf/36-09**

Competition and Markets Authority (2014) *Competition Law Compliance: Guidance for Businesses* (last accessed 20 July 2017) **https://www.gov.uk/government/collections/competition-and-consumer-law-compliance-guidance-for-businesses**

Competition and Markets Authority (2015) 'Competing fairly in business: at-a-glance guide to competition law' (last accessed 20 July 2017) **https://www.gov.uk/government/publications/competing-fairly-in-business-at-a-glance-guide-to-competition-law**

Cooperative Bank (2008) *The Ethical Consumerism Report 2008* (last accessed 20 July 2017) **http://www.ethicalconsumer.org/portals/0/downloads/ethical%20consumer%20report.pdf**

Department for Business, Energy & Industrial Strategy [no date] Consumer Rights Act 2015 (last accessed 20 July 2017) **https://www.gov.uk/government/publications/consumer-rights-act-2015/consumer-rights-act-2015**

Department for Business, Energy & Industrial Strategy (2017) *Trade Union Membership 2016: Statistical Bulletin* (last accessed 20 July 2017) **https://www.gov.uk/government/uploads/system/uploads/attachment_data/file/616966/trade-union-membership-statistical-bulletin-2016-rev.pdf**

Ethical Consumer (2016) *Ethical Consumer Markets Report 2016*, Ethical Consumer/Triodos Bank (last accessed 20 July 2017) **http://www.ethicalconsumer.org/portals/0/downloads/ethical%20consumer%20markets%20report%202016.pdf**

Ewalt, D. M. (2016) 'The world's most powerful people 2016', *Forbes* (last accessed 20 July 2017) **https://www.forbes.com/sites/davidewalt/2016/12/14/the-worlds-most-powerful-people-2016/#67f2ba741b4c**

Forbes (2016) 'The world's most powerful people 2016 ranking' (last accessed 20 July 2017) **https://www.forbes.com/powerful-people/list/#tab:overall**

Gallup (2016) 'Majority of Americans dissatisfied with corporate influence' (last accessed 20 July 2017) **http://www.gallup.com/poll/188747/majority-americans-dissatisfied-corporate-influence.aspx?g_source=corporate+influence&g_medium=search&g_campaign=tiles**

GCA (2016) *Investigation into Tesco plc* (last accessed 20 July 2017) **https://www.gov.uk/government/uploads/system/uploads/attachment_data/file/494840/GCA_Tesco_plc_final_report_26012016_-_version_for_download.pdf**

Goodrich, S. (2015) 'Lobbying reform: we need political will not gesture politics', Transparency International (last accessed 20 July 2017) **http://www.transparency.org.uk/lobbying-reform-we-need-political-will-not-gesture-politics**

Gow, D. (2006) 'Fears for UK car plants as factories shift east', *Guardian*, 2 March

Harmston, S. (2017) 'One in five consumers have boycotted a brand', YouGov (last accessed 20 July 2017) **https://yougov.co.uk/news/2017/04/07/one-five-consumers-have-boycotted-brand**

Hertz, N. (2001) *The Silent Takeover: Global Capitalism and the Death of Democracy* (London: Heinemann)

Houlder, V. (2014) 'UK Uncut to stage tax avoidance protests', *Financial Times*, 15 May (last accessed 20 July 2017) **https://www.ft.com/content/1355daf4-db7f-11e3-b112-00144feabdc0?mhq5j=e1**

Hutton, W. (1996) *The State We're In* (London: Jonathan Cape)

Hutton, W. (2015) *How Good We Can Be: Ending the Mercenary Society and Building a Great Country* (London: Little, Brown)

Insley, J. (2013) 'British farmers wilting as supermarkets pile on the promotions', *Observer*, 12 August (last accessed 20 July 2017) **http://www.guardian.co.uk/business/2012/aug/12/farmers-wilt-under-supermarket-promotions**

Kay, J. (2004) *The Truth About Markets* (Harmondsworth: Penguin)

Levitt, T. (2016) 'Three years on from the horsemeat scandal: 3 lessons we have learned', *Guardian*, 7 January (last accessed 20 July 2017) **https://www.theguardian.com/sustainable-business/2016/jan/07/horsemeat-scandal-food-safety-uk-criminal-networks-supermarkets**

Lindblom, C. E. (1980) *The Policy Making Process* (Harlow: Prentice-Hall)

Luger, S. (2000) *Corporate Power, American Democracy, and the Automobile Industry* (Cambridge: Cambridge University Press)

May, T. (2016) '2016 speech to launch leadership campaign', available at UKPOL (last accessed 20 July 2017) **http://www.ukpol.co.uk/theresa-may-2016-speech-to-launch-leadership-campaign**

Moran, M. (2009) *Business, Politics and Society: An Anglo-American comparison* (Oxford: Oxford University Press)

Office of Fair Trading (2013) 'OFT issues five infringement decisions in the distribution of Mercedes-Benz commercial vehicles investigation' (last accessed 20 July 2017) **http://oft.gov.uk/news-and-updates/press/2013/30-13#.UWZ6DbXWZjU**

Pegg, D. (2015) 'Lobbying register covers fewer than one in 20 lobbyists—report', *Guardian*, 21 (September last accessed 20 July 2017) **https://www.theguardian.com/politics/2015/sep/21/lobbying-register-transparency-international-report**

Peston, R. (2008) *Who Runs Britain?* (London: Hodder & Stoughton)

Prince, R. (2010) 'MPs for hire: three former Labour ministers banned from Parliament', *Telegraph*, 9 December (last accessed 20 July 2017) **http://www.telegraph.co.uk/news/politics/labour/8191301/MPs-for-hire-three-former-Labour-ministers-banned-from-Parliament.html**

Reich, R. (2008) *Supercapitalism* (Cambridge: Icon Books)

Seely, A. (2015) 'Supermarkets: the Groceries Code Adjudicator', House of Commons Library Briefing Paper Number 6124 (last accessed 20 July 2017) **researchbriefings.files.parliament.uk/documents/SN06124/SN06124.pdf**

Simms, A. (2007) *Tescopoly: How One Shop Came out on Top and Why It Matters* (London: Constable)

Transparency International UK (2015a) 'Accountable influence: bringing lobbying out of the shadows' (last accessed 20 July 2017) **http://www.transparency.org.uk/publications/accountable-influence-bringing-lobbying-out-of-the-shadows**

Transparency International (2015b) 'International standards for lobbying regulation' (last accessed 20 July 2017) **http://lobbyingtransparency.net/lobbyingtransparency.pdf**

Transparency International (2015c) 'Lobby meetings with EU policy-makers dominated by corporate interests' (last accessed 20 July 2017) **https://www.transparency.org/news/pressrelease/lobby_meetings_with_eu_policy_makers_dominated_by_corporate_interests**

Treanor, J. and Davies, R. (2016) 'Ticket resale websites run risk of fines after CMA launches inquiry', *Guardian*, 19 December (last accessed 20 July 2017) **https://www.theguardian.com/business/2016/dec/19/ticket-resale-websites-run-risk-of-fines-cma-launches-investigation-competition-and-markets-authority**

Unlock Democracy (2016a) '5 lobbying firms with more influence over the Brexit process than you' (last accessed 20 July 2017) **http://www.unlockdemocracy.org/blog/2016/10/13/5-lobbying-firms-with-more-influence-over-the-brexit-process-than-you**

Unlock Democracy (2016b) 'NGO lobbying transparency briefing June 2016' (last accessed 20 July 2017) **http://www.unlockdemocracy.org/publications/lobbying-transparency-bill-briefing?rq=lobbying**

Wheatley, H. (2017) 'Fracking in the UK: opposed nationwide, overruled in Westminster', New Economics Foundation (last accessed 20 July 2017) **http://neweconomics.org/2017/03/fracking-in-the-uk**

Wilks, S. (2013) *The Political Power of the Business Corporation* (Cheltenham: Edward Elgar)

Wilson, G. K. (2003) *Business and Politics* (Basingstoke: Palgrave)

Winnett, R. (2010) 'Stephen Byers, Patricia Hewitt and Geoff Hoon suspended over lobbying allegations', *Telegraph*, 24 June (last accessed 20 July 2017) **http://www.telegraph.co.uk/news/politics/labour/7500906/Stephen-Byers-Patricia-Hewitt-and-Geoff-Hoon-suspended-over-lobbying-allegations.html**

World Health Organization (2017a) 'Tobacco Fact Sheet' (last accessed 20 July 2017) **http://www.who.int/mediacentre/factsheets/fs339/en**

World Health Organization (2017b) 'WHO report finds dramatic increase in life-saving tobacco control policies in last decade' (last accessed 20 July 2017) **http://www.who.int/mediacentre/news/releases/2017/tobacco-report/en**

Chapter 12
Is inequality bad for business?

Dorron Otter and Paul Wetherly

Learning objectives

When you have completed this chapter, you will be able to:

- Explain what is meant by 'equality of opportunity', 'social mobility', and 'equality of outcome'.
- Identify developments in the business environment which have pushed equality up the political and business agendas.
- Use relevant data to analyse patterns of inequality in the UK and examine recent trends.
- Reflect on the values and interests that inequality raises and their relevance and implications for business.

THEMES

The following themes of the book are especially relevant to this chapter

- **DIVERSITY** Inequality is an issue that confronts all countries, but some societies are more unequal than others and it calls into question the varied nature of capitalism. Similarly, the extent of inequality, and the response to it, varies between businesses.
- **INTERNAL/EXTERNAL** Equality issues have an important internal dimension in respect of organization culture and business decisions. For example, growing inequality has been attributed in part to a culture of greed in boardrooms and barriers to women progressing may be attributable, in part, to a 'macho' culture.
- **COMPLEXITY** Inequality is a complex issue and many causal factors are involved.
- **LOCAL TO GLOBAL** This chapter focuses mainly on the UK, but we will view the UK in comparative terms and inequality in the UK is partly influenced by international and global factors.
- **DYNAMIC** Inequality varies over time, so it is important to analyse trends.
- **INTERACTION** Inequality is not just part of the business environment but is rooted in the nature of the political and economic system.
- **STAKEHOLDERS** Inequality concerns the basic stake that people have in business and the economic system: whether they have fair chances and fair rewards.
- **VALUES** Whether inequality is a 'problem' and, in particular, whether it is 'bad for business' are questions which are largely concerned with values about the kind of economic system we want and what benefits it should provide for society.

Introduction

LOCAL TO GLOBAL Growing inequality has recently moved up the national and global political agendas and is recognized as a problem *between* as well as *within* countries. It has also become a major concern within the wider business community and from outside it has become an important focus for criticism of capitalism and a catalyst of vocal protest movements. Political and business leaders share the concerns about lack of fairness, but they have also become concerned about the damage to the legitimacy of market economies and democratic political systems, and the potential for political instability.

This chapter will explore the key issues and questions that inequality raises. What do we mean by equality/inequality, and how do we measure it? To what extent have Britain and other societies become more unequal? What are the main drivers of increased inequality, and what policy responses are on offer? What's wrong with inequality? Is inequality bad for business?

What is equality?

VALUES There are sharply divided opinions on the question of inequality. For neoclassical critics inequality is both the natural and desirable outcome of the market while those from within the structuralist/institutionalist and Marxist perspectives see it as the most damaging social problem. Equality is a contested term or concept and in debates about equality and inequality quite distinct meanings of the terms can be in play, and the argument is often not along the lines of 'equality versus inequality' but how much inequality is acceptable or fair. Should we accept whatever pattern of income distribution the market throws up? Is it sufficient to ensure that there are equal opportunities in the market? Or should we seek to narrow the gap between rich and poor?

Equality of opportunity versus equality of outcome

An important distinction within this debate is between equality of *opportunity* and **equality of outcome**. Some argue that what matters is that people should have the same opportunities to get on in life and earn as much as they can on the basis of their own talents and efforts, if that is what they want to do. As long as opportunities are equal, it is fair enough if some get ahead and others fall behind. For example, if jobs such as chief executive positions are appointed on the basis of merit, then it is fair enough that individuals who have succeeded in being appointed in competition with others benefit from the higher rewards that come with the position. Others argue that we should still be concerned about the outcome, to ensure that some don't get left too far behind or that some don't pull too far ahead. Perhaps individuals who are appointed, on merit, as chief executives deserve higher rewards than their unsuccessful counterparts who are less talented or have made less effort (or, perhaps, been less lucky), but there is still a question about whether the ratio between the pay of chief executives and the rest of the workforce is fair. Equality of opportunity is really concerned with ensuring that the competition for advantage is fair, whereas equality of outcome is really concerned with the extent of advantage and disadvantage that is tolerable in society.

We can clarify this distinction using the example of the salaries paid by the BBC to its top talent. As required by its charter, in July 2017 the BBC produced a list of the salaries of all ninety-six 'stars' who are paid more than £150,000. It turned out that two-thirds of these high earners, and all of the top seven, were men. There were two types of critical reaction to the data published by the BBC. One reaction raised equal opportunity concerns: here the argument was that there should be more women in the list and, perhaps, parity between men and women. The data seemed to show that the BBC is not ensuring equal opportunities for women. A second reaction focused on whether the BBC was paying too much for 'top talent': was it getting good value for licence fee payers, and were these very high earnings in comparison with average earnings consistent with a social norm of fairness. This last concern is about equality of outcome (BBC 2017).

Stop and Think

If the BBC is producing programmes that are rated highly by viewers, should it matter how much the corporation pays its top stars?

Both conceptions of equality have implications for the role of government. The first view is consistent with, for example, having laws to ensure equal opportunities through education (to ensure that all children have the same opportunity to gain skills and qualifications), and by prohibiting discrimination in the labour market (e.g. the 2010 UK Equality Act). The second view suggests the need for government to do more than this, such as using the tax and benefit system to redistribute income or using the law to set minimum and even maximum wages and salaries.

However, it can be argued that these two concepts of equality are closely related, as suggested by the Milburn report:

> It is no coincidence that countries such as Australia, Japan, Sweden and the Netherlands, which are the most socially fluid in the world, are also among the most equal. The fact that the UK remains such a persistently unequal society is in large part the reason why social mobility is lower than in other less unequal nations. Greater equality and more mobility are two sides of the same coin.
>
> (Panel on Fair Access to the Professions 2009)

The point is that if economic inequality (the gap between rich and poor) is allowed to become too large it undermines equality of opportunity. Structuralists in particular will highlight examples such as the well-off being able to use their resources to provide advantages to their children which the poor cannot, such as moving to an area with a 'good' school, paying for private tuition, or paying for a private school. In addition, in highly unequal societies there is more of an incentive for parents to provide advantages for their children since the consequences of failure are much worse than in a more equal society (i.e. people have further to fall).

Equality of opportunity

VALUES **COMPLEXITY** **Equality of opportunity** can be seen as a core value of western societies, related to ideas such as freedom and individualism (see Chapter 4). The basic idea is that individuals should be, as far as possible, free to live as they choose and, in particular, should have equal opportunities to use their talents and energies in the way that they see fit to get on in life and achieve the goals and aspirations that they set for themselves. This doesn't mean that we all do or should have the *same* goals and aspirations. On the contrary, the value of freedom is associated with the idea that individuals make different choices about how they want to live their lives. For example, some people might think of a good life in terms of earning as much money as they can, while others think in terms of doing good for others (or we might have different ideas about how we balance these goals).

However, the idea of equality of opportunity is quite complex and involves two types of question: what kinds of opportunities are we concerned with, and, how can we make them equal? Although we could think of endless kinds of opportunities in terms of different goals or aspirations, the discussion tends to focus on a more limited range of opportunities that are recognized as being important for everybody. High among these are education and employment. Education is important for everybody no matter what kind of life they choose to live, and therefore it can be argued that everybody should have the same opportunity to benefit from education to a certain standard. Employment opportunities are important for a number of reasons:

- For most people in capitalist societies the extrinsic benefit of employment is the wage or salary earned which is the primary source of livelihood.
- Employment though also brings a range of intrinsic benefits such as social contact and job satisfaction and is an important source of social status and self-respect.

Since paid work defines our ability to buy goods and services it could be seen to be wrong if some people have a greater opportunity than others to work or to access higher positions within the occupational hierarchy just, say, because they are well-connected or are the preferred sex or ethnicity. In this sense equal opportunity is a universalist principle—everyone should be treated equally in respect to the opportunities that are open to them. For example, women should have the same opportunity as men to become company directors, and the same can be said in relation to other characteristics such as ethnicity or race, age, sexuality, and disability. Martin Luther King expressed the principle of equal opportunity in the context of the civil rights struggle in the US when he demanded that people should be judged not on the colour of their skin but on the content of their character (King 1963).

Why has equality of opportunity moved up the agenda?

VALUES **DYNAMIC** Attitudes about women and their place in society have shifted considerably in recent decades, driven largely by women's campaigns and the growing influence of feminism. In the middle of the last century a widely held view could be summed up in the phrase: 'A woman's place is in the home', referring to a division of labour (that may have been thought of as 'natural') in which men worked to earn a family wage while women stayed at home as mothers and 'housewives'. In the UK it was entirely usual up until the 1970s for employers to have separate pay scales for their male and female employees and very common for women to leave their jobs altogether when their first child was born. In recent years this view had been replaced by support for the idea of equal opportunity—that women should have the same opportunities (and rights) to engage in paid employment as men—as many traditional ideas or norms about the nature of 'masculinity' and 'femininity' were increasingly questioned and challenged. See Mini-Case 12.1.

Mini-Case 12.1 The expansion of the equal opportunities agenda

DYNAMIC. In the 1970s the focus of campaigning and legal reform was on race and sex, but in the succeeding decades the equal opportunity agenda has been extended. In the UK, the Equality and Human Rights Commission (EHRC), established by the 2006 Equality Act as a national equality body, now has statutory responsibility to protect, enforce, and promote equality across nine 'protected' characteristics (https://www.equalityhumanrights.com/en/equality-act/protected-characteristics):

- age;
- disability;
- gender reassignment;
- marriage and civil partnership;
- pregnancy and maternity;
- race;
- religion and belief;
- sex; and
- sexual orientation.

This is a remarkable process of social change. Forms of discrimination that were regarded by many as natural or acceptable a generation ago are now prohibited in law. (Table 12.1 shows a timeline of the key equal opportunity Acts and regulations.) The series of legal enactments may be seen as both reflecting and promoting the changing values and attitudes within modern society. Although prejudicial and discriminatory attitudes and behaviours may have receded, changes in the law have been required because:

(a) the law is a powerful *public statement* of values and gives authoritative expression to the principle that discrimination is unacceptable; and

(b) law enables *enforcement* of non-discriminatory behaviour and thus protection of vulnerable and disadvantaged groups.

In other words, government action in the form of making and enforcing law is necessary because experience shows

Table 12.1 Timeline of equal opportunities—key Acts and regulations

1970	Equal Pay Act	To prevent discrimination, as regards terms and conditions of employment, between men and women.
1975	Sex Discrimination Act	To render unlawful certain kinds of sex discrimination and discrimination on the ground of marriage, etc.
1976	Race Relations Act	To make fresh provision with respect to discrimination on racial grounds and relations between people of different racial groups, etc.
1995	Disability Discrimination Act	To make it unlawful to discriminate against disabled persons in connection with employment, etc.
1998	Human Rights Act	Enshrined rights and freedoms under the European Convention on Human Rights in UK law.
2001	Special Educational Needs and Disability Act	Amends the Education Act 1996 to make further provision against discrimination on grounds of disability in schools and other educational establishments.
2003	Employment Equality (Religion or Belief) Regulations	To prevent discrimination on the grounds of religious or philosophical beliefs, etc.
2003	Employment Equality (Sexual Orientation) Regulations	To prevent discrimination on grounds of sexual orientation, etc.
2005	Disability Discrimination Act	Amends the 1995 DDA, e.g. extends the definition of disability and introduces a public sector disability duty, etc.
2006	Employment Equality (Age) Regulations	To prevent discrimination on the ground of age, etc.
2006	Equality Act	Established the EHRC, etc.
2006	Racial and Religious Hatred Act	To make provision about offences involving stirring up hatred against persons on racial or religious grounds.
2010	Equality Act*	• Replaces previous anti-discrimination laws with a single Act, including most of those listed above. • Rstablishes a Single Public Sector Equality Duty covering the protected characteristics.

Note: * For further information go to the EHRC website: What is the Equality Act? https://www.equalityhumanrights.com/en/equality-act-2010/what-equality-act and see Equality Act 2010: guidance at https://www.gov.uk/guidance/equality-act-2010-guidance

that discrimination will otherwise persist—the market will not eliminate the problem if left to itself. However, passing a law does not by itself solve a social problem. To be effective a law must introduce measures that are appropriate and adequate, and there has to be compliance. Has the law been effective in realizing the goal of equality of opportunity between men and women in business?

Question

Why has the equal opportunity agenda been extended?

Do women have equal opportunities in business?

What does it mean for men and women to have, say, the same or equal opportunity to become a company director? How can we make opportunities equal? These questions can be answered in different ways, and this means that there can be strong disagreements between people who are in favour of equal opportunity. A generally accepted limited conception of equal opportunity is meritocratic, meaning that appointment to positions in the occupational hierarchy should be determined by the talents of the applicants and how well they match up to the employee specification so that employers should choose or discriminate between applicants only on these grounds. That would seem to be the best way to choose between candidates since the employer presumably wants the best person for the job. If the employer were to choose on other grounds, such as having a preference for men over women for particular jobs, it would constitute unfair discrimination because, other than in exceptional circumstances, whether an applicant is male or female is irrelevant to their ability to perform a role. Thus, ensuring equal opportunity for men and women in the labour market requires that sexual discrimination is prohibited. This requires the removal of both direct and indirect discrimination such as: explicitly stating a preference for male applicants (direct discrimination) and imposing a requirement that women on average are less able to satisfy and that is not relevant to the job (indirect discrimination). Unfair discrimination on grounds of gender has now been outlawed in most industrialized countries. In the UK this has been the case since 1975 when the Sex Discrimination Act was passed.

STAKEHOLDERS INTERNAL/EXTERNAL Unfair sexual discrimination is a barrier to women doing the kinds of jobs they want to do as an aspect of the kinds of lives they choose to lead. But we can see why it can be argued that removing this structural barrier is not enough to ensure equal opportunity, and more has to be done. Even if all employers implemented best equal opportunity practice they might find that it is difficult to recruit women because of a shortage of suitably qualified female applicants. This could be addressed through institutional change in the form of 'positive action' such as recruitment drives targeted at women, mentoring, or the provision of training to increase the pool of female applicants. However, there may be barriers or constraints external to the workplace that make it harder for women to compete in the labour market and apply for jobs on equal terms with men. In other words, discrimination in the labour market is not the only problem. Most obviously, if males and females do not enjoy the same opportunities in education they cannot have equal opportunities in the labour market. On a global scale, lack of access to education for girls remains a major challenge (UNESCO 2015) and the wider issue is of educational outcomes. In this respect in the UK it is apparently boys rather than girls who are lagging behind as there is an attainment gap in favour of girls. For example, more girls than boys achieve at least five A*–C GCSEs or equivalent, including English and Mathematics, at state schools in England (Equality and Human Rights Commission 2016, Department for Education and Skills 2007). However, there are gender differences in subject choices: at GCSE 'many subjects show gender stereotypical biases', and 'Gender differences in subject choice are greater at A-Level' (Department for Education and Skills 2007). There is also a gender gap in higher education in England—at age 18 women are 35 per cent more likely than men to go to university. Here again, though, there are clear gender differences in subject choices along stereotypical lines:

> in nursing . . . women outnumber men by nine to one . . . Psychology has the second biggest gender divide, followed by social work, education and design. Women are also ahead in areas such as history, philosophy, English, law and biology. Among the subjects with more men, the biggest gap is in computer science . . . followed by mechanical engineering, sports science, electrical engineering and economics.
>
> (*Guardian* 2016)

So, women are ahead of men in terms of educational attainment, but gender differences in subjects studied from GCSE through higher education lead to gender differences in occupational opportunities and choices, reflected in the persistence of 'occupational segregation'. These differences can be seen as part of a more general pattern of gendered socialization and social norms governing what are seen as typical masculine or feminine characteristics and behaviours. Thus, gender differences in higher education follow conventional ideas of 'male' and 'female' subjects. These norms are also reflected in the household and the gendered '**domestic division of labour**': women are disadvantaged in relation to men in the labour market in so far as it is usually women that continue to accept prime responsibility for domestic roles including childcare and eldercare. This means that economic opportunities for women are tied up with men's roles in the household, and specifically their choices as fathers in relation to childcare responsibilities.

These considerations about societal barriers and constraints suggest that, though tackling discrimination in the labour market is important, the equal opportunity agenda must be widened considerably. Whereas the meritocratic view focuses on appointment on the basis of merit, a wider view looks at the societal context and the barriers and constraints that influence women's entry into the labour market. What may be termed a 'substantive' conception of equality of opportunity can be used to support the goal of 'proportional equal opportunity'. In this view 50 per cent of, say, chief executives ought to be women because women make up 50 per cent of the population. If only one in four chief executive officers (CEOs) are female, then, in this view, women are 'under-represented'. The proportional representation goal is based on the underlying assumption that, on average, women have the same natural talents and aspirations as men and therefore, in a genuinely equal opportunity society in which all barriers and constraints were removed, a 50:50 balance between men and women in chief executive roles would result.

Stop and Think

What is a meritocratic conception of equality of opportunity? Why is it rational for businesses to be equal opportunity employers in this sense? Is a meritocratic approach enough to ensure that women really do have the same opportunities in business as men?

A woman's place?

DYNAMIC **VALUES** The shift away from the traditional idea that a woman's place is in the home is reflected in the changing sexual composition of the labour market resulting from a long-term trend of increasing economic activity among women, narrowing the gap with men.[1] In the UK in 2014 (Q4) '83.3% of men and 74.5% of women were either in employment or actively seeking it and therefore participating in the labour market', a gap of 8.8 per cent. However, the gap twenty years earlier, in 1994, was 14.5 per cent. Over the period, the participation rate for women increased from 71.3 per cent while the participation rate for men has been gradually decreasing from 85.8 per cent (Office for National Statistics 2015).

LOCAL TO GLOBAL The employment rate (the proportion of people who are in work) is lower for women in all EU member states, though with marked differences in the size of the gap. The employment rate for women aged 20–64 in 2015 was higher in the UK (71.3 per cent) than for the EU28 as a whole (64.3 per cent), though this largely reflects a higher employment rate for both men and women aged 20–64 in the UK (with the employment rate for men being 82.5 per cent in the UK and 75.9 per cent for the EU28). The gender gap in the employment rate for ages 20–64 in 2015 was slightly lower in the UK than for the EU28 as a whole (11.2 per cent compared to 13.6 per cent). Finland has achieved near parity with a gender gap of just 2.1 per cent (Eurostat 2016). In 2016 (Q4) women made up 49 per cent of all employees aged 16 and over in the UK (Powell and Mor 2017).

DYNAMIC Yet this apparent evidence of a trend towards equalizing opportunities between men and women conceals some marked and persistent differences in male and female experiences of paid work. These differences can be analysed in terms of:

- the distinction between 'traditional' and 'flexible' patterns of working;
- the types of jobs that men and women do (occupational segregation); and
- the amount that men and women, on average, are paid.

Flexible work

Flexible work includes temporary and part-time work, and is often contrasted with 'traditional' full-time, 'permanent' (i.e. of indefinite duration) jobs. Attention is increasingly focused on the expansion of the '**gig economy**' in which, 'instead of a regular wage, workers get paid for the "gigs" they do, such as a food delivery [e.g. Deliveroo] or a car journey [e.g. Uber]' and are generally not treated as employees but 'independent contractors', and the growth of 'zero-hours' contracts in which employees have no guaranteed minimum hours (BBC 2017). Although the gig economy is male dominated, women are more likely than men to be employed on zero-hours contracts (Balaram et al. 2017, Office for National Statistics 2017). More generally, women predominate in part-time and temporary work. Figure 12.1 shows that in 2016 (Q4) the number of women working part-time was 6.3 million, compared to 2.3 million men. In other words, 42 per cent of females were in part-time work compared to just 14 per cent of males—a female employee is three times as likely as a male to work part-time (Powell and Mor 2017). In other words, part-time employment is a common experience for women but remains rare for men.

Flexibility and parenthood

So far we have considered men and women in general, but another way we can examine how far their participation in the labour force differs is in terms of parenthood. If we look more

[1] The labour market is made up of the population aged 16 years and over, divided into three main groups: employed, unemployed (which together comprise the economically active, or the 'labour force'), and the economically inactive (including those looking after a home, retirees (the largest proportion), and those unable to work due to long-term sickness or disability).

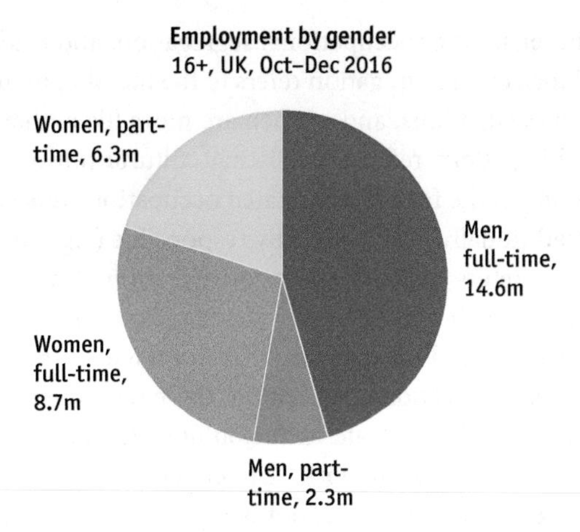

Figure 12.1 Employment by gender: 16+, UK, Oct–Dec. 2016
Source: Powell and Mor 2017.

closely at increased female economic activity it is particularly noticeable among mothers with dependent children (age 0–18 years). Between 1975 and 2010 this increased from half to 67 per cent. However, 'the presence of a dependent child in the family continues to have a major effect on the economic activity of women of working age' (Office for National Statistics 2009: 47), in contrast with men. Women of working age with dependent children are less likely to be in employment. For example, 89 per cent of women in the 25–34 age group without dependent children are in employment, as against 61 per cent of those with dependent children, whereas for men in this age group having dependent children makes virtually no difference to the employment rate. This contrast does seem to reflect the persistence of the 'traditional' idea of the male 'breadwinner' and the domestic division of labour. The gap in the employment rate between women with and those without dependent children is greatest in the 16–24 and 25–34 age groups, and this is consistent with the employment rate being correlated with the age of the youngest dependent child. For example, 63 per cent of married or cohabiting mothers whose youngest child is under 5 are in employment and this rises to 82 per cent where the youngest child is 16–18 (the corresponding figures are lower for lone mothers). In other words, mothers are more likely at all ages than fathers to be looking after children (and less likely to be in employment), and mothers with younger children are more likely to be looking after them and less likely to be in employment than mothers of older children. The employment rate of mothers increases as they and their children get older.

We have also seen that women are more likely to work part-time than men, and we can now add that working part-time is closely associated with motherhood. In 2011, 37 per cent of working women with dependent children worked part-time, whereas the figure for working women with no dependent children was 30 per cent (Equality and Human Rights Commission 2013). By contrast, having dependent children makes it *less* likely that men work part-time. In 2011 just 6 per cent of working fathers worked part-time, whereas the figure for working men with no dependent children was 13 per cent (Equality and Human Rights Commission 2013).

Occupational segregation

Occupational segregation refers to the fact that men and women are not equally represented throughout the labour force, and this is another persistent but slowly changing difference in the experience of work that may be seen as part of the pattern of disadvantage faced by women. There are two dimensions of occupational segregation, and evidence for both can be gained from Table 12.2. Horizontal segregation refers to the fact that men are more likely than women to work in certain occupations, and women are more likely than men to be found in others. To some extent this pattern reflects persisting cultural norms concerning 'women's work' and 'men's work'. Some of the female dominated occupations reflect the household tasks for which women have traditionally been primarily responsible (e.g. caring, cleaning, and catering). Vertical segregation refers to the greater representation of men at more senior levels in the occupational hierarchy, such as in managerial and professional roles. The phenomenon of segregation is sometimes referred to by saying that women are 'under-represented' in certain types of work and in senior positions, but both of these terms must be treated with some caution. 'Segregation' may suggest deliberate exclusion of women but, while this may be part of the story, there may be other factors at work. 'Under-representation' implies some desired or appropriate level of representation which is not being achieved, but there may be different views of what that level is. For example, what level of female representation would be appropriate on the boards of major companies? (See Mini-Case 12.2.)

Table 12.2 shows all in employment by sex and occupation for the UK in 2016, based on the Standard Occupational Classification. There are some occupations in which men and women are equally (or nearly equally) likely to be represented ('professional', 'associate professional and technical', and 'elementary'), although closer inspection reveals differences within these broad categories. For example, within 'professionals', women are a majority of 'nursing & midwifery' (89 per cent) and 'teaching and education' (68 per cent) professionals, while men dominate in 'IT & telecommunications' (82 per cent) and 'engineering' (92 per cent). Looking

Table 12.2 All in employment by sex and occupation, UK, 2016 Q2 (no. (000s), % and (rank)). Standard Occupational Classification (SOC 2010)

	Males	Females	All
1 MANAGERS, DIRECTORS AND SENIOR OFFICIALS	2,205 13.1% (4)	1,176 7.9% (7)	3,381 10.7% (4)
2 PROFESSIONAL OCCUPATIONS	3,274 19.4% (1)	3,173 21.4% (1)	6,447 20.4% (1)
3 ASSOCIATE PROFESSIONAL AND TECHNICAL OCCUPATIONS	2,455 14.6% (3)	1,941 13.1% (4)	4,395 13.9% (2)
4 ADMINISTRATIVE AND SECRETARIAL OCCUPATIONS	778 4.6% (8)	2,461 16.6% (2)	3,239 10.2% (6)
5 SKILLED TRADES OCCUPATIONS	3,079 18.3% (2)	334 2.3% (8)	3,413 10.8% (3)
6 CARING, LEISURE AND OTHER SERVICE OCCUPATIONS	499 3.0% (9)	2,397 16.2% (3)	2,897 9.2% (7)
7 SALES AND CUSTOMER SERVICE OCCUPATIONS	925 5.5% (7)	1,529 10.3% (5)	2,454 7.8% (8)
8 PROCESS, PLANT AND MACHINE OPERATIVES	1,775 10.5% (6)	234 1.6% (9)	2,009 6.3% (9)
9 ELEMENTARY OCCUPATIONS	1,808 10.7% (5)	1,526 10.3% (6)	3,334 10.5% (5)
All occupations	16,856 100%	14,805 100%	31,661 100%

Source: Office for National Statistics 2016b.

in finer detail, within 'teaching and education professionals' men are more than half (51.4 per cent) of 'higher education teaching professionals' but are a small minority in 'primary and nursery teaching professionals' (15 per cent) where women dominate (85 per cent).

There are three occupational groups in which women are more likely to work than men ('Administrative and Secretarial Occupations'; 'Caring, Leisure and Other Service Occupations'; and 'Sales and Customer Service Occupations'). One in six women work in administrative and secretarial occupations compared to less than one in twenty men. Looked at another way, of 3.2 million in employment in this occupational group in 2016, three out of four (76 per cent) were women. A similar gap is apparent in personal service occupations. Conversely, men predominate in skilled trades, this being the second highest ranked occupation for men (18.3 per cent) and the second lowest for women (2.3 per cent): skilled trades are virtually a male preserve.

Table 12.2 also shows a pattern of vertical segregation, in which women are less likely than men to be found in managerial positions. More than one in eight men is a manager or senior official compared to less than one in twelve women. This 'under-representation' of women is often referred to as the 'glass ceiling', meaning that women face a barrier to their progression to the most senior positions in organizations. Vertical segregation is most pronounced at the very top: less than 10 per cent of executive directors of the UK's top 100 companies are women (Sealy et al. 2016).

Stop and Think

Do you find it surprising that less than 10 per cent of executive directors of the UK's top 100 companies are women? Is it plausible that women have equal opportunities with men when so few at the top are female? Do you think that the figure should be greater than 10 per cent? How much greater?

The gender pay gap

LOCAL TO GLOBAL Across the world there is a **gender pay gap** which has narrowed over time, but which remains substantial. In the UK the gender pay gap based on median hourly earnings for all employees decreased from 22 per cent in 2008 to 18.1 per cent in 2016. The gap for full-time employees was substantially lower at 9.4 per cent. In other words, on average men were paid 9.4 per cent more per hour than women (expressed as a percentage of male median hourly earnings). The overall difference is explained by part-time work. For part-time employees there is actually a gender pay gap in favour of women, or a 'negative' gender pay gap. However, on average part-time jobs are less well-paid than full-time jobs, so the fact that women are more likely than men to work part-time means that the earnings gap is greater for all employees than for full-time employees only. Women who work part-time, e.g. to balance employment with care of dependent children, are disadvantaged by the scarcity of well-paid part-time jobs (McGuinness 2016, Office for National Statistics 2016a).

The gender pay gap is largest for the highest paid occupations. For the top 10 per cent of high earners (top decile), the gap for full-time employees was 18.8 per cent in 2016, whereas for the bottom 10 per cent of low earners (bottom decile) it was 4.9 per cent. The narrower gap for low earners may be explained by the equalizing effect of the introduction of the National Living Wage, as women tend to work in lower paid occupations and so have benefited most (Office for National Statistics 2016a).

Comparing weekly or annual earnings shows a bigger gender pay gap because men, on average, work longer hours and are more likely to receive overtime pay and bonuses. For example, the gap in weekly earnings is twice the hourly gap for all employees, at 36 per cent (Johnson 2016). The average hourly pay gap conceals differences over the life cycle, which may be explained in terms of a 'motherhood pay penalty'. The gap is smallest among the youngest cohorts and widens after women have children. From the first child being born to reaching 12 years of age, the pay gap widens from 10 per cent to more than 30 per cent. This wage penalty is associated with women losing out on work experience through time out for childcare and returning part-time (Institute for Fiscal Studies 2016). Obviously, the gender pay gap accumulates over women's working lives so that women experience a lifetime earnings shortfall compared to men. On the basis of the gender gap in weekly earnings for full-time employees in 2015, and assuming a working life of fifty-two years, this shortfall has been calculated as nearly £300,000 (Allen 2016b).

Although the wage gap appears to be closing, progress is slow. In fact, it is slower than appears from just comparing hourly earnings, since the gains are partly attributable to more women being educated to degree level and accessing higher-earning jobs. This has raised women's median hourly earnings, but 'among the university educated the wage gap between men and women has barely shifted . . . [since] the mid-1990s. The same is true of women educated to A-level standard' (Johnson 2016). It has been calculated that, at the current rate of progress, the gender pay gap will not be eliminated until 2069 (Allen 2016a, Deloitte 2016). The United Nations has projected that it will take seventy years to close the gender pay gap on a global scale (Topping 2015).

COMPLEXITY The gender pay gap has a number of causes and therefore requires a range of solutions. It is clearly bound up with occupational segregation since the occupational areas in which women are clustered are low paid compared to those occupations where women are under-represented. The 'pay gap' and 'opportunity gap' are closely related. It is also related to the higher proportion of women than men who work part-time and the 'motherhood penalty'. Of course, these factors point to deeper causes including social norms, stereotypical ideas of 'male' and 'female' work, childcare provision, and the domestic division of labour. However societal factors should not distract attention away from steps that can be taken within businesses and employers' responsibilities. Knowing who are the 'best' and worst' employers might stimulate action by businesses.

INTERNAL/EXTERNAL In this spirit the UK government has introduced mandatory gender pay gap reporting from April 2017 for all employers in Great Britain with more than 250 staff. Businesses are required to publish the following four types of figures annually on their own website and on a government website:

- gender pay gap (mean and median averages);
- gender bonus gap (mean and median averages);
- proportion of men and women receiving bonuses; and
- proportion of men and women in each quartile of the organization's pay structure.

The snapshot date each year is 5 April for businesses and charities, so the first data will have to be published within a year of 5 April 2017 (Gov.uk 2017). There are concerns that businesses might attempt to manipulate the data and, crucially, there are no targets that employers have to meet or requirements for action of any kind other than to publish the data. However, producing the data might stimulate discussion within businesses and action to close gender gaps, motivated either by a genuine desire to tackle the problem or the aim of avoiding reputational damage and the potential negative effects on sales and recruitment—see Mini-Case 12.2.

Mini-Case 12.2 Women in the City and on boards

A report by the Equality and Human Rights Commission (EHRC 2009) examined the extent of sex discrimination and the gender pay gap in the financial services sector. It found that although 'men and women make up almost equal proportions of employees within the sector' (p. 9), there is a persistent pattern of occupational segregation and a related marked pay gap. These problems are more marked in the financial services sector than in the economy as a whole.

Gender pay gap

The overall gender pay gap is 55 per cent based on mean full-time gross annual earnings, and 'there is evidence of gender bias in the distribution of bonuses and performance-related pay' (p. 10).

Occupational segregation

Women are concentrated in the lower paid jobs, and under-represented in revenue-generating functions for which basic and performance-related pay are much higher. Hence the opportunity and pay gaps are closely related. 'Men occupy two-thirds of managerial and senior jobs and nearly three-quarters of professional jobs' (p. 11).

Work culture

INTERNAL/EXTERNAL Some important aspects of work culture are seen to disadvantage women. Client networking activities play an important role in the sector and tend to be male-oriented, serving to 'exclude women (such as a focus on male-dominated sports) or even demean women (such as socializing at lap-dancing clubs or hostess bars)' (p. 12). The characteristic long-hours culture is an obstacle to improved work–life balance and disadvantages employees trying to balance work and family responsibilities, particularly women. Furthermore, requests for flexible working for senior employees are not regarded positively and may involve demotion, and women taking maternity leave are disadvantaged by reallocation of their clients and other negative consequences.

The EHRC put forward a number of recommendations to improve the opportunities for women in the financial services sector on the basis not only of fairness but also the benefits to business. Trevor Phillips, chair of EHRC, argues that through such improvement 'financial firms have the chance to boost morale, bring on new talent, and maximize the potential of their existing employees' (quoted in the *Guardian* 7 September 2009).

Similar arguments have been made in favour of greater female representation on the boards of directors of large companies. In 2011 Lord Davies published the findings of an independent review *Women on Boards*. This showed that in 2010 only 12.5 per cent (one in eight) of directors of FTSE 100 companies were women and eighteen companies had no female board members, a clear example of 'vertical segregation'. Davies recommended that these companies should be aiming for a minimum of 25 per cent female board member representation by 2015. According to the report:

The business case for gender diversity on boards has four key dimensions:

- *improving performance*
- *accessing the widest talent pool*
- *being more responsive to the market*
- *achieving better corporate governance*

(Davies 2011)

Davies commented 'This is not . . . just about promoting equal opportunities but it is about improving business performance. There is growing evidence to show that diverse boards are better boards, delivering financial out-performance and stock market growth.' By October 2015 the five-year review reported that women made up 26.1 per cent of all directorships in FTSE 100 companies, as shown in Figure 12.2. Davies extended the target, calling on all FTSE 350 companies to achieve 33 per cent female representation by 2020.

However, in 2016 women only held less than 10 per cent of executive directorships compared to more than 30 per cent of less powerful non-executive directorships, and the UK is behind many other European countries. For example, Norway, which has a mandatory target of 40 per cent, is the leading country with 37 per cent female representation on boards (European Women on Boards 2016, Sealy et al. 2016—and see Mini-Case 12.3).

Question

Some people argue that when a woman chooses to be a stay-at-home mother, this 'choice' simply reflects the way girls are socialized. In this view, males and females are equally capable of performing high-flying roles in the City and would be equally likely to choose this path if it weren't for their upbringing or other factors. Do you agree?

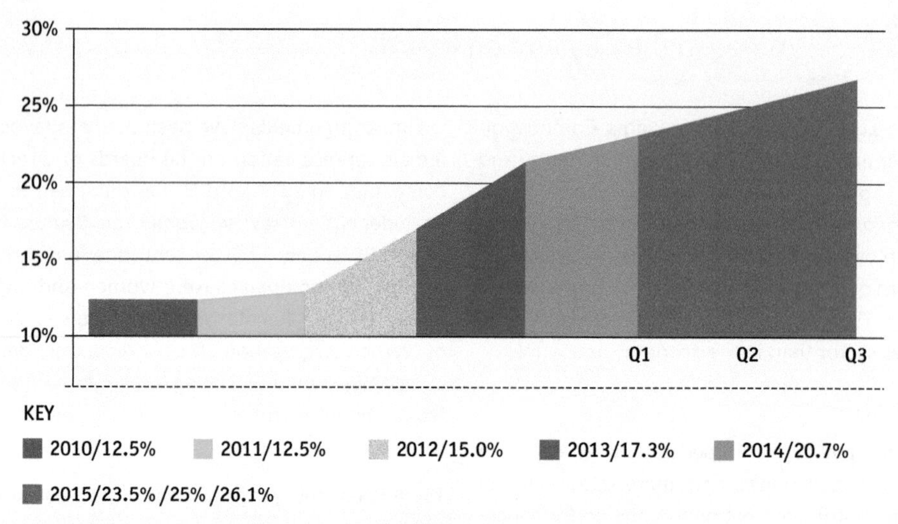

Figure 12.2 Women on boards of FTSE 100 companies (%), 2010–15
Source: Davies 2015.

Mini-Case 12.3 Can opportunities ever be equal?

The idea of equal opportunity is that men and women, on average, should have the same chances of, say, becoming the chief executive of a FTSE 100 company, or of pursuing careers in management at all levels. What individuals make of their lives should depend on their talents, choices, and efforts, not on artificial barriers such as sexual discrimination. We might expect that equal opportunities will lead to roughly equal representation of men and women in management, or at least that representation at this level will reflect the balance between males and females within the workforce. Should we expect 50 per cent of managers to be women? If so, British business is clearly a long way short of the mark. However, this outcome should only be expected if men and women have, on average, the same talents and make the same choices. It can be argued that part of the 'under-representation' of women in management is a reflection of women having, as a group, different attitudes to work and careers than men. In particular, if a proportion of women choose home (i.e. being a stay-at-home mother looking after young children) over career then we would expect men, on average, to be more successful in their careers than women.

'Mummy, I want to be a housewife' (Hakim 1996)

VALUES Hakim's research suggests that some women choose to prioritize 'home' over 'career', and that these choices go some way to explain occupational segregation and pay differences: 'sex differentials in employment experience . . . are . . . due to personal choice as much as to sex discrimination'. She claims that there is a polarization of the female population between 'career women' and 'home-centred women'.

This research suggests that we need to distinguish between support for the principle of equal opportunity and approval of working wives/mothers among women, and the personal choices of many women about their own lives.

However, this argument is controversial because, it can be argued, we need to consider the pressures and constraints that influence women's 'choices'. These choices might be explained by cultural norms concerning femininity or by the refusal of men to take on a fair share of childcare and household chores.

Question

What steps can businesses take to promote more equality of opportunity for women?

Social mobility—is Britain a mobile society?

Another way of looking at equal opportunity is to look at the relative chances of people from different social backgrounds in terms of income level, achieving high-earning jobs, or moving up the occupational class hierarchy (see Chapter 6). How far does class position limit opportunities in life? In particular, what are the chances of children from 'working class' backgrounds gaining entry to 'middle class' occupations? These are questions of social mobility.

DYNAMIC In the last century there appeared to be a good deal of upward mobility, due largely to the expanding, non-manual, occupations recruiting employees from working class backgrounds (there was more room in the middle and at the top). However, the general picture is one in which social mobility is restricted and limited in range. In other words, the chances of working class children entering middle-class professions are not good.

Adding together the data on social mobility of men from a number of generations spanning much of the last century, Heath and Payne show that sons of working class fathers were likely to follow in their footsteps. For example, 70 per cent of sons whose fathers were semi-skilled or unskilled manual workers ('lower working class') either remained in the same class (38 per cent) or moved up only into the 'higher working class', including skilled manual workers (32 per cent). Only 18 per cent made it into the 'higher and lower salariat' of professionals and managers. Conversely, 69 per cent of sons whose fathers were in the highest class (the higher salariat) themselves remained in that class (46 per cent) or the lower salariat (23 per cent) (Heath and Payne 2000: 262–5). The odds of a child making it into the middle class, as opposed to ending up in the working class, are much better for a middle-class child than one from the working class. The ratio of these odds across modern societies (i.e. not just in Britain) has been calculated to be 15:1 (Aldridge 2004). These findings indicate that class background exercises a strong influence on life chances or opportunities in terms of the labour market (see end of chapter case study).

What has inequality got to do with business?

In recent years, survey evidence has indicated widespread public concern that the gap between rich and poor is too wide, and the question of inequality has moved up the political agenda.

To judge whether income inequality is a problem we need to consider its economic and social impacts. These impacts can be both positive and negative. As we have seen, the main debate is about the degree of inequality that is acceptable. Most people agree, for example, that chief executives should be paid more than their employees in the business, but they are likely to disagree about whether the widening gap can be justified. The debate is often framed in terms of two key principles: efficiency and fairness (or social justice).

Incentives

Advocates of the free market argue that inequality can be seen as good for efficiency, on the basis that incentives are required to attract talent and motivate performance. In other words, the very high rewards of chief executives are needed to attract the best people to perform these important jobs. Having the most talented people running our companies means that they are more likely to be efficient and successful. This argument has also been used to defend bankers' bonuses in response to widespread public criticism in the context of the financial crisis and economic recession. The high rewards available at the top will motivate others to perform to a high level in order to progress up the career ladder.

The going rate

From the perspective of neoclassical economics, the scarcity of talent bids up the price of chief executives and of other highly rewarded occupations. For example, being a medical practitioner is one of the best rewarded occupations, and the same logic applies here: high earnings attract talented people into these jobs. Against the accusation that CEOs are 'fat cats' awarding themselves excessive pay, it can be argued that companies have to pay the 'going rate' in a competitive market. Just as football clubs have to pay huge sums in transfer payments and salaries to attract top players such as Gareth Bale, they also, like all other businesses, have to pay whatever is necessary to recruit the best manager. The alternative is to risk loss of competitiveness and the prospect of sliding down the league table.

The same argument applies at the other end of the scale. In other words, checkout operators are low paid because their wages are also determined by competition in the labour market. Only in this case there is no scarcity to bid up the price, rather a plentiful supply of workers able to do this job holds wages down. Again, companies have to pay the going rate since if one company pays more than its rivals it puts itself at a competitive disadvantage by increasing its costs.

Trickle down

For some people the gap between the top and bottom of the earnings distribution seems like an obvious case of unfairness. In fact this seems to be a view that is held widely: a large majority of the British population agrees that 'the gap between those with high incomes and those with low incomes is too large' (British Social Attitudes survey, quoted in Hills 2004: 32). This suggests that there may be a trade-off between efficiency and fairness: if we want to promote efficiency through incentives this will involve inequalities in earnings that are perceived as unfair, but reducing such inequalities in the name of fairness may reduce incentives and so damage efficiency.

Against this, it can be argued that efficiency and fairness go hand in hand through what is sometimes referred to as the **trickle-down** effect. The economist Simon Kuznets argued that while in the short run inequality might widen in societies that are growing this is the natural result of the talented members of the economy powering it forward and reaping their just rewards. However, over time everyone will benefit because the successful businesses that are built both provide employment for the rest of the society and the tax base to provide for the education and training and benefits for those seeking employment as well as other forms of spending to help the poor.

Social cohesion

For Marxist critics, the defining characteristic of capitalism is that income and wealth will not be distributed in any way that can be seen as fair, and for structuralist and institutionalist critics there are clear obstacles that prevent both equality of opportunity and outcome. They will point out that there is no really convincing evidence to support the natural trickle-down effect and the Kuznets hypothesis. Even if it were true, those at the bottom end of the earnings distribution, though better off than in the past, are still likely to feel a sense of unfairness. This is because people tend to care not only about their absolute level of earnings but also their position relative to others in the hierarchy. In this view inequality is a social problem because being at the bottom of the hierarchy, in a society that celebrates affluence and consumption, is associated with failure and low status. For example, those who can afford luxury cars and other forms of 'conspicuous' consumption are sending out a signal that they are successful whereas an extension of this outlook suggests that those who use public transport must have failed in life. Critics of inequality say that it is difficult to sustain social cohesion—the sense that we are all members of a shared society—in the context of a division between rich and poor and a perception of unfairness.

Morale

VALUES This dimension of social cohesion has important implications for business in the sense that employees are encouraged to see themselves as working for the good of the team. This sense of team membership may be undermined by a feeling among employees that executives are taking more than their fair share out of the business and are motivated more by greed than the benefit of the team. Because this feeling may undermine morale and work performance it can be argued that a greater sense of fairness in business is a key ingredient of efficiency.

Greed and social responsibility

VALUES While it is true that firms operating in competitive markets have to respect the going rate for various types of jobs, institutionalists argue this does not mean that firms have no discretion or choice in relation to pay, and that furthermore, pay is often simply not linked to market conditions. There is increasing agreement that major companies operate in effect as a cartel and the boardroom pay is pushed up by a small number of remuneration consultants. This may reflect in part a shift in the culture of business especially in the US and the UK in which, according to critics, greed has replaced the moral restraints that previously maintained a lower ratio of boardroom pay to workforce earnings. Critics also maintain that there is now increasing empirical evidence that increases in boardroom pay are not justified on the basis of excellent performance, but occur despite mediocre or poor performance.

Reputation

If ethical restraints on executive pay have weakened, companies might still be concerned about the risk to reputation posed by public criticism of greed. Public criticism takes up management time, can adversely affect the morale and performance of employees whose sense of working for a good employer is undermined, could damage relations with clients who are keen to maintain their own ethical reputations, and could encourage greater political and regulatory scrutiny.

Stop and Think

Is there a trade-off between efficiency and fairness in business, or do the two go hand in hand?

Income inequality

Complexity

When examining trends in global inequality over the last thirty years we need to draw a distinction between two measurements of inequality. Absolute inequality measures the quantitative difference between the amounts that people earn, e.g. assume that one person earns $1 a day and another earns $10 a day. Here the absolute gap in earnings is clearly $9 and there is a relative inequality ratio of 10:1 in terms of what the richest person earns compared to the poorest. Let us now assume that there is a general rise in the economic growth of the country and in ten years the poorest person now earns $10 a day and the richest person earns $90.

Stop and Think

What is the relative gap between the rich person and the poor person? What is the absolute gap? Which measure of inequality is the most important?

So, in the example above, the relative gap has closed to 9:1, but the absolute gap has clearly risen from $9 a day to $80 a day.

LOCAL TO GLOBAL **VALUES** If we look at global trends, this distinction between relative and absolute inequality is important. Everyone would agree that the most important economic goal must be to lift people out of absolute poverty, which is defined as the level at which it is impossible to fulfil even the most basic of human needs. Despite many reservations as to the universal applicability of this figure the World Bank defines this level of income as being $1.90 per day. The good news for the global community is that the 1990 Millennium Development Goal target of reducing global extreme poverty in 2015 by 50 per cent compared to 1990 levels was achieved in 2010, meaning that 1.1 billion people had been lifted out of extreme poverty. This has been mainly because of the rapid economic growth in countries such as India, China, and Brazil but while these growth rates have indeed led to reductions in extreme levels of poverty there has been a general tendency for inequality to rise. In Latin America generally, relative inequality has fallen but absolute inequality has still risen, whereas in South Asia, both have risen which mirrors the rising levels of both relative and absolute inequality in Europe and North America. Globally, inequality has been both relatively and absolutely increasing for the last thirty years. Across the OECD countries on average the gap between the top 10 per cent and the bottom 10 per cent has risen from 7:1 in the 1980s to 9:1 today.

For global organizations like the World Bank, the Organisation of Economic Co-operation and Development, the United Nations, and in recent years the IMF and the World Economic Forum, existing levels of absolute inequality pose a real barrier to the new 2030 Sustainable Development Goal of an end to all extreme poverty being realized. Furthermore, persistent inequality may even see a rise in people falling back into extreme poverty and also pose a wider range of economic and social problems examined above.

Income and wealth inequality is conventionally measured using a statistical device known as the Gini coefficient. This can be either expressed as a percentage e.g. 45 per cent or as a decimal in the range 0 to 1 e.g. 0.45. If we imagine a population size of 100 and only one person owned all the income, then the Gini coefficient would be 1 or 100 per cent. If every person earned exactly the same (or 1 per cent of total income), then it would be 0 or 0 per cent. Table 12.3 shows the Gini coefficients for selected countries in the period 2000–15.

DYNAMIC Table 12.4 shows how the Gini coefficient for the UK has changed over the last four decades. The Gini coefficient in 1945 was approximately 0.41 and fell dramatically in the post-war period which was a common trend across the developed countries.

Table 12.3 Average Gini coefficients for selected countries, 2010–15

Country	Average Gini coefficient 2010–15 (rounded to 2 decimal places)
Norway	0.26
Germany	0.30
UK	0.33
India	0.35
US	0.41
Russia	0.42
China	0.42
Nigeria	0.43
Brazil	0.52
South Africa	0.63

Source: adapted from *United Nations Development Programme Human Development Report 2016* http://hdr.undp.org/en/composite/IHDI

Table 12.4 The Gini coefficient for the UK by decade, 1977–2017

UK Gini coefficient	Year
0.24	1977
0.29	1987
0.33	1997
0.36	2007
0.37 (est.)	2017

Sources: adapted from 'How has inequality changed?' (Equality Trust) https://www.equalitytrust.org.uk/how-has-inequality-changed
Note: At the time of writing, the most recently reported figure for the UK was for 2016 and the Gini coefficient had been reported as having fallen to 0.34. However, research by the Resolution Foundation showed that while inequality appeared to have fallen back in the years following the financial crisis of 2008 onwards, this has now reversed, and so the figure for 2017 is estimated. See http://www.resolutionfoundation.org/publications/the-living-standards-audit-2017

Stop and Think

Which of the developed countries in the list in Table 12.3 are the most equal and which is the most unequal?

What might explain the difference in the Gini coefficients between the BRICS countries? (Brazil, Russia, India, China, and South Africa)?

In the long run what has happened to the degree of inequality in the UK in the period 1977 to 2017?

VALUES While an analysis of Gini coefficients allows us to gauge the levels and trends in inequality it is often difficult to really appreciate the scale and qualitative nature of inequality. Using the UK as an example, what lies behind the Gini coefficient? We can break down the

Table 12.5 Distribution of earnings per quintile

Quintile (each 20% of income earners)	Percentage share of income (original income before taxes and transfers)
Top Fifth	40
Fourth Fifth	23
Third Fifth	17
Second Fifth	13
Bottom Fifth	7

Source: Adapted from 'The scale of economic inequality in the UK' (Equality Trust) https://www.equalitytrust.org.uk/scale-economic-inequality-uk

overall inequality figure by focusing on the actual dispersion of earnings. Using data from the Equality Trust, who in turn derived this from the UK National Office of Statistics in 2015/16, Table 12.5 shows the distribution of earnings across the working population disaggregated into each quintile, or 20 per cent of the working population.

Clearly, this shows an unequal share of income in the UK, with the 'top' fifth quintile of income earners owning 40 per cent of the total income. When incomes are distributed in such an unequal way it is meaningless to give a figure for what the 'average' person might earn as the high proportion of income earned by the top quintiles raises the average so that in fact the majority of the working population earn less. In 2014–15, three-fifths of UK households received less than the average. Instead it is often the 'median' income that is quoted in statistics which is the income that the person earns who is in the middle of the earnings distribution (the fiftieth percentile). In the UK this was £19,000 in 2016.

The National Living Wage replaced the former National Minimum Wage in the UK in 2015, and in 2017 it was set at £7.50 an hour and is meant to be applied to all those who are 25 or over. For campaign groups seeking to reduce poverty and reduce inequality the National Living Wage is set at too low a figure so to again add some perspective, the Joseph Rowntree Foundation (JRF) uses a Minimum Income Standard (MIS) to measure what is seen as a minimum acceptable standard of living and in 2017 this was set at £17,900 for a single person with no children and for a couple with two children they would need to earn at least £20,400 each. It was estimated by the JRF that 15 million people were earning less than the MIS (https://www.jrf.org.uk/report/minimum-income-standard-uk-2017 a minimum income standard for the UK 2017).

Again, using data from the Office of National Statistics 2015–16, the Equality Trust calculated that for the bottom 20 per cent, total household average disposable income (which allows for the impact of taxes and benefits) was £9,644 and for the top 10 per cent their incomes of an average £83,875 were almost nine times greater. If we looked at pre-tax and benefit incomes the average income for the bottom 10 per cent would have been £4,436 and for the top 10 per cent £107,937 which is twenty-four times greater (https://www.equalitytrust.org.uk/scale-economic-inequality-uk).

Stop and Think

Before the effects of the redistribution effects of the tax and benefit system in the UK the relative inequality between the top 1 per cent and the bottom 10 per cent was 24:1 and after income tax, council tax, and benefits are applied it fell to 9:1. Do you think this gap is too low, too high, or about right?

COMPLEXITY Of course this covers a wide dispersal of earnings and we must also allow for the fact that simple monetary figures do not completely capture the true standard of living and that how much money there is to go round in a household will depend on the numbers in that household. However, it is when we break down the income distribution in the last 10 per cent, the last 5 per cent, and the last 1 per cent that both the levels of relative and absolute inequality begin to really hit home.

Moving away from household figures to individual incomes in 2016 in the UK the average annual income of the 95th percentile was £70,000. Once we explore the incomes of people above this, both absolute and relative levels of inequality begin to soar and this is especially marked when we enter the world of the top 1 per cent of income earners. The way in which incomes take off after the 99th percentile gave rise to the popular slogan 'We are the 99 per cent' coined by the US academic and activist David Graeber in 2011. While there is indeed a big difference between earnings in the 99 per cent it is relatively smaller compared to what happens after we reach the 99th percentile, and by far the biggest increases in inequality in many countries is because of the rapid rise in the incomes of this 1 per cent group.

In 1971 the Dutch economist Jan Pen tried to cut through the dry statistics of income distribution to paint a visual picture of inequality in modern economic systems and he chose to focus on Britain. Pen asked the reader to imagine that they were about to see all income earners in Britain parade past (in 2015/16 this was 30.6 million people) in one hour but that their height would be decreased or increased in relation to their incomes. You the viewer would be earning the average income which in 2015/16 was £27,615. So, what would a modern day's 'Pen's parade' look like?

Using figures for 2015/16 (see https://www.gov.uk/government/statistics/percentile-points-from-1-to-99-for-total-income-before-and-after-tax) the first half of the parade would be a gradual procession of very small people. The first per cent of the population which would pass by you at the 36th second would be around 2 feet tall and then from then until the 36th minute heights would gradually rise until people your height pass by. Clearly then there is inequality but this is only a ratio of 1:3. You might have expected people of your height to pass by at the half way mark of 30 minutes but in fact the 50th percentile would be 5 feet 7 inches. People your height do not pass until the 36th minute and after this the parade would trundle on and the people that you see now get bigger and bigger so that by the 54th minute you will see people earning £51,400 and they would be just over 11 feet tall. Now 90 per cent of the parade has passed. At the 57th minute come the people who are earning over £70,000 and who would be 15 feet tall. You would indeed be looking up to them as we are now at the 95th percentile. After this in the last three minutes things start to escalate. With 24 seconds left on the clock the 99th richest percentile of people pass, and they are now relative giants compared to you at a height of 35 feet. What happens next is what exercises the attention of most researchers into levels of inequality.

In 2016 the average annual income of the top 1 per cent was £267,000 (which equates to a height of 58 feet) but the average annual income of those in the top 0.1 per cent was £990,000 (215 feet). However, there is an elite group within the elite group of the 1 per cent whose earnings are simply astronomical and whose heights would cause trouble to aircraft controllers if they lived anywhere near an airport!

Given this concentration of incomes at the top it is not surprising then that there is scrutiny as to who makes up this group. Some of this group have made it there as the superstars of sport, music, and film and some are there because of inherited wealth from which they derive substantial unearned income. However, by far the biggest group is people who have earned their incomes in a narrow range of business occupations. There will be a few very well-paid private doctors and lawyers, but the most significant groups are the chief executives of large corporations and in the last thirty years in those countries like the US and now followed by the UK people who work at the top levels of finance and banking.

In 2017 using figures from 2015/16 the Equality Trust in the UK reported that the average chief executive of the top 100 UK businesses earned 386 times more than a worker on the National Living Wage. On average each CEO earned £5.3 million compared with £13,662 for someone on the National Living Wage (https://www.equalitytrust.org.uk/sites/default/files/Pay%20Tracker%20%28March%202017%29_1.pdf Pay Tracker).

Danny Dorling argues that the most significant fact in both the relatively and absolutely higher levels of the US and UK compared to other OECD countries has been the rising proportion of bankers in the top 1 per cent and that this is especially true of the top 0.1 per cent of income earners. According to Dorling (2015a), the UK has ten times more highly paid bankers than Germany and in 2014 there were more bankers being paid over £1 million pounds in one bank in London alone compared to all people earning over £1million in all sectors in Japan.

A major reason for both the rapid rise in absolute and relative inequality of the top 1 per cent is that as well as earning very large salaries part of their compensation packages are often made up of shares in financial assets and they are also able to use their large incomes to invest in ownership of property and land as well as stocks and shares so building up very large wealth holdings which further yield large incomes in the form of unearned incomes from rents, shares, and dividends. While we have so far explored income inequality when it comes to wealth inequality the scale is very much higher.

Wealth inequality

Measuring wealth is very difficult for the simple reason that the wealthy are very adept at hiding it and employ (some very well paid) accountants and legal advisers to enable them to legally avoid tax liabilities and in many case to illegally evade them. However, every year Credit Suisse publishes its *Global Wealth Report* which is seen as a highly reliable guide to who owns wealth globally and from where their wealth is derived. Table 12.6 shows the global distribution of wealth in 2016.

Table 12.6 clearly shows an extraordinarily high level of unequal wealth ownership and as we discussed earlier in this chapter there are severe concerns of the effect that this has on social mobility with considerable advantages of economic capital given to the sons (and it would seem especially the sons) and daughters of those with wealth and the accompanying

Table 12.6 Global distribution of wealth 2016

Wealth range	Number of people	% global population	Amount of wealth ($US trillions)	% global wealth
>$1m	33m	0.7	116.6	45.6
$100,000–$1m	365m	7.5	103.9	40.6
$10,000–$100,000	897m	18.5	29.1	29.1
< $10,000	3.546	73.2	6.1	2.4

Source: Adapted from James Davies, Rodrigo Lluberas, and Anthony Shorrocks, 'The global wealth pyramid', *Credit Suisse Global Wealth Databook 2016* https://www.credit-suisse.com/corporate/en/articles/news-and-expertise/the-global-wealth-report-2016-201611.html

Mini-Case 12.4 It's a billionaire's world

It was Oxfam's report into wealth inequality in 2014 that was widely discussed in that year at the annual meeting of the World Economic Forum at Davos which focused on the threat that inequality posed to the business community. The irony was not lost on many commentators that it was the world's richest business people who were now acknowledging that they were the problem! Oxfam hit on the effective strapline to publicize their report by reducing all the facts and figures down to one eye-catching headline that was eighty-five people owned as much as half the world's population. Since 2014, Oxfam has continued to keep up the pressure to bring wealth inequality to the attention of the business and political community. By 2016 the headline figure was that it was now sixty-two individuals that owned as much as half the world's people and by their 2017 report they argued that careful checking of wealth figures did reveal considerable underestimates in the Credit Suisse report and that in fact it was now only eight individuals. According to an Oxfam press release these were the eight richest individuals in 2017:

1. Bill Gates: US founder of Microsoft (net worth: $75bn).
2. Amancio Ortega: Spanish founder of Inditex, Zara fashion chain (net worth: $67bn).
3. Warren Buffett: US CEO, largest shareholder in Berkshire Hathaway (net worth: $60.8bn).
4. Carlos Slim Helu: Mexican owner of Grupo Carso (net worth: $50bn).
5. Jeff Bezos: US founder, chairman, chief executive of Amazon (net worth: $45.2bn).
6. Mark Zuckerberg: US chairman, CEO, co-founder of Facebook (net worth: $44.6bn).
7. Larry Ellison: US co-founder, CEO of Oracle (net worth: $43.6bn).
8. Michael Bloomberg: US founder, owner, CEO of Bloomberg LP (net worth: $40bn).

During the period 1988–2011 the income of the poorest 10 per cent in the world rose in total by $65 and that of the richest 1 per cent by $11,800.

Source: Oxfam (2017)

Questions

1. **What do all the people in the list have in common?**
2. **What do all the businesses they lead (or have led) have in common?**
3. **To what extent did the poorest 10 per cent improve their economic well-being in this period?**

deterioration in the prospects of upward social mobility into high paying occupations of those without it. In 2016 Credit Suisse looked at the share of the top 1 per cent of wealth earners and estimated that this was 89 per cent but in 2017 the UK development charity Oxfam argued that in fact this was a share of 99 per cent. See Mini-Case 12.4.

COMPLEXITY Dorling argues that we again need to be careful when examining wealth inequality because of the huge variance within the top 1 per cent of wealth owners. Globally there are 12 million people classified as being high net worth individuals (HNWIs) and to be in this group you would need to have at least a net worth of $1 million excluding ownership of the property in which you live. The vast majority of these do not earn much more than this and they live in the US, Germany, and Japan. A large number of HNWIs own second homes in the UK, without being officially UK residents, but there were 465,000 HNWIs living in the UK making up 1 per cent of the adult population. In 2012 the top 1 per cent of HNWIs (known as ultra or UHNWIs) owned above £30 million and there were 111,000 of these who owned one-third of all the wealth of the HNWIs. London was the preferred home for more UHNWIs than any other city in the world (Dorling 2015b). For critics such as Chrystia Freeland (2013) the global business environment is now dominated by the rise of these plutocrats.

We have seen that not all countries experience the same levels of inequality but that in recent years there has been a general drift towards greater degrees of inequality in developed and developing countries alike. This is almost always because of an increasing share in the income and wealth of the top 1 per cent. In the case of the developed world it is the US in which the greatest shift to more inequality has been seen, then followed by the UK and in both cases this is as a result of an increasing proportion of the 1 per cent being occupied by people in banking and finance. In the US, Stiglitz (2013) has shown that while growth has picked up after the financial crisis most of the gains have been captured by the 1 per cent and those at the bottom and the middle of the income and wealth distribution are worse off in real terms than they were at the beginning of the century and for those at the bottom, life is particularly harsh. Similar results are found in the UK. Research conducted by sociologists at the London School of Economics into the changing nature of class in the UK confirm the existence of what Guy Standing referred to as a 'Precariat' group of people at the bottom of the economic ladder. In this research this was estimated as being 15 per cent of the population (Savage et al. 2015), but Will Hutton, Master of Hertford College at the University of Oxford argues that in the UK the bottom 30 per cent of the workforce are what he terms the 'disadvantaged'. Above this there is another, the middle 30 per cent who are the 'marginalised and insecure' (Hutton 2015). We have seen that even people towards the middle and upper ends of the income distribution have seen their living standards decline or at least not recover to the levels that they experienced before the financial crash of 2008. Even for those entering full-time employment it is harder to find jobs offering the secure pension rights offered to previous generations and with the pressure on public finances in many developed countries state pension ages are rising. What has been remarkable in many developed countries is that despite the recessionary effects of the financial crisis unemployment has not fallen but that has been partly because workers have been prepared to accept lower wages but also because of the significant rise of part-time, temporary work, the rise of self-employment, and the rise of the so-called 'gig' or 'task rabbit' economy. One significant area of concern since the global financial crisis has been the reduction in secure opportunities for people under 35 and the gradual erosion of in-work benefits such as pensions.

Why has inequality increased?

INTERNAL/EXTERNAL The most significant impact of the rise in inequality in recent years across the globe has been on the growing polarization between the top 1 per cent and everyone else, and within the 99 per cent most people seeing no appreciable increase in living standards and for the majority actual declines which has been worse for the those in the precariat. It would also appear that there is a growing consensus across the political divide, from a range of pressure and religious groups and even from within the business community that something needs to be done to reverse this but before we examine these proposals we need to briefly examine the reasons for the growth in inequality.

Changes in labour markets—'flexibility' for the 99 per cent, protected markets for the 1 per cent

There are very few people who now argue that the soaring high pay for the elite group at the top is a result of market forces rewarding the exceptional talented few. The pay of CEOs is determined in a 'closed shop' way of senior remuneration committees composed of the people drawn from the same economic class who operate in a self-reverential and self-serving way that ensures that pay remains high. There is little evidence that pay is in any way related to performance with the rise in pay often rising well above rise in profits and in some cases despite clear company underperformance.

Labour markets in the developed world did develop strong institutions to protect pay and conditions with strong trades unions and the provision of extensive welfare systems but in the last thirty years these have been under pressure. Not all countries have dismantled these to the same extent and in those countries which still retain worker protection and there is a strong commitment to welfare services such as in the Nordic countries and Germany there has not been such a rise in inequality as has occurred in the UK and the US. In the UK the change in the funding of higher education means that for all but those destined to get to the top of the executive pay ladder or enter the City, there will be a lifetime burden of student debt.

The global financial crisis

LOCAL TO GLOBAL It has been a remarkable feature that the effects of the financial crisis in most developed economies has not led to increases in unemployment (although this has been the case in countries such as Greece, Spain, Portugal, and to some extent in Spain). However, the reason for this has been that workers have clearly been prepared to either accept cuts in wages or have been seeking to find temporary work or earn some money through a form of enforced self-employment. For the member of the 1 per cent there was some deterioration of their incomes in the immediate aftermath of the crisis but since 2015 this has been reversed and as we have seen they continue to capture the lion's share of the increases in growth.

Globalization

Chapter 10 shows that advocates of globalization argue that it brings universal benefits to all, but critics argue that in some cases there can be losers, and this will be particularly people in less skilled jobs who either come into competition with foreign imports or from migrant workers taking the opportunity to move across borders. There have been a number of recent empirical studies to show that this has indeed been the case and to show why there has been an apparent 'backlash' against globalization, from the so-called 'rust belts' of the US to the voices of those who argued for Brexit in the UK.

Technology

INTERACTION We saw in Chapter 3 that there has been growing evidence that the desirable benefits of growth in ICT, the digital revolution, and the rise of AI and robotics has already led to a polarization between those who have the higher level managerial and creative skills and those who do not.

Financialization

In the UK and the US in particular the rise in the power and importance of the financial sector as a result of both the deregulation of many of the previous controls and globalization has seen the rise of a new financial elite earning huge bonuses on top of their standard salaries.

Capital in the twenty-first century

The French economist Thomas Picketty's book *Capital in the 21st Century* attracted widespread attention and despite some criticisms over his use of data, a large amount of agreement with his central idea. For Picketty, there is a long-run tendency for the rate of return on capital to outstrip the rise in economic growth. We have seen that while income can be unequally distributed this is much more so in the case of wealth. Owners of capital are always going to earn more than those who do not possess capital (and for most this is simply the house in which they live). Societies where there is a high concentration of ownership of capital will tend to experience rising levels of inequality (Picketty 2013). The former World Bank economist Branko Milanović agrees that inequality will continue to rise as a result of the concentration of income and wealth to a small global elite and that unless action is taken this will lead to future political instability (Milanović 2016).

What can be done?

We have seen that since the late 1970s absolute inequality within many countries has increased despite some modest relative global reductions between developing and developed countries. However reducing inequality is not inevitable unless action is taken to address it. We have also seen that there is now a widespread recognition that such action needs to take place, although it remains to be seen if these warm words will be translated into policy. For Picketty, the answer would lie in some form of global wealth tax but in a world of globalized financial markets and where there is a lack of a strong system of global scrutiny and regulation he is not unaware of the problems of tax avoidance and evasion. There is a consensus in both the developed and developing world that corruption and tax evasion is extensive and needs to be prevented, but while this is easy to say it is much more complex to solve.

LOCAL TO GLOBAL **INTERACTION** It is clear that the forces of globalization and technological change have undermined the economic power of people with either a low level of skill or poor access to education and training. For critics like Atkinson (2015) the answer then lies not in trying to resist these forces but tackling head on the need to acknowledge their downsides by strong state action to support redistribution of income as well as raising the incomes of both those in precarious labour markets as well as those in low wage ones.

There is a clear need to address redistribution through raising income taxes and exploring how to levy wealth taxes on the rich. There is also the concomitant need to lower tax rates for the less well paid. We have seen that governments can seek to support wage levels through the introduction of a national minimum wage. In the UK supporters of the Living Wage were quick to see the UK government's change of the name of this to the National Living Wage as a cynical ploy to steal the clothes of genuine campaigners for what is seen as the true level of what is required. In 2017, it was argued that the 'Real Living Wage' should be higher than the UK Living Wage of £7.50 an hour (see https://www.livingwage.org.uk/what-is-the-living-wage). Other groups argue that while this may or not afford some measure of raising the income of the in-work poor a better policy would be to design a Universal Basic Income or Citizen's Income available to all adults as a right (see http://citizensincome.org).

In the absence of such a policy at the very least it is argued by anti-poverty campaigners that cuts in benefits and allowances need to be reversed and instead there should be increases in these and the bureaucratic obstacles that benefit seekers face should be simplified. Given the predominance of women among the poorly paid, it is also important that the gender pay gaps are addressed.

In relation to addressing runaway executive pay, a number of proposals have been put forward. In April 2017 the UK Business, Energy and Industrial Strategy Committee published a report arguing for a strengthening of the codes of conduct of British companies and in relation to executive pay it proposed giving more power to shareholders to reject pay deals, having employee representation on boards and requiring businesses to report on the pay ratios between the top and bottom of their organizations. Some businesses already do this and have set a limit to these ratios. For many a ratio of 20:1 might be seen to be acceptable. In 2015, Sacha Romanovitch, the CEO of Grant Thornton, a leading UK accountancy firm, announced that her pay would be fixed at twenty times the pay of the average earnings of all employees and that there would also be a profit sharing scheme for all employees modelled on the existing scheme at the John Lewis partnership. Mondragon, a Spanish cooperative of over 75,000 employees, goes even further with a pay ratio of 9:1.

We explored the rise of financialization in Chapter 2 and while there have been some control measures to try and prevent the type of reckless lending policies that caused the financial crisis that exploded in 2008, there is still official disquiet about the inability of banks to limit and address the bonus culture that was so harmful in the past.

Looking ahead

- Inequality is likely to remain high on business and political agendas for the foreseeable future.
- Equality is both a key value in the UK and other western societies and a deeply contested one. For both of these reasons it will continue to be part of the debate about the kind of economic system we want and the role and responsibilities of business.
- There is a considerable head of steam behind achieving ever greater equality of opportunity for women, and in relation to the other protected characteristics.
- There is also increased acceptance of the need to ensure that the benefits of globalization and economic growth are shared more widely and create an economy that 'works for everyone'. Thus, equality of outcome looks set to remain a key focus of debate in politics and business.
- Inequality is a complex issue. The prospects for reducing inequality in the next five years are uncertain. They depend on an understanding of the drivers of inequality in recent decades and the will within business and politics to turn rhetoric into reality.

Summary

- Inequality has moved up the agendas of politics and business in recent years, reflecting growing awareness and societal concern.
- This issue has relevance on a global scale, not just in the UK.
- In this chapter we have examined the related concepts of 'equality of opportunity', 'social mobility', and 'equality of outcome'.
- There is substantial evidence that women have not achieved equality of opportunity in business with men. There has been progress, but it is slow.
- Social mobility has historically been lower in the UK than in many other countries, and access to professional occupations remains socially exclusive.
- Equality of opportunity and achieving an 'open society' can be seen as both fair and beneficial for business.
- There has been increasing disquiet about the rise in the income and wealth gap between the top 1 per cent and the rest of society, and increasing attention paid to how to reduce this.

Case Study: Breaking open the closed-shop society?

In recent years the problem of a low rate of social mobility in the UK has become a focus of renewed debate, an important contribution to which was the Milburn report, focused on fair access to the professions (Panel on Fair Access to the Professions 2009). The report argues that the professions have come to play an increasingly important role in the UK economy over the last century, and will continue to do so in the context of the growth of highly professionalized knowledge-based services.

DYNAMIC Whereas only one in fourteen jobs were classed as professional in 1911, this had increased to more than one in three by 2001. This growth facilitated social mobility in the twentieth century as children from poorer backgrounds moved up into professional occupations. However, despite this, social mobility has historically been lower in the UK than in many other countries, and access to professional occupations remains socially exclusive. In other words, there is not an equal chance of access to professional occupations for people from across the whole of society and from different class backgrounds. Rather, the professions tend to recruit people from wealthy and privileged backgrounds. For example, more than 50 per cent of CEOs of companies attended independent schools, even though only 7 per cent of the population as a whole attend the independent sector. In other words, going to an independent school appears to afford a much greater chance of becoming a CEO or other professional. Furthermore:

> *the professions have become more, not less, socially exclusive over time. Despite a sharp growth in professional employment opportunities over recent decades, access to the professions is becoming the preserve of those from a smaller and smaller part of the social spectrum.... If action is not taken to reverse the historical trend, the typical professional of the future will be growing up in a family better off than seven in ten of all families in the UK.*
>
> *(Panel on Fair Access to the Professions 2009; see also Social Mobility and Child Poverty Commission 2014)*

The report makes clear that this is not just a problem of fairness. It is in the interests of the professions, and the wider economy, to draw on a wider pool of talent to ensure that the best people are recruited. It can also be argued that professions need to reflect the diversity of the society they serve in order to do so effectively.

In a subsequent 'progress report', Milburn (2012) states that the professions will account for over 80 per cent of new jobs in the UK over the next decade, and 46 per cent of all employment in the UK by 2020. Thus, the professions 'hold the key to improving social mobility', but because of slow progress in ensuring fair access 'Britain risks squandering the social mobility dividend that the growth in professional employment offers our country' (Milburn 2012: 1). One of the barriers to fair access identified by Milburn is the increasing importance of internships, which are often arranged informally using personal contacts rather than through an open process. Further, 'unpaid internships clearly disadvantage those from less affluent backgrounds who cannot afford to work for free for any length of time' (Milburn 2012: 5). Internships are, in practice, not drivers of social mobility but barriers, providing restricted routes to careers for the privileged few (Roberts 2017). Milburn recommends that internships 'should be subject to similar rules to other parts of the labour market. That means introducing proper, transparent, and fair processes for selection and reasonable terms of employment, including remuneration for internships' (2012: 5).

An assessment of government policies on social mobility over a twenty-year period, 1997–2017, by the Social Mobility Commission argues that there has been inadequate progress and that British society is characterized by deep divisions in terms of class, regions, and generations. For example, educational attainment gaps between poor and rich students starting in early years persist, and high-earning jobs remain elitist (Social Mobility Commission 2017).

Another way to look at social mobility is within a generation rather than between generations (intra- as opposed to intergenerational mobility). Here the question is the extent to which people move up or down the occupational order or earnings distribution within their working lives. To measure this, a study by the Resolution Foundation looked at movements within the earnings distribution for a group of individuals during the 1990s who were in their early thirties at the start of the decade, and for a comparable group in the 2000s. For this purpose, individuals are allocated to decile or quintile groups within the earnings distribution at the start and finish of the decades being studied. The results showed that around two-fifths stayed in the same quintile in the earnings distribution in each decade—their relative position was stable. This means that more than half experienced movement up or down the distribution. But such movement is predominantly short-range (one or two deciles) with limited impact on living conditions or place in the 'pecking order'. Conversely, long-range mobility is infrequent. The study also shows that mobility is higher for those in the middle of the distribution, and more limited for those at the top or bottom. In other words, those at the top or bottom are likely to stay there or only move a short distance up or down. For example, 'in the 1990s, less than 3 per cent of people who started the decade in the lowest quintile were in the top earning quintile by the end of the decade' (Resolution Foundation 2011: 3).

LOCAL TO GLOBAL Barriers to social mobility, or fair access to professional and managerial occupations, is not just an issue for the UK economy. That is because inequality tends to mean that the sons and daughters of better-off parents have advantages in life that are not enjoyed by those from poorer backgrounds. Thus, an OECD study shows that 'the relationship between parental or socio-economic background and offspring educational and wage outcomes is positive and significant in practically all countries for which evidence is available' (Causa and Johansson 2010: 1). However, the strength of this relationship varies between countries, being tighter or looser. The OECD study finds that 'low mobility across generations, as measured by a close link between parents' and children's earnings, is particularly pronounced in the United Kingdom, Italy, the United States and France, while mobility is higher in the Nordic countries, Australia and Canada' (Causa and Johansson 2010: 3). In the UK about 50 per cent of the economic advantage enjoyed by high-earning parents compared to low earners is passed on to the next generation, compared to less than 20 per cent in Norway and Finland. In other words, there is a high level of intergenerational persistence of earnings differentials in the UK, or low social mobility, compared to other rich countries.

Questions

1. **What is social mobility? How is it measured?**
2. **Would it be a good thing if more CEOs of major UK companies were educated in state schools?**

Review and discussion questions

1. Is inequality bad for business?
2. Using relevant evidence, examine how far women have achieved equality of opportunity in the labour market. To what extent is the evidence, such as relating to the gender pay gap, open to different interpretations?
3. Is fairness or social justice an issue that business should be concerned about, or should it be concerned only with efficiency and profitability?

Assignments

1. It has been claimed (Deloitte 2016) that the gender pay gap in the UK won't close until 2069. Produce a report identifying the main obstacles to closing the gender pay gap and make recommendations to speed up progress.
2. Prepare a brief written or verbal presentation on what steps a business should take to be an equal opportunity employer. You should refer to good practice guidance from the EHRC.
3. Identify key arguments that could be used from a trade union perspective to criticize recent trends in boardroom pay, and arguments that might be used from a business perspective to defend these trends.

Further reading

Powell and Mor (2017) *provides an overview of women in the economy.*

On women on boards, see Davies (2015) and European Women on Boards (2016)

Institute for Fiscal Studies (2016) and McGuinness (2016) *provide thorough analyses of the gender pay gap.*

Social Mobility Commission (2017) *assesses government policies on social mobility.*

Test your understanding of this chapter with online questions and answers, explore the subject further through web exercises, and use the weblinks to provide a quick resource for further research. Visit the online resources at www.oup.com/uk/wetherly_otter4e/

Useful websites

www.statistics.gov.uk
Office for National Statistics

https://www.gov.uk/government/organisations/government-equalities-office
Government Equalities Office

www.fawcettsociety.org.uk
Fawcett Society

http://www.ifs.org.uk
Institute for Fiscal Studies (IFS)

http://www.equalityhumanrights.com/en
Equality and Human Rights Commission (EHRC)

http://highpaycentre.org
High Pay Centre

https://www.equalitytrust.org.uk
Equality Trust

References

Aldridge, S. (2004) *Life Chances and Social Mobility: An Overview of the Evidence*, Cabinet Office (accessed 30 June 2017) **https://www.cabinetoffice.gov.uk**

Allen, K. (2016a) 'Gender pay gap won't close until 2069, says Deloitte', *Guardian*, 24 September (accessed 30 June 2017) **https://www.theguardian.com/society/2016/sep/24/gender-pay-gap-wont-close-until-2069-says-deloitte**

Allen, K. (2016b) 'Gender pay gap: women earn £300,000 less than men over working life', *Guardian*, 7 March (accessed 30 June 2017) **https://www.theguardian.com/money/2016/mar/07/gender-pay-gap-uk-women-earn-300000-less-men-lifetime**

Atkinson, A. (2015) *Inequality—What Can Be Done?* (Cambridge, MA: Harvard University Press)

Balaram, B. et al. (2017) *Good Gigs: A Fairer Future for the UK's Gig Economy* (London: Royal Society for the Encouragement of Arts, Manufactures and Commerce) (accessed 30 June 2017) **https://www.thersa.org/globalassets/pdfs/reports/rsa_good-gigs-fairer-gig-economy-report.pdf**

BBC (2017) 'BBC pay disclosures' (accessed 30 June 2017) **http://www.bbc.co.uk/aboutthebbc/insidethebbc/howwework/accountability/bbc_talent_pay**

Davies, M. (2011) *Women on Boards* (London: Department for Business, Innovation & Skills) (accessed 30 June 2017) **http://www.bis.gov.uk//assets/biscore/business-law/docs/w/11-745-women-on-boards.pdf**

Davies, M. (2015) *Improving the Gender Balance on British Boards—Women on Boards Davies Review Five Year Summary October 2015* (accessed 30 June 2017) **https://www.gov.uk/government/uploads/system/uploads/attachment_data/file/482059/BIS-15-585-women-on-boards-davies-review-5-year-summary-october-2015.pdf**

Deloitte (2016) *Women in STEM: Technology, Career Pathways and the Gender Pay Gap* (accessed 30 June 2017) **https://www2.deloitte.com/content/dam/Deloitte/uk/Documents/Growth/deloitte-uk-women-in-stem-pay-gap-2016.pdf**

Department for Education and Skills (2007) *Gender and Education: The Evidence on Pupils in England* (accessed 30 June 2017) **http://webarchive.nationalarchives.gov.uk/20090108131527/http://www.dcsf.gov.uk/research/data/uploadfiles/RTP01-07.pdf**

Dorling, D. (2015a) 'Income inequality in the UK—comparison with five large Western European countries and the USA', *Applied Geography*, 61: 24–34 (accessed 30 June 2017) **http://www.dannydorling.org/wp-content/files/dannydorling_publication_id4756.pdf**

Dorling, D. (2015b) *Inequality and the 1%* (London: Verso)

Equality and Human Rights Commission (2009) *Financial Services Inquiry: Sex Discrimination and Gender Pay Gap Report of the Equality and Human Rights Commission* (London: Equality and Human Rights Commission)

Equality and Human Rights Commission (2013) *Women, Men and Part-time Work* (London: Equality and Human Rights Commission)

Equality and Human Rights Commission (2016) *Is England Fairer? The State of Equality and Human Rights 2016* (London: Equality and Human Rights Commission) (accessed 30 June 2017) **https://www.equalityhumanrights.com/sites/default/files/is_england_fairer.pdf**

European Women on Boards (2016) *Gender Diversity on European Boards* (accessed 30 June 2017) **http://european.ewob-network.eu/wp-content/uploads/2016/04/EWoB-quant-report-WEB-spreads.pdf**

Eurostat (2016) 'File: employment rates for selected population groups, 2005–2015(%) YB16 III.png' (accessed 30 June 2017) **http://ec.europa.eu/eurostat/statistics-explained/index.php/File:Employment_rates_for_selected_population_groups,_2005%E2%80%932015_(%25)_YB16_III.png**

Freeland, C. (2013) *The Rise of the New Global Super Rich* (London: Penguin)

Gov.uk (2017) *Guidance: Gender Pay Gap Reporting: Overview* (accessed 30 June 2017) **https://www.gov.uk/guidance/gender-pay-gap-reporting-overview**

Guardian (2016) 'Gender gap in UK degree subjects doubles in eight years, UCAS study finds', 5 January (accessed 30 June 2017) **https://www.theguardian.com/education/2016/jan/05/gender-gap-uk-degree-subjects-doubles-eight-years-ucas-study**

Hakim, C. (1996) 'Mummy, I want to be a housewife', *Times Higher Education*, 26 April

Heath, A. and Payne, C. (2000) 'Social mobility', in A. H. Halsey (ed.), *Twentieth Century British Social Trends* (Basingstoke: Palgrave)

Hutton, W. (2015) *How Good We Can Be—Ending the Mercenary Society and Building a Great Country* (London: Abacus)

Institute for Fiscal Studies (2016) *The Gender Wage Gap* (accessed 30 June 2017) **https://www.ifs.org.uk/uploads/publications/bns/bn186.pdf**

Johnson, R. (2016) 'The first step to tackling the gender pay gap is to understand it', Institute for Fiscal Studies (accessed 30 June 2017) **https://www.ifs.org.uk/publications/8435**

King, M. L. (1963) 'I have a dream' (speech), in B. MacArthur (1999) *The Penguin Book of Twentieth Century Speeches* (London: Penguin) (accessed 30 June 2017) **http://news.bbc.co.uk/1/hi/world/americas/3170387.stm**

McGuinness, F. (2016) *Gender Pay Gap*, House of Commons Library Briefing Paper Number 7068, 26 October (accessed 30 June 2017) **http://researchbriefings.parliament.uk/ResearchBriefing/Summary/SN07068**

Milanović, B. (2016) *Global Inequality—A New Approach for the Age of Globalization* (Cambridge, MA: Harvard University Press)

Milburn, A. (2012) *Fair Access to Professional Careers: A Progress Report by the Independent Reviewer on Social Mobility and Child Poverty* (accessed 30 June 2017) **https://www.gov.uk/government/uploads/system/uploads/attachment_data/file/61090/IR_FairAccess_acc2.pdf**

OECD (2015) *In It Together: Why Less Inequality Benefits All* (Paris: OECD Publishing) (accessed 30 June 2017) **http://dx.doi.org/10.1787/9789264235120-en**

Office for National Statistics (2009) *Social Trends* 39 (London) (accessed 30 June 2017) **www.ons.gov.uk**

Office for National Statistics (2015) *Participation Rates in the UK Labour Market: 2014* (London) (accessed 30 June 2017) **https://www.ons.gov.uk/employmentandlabourmarket/peopleinwork/employmentandemployeetypes/compendium/participationratesintheuklabourmarket/2015-03-19**

Office for National Statistics (2016a) *Annual Survey of Hours and Earnings: 2016 Provisional Results* (London) (accessed 30 June 2017) **https://www.ons.gov.uk/employmentandlabourmarket/peopleinwork/earningsandworkinghours/bulletins/annualsurveyofhoursandearnings/latest#gender-pay-differences**

Office for National Statistics (2016b) *Dataset: EMP04: Employment by Occupation, April–June* (London) (accessed 30 June 2017) **https://www.ons.gov.uk/employmentandlabourmarket/peopleinwork/employmentandemployeetypes/datasets/employmentbyoccupationemp04**

Office for National Statistics (2017) *Article: Contracts that Do not Guarantee a Minimum Number of Hours: May* (London) (accessed 30 June 2017) **https://www.ons.gov.uk/employmentandlabourmarket/peopleinwork/earningsandworkinghours/articles/contractsthatdonotguaranteeaminimumnumberofhours/may2017**

Oxfam (2017) 'An economy for the 99%: it's time to build a human economy that benefits everyone, not just the privileged few' (accessed 22 July 2017) **http://policy-practice.oxfam.org.uk/publications/an-economy-for-the-99-its-time-to-build-a-human-economy-that-benefits-everyone-620170**

Panel on Fair Access to the Professions (2009) *Unleashing Aspiration: The Final Report of the Panel on Fair Access to the Professions* (London: Cabinet Office) (accessed 30 June 2017) **http://webarchive.nationalarchives.gov.uk/+/http:/www.cabinetoffice.gov.uk/media/227102/fair-access.pdf**

Picketty, T. (2013) *Capital in the Twenty-First Century* (Cambridge, MA: Harvard University Press)

Powell, A. and Mor, F. (2017) *Women and the Economy*. House of Commons Library, Briefing Paper Number CBP06838, 1 March (accessed 30 June 2017) **http://researchbriefings.parliament.uk/ResearchBriefing/Summary/SN06838**

Resolution Foundation (2011) *Moving on Up? Social Mobility in the 1990s and 2000s Summary* (accessed 30 June 2017) **http://www.resolutionfoundation.org/app/uploads/2014/08/Moving-on-up-Social-mobility-in-the-1990s-and-2000s.pdf**

Roberts, C. (2017) *The Inbetweeners: The New Role of Internships in the Graduate Labour Market* (London: IPPR) (accessed 30 June 2017) **http://www.ippr.org/publications/the-inbetweeners**

Savage, M., Cunningham, N., Devine, F., Friedman, S., Laurison, D., McKenzie, L., Miles, A., Snee, H., and Wakeling, P. (2015) *Social Class in the 21st Century* (London: Pelican)

Sealy, R. et al. (2016) *The Female FTSE Board Report 2016* (accessed 30 June 2017) **http://30percentclub.wardourdigital.co.uk/assets/uploads/UK/Third_Party_Reports/Female_FTSE_Board_Report_2016.pdf**

Social Mobility and Child Poverty Commission (2014) *Elitist Britain?* **https://www.gov.uk/government/uploads/system/uploads/attachment_data/file/347915/Elitist_Britain_-_Final.pdf**

Social Mobility Commission (2017) *Time for Change: An Assessment of Government Policies on Social Mobility 1997–2017* (accessed 30 June 2017) **https://www.gov.uk/government/uploads/system/uploads/attachment_data/file/622214/Time_for_Change_report_-_An_assessement_of_government_policies_on_social_mobility_1997-2017.pdf**

Stiglitz, J. (2013) *The Price of Inequality* (London: Norton)

Topping, A. (2015) 'Gender pay gap will not close for 70 years at current rate, says UN', *Guardian*, 5 March (accessed 30 June 2017) **https://www.theguardian.com/money/2015/mar/05/gender-pay-gap-remain-70-years-un**

UNESCO (2015) *Education for All 2000–2015: Achievements and Challenges* (Paris: UNESCO Publishing) (accessed 30 June 2017) **http://unesdoc.unesco.org/images/0023/002322/232205e.pdf**

Chapter 13

Creating effective trading blocs: what lessons does the European Union provide?

Stratis Koutsoukos and Dorron Otter

Learning objectives

When you have completed this chapter, you will be able to:

- Explain the different levels of economic and political integration at the regional level and assess the relative advantages and disadvantages of these.
- Describe the institutional and policymaking framework of the European Union (EU), including the European Parliament (EP), European Commission (EC), European Council, and European Central Bank (ECB) and their significance and impact on business.
- Analyse the differing forms of economic integration relevant to EU development and issues arising from successive enlargements.
- Explain the recent development in the EU.

THEMES

The following themes are particularly relevant in this chapter

INTERNAL/EXTERNAL There Is a very strong case for countries at the same level of economic development and in geographical proximity to push ahead and forge greater levels of integration for the mutual benefit of all. But there are also problems in that greater integration involves close cooperation and, indeed, a pooling of sovereignty that may fit uneasily with the desire to have national independence.

COMPLEXITY Ironically, trying to create a 'level playing field' where there is open and free competition between members in regional trade groups requires complex political and economic structures with which businesses will need to deal. Regulatory shifts in areas such as competition, agriculture, or financial services policy mean businesses have to constantly re-evaluate their strategies.

LOCAL TO GLOBAL Integration can take place at different levels, with each level requiring an appropriate structural framework to support its aims.

DYNAMIC A key theme in this chapter is the extent to which the movement towards greater regional integration is leading to a deeper or wider integration among the members of these groups and is taking the world towards or away from greater global integration.

Introduction

INTERNAL/EXTERNAL We explored the contrasting views about the nature of globalization in Chapter 10 and we saw that in reality while it potentially has great benefits, trade across national boundaries, especially when nations are at different stages of development, can be problematic. The major fault line in creating closer global cooperation in relation to trade has been the conflicting interests between the developed and the developing world. And, in the absence of a completion of the last round of world trade negotiations (the Doha 'development' round), there has been an increased focus on the plethora of regional trade associations that exist.

LOCAL TO GLOBAL In this chapter we will explore the different types of regional trade agreements that can exist and how the nature of these affects the business environment and, in turn, the implications for business behaviour. The EU will be a particular focus.

The themes and issues surrounding the impact of the EU, one of the world's most influential trading blocs, on business activity, strategy, and performance are many and varied. From labour law to immigration law, competition policy and law to environmental policy and law, economic restructuring policies, trade agreements, and many more areas this makes it a unique case study of an economic union and trading bloc.

At the heart of the debates about the current state of affairs in the EU is the political level and the issue of **sovereignty**. Inevitably, by being members of an economic union, individual nation states have had to accept a transfer of political influence to the governing institutions at the regional level, which we will explore later in this chapter. This has provoked intense disagreements between those who see this as 'ceding', or giving up power or sovereignty over national self-interest, and those who see this as a 'pooling' of power for collective and shared responses in the context of a global world economy facing global challenges (e.g. the environment, financial crisis, conflict resolution).

Chapter 2 examines the debates in relation to how economic policy should be conducted, and the experience of the EU shows that in order to build economic cooperation there are pol itical changes that need to occur, which have the potential to create tension across the politic al divide. For neoliberal critics, the EU's mission is primarily to produce a single free market across the European continent whereas others argue that for this to work effectively there needs to be more integrated political and economic structures to support the market. In fact for some Europeans, the Union represents more than a market, a convergence and symbiosis of national identities, histories, and cultures. For many people, while there is a desire to see the widening of free trade within regions, there is a reluctance to accept the need for the deepening of this integration beyond the formation of simple Free Trade Areas (FTAs) or the continued use of Preferential Trading Areas (PTAs which normally encompass relationships between developed and developing countries which formerly were conjoined through colonization). For structuralist writers, a deepening integration is vital if there is to be genuine free trade that works in a way that is really inclusive to all parties.

The political battles over sovereignty are illustrated in this chapter through the applied example of the EU engaged in the economic 'haggling' relating to the nature of the 'European Union development project'. Furthermore, working across so many national boundaries involves the assimilation of different business cultures. While a widespread cultural diversity exists within the Union, it is acknowledged that there is a shared lowest common denominator describing the notion of European identity. The prospect of future **enlargement**, including possible entrants such as Turkey, raises the prospect of introducing Asian cultures into the EU mix, further questioning the nature of a unified concept of a European identity (see

Mini-Case 13.1 on Turkey and the EU). Others argue that perhaps the biggest cultural export and trademark of Europe Inc. is the spread of democracy, respect of law, and inclusion of minority groups, what is often termed as 'the European values'.

The global economy and the EU are at a critical stage of their development and this chapter seeks to evaluate business and decision-making in this context and explore the potential lessons that may be learned from the EU experience for other regional trading blocs.

Forms of integration and trade in theory

LOCAL TO GLOBAL We have seen in Chapter 10 that international trade can potentially be hugely beneficial for individual countries. Trade can take place at three spatial levels: bilateral trade occurs when two countries agree preferential trade arrangements between each other; regional trade occurs when groups of countries in a particular geographical area develop trade relationships common across all members; and global trade relationships which are negotiated through the World Trade Organization (WTO). Given the inability of the WTO process to conclude the latest round of trade negotiations, there is a feeling that in the medium term it is regional trade agreements that will continue to shape the future of the global business environment. For advocates of globalization this tendency for the increased importance of regional trade is seen as regrettable, as it prevents the creation of a genuine global free market and may result in future potential economic and political rivalry and even conflict between big separate power blocs.

Economists distinguish between the **static gains from trade** that stem from the ability to exploit comparative advantages and the wider **dynamic gains from trade** such as the ability to exploit larger markets and thus benefit from economies of scale, the exposure to higher levels of competition that opening up trade might create, the opportunities for technology transfer, and simply consumers having the benefit of a greater choice of goods and services. However, closer integration may also bring political advantages such as creating closer relationships for peace and security or allowing a greater political voice at global economic and political negotiations. Table 13.1 shows a spectrum of economic linkages encompassing ever closer integration.

A **free trade area** such as the European Free Trade Area (EFTA) that covers countries Iceland, Norway, Liechtenstein, and Switzerland extends preferential tariff treatment to all members (see http://www.efta.int). It is a loose association in which members eliminate trade barriers between themselves but retain their own trade policies with respect to outsiders. Tariffs are taxes that are levied on goods coming into a country and traditionally were a way for nation states to protect themselves from trade.

Table 13.1 Different types of economic integration

	No internal trade barriers	Common external tariff	Factor and asset mobility	Common currency	Common economic policy
Free trade area	✓				
Customs union	✓	✓			
Single market	✓	✓	✓		
Monetary union	✓	✓	✓	✓	
Economic union	✓	✓	✓	✓	✓

A **customs union** is where a joint external trade policy exists with the imposition of a common external tariff (CET) on non-member imports. The customs union shares revenue from this CET as part of the common budget. A customs union creates trade among its members but diverts it from those excluded. While trade might grow substantially, much of this may be internally within the regional bloc. While this might be successful in terms of boosting regional integration, it might not actually lead to an increase in world trade overall as it will simply divert trade from non-group members. In some cases, these other countries might have had strong historical, cultural, or political links with members inside the group and in others might actually prevent future beneficial trading links being established on a bilateral basis. Such has been one of the arguments of those who opposed the UK's continuing membership of the EU. British business is prevented from fully pursuing its traditional links with countries with which it had former colonial links or as in the case of the US, one with whom they feel there is a 'special relationship'.

Stop and Think

Assume German footwear manufacturers produce trainers for domestic consumption that retail at €60 per pair. In Spain these shoes can be produced and delivered to Germany for €40 but when Germany imposes a €25 tariff on such imports, Spain cannot compete effectively. If, however, Germany and Spain become part of a customs union and abolish all trade barriers between them, German shoe imports from Spain will increase to the extent that this replaces expensive German production and contribute to 'trade creation'.

However, suppose China can produce and ship trainers to Germany for €30 per pair. Before the customs union China sold trainers to Germany for €55 (€30 + €25 tariff) but the tariff reduction only applies to Spain. Thus, Spanish trainers also replace German imports from China. Since China is a lower cost producer than Spain, this part of the increased Spanish exports is 'trade diversion'.

DYNAMIC Both a free trade area and a customs union can essentially be seen as being essentially examples of negative integration that simply remove barriers to trade. Higher levels of integration involve positive integration, implying the building of an institutional framework and policy harmonization, as in monetary union. A common or single market abolishes all trade barriers—not just tariffs but non-tariff barriers (NTBs) and mobility restrictions, embracing the free movement of:

- goods—consumers and companies can buy and sell their products anywhere in member states;
- people—individuals are free to move and work within the common market;
- capital—seen as facilitating the free movement of people, services, and goods; and
- services—encompasses both the freedom to establish a business and the right to offer services in another member state.

The highest order of integration would be to have a monetary union and as we shall see, in practice, this has come to be a difficult undertaking of the EU project. Even with the removal of all the trade barriers as outlined above one major obstacle to trade would be the continued existence of national currencies within the common market. If trade is conducted across national boundaries with different currencies this means that for exporters and importers the actual value of the costs or revenues received will depend on the value of the currency in which they are making or receiving payment compared to the value of their home currency. The problem is that in reality exchange rates are very volatile especially as a result of speculation on the international money markets. This volatility can increase business risk.

To avoid this damaging uncertainty which might deter businesses from 'getting their fingers burned' in this way by trading, there is a strong case for fixed rates and ultimately having a common currency. If the logic for greater integration is that it will create more trade, then it seems illogical to stop short of full monetary integration and allow a major obstacle to trade to remain. If all countries within the full union had the same currency, then this would mean that national governments would need to coordinate monetary and fiscal policies which would provide a common stable macroeconomic environment across the union. This favourable business environment would encourage trade and greater competition as the costs and prices charged by all firms throughout the region would be subject to greater transparency. In this way, for many proponents of the benefits of monetary union the inevitable consequence of this is that there will need to be a full economic union with close coordination of economic policy. As we shall see, the strength of this argument has propelled many members of the EU to accept the need for a common currency and adopt the euro, including Spain, but not the UK.

However, there are a range of economic and political arguments that urge caution in the belief that greater integration automatically implies monetary union. A common currency requires cooperation between different countries over macroeconomic policies and such collective action diminishes the individual nation's sovereignty over domestic policy. It can be argued that once the step towards an economic union is taken then this implies a political union. While opponents of this possible move toward political integration may deem this action to be appropriate within an individual country such as the US, it is regarded as inappropriate across separate countries, such as within the EU, and they may resist any attempt to indeed create a 'United States of Europe'.

The decision to do away with individual currencies and adopt a common currency is intimately tied to the arguments over whether it is better for the exchange rate of a country to float freely and be determined by market forces or for governments to intervene and determine the external value of the currency by having 'fixed' exchange rates. The possible adoption of monetary union is the extreme version of this. No longer do you need to swap your currency for that of another's if you wish to trade; by using the same common currency, all businesses across the union would have the certainty of what they would receive through trade and the common currency would have the further advantage of ensuring that prices across all countries and goods and services are immediately transparent. The downside of this, though, is that each country now loses the power to determine the value of its currency externally.

Floating rates offer autonomy to nations (so-called economic sovereignty). If, for example, the UK was to find that as a result of a decline in competitiveness compared to other countries it was seeing its exports declining but that consumers in the UK were still buying imports this would be reflected in an adverse balance of payments. However, under a floating exchange rate regime it could allow its currency to float downwards in value. This drop in the exchange rate would mean that people abroad could now buy goods valued in the weaker pound more cheaply and conversely as consumers in the UK would now have to pay more for imports, the demand for these would fall. The floating exchange rate thus 'disguises' the short-term loss in competitiveness and might allow the government the breathing space to address the underlying competitive weakness. In response to what they hope would be a temporary loss of economic competitiveness, governments might use fiscal policy to provide for social security assistance, Keynesian demand management policies to boost the economy, and direct support for ailing industries.

In a fixed rate system or a monetary union this option would not be available to the national government and the country would now face a recessionary situation. Without the ability to allow the currency to depreciate in order to restore macroeconomic stability in the long run, the country would have to undertake draconian microeconomic measures such as cutting wages, welfare benefits and, in return for attracting the short-term borrowing needed to finance the balance of payments deficit, the government would have to accept high levels of interest and commit to reducing public expenditure. The end of chapter case study in Chapter 9 illustrates the problems that have been faced by certain members of the EU that signed up to monetary union and we will return to this later in this chapter. However, certainly if a country were to try to 'tough it out alone', relying simply on these microeconomic austerity measures, the result would be severe short-term declines in living standards and jobs until the long-term restructuring of the economy occurred.

Economists have always warned that, if full monetary union is to be achieved, it would be necessary to ensure that there was a large stability fund at the central or federal level so that when countries find themselves under competitive pressure, funds would be available to help lessen the economic hardship. If there are deficit countries in the Union, then it is likely that such sovereign funds would be available from the surplus countries. Since it is in the strategic interests of surplus countries to restore growth for less competitive regions, then surely it would be beneficial to release these? As a way of ensuring that this was the case, it would be advisable if all members of a monetary union were to pool some of their reserves into a central fund which could be used for precisely this purpose. These funds would then be viewed as a common insurance fund to help in those individual cases of temporary hardship, but in such a way as to benefit the union as a whole. Ultimately, monetary integration would involve full economic union, implying macroeconomic policy coordination and including both fiscal and monetary policy. Members forgo their economic independence and a central federal government would dominate macroeconomic policymaking.

If it were the case that generally all nations in the bloc were at a similar level of development in terms of competitiveness, then the likelihood of these funds being needed would be small, but as we shall see in the case of the expansion of the EU, this does not seem to have been the case. While careful conditions are placed on countries seeking accession and there have been careful plans in place to ensure that the process to European Monetary Union (EMU) was achieved, it would appear that the safeguards were insufficient and what resulted was an EU that was some way from a full economic union, with members retaining fiscal sovereignty whilst simultaneously being tied into a monetary union.

Thus, integration is wide in scope and, while depicted here in economic terms, also requires political will, as progressive interdependence requires the release of ever more sovereignty over domestic decision-making.

Trading blocs in reality

There are a huge number of regional and preferential trading associations, and to keep track the WTO maintains a database at wto.org/english/tratop_e/region_e/rta_pta_e.htm. Often these trading blocs aim to achieve cooperation across a wider range of political, strategic, and cultural objectives than the narrow economic arguments detailed above. The fact that the WTO has to request signatories of the various agreements to permit them to catalogue these deals shows the extent to which it is this regional trade expansion that is driving the global trading environment. The patchwork nature of these individual trading agreements is seen by some critics as an obstacle to the eventual goal of a global free trade system. However, for others it is seen as an inevitable consequence of the economic and political sovereignty problems that too rapid or deep an integration might produce.

We will discuss the EU in detail later in this chapter. As the most integrated trading bloc, it helps to shed light on the contrasting views about the benefits of integration outlined above (for the official EU view about the European integration, see http://europa.eu/index_en.htm).

In North America NAFTA is an example of a trading bloc which brings together a developing nation, Mexico, with its developed northern partners, the US and Canada (see www.nafta-sec-alena.org). This is unusual because, as we saw in Chapter 10, structuralist and dependency critics warn of the potential problems in opening up trade between the developed countries in the 'Global North' and the developing countries in the 'Global South'. They argue that until the appropriate supporting institutions are put in place to ensure that free trade is equitable, greater South-South trading relationships are needed instead of North-South models of trade. As recent American policy demonstrates the model does pose some challenges, notably it can polarize manufacturing and foreign direct investment (FDI) flows and challenges the partnership at its core. Chapter 16 will explore recent developments in relation to China's increasing trade links with other developing countries and the attempts by the BRICS to take the lead role in development away from organizations like the World Bank.

In Latin America in the 1990s there was an attempt to build a free trade area for the Americas (FTAA) which sought to bring together all the Latin American countries, the Caribbean countries, Canada, and the US. However, suspicions amongst many countries that it would be a trading bloc primarily benefiting the US led to its failure. Over the years there have been many expressions of interest for further regional integration, but intraregional trade is relatively low, and progress has been slow. The main trading blocs are: the common market CAN (or the Andean Pact) which includes Columbia, Bolivia, Ecuador, and Peru; and MERCOSUR, which is now a full customs union consisting of Brazil, Argentina, Uruguay, and Venezuela (see http://en.mercopress.com/about-mercosur).

The main obstacles to greater integration in Latin America have been: a tendency for countries to react to unfavourable external economic shocks, such as the 1997 Asian crisis, by resorting to non-tariff trade restrictions; an unwillingness to implement agreements that could be politically contentious in a national context; and a lack of coordinated macroeconomic policy. Political and ideological differences can often be profound. In South East Asia the ASEAN bloc has expanded quickly and looks to be moving fast towards greater regional integration. The way it is developing, is in part in a response to the problems faced by the EU. We explore this in detail in the case study at the end of this chapter.

In Africa the most notable bloc is the Southern African Development Community (SADC), a free trade area comprising the following countries: Angola, Botswana, Lesotho, Malawi, Mozambique, Namibia, South Africa, Swaziland, Zambia, and Zimbabwe (see http://www.sadc.int).

SADC is trying to deepen its levels of integration though progress is difficult because some members were also members in other African trading groups, such as the East African Community and the Common Market for East and Southern Africa. Since 2008 integration has been made easier by the formation of the African Free Trade Zone, which is seeking to create a free trade area across all three of the existing groups.

In reality, there is a broad range of regional economic blocs, all with different and sometimes overlapping principal objectives. The implications for businesses are profound, as trading within regional blocs requires knowledge of the rules and regulations within each bloc and, if businesses are trading across these regional boundaries, they have to cope with different regulatory frameworks and institutional structures. The rest of this chapter will focus primarily on the issues relating to European integration, which currently is experiencing economic slowdown (blamed by some on the integration process itself). The case study at the end of the chapter will profile South East Asia, a region that is leading the way in terms of economic growth.

The EU: a deepening, widening, or fragmenting union?

COMPLEXITY The modern history of Western Europe covers two contrasting periods of the twentieth century. The first half was plagued by the horrors of two world wars and national fervour; the second half attempted to build peace through economic and social integration. There has been a lively debate about how best to achieve the latter. At the heart of this debate is the broad ideological divide between those who see the EU as providing a means of expanding the free market and those who believe that structural economic and political interventions are needed. Furthermore, key members have sought different outcomes from participation in the European Economic Community (EEC) and later EU.

For example, Germany and France, for many years the dominant powers, favour a **federalist**, long-term, and politically integrated Europe. A federalist Europe would mean that the institutions of the EU would have a wider range of power to determine policies which would then become binding on the individual countries. Moreover, France is often perceived as being implicitly protectionist, for example, seeing the EU as a means of giving help to its agricultural sector, with a particular focus on preserving the Common Agricultural Policy (CAP). Spain has sought cohesion and funding support for the southern states, while the Italians desire improved governance. The new central and Eastern Europe accession states see membership as a means to overcome the legacy of centrally planned communist rule and embark on sustained development. Denmark and Sweden have sought a loose union; an anti-federalist, free trade, 'cafeteria' approach in which it could pick and choose policies to suit its needs. Successive UK governments have argued for the development of an enlarged Europe, focusing on a large single market rather than proceeding with further political and social integration. Thus, although the EU represents a partnership of twenty-eight sovereign nations, it contains a diverse set of countries with differing aspirations that complicate decision-making and consensus (see Table 13.2).

Table 13.2 EU membership development: new members, leavers, stalled progress, and potential developments

Date	Country
1958	**EU founding**: Belgium, France, Germany, Italy, Luxembourg, Netherlands
1973	**1st enlargement:** Denmark, Ireland, UK (withdrawal of French veto allows UK entry)
1981	**2nd enlargement:** Greece
1985	**1st exit:** Greenland (gains autonomy from Denmark in 1979 and leaves following a 1982 referendum over a dispute over fishing rights)
1986 & 1995	**3rd & 4th enlargements:** Portugal and Spain/Austria, Finland, and Sweden
2004/2007/2013	**5th, 6th, & 7th enlargements:** Cyprus, Czech Republic, Estonia, Hungary, Latvia, Lithuania, Malta, Poland, Slovakia, Slovenia/Bulgaria, and Romania/Croatia
2017-present	**Stalled entries:** Ukraine, Turkey, FYROM, Serbia, Montenegro, Albania
2020+	**2nd exit:** UK
2025+	**Potential new entries:** Norway, Iceland, Switzerland

Table 13.3 Key European treaties

1951	Treaty of Paris–European Coal and Steel Community (ECSC)
1958	Treaties of Rome–European Economic Community (EEC) and European Atomic Energy Community (Euratom)
1986	Single European Act–Single Market creation
1992	Treaty of Maastricht–European Union (EU)
1997	Treaty of Amsterdam–amended EEC treaty and paved way for completion of the Single Market
2001	Treaty of Nice–amended earlier treaties and streamlined the EU's institutional system
2004	Treaty of Rome–Treaty establishing a Constitution for Europe
2007	Treaty of Lisbon–the Reform Treaty establishing the 'rebranded' EU constitution

Note: The text of these treaties can be found at http://europa.eu

The modern EU is based on treaties agreed by member governments and, ultimately, their electorates. Once agreed, the treaties form the 'EU club' rules and the foundation for everything the EU undertakes. In drafting the original Treaty of Rome, the EEC was charged with:

> Establishing a common market and progressively approximating the economic policies of the Member States, to promote throughout the Community a harmonious development of economic activities, a continuous and balanced expansion, an increase in stability, an accelerated rise in the standard of living and closer relations between the states belonging to it.
>
> (Article 2 of the Treaty of Rome 25 March 1957 (<ec.europa.eu/economy_finance/emu_history/documents/treaties/rometreaty2.pdf>)

The key **European treaties** are shown in Table 13.3. Under the treaties, the EU members delegate some national sovereignty to shared institutions representing their collective interest. The treaties represent 'primary' legislation, from which regulations, directives, decisions, opinions, and recommendations are derived.

There are four types of legislative instruments as established by the Treaty of Amsterdam:

1. A **regulation** has a general application. It is binding in its entirety and directly applicable in all member states.
2. A **directive** is binding, as to the result to be achieved, upon each member state to which it is addressed, but leaves to the national authorities the choice of form and methods.
3. A **decision** is binding in its entirety upon those to whom it is addressed.
4. **Opinions** and **recommendations** have no binding force.

These legislative instruments, and EU policies generally, result from discussions among the **institutional triangle**—the Council of the European Union, the European Parliament, and the European Council. This institutional triangle only functions effectively with mutual cooperation and trust.

EU expansion and challenges from globalization and terrorism led the member nations to consider revising the EU's rules. Following the initial rejection of the EU Constitution Treaty (Treaty of Rome) in referenda in France, the Netherlands, and Ireland, eight years of intense negotiations and amendments, and the Berlin Declaration of common intent, in 2007 EU leaders came to an agreement. The outcome was the 2009 Treaty of Lisbon which established a Reform Treaty.

This Treaty consolidates and simplifies existing treaties, clarifies the powers of members, and sets out to modernize the EU's institutions and streamline its decision-making. It established the posts of full-time president of the EU Council and an EU 'High Representative' who heads a new European Diplomatic Service. The Reform Treaty also enshrines a Charter of Fundamental Rights which requires national parliaments to check whether proposed laws could be better implemented at national level or EU level, and makes decision-making easier by removing the national veto in areas such as climate change, energy security, and emergency aid. Unanimity will still be required in the areas of tax, foreign policy, defence, and social security. The Reform Treaty also introduces a redistribution of voting weights between member states phased in by 2017, meaning more qualified majority voting decisions (achieved by a 'double majority' of 55 per cent of member states and representing a minimum of 65 per cent of the EU's population).

Stop and Think

Discuss your views about a further EU enlargement post-2020 by identifying the potential new entrants and the arguments for and against them joining the EU.

Enlargement

EU enlargement is not a new concept (see Tables 13.2 and 13.4), but in 1993 the European Council set out accession conditions (the 'Copenhagen criteria'):

- *political*: stable institutions guaranteeing democracy, the rule of law, respect for and protection of human rights and minorities;
- *economic*: a functioning market economy and capacity to cope with competitive pressures and market forces within the EU; and
- *acquis communautaire*: the implementation of EU legislation via an appropriate administrative and judicial structure. It implies the ability to assume the obligations of membership, including meeting the aims of political, economic, and monetary union.

The precise implications of enlargement remain uncertain (see Table 13.4). General political and social benefits are assumed to flow from the extended zone of peace, stability, and

Table 13.4 Economic advantages and disadvantages of enlargement

Advantages	Disadvantages
Market: enlargement increases the internal market, raising demand for EU goods.	***Budget:*** enlargement costs for the financial perspective 2000–6 were estimated at 40.8 billion euros.
Economic growth: effective 1.5% rise in GDP among new members raises spending power and job growth.	***Regional policy:*** 'statistical effect' on existing structural fund recipients who lose relative to the new members.
Investment: new members offer new FDI opportunities and skilled but cheaper labour.	***Overstated benefits:*** many trade and investment effects are due to global forces and restructuring not enlargement.
Allocation effects: encourages competition, trade, and greater consumer choice and reduces barriers in previously protected markets.	***Transition costs:*** expense of social, political, and economic changes to meet the Copenhagen criteria and balance of payments deficits resulting from 'catch-up' expenditure.
Accumulation effects: furthers the process of liberalization in progress since the start of the 1990s.	***Uncertain migration:*** tensions and costs might arise from widespread migration from the new member states as well as unsecure external borders.

Mini-Case 13.1 Turkey and the EU

With a relatively young population of 70 million, an export-oriented economy, and a developing information society, Turkey's accession has the potential to increase the size and competitiveness of the single market. The elimination of technical and non-technical barriers to trade and Turkey's adoption of EU legislation and standards are gradually increasing competitiveness and product quality. With a services sector constituting 65 per cent of its GDP, a public procurement market of over 30 billion, and FDI opportunities, Turkey offers huge potential for European firms.

However, Turkey's standard of living is barely half that of Poland; only 45 per cent of Turkish people of working age have a job. The female employment rate is only 25 per cent and educational standards are low. The economy has also suffered from high and variable inflation, erratic growth, and high levels of public debt.

Economic improvement is a necessary, but not sufficient, condition for membership. Turkey must prove it can meet the Copenhagen criteria in terms of the rule of law, democracy, and respect for human rights. Recent events have highlighted how significant a challenge this is for Turkey. Additionally, Turkish borders are not secured, and many European nations fear the inflow of immigrants as was demonstrated with the Syrian civil war. If accepted, Turkish entry offers the EU an opportunity to absorb a large and growing economy, and overwhelmingly Muslim country as well as culturally different to the rest of the EU. Above all, Turkish accession rests on European political consensus and European citizen support. At present there are a number of significant challenges that have to be overcome for a Turkish accession to become a practically and acceptable reality. Perhaps this would explain why it has taken Turkey almost fifteen years to ratify thirty-five out of the sixty-nine chapters needed to join the EU.

Question

What are the main benefits and costs of Turkey joining the EU?

prosperity which enhances security, offers political reunification of the EU, and links with states to the south and east. Improvements in the quality of life for citizens occur as new members adopt common policies for protecting the environment and fighting crime, drugs, and illegal immigration. New members enrich the EU through increased diversity, the interchange of ideas, and better understanding of other peoples.

In the case of Eastern European countries, there are many who argue that enlargement has been a success (Foxley 2010). Prior to the collapse of the Soviet Union most Eastern European trade had taken place within the Soviet economic bloc, the Council for Mutual Economic Assistance (COMECON). By the 1980s growth rates across the region were low and there was widespread dissatisfaction with the lack of consumer goods. After the demise of Soviet-style communism, Eastern European countries quickly sought to strengthen their links to the EU. They endeavoured to develop strong democratic structures, reorient their economies, and build the appropriate institutions and structures to bring their living standards up to Western European levels. The convergence criteria acted as a standard to aspire to and, in turn, the EU allowed countries access to the structural and cohesion funds that previously were available for EU members only. In the period from accession until the 2008 crisis, generally, economic growth rates in the former Eastern Europe countries were increasing, as were their exports as a percentage of their GDP (Foxley 2010).

The mere prospect of joining the EU does seem to provide countries with the ability to develop their economic and political systems and enjoy increased growth. Turkey is widely seen as being one of the next generation of countries to follow in the footsteps of the BRICS, and, in part, its recent surge in terms of development has been fuelled by its objective to join the EU.

Institutions and decision-making in the EU

Council of Ministers of the European Union

The Council of Ministers, 'the Council', consists of ministers from each member state, who vary with the subject under discussion. Hence, transport ministers attend transport-related discussions, and so on. It is the champion of national interests, with a European Council President appointed by EU member states for a period of two and a half years (and renewable once as established by the Lisbon Treaty). In 2009 EU leaders chose the Belgian Prime Minister Herman Van Rompuy to be the first permanent Council President, replacing the system where countries take six month turns leading the Council Presidency. European 'summits' involve heads of state, governments of the member states, and the president of the Commission and occur twice yearly. In 2017 the President of the Council is the former Polish Prime Minister, Donald Tusk. The Council has a decisive role in legislation, co-decision-making with the EP. Following the Amsterdam Treaty, most legislative decisions are taken by qualified majority voting with unanimity required in a few areas.

European Parliament

Following Eastern enlargement, the EP has 751 members, elected for a five-year term. It is the champion of the interests of the EU people. Its roles are to: approve the member states' choice of president of the EC and endorse the appointment of commissioners; amend and adopt the community budget; amend and approve legislative proposals in co-decision with the Council; and investigate complaints of maladministration in other institutions. With EU decision-making increasingly in the hands of members of the EP (MEPs), the EP has acquired almost equal legislative powers (boosted by the Lisbon Treaty) with the Council (co-decision procedure including agriculture, energy policy, immigration, and EU funds). It can use its position to delay reports or extract concessions from the Commission or Council. Seats are distributed among countries according to 'degressive proportionality', i.e. smaller countries are allocated a higher number of MEP representatives than their relatively smaller size in proportion to larger countries. No country has fewer than six or more than ninety-six MEPs.

European Commission

The EC is, in effect, the European civil service and the champion of European integration. It is responsible for: initiating and drafting legislative proposals; formulating policy; implementing decisions taken by the Council of Ministers and the EP; administering the EU's various funds; and monitoring law implemented by the member states.

Increasingly, the EC focuses less on legislation and more on encouraging the member states to align their own policies to common guidelines. The Commission comprises twenty-eight members (one per member state, a condition reaffirmed by the Lisbon Treaty); a president, vice president, and twenty-six commissioners, known as the College of Commissioners, nominated by member states. The whole Commission must be approved by the EP. The main part of the Commission comprises thirty-seven departments, or Directorates-General (DG) responsible for policy areas.

Decision-making in the EU

The Council of Ministers is generally perceived as the most influential decision-making body, tasked with approving EU laws. The EP monitors laws and the other bodies and is gradually assuming a higher profile. The EC proposes new laws for the Council and Parliament to consider. These three institutions work together to formulate policies, the most important of which include:

- enabling businesses and people to trade and work freely (trade, industry policies);
- creating an area of freedom, security, and justice across the EU (security policy);
- helping poorer regions (regional policy);
- improving the environment (environmental policy);
- supporting EU agriculture (CAP);
- giving the EU a stronger global voice (external policy); and
- helping nations coordinate their policies to boost growth, stability, employment, and the single currency (macroeconomic and euro policies).

As established by the Treaty of Lisbon, the EU shares sovereignty with member states on a number of areas ('shared competencies' and, in some cases, provides a consultative role in areas of 'limited or supporting EU competencies') and has exclusive sovereignty in some areas defined under the 'exclusive competencies clause' (Table 13.5).

Stop and Think

With reference to the main three EU institutions, where does the balance of power lie and why? How do you think the main EU institutions differ from those governing your country and what are the similarities? Argue the strengths and weaknesses of a shared EU competencies system of governance.

Table 13.5 Dimensions of sovereignty between the EU and member states

Exclusive EU competencies	Shared EU competencies	Supporting or limited EU competencies
The Union has exclusive competence to issue directives and conclude international agreements as stipulated in the EU treaties and legislative acts. • the customs union • common commercial (trade) policies • conservation of marine biological resources (common fisheries policy) • common market policies • monetary policy for the member states whose currency is the euro	Shared competence between the EU and member states, however, the latter cannot exercise competence in areas where the Union has done so. • agriculture and fisheries, excluding the conservation of marine biological resources • consumer protection • economic, social, and territorial cohesion (EU regional policy) • environment • social policy, for the aspects defined in the Lisbon Treaty • the internal market (inc. competition policy) • energy • transport • external relations • trans-European networks • the area of freedom, security, and justice • common safety concerns in public health matters • common foreign and security policy	The Union can carry out actions to support, coordinate, or supplement member states' actions. • education, youth, sport, and vocational training • public health policy • industrial policy • culture • tourism • civil protection (disaster prevention) • administrative cooperation

Table 13.6 Suggested cultural groupings

• Anglo-Saxon	UK, Ireland
• Baltic	Estonia, Latvia, Lithuania
• Central & Eastern European	Bulgaria, Czech Republic, Hungary, Slovakia, Slovenia, Poland, Romania
• Germanic/N. European	Austria, Belgium, France, Germany, Netherlands, Luxembourg
• Mediterranean	France, Spain, Portugal, Italy, Greece, Cyprus, Malta
• Nordic/Scandinavian	Denmark, Finland, Sweden

Cultural diversity and business implications

DIVERSITY Chapter 5 showed us that culture is the glue that binds a society together; it is about people and their behaviour stemming from their backgrounds, group affiliation, values, and practices. Cultural traits derive from various factors, such as: language, social organization, the law, religion, education, and political ideology.

Europeans share a common heritage but the integration and administration of an enlarged EU, comprising almost 500 million people of diverse cultures, is an enormous task. At a basic level, there is no single European language and relatively few people can follow a conversation in a language other than their own.

For businesses, such cultural aspects impinge on decisions to take a pan-European perspective, treating Europe as a relatively uniform market, or targeting specific nations or cultural groups. If the latter, the diversity of the EU might suggest groupings such as those in Table 13.6.

Stop and Think

What is a European citizen? What other groupings can there be (history, language, geography, etc.)?

What are the main cultural and globalization challenges facing operating companies in the new Europe?

The euro and business—one step too far or one step short of a full ladder?

DYNAMIC **INTERACTION** We discussed the macroeconomic aspects of EMU in Chapter 9's end of chapter case study, and we have explored the arguments for and against having a single currency above.

With the advent of the single market programme, it became clear that transaction costs linked to currency conversion, and high-risk premiums associated with exchange rate fluctuations, would hinder realization of the internal market potential. Hence, a three-stage approach (Mini-Case 13.2) was formulated for the introduction of a single currency, enshrined in the 1992 Maastricht Treaty. This shows clearly that the theoretical problems of creating monetary union were appreciated, but, for many members of the EU, these dangers could be negated with coordination and careful planning, thus ensuring the prize of a single currency with all the associated benefits.

Central to the introduction of the euro was the need to avoid destabilizing inflation that would undermine competition, confidence, and purchasing power. Accordingly, an independent ECB was formed in 1998 tasked with controlling interest rates to effect monetary policy; mainly interpreted as a 'year on year' increase in the Harmonized Index of Consumer Prices (HICP) of less than 2 per cent. During 1997 the European Council adopted three supporting resolutions covering:

- economic growth—to ensure that employment was a key objective;
- economic coordination—closer ties between members to embrace financial, budgetary, social, and fiscal policies; and
- the revised Stability and Growth Pact—a commitment to budgetary discipline.

The **Stability and Growth Pact** set legally binding ceilings of 3 per cent GDP on eurozone members' budget deficits, a breach of which would incur fines of up to 0.5 per cent of GDP. However, the pact was widely considered too rigid for countries struggling to grow. The rules were relaxed but, with hindsight, this was not enough. Critics point out that this was a crucial mistake, as it effectively forced member states to undertake unpopular reforms necessary to structurally readjust their economies and make them more competitive. This measure was

Mini-Case 13.2 The Trojan horse of Europe? The case of Brexit and Europe's transformation

In 2016, the EU faced its biggest challenge yet since the 2004 and 2007 EU enlargements and even the 2010 Greek debt and eurozone crisis. Following a UK referendum in 2016, the third such to have ever been held in the country and second on the question of EU membership, 52 per cent of participants voted for the UK to leave the EU. Named the 'Brexit referendum', the result surprised politicians, business leaders, and industry associations as well as many citizens. It demonstrated a big societal divide, juxtaposing the elderly against youth, affluent communities against impoverished ones, Scotland and Northern Ireland against the rest of the UK, and large cities against smaller ones and rural areas. Fundamentally, what was dubbed to be a 'protest vote', united a diverse set of protests with a common cause. The two issues that pro-Brexit voters perceived to be at the centre of the referendum result were perceptions on sovereignty and immigration, although there were many diverse and complex reasons for the result (Jessop 2017).

Economists, experts, politicians, and other commentators faced both sides of the arguments for the referendum and subsequent preparations for exit with uneven arguments and unprepared plans for the eventuality of an exit, leading to speculation and amassed uncertainty bordering on paranoia. The 'Brexiteers' (supporting the leave the EU campaign) would argue about the added benefits of British sovereign decisions and Britain's ability to negotiate trade deals directly with the US and growing nations such as BRICS and others. The 'Remainers' (supporting for Britain to remain in the EU) predicted catastrophic outcomes, mostly spelled around the notion of economic and cultural isolationism. Ironically, both campaigns failed to highlight what was good and worth celebrating about the EU altogether. One focused on doom-and-gloom scenarios of leaving and the other on hyperbolic expressions of national pride and jingoism in going it alone! Irrespective of the authors' own views, it can objectively be said that both the surprising decision to exit the EU combined with the apparent complete lack of any plans to prepare for the eventuality have significantly contributed to a growing sense of volatility and growing uncertainty.

The nature of the British exit from the EU can be divided into two categories. A 'soft Brexit' would represent a set of possible scenarios where Britain negotiated a deal short of a full withdrawal from the EU. Best achieved through a negotiated form of a strategic partnership agreement, where the UK would resume control of its own immigration rules and both the EU and UK would maintain mutual market access and the UK would continue its financial contributions in the EU budget. A 'hard Brexit' agreement represents a full withdrawal from the EU where the UK would give up participation in the EU single market and its legal rules. Essentially the above could be summarized in five trading options post-Brexit for the UK:

- an EEA-type arrangement with the EU, similar to that of Norway's, that gives access to the single market in return for financial contributions, EU regulations, and free labour mobility;

- an EFTA-type arrangement, similar to that of Switzerland's, where trade deals are agreed on a sector-by-sector basis, a UK financial contribution, free labour mobility, and better access for financial services;
- a customs union, e.g. like in the case of Turkey, establishing a customs union with the EU with no barriers in manufactured goods;
- a bilateral agreement, e.g. like with Canada, establishing a bilateral trade deal, eliminating tariffs, offering better intellectual property protection and investor-state dispute settlement (ISDS) provision; and
- trading under the unilateral approach as a WTO member.

The impact of the British exit itself on the EU has also been subject for speculation. Projected to be as stable as an 'economic house of cards', many projected the Union to collapse. This is because, beyond a strong mere economic impact, Brexit has a more significant political impact too on the Union. Within the Union anti-EU factions wait with anticipation to see the state of the Union following the British exit. Protest parties throughout the EU are beginning to challenge EU membership with populist arguments building momentum. Consensus has been reached on the level of uncertainty the exit has placed. Three facts have been commonly seen as guiding parameters to the outcome of Brexit for Europe:

1. A speedy exit negotiation following the referendum will minimize the negative impact on the European Union: article 50 itself is set to take two years to complete the exit with a year to six months following this to finalize arrangements. It is quite easily imaginable that the EU might agree to a transitional exit arrangement for Britain. This would be a mistake as giving Britain more time to find alternatives to EU trade will only strengthen the success for its exit (see second point). Additionally, the balance of power is in the EU's favour as export trade with the EU is linked to about 12.5 per cent of British GDP, while the EU's trade with Britain is linked to only about 3 per cent of its GDP (*Guardian* 2016). Not aiding Britain's recovery of its market loss would send a strong message to other EU members and citizens, that membership is preferable to economic damage.
2. A 'hard' Brexit outcome would have more pronounced negative effects for the Union if it is seen to deliver benefits and successes for the British economy in the short and medium term.

In the medium to long term, Brexit also presents opportunities for Europe such as further progress with political integration and policy development agendas. Similarly, the EU could adopt more flexible and smaller group participatory initiatives creating a 'Europe à la carte' post-Brexit so that those nations that wish to integrate more can be allowed to do so while others stay where they are. Perhaps, this could see the rise of the eminence of the central and Eastern European axis as a balancing power against the German and French dominant positions.

In conclusion, the impact of Brexit on the EU cannot easily be predicted or understood in simple economic or political terms. Perhaps for the best way to gain an understanding of what could happen, it is necessary to comprehend what the EU is about. To achieve this, we can borrow an analogy of a definition of the ontological essence of organizations (Arrigoni 2017). Thus, in an attempt to define what the EU is, we move beyond the expressions and meanings of the series of the treaties that define it, but instead we look in detail to the interaction and influence of the principal architects of the development of the EU as well as its principal actors and beneficiaries, its members states.

Without a doubt, the core idea behind the purpose of the EU evolved a long way from the need for the development of peace and security in the continent that had seen two world wars. A strong component of the later stages of the development of the Union saw the establishment of further economic integration and political integration, standardization practices and a drive to boost EU competitiveness at a global stage, transnational and global perspectives and priorities on the preservation of the environment, major interventions on establishing the EU as a global technological innovator, and many more often contradicting perspectives. The majority of these decisions, adjustments of future development perspectives of the EU have been agreed across its nations through intense dialogue, compromises, and in some cases conflict and resolution negotiations. Figure 13.1 encapsulates these expressions in an attempt to better define what the EU represents.

Thus, we could define the EU as 'the expression of the outcome of the interaction of its member states'. In other words, the EU is not simply an economic union in the same way that a company is not simply a building and its factories and machinery, but something greater than the simple sum of its parts. In this way, we can understand that the exit of Britain, while it has a significant impact, simply alters the membership of the EU and by implication the balance of interactions of its twenty-seven members, in itself generating a new evolving expression of what Europe is developing to be.

Questions

1. **What negotiating stance do you think the twenty-seven EU member states should adopt in relation to the UK?**
2. **What stance do you feel the UK should adopt in its negotiation with the EU?**
3. **What should the UK aim towards as it charts a future away from the EU?**

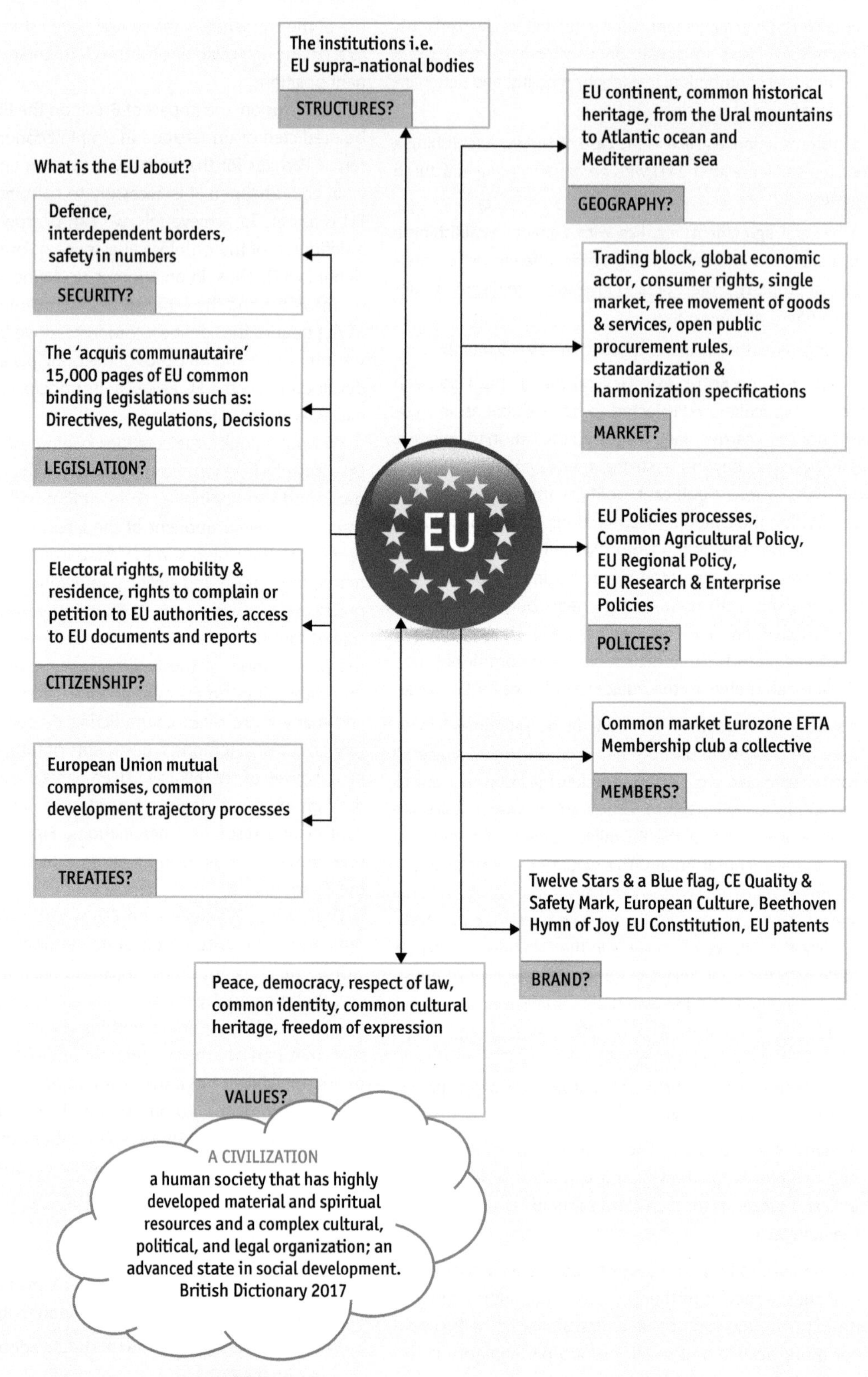

Figure 13.1 What is the EU?

needed to allow for a stable and sustainable eurozone but might be impossible to achieve. However, the counterargument holds that such conditions act as a huge incentive for countries, especially the less competitive ones, to improve their economic performance and, thus, can actually speed up convergence.

The performance of the euro

On the one hand, the EMU can be seen as representing a remarkable achievement. Only ten years elapsed between the Treaty of Maastricht, which laid the foundations for the single currency, and the 2002 introduction of euro notes and coins in twelve nations. The euro replaced individual currencies that were long-standing instruments, and crucially, symbols of national identities. People now travel and trade across large swathes of Europe using a single currency. In 2011, Estonia became the latest member state to join the eurozone, bringing the total to seventeen out of twenty-eight member states, with approximately 331 million EU citizens using the euro.

However, as we saw in Chapter 9's end of chapter case study, all is not well in the eurozone, especially in relation to what have come to be referred to as the PIGS (Portugal, Ireland, Italy, Greece, and Spain).

It is important to distinguish between cause and effect here, as it is not the euro itself that caused the crisis, nor indeed is it primarily the countries mentioned above. The roots of the problem lie in the global recession of 2008 which was the result of irresponsible financial practices and the lack of an effective global regulatory environment. We explored the immediate causes of this in Chapter 2 and the possible global responses in Chapter 10, but it is clear that there has, as yet, not been an effective global response.

Consequently, individual countries have responded to the crisis in different ways. In the US there has been a measure of old-fashioned Keynesian fiscal and monetary expansion and, in the view of structuralist critics, this has both prevented the US from experiencing a collapse and brought the beginnings of the restoration of growth. In Europe the main model adopted has been one of austerity. Here the fault lines of the euro become horribly exposed. The UK and other non-eurozone countries feel vindicated in their decision not to join the euro as they can exercise their own response. Instead, in the UK, to the frustration of most of the academic economics community and a wide range of economic commentators who would advocate a Keynesian expansionary programme, an austerity programme has been instituted, albeit accompanied by a very large increase in the money supply supported by its ability to borrow short term at very low interest rates.

For the relatively strong countries in the Union, even where growth rates are slowing or even dipping, their good credit ratings mean that they can continue to borrow to offset the worst effects of the recession as they seek to restore their competitive positions. There is also the belief that, while the PIGS may not have caused it, the 2008 crisis simply exposed the fact that they had allowed budget deficits to rise too far and not done enough to restructure their economies to become competitive.

The richer countries within the eurozone do recognize the danger of a financial crisis being precipitated by the default of a struggling country. And there have been attempts to ensure there are sufficient funds in place to rescue a country should there be a speculative attack on one. In this the EU central bank has been supported by the IMF. However, essentially, the long-term burden to address the large budget deficits does fall on each country and, in return for the funds they are receiving from the IMF and ECB, they are forced to enact deep austerity measures. Currently, as we have seen in Chapter 9, this is creating huge social and political tensions in Greece and Spain in particular.

There are plenty of critics of the policy of the EU, and the eurozone specifically, and they come from all sides of the economic and political divide. For Keynesian critics, the immediate blame has to be with the EU itself and its austerity policies. While it might be a logical tactic for one country alone to undertake microeconomic adjustment at the macroeconomic level, the reduction in aggregate demand collectively brings everyone down and is, ultimately, self-defeating. What is needed is a fiscal expansion in all countries, which if led by the stronger countries, would restore confidence in the European economy and still allow borrowing to occur at low interest rates.

When it comes to the role of the euro, opponents simply see the current pressures as evidence that the euro is a step too far, and the edifice of European unity is now crumbling. For free market critics, the PIGS may have got themselves into this mess, but they cannot do anything else but undertake drastic measures to bring their economies under control now that they are deprived of the ability to use the exchange rate to buffer their economies. For left-wing critics, there are strong objections to the loss of democracy as citizens and elected national governments are essentially forced to comply with the conditions attached to the loans.

For those who firmly believe in the long-term benefits of a full economic union, what this situation reveals is that there must be much greater economic and political integration, involving a greater role for an independent central bank with access to larger stability funds contributed by members. Members would have to agree to allow much greater central scrutiny of their government spending plans, and fines for non-compliance would be necessary. It is not that the current situation shows the ultimate and complete failure of the euro project, it is simply that the process towards an effective eurozone is incomplete. It seems that what is needed is a 'two-speed' Europe, with those who wish to join and remain in the eurozone agreeing to undertake more overarching political and economic cooperation and those who do not wish to participate remaining part of the negotiations but not signing up to the agreements.

Doing business in Europe

INTERNAL/EXTERNAL Having explored the main external issues that are affecting the European business environment, in this next section we look at some of the ways in which operating in Europe may affect the internal decisions of businesses.

The Lisbon Summit in 2000 set the following business goals for Europe (the Lisbon Agenda):

> that the EU should become the most competitive and dynamic knowledge-based economy in the World, capable of sustained economic growth, with more and better jobs, and greater social cohesion.

The agenda aimed to create an effective internal market with an improved infrastructure and more investment in research and development (R&D), leading to a strong industrial base, characterized by an adaptable workforce, free and fair trade, and innovation. Almost twenty years following the setting out of the Lisbon Agenda, the EU has yet to fully achieve its objectives and is in danger of being irreversibly overtaken by emerging economies. To meet these aims the EU requires efficient business-related policies and relentless investment in education, R&D, and enterprise creation.

Stakeholder management in the EU

STAKEHOLDERS Decisions made in Brussels affect businesses, consumers, and citizens in many different ways. Often these decisions must reconcile the needs of the various stakeholders through open debate and examination of the opposing and conciliatory arguments. Understanding and compromise are key to delivering decisions acceptable to all. It is crucial for businesses to be involved and have an influence at an early stage in the formulation of EU regulations and legislation.

This has given rise to a large lobbyist body in Brussels, representing large companies, industrial and economic sectors, trade associations, employer and union representatives, consumers, chambers of commerce, city and regional representatives, and think tanks. They all seek to influence and contribute to EU decision-making.

> ***Stop and Think***
>
> What drives businesses to pay attention to EU decision-making? Use examples to argue your case.

Competition and industry policy

EU competition policy follows the neoclassical free market philosophy now prevalent in all member states; a liberal economic vision contrasting with the centrally planned approach previously experienced by the new eastern members. Competition policy follows articles 81 and 82 of the Treaty of Rome and seeks to ensure the internal market is not distorted. Areas which hinder efficiency and competitive forces (e.g. monopoly, oligopoly, cartels, restrictive practices, subsidies, state procurement, and protection) are targeted. EU competition policy has grown in significance, boosted by the Lisbon 2000 economic reform and competitiveness agenda.

There are broadly five components:

Anti-trust agreements prohibit concerted or restricted practices or agreements among firms that limit competition, unless special circumstances exist to promote technical or economic progress. Enforcement of anti-trust legislation has gathered momentum with actions against cartels covering beer, banking, and vitamins.

Anti-trust abuse of a dominant position targets monopoly and oligopoly situations where abuse occurs, such as low pricing to eliminate the competition, discriminatory pricing (the charging of different prices for the same commodity) within or between member states, and limits imposed on production, markets, or technological development to raise prices and/or profits. The main tests are: a market share of 40 per cent or more; the degree of independence from competitors; the ability to eliminate the competition; or a dominant relationship with suppliers or customers. However, prosecutions are rare, partly because many people feel there is a need for large, globally competitive corporations that are EU and national 'champions'.

Mergers can create or strengthen a dominant position which may lead to abuse. A Merger Regulation was adopted in 1989 (No. 4064/89) which established exclusive commission jurisdiction for mergers between firms with a joint global turnover of €5 billion and within the EU of €250 million each, below which national legislation prevails. During the 1990s the EC became more interventionist and accordingly was criticized, for example, for having prohibited the GE/Honeywell merger and having decisions overturned by the Court of

Justice (Airtours/First Choice; Schneider Electric/Legrand; and Tetra Laval/Sidel). In 2004 a new Merger Regulation (No. 139/2004) placed greater responsibility on firms to assess the impact of any merger or acquisition.

State aid refers to financial assistance from public funds that distort competition and efficient resource allocation. It applies to subsidies, tax breaks, soft loans, preferential procurement, and guarantees. Article 87 (2, 3) of the EC Treaty allows for state aid under circumstances compatible with the internal market, for example, social aid or that given to overcome the effects of natural disasters.

A total ban on state aid is impossible; indeed, a fundamental EU tenet is that intervention is necessary for balanced and sustainable economic development. Consequently, a history of state aid support exists, notably rescue subsidies for shipping, car, coal, and steel industries. These subsidies have been substantially reduced and redirected via regional policy. Despite progress, state aid issues remain; indeed, they have re-emerged with the accession of former centrally planned economies. As our case study demonstrates state aid remains an area that requires vigilant oversight and supranational intervention for the benefit of all.

Utilities have been liberalized throughout the EU, boosted by privatization drives and single market reforms. Key sectors are 'network' industries or natural monopolies such as energy, water, postal services, telecommunications, railways, and airlines. For years these public interest monopolies were protected, but technological developments have exposed operating weaknesses. The Commission's liberalization policy based on article 86(3) has created complex packages of directives, restrictive practice, and merger case law to open up these areas.

Competition legislation has a special place in EU policy as it defends the collective interest in economic efficiency secured through the single market. Nevertheless, it faces radical challenges. National competition agencies have grown in stature, with often better analytical and legal bases, and the European Court of Justice has often expressed concern about Directorates-Generals' competition interpretations. Moreover, member nations are often reluctant to reduce state support for their companies. The test will be whether policy can be flexible enough to meet national concerns and lead to the gains in EU competitiveness and growth required by the Lisbon Agenda.

Industry policy

Competition policy has played a central role in the 'economic EU constitution', in shaping and giving birth to an industrial policy for the EU. The concept of an EU industrial policy in itself has been, and remains, contentious in the EU. Taken literally, industrial policy entails all acts and policies of the state relating to industry. This would include instruments and measures designed to control and influence the performance of firms within particular sectors of the economy as well as passive or active measures (i.e. relating to liberalization of markets or correction of market failure), tasks usually associated with the sovereignty of the national state. Therefore, the original Treaty of Rome did not provide a legal basis for active sectoral policies to be pursued and left industrial policy within the competence of member states. However, with the liberalization of global trade, increased attention was placed on whether member states' national, often protectionist, industrial policies could distort economic competition between states and ultimately harm the ability of the trading bloc to compete globally. Therefore, an EU industrial policy was first introduced in 1991 in the Treaty of the European Union (TEU) Article 3 (1) which states that activities of the Community shall 'strengthen the competitiveness of Community industry'. Under the Treaty the Commission was tasked with the coordination of member states in this matter. Subsequently, the Maastricht 1992 (article 129b) and Amsterdam 1997 (article 157) treaties provided a further basis for solidifying an EU industrial policy. The intention has been to promote structural adjustment, encourage small and medium-sized companies, and stimulate innovation. Maastricht also emphasized trans-European network developments in areas of transport, telecommunications, and energy.

EU industrial policy is being developed with the principles of an integrated approach across sectors and member states and a non-interventionist ethos. The main strategies applied are, firstly, the creation of a business environment conducive to developing new technologies and entrepreneurial activity. This includes promoting institutional measures such as venture capital provision, a European patent system, and boosting R&D by strengthening links between universities, research organizations, and businesses. Second, a key focus has been to provide a framework for pan-EU mergers and takeovers via approval of a takeover directive, seen as critical to cementing the single market and enlargement.

VALUES However, EU industry policy is a collection of often conflicting programmes. For example, there are diverse views about the benefits of allowing cross-border takeovers, hence debate in the EP has held up the takeover directive. One perspective favours a robust competition policy backed by deregulation to overcome protectionist tendencies that have prevented EU-wide competition. Policies to raise productivity in key technologies (e.g. biotechnology, information technology, and creative industries) (see Chapter 3) would support this approach. An alternative view emphasizes restructuring the industrial base with less concern for internal EU competition. This approach takes a more global view, arguing that Europe needs large efficient businesses which would be competitive with the US and Far East, such as airbus industries in the aviation sector. Such issues are debated at European summits, but there is still reluctance to abandon protectionism as a tool of industrial policy.

For EU business leaders, there is often considerable frustration at the policy hurdles faced. They helped to shape the Lisbon Agenda and communicate their views via trade associations, chambers of commerce, and the thousands of lobbyists in Brussels; yet they struggle to see tangible industrial policy benefits. However, the close connection between competition policy and industry policy is now better understood in the EU, and the value of a coordinated approach within the context of globalized market economies is recognized. (See Mini-Case 13.3.)

Mini-Case 13.3 Apple vs. the EC: competition and the complexities of multilevel governance

For a common market to truly work, there is a need for vigilantly ensuring member states abide by the rules that bind their union. The power of the 'supranational triumvirate', represented by the EC, EP, and the Council is in most cases subtle and rarely makes the headlines. However, in August 2016, in a surprise announcement the EC challenged the world's largest tech company, Apple, over two decades of €13bn plus interest in what was claimed to be unpaid taxes. Competition Commissioner Margrethe Vestager summarized the EU's position as follows: 'EU Member states cannot give unfair tax benefits to selected companies'.

The case follows a 2013 EC investigation covering the period 2003–14. Apple set up a subsidiary company called Apple Sales International (ASI) based in Cork, Ireland. It acted as an intermediary of the Apple corporation, by purchasing Apple products from Apple's manufacturers to resell them to consumers in Europe, the Middle East, Africa, and India (EMEAI). The Irish-based subsidiary was subject to nominal corporation tax (12.5 per cent, the lowest in Europe). Its headquarters in Ireland had no employees. In this way, Apple took advantage of the 1991 and 2007 Irish tax rulings that allowed for 'stateless companies' to pay no tax in Ireland. This legislation was unique in Europe and was subsequently repealed in 2015. As a result of these rulings, the vast majority of profits made by ASI through sales in its European and other international markets were attributed to its 'virtual' and 'stateless' head office.

This meant Apple was paying a negligible amount of taxes, well below the Irish corporate tax rate of 12.5 per cent. For example, in 2011 alone, for a staggering €16bn in profits in the EMEAI region, fewer than €15m were allocated to the Irish ASI branch and the rest was exempt from tax as it was attributed to the headquarters. By 2014, Apple lessened its tax payments to the Irish state further and was paying €50 in taxes per €1 million in profit made, enjoying effectively a 0.005 per cent corporation tax.

There are four principal protagonists in this case, which has been referred to the European Court of Justice. The first, the EC, acts as the guardian of the treaties governing the Union of twenty-eight states. Under European common market competition rules, no special arrangements can be made for a selected company thus allowing for uniform rules and treatment across the common market. According to the Commission, sales that had a contractual base in an EU headquartered company have to be matched by the respective tax paid within the trading bloc. By extension also it does act to protect the interests of European corporations by ensuring competition is fair both within the trade bloc as well as in others where they operate.

Apple is the party accused of evading tax. From its perspective, it claims to have followed the legal advice given by the Irish government in its 1991 and 2007 rulings. It also claims that the distribution arm of its corporations does not 'add value' to essentially a product developed in the US and should not be taxed.

EU legislation allows for member states charging different levels of corporation tax as it is seen as a sovereign right of nations maintaining autonomy over their fiscal policies. Ironically, the Irish government does not want to collect the €14.5bn in taxes and supports Apple's appeal to the European Court of Justice. Ireland could pay a large number of its debts through these receipts, however not only are the Irish authorities worried about the 6,000 Apple jobs based in Ireland but more importantly of the negative impact such a case could have on Ireland's credibility as an inexpensive place to do business, where tax legislation is well established and stable. Ireland denies it effectively gave state aid to Apple. Other EU member states have employed low corporation tax as a means to attract FDI and jobs such as Netherlands and Luxembourg for example as opposed to France whose corporation tax stands at 33.5 per cent.

Paradoxically, one would expect the US government to encourage efforts to collect tax from US-based multinationals using non-US based subsidiaries to pay less or almost no tax. Yet the US Treasury department is fighting the case against Apple for two reasons. First, to protect the rights of US businesses abroad but also to preserve hopes in potentially recovering tax revenue at a later time. Yet this is not a new story. The US Treasury is well aware of large US corporations engaging in 'inversion' practices to avoid paying high US corporation taxes. The practice refers to a US corporation acquiring a subsidiary abroad and transferring its legal headquarters there in order to challenge its identity as a US company and related tax obligations.

The case of Apple is not unique: the Commission is flexing its muscles and is currently bringing a case against Starbucks over unpaid taxes in Luxembourg. Yet it also raises questions about the treatment of large businesses in the trading bloc. While these account for a meagre 1 per cent of all businesses they account for one third of employment and approximately 40 per cent of the Gross Value Added (GVA) generated in the EU. In light of such contributions, should the EU adopt less strict competition legislation towards large businesses in the EU in the same way the US does?

Questions

1. **What do you think is the EC set to gain in its action against Apple?**
2. **Is EU competition policy fair as it is centred on large companies and exempts small businesses from receiving state subsidies?**
3. **Is Apple's stance justified?**
4. **Did Ireland make 'unfair' arrangements with Apple?**
5. **What are the strengths and weaknesses of EU competition policy?**

Looking ahead

In all the current doom and gloom about the low rates of growth in Europe, and in light of the particular problems faced by Greece and other Southern European countries, advocates of the EU project remind us that prior to 2008 huge gains were made across all countries, and that especially the new accession countries in Eastern Europe have been dramatically transformed. In recent months there are now encouraging signs that growth and recovery are happening across the EU27 while the uncertainty caused by Brexit does seem to be slowing growth in the UK.

There are undoubted economic benefits derived from the greater trade opportunities and competition that the EU has brought, and it is still the case that the EU provided a role model for other aspiring trading blocs.

Politically, enlargement has been one of the EU's most successful policies and a powerful foreign policy tool. The zone of peace and democracy has been progressively extended and, in this 'democratic' sense, a closer union of member states exists, stretching from the Atlantic to the eastern Mediterranean, from Lapland to Malta.

Given the problems that the WTO is facing in forging ahead with the latest round of trade talks, it is clear that the pattern of world trade is being heavily influenced by regional trade agreements. Across the globe more and more countries want to join such trading blocs. One interesting development is how these blocs relate to each other—something we look at in Chapter 16.

As we will see in the ASEAN case study at the end of this chapter, FTAs can be mutually beneficial even for countries at moderately different levels of development. But it is South–South cooperation that will have the best chances of success. The reservations of structuralist and dependency writers that we saw in Chapter 10 regarding trade between the developed and developing world still remain. If integration is to proceed beyond the FTA level, then it is clear that there must be much greater political and economic integration, as well as attention paid to the need for realistic convergence between members. The experience of the EU shows the danger of too rapid an integration, and that some members might not be able to bring their economies up to the levels required to benefit from the free competitive conditions. As the recent experience with the euro shows, the jury is still out on the issue of the feasibility of a full economic union. For many, the only way this could be achieved is through much closer political and economic cooperation in a federal model (see European Council 2017 for the ongoing strategic vision of the EU). As the case of Britain shows, this may be a step too far for some members and one which indeed leads to calls for a fundamental reassessment of what closer trading links might entail.

Summary

- The process of globalization is being heavily influenced by the development of regional trading blocs and there is a range of levels of integration possible within these blocs. The rise of social as well as environmental concerns and the recognition of the resource limited imperfect capitalist governing economic model mean that globalization is also challenged at citizen levels across nations around the world. Increasingly, there is a limited appetite for adjustment to the world's global economic shift.
- The EU provides an instructive model in managing integration. The EU involves complex decision-making based on treaties and the 'institutional triangle'. Integration has progressed from removing trade barriers to positive building and harmonization of policies, the most significant of which is the experiment with monetary union and the creation of the eurozone.
- Expediency, effectiveness, and individual vs. collective added value emerge as key factors in building trust and loyalty from trading bloc members in turbulent global financial

settings. The poor eurozone response to shocks like the Greek debt crisis, the perceived meddling of the EU in common market affairs as illustrated by the case of Apple and Ireland, and the poor collective EU response to the Syrian migrant crisis raised issues about the sustainability of the incomplete monetary union in Europe and more generally its continued evolution.

- Doing business in Europe is strongly influenced by the EU policy environment, especially industry and competition policies. These are influenced by the neoclassical free market philosophy dominant in member states to enhance the single market and prevent distortion of competitive forces. Key industries such as the utilities, car, telecoms, and airlines have all changed radically under such influences.
- In attempting to become an ever closer union of member states, Europe faces future challenges in implementing the essence of the Lisbon Agenda and making a success of enlargement. Efforts to both deepen and widen integration will create tensions among existing members with differing objectives. It requires businesses to appreciate different scenarios that may impinge on their operating environment, ranging from operating in a two-speed union to the possibility that certain countries might break away. At the same time following Brexit, it is unlikely a strong proponent of opposition will emerge to replace the UK, and as the balance of power shifts to more traditional founding European member states, it is likely Europe will begin developing with the emergence of new treaties aimed at integration.

Case Study: The development of the ASEAN trading bloc

We saw in Chapter 10 that trade has been the most important engine for growth in South East Asia, but the way in which these countries developed their trade strategies owed little to the idea of free market orthodoxy. Initially, Japan's model was one of state-led industrialization exploiting its comparative advantage in low-cost but skilled labour to export to Europe and the US. With the state and other financial institutions directing investment into designated export activities and fostering technology transfer, Japan was able to move up the value chain—away from low-cost labour intensive goods to capital-intensive intermediate goods and then to high-tech manufacturing goods.

The Association of Southeast Asian nations or ASEAN started in 1967 with a membership of Singapore, Indonesia, Malaysia, the Philippines, and Thailand. It was initially for political cooperation, acting as a bulwark against the many communist countries that they bordered. The Japanese economist Akamatsu published his 'Flying Geese' model of economic development in 1962 (Akamatsu 1962). For Akamatsu, the pattern of regional economic development in areas such as South East Asia would resemble the formation of a flock of geese with a lead member pulling all the others forward but with a constant process of leadership rotation. In this model, Japan would provide the initial leadership for the region and, as it developed, it would progressively move up the value chain and directly outsource, or vacate, the labour intensive activities to allow countries in the region to exploit their comparative advantages in these areas. Foxley shows that indeed countries such as South Korea, Singapore, Taiwan, and Hong Kong did initially become part of a vertically integrated supply chain to enable Japanese business to continue its process of export expansion (Foxley 2010). As we have seen in Chapter 10, the type of industrial policies that each country had developed by concentrating on certain sectors with a large amount of state directed support, enabled them to trade up the value chain, providing room for other countries to follow in their paths, e.g. Indonesia, the Philippines, Thailand, Malaysia, and, of course, China which was more recently followed by Vietnam, Laos, and Cambodia. In the process, South Korea, Singapore, Taiwan, and Hong Kong all became economic powerhouses in their own right.

The ASEAN nations were reluctant to undergo trade liberalization within their bloc, which would increase intraregional trade, as the prime focus of their economic activity was on exporting to the developed world of North America, Europe, and Japan. However, a number of important changes in the external environment have led to increasing integration and a widening of its present and potential membership. The changes in the orientation of the communist economies, and especially the rise of China with its huge numbers of low-cost workers, has given further impetus to the shifting of comparative advantages in the region and encouraged an acceleration of the ASEAN members' movement towards higher technology manufacturing industries. The 1997 South East Asian crisis demonstrated the need for greater cooperation in terms of coordinated fiscal and monetary policies to avoid the contagion spreading so rapidly. And, finally, the global recession and ensuing slow growth in the West has shown the Asian economies that there is a need to diversify their trading relationships to avoid over concentration in certain markets. While this might be seen as a negative defensive response which is encouraging closer integration, the sheer speed with which living standards in the region have risen, and the creation of large urban middle-class consumers, means that there is now a positive interest in this large and growing intraregional market.

In 1992 the ASEAN free trade area (AFTA) was established with the intention of phasing out all tariffs between members and in recent years the ASEAN bloc has grown to include: Brunei Darussalam, Lao PDR, Myanmar, Cambodia, and Vietnam (see www.asean.org).

Prior to the currency turmoil of the 1997 South East Asian financial crisis, ASEAN+ 3 (APT) was formed to provide a platform for regular meetings between ASEAN and China, Japan, and South Korea in coordinating trade relationships with Europe. But after the crisis it became clear that APT would increasingly be needed to strengthen mutual interests. Two direct examples of this cooperation are the signing of the Chiang Mai Initiative, which provides a forum for currency swaps to build up funds to use in the event of future currency instability, and the creation of the Asian Bonds Market Initiative, which seeks to channel domestic savings into targeted areas of regional investment. APT has also now broadened the areas of cooperation to include a range of political, social, and strategic objectives (see ASEAN 2017).

More recently the ASEAN+6 has developed, adding India, Australia, and New Zealand. All of the +6 countries have already negotiated FTAs with ASEAN, but now the proposal is to create a FTA across all sixteen countries which would create a free trade area of 3.6 billion people.

Questions

1. **How have the nations of South East Asia sought to integrate themselves into the global economy?**
2. **What role did geographical proximity play in developing trading links?**
3. **How, prior to the formal development of ASEAN, were the development strategies of their members influenced both domestically and regionally?**
4. **What have been the external and internal factors that have encouraged the more recent forms of integration for the ASEAN bloc?**

Review and discussion questions

1. What are the advantages for a business of being able to operate within a regional trade area?
2. Critically assess the argument that the EU is merely a protectionist trade bloc.
3. Examine whether a single currency is necessary for the efficient working of the European single market.
4. Is the development of regional trading blocs an example of the possible fragmentation of the world trade system or the inevitable consequence of a global business environment consisting of countries at different levels of development and with different historical and cultural determinants?

Assignments

1. (a) Imagine that there is going to be a referendum in the UK in 2019 to decide whether the UK should accept the terms of the negotiated Brexit agreement or reject it. Research into the opposing views and decide which way you would advise British people to vote. Would you be pro or anti advising the UK accepting the Brexit terms?

   (b) Depending on your answer to the question above, imagine that you have been recruited by one of the campaign organizations to help them in their pro or anti campaign by producing a two-page campaign leaflet to be distributed to your local business community (for useful research material, see the websites below).

2. Write a report which compares and contrasts two of the following trading blocs, in terms of their scope and levels of integration, and identify the likely areas of development in these blocs in the next ten years.

ASEAN
EU
MERCOSUR
NAFTA

Further reading

De Grauwe (2016) *a comprehensive evaluation of the costs and benefits of monetary union followed by its present workings covering the ECB, monetary and fiscal policies, and the international role of the euro.*

Bickerton (2016) *profiles the functions and scope of the EU.*

Dunton (2017) *a commentary from a 'Bremainer' who argues that Brexit will not be in the best interests of the UK or the EU.*

Test your understanding of this chapter with online questions and answers, explore the subject further through web exercises, and use the weblinks to provide a quick resource for further research. Visit the online resources at www.oup.com/uk/wetherly_otter4e/

Useful websites

https://www.gov.uk/government/organisations/department-for-exiting-the-european-union
The home page of the UK's Department for Exiting the EU

http://europa.eu/index_en.htm
The official home page for the EU

http://www.efta.int
The home page for EFTA

wto.org/english/tratop_e/region_e/rta_pta_e.htm
The WTO database of all RTAs and PTAs

www.nafta-sec-alena.org
The home page for NAFTA

http://en.mercopress.com/about-mercosur
The home page for MERCOSUR

http://www.sadc.int
The home page for SADC

www.european-voice.com
A useful source of news and views about the EU

www.gov.uk/trading-in-the-eu
An advice site run by the UK government for doing business in Europe

www.cer.org-uk
The home page for the Centre for European Reform, a leading EU research think tank

www.euromove.org.uk
The home page for the European Movement which campaigns to present the positive case for UK membership

www.brugesgroup.com
The home page of the Bruges Group which is a UK all-party think tank which campaigns to stop deeper integration for the UK within the EU

References

Akamatsu, K. (1962) 'A Historical Pattern of Economic Growth in Developing Countries', *Journal of Developing Economies*, 1(1): 3–25

Arrigoni, A. (2017) 'Social alterity and articulation: the deep roots of sociological realism', in Emmanuele Morandi (ed.), *Experiencing Society: Eric Voegelin's Criticism of Sociologism* (Milan: Mimesis Edizioni), 11–18

ASEAN (2017) 'Overview of ASEAN Plus 3 Co-operation' (accessed 4 August 2017) **http://asean.org/storage/2017/06/Overview-of-APT-Cooperation-Jun-2017.pdf**

Bickerton, C. (2016) *The European Union: A Citizen's Guide* (London: Pelican)

De Grauwe, P. (2016) *Economics of Monetary Union* (10th edn, Oxford: Oxford University Press)

Dunton, I. (2017) *Brexit: What the Hell Happens Now?* (Surrey: Canbury Press)

European Council (2017) The European Council (accessed 4 August 2017) **http://www.consilium.europa.eu/en/european-council**

Foxley, A. (2010) *Regional Trade Blocs: The Way to the Future?* (Washington, DC: Carnegie Endowment for International Peace) (accessed 4 August 2017) **http://carnegieendowment.org/files/regional_trade_blocs.pdf**

Guardian (2016) 'Hard Brexit will cost Treasury up to £66bn a year, ministers are told', 11 October (accessed November 2017) **https://www.theguardian.com/politics/2016/oct/11/hard-brexit-treasury-66bn-eu-single-market**

Jessop, B. (2017) 'The organic crisis of the British state: putting Brexit in its place', *Globalizations*, 14(1): 133–41

Chapter 14
What role for the public sector?

Paul Wetherly

Learning objectives

When you have completed this chapter, you will be able to:

- Define the **public sector** and explain its nature and scope.
- Explore the concept of the state as an 'economic actor' and understand why this is a subject of political controversy.
- Assess the concept of a public corporation and examine arguments for and against **nationalization** of business.
- Evaluate the concept of social or welfare rights and assess arguments for and against the **welfare state**.
- Examine challenges to the future of welfare states.

THEMES

The following themes of the book are especially relevant to this chapter

- **DIVERSITY** This chapter exemplifies the broad definition of business by analysing the role of the state or public sector as an economic actor.
- **INTERNAL/EXTERNAL** This chapter considers the claim that the public sector is characterized by a distinctive ethos of public service, in contrast with the profit motive of the private sector.
- **COMPLEXITY** The public sector is an important part of the business environment and makes an important contribution to the economy.
- **LOCAL TO GLOBAL** The size of the public sector varies between countries.
- **DYNAMIC** The role of the public sector in a capitalist economy is a focus of political controversy and ideological debate. Changes in government and the prevailing ideology have been reflected in shifts in the nature and size of the public sector.
- **INTERACTION** The public and private sectors are not separate but interconnected, e.g. through contractual arrangements.
- **VALUES** The debate about the role of the public sector reflects competing values and alternative models of capitalism.

Introduction

DIVERSITY This chapter will focus on the state as an economic actor and the public sector of the economy. Although the essential role of government or the state can be seen as the exercise of authority (see Chapter 4), we encounter the state not just as a law-enforcer but also as a provider of a range of goods and services. Today, according to Kay:

> we look to government to secure the provision of education and a transport infrastructure, to guarantee us medical treatment and security in old age, to organise the collection of rubbish and assure unfailing supplies of electricity. The main role of government today is in the provision of goods and services, rather than the exercise of authority.
>
> (2004: 75)

In a democracy the members of society use the state to make and enforce rules, provide some goods and services, and decide who should pay for these functions through the tax system. Clearly, just as the exercise of authority is often controversial because it impinges on individuals' freedoms, the provision of goods and services by the state is also controversial because it involves using resources for purposes that individuals might not otherwise choose—having to pay a portion of their income as tax to finance public services which they might prefer to retain in order to finance private consumption. Indeed, Kay claims that 'it is the delivery of goods and services by the public sector, not the private sector, which is at the centre of political debate today' (2004: 76). We will examine this debate in the chapter.

DIVERSITY The provision of goods and services involves the state as an economic actor or, we might say, performing the role of business. Thus government (the public sector), the market (private sector), and voluntary organizations (third sector) constitute alternative mechanisms for allocating resources, that is, for deciding what is produced with the resources available to society, how it is produced, and for whom (see Chapters 1 and 2). The collection of rubbish, to take one of the examples given by Kay, can be organized as a public service funded by taxation, as a service provided by profit-making firms for paying customers in a market, as a voluntary service provided by charities, or even through a combination of these mechanisms. The same can be said for medical treatment and security in old age, including adult social care.

INTERACTION In the UK, the collection of rubbish from private households is organized as a public service, financed through taxation, and organized by local councils. Households do not have to pay private companies to empty their bins, or rely on the efforts of voluntary organizations. Yet the bin lorry is likely to be owned by a private company which employs the 'bin men'. Rubbish collection is a public service but the taxes that pay for it are used to hire a private company which provides the service for profit. Adult social care, apart from the importance of household production, is managed by local authorities in England, but most services are commissioned (i.e. bought in) from the private and voluntary sectors. 'Local authorities typically only pay for individual packages of care for adults assessed as having high needs and limited means', and 'many adults pay for some or all of their formal care services' (National Audit Office 2014).

These examples illustrate the difficulty of defining the public sector and distinguishing it clearly from the private sector. How do we define the public sector?

What is the public sector?

According to the OECD 'The public sector comprises the general government sector plus all public corporations including the central bank' (2014). 'General government' refers to central and local government. Similarly, the International Monetary Fund states that 'The public sector is comprised of 'general government'—central and local governments . . .—and all public corporations' (IMF 2009). Thus, there are different types of organizations within the public sector, the difference being that a public corporation is a 'market body' that is controlled by central or local government but has substantial day-to-day operating independence. A market body is an organization 'that derives more than 50% of its production cost from the sale of goods or services' (i.e. it operates in a market environment) (HM Treasury 2016: 105). General government organizations are not market bodies. For example, the BBC (British Broadcasting Corporation) is not, in spite of its name, a public corporation since it does not sell services in the market, but is part of general government. 'However, its commercial arm, BBC Worldwide, does sell services, and is therefore a public corporation' (Institute for Fiscal Studies 2014: 5–6). Another example of a public corporation is London Underground Ltd.

DIVERSITY The public sector comprises a vast and complex set of organizations, there being nearly 4,000 public sector bodies, of which more than 1,500 are in general government (825 in central government and 737 in local government) (Office for National Statistics 2017). More than half of public sector bodies are public corporations but, as we will see shortly, public corporations now constitute a relatively small part of the public sector in the UK by employment due to **privatizations** since the 1980s.

In contrast with the public sector, 'The private sector comprises households, private corporations, and privately-owned nonprofit organizations' (IMF 2009). Everything that is not in the public sector is by definition in the private sector (thus it includes what is often defined separately as the 'third sector'—see Table 14.1).

To clarify the scope of the public sector further, let's return to the example of rubbish collection which, as stated earlier, is organized as a public service—it is financed through taxation, organized by local councils, but ownership is in the hands of private contractors. Here we can see that there are three potential criteria for including an organization or service within the public sector: financing, control, and ownership. The difficulty is that, as shown by the example of rubbish collection, these criteria do not always go together—in this case we have public funding and control together with private ownership. We could conclude that rubbish collection is semi-public and semi-private, but in official statistics everything is either public or private. This requires a strict definitional criterion. For this purpose, 'the difference between the public and private sector is determined by where control lies, rather than by ownership or whether or not the entity is publicly financed' (Office for National Statistics, in Institute for Fiscal Studies 2014: 4).

Table 14.1 The distinction between the public and private sectors

Public sector	Private sector		
'general government' (central and local governments) and all public corporations	households	private corporations	privately owned non-profit organizations

Source: Derived from IMF 2009.

VALUES Control matters because it is about being able to make things happen and therefore to decide on what basis a service is provided, and who benefits. For example, public support for the National Health Service (NHS) in the UK is based on the preference for central government control to ensure that access to healthcare is based on the principle of equal treatment for equal need.

Thus, the public sector comprises all activities that are controlled by government, in contrast to those that are undertaken in the private sector by households, businesses, and non-profit organizations outside of government control. Another way of making this distinction is in terms of public or collective decisions or choices as opposed to private or individual ones. In other words, the public sector consists of those activities which society has decided to control collectively through government rather than leave to individuals. For example, as a public sector activity, we have chosen to finance rubbish collection together through the tax system and to make decisions about the way the service is run as a community through our elected representatives in local government. Is this a good arrangement? How should we decide, more generally, which activities should be public or private? The answers to these questions are contested. We will examine arguments for and against the state later in the chapter, but first we need to have an understanding of the size of the public sector and what it does.

Getting the measure of the public sector–size and functions

The size of the public sector can be measured in terms of employment and spending. To get an idea of the importance of the public sector in the whole economy it is useful to look at measures of employment and spending not only in absolute but also in relative terms, as shares of total employment and output (GDP). We can also get a better idea of what the public sector does by breaking down employment and spending into the main spending areas or functions.

Public sector employment

The public sector constitutes a small but significant part of the UK economy in terms of employment. In September 2016 total UK public sector employment stood at 5.442 million (17.17 per cent of total employment), compared to 26.32 million in the private sector (82.83 per cent) (Office for National Statistics 2016b). Table 14.2 shows that almost all public sector employment is in the 'general government' sector (central and local), with only one in eighteen (5.7 per cent) employed in public corporations.

Table 14.2 Public sector employment, September 2016

	Millions	% of total public sector **% of total employment**
Local government	2.18	40.1
Central government	2.95	54.2
Public corporations	0.312	5.7
Total public sector	**5.442**	**100/17.17**
Total private sector	**26.32**	**82.83**
Total employment	**31.762**	**100**

Source: Office for National Statistics 2016b.

DYNAMIC Public sector employment in September 2016 was a lower share of total employment than in the recent past, having fallen from a peak of 6.44 million in 2009, a decline of nearly one million or nearly one in six (15.5 per cent) of the public sector workforce (Office for National Statistics 2016b). This fall reflects the policies of 'austerity' that have been implemented by UK governments since 2010, involving cuts to public spending and employment. This overall decline conceals contrasting trajectories in central and local government: employment in the former has risen slightly while it has fallen sharply in the latter (Office for National Statistics 2016b). This largely reflects the burden of austerity falling mainly on local government, while some areas of central government, notably the NHS, have been relatively protected.

DYNAMIC VALUES Putting this decline in a wider historical context, public sector employment has fluctuated over the period since the Second World War (i.e. post-1945), reflecting changing social and economic circumstances and ideological shifts brought about by changes of government. The post-war period can be divided into four phases.

- The first phase, up to the end of the 1970s, was one of growth of the state in the UK. The public sector workforce expanded under successive Labour and Conservative governments, reflecting both a bi-partisan commitment to a more interventionist role for government in social and economic life, particularly through expansion of the welfare state, and a sustained period of economic growth generating rising tax revenues. Public sector employment increased from 5.9 million in 1961 to a peak of 7.4 million in 1979, with this growth mainly accounted for by general government.
- In the second phase, during the 1980s and through to the late 1990s, public sector employment fell under Conservative governments committed to 'rolling back the state' against the background of deteriorating economic performance, including a major recession during the 1970s. The fall in public sector employment in the 1980s was largely due to the privatization of state owned industries (public corporations) which shifted jobs from the public to the private sector. By 1998/9 public sector employment had fallen to 5.4 million.
- From this point and through the 2000s, the third phase, public sector employment expanded again under a 'New Labour' government in the context of a buoyant economy to reach a peak of 6.1 million in 2010, though not regaining the peak of the 1970s.
- In the fourth phase from 2010, in the aftermath of the global economic crisis (GEC), the size of the public sector workforce has again fallen as a result of austerity, as already noted. Looking ahead, further cuts to the public sector workforce have been forecast by 2018–19 that 'would take the share of the workforce working in general government to just 14.8%, compared with 19–20% during the late 1990s and 2000s' (Institute for Fiscal Studies 2014: 2).

Composition of the public sector workforce

The public sector workforce is concentrated in three main industries which together accounted for about 75 per cent of all employment in 2016: the NHS (1.59 million, 29 per cent), education (1.525 million, 28 per cent), and public administration (1.002 million, 18 per cent). We can see from these data that the welfare state looms large in public sector employment, with two of the main areas of welfare provision—health and education—together accounting for 57 per cent of the total (Office for National Statistics 2016b). This reflects the fact that these were the principal growth areas during the periods of expansion of public sector employment in the 1960s and 1970s and again in the 2000s, and that they have tended to be relatively protected during periods of falling public sector employment in the 1980s and since 2010 (Institute for Fiscal

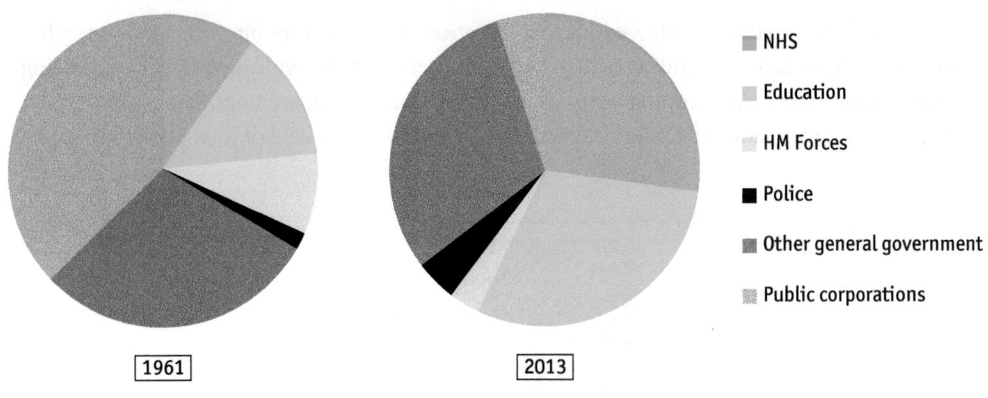

Figure 14.1 Proportion of public sector workforce in each area, 1961 and 2013

Source: Institute for Fiscal Studies 2014: 14, figures 3(a) and 3(b).

Table 14.3 Proportion of public sector workforce in selected areas, 1961 and 2013

	1961	2013
Education	14	30
NHS	10	27
Public corporations	37	5

Source: Institute for Fiscal Studies 2014: 14.

Studies 2014). Since the early 1960s, the NHS and education have accounted for a growing share of both total public sector employment and general government, as shown in Figure 14.1 and Table 14.3. While employment in public corporations has declined from 37 per cent to just 5 per cent, employment in education and the NHS combined has increased from 24 per cent to 57 per cent.

Thus, when looking at changes in the composition of the public sector workforce, 'the most important long-run trend seems to be the increasing dominance of the education and NHS workforces' (Institute for Fiscal Studies 2014: 14).

Public spending

In 2016–17 the UK government was expected by the independent Office for Budget Responsibility (OBR) to spend almost £780 billion (Office for Budget Responsibility 2016). To make this large number more meaningful, it is equivalent to 39.9 per cent of national income, which means that public spending accounts for £4 out of every £10 of income received by the UK population. It is also equivalent to £28,000 per household in the UK. To help to make sense of this number, 'In the financial year 2014/15 median household income was £25,660' (Office for National Statistics 2016a), which means that this was the income of the household at the halfway point if all households were ranked from the poorest to the richest. Thus, when we use spending as a measure of the size of the public sector it accounts for a larger part of the economy than when employment is used—around 40 per cent in contrast to approximately 20 per cent.

Composition of public spending

Cash transfer payments in the form of state pensions, tax credits, and 'other welfare payments' account for 28 per cent of all public sector spending (Figure 14.2 and Table 14.4). Central government departments—health, education, defence, and 'other public services'—together account for 40.5 per cent of spending, with health (14.7 per cent) and education (7 per cent) being the biggest departments in spending terms as well as in terms of employment. Thus, welfare payments (social security) and public services account for nearly 70 per cent of total public spending.

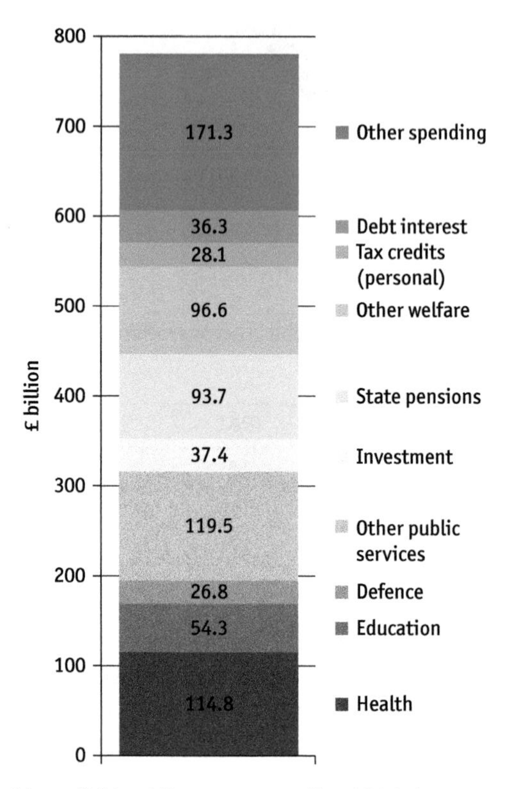

Figure 14.2 The composition of UK public sector spending 2016–17

Source: Office for Budget Responsibility 2016: 4.

Table 14.4 The composition of UK public sector spending 2016–17 (% of total)

Other spending	**22**
Debt interest	**4.7**
Tax credits (personal)	3.6
Other welfare	12.4
State pensions	12
Total welfare (tax credits (personal), other welfare, state pensions)	**28**
Investment	**4.8**
Other public services	15.3
Defence	3.4
Education	7.0
Health	14.7
Total public services (other public services, defence, education, health)	**40.5**
Total	**100.0**

Source: Office for Budget Responsibility 2016: 4.

DYNAMIC These data provide a 'snapshot' of public spending for one year. Figure 14.3 puts this in a long-run perspective, depicting general government expenditure (i.e. excluding public corporations) as a share of national income over the course of the twentieth century. It shows a long-run increase in public spending as a share of the economy from around 10 per cent at the start of the last century to around 40 per cent by its end. This growth of the state constitutes one of the main processes of social and economic transformation during the century.

Within this long-run trend, Figure 14.3 shows short-run fluctuations. Most obvious are the spikes in public spending associated with the two world wars (1914–18 and 1939–45). It can be seen that after each war public spending fell back but to a higher level than before the war. During the period since the Second World War (post-1945) public spending fluctuated as a percentage of the economy between the low 30s and the high 40s within a rising trend.

Figure 14.4 shows total public spending (including public corporations) during the post-war period and projections up until 2020–1. It shows a rise of public spending in the 2000s

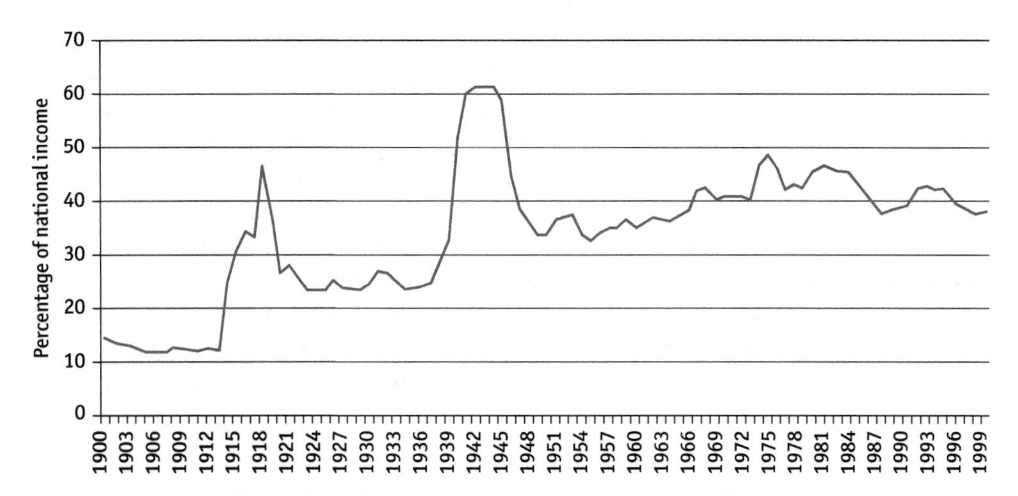

Figure 14.3 UK general government expenditure as a share of national income, 1900–99

Source: Institute for Fiscal Studies 2009.

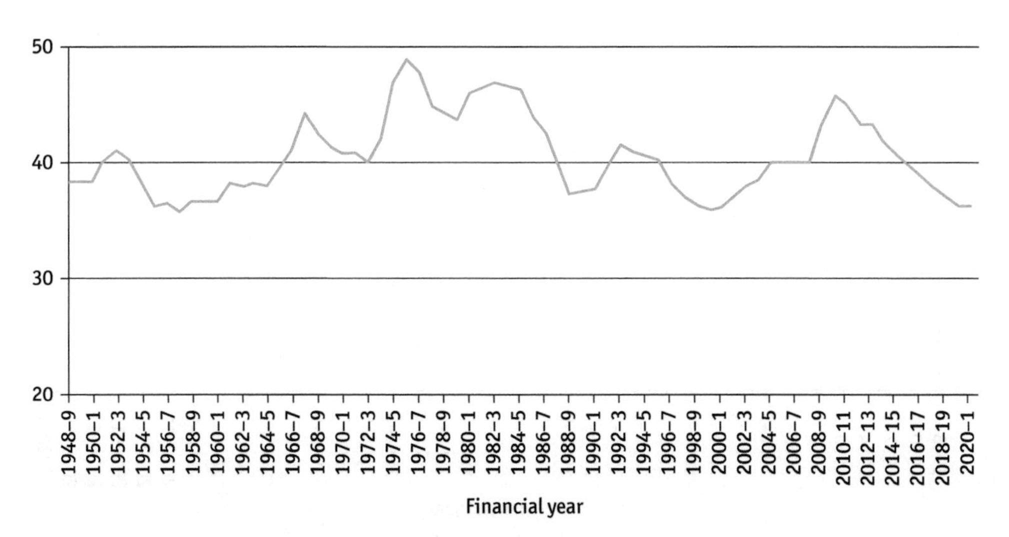

Figure 14.4 Total UK public spending (total managed expenditure) as a share of national income, 1948–9 to 2020–1 (%)

Source: Institute for Fiscal Studies 2015a: figure 1b.

followed by a sharp fall from 2009–10 which is projected to continue through to 2020–1, bringing public spending back down to the share at the beginning of this century.

Figure 14.5 shows that the fluctuations in public spending when measured as a share of national income conceal a fairly steady increase in real terms (i.e. in cash terms adjusted for inflation) over the sixty-year period from 1948–9 to 2008–9, after which it more or less levelled off.

'Between 1948–49 and 2008–09 the average annual real increase in TME has been 3.4 per cent' (Institute for Fiscal Studies 2009: 4). During this period the average annual rate of growth of public spending was higher than the rate of growth of the economy (GDP), hence public spending increased as a *share* of national income. How can we account for the short-run fluctuations in the share of public spending as a share of national income? Aside from the exceptional periods of the two world wars, there are two main factors: attitudes to public spending by the party in government (ideology—see Chapter 4), and the performance of the economy (economic cycle). Public spending as a share of the economy tends to fluctuate with the economic cycle of growth and recession. 'Real GDP has grown considerably since the end of the Second World War. The quantity of goods and services produced in the economy [in 2012 was] . . . approximately four times larger than in 1948' (Office for National Statistics 2013). This has resulted from an average annual growth of GDP of 2.6 per cent. However, the average conceals year-on-year fluctuations in the rate of growth and periods of recession when national income has declined. After sustained (though variable) year-on-year economic growth between the late 1940s and early 1970s, there were recessions in the UK economy in the mid 1970s, early 1980s, early 1990s, and the late 2000s. Figure 14.4 shows that increases in public spending as a share of national income have corresponded with these periods. That is because when national income falls a given *level* of public spending represents an increased *share* of the smaller economy. In addition, there are upward pressures on some elements of public spending, notably spending on benefits due to an increase in unemployment. Conversely, we might expect public spending to fall as a share

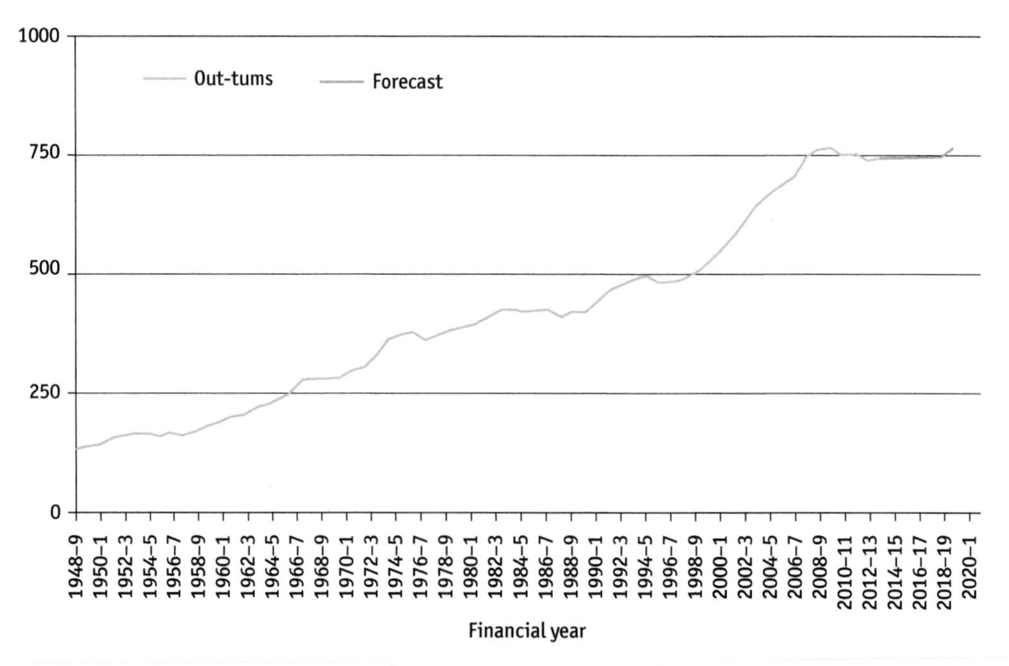

Figure 14.5 Total UK public spending (total managed expenditure) in real terms, 1948–9 to 2020–1 (£ billion, 2015–16 prices)

Source: Institute for Fiscal Studies 2015a: figure 1a.

of national income when the economy is growing, and Figure 14.4 shows this association during the periods of economic growth in the late 1980s and late 1990s (Institute for Fiscal Studies 2009: 4).

VALUES However, ideology is also an important factor since it involves ideas about the desirable size of the state and therefore guides political decisions about public spending in both phases of the economic cycle—growth and recession. For example, recession tends to create a deficit in the public finances as a result of tax revenue falling at the same time as some components of spending are increasing. In these circumstances ideology will guide the policy response: whether to try to reduce the deficit and 'balance the books' through public spending cuts, or allow the deficit to grow and even increase public spending in order to sustain or increase aggregate demand (see Chapter 9). In Figure 14.4 three periods can be identified which show the effects of ideology in favour of increasing or decreasing public spending. In the post-war period from the mid 1950s up to the early 1970s and again in the 2000s public spending increased as a share of a growing economy, in contrast with the late 1980s and late 1990s. The post-war decades were characterized by a broad consensus between the two governing parties (Labour and Conservative) concerning the desirability of a mixed economy and increased spending on the welfare state. In the 2000s, under a 'New Labour' government (1997–2010), public spending accelerated, with notable increases in spending on health and education. 'Total spending . . . increas[ed] at an average annual rate of 4.3 per cent between 1999–2000 and 2009–10' (Institute for Fiscal Studies 2015a: 2). In between these two periods of growth of the state, from the mid 1970s until the end of the century, public spending fell as a share of national income (though with increases associated with the recessions in the early 1980s and 1990s, as already noted). This can be seen to reflect an ideological shift away from the post-war consensus in favour of 'rolling back the state', particularly under successive Conservative governments (1979–97).

The UK in an international context

LOCAL TO GLOBAL How does the UK compare to other economies? Is public spending in the UK high by international standards? International comparisons of public spending give us a rough idea of how big government is in different countries.

VALUES Figure 14.6 shows public spending as a share of national income in thirty-one members of the Organisation for Economic Co-operation and Development (OECD), which is an association of developed countries (the OECD uses a slightly different measure of public spending). Figure 14.6 shows that the range of choices about public spending as a share of national income is substantial: from 31.5 per cent (Korea) to 58.7 per cent (Finland). We can also see that the UK is a mid-table country in these terms, in 14th position, not a particularly high or low spender at 44 per cent.

Figure 14.6 provides a snapshot, but Figure 14.7 compares the UK with six other rich countries over time. We can see how the position of the UK in this 'mini-league' has changed. In 2000 the UK was at the bottom but had moved up to third by the end of the 2000s. This was the result of the increase in public spending under 'New Labour' that we have already referred to, and, between 2007 and 2009, a rapid increase as a result of the recession following the financial crisis. The increase in public spending as a share of national income between 2007 and 2009 in the UK (6.8 per cent) was higher than any of the countries shown (Institute for Fiscal Studies 2015b). Thus, the UK would occupy a lower place in the international league table if not for the more severe impact of the recession.

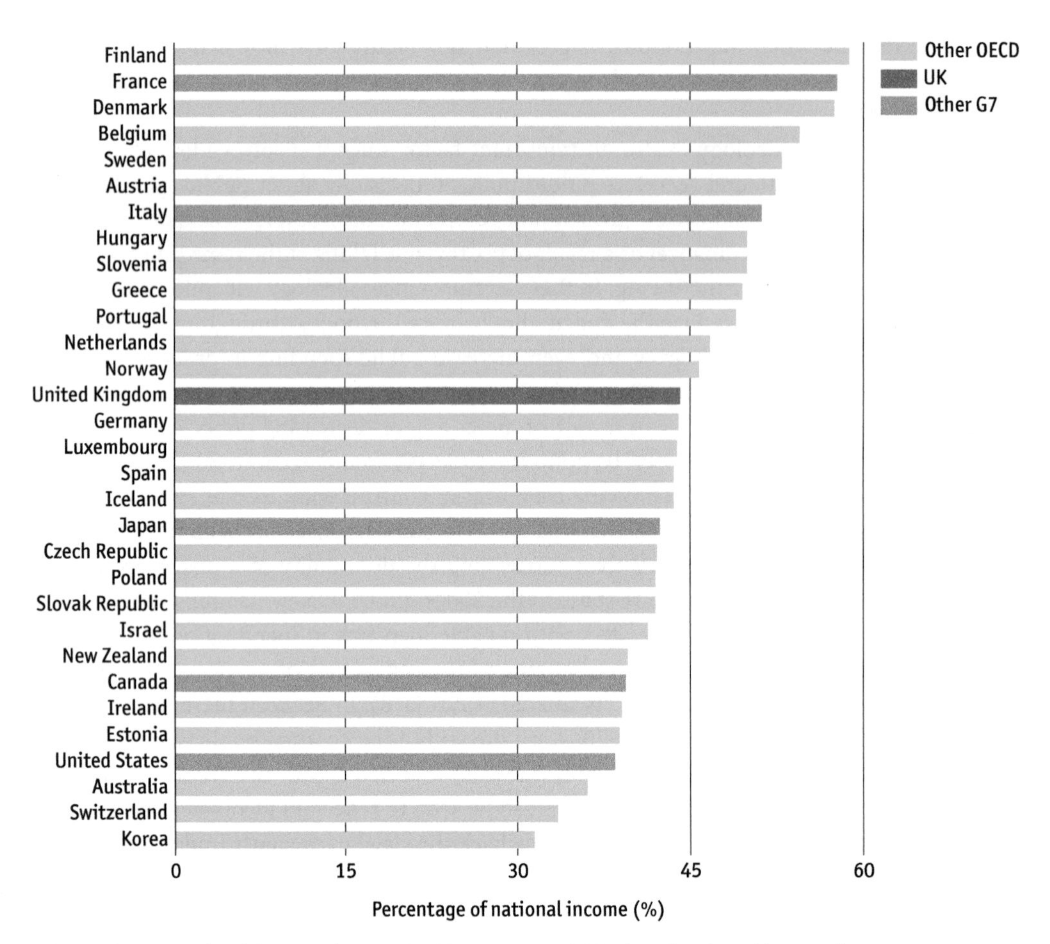

Figure 14.6 Total public spending in OECD countries, 2014 (% of national income)
Source: Institute for Fiscal Studies 2015b: figure 1 (using OECD data).

Comparing total public spending as a share of national income provides only a superficial indication of the different choices made by countries, for it does not tell us about public spending priorities—what the money is spent on. As we have seen, health accounts for a sizeable proportion of UK public spending, but how does the UK compare with other countries in this area? (See Mini-Case 14.1.)

International comparisons are important because they give us an idea of the different choices that countries make about the role of government and the balance between the public and private sectors. And awareness of these differences between countries can inform the choice within any particular country. For example, the claim that public spending is too high (or too low) in the UK might be responded to by pointing out that it is lower (or higher) in other comparable countries.

VALUES Of course, such comparisons cannot tell us what the 'right' choice is. Some people might say that we should aim to be towards the bottom of an international league table of public spending (or employment), while others would aspire to be near the top. Our choice will depend on our values and our beliefs about the effectiveness of government: what kind of society do we want to live in? And how effective is the public sector in creating such a society? These are questions of ideology, contesting the role of the public sector.

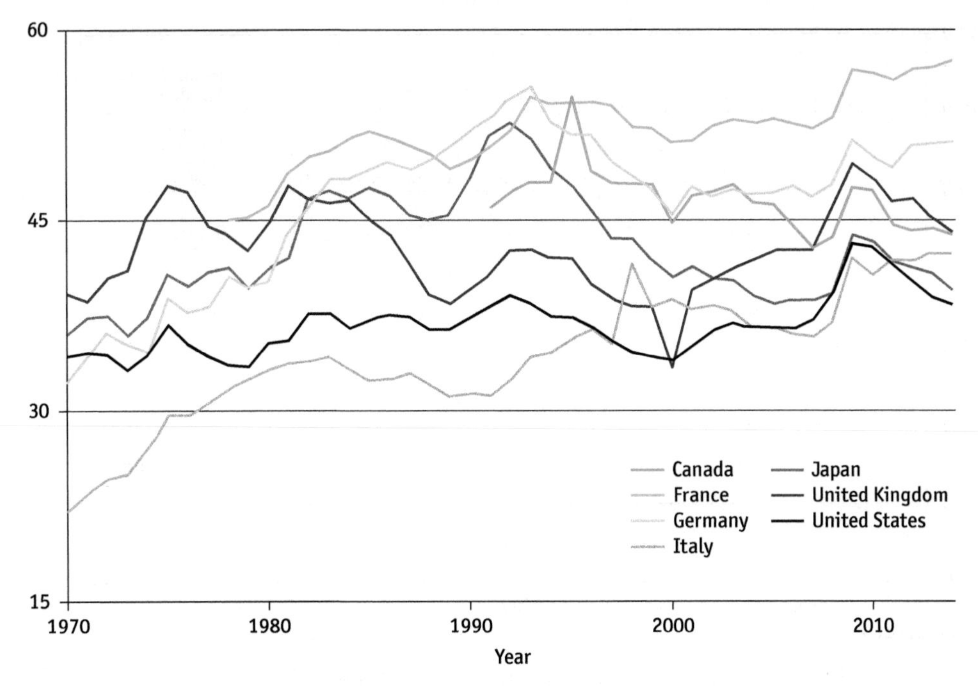

Figure 14.7 Total public spending as a share of national income in selected countries, 1970–2014
Source: Institute for Fiscal Studies 2015b: figure 2 (using OECD data).

Mini-Case 14.1 UK spending on health compared to other countries

VALUES The share of national income devoted to spending on health varies between countries, and they also vary in the division of health spending between the public and private sectors. In other words, they have different models of healthcare.

Figure 14.8 shows that, with the exception of the US, the G7 group of rich countries devote roughly 9–11 per cent of their national income to healthcare, and most of this is 'government/compulsory' spending (i.e. government-financed expenditure

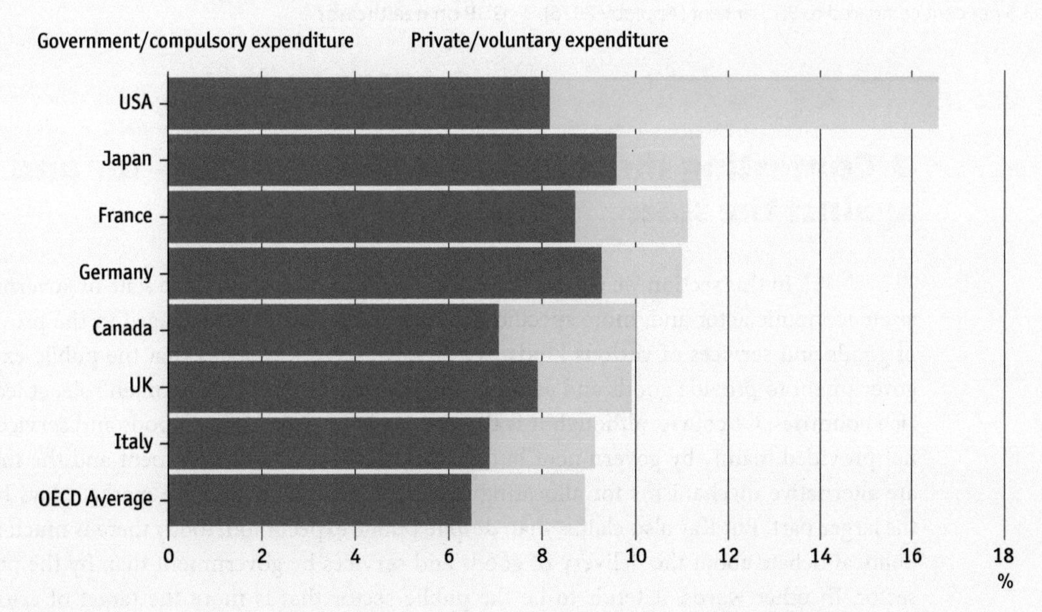

Figure 14.8 Current healthcare expenditure as a percentage of GDP for G7 countries, 2014
Source: Office for National Statistics 2016c.

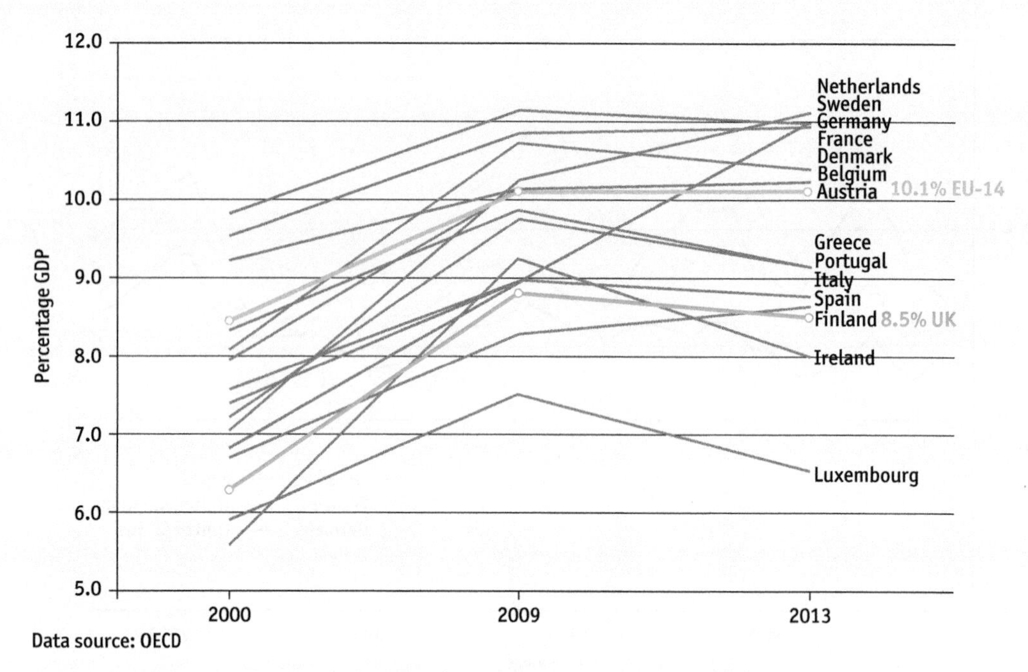

Figure 14.9 Total healthcare spending (public and private) as a share of GDP
Source: Appleby 2016.

and compulsory insurance). In contrast, the US devotes a much higher share of GDP to healthcare and about half of this is 'private/voluntary' spending. Among the G7 only Italy has lower spending on healthcare as a share of GDP than the UK. Figure 14.8 shows that all the G7 countries are above the OECD average. However, if the US is excluded as an outlier that distorts the average, total healthcare spending as a share of GDP in the UK is lower than the OECD average in 2013–8.5 per cent compared to 9.1 per cent (Appleby 2016). The UK is also below the EU14 average of 10.1 per cent of national income, and quite far behind the highest spending EU states (Netherlands, Sweden, Germany, France), as shown in Figure 14.9. Thus 'it's clear the UK is currently a relatively low spender on health care' (Appleby 2016).

Question

Do you think that the UK spends a large enough share of GDP on healthcare?

Contesting the role of the public sector—for and against the state

VALUES In this section we will focus on arguments for and against the state or government as an economic actor and, more specifically, as an owner-producer engaged in the provision of goods and services of various kinds. As we have seen, Kay states that the public expects government to provide goods and services and that this has become its main role, at least in rich countries. Of course, although it is the main role of government, goods and services are not provided mainly by government but by the private sector. Government and the market are alternative mechanisms for allocating resources between which the market plays by far the larger part. But Kay also claims that, despite public expectation, today there is much more political debate about the delivery of goods and services by government than by the private sector. In other words, it tends to be the public sector that is more the target of criticism than the private sector in political debate. We will examine this debate in this section and see whether this claim is justified. The debate is broadly about the best mix of government and the private sector—when is it better to leave the provision of goods and services to the market and the private sector, and when is it better for government to step in as an economic actor?

There is a very long history of states taking charge of the production of some goods and services, notably in relation to the basic tasks of government to ensure order and security. It is conventional political wisdom that the first duty of government is to protect its citizens from threats to their lives and property. Thus, even most advocates of minimal government accept that the state has a responsibility to provide a police force and armed services. We all benefit from these services provided by the state which secure the basic conditions in which people can get on with their lives and which, it is generally accepted, cannot be left to the private sector.

But much more controversial than the responsibility of government to protect its citizens is when the government steps in as an economic actor on a much wider front and which takes two forms: the creation of public corporations, and provision by government of a range of goods and services which make up the 'welfare state' (part of 'general government'). Among the goods and services mentioned by Kay, the supply of electricity was the responsibility of a public corporation before privatization in the 1980s, while others are conventionally included in the welfare state—education, medical treatment, and security in old age (i.e. pensions). The basic difference, as we have seen, is that public corporations are market bodies whose funding mainly comes from the sale of goods and services, whereas the public services that constitute the welfare state do not operate in a market environment. But in both cases government takes over the responsibility of providing goods and services rather than leaving it to private sector businesses.

The market versus the state: the ideological contest

VALUES In the twentieth century, arguments about the role of government as an economic actor and the relative advantages of the public sector compared to the private sector were bound up with the ideological contest between liberalism and socialism as rival accounts of the nature of capitalism and alternative visions of the good society. 'Differing attitudes to the question of state and economy have . . . helped to define what is probably the single most important cleavage in political opinion of the past 200 years' (Pierson 2011: 81). In essence, socialism is an anti-capitalist ideology that views the systemic flaws of capitalism as so serious that nothing less than its replacement by an entirely different economic system is required. In this view the basic problem with capitalism is that the private ownership of business creates a class-divided society in which there is a conflict of interest between the class of owners and managers of business (capitalists) and the class of workers. Profits are a form of unearned income derived from the workforce adding more value to output than is returned to them in wages—'reaping without sowing'. The capitalist labour market produces large inequalities not only between workers and capitalists but also between different occupations, with poverty at the bottom end due to low pay and unemployment. Private ownership involves a form of unaccountable economic power: workers have little say or control in the workplace, and private firms make investment and other decisions that are highly consequential for society without being effectively accountable to the people. There are other problems too, such as capitalism's tendency to develop through a pattern of boom and slump. Capitalism is thus seen as an intrinsically unjust, unstable, and undemocratic system. Because private ownership of business is the basic problem, the socialist alternative involves replacing this with some form of social or public ownership. This can take a number of forms but typically involves ownership and control by government. Thus, in its most radical form, socialism envisages replacing private ownership and markets with public ownership and economic planning.

On the other hand, liberalism is in essence a pro-capitalist ideology. (Before going further, it is important to clear up the confusion that arises from political labels in both the UK and the US. In both cases the label 'conservative' tends to be used to refer to people whose economic beliefs and principles are basically liberal. For example, the Conservative Party in Britain has since the 1970s embraced a strand of liberal thought that is often referred to as 'neoliberal'. Similarly, in the US, Republicans who advocate liberal ideas tend to be described as 'conservative', while the label 'liberal' is often attached to beliefs and principles that are more socialist.) Whereas socialism emphasizes equality as its prime value, liberalism emphasizes freedom and individualism. In this view the good society is one in which individuals decide for themselves how to live their own lives but are also self-reliant. This aligns with support for the market because it is seen as a system of voluntary exchange in which individuals make choices about how to use their own resources. Competition and the profit motive lead firms to strive to improve efficiency, to develop new products and services, and to be highly customer-focused. This accountability to consumers—'consumer sovereignty'—works well to ensure that although firms are motivated by self-interest (profit) they act in the common interest. Thus, the key virtues of markets are freedom, innovation, and efficiency. In its most radical form of neoliberalism, sometimes referred to as 'market fundamentalism', a pure form of free market capitalism is advocated with a minimal role for the state as a kind of 'night watchman' that focuses on a few key tasks to enable markets to function such as ensuring law and order, property rights, and the enforcement of contracts.

These two ideological positions are important because they continue to frame debate about the role of government and the private sector in the good society. Socialism sets out the criticisms of markets in their strongest form, while liberalism provides the strongest advocacy of markets. To put it simply, whereas socialists look to the state to replace the fundamentally flawed market, for neoliberals 'government is the problem, not the solution'. However, in between these two positions there is a range of arguments that reject free markets or a state-run economy and look for ways to mix the public and private sectors. In place of the general views that either the private sector or the public sector is 'good' or 'bad' this involves a more case-by-case assessment. Rather than a dichotomy—liberalism versus socialism, the market versus the state—there is a spectrum of views contesting the balance or mix of public and private. In practice, since the Second World War (i.e. post-1945) political debate in western societies, with national variants, has involved a spectrum from more limited versions of socialism, that seek to reform what would remain a largely capitalist economic system through a greater role for the state, to neoliberalism, which was a reaction against this reform agenda and sought to roll back the state (see Chapter 4). Although there are differences between European countries, the European 'social model' is often contrasted with the more liberal model adopted in the US. In the post-war decades through to the 1970s Britain adopted a version of the European social model often referred to as the Keynesian–welfare consensus. This combined Keynesian policies of economic management, the welfare state, and a mixed economy including a substantial element of 'nationalized' industries. After the 1970s this consensus broke down and neoliberal ideas have been dominant.

Stop and Think

What are the main points of difference between liberalism and socialism in their view of the role of the public sector?

Nationalization, denationalization, renationalization? Arguments over the mixed economy

DYNAMIC Public ownership of business has come back on to the political agenda in recent years. In the 2017 UK general election campaign the Labour Party under the leadership of Jeremy Corbyn made a commitment to 'renationalize' the railways, water companies, and the post office and to establish regional energy companies under public ownership. Public ownership had been part of the post-war consensus championed by the Labour Party but, starting in the 1980s, returning nationalized industries to the private sector (privatization or **denationalization**) became a key element of the neoliberal agenda to 'roll back the state'. In Britain most of the nationalized industries were privatized between 1979 and 1997 under successive Conservative governments. This pattern—advance of public ownership in the post-war decades followed by retreat from the 1980s—can be seen in other European states, though with national variations in scale and timing. Indeed, 'privatisation . . . has been a world-wide phenomenon' (Pierson 2011: 85). Britain was a privatization pioneer—by 1997 the UK was at the bottom of the league of EU15 states in terms of 'public undertakings' as a share of the overall economy, at less than 3 per cent compared to an EU average of 10 per cent and more than 14 per cent in Italy, France, Greece, and Finland (European Parliament 1997). Feeling that the tide had turned (and gone out a long way), the British Labour Party in the 1990s overturned its historic commitment to public ownership, including any renationalization of industries privatized by the Conservatives. So, what is the case for nationalization, and the opposing case for privatization?

Reasons for nationalization

'Nationalization' refers to the process of taking private sector businesses or industries into public or 'common' ownership. As we have seen, public ownership is a key element of socialism, involving as it does overturning the foundation of capitalism in the private ownership of business. The commitment to public ownership was proclaimed in clause IV of the constitution of the British Labour Party, adopted in 1918:

> To secure for the workers by hand or by brain the full fruits of their industry and the most equitable distribution thereof that may be possible upon the basis of the common ownership of the means of production, distribution, and exchange, and the best obtainable system of popular administration and control of each industry or service.
>
> (in Gani 2015)

This clause is often interpreted as a commitment to the aim of replacing capitalism with a socialist economic system in which all production is in the hands of the people through public ownership, enabling democratic planning ('popular administration') of the economy so as to achieve fairness or equality of living standards ('equitable distribution'). However, the Labour Party has never attempted to carry out such a wholesale economic transformation when in government, and it has not been attempted by any western government. Clause IV was repealed in the 1990s under the leadership of Tony Blair as part of the shift to 'New Labour'.

In considering the case for nationalization we can distinguish between the vision of the whole economy being organized on the basis of common ownership (the socialist ideal) and the case for specific measures of nationalization, creating a small but significant public sector within a mixed economy that remains predominantly capitalist. Such piecemeal measures might be seen as part of a strategy for the gradual transformation of capitalism (i.e. to be extended over time), but it is important to recognize that public ownership is not necessarily a socialist measure and that it can be supported for non-socialist reasons. Nationalization is not necessarily 'anti-business'. Thus, there are general reasons in favour of public ownership and specific considerations that are made on a case-by-case basis. The principal reasons for nationalization are as follows:

- enable democratic control of business and accountability to the public;
- transform the employment relationship and institute workers' control or industrial democracy;
- ensure universal access to essential services (public utilities);
- provide infrastructure;
- prevent abuse of market power by natural monopolies;
- enable control over industries deemed to be of strategic importance for the economy, and prevent foreign ownership; and
- rescue firms or industries in competitive difficulties or that are 'too big to fail'.

Of these, the first two are general reasons for public ownership related to socialist principles. The ideal of putting economic power into the hands of workers or the people applies in principle to any and all firms and industries. Socialist ideology motivated the major programme of nationalization undertaken by the post-war Labour government (1945–51)—the nationalized industries were to be run for the benefit of the people rather than the benefit of private owners. When the National Coal Board took control of the mines in 1947 signs put up at collieries stated that they were now 'run by the National Coal Board On Behalf of the People' (National Archives [no date]).

The other reasons are more case by case. Ensuring universal and fair access to essential services that meet people's basic needs can also be seen as reflecting a socialist argument that access cannot be left to be determined by ability to pay in the market since this would mean that people on low incomes would not be able to meet their basic needs. What counts as an essential service is open to some debate, but typically includes the 'public utilities' (gas, electricity, and water supply) and may include public transport and communications. The argument for public ownership in these cases is therefore akin to the argument for the welfare state. However, there can also be a business case in terms of providing an infrastructure vital to economic activity and competitiveness.

Public ownership can be justified on grounds of market failure (natural monopoly), or where an industry or firm is not economically competitive or viable and where the economic and social impact of allowing it to fail is deemed to be unacceptable. A natural monopoly exists where efficient supply cannot be organized on the basis of market competition. In other words, having a single supplier is the most efficient solution. But in private hands consumers are at risk of abuse of market power involving restricted output and higher prices. So in this case public ownership is a remedy for market failure (the inherent incapacity of the market to achieve socially desirable outcomes), and this case can be supported by economic liberals who advocate 'the market where possible, the state where necessary'. In other words, public ownership is seen as the exception to the norm of the private sector, in contrast with the socialist principle. However, the 'natural monopoly' (efficiency) and 'essential services' (fairness) arguments often go together. Thus, Hutton argues that the case for public ownership of companies should meet four tests: there has to be a natural monopoly, the good or service must be available to everyone because it is a necessity, there needs to be fair access, and there needs to be accountability to 'citizen consumers' to prevent abuse of market power (Hutton 2015: 147) For example, the rail network meets these tests—it is

> a natural monopoly (it is absurd to have more than one railway line between one destination and another); it must connect all major population centres; it must be fairly accessible; and to ensure legitimacy that the network is as safe and as modern as possible requires ongoing dialogue with citizen passengers.
>
> (Hutton 2015: 147)

On these grounds Hutton argues that there is a case for public ownership of 'all the country's varying national networks' (Hutton 2015: 147) such as 'the National grid, the mobile telephone network, the money transmission system, the optical fibre and fixed line telephone system, and the water collection, distribution and sewer system' (Hutton 2015: 148). Notice that public ownership of a network is consistent with private companies competing to supply services through the network. For example, in advocating public ownership of the rail network Hutton leaves open the question of whether the companies operating the trains on the network should be renationalized.

In theory markets encourage firms to be well managed and efficient in order to remain competitive and make profits. Markets work not by ensuring that all firms are well run but by eliminating those that are not. But sometimes the social and economic consequences of firms not being well managed and threatened with closure are judged to justify public ownership or other intervention. The post-war Labour government in the UK nationalized the coal mining industry in the face of deep financial problems and poor industrial relations. Rolls-Royce was nationalized by a Conservative government in 1971 to rescue it from financial difficulties. In 1975 a Labour government nationalized the car maker British Leyland in response to the company's failure to meet the challenge of growing international competition. Railtrack, the private company set up to manage the rail network as part of railway privatization in 1993, was effectively nationalized in 2002 after it became overburdened with debt.

Banks or other firms may be judged 'too big to fail' when bankruptcy would have catastrophic systemic consequences, for the financial system as a whole and the wider economy. This risk can justify state 'bailouts' (e.g. providing extra capital into the banking system) and public ownership of banks at risk of closure. The 'too big to fail' logic was expressed during the global financial crisis in the public commitment by the G-7 group of rich states in 2008 to 'take decisive action . . . to support systemically important financial institutions and prevent their failure' (in Wolf 2014: 27). In the UK the government carried out a £1 trillion bailout of the banks by 2009 and effectively took the Royal Bank of Scotland (RBS) and Lloyds HBOS into public ownership through large equity stakes (82 per cent and 43 per cent respectively) (Hutton 2015, Wolf 2014). Although there were arguments for retaining these banks in the public sector, public ownership was always intended as a temporary emergency measure with sales of the shares seen as getting the money back for tax payers. Indeed, the government sold all its shares in Lloyds in stages between 2013 and 2017 (Treanor 2017).

The turn to privatization

The return of Lloyds to the private sector was, from the government's point of view, a return to normality since nationalization had only been seen as a temporary fix to prevent closure and allow the bank to turn itself around. The government never took any operational control over the bank. For these reasons it might be argued that it was not a proper case of nationalization or, therefore, of privatization. In contrast the programme of privatizations pioneered in the UK and starting in the 1980s was not a return to normality but a break with what had come to be regarded as the normal 'mixed economy' character of modern capitalism. Indeed, the major programme of privatization that was to come was not set out in the Conservative

Party manifesto ahead of its victory in the 1979 general election that commenced the era of 'Thatcherism' or 'neoliberalism'. Privatization can be defined simply as 'the transfer of responsibility for an industry or the ownership of a company from the public to the private sector' (House of Commons Library 2014). What was the rationale for privatization?

In general terms privatization has to be seen as an integral part of a neoliberal agenda to disengage the state from the economy and, more broadly, roll back the state, including in relation to the welfare state. Privatization obviously involved a rejection of socialism and its motto was, in effect, 'private good, public bad'. In this sense it rejected the case-by-case appraisal of whether the public or private sector was preferable in favour of the assumption that markets are always better, even in the case of natural monopoly. Thus all nationalized industries were to be privatized. Within the context of this pro-market ideology, the principal reasons for privatization are as follows:

- to increase efficiency;
- to raise revenue through the proceeds of sales;
- to extend share ownership through sales of shares to members of the public;
- to weaken public sector unions;
- to expand opportunities for private sector businesses; and
- to increase electoral support.

Of these reasons, the first was generally stated as the most important—'the primary aim of the privatisation programme was to improve performance of the former state-owned industries' (Conservative Chancellor Nigel Lawson, in House of Commons Library 2014). The idea here is that the private sector is preferable to the public sector because the profit motive and competition incentivize continual improvements in efficiency. Whereas these incentives do not operate in the public sector and, it was argued, the methods of political control and accountability were ineffective. Worse, 'political interference by ministers in the running of nationalized industries had undermined their ability to take strategic decisions and operate efficiently' (House of Commons Library 2014). The aim of weakening public sector unions is also part of the efficiency argument. In the neoliberal view trade unions are seen as an obstacle to the efficient operation of markets because they can resist managerial attempts to respond to market conditions and maintain competitiveness. Hence tackling trade union power and restoring the 'right to manage' was a key aspect of the neoliberal agenda (but for a different view see Chapter 12). One of the problems of nationalization, in this view, was that it had created large and powerful public sector unions. Privatization could help to solve this problem because private sector employers would be less accommodating, and union members would no longer all be employed by the same firm on the same contract so bargaining and union power would be fragmented (House of Commons Library 2014).

The goal of extending share ownership was often characterized in terms of 'popular capitalism' and 'encouraging the "entrepreneurial society" in which individuals became actively engaged in the economy by taking ownership of key assets' (House of Commons Library 2014). It was claimed that, in contrast with nationalization, shares would give people real ownership. Against this, critics argued that owning a few shares would not give people any influence in the management of the businesses and, in any case, most shares sold to the public soon ended up with institutional shareholders as individuals sought to gain from short-term increases in the share price. The offer of shares to the public was expected to be popular with voters and therefore part of the Conservative Party's electoral strategy, just as Labour's commitment to limited measures of renationalization in 2017 was popular with the public. Just as nationalization is not necessarily anti-business, privatization is not necessarily pro-business. From a business point of view, the railway system, for example, is critical infrastructure so whether it is in public or private ownership ought to be a pragmatic judgement on the basis of the best way of ensuring that it is well managed. Similarly, if public ownership is more likely to ensure continuity of energy supplies than private ownership that is a key issue for business. However, privatization is clearly in the interests of those companies for whom it creates opportunities to take over profitable assets or bid for contracts. Thus, powerful business lobbies advocate privatization and expanding opportunities for private sector businesses can be seen as one of the motives (see Chapter 11).

We have seen that the efficiency argument is used on both sides of the debate. Privatizers argue that market incentives and motives provide the best assurance of well-managed businesses, but nationalizers can point to examples where the market does not induce the right behaviour, and in the worst case induces behaviour that can threaten the whole system (the financial crisis). It can be argued that the case of British Leyland provides ammunition for both sides. It was not well managed in the private sector and nationalization was necessary to avert the large-scale negative economic and social impacts of allowing it to close down, particularly large-scale job losses. But the firm did not fare well in the public sector, becoming 'one of the biggest disasters in the history of nationalisation' (Schifferes 2008). Privatization in the 1980s did not reverse the decline and the company was broken up and taken over. Today, although some of the brands remain (e.g. Mini), they are all under foreign ownership. Although making cars is still an important industry in Britain there is no British car maker.

In cases of natural monopoly, although privatization introduced some elements of competition, it has not been possible to create a normal competitive market environment and firms are able to exercise considerable market power. This meant that there was now a need for

> regulatory regimes and regulatory bodies to enforce acceptable market behaviour. For example Oftel was set up to regulate the new telecommunications industry when BT was privatised, and Ofgas was created when British Gas was privatised.
>
> (House of Commons Library 2014)

Hence privatization was meant to 'roll back' the state but meant that it also had to 'roll forward' through the creation of the 'regulatory state' (see Chapter 4).

Stop and Think

Nationalization is often seen as anti-business. Do you agree?

Social justice and the welfare state

STAKEHOLDERS In liberal democracies people are citizens with rights. Rights are closely bound up with the liberal ideal that people should be free to live as they choose so long as they don't harm other individuals. Thus, *civil* rights or liberties can be defined as 'The rights necessary for individual freedom—liberty of the person, freedom of speech, thought and faith, the right to own property and to conclude valid contracts, and the right to justice' (Marshall 1992). These rights protect citizens from interference by the state (e.g. censorship, banning trade unions or other voluntary associations, arbitrary arrest, or imprisonment without trial) and also create important conditions for markets to function (rights to own and exchange property). Civil rights also curb some market freedoms by protecting people from being discriminated against as customers or employees, on grounds of race, sex, and other protected characteristics (see Chapter 4). *Political* rights establish 'the right to participate in the exercise of political power' (Marshall 1992), particularly through the rights to vote and stand for election. A key aspect of citizenship is the idea of equal treatment—everybody has the same set of rights.

VALUES In this context the welfare state can be seen as another dimension of citizenship involving *social* (or welfare) rights. These rights are more controversial than civil and political rights, and in this section we will examine that controversy in relation to the state's role in a market economy. What is the welfare state? What is the rationale for welfare rights? The welfare state involves a particular conception of 'the state's responsibility to its citizens' (Begg et al. 2015: 4). This responsibility is captured in Lister's statement that 'The term "welfare state" refers . . . to those of the state's functions that promote the welfare and social protection of its members through a range of benefits and services' (2010: 18). Further, 'The idea of welfare rights . . . involves the idea of a just distribution of resources and, therefore, a correction of market outcomes' (Plant 1992: 16).

The idea of 'social protection' involves two aspects: that there are risks that are inherent in the operation of markets *and* that individuals cannot be left to bear these risks on their own. A market is a system of voluntary exchange and in a free market (without a welfare state) individuals would be free to use their own resources (property) to live as they choose, to enter into contracts with others (e.g. to earn a wage or salary), and their living standards would depend on their own efforts and choices—they would be free and self-reliant. This is essentially the neoliberal ideal. But, critics of this ideal argue, the problem is that individuals may face circumstances in which, through no fault of their own, they are unable to maintain a decent living standard through their own efforts or self-reliance. They would then no longer be free to live the life they choose in a meaningful sense if their lack of resources severely restricts the choices open to them. Therefore, they need protection against these risks, and this has to be the responsibility of the state on behalf of society. The market, left to its own devices, is not intrinsically fair and the correction of market outcomes by the state is necessary to create a just distribution of resources.

In his famous blueprint for the post-war welfare state—*Social Insurance and Allied Services* (1942)—Beveridge characterized these risks as 'five giant evils': want, ignorance, squalor, idleness, and disease (Marquand 2008: 107, Marquand and Seldon 1996). You are at risk of want if you are poor, at risk of ignorance, squalor, or disease if you are unable to gain access to education, decent housing, or adequate healthcare, and at risk of idleness if you cannot find a job. Thus, as defined by Lister, a broad Beveridgean conception of the welfare state involves a range of benefits and services to remedy these 'evils', coupled with macroeconomic policies to ensure full employment. These benefits, services, and policies are connected by the idea that these are all basic needs essential to individual well-being (welfare) and must be the responsibility of the state because if left to themselves in markets individuals might not be able to satisfy these needs. Individuals should not be left to 'sink or swim'. (This broad definition, used in this chapter, may be contrasted with a narrow use of the term 'welfare' to refer specifically to the system of cash benefits.)

LOCAL TO GLOBAL The development of welfare states was 'one of the most remarkable social transformations of the twentieth-century world' (Gamble 2016: 86). It was, however, a development that was restricted to the developed world, and Europe in particular. Although the origins of welfare states can be traced to earlier social reforms, they largely developed after the Second World War (post-1945). In the UK the structure of the post-war welfare state was created by the 1945–51 Labour government and became the basis for the Keynesian–welfare consensus (including the 'mixed economy') that endured until the 1970s. The development of the British welfare state can be seen as part of a European trend and, although there are differences between European states—different welfare regimes—it is possible to speak of a distinctive 'European social model'. Indeed, 'the values and norms that underpin the continent's social model are at the heart of what it means to be European' (Begg et al. 2015: 3). (The European 'social model' also includes legal protections such as employment rights, but in this chapter we are focusing primarily on the state as an owner-producer—see also Chapters 4 and 5.)

Stop and Think

Why are social rights an important part of citizenship? How is being a 'citizen' different from being a 'consumer'?

A welfare state entails commitment to a high level of public spending and a correspondingly high level of taxation. As countries grow richer they can afford to devote a higher share of their GDP to welfare spending, so social spending is generally a higher share of GDP in higher income countries. According to the Office for Budget Responsibility (OBR):

> in 2015–16 . . . [the UK public sector] spent around £486 billion (about 26 per cent of GDP) on the 'welfare state', broadly defined, including health, education, social services, public service pensions and housing, as well as social security and tax credits.
>
> (OBR 2017: 5)

Spending on the welfare state accounted for about 65 per cent of total public spending in that year. Figure 14.10 shows the breakdown of spending on the welfare state in the UK into its various components.

Figure 14.10 shows, in the second column, that the largest single component of the welfare state is welfare in the narrow sense of cash benefits (social security and tax credits), amounting to about 45 per cent of all spending on the welfare state. In other words, much welfare state spending involves the transfer of money between people in society—taking money in through taxes and paying it out in cash benefits or credits—to tackle want. The third and fourth columns give an idea of the range of risks that the benefits system protects against—loss of income due to unemployment, sickness, or retirement; additional needs arising from disability; being unable to afford to pay the rent; and incurring additional expenses to bring up children. Beveridge referred to this kind of system as providing 'cradle to grave' protection.

One way of thinking about the welfare state is as a 'piggy bank' (Begg et al. 2015: 7) which individuals pay into through the tax system and from which they draw in times of need. For example, individuals pay taxes during their working lives and then receive a state pension when they retire. However, this conception is misleading as a way of thinking about the welfare state in broad terms since individuals do not accumulate a personal fund—they do not get out what they have paid in. If they did the welfare state would not protect individuals who are unable to pay in very much because of low incomes. It is more accurate to say that in general all

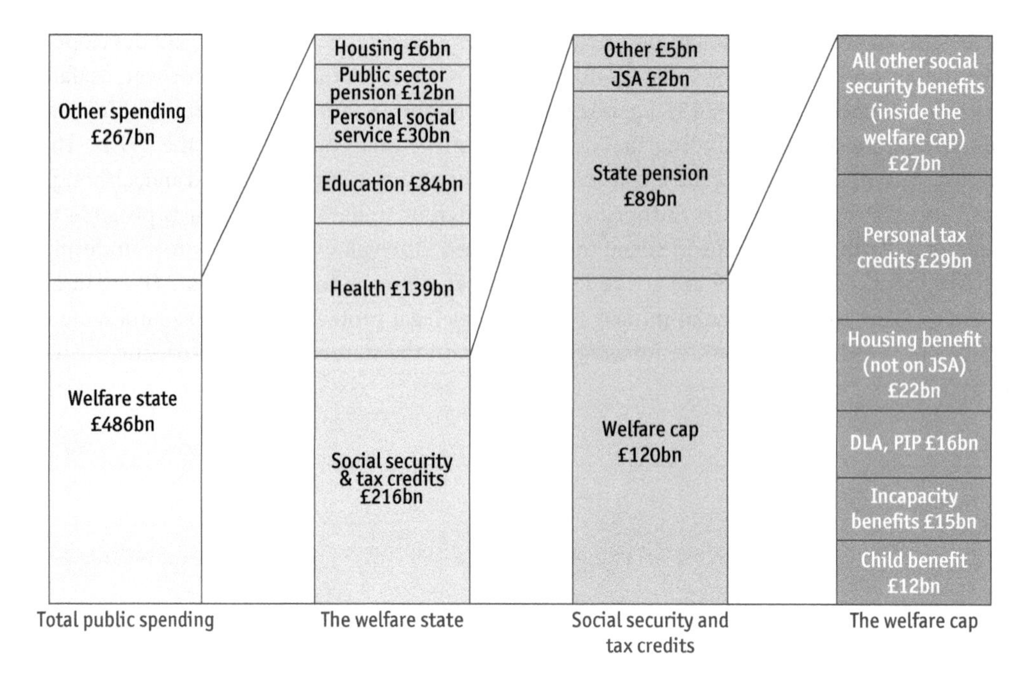

Figure 14.10 Welfare spending in the UK in 2015–16
Source: OBR 2017: 5.

individuals pay into a common fund and their rights to draw from the fund are determined not by what they have paid in but by their needs. For example, the NHS is based on the principle that treatment is free at the point of use (aside from means-tested prescription charges) and that all individuals are treated equally according to their needs. This means that some people will pay in more than they draw out and that, on the whole, this involves redistribution from those who are better-off to those who are less well-off. This 'Robin Hood' (Begg et al. 2015: 7) function of the welfare state depends on how progressive the tax system is overall, and the share of services and benefits received by different income groups. For example, the better-off enjoy greater life expectancy on average than the poor and therefore enjoy greater benefit from the state pension.

VALUES Clearly then, the welfare state has, ideally, a very different motivational basis than the market which is based on exchange of equivalents. In contrast, when we contribute to the welfare state, rather than getting an equivalent return it may be others that benefit. It can be argued that 'welfare provision is a matter of strict obligation for those who hold resources and . . . those who are in need have strict moral claims on those better off in society. Their needs create a right to welfare and a duty on the part of the better endowed to grant welfare benefits to meet such needs' (Plant et al. 1980: 39). It can also be argued that the sharing of resources through the welfare state tends to both reflect and foster a sense of community, or fellow-feeling, in contrast with the individualism of the market.

The question of motivation is also relevant to the public sector employees who deliver services and benefits. Advocates of the welfare state argue that the absence of a profit motive in the public sector means that welfare professionals are motivated instead by a public service ethic. Where healthcare is provided through a market there might be a temptation for the private clinic to over-treat patients—to sell them treatments that they do not really need but are profitable. This is compounded by the problem that patients typically do not have the necessary knowledge to make good decisions in their own interests (a form of market failure).

In contrast, where healthcare is provided as a public service it is argued that professionals can have regard only for the needs of patients and this creates the basis for trust. This type of argument is behind the idea that it is immoral to make a profit from healthcare—the motive should be care not making money.

> *Stop and Think*
>
> Explain what is meant by the 'piggy bank' and 'Robin Hood' functions of the welfare state.

We can see that the rationale for the welfare state as a correction of market outcomes has a number of elements:

- The state has a responsibility to meet the basic needs of all citizens as social rights.
- Individuals face risks in markets which they cannot be left to bear on their own—in a market not all individuals would have sufficient resources to meet their needs and live a decent life.
- Individuals are not always the best judges of their own welfare and are vulnerable to being taken advantage of in markets.
- Public service ideally embodies superior ethics of care and community.

This broad conception leaves open many questions about the scope of the welfare state and its institutional design or delivery mechanisms. These are the classic what, for whom, and how questions. The 'what' question concerns the range of risks or needs that the welfare state is intended to meet and the standard at which it meets them. This is a question that concerns balancing ideas about what is required for all citizens to have a reasonable standard of living and what is affordable in terms of public finances. The 'for whom' question concerns eligibility for benefits and services—whether they are based on a contributory principle (e.g. eligibility for the UK state pension depends on national insurance contributions), and whether non-contributory benefits and services are provided for all citizens (universality) or on the basis of selectivity (for example, before 2013 child benefit was paid as a universal non-contributory benefit to all families but since then eligibility is restricted for higher earners). This is a question about whether the state takes responsibility entirely away from individuals or individuals still bear some responsibility. The 'how' question concerns the methods of delivery of benefits and services and questions of efficiency.

Health and social care services certainly meet basic needs (Beveridge's giant evil of 'sickness', broadly conceived) and are conventionally seen as parts of the welfare state. In the UK the NHS is intended as a comprehensive healthcare system providing free treatment to all on the basis of need. But there is continual political debate about the level of funding that the NHS needs (and its affordability), and there is acceptance that the NHS cannot meet all needs so there has to be rationing. In contrast, social care (in a residential setting or home care) is provided on a selective basis, according to a wealth threshold. In other words, only those with very limited wealth (up to £23,500 in May 2017) do not have to pay for their social care. In spite of this strong element of self-reliance it is generally accepted that social care is not adequately funded by local authorities. As a result, it was calculated by the charity Age UK that 'there are 1.2 million people who need help with the activities of daily living who are not getting it' (Collinson 2016; see also Mini-Case 14.2).

Mini-Case 14.2 Overcoming Beveridge's 'giant evil' of ignorance—the right to education?

What is required to overcome the risk of 'ignorance' and meet the need for education? The obvious answer is that it requires a tax-funded school system with every child being provided a place in a good school. Nobody should have to pay for their child's education because it is a social right. But that answer leaves many questions, including: how much should the state spend per pupil in order to, say, attract talented individuals into teaching, reduce class sizes, and provide better IT equipment? At what ages should schooling begin and end? Should the state provide pre-school care and education? Should the right to free education provided by the state include going to university? These are questions about how we understand the 'need' for education and balance this with what is affordable in terms of public finances. The difficulty comes if need clashes with affordability.

Should higher education (HE) be a right? Not everybody goes to university but before the introduction of tuition fees in England and Wales there was a 'right' to HE in the qualified sense that it was free to all those who wanted to go and were accepted on the basis of their qualifications for the places that were available. But it was never seen as a basic need for all people like school. Tuition fees were introduced in 1998 (at £1000 per year) in order to make the expansion of HE more affordable in terms of the public finances. More people who qualified could go to university, and in this sense it was recognized that more people could benefit from HE, but they would have to contribute to the costs. Tuition fees were then increased to £3000 in 2006 and to a maximum of £9000 in 2012. Critics argued that fees eroded the 'right' to HE because they introduced a payment element that would be a barrier for would-be students from lower-income backgrounds (Full Fact 2016, O'Carroll and Fishwick 2016), though against this it was argued that tax-funding was unfair to low-income groups because they were effectively paying towards the benefits of HE for children from well-off families who dominated universities.

When fees were introduced in 1998 HE was still mainly tax-funded, and fees were a fairly small proportion of costs. But when fees were raised to £9000 they replaced tax-funding through teaching grants paid to universities by government. Although this looks as though the cost was shifted entirely from tax-payers to students, in fact a substantial public subsidy was still involved because of the design of the tuition fee system (Crawford et al. 2014).

In particular, students did not pay fees 'up front' and repayment was contingent on income after graduation and time-limited, and this meant that many students would not repay some or all of the loan. The lowest paid graduates (earning less than the threshold of £21,000) would pay nothing and high paid students would repay their loans in full (though in fact the highest paid would not pay back most because they would repay the loan over a shorter period and therefore pay less interest).

In principle universities can charge variable fees within the cap. This provision, and allowing them to recruit as many students as they like (moving away from a centralized system of planned numbers) was intended to make the HE sector more like a market where universities compete to attract students. This marketization was taken further by the Higher Education and Research Act (April 2017) which provides for new private providers to obtain degree-awarding powers, including profit-making organizations.

Is HE part of the welfare state?

The answer is not clear-cut. There has never been a universal right to HE but it used to be free to those who got in. But under this arrangement it did not perform a 'Robin Hood' function and transfer resources from well-off to least well-off households but the opposite. Students now have to pay tuition fees, and this seems to make HE less of a right available to all. But many students are not in practice liable for some or all of their fees because repayment is linked with income, and so HE has arguably become more of a Robin Hood system (especially if graduates with less well-paid jobs are more likely to have come from less well-off families).

Universities are not part of the public sector but private organizations (non-profit institutions serving households), and in future there may be more profit making organizations. They compete in an increasingly market-like environment. But universities and academics may still think of themselves as providing a public service and conforming to a public service ethic.

Question

Is there, or should there be, a right to HE?

Neoliberalism and the critique of the welfare state

As we have seen, the welfare state was part of the post-war consensus in Britain—it was broadly accepted as a necessary part of a form of managed capitalism, and it enjoyed broad popular support. The economic context during these decades was arguably conducive to the expansion of social spending. 'European countries developed their welfare systems during a period when the region's benign demographic profile could support extensive social spending and when solid economic growth made it affordable' (Begg et al. 2015: 6). However, in the 1970s this period of sustained economic growth came to an end and this led to questioning of the post-war consensus and the welfare state. A new political ideology came to the fore which saw 'big government' as the main problem and declared that 'Public expenditure is at the heart of Britain's present economic difficulties' (Dean 2013, Hills 1998).

If this was the case then, since the welfare state accounted for the major part of public spending, it was obvious that reducing spending on welfare would be necessary. Thus, the neoliberal critique of the welfare state was largely driven by the aim of rolling back the state. Overall, what is involved is a recasting of the European social model's conception of 'the state's responsibility to its citizens'. This responsibility was to be scaled back, shifting responsibility from the state to the individual, from the state to the market, and from the public to the private sector.

VALUES **DYNAMISM** Neoliberalism (sometimes referred to as Thatcherism in the UK context after the Prime Minister Margaret Thatcher (1979–90)) represented a philosophical or ideological challenge to all the main elements of the post-war Keynesian–welfare consensus (Table 14.5) (see also Chapters 4, 9, and 12). It can be argued that neoliberalism remains the dominant approach framing arguments about the role of the public sector nearly forty years later—it has arguably become the new consensus.

The case against the welfare state involved a range of interrelated criticisms and drivers (see also Chapter 4):

- The aim to control and reduce public spending and taxation.
- The moral case for lower taxes in terms of liberty.
- The public sector is less efficient than the private sector.
- The need for greater selectivity or targeting.
- Welfare creates dependency (see Mini-Case 14.3).

Table 14.5 Neoliberalism versus the Keynesian–welfare consensus

Keynesian–welfare consensus	Neoliberalism
Keynesian macroeconomic policy (demand management) to secure 'full employment'	Macroeconomic policy (monetarism) rejected deficit financing of public spending and focused on control of inflation. Supply-side economics to increase competitiveness.
Mixed economy including a significant public sector (public corporations)	Privatization
Trade unions have an important role representing the voice and interests of employees with employers and government	Tackle 'excessive' trade union power and restore the 'right to manage'
High levels of public spending and taxation to provide a range of benefits and services—the welfare state	'Public expenditure is at the heart of Britain's present economic difficulties'

The idea that public spending was too high, and a prime cause of economic difficulties was largely an argument about the 'tax burden'. In other words, the need to reduce spending was a consequence of the need to reduce taxation. In particular, it is claimed that high taxation can undermine economic incentives and, through taxes on business, take away resources that could otherwise be used for investment. In a globalizing world high rates of income tax and corporation tax can encourage talented individuals and corporations to go elsewhere. Thus, it is argued that lower *rates* of taxation can lead to higher tax *revenues* because of the positive effects in terms of incentives, investment, and growth (and vice versa).

In addition to the economic case for lower taxation, the moral argument is that individuals and companies are entitled to the money that they have earned through their own efforts involving voluntary exchanges in the market. People should be free to decide how to spend their own money and therefore taxes, which are necessary to finance essential government activities, should be kept to a minimum. Therefore, government activities should be kept to a minimum.

It is claimed that, as a general rule, the private sector is always more efficient than the public sector because competition and the profit motive act as powerful drivers. It is claimed that in the public sector, where consumers have to take what they are given and cannot shop around, services will tend to be managed for the convenience of the producers ('producer-led') rather than the consumers. The claim that public sector employees are motivated to act in the best interests of users by a higher public service ethic is treated with scepticism. The implication of this argument is that, where government has a continuing responsibility for benefits and services, it should seek to 'contract out' the delivery to private or voluntary sector organizations where possible, or introduce market-like mechanisms (internal or quasi-markets) and private sector management methods (**new public management**) into the public sector (see Flynn 2012).

The neoliberal belief in individualism and self-reliance means that individuals should look after themselves and the state should step in on a selective basis only to help those who are in real need and cannot help themselves. For example, as we have seen, child benefit was switched from a universal (paid for all children regardless of the family income) to a selective benefit (not paid for children with a high-earning parent). In the 2017 general election campaign the Conservative Party announced a plan to switch the winter fuel allowance from a universal payment to all pensioners to a selective payment for poorer pensioners only. Selectivity is justified on grounds of controlling public spending and fairness (i.e. that it is both wasteful and unfair to taxpayers to go on spending tax-payers' money on a winter fuel allowance for wealthy pensioners who don't need it). Against this, supporters of universal benefits argue that selectivity involves administrative costs, that means-testing creates stigma and can lead to people not claiming benefits they are entitled to, and that universalism embodies the ideal of community.

We can see that contesting the role of the public sector involves a debate not only about the *size* of the state but also about the *organization and management* of the public sector and the primary *purpose* of the state. These differences are summarized in a simplified and stylized way in Table 14.6.

Table 14.6 Neoliberalism versus the Keynesian-welfare consensus

	Keynesian-welfare consensus	Neoliberalism
Size of the state—basic attitude to the state and the market	'Public good, private bad', Expand the state	'Private good, public bad'. Roll back the state
Organization and management	State provision—centralized, top-down, bureaucratic	Separate purchaser and provider (finance and delivery)—privatization, contracting out, internal markets
Principal purpose	Social justice	Efficiency and competitiveness

Mini-Case 14.3 Does welfare create a 'dependency culture'?

The neoliberal belief in individualism and self-reliance is also reflected in a concern, particularly in relation to cash benefits, that when the state steps in to meet people's needs it may have the unintended and undesirable effect of undermining their own drive to help themselves. In short, individuals might become habituated to a life on benefits and a culture of dependence might be created, particularly if benefits are 'too generous' or not made conditional on unemployed claimants looking for work. This problem is often referred to as a form of 'moral hazard' since the benefits system is being seen as creating a hazard for the morality of claimants. This criticism of welfare was expressed by Margaret Thatcher when she was UK Prime Minister:

> *The welfare state 'undermines the spirit of enterprising self-reliance without which the freedom we so much treasure in Britain cannot be assured. . . . [The neoliberal view] emphasizes particularly the destructive effects on character and social behaviour of welfare dependency. The underclass life created by misconceived state welfare poses a grave threat to freedom and civility . . . The majority of the population should be encouraged to provide for themselves through market and mutual agencies, for the whole range of their welfare needs'.*
>
> (Thatcher, in Lister 2010: 44)

Critics argue that the problem of welfare dependency is exaggerated and that the vast majority of people who are unemployed want to work. It is the experience of unemployment that can have severe effects on well-being and mental health. From this point of view government needs to ensure full employment and that all jobs pay a decent wage.

There are several problems with the proposal that most people should provide for themselves through the market:

- The market only caters for those who can afford to pay insurance premiums—this problem of affordability is the basic one that the welfare state solves by pooling risk.
- Even if individuals can afford to buy insurance it might be unrealistic to expect people to foresee and insure against long-term risks such as income in retirement or the need for care.
- There is a risk of individuals making bad decisions or being victims of mis-selling where they do not have the knowledge to assess the value for money of financial products.
- A final problem is whether insurance markets exist for all the risks that individuals face. For example, 'insurance markets don't exist that will let [individuals] buy social care insurance' early in life that would protect them from the 'low but meaningful risk of incurring very high care costs' in old age (Institute for Fiscal Studies 2017).

Question

What is meant by 'welfare dependency'?

Is the welfare state bad for business?

We saw earlier that, according to Kay, there is more controversy about the role of the public sector in the provision of goods and services than about the private sector. This is partly about public expectations of the quality of services provided by the welfare state, but it is also about the economic impact. Neoliberalism asserts that spending on the welfare state has negative economic effects—that it is bad for business. It was also suggested that neoliberalism may be considered as a new consensus. Has neoliberalism triumphed? In fact there is a considerable gap between the rhetoric of 'rolling back the state' and the reality of what has happened to public spending on the welfare state.

> In its last year in office, 1996–97 (the financial year starting in April 1996), the Conservative Government devoted almost the same share of national income to the main welfare services as its Labour predecessor had twenty years before . . . The balance of welfare spending changed between services—towards health and social security at the expense of housing and education—but the overall total remained at or around a quarter of national income.
>
> (Hills 1998: 2)

In some ways 'New Labour', in government after the Conservatives (1997–2010), represented something of a return to support for expansion of the welfare state, notably through commitments to major increases in spending on health and education and to reducing relative poverty (setting the ambitious target of eliminating child poverty by 2020). Between 2000 and 2010 spending on four key areas of the welfare state (education, health, welfare, and pensions) increased as a share of GDP from 22.23 per cent to 28.83 per cent (http://www.ukpublicspending.co.uk/spending_history). On this basic measure it appears that the welfare state is still intact, though it has faced new pressures in the context of 'austerity' since 2010 (see case study at end of chapter).

VALUES Still, it can be argued that neoliberal ideas have altered the terms of the ongoing debate about the role of the public sector and the welfare state. It has arguably fostered a more sceptical view of the efficiency and effectiveness of the public sector and of the motives of politicians and public officials. It has also encouraged a more individualistic society. These shifts are reflected in the perception of '**tax resistance**', or the reluctance of voters to support higher taxes to fund increased spending on public services.

The 'old' model of the state as a provider of a monopoly service has been displaced by the model of the 'enabling' state and ideas of choice. The enabling state is characterized by the idea that the state retains responsibility for ensuring citizens have access to services through financing but doesn't have to be the provider. In this way financing is separated from delivery which can be contracted to private or third sector organizations. Arguably, this has the advantage of maintaining the basic rationale of the welfare state of meeting needs through a range of benefits and services while allowing the skills of the private and voluntary sectors to be utilized. The reasoning is that users care whether they are getting a good service and not whether the person providing it works for the public sector or the private sector. However, increasing the role for the private sector and the profit motive in areas like the NHS remains controversial. This reflects concerns about 'cherry picking', transaction costs of drawing up and monitoring contracts, and that the risk still remains with the public sector if the private provider fails or walks away from the contract. However, there is also a basic moral concern that the profit motive should not have a role in healthcare.

The idea that users of public services should be treated more like consumers and be able to exercise choice between providers as in a market has also become established, notably in education through the idea of a range of different types of schools competing to attract pupils and universities competing for students. However, there are concerns about the fragmentation of the school system and the loss of democratic accountability and control, the phenomenon of winners and losers and the undermining of educational equality with the emergence of a 'two-tier' system.

It has been argued that a transition has taken place from the welfare state to the '**competition state**' with a focus on policies that will enhance the competitiveness of the UK economy (see case study at end of chapter). Though this shift might be exaggerated, the social justice rationale of the post-war welfare state has been tempered by the emphasis on efficiency and competitiveness in neoliberalism. Under New Labour there was an attempt to move beyond the 'state versus market' debate and to emphasize that social justice and competitiveness should be seen as complementary rather than as a dichotomy. This was reflected in the way education was framed as both a social policy (education as a basic need and right of citizenship) and an economic policy (education as the basis for creating a 'knowledge economy' and competing in a globalizing world). This idea of the complementarity of fairness and efficiency has become accepted by mainstream political parties.

The endurance of the welfare state arguably reflects not only the continued popularity of public services (especially health, education, and pensions) which has constrained public spending cuts, but also the benefits to business and the economy. Neoliberalism highlights the idea of a 'tax burden' but, in the same way that it is argued that 'taxes are the price we pay for a civilised society' (attributed to US judge Oliver Wendell Holmes Jr and acknowledged by Theresa May during her campaign to become leader of the Conservative Party (PoliticsHome 2016)), it can be argued that taxes are a price paid for a successful economy.

- The correction of market outcomes by the welfare state can be seen as an important source of legitimacy for the market system. The tendency of unchecked markets to create problems of insecurity, poverty, and inequality can generate a feeling that the economy isn't working for everyone and lead to political opposition and unrest. Thus 'welfare states were accepted . . . as a crucial component of a legitimate market order' (Gamble 2016: 20).
- The welfare state produces goods and services many of which, either directly or indirectly, provide inputs for business and contribute to competitiveness. As we have seen, education can be regarded as both a social and economic policy—all businesses benefit from an educated workforce. Likewise, healthcare is an important individual need, but the economy also needs a healthy workforce. This function of the welfare state can be characterized in terms of 'social investment' (in addition to the 'piggy bank' and 'Robin Hood' functions). This function 'enables the state to invest in the nation's human and . . . social capital. This includes kindergarten care, state education from primary level through university, out-of-work training and various types of work-related tax benefits' (Begg et al. 2015: 7).
- For some sectors, such as pharmaceuticals and medical equipment, the welfare state is an important customer. Contracting out has, controversially, expanded opportunities for private sector businesses.
- State welfare budgets constitute 'automatic stabilizers' for the macroeconomy, for example helping to moderate economic downturns as cash benefits protect the living standards and thus spending power of the unemployed. There is also evidence that more unequal societies are more prone to economic cycles (see Chapter 12).
- These beneficial effects of welfare states may influence companies' location and investment decisions positively. Companies are not just interested in low corporation taxes.

Stop and Think

What is meant by the 'social investment' function of the welfare state?

Looking ahead

There is no such thing as a free market and therefore the public sector will continue to be an important feature of capitalist economies.

However, the size, organization and management, and purpose of the public sector will continue to be contested, as it has always been. Therefore, looking ahead is fraught with uncertainty.

In the twentieth century, the growth of the public sector—the mixed economy and the welfare state—was (though with national variations) a universal feature of advanced capitalist economies, especially in Europe (the 'European social model'). Capitalist development and public sector expansion seemed to go hand in hand.

However, since the 1980s this association has been challenged by a set of related developments: less favourable economic and demographic circumstances, the shift to neoliberalism, austerity, and globalization.

For the foreseeable future, at least in the UK, the prospects for the public sector will continue to be set within a framework of 'austerity'. The initial plan to eliminate the budget deficit by 2015 has now been pushed back into the 2020s. Although framed by the UK government as an economic necessity, austerity should be seen as a political choice and can be seen as a continuation of neoliberalism. Political choices can, of course, change, and the UK general election in 2017 seemed to indicate public weariness with ongoing austerity. Arguments for a more positive role for the public sector might make a comeback.

The future of the public sector involves a range of possible scenarios involving political responses to changing economic and social circumstances. The future of the welfare state will depend on balancing the three functions identified in this chapter—'piggy bank', 'Robin Hood', and 'social investment'.

Summary

- 'The public sector is comprised of "general government"—central and local governments . . .—and all public corporations.'
- The public sector, measured in terms of employment and spending, is a relatively small but significant part of the economy. The UK public sector is not large by international standards.
- The state's role as an economic actor is a key issue of political controversy. This debate concerns the best mix of the state and the market—the size, organization, management, and purpose of the public sector.
- Debate about the role of the public sector has been bound up with the ideological contest between liberalism and socialism as rival accounts of the nature of capitalism and alternative visions of the good society.
- A consensus embracing the mixed economy and the welfare state broke down in the 1970s, challenged by the neoliberal aim to roll back the state.
- There is debate about the future of welfare states in the context of austerity and questioning of their affordability.

Case Study: Austerity and the future of the welfare state

We have seen that the context in which welfare states expanded during the post-war period was benign in terms of economic and demographic conditions. In short, strong economic growth generated buoyant tax revenues to finance public spending, and the balance between the working population (whose incomes provided the tax base for public spending) and the dependent non-working population was also favourable. In this context, coupled with popular support for the welfare state and a political consensus, governments found it relatively easy to increase spending on the welfare state. However, the 'era of expansion [of welfare states] came to an end in the 1970s, and since then they have entered an era of permanent austerity' (Gamble 2016: 2).

As we have seen, what changed in the 1970s was the economic environment with the coming to an end of the long period of sustained post-war economic growth. This economic change prompted questions about the affordability of the welfare state, the ascendancy of neoliberalism and the introduction of 'austerity' in the form of attempts to reduce public spending. If New Labour marked a return to welfare state expansion, 'since the financial crash in 2008 . . . [welfare states] have had to confront a new era of retrenchment and austerity' (Gamble 2016: 2) and, in the UK, this has been more severe than in the 1980s.

DYNAMISM Austerity is one of a number of interrelated contemporary challenges confronting the welfare state, which can be identified as follows (Begg et al. 2015, Gamble 2016):

- demographic change–ageing of the population;
- globalization;
- austerity/affordability; and
- social change creating new risks.

In considering these challenges, the key question is whether they are short term and manageable or bring into question the long-term sustainability of the 'European social model'.

Affordability/austerity

The challenge of affordability suggests that there is a fiscal gap or deficit–between welfare state spending and the ability of governments to raise taxes to finance this spending–or that raising the necessary tax revenues will have unacceptable negative economic effects. In 2015 the then UK Chancellor of the Exchequer, George Osborne, stated that the UK has got '1% of the world's population, 4% of its GDP, but we undertake 7% of the world's welfare spending' (referring to welfare in the narrow sense) and characterized this spending as 'completely unsustainable', i.e. unaffordable (in Mason and Nardelli 2015).

But even assuming these data to be correct (Full Fact 2015), it is not clear why this is unaffordable. As we have noted, welfare spending is higher in rich countries–as GDP increases countries tend to spend a higher share on welfare. So, the question is not really whether the spending is affordable but the collective choices that nations make about the generosity of their welfare systems. Osborne claims that reducing welfare spending would ensure 'a fair deal to the people, the taxpayers of this country, who pay for it' (in Mason and Nardelli 2015). This misleadingly implies that taxpayers and recipients of welfare benefits are different groups of people, but the point is that fairness is a political judgement. If people are willing to pay through the tax system to finance welfare spending, then it is sustainable.

Of course, it could be true that there is not a high level of support for existing levels of welfare spending and that could make the spending difficult to sustain. It is the case that some elements of the welfare budget (e.g. benefits to the unemployed) do not have high popular support, although that is not true of pensions which accounts for a large share of the 7 per cent. More generally, Gamble characterizes the affordability challenge in terms of reconciling expectations with willingness to pay tax. There is a mismatch between increases in spending, as 'governments . . . promise too much' and 'bend to . . . pressures' to spend more, and 'the amount governments are able to raise in taxes' (Gamble 2016: 58). 'Voters in Western democracies vote for parties that promise them more spending on public services and lower taxes. They want Swedish-style public services and American-style taxes' (Gamble 2016: 59). But, as Gamble acknowledges, the problem is not strictly one of affordability but of 'political will'. Tax resistance might be in part a reflection of the influence of neoliberal ideas and does not need to be seen as a fixture of political attitudes but as potentially amenable to change through political argument and engagement. It can be argued that Sweden shows the possibility of voters wanting Swedish-style public services and being willing to pay Swedish-style taxes. The question then is, could Britain become more like Sweden?

Since 2010 the problem of affordability has been framed in terms of austerity. The argument here is that cuts to public spending are necessary to bring down the deficit and, ultimately, start to reduce government debt (see Anderson 2014 for explanations of these terms). In other words, the unsustainability of the deficit means that current levels of public spending are unaffordable. However, it is important to recognize that 'austerity' was a political choice resting on a contested theory of how the economy works. Critics of the government, using a different theoretical approach, argued that austerity was not necessary and would prove to be counterproductive in its own terms. In this view austerity would hamper economic recovery and thus slow down the growth of tax receipts, making it harder to achieve the targets of reducing the deficit and the stock of debt (e.g. see Krugman 2015). Policy choice was also evident in the balance between tax increases and public expenditure cuts, and the decisions about which areas of spending to cut. In any case it can be argued that austerity reflected a neoliberal ideological choice in favour of a smaller state, with the financial crisis providing a pretext for this policy.

Two other challenges also have implications in terms of affordability: demographic change and globalization. The ageing of the population has implications for affordability because of an increasing old-age dependency ratio–the ratio between the population of working age who constitute the tax base to finance spending on the welfare state and the retired population who depend on welfare services such as pensions and health and social care. This demographic change is examined in Chapter 6.

Globalization

One of the ways in which globalization can have implications for the sustainability of spending on welfare states is through tax competition. The argument here is that multinational corporations make decisions about where to locate their operations based partly on 'locational advantage' such as the costs of production in different countries. Thus, by lowering corporation taxes states can potentially attract and retain investment–part of the 'competition state' strategy. By the same reasoning, reducing the rate of income tax for very high earners can encourage key personnel to move to or remain in a country. However, these moves may erode the tax base and therefore the sustainability of welfare state funding. Another problem is that globalization offers mobile companies and individuals increased opportunities to evade taxation (see Chapter 1). Finally, rich countries face increased competition from low-wage emerging economies such as the BRIC group (Brazil, Russia, India, and China) and this puts in question the sustainability of high wages in internationally traded sectors of the economy, including a high 'social wage' (welfare services and benefits).

Does this mean that rich countries will have to scale back their welfare states in order to remain competitive? In recent years the UK has vigorously implemented a tax competition policy and justified it on the grounds of making the UK an attractive location for business. However, corporation tax is only one element in 'locational advantage' and we have seen that the 'social investment' function of welfare states affords important benefits to business. And the social investment state is key to meeting the challenge of low wage competition, enabling western economies to remain competitive not by lowering wages but moving up the value chain into high-skilled knowledge-based activities (Gamble 2016: 81).

Questions

1. **What is 'austerity'?**
2. **Is spending on the welfare state unsustainable, or is it just a question of political will?**
3. **Do countries have to scale back welfare spending due to tax competition?**

Review and discussion questions

1. Using data on spending and employment, examine the size and functions of the public sector in the UK and compare it with other countries.
2. Assess the claim that 'Public expenditure is at the heart of Britain's present economic difficulties'.
3. Critically examine arguments for and against public ownership of business.
4. Critically examine arguments for and against the welfare state.
5. Have welfare states become unaffordable?

Assignments

1. You have been commissioned by the National Union of Rail, Maritime and Transport Workers (RMT) to write a briefing paper identifying the main arguments for renationalization of the railways.
2. You have been commissioned by the Association of Independent Healthcare Organisations (AIHO) to write a briefing paper identifying the main arguments in support of the use of private providers in the NHS.

Further reading

For useful discussions of the challenges facing welfare states see:

Begg, Mushövel, and Niblett (2015)

Flynn (2012)

Gamble (2016)

Taylor-Gooby (2013)

For an overview of the policy of privatization in the UK see:

House of Commons Library (2014)

LeGrand et al. (2008) *provides an economic framework for thinking about public policy responses to social problems.*

Pierson et al. (2014) *provides a useful set of readings on the welfare state.*

Test your understanding of this chapter with online questions and answers, explore the subject further through web exercises, and use the weblinks to provide a quick resource for further research. Visit the online resources at **www.oup.com/uk/wetherly_otter4e/**

Useful websites

For UK public spending data and analysis go to:

Institute for Fiscal Studies
www.ifs.org.uk

Office for Budget Responsibility
http://budgetresponsibility.org.uk

Office for National Statistics
https://www.ons.gov.uk

Full Fact
https://fullfact.org

King's Fund (healthcare think tank)
https://www.kingsfund.org.uk

References

Anderson, R. (2014) 'UK debt and deficit: all you need to know, 21 February, BBC **http://www.bbc.co.uk/news/business-25944653**

Appleby, J. (2016) *How Does NHS Spending Compare with Health Spending Internationally?* (London: King's Fund) **https://www.kingsfund.org.uk/blog/2016/01/how-does-nhs-spending-compare-health-spending-internationally**

Begg, I., Mushövel, F., and Niblett, R. (2015) *The Welfare State in Europe: Visions for Reform* (London: Chatham House) **https://www.chathamhouse.org/sites/files/chathamhouse/publications/research/20150917WelfareStateEuropeNiblettBeggMushovelFinal.pdf**

Collinson, P. (2016) 'Social care: why are we "beyond the crisis point"?', *Guardian*, 12 December **https://www.theguardian.com/society/2016/dec/12/social-care-crisis-funding-cuts-government-council-tax**

Crawford, C. et al. (2014) *Estimating the Public Cost of Student Loans (IFS Report R94)* (London: Institute for Fiscal Studies) **https://www.ifs.org.uk/comms/r94.pdf**

Dean, M. (2013) 'Margaret Thatcher's policies hit the poor hardest—and it's happening again', *Guardian*, 9 April **https://www.theguardian.com/society/2013/apr/09/margaret-thatcher-policies-poor-society**

European Parliament (1997) *Public Undertakings and Services in the European Union*, Working Paper, Economic Series W-21 **http://www.europarl.europa.eu/workingpapers/econ/w21/default_en.htm**

Flynn, N. (2012) *Public Sector Management* (London: Sage)

Full Fact (2015) 'Does the UK make up 7% of the world's welfare spending?', 17 June **https://fullfact.org/economy/does-uk-make-7-worlds-welfare-spending**

Full Fact (2016) 'Are there record numbers of young people going to university?', **https://fullfact.org/education/are-there-record-numbers-young-people-going-university**

Gamble, A. (2016) *Can the Welfare State Survive?* (Cambridge: Polity)

Gani, A. (2015) 'Clause IV: a brief history', *Guardian*, 9 August **https://www.theguardian.com/politics/2015/aug/09/clause-iv-of-labour-party-constitution-what-is-all-the-fuss-about-reinstating-it**

Hills, J. (1998) *Thatcherism, New Labour and the Welfare State* (London: Centre for Analysis of Social Exclusion, LSE) **https://core.ac.uk/download/pdf/93746.pdf**

HM Treasury (2016) *Public Expenditure Statistical Analyses 2016* **https://www.gov.uk/government/uploads/system/uploads/attachment_data/file/538793/pesa_2016_web.pdf**

House of Commons Library (2014) *Privatisation.* Research Paper 14/61 **http://researchbriefings.parliament.uk/ResearchBriefing/Summary/RP14-61**

Hutton, W. (2015) *How Good We Can Be: Ending the Mercenary Society and Building a Great Country* (London: Little, Brown)

IMF (2009) 'IMF Working Paper—Where does the public sector end and the private sector begin?' **http://www.imf.org/external/pubs/ft/wp/2009/wp09122.pdf**

Institute for Fiscal Studies (2009) *A Survey of Public Spending in the UK* (London: IFS) **https://www.ifs.org.uk/bns/bn43.pdf**

Institute for Fiscal Studies (2014) *The public sector workforce: past, present and future* (IFS Briefing Note BN145) (London: IFS) **https://www.ifs.org.uk/bns/bn145.pdf**

Institute for Fiscal Studies (2015a) *Total UK Public Spending* (London: IFS) **https://www.ifs.org.uk/tools_and_resources/fiscal_facts/public_spending_survey/total_public_spending**

Institute for Fiscal Studies (2015b) *UK Public Spending Compared with Other Countries* (London: IFS) **https://www.ifs.org.uk/tools_and_resources/fiscal_facts/public_spending_survey/uk_spending_in_an_international_context**

Institute for Fiscal Studies (2017) 'Social care—a step forwards or a step backwards?', 19 May (London: IFS) **https://www.ifs.org.uk/publications/9243**

Kay, J. (2004) 'The state and the market', *Political Quarterly*, July, suppl. 1, vol. 75

Krugman, P. (2015) 'The austerity delusion', *Guardian*, April 29 **https://www.theguardian.com/business/ng-interactive/2015/apr/29/the-austerity-delusion**

LeGrand, J. et al. (2008) *The Economics of Social Problems* (Basingstoke: Palgrave Macmillan)

Lister, R. (2010) *Understanding Theories and Concepts in Social Policy* (Bristol: Policy Press)

Marquand, D. (2008) *Britain Since 1918: The Strange Career of British Democracy* (London: Phoenix)

Marquand, D. and Seldon, A. (1996) *The Ideas that Shaped Post-War Britain* (London: Fontana)

Marshall, T. H. (1992) *Citizenship and Social Class* (London: Pluto)

Mason, R. and Nardelli, A. (2015) 'Britain responsible for "unsustainable" 7% of world's welfare spend—Osborne', *Guardian*, 17 June **https://www.theguardian.com/politics/2015/jun/17/britain-responsible-unsustainable-worlds-welfare-spend-osborne**

National Archives [no date] *The Cabinet Papers: Post-war nationalisation*. **http://www.nationalarchives.gov.uk/cabinetpapers/themes/post-war-nationalisation.htm**

National Audit Office (2014) *Adult Social Care In England: Overview* (London: NAO) **https://www.nao.org.uk/wp-content/uploads/2015/03/Adult-social-care-in-England-overview.pdf**

O'Carroll, L. and Fishwick, C. (2016) 'Fall in state-school university entrants since tuition fees hit £9,000', *Guardian*, 3 August **https://www.theguardian.com/education/2016/aug/03/tuition-fees-state-school-university-education-jo-johnson**

OECD (2014) 'Glossary of statistical terms: public sector'. **https://stats.oecd.org/glossary/detail.asp?ID=2199**

Office for Budget Responsibility (2016) *A Brief Guide to the UK Public Finances* (London: OBR) **http://budgetresponsibility.org.uk/docs/dlm_uploads/BriefGuideAS16.pdf**

Office for Budget Responsibility (2017) *An OBR Guide to Welfare Spending* (London: OBR) **http://budgetresponsibility.org.uk/forecasts-in-depth/brief-guides-and-explainers/an-obr-guide-to-welfare-spending**

Office for National Statistics (2013) *Long-term Profile of Gross Domestic Product (GDP) in the UK* (London: ONS) **http://webarchive.nationalarchives.gov.uk/20160105160709/http://www.ons.gov.uk/ons/rel/elmr/explaining-economic-statistics/long-term-profile-of-gdp-in-the-uk/sty-long-term-profile-of-gdp.html**

Office for National Statistics (2016a) *UK Perspectives 2016: Personal and Household Finances in the UK* (London: ONS) **http://visual.ons.gov.uk/uk-perspectives-2016-personal-and-household-finances-in-the-uk**

Office for National Statistics (2016b) *Statistical bulletin: Public Sector Employment, UK: September 2016* (London: ONS) **https://www.ons.gov.uk/employmentandlabourmarket/peopleinwork/publicsectorpersonnel/bulletins/publicsectoremployment/september2016**

Office for National Statistics (2016c) *How Does UK Healthcare Spending Compare Internationally?* (London: ONS) **http://visual.ons.gov.uk/how-does-uk-healthcare-spending-compare-internationally**

Office for National Statistics (2017) *Public Sector Classification Guide* (London: ONS) **https://www.ons.gov.uk/economy/nationalaccounts/uksectoraccounts/datasets/publicsectorclassificationguide**

Pierson, C. (2011) *The Modern State* (Abingdon: Routledge)

Pierson, C. et al. (2014) *The Welfare State Reader* (London: Polity)

Plant, R. (1992) 'Citizenship, rights and welfare', in A. Coote (ed.), *The Welfare of Citizens* (London: IPPR/Rivers Oram Press)

Plant, R., Lesser, H., and Taylor-Gooby, P. (1980) *Political Philosophy and Social Welfare* (Abingdon: Routledge)

PoliticsHome (2016) 'Theresa May rails against tax avoidance and says big businesses "need to change"', 11 July **https://www.politicshome.com/news/uk/political-parties/conservative-party/news/77180/theresa-may-rails-against-tax-avoidance-and**

Schifferes, S. (2008) 'The lessons of nationalisation', BBC **http://news.bbc.co.uk/1/hi/business/7250252.stm**

Taylor-Gooby, P. (2013) *The Double Crisis of the Welfare State and What We Can Do about It* (Basingstoke: Palgrave Macmillan)

Treanor, J. (2017) 'Final taxpayer shares in Lloyds Banking Group to be sold off', *Guardian*, 14 May **https://www.theguardian.com/business/2017/may/14/final-taxpayer-stake-lloyds-banking-group-sold-off**

Wolf, M. (2014) *The Shifts and the Shocks: What We Have Learned—And Have Still to Learn—From the Financial Crisis* (London: Allen Lane)

Chapter 15

From starting to scaling and beyond: how do entrepreneurs and SMEs innovate and grow?

Simon Raby and Geoff Gregson

Learning objectives

When you have completed this chapter, you will be able to:

- Define small and medium-sized enterprises (SMEs) and explain why they are important.
- Identify the pros and cons associated with working for a smaller enterprise.
- List the stages of growth, and name some of the factors that influence growth.
- Explain the concept of entrepreneurship and what defines an entrepreneur.
- Describe how entrepreneurship applies across different business environments.
- Recall the key processes involved in forming a new venture.
- Evaluate some of the critical debates surrounding entrepreneurship and SMEs.

THEMES

The following themes of this book are especially relevant to this chapter

- **DIVERSITY** The domain of entrepreneurship and organizations that operate as SMEs are distinct and each worthy of attention.
- **COMPLEXITY** An array of factors, internal and external to the firm, influence the operation and success of start-up and SME ventures.
- **LOCAL TO GLOBAL** Entrepreneurs and SMEs operate within local settings and across global markets.
- **DYNAMIC** It is the very nature of entrepreneurs, and the organizations they build, that they constantly evolve and develop their thinking as new opportunities emerge.
- **INTERACTION** Entrepreneurs and SMEs are influenced by, and can influence, the environment within which they operate. They play a vital role in boosting the competitiveness, innovation, and wealth creation of economies around the world.
- **STAKEHOLDERS** While the majority of smaller enterprises are privately owned and managed, entrepreneurs and SMEs do need to effectively manage stakeholders who will include investors, customers, suppliers, and regulators (e.g. government).
- **VALUES** What entrepreneurs and business owners believe is important has a profound impact on the way in which their organizations develop.

Introduction

The purpose of this chapter is to provide an overview of SMEs and entrepreneurship. While 'enterprise' and 'entrepreneurship' are related themes, they are not the same in many respects. The term 'entrepreneur' can refer to a broad range of individuals within the business environment who identify new market opportunities and act upon them. Although entrepreneurship is often associated with starting a new business, entrepreneurial activity occurs across different business domains, which include the new enterprise, SMEs, large corporations, family firms, public organizations, academic institutions, and not-for-profits.

A common theme of entrepreneurship is a level of opportunistic, risk-taking thinking and action that brings new products, services, processes, or ways of doing business to the market. Not all SMEs originate from entrepreneurial activity and some SMEs display less innovative or opportunistic tendencies that would suggest they are not 'entrepreneurial'. This debate, as to whether small business owners are entrepreneurs, will be addressed in this chapter.

The first part of the chapter considers different approaches in defining the SME, discusses the importance of SMEs to the economy, describes common SME characteristics and how they compete against large firms, and considers factors influencing SME growth. The second part of the chapter defines entrepreneurship, describes common characteristics of the entrepreneur, considers the different domains of entrepreneurship, and focuses attention on new venture creation.

Understanding SMEs

Defining the SME

DIVERSITY There is no universal or commonly accepted **definition** for what constitutes an SME. SMEs are often defined in relation to where they are globally located, and are typically privately owned and managed. Table 15.1 outlines how the SME definition changes across different jurisdictions such as Europe, North America, China, and India.

The European Union (EU) and its twenty-eight member states share a common definition of micro, small and medium enterprises (MSMEs) which makes it easier to apply EU-wide finance and support programmes for MSMEs (Recommendation 2003/361). The EU defines MSMEs based on three measures: headcount, revenue, and balance sheet values.

In the US, the Small Business Administration (SBA) (2015) has adopted a size standard for small enterprises, using as a measure the level of revenue ($ millions) or number of employees. Being defined as 'small' in the US allows an enterprise to register and tender for government contracting. However, the size standard in the US also varies, in contrast to the EU definition, by the activity of the business (i.e. sector) as defined by the North American Industrial

Table 15.1 Contrasting SME definitions

Company category	Employees				Annual revenues			
	EU	US	Canada	China	EU	US	India	China
Micro	< 10	-	–	–	≤ 1.7m	–	< 230k	–
Small	< 50	100–1500	< 100	100–600	≤ 8.6m	< 31m	230–600k	75–220k
Medium	< 250	–	< 500	100–3000	≤ 43m	–	600k-1.2m	220k-2.2m

Notes: All values in pound sterling, rounded up, and valued at November 2015. India does not recognize an SME by employee size and Canada does not recognize an SME by revenue.

Classification System (NAICS). In addition, while the EU definition has remained unchanged, the US definition is regularly updated.

INTERACTION For example, on 26 February 2016 the size for a small manufacturing business (NAICS 31–3) operating in the US petroleum refining sector was amended to include those businesses with a refining capacity of no more than 200,000 barrels per calendar day. This was estimated to bring a further 1,250 enterprises under the 'small' classification. This particular change is an interesting development when one considers that the US has become a net oil and gas exporter, having been previously reliant on oil and gas imports from other countries. Adjusting the definition for what constitutes a small enterprise may well have allowed small enterprises access to government funding helping them to establish a foothold in the home market, prior to exporting their products.

Canada's definition of what constitutes an SME is different to that of the US, despite the two countries sharing close economic ties. Canada simply defines an SME by headcount, with 'small' employing between 1 and 99 employees, and 'medium' employing between 100 and 499 employees. Canada also defines SME using a 'financial institution' definition, with small referring to a loan size of $1 million or less, medium referring to loans of $1–5 million (and large being anything over $5 million).

In India, the Micro, Small and Medium Enterprises Development Act was passed in 2006, and resulted in enterprises being split into either products/goods or service industries and then aligned by size in revenues. For enterprises operating within the goods industry, micro enterprises are twenty-five lakh rupees, small are five crore rupees, and medium are ten crore rupees. For services, micro are ten lakh rupees, small are two crore rupees, medium are five crore rupees. At today's exchange rate, this would mean that a *small* manufacturing enterprise would have a revenue that equates to £600,000, and a *medium* enterprise £1.2m.

China's definition of SME is based on their Promotion Law enacted in 2003. Much like the EU, the Chinese definition is based on headcount, revenue, and total assets, and the assets definition tends to vary by sector. What China refers to as an 'industrial' (i.e. goods producing) SME can employ up to 2,000 people, and have an annual revenue not exceeding RMB300 million (*c*.£35m). Medium-sized enterprises should employ a minimum of 300 people, and have revenues not exceeding RMB30 million (*c*.3.5m).

INTERACTION Enterprises are also described according to levels of growth. *High-growth firms*, as defined by the OECD, are those with average annualized growth rates greater than 20 per cent per year, over a three-year period, and with ten or more employees at the beginning of the period. Their growth can be recorded in terms of revenue or number of employees. If growth of 20 per cent over three years takes place in the first five years of the enterprise's existence, the enterprise is defined as a 'rapidly growing' start-up—or commonly referred to as a 'gazelle'. We will return to the topic of enterprise growth later in the chapter.

> ***Stop and Think***
>
> How are SMEs defined in your local context?

Why are SMEs important?

Small business[1] is big business, and statistics across different countries highlight the critical contribution of SMEs to the global economy. In the UK, 99.3 per cent of all 5.5 million enterprises are small (Department for Business, Energy and Industrial Strategy 2016). In the US,

[1] Here, 'small' is defined as between one and forty-nine employees.

95.6 per cent of 5 million private enterprises are small (US Census Bureau 2015). Small enterprises also account for a significant proportion of a country's gross domestic product (GDP) and employed labour. In the UK, small enterprises make up 60 per cent of all private sector employment and 47 per cent of private sector GDP (£1.8 trillion) (Department for Business, Energy and Industrial Strategy 2016). In the US, small enterprises make up 42.7 per cent of all private sector employment and 44.6 per cent of private sector GDP (Kobe 2012).

INTERACTION Small enterprises became the focus of public attention through the seminal work of David Birch (1979) who published a research paper entitled *The Job Generation Process*. Birch's research identified small enterprises as influential **job creators** in the US, and identified a set of rapidly growing enterprises that he labelled 'gazelles' (we will revisit this shortly). In addition to size, age has also been found to be a key determinant of job creation, with contrasting results. In the US, young start-up enterprises have been found to be significant job creators (Haltiwanger et al. 2013) while more established small enterprises are heralded in Canada (Parsley and Halabisky 2008).

Stop and Think

Why are high-growth firms attractive to policymakers?

Use of job creation as the primary measure of SME economic contribution is criticized for a number of reasons. First, job creation does not tell the full story, as job losses or 'job destruction' is not always included within calculations. For this reason, economists now use *net* job creation as a key measure, subtracting job losses from jobs created. Net job creation varies by year, and is influenced by the economic conditions of the time.

For example, Figure 15.1 highlights in the US that 19.1 million jobs were created in 2006, 13.5 million in 2009, and 15.7 million in 2011. As you can see, this figure clearly depicts the economic downturns of 1982–3 and 2007–9, and the impact they had on job creation and destruction rates. What is stark about the period 2007–9 (known as the 'global financial crisis', or 'GFC'), when compared to the recession of 1982–83, is the speed of recovery. The 1980s

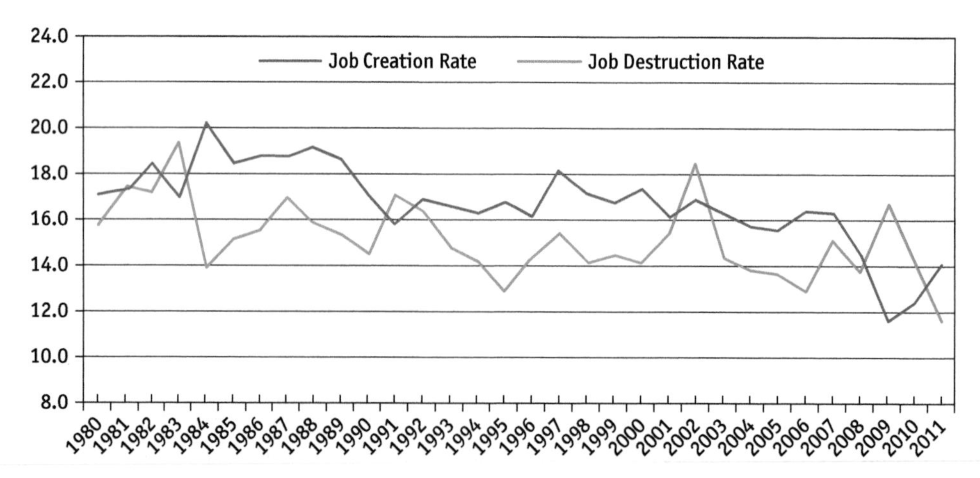

Figure 15.1 Annual Job Creation and Destruction Rates in the U.S.

Source: Haltiwanger, Miranda and Jarmin 2013.

recession was characterized by a rapid recovery, while the GFC led to high levels of job destruction, which remained high for a prolonged period of time, with job creation remaining subdued (Haltiwanger et al. 2013).

STAKEHOLDERS Second, the allure of high levels of job creation via 'high-growth' firms or 'gazelles' has biased public support for such firms in many regions. However, such enterprises represent a small proportion of firms; typically, between 5 and 7 per cent of enterprises in most developed economies (e.g. Industry Canada 2015, NESTA 2009).

VALUES Third, many business owners do not set up an enterprise with the sole purpose being job creation, even though collectively, SMEs are major contributors to new jobs in the economy (take a look at Mini-Case 15.3). Supporting the majority of enterprises not defined as high growth to achieve, or even be committed to growth is often overlooked by policymakers. We will revisit this point later when we consider the models of growth.

DYNAMIC In addition to job creation, small enterprises play a crucial role in **innovation** (ERC 2016). 'Innovation' enables enterprises to respond to, and compete in an ever-changing marketplace. Figure 15.2 reveals the top ten innovative countries measured by the number of patents granted (a typical innovation measure). This data highlights that the US would be classed as the most innovative country on this metric. In 2014, the whole of European granted one-fifth of the number of patents when compared to the US.

While patents can be used to assess a country or enterprise's volume of innovation, they relate solely to forms of new technical innovation, and can overlook other outcomes. It is well known that SMEs can be resource poor; and suffer from what is often referred to as the *liability of smallness* (Welsh and White 1981). This means that SMEs can lack the resources to invest in R&D activity (Hewitt-Dundas 2006, Rammer et al. 2009). Using the number of patents as a measure is not necessarily the most appropriate method to understand how innovations emerge in most small enterprises (Lundvall 2010).

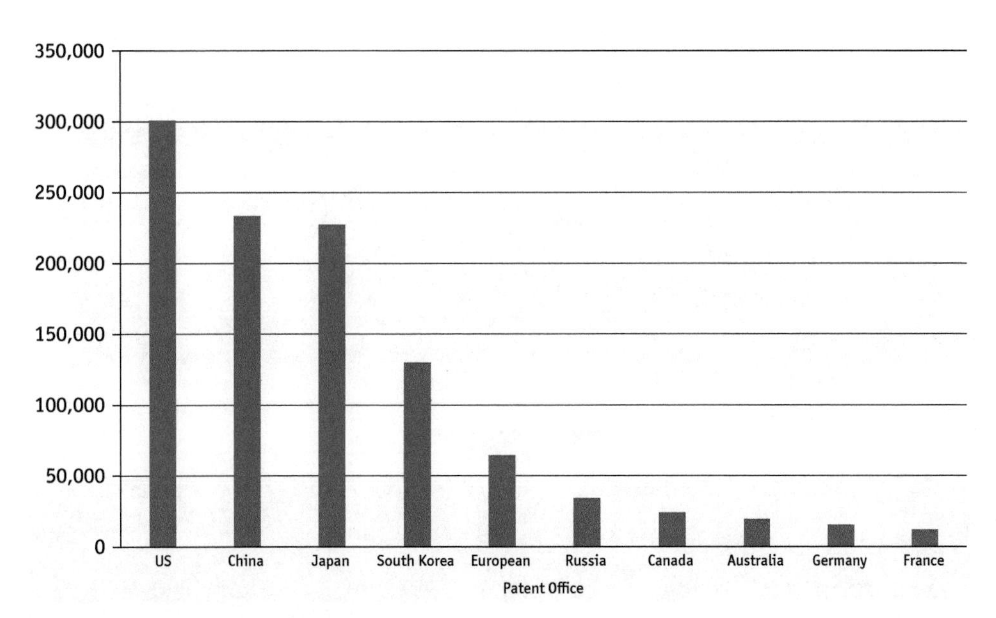

Figure 15.2 Number of patents grants, 2014

Source: World Intellectual Property Organization 2015.

DIVERSITY In their review of the innovation literature, Edison et al. (2013) found forty different ways to define innovation. The relationship between innovation and entrepreneurship is believed strong, and it was Drucker (1985) who said that innovation is 'the specific instrument of entrepreneurship . . . the act that endows resources with a *new* capacity to create wealth' (p.36) [emphasis added]. Here, 'new' can mean to the world, an industry, an enterprise, or even a group within an enterprise.

Other scholars have postulated that innovation can, and should be classified on different axes. Edison et al.'s review identified two dimensions against which innovations can be aligned, that of *novelty* (i.e. degree of newness) and *type* (i.e. product, service, market). This speaks to the existence of typologies that can be used to analyse innovation activities. For example, Damanpour (1991) highlight three contrasting dichotomies: technological vs. administrative, product vs. process, and radical vs. incremental. We will explore how innovation differs to entrepreneurship later in this chapter.

One of the largest studies of innovation across Europe, the Community Innovation Survey (CIS), defines innovation as 'the creation and/or introduction of new products, services, processes, support systems or methods'. Mini-Case 15.1 describes key findings from their 2015 study. Perhaps the simplest definition of innovation is 'creating new value and/or value in new ways' (Patel and Frey 2015), which broadens innovation to encompass value-creating activities such as an enterprise's business model, networks, partners, and pricing (see Figure 15.3).

> *Stop and Think*
>
> Which definition of innovation resonates most with you? What example comes to mind when adopting this definition?

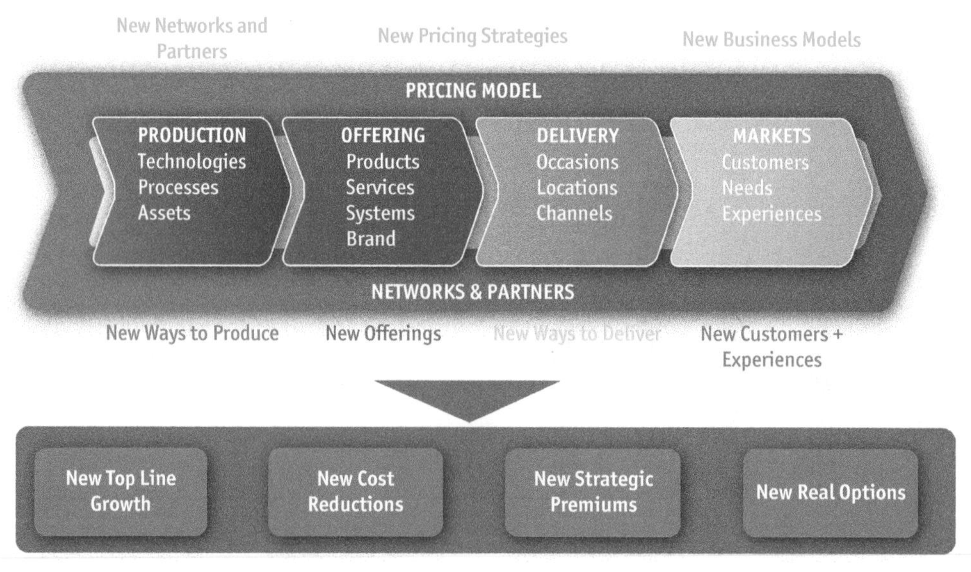

Figure 15.3 Where innovations come from

Source: IXL Center and Global Innovation Management Institute.

Mini-Case 15.1 The EU Community Innovation Survey

INTERACTION The Community Innovation Survey provides statistics on innovation across EU member states. Innovation in this context is defined as 'the introduction of a new or significantly improved *product, process, organisational method,* or *marketing method* by an enterprise' (emphasis added).

Analysis of innovation taking place across the EU between 2010 and 2012 indicates that close to half (48.9 per cent) of all enterprises innovated in some way. The most innovative locations were Germany (66.9 per cent), Luxemburg (66.1 per cent), Ireland (58.7 per cent), and Italy (56.1 per cent). The least innovative locations were locations in Eastern Europe including Bulgaria (27.4 per cent), Poland (23.0 per cent), and Romania (20.7 per cent). Across the EU, enterprises were most likely to report implementing some form of organizational innovation (new business practices, workplace organization, and external relations), then marketing innovations (new marketing concept or strategy), and product innovations (new or significantly improved goods or services). Enterprises were least likely to implement process innovations (production processes, distribution methods, or supporting activities).

When considering innovation, enterprises were most likely to access information from their suppliers, followed by their own staff, and customers/consumers. Universities or other higher education institutions were less likely to be used, however their use differed quite widely across the member states. As many as three out of five innovative enterprises in Austria and Finland used information from these sources. Government, public, or private research institutes were least likely to be used as a source of information for innovation.

Source: Eurostat 2015.

Questions

1. **What factors do you think might explain differences between the most and least innovative locations in the EU?**
2. **What barriers could impede the successful transfer of information and knowledge between universities and enterprises? How might these barriers be overcome?**

The SME work environment

STAKEHOLDERS The working environment of small enterprises is quite different compared to larger enterprises. Early studies of small enterprises portrayed the working environment as relatively conflict-free and harmonious:

> In many respects small firms provide a better environment for the employee than is possible in most large firms. Although physical working conditions may sometimes be inferior in small firms, most people prefer to work in a small group where communication presents fewer problems: the employee in a small firm can more easily see the relation between what he is doing and the objectives and performance of the firm as a whole . . . No doubt mainly as a result of this, the turnover of staff in small firms is very low and strikes and other kinds of industrial disputes are relatively infrequent.
>
> (Bolton 1971: 22)

The findings of the seminal Bolton Inquiry into small enterprises have since been contested. The harmony thesis or 'small is beautiful' image of smaller enterprises is to be contrasted with the bleak house thesis or 'small is brutal' image. As Table 15.2 reveals, some scholars have

Table 15.2 Contrasting perspectives on small enterprise working environments

Harmony thesis/small is beautiful	*Bleak House thesis/small is brutal*
Contributions more readily recognized	Poor working conditions
Higher levels of personal autonomy	Low wages
Unimpeded communication	Longer working hours
High proximity to leader/decision-maker	Higher levels of health and safety incidents

Sources: Bolton 1971, Barrett 1999, Rainnie 1989, Scase 2003, Storey 1994.

found evidence of poor working conditions, low wages, and long working hours (e.g. Rainnie 1989, Storey 1994), while others believe small enterprises provide an attractive work environment due to the proximity to leadership, simpler lines of communication, and the ability to see one's contributions more readily recognized (e.g. Barrett 1999, Scase 2003).

COMPLEXITY Research highlights the influence of the 'product market' environment on small enterprise competition, the strategic choices they have available, and how they manage their labour. For example, research undertaken on small enterprises surviving on the margins of the economy found that workers within these enterprises found it difficult to 'break out' due to the level of skills demanded by larger enterprises (Scase 1995, Storey 1994). In his study of ethnic minority workplaces, Ram (1994) found that Asian workers became trapped in smaller enterprises in the clothing sector because few other employment opportunities presented themselves. In contrast, in their case study analysis of the employee voice practices across five established small enterprises, Gilman et al. (2015) did not find evidence of a bleak house scenario. Mini-Case 15.2 provides further insight into the nature of voice in these enterprises.

VALUES Research highlights the dynamic nature of enterprise ownership, power, and control. It was Goss (1991) who developed a typology of employer control strategies, drawing attention to: 'the dependence of the employer upon particular employees and vice versa; and the power of workers individually or collectively to resist the exercise of proprietorial control' (see Figure 15.4). Employers that exhibit a *fraternal* approach allow employees to have greater discretion and autonomy, while *benevolent autocracy* or *sweating* is when employers make few concessions for employees. In an environment akin to a 'sweat shop' labour is seen as cheap and plentiful, and employee skills are not believed central to competitive advantage.

Stop and Think

What type of leader are you? Do you have a preference for delegating or taking responsibility?

Those business owners who take on too much responsibility and control over decision-making can find it hard to 'let go' and grow their team, and in turn their businesses.

Do not however become fooled that employees do not have a degree of power in the workplace! For instance, scholars (e.g. Moule 1998, Ram 1994) have found evidence that power and control are complex and contested constructs, they change and evolve in different ways and in different contexts. Employees have been found to alter the terms of the 'work effort–bargain'

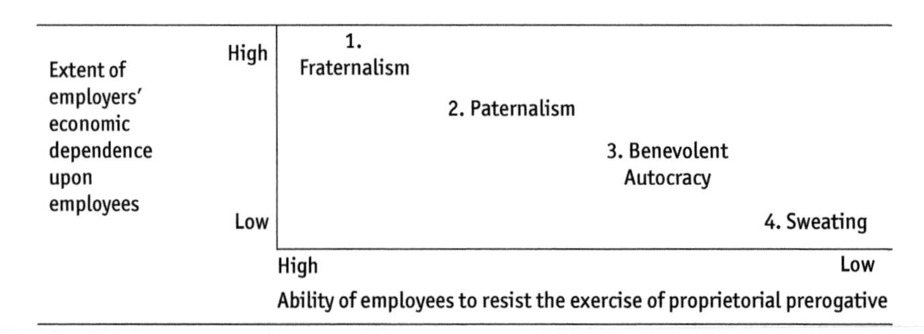

Figure 15.4 Types of employer control in small enterprises

Source: Goss 1991: 73.

(the reward an employee gets from the effort they invest) by taking opportunistic and pragmatic actions (e.g. stockpiling work, modifying the role of the supervisor); actions that can afford a degree of leeway in how work is performed.

Growth at all costs?

DIVERSITY Different growth models have been developed that attempt to explain enterprise growth. 'Organizational life cycle models', which take their origins from biological life cycles, emerged in the 1980s and 1990s and are among the most referenced growth models. They postulate that growth is a function of age and occurs as a sigmoid shape (Steinmetz 1969) whereby one gets bigger as one grows older (Davidsson et al. 2005). While these models suggest that enterprises pass through particular stages or states, there is little consensus on how many stages an enterprise actually experiences; which can range from three to ten. Life cycle models do share four common stages through which an enterprise progresses over time: birth, growth, maturity, and decline (Raby 2013).

COMPLEXITY In addition to age, SME growth is influenced by other factors that include: *crises experienced by the enterprise* (Lippitt and Schmidt 1967); *management style* (Adizes 1979); *effectiveness* (Cameron and Whetten 1981, Quinn and Cameron 1983, Smith et al. 1985); *organizational complexity* (Hanks et al. 1993, Hanks and Chandler 1994, Churchill 1997), or the approach taken towards *strategic planning* (Robinson et al. 1984). Both Greiner's

Mini-Case 15.2 An opportunity for having your voice heard?

STAKEHOLDERS Employee voice relates to the practices that exist in enterprises, large and small, to afford employees a degree of opportunity to contribute towards decision-making. Decision-making can occur at many different levels in an enterprise. For example, one may have a degree of choice in the way their work is organized, but not have much say in their team or group work environment. While other employees may be integrally involved in supporting senior leaders with strategic decisions; decisions that have the potential to affect the course of the enterprise.

Gilman et al. studied the way in which employee voice played out in a set of five relatively well established small enterprises. As noted earlier, established small enterprises create the majority of jobs. To summarize, the authors found the following three key points:

1. Voice practices differed across enterprises and this was largely due to the exposure of employees and managers to different working environments. Those employees and managers who lacked exposure to the practices of voice held limited understanding of the benefits, or desire to implement said practices.
2. The ability for owner-managers to step up to a strategic role determined the degree to which employees became involved in decision-making. Those leaders that retained more operational roles constrained the opportunity for employee voice at a strategic level.
3. The collective belief in the power of voice was essential if employees were to play a role in decision-making. In some enterprises, employees were disinterested in playing a more influential role in decision-making. Coupled with the inability for some owner-managers to 'let go' of the operational reins, this resulted in a 'missed opportunity for employees and managers'.

So, employee voice was heavily influenced by the owner-manager, with some enterprises having a high degree of involvement and participation in decision-making, and some less so. Aside to having their voices heard, employees reported that the 'family feel', 'personal fit', and the 'quality of the working environment' played crucial roles in sustaining their satisfaction for working for a small enterprise.

Source: Based on Gilman et al. 2015.

Questions

1. **What types of business are most likely to benefit from giving a stronger voice to employees in decision-making?**
2. **If you were an owner-manager, what strategies or methods would you use to stimulate employee involvement and participation in decision-making?**

(1972) model, that depicts the *evolutions* and *revolutions* that occur as an enterprise grows, and Churchill and Lewis's (1983) staged model of growth are often well cited.

Table 15.3 provides a summary of Churchill and Lewis's depiction of the five stages of enterprise growth. Between each stage, the model suggests that an enterprise is faced with four possible options: exit (i.e. close down), sell, stay, or move to the next stage. Moving to the 'take-off' stage is seen as an essential step, one that requires an owner to choose to either build from the stable platform for growth, or not:

> This [success stage] is a pivotal period in a company's life. If the owner rises to the challenges of a growing company, both financially and managerially, it can become a big business. If not, it can usually be sold—at a profit—provided the owner recognizes his or her limitations soon enough.

Although staged models of organizational growth are popular, they are subject to a number of criticisms. First, few models have been empirically validated as to provide a generalized theory that explains enterprise growth. Second, most models assume that each enterprise will sequentially pass through a set of discrete events; one forming a precondition for the next. In reality, most enterprises are in transition through growth stages, as opposed to being in a stable state, and will progress through the stages at a different rate (Dodge et al. 1994). Third, growth is typically discontinuous and a short-lived event (Smallbone et al. 1995) and luck and chance play an important role (Storey 2011). The growth process is unpredictable and involves a number of disconnected jumps, as a consequence of the reaction to critical events (Deakins and Freel 1998).

DYNAMIC Another model used to explain enterprise growth is the 'dynamic states of growth model' (Levie and Lichtenstein 2010). This model moves beyond the focus on 'how much' enterprises grow by, towards understanding the process of 'how' enterprises grow (Leitch et al. 2010). The model is characterized as multilevel, dynamic, and contextually specific and identifies a number of factors that can influence the process of growth, such as:

- *The Industry level:* policy, taxation, regulation, support (e.g. Smallbone and Wyer 2000, Storey 1994)
- *The enterprise level:* age, location, nature of family/kinship relations (Battitsti et al. 2013)

Table 15.3 Churchill and Lewis's growth stage model

Stage	Enterprise focus	Planning	Role of the owner
Existence	Obtaining customers	Non-existent	Do everything directly
Survival	Appreciating relationship between revenues and expenses	Minimal, cash forecasting	Delegate certain orders to a supervisor
Success-disengage	Earning above-average profits and avoiding overspending	Exists to maintain the status quo	Delegate to functional managers for certain duties
Take-off	Achieving rapid growth and how to finance	Nascent strategic and operational planning	Delegate, separate self from business
Resource maturity	Controlling growth and preserving entrepreneurial spirit	Detailed strategic and operational planning	Innovate, take risks, nurture the entrepreneurial spirit

Source: Churchill and Lewis 1983.

- *The entrepreneur's characteristics:* age, gender, commitment/willingness to grow, education attainment, prior management experience, top team composition (e.g. Barbeo et al. 2011, Price et al. 2013)
- *The strategies used by management:* e.g. cost, differentiation, customization, internationalization (e.g. Bamiatzi and Kirchmaier 2014, Hilmersson 2014)

An important factor which is not well recognized in existing enterprise growth models is the level to which founder(s) and senior managers are committed to growth. However, the notion that growth is the only reason why individuals set up their own enterprise can, and should be questioned. Read Mini-Case 15.3.

Stop and Think

Are there any other factors that you believe influence firm growth?

Mini-Case 15.3 Growth: not the only reason?

VALUES One of the authors of this chapter was invited to run a workshop with business owners on how they achieve their aspirations for growth. In planning for the session, the following questions emerged:

- How do we each define success?
- What are the key challenges getting in the way of achieving our aspirations?
- How can we think differently about the way we, and our businesses, work?

What success means to me—not just profits, a whole range of factors personal to me!

Success for participating SMEs was not just about profit. Participants noted success to be a very personal thing founded on expectations that 'we set for ourselves'. Making reference to Maslow's hierarchy of needs, participants spoke about first fulfilling 'basic needs'; the ability to put food on the table and pay the bills. From there, success focused on building and sustaining relationships, a desire for belongingness and satisfying others, such as fellow business owners and customers. The distinction between profit and wider prosperity was made, alluding to the belief that business was more than just a vehicle through which to achieve our own goals; business holds the potential to drive social good and change. The ability to think and look differently at the way we deliver our work, be creative and continuously seek better ways of doing things rounded off this piece of the discussions.

Achieving our aspirations—working 'on' not just 'in' the business

Common challenges to achieving participants' aspirations surfaced. Initially there was a focus on the 'here and now issues', such as the challenge of navigating government systems and policies. Participants commented that it 'Often feels like we're trying to run with our shoelaces tied together . . . it's not easy or graceful and often a struggle!' Observations were made of the need for strategic thinking to allocate finite resources. Of particular importance was finding, selecting, and retaining the right people in order to release time for owners to work 'on' the business, not just 'in' the business.

Time to think differently about the way we work—reflecting on 'what works'

Through exploring the BIG Ten characteristics [Table 15.4], participants observed:

- 'I recognize that there are some things I like doing and have a preference for, and others less so!'
- 'I need to build a team around me that has an eye on each of these areas.'
- 'It's opened further questions that I need to take away and work on with my team.'

Source: Excerpt from 'Create' event at Fruitworks co-working space, Canterbury, UK.

Questions

1. **How might you define 'success' for your own business? What measures of success would you adopt for your company?**
2. **What are the potential advantages and disadvantages of hiring more people to achieve business growth?**
3. **As a business owner, what things would you prefer to work on, and what areas of the business would you delegate to others?**

SME growth in practice

COMPLEXITY Researchers at the University of Kent in the UK undertook a rigorous applied programme of research—Promoting Sustainable Performance (PSP)[2]—that investigated the determinants of sustainable growth for SMEs. This programme of research moved beyond traditional functional organizational silos by identifying a set of capabilities that leaders of better performing SMEs were using to strategically develop and grow their businesses (see: Gilman et al. 2012).[3] This research provides an opportunity for those working with SMEs, whether they be academics, leaders (both mature and next generation), practitioners and policymakers, to identify and develop individual and organizational good practice. The 'BIG Ten'™ capabilities are detailed in Table 15.4 and can be explored through a short video cartoon.[4]

Stop and Think

Which capabilities do you believe you have and, if you were establishing your own venture, which would you need to find elsewhere?

Table 15.4 The BIG Ten™ characteristics of successful SMEs

	Lens	Summary of attribute
	Enthusiast	Channel passion and effort through purpose
	Transformer	Manage change and transition, sustain a unique advantage
	Strategist	Develop and execute growth strategy
	Delegator	Clarity in tasks, roles, and capabilities
	Innovator	Generate new ideas and new products/services
	Integrator	Understand value and promote supply/value chain collaboration
	Calculator	Apply a holistic set of evidence-based performance measures

[2] PSP utilizes a mixed method approach to understanding SME growth. Data is collected and synthesized through quantitative and qualitative instruments (e.g. surveys, personal interviews, detailed case studies, and focus groups) with leaders and SMEs. The research model is guided by a multidisciplinary team of researchers at Kent Business School, University of Kent representing a wide range of business and management disciplines.

[3] Contact simon@big-associates to obtain a full copy.

[4] Navigate to 'BIG Ten' at www.time2thinkbig.com

Table 15.4 *(Continued)*

	Lens	Summary of attribute
	Systemizer	Build repeatable, reliable, and scalable processes
	Engager	Embed practices that engender commitment
	Sponge	Absorb, assimilate, and exploit new knowledge

These capabilities help us to develop an awareness of the broader issues central to SME growth, and their interaction with strategy. Within the research, those SMEs that demonstrated an awareness of, and were taking action across a range of these capabilities were achieving higher and more sustained levels of economic growth. Each of these ten capabilities were explored in greater detailed by the research team in partnership with business leaders across the south of England. Hosted by the digital radio show the *Business Bunker* the research team (2014) led a discussion on the essence of each capability and the way in which they could be applied in an SME context.[5]

Entrepreneurship

In the past few decades, entrepreneurship has captured the imagination of people across the globe. Entrepreneurs are the new business super-heroes and their ventures have become household names, such as Tory Burch of Tory Burch fashion, Mark Zuckerberg of Facebook, Anita Roddick of the Body Shop, Richard Branson of Virgin, and Elon Musk of Tesla.

VALUES The rise of the 'entrepreneurial society' can be understood by a number of underlying factors. Entrepreneurship is opportunity-centred and rewards talent, performance, and ambition over social class or educational credentials. Entrepreneurship creates economic and social mobility and does not discriminate according to skin colour, religion, gender, or national origin. Indeed, ethnic minorities and immigrants in many OECD countries are shown to excel at entrepreneurship. The Global Economic Monitor (GEM) now provides data on entrepreneurial behaviour and attitudes across over 100 countries.[6]

Entrepreneurship can be described as a social phenomenon with its roots deeply embedded in US culture. Yet, entrepreneurship is not unique to any country and occurs everywhere. Studies on entrepreneurship have yet to identify a particular set of personal traits essential for entrepreneurial success. This suggests that certain skills and behaviours of the entrepreneur can be learned and applied, although some personal traits, such as ambition and passion, are common among successful entrepreneurs.

[5] To listen to a short podcast on 'The Strategist' navigate to: http://www.kentbusinessradio.co.uk/b-g-insights

[6] http://www.gemconsortium.org

DIVERSITY Entrepreneurship has also emerged as a focal point for economic growth, sustainable job creation, and competitiveness in global markets, as entrepreneurs start up and grow new enterprises and introduce new innovations to the market. The critical role played by SMEs in the economy was described in the previous section. SMEs that are innovative and growth-oriented are 'market catalysts' that in time will contribute disproportionately to economic development and future prosperity for the global economy. Such SMEs are often led by ambitious entrepreneurs and are often referred to as 'gazelles'. This highlights the direct relationship between enterprise and entrepreneurship.

While entrepreneurship is often associated with new venture creation, the term 'entrepreneur' can also refer to a broad range of individuals within the business environment who identify new opportunities and act upon them. Entrepreneurship occurs across different business domains, which include new enterprise, large corporations, family firms, public organizations, academic institutions, and other non-profits. We now turn our attention to defining entrepreneurship.

Stop and Think

Reflect on successful entrepreneurs that you may know personally. What particular traits, capabilities, or ambitions do they display which could explain some of their success?

Defining entrepreneurship

DIVERSITY There is no generally accepted or universal definition for 'entrepreneur', as we found in attempting to define 'SME'. The word 'entrepreneur' is derived from the French words *entre* ('between') and *prendre* ('to take'). Translation into English suggests the entrepreneur is someone who takes on the risk of working between buyers and sellers. Over the past few hundred years, a variety of different definitions of entrepreneur have been proposed, with more common definitions presented in Table 15.5. Observe how definitions of entrepreneurship and

Table 15.5 Definitions of entrepreneurship

Source	Definition
Richard Cantillon (1680–1734)	the act of purchasing, repackaging, and marketing of products at an unpredictable and uncertain price
Jean Baptiste Say (1767–1832)	the individual who acts as a 'broker' in the production and selling of a product
Frank Knight (1882–1972)	the individual who 'handles' the uncertainty that exists in the market
Joseph Schumpeter (1888–1950)	the individual who 'disrupts' the equilibrium of the economic system by introducing new combinations (i.e. innovations) into that system
Israel Kirzner (1930–)	a 'pure' entrepreneur observes the opportunity to sell a product at a higher price than that at which he can buy it
Jeffry Timmons (1941–2008)	a way of thinking, reasoning, and acting that is opportunity obsessed, holistic in approach, and leadership balanced
Howard Stevenson (1941–)	'entrepreneurship is the process by which individuals—either on their own or inside organizations—pursue opportunities without regard to the resources they currently control' (Stevenson and Jarillo 1990).

Table 15.6 Distinctions between invention, technology, and innovation

Invention	• A synthesis of new knowledge derived from a sequence of acts of independent insight • Creation of a new idea or concept
Technology	• '*Utilitarian invention* socially constructed, interpreted & used by people', and reflecting a 'cultural system concerned with the relationships between humans and their environment' (Cohen and Levinthal 1990)
Innovation	• New ways of doing things • New product, process, service, or method • New commercial application of technology

entrepreneur have evolved from the French meaning to include concepts of risk-taking, opportunity identification, and resources required for pursuing the opportunity.

From Table 15.5, we observe that entrepreneurship is defined as a process, whereby individuals identify and pursue new opportunities, and as a way of thinking and acting. Entrepreneurship is also associated with the concept of innovation. Earlier discussion described the important role played by SMEs in introducing innovations to the market and how innovation provides SMEs with a competitive advantage.

While the basis of innovation may be a new 'invention' or new 'technology', it is important to distinguish these concepts from innovation, as shown in Table 15.6. One can think of innovation as the process by which entrepreneurs apply invention or technology in new ways to create value.

DIVERSITY A strong relationship between innovation and entrepreneurship was identified earlier, drawing on the work of management guru Peter Drucker (1985). Joseph Schumpeter (1934), the economist best known for highlighting innovation as the basis for economic growth, describes entrepreneurs as those who introduce new 'combinations' that disrupt the status quo of the market. Schumpeter suggests five types of innovations, described further in Table 15.7.

Table 15.7 Types of innovation

Type of innovation	Description	Example
New good or service	One in which users are not yet familiar; or new level of quality of a good or service	Mobile phone, digital camera, MP3 player, microwave oven
Process innovation	New method of production or new way of handling a commodity commercially	Lean production, computer-aided design, software
New market	Entirely new market; for example, a market in which users are not yet familiar with a new product, service, or process	Foreign market entry, repositioning of product for a new customer category
New source of raw material	Or half-manufactured good	Silicon, plastics, steel, nanoparticle, stem cell
New organizational form	New business models, organizational structure, and so forth	Lean start-up, self-organization (e.g. *Wikipedia*), collaborative organization (e.g. Procter & Gamble)

DYNAMIC The impact of innovation in the market is often described by the terms 'incremental' innovation and 'radical or disruptive' innovation. Most innovations are incremental, offering improvements on the previous innovation. Radical innovation refers more to Schumpeter's suggestion that such innovations disrupt the status quo of the market, by making existing offering (e.g. products, services, processes) less attractive and contributing to the decline of enterprises that do not innovate. Schumpeter called this process 'creative destruction'. Drucker (1985) describes innovation in terms of the change that creates a new dimension of performance.

> *Stop and Think*
>
> What innovations can you identify that have created a new dimension of performance when introduced to the market? What has been the impact on competitors in that market?

This continuous generation of new ideas, innovations and the birth and decline of businesses is an accepted ethos of a capitalist market and the infinite source of entrepreneurial opportunity. But innovation does not occur as a random event, and central to the innovation process is entrepreneurial activity.

Are small business owners also entrepreneurs?

DIVERSITY The question of whether a small business owner is also an entrepreneur has attracted much debate among entrepreneurship scholars. A distinction between the entrepreneur and types of small business owners is made by Stokes et al. (2010), as described below:

- **The craftsman/owner manager:** this refers to occupations that include: carpenter, plumber (tradesperson), hairdresser, baker, butcher, shopkeeper, etc.
- **The professional manager:** this refers to individuals who build a 'little big business' and includes accountants, lawyers, doctors, and other professionals who establish their own enterprises.
- **The promoter/entrepreneur:** this refers to the 'wheeler-dealer' who starts, grows, buys, and often sells businesses. This category suggests entrepreneurs as risk-taking, opportunity-seeking individuals.

A further distinction—between entrepreneur, promoter, manager (and inventor)—is made by Spinelli and Adams (2012), who suggest that entrepreneurs combine high levels of creativity and innovation with high levels of general management skills, know-how, and networks (see Figure 15.5).

Spinelli and Adams (2012: 46) contend that 'the making of an entrepreneur occurs by accumulating the relevant skills, know how, experiences and contacts over a period of years and includes large doses of self-development'. This suggests that the business environment for nascent (new) entrepreneurs is much different to that for experienced entrepreneurs. The concept of *liability of newness* is used to refer to a lack of market credibility for a new entrepreneur or enterprise, whereby customers, potential business partners, or employees may be reluctant to buy, engage, or join the business because of lack of track record and uncertainty over

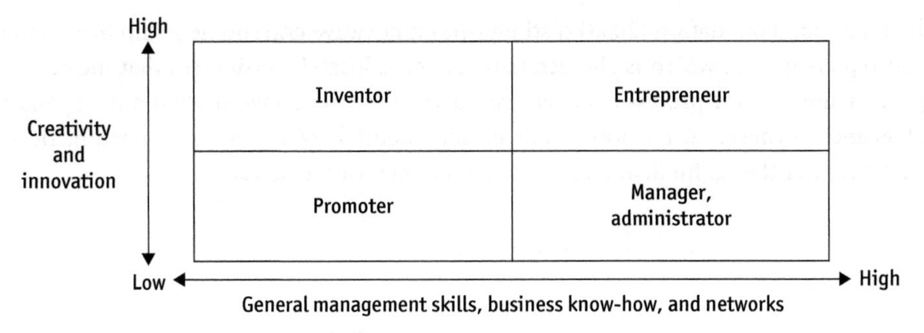

Figure 15.5 Distinguishing characteristics of the entrepreneur

Source: Spinelli and Adams 2012. Reproduced with the kind permission of McGraw-Hill Education.

market acceptance (e.g. Stinchcombe and March 1965). Existing businesses have already validated market acceptance by customers while new enterprises have not, and their very survival remains in doubt.

Reluctance in the market by customers to engage with nascent entrepreneurs and enterprises is not unfounded, given the high failure rates of new businesses. Gage (2012) suggests that 60 per cent of start-ups survive to three years, and only 35 per cent of start-ups survive to ten years, with high mortality rates identified across other studies. Because innovative entrepreneurs try to do things that haven't been done before (versus imitating or copying others), this significantly increases their chances of failure.

Some scholars suggest that entrepreneurs differ from small business owners not only by their innovative behaviour but also by their 'high achievement motivation' (Carland et al. 1984, Lumpkin and Erdogan 1999). Although no single psychological model of entrepreneurship has been identified, psychological motivation is a common characteristic of successful entrepreneurs, which include the need for achievement, power, and affiliation (Spinelli and Adams 2012).

Schumpeter's definition of the entrepreneur as innovator—who introduces novel combinations to the market—would appear to apply less to an individual who imitates another business, buys into a franchise operation, or chooses self-employment in the same line of business previously undertaken as an employee.

DIVERSITY Self-employment is defined as working for oneself rather than for an employer and directly operating and profiting from one's own business. Independence and self-fulfilment are identified as prime motivators for becoming self-employed (Parker 2004) and two expressions of self-employment are lifestyle enterprises and participation in the 'gig economy'.

Lifestyle enterprises provide the founder/owner (and his/her family) with a particular lifestyle and income. Such enterprises will usually remain small and may remain geographically bound, due to a conscious decision on the part of the owner. However, lifestyle enterprises can reach a global audience (e.g. launching an ebook) and also evolve into profitable businesses, depending on the motivation and capabilities of the owner.

The gig economy refers to temporary, flexible work provided by the self-employed to other organizations. The gig economy reflects a shift in the concept of long-term, full-time employment that characterized previous decades (Friedman 2014). While some activities, such as driving for Uber or offering professional services from home, respond to changing demands of the market, small-scale entrepreneurship is evident in new services made possible by identifying new opportunities and leveraging technology.

The Kauffman Foundation (2008) distinguishes innovative entrepreneurship from 'replicative' entrepreneurship, which is characteristic of small lifestyle businesses that include small shops, restaurants, and professional service businesses. The above discussion suggests that small business owners may be more or less 'entrepreneurial' by the level of opportunistic, risk-taking behaviour they exhibit, and innovative outcomes they generate.

Stop and Think

How would you respond to the suggestion that small business owners are 'less entrepreneurial' if they replicate an existing business concept or buy into a franchise business—compared to someone who introduces a novel business idea to the market?

Domains of entrepreneurship

LOCAL TO GLOBAL Although entrepreneurship is often associated with new enterprise creation, entrepreneurial activity can be found across different business domains, with some of these domains described in Table 15.8.

VALUES How does entrepreneurship manifest itself across different business domains? High achievement motivation, a distinguishing entrepreneurial characteristic noted above, aligns with the concept of 'entrepreneurial orientation' (EO), which has been shown to be a strong predictor of enterprise performance (Lumpkin and Dess 1996, Rauch et al. 2009). The EO model proposes five dimensions of entrepreneurial behaviour and actions that enhance enterprise performance, as described in Table 15.9.

Table 15.8 Entrepreneurship in different domains

Domain	Description
Corporate entrepreneurship	A means of taking the skills of a successful entrepreneur and incorporating these characteristics into the culture of a large organization in an attempt to combat stagnation and lack of innovation that organizations often develop as they grow (Thornberry 2003) • **Intrapreneurship**: how individuals act in an entrepreneurial way in larger organizations • **Corporate venturing**: how larger organizations manage new, entrepreneurial ventures from their mainstream activity (Burns 2013)
Family enterprising	'The proactive & continuous search for opportunistic growth when expansion is neither pressing nor particularly obvious' (Jeffry Timmons)
Social entrepreneurship	The entrepreneur sees embedded in a particular context a suboptimal situation/problem and seeks to provide a new solution, product, service, or process. The entrepreneur applies a unique set of personal characteristics to the situation–inspiration, creativity, direct action, courage, and fortitude (Martin and Osberg 2007)
Sustainable entrepreneurship	Entrepreneurship can help resolve environmental problems through the exploitation of opportunities inherent in environmentally relevant market failures and thereby help move global economic systems towards sustainability (Dean and McMullen 2007)

Table 15.9 Dimensions of entrepreneurial orientation (EO)

Dimension	Definition	Behaviour/actions
Autonomy	Independent action by an individual or team to bring forth and implement a business concept	• Opportunity recognition and formulation • Strategic positioning • Securing resources
Innovativeness	Through experimentation and creativity, develop new and novel products, services, processes	• Continuous innovation • User-led and open innovation
Proactiveness	A forward-looking perspective characteristic of a market leader who has foresight	• First-mover advantage • Benchmarking competitors
Competitive aggressiveness	An intense effort to outperform rivals, characterized by a combative posture or aggressive response	• Introducing new products before competitors • Copying and adopting leading-edge practices and technique
Risk-taking	Making decisions and taking action without certain knowledge of probable outcomes	• Venturing without knowing probability of success, e.g. due to untested markets, technology • Risk-return trade-off, which may include heavy borrowing and large resource commitments • Risks to personal reputation, career, and enterprise that occur by taking some actions

Although EO appears as a well-established concept in the entrepreneurship literature, different situations or business contexts will influence the extent to which EO enhances enterprise performance. For example, EO is shown to be significantly more important for micro-businesses (e.g. 1–9 employees) than for small businesses (e.g. 10–150 employees) and for high-tech industries than for non-high-tech industries (Rauch et al. 2009). This suggests that entrepreneurial behaviour and actions, as represented by the five dimensions of EO, are more important for tech-based, micro-businesses.

Another concept which explains entrepreneurship within existing enterprises is known as 'dynamic capabilities', and refers to the ability to *sense and then seize* new opportunities and to reconfigure and protect know-how assets, competencies, and technologies to achieve sustainable competitive advantage (Teece 1998). Deployment of dynamic capabilities is a central function of successful entrepreneurial leaders within innovative firms and emphasizes the role of strategic management in adapting and reconfiguring knowledge and other assets to match the requirements of a changing internal and external business environment.

Enterprises that can respond quickly and flexibly to changing conditions will be more successful, which was earlier identified as an advantage of SMEs over larger firms, particularly in dynamic and competitive business environments. The concept of dynamic capabilities is also highly relevant in public sector organizations, where strategic management capabilities may be more appropriate than dimensions of behaviour and action suggested by EO.

Entrepreneurship and new ventures

STAKEHOLDERS Each year, millions of people around the globe make the decision to start a new venture. The majority of these new ventures are lifestyle or 'necessity-driven' businesses, as much as 90 per cent by some estimates (Davis 2003). Funding will come primarily from the founders themselves, supplemented by family and friends, the aptly named '3F' funding source. Lifestyle or necessity-driven enterprises are less likely to face high start-up capital requirements. Many will be service based, typically employ only the founder or a small number of employees, and remain small. New ventures that can generate early sales and free cash flow (e.g. cash left over after expenses are paid) are not likely to require any external investment (Gregson 2014).

A smaller proportion of new ventures will be growth oriented, more innovative, and led by visionary and ambitious entrepreneurs. These ventures are market catalysts that in time will contribute disproportionately to economic development and future prosperity for the global economy, and we have previously described these as 'gazelles'. Their early funding requirements will typically take them beyond the limits of 3F sources and to seek external sources of investment. Sourcing adequate capital is a major obstacle to growth oriented new ventures—particularly seed capital for product development, prototyping, and testing the idea in the market. Many early stage ventures are not yet profitable—some have yet to make their first sale.

For new ventures led by nascent (i.e. new) entrepreneurs, the absence of a business track record—along with an unproven product, service, or market need—makes these risky investments (Gregson 2014). We discussed earlier the challenges of 'liability of newness' for the nascent entrepreneur. Debt financing from banks is usually not an option, given the lack of built-up assets to offer as collateral against the debt. So, although the entrepreneur has identified a promising new business opportunity and is passionate about pursuing it, the dream may not become a reality because of a lack of funding or difficulty in accessing capital markets.

COMPLEXITY Different market conditions will influence the entrepreneur's ability to develop a new venture. Successful growth-oriented entrepreneurial venturing tends to be concentrated in locations where there is an abundance of talent, related services, large markets to sell products and services, less barriers to doing business, and access to different sources of finance. This usually favours large metropolitan cities as hotbeds for entrepreneurial activity, but there are exceptions—no better illustrated than by Internet-based start-ups which can be launched into the World Wide Web from almost anywhere.

New venture formation

In this section, we discuss what it takes to start a new enterprise and provide a holistic picture of the process of new venture formation—where the entrepreneur is the central figure in forming a new business. Here, we use the term 'entrepreneur' to acknowledge the *opportunistic* and *risk-taking* behaviour and actions required to start one's own business. While we have already discussed potential distinctions between high-growth and non-high-growth entrepreneurship, we will discuss new enterprise formation here in general terms.

The entrepreneur starting a new business must overcome a different set of challenges compared to existing SMEs, as noted earlier. The new business is unknown and its market value unproven—making its survival, let alone prospects to thrive and grow, highly uncertain.

COMPLEXITY Most new businesses engage in six key 'business formation' activities, as suggested in Figure 15.6: opportunity identification; securing resources; management and team building; company formation; refining service or product for market; and financial feasibility.

Business formation activities are not the same as 'business planning' activities—which are detailed plans unique to a particular business. There are six common business formation activities, shown in Figure 15.6, that entrepreneurs engage in when setting up their ventures. Each activity is described further below.

Opportunity

The ideas behind new ventures are as varied as the entrepreneurs who create them; from social media sites to medical devices, to speech and language recognition software, to new distribution platforms, new value chains, new linkages between consumer markets, and so forth. New businesses are typically formed when an entrepreneur, or founding team, applies their know-how to offer a new service or product, or better solve an existing problem in the market. In rare cases, entrepreneurs create entirely new markets with novel services or products.

Many new ventures are based on leveraging an individual's previous experience and his/her domain expertise in a particular field. In these cases, a trigger event may compel the individual to leave a salaried position and venture out on his/her own. This trigger event could include a desire to be self-employed and work for oneself or to pursue an opportunity that might not otherwise be developed. Mini-Case 15.4 identifies how vision and personal values also shape the entrepreneurial opportunity.

Alternatively, opportunities may emerge through research or academic study, where recognition of the potential to commercially develop research results stimulates the formation of a new business to realize value from the research. However, academic entrepreneurship, as it is commonly referred to, is often challenging for academic researchers because key entrepreneurial behaviours and actions required to transform invention to innovation are absent. In some cases, the vision to exploit potential opportunities comes from others, such

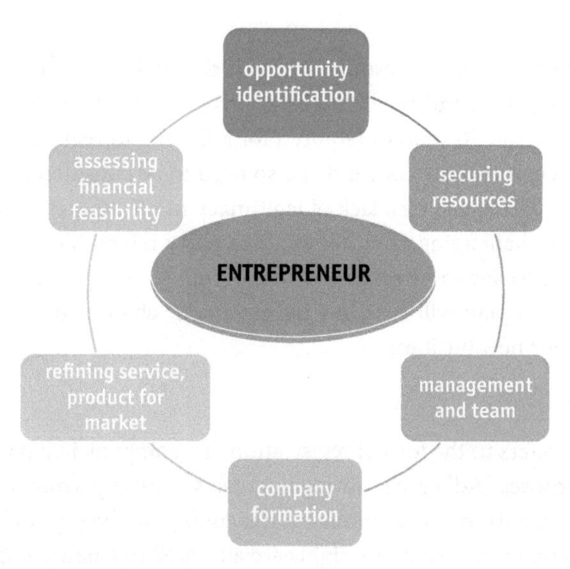

Figure 15.6 New venture formation activities

Source: Gregson 2014.

Mini-Case 15.4 How vision shapes the entrepreneurial opportunity

Some opportunities are based on a particular vision or set of values that shape the subsequent venture. A vision sets out what the venture aspires to become, acts as a reference point for every decision and guides future behaviour of people in the venture. A vision gives purpose to the pursuit of the opportunity and should be bold but simple. Many ventures that have grown into large corporations have been guided by an ambitious vision. Google's vision is 'to organize the world's information and make it universally accessible and useful'. Nike's vision is 'to bring inspiration and innovation to every athlete in the world', while Tesla's vision is 'to accelerate the world's transition to sustainable energy'. A vision is important because it forces the entrepreneur to really know the ambitions for the business and what outcomes it will create.

For some entrepreneurs, this vision reflects their personal values. For example, Anita Roddick, founder of the Body Shop, established a clear set of values that defined her company and attracted customers who shared these values. These values included no animal testing on products; support for community fair trade; defending human rights; and protecting the planet.

Questions

1. **What other companies can you identify where personal values of the entrepreneur/founder have clearly shaped how the business has developed?**
2. **How would your personal values shape the development of your own entrepreneurial opportunity?**

as the university technology transfer office or from advisers, rather than from the academic inventor.

Entrepreneurs have been shown to spend little time actually researching and analysing opportunities; rather, entrepreneurs screen opportunities quickly, focus on a few important issues and are ready to adapt original plans, even when they are not entirely sure of the outcomes (Bhide 1994). Flexibility and acceptance of the need to adapt original plans will be expected of entrepreneurs by most investors. However, this will vary, depending on the type of business. Forming a medical device venture, for example, will require more considered planning compared to a web-based start-up.

Securing resources

To pursue an opportunity requires resources, which can include funding, specialized equipment, property or land, skills and capabilities not possessed by the entrepreneur, and critical partnerships or agreements. Resources required for adhering to regulatory or compliance requirements in a particular industry or market also need to be considered.

New businesses are challenged by a lack of legitimacy in the market, which makes securing resources from others challenging. The role of third party referrals can be valuable, particularly when attempting to secure investment. Identifying a very promising opportunity and having a strong business plan will certainly improve your chances of securing necessary resources to develop your new business.

Company formation

Company formation refers to the formal registration of a company in a particular jurisdiction for legal and tax purposes. Adherence to regulations, securing permissions and permits are also required before operations can commence, depending on the type of business.

In this process of company formation, rights are allocated to a new company and owners of the business receive shares or an ownership stake to compensate them for the knowledge and assets brought in to the company. These are referred to as 'founder shares'. If the business raises external investment, then subsequent investors represent another type of share—'financial shares' which are directly related to the capital they invest in the business.

Refining the value proposition

Many new businesses are formed while the entrepreneur continues to refine or further develop the primary product or service. Often, refinement occurs as first customers are engaged, and critical feedback from such engagement results in refining, fine-tuning and in some cases, repositioning the service or product in that market segment.

New ventures seeking external funding need to offer something to the market that has high potential to build business value, which often equates to market growth. Investors seek businesses with strong 'value propositions' that meet a clearly defined market need and can expand beyond a single product or service. Investors such as business angels will invest in businesses that offer an exit—so that they can get a return on their investment. This may require the entrepreneur to eventually sell their business.

Management and team

Many new ventures are sole proprietorships or 'lifestyle'-oriented businesses, where requirements for additional management capabilities are not always necessary. For larger, growth-oriented businesses, there may be a requirement to complement the entrepreneur's skills to develop a wider management skill set. Studies show that new businesses founded by a team tend to be more successful than those founded by a sole entrepreneur (Birley and Stockley 2000).

A complementary balance of people skill sets, capabilities, and experiences determine the knowledge or 'intellectual' base of the business from which competitive advantages arise. Running a four-star resort, for example, will require a strong team that demonstrates capabilities in finance and accounting, operations management, and marketing and sales.

Assessing financial feasibility

Starting your own business, as any experienced entrepreneur will tell you, is a highly personal career choice. Every entrepreneur must make a personal case for themselves—in deciding to pursue a new business opportunity or not. For some, it is the logical choice, but for others, it is a much more measured decision.

An objective assessment of the feasibility of your own business opportunity is often difficult, given the level of emotional, intellectual, and often financial capital that may already be committed. It is often the case that the process of generating a business plan—requiring more formal financial data—clarifies the financial feasibility of the opportunity.

Summarizing new venture formation

- ✓ The new venture formation process shown in Figure 15.6 is *iterative in nature*, reflecting the fact that there is no one best method for creating a new business. Although opportunity identification is likely a first step in the process, some entrepreneurs may form a company prior to building a team, or refine their services for the market only after securing resources.
- ✓ New business formation is very much a learning process, particularly for first-time entrepreneurs (referred to as 'nascent' entrepreneurs). Each of the activities in Figure 15.6 generates new information and insights that informs the viability of the opportunity. This learning process will be very much evident as the entrepreneur proceeds through a business planning process.

Financing the new venture

Entrepreneurs usually need to spend money before they make money—to cover expenses in the absence of any sales revenues. Such expenses may include purchasing, renting, or leasing equipment and business space, paying suppliers, and paying staff salaries. This investment is known as start-up capital or seed funding. The level of start-up capital required is influenced by the nature of the market and industry, including:

- Capital intensity of the particular business sector. Capital costs to launch a web-based business are significantly less than developing a biotech company. High start-up costs, along with the need for specialized know-how, equipment, property, or locations can be significant entry barriers for new ventures.
- Size and growth of the market. A large market of customers with a similar profile may allow a new business to gain rapid market share; however, this usually requires an exceptional product or service, secured channels to sell to them, and money spent on marketing.

Market and industry factors also affect the level of external financing sought by the business. External investors usually expect the entrepreneur to treat their investment as growth capital rather than business development funding. For example, funding requests to increase sales, such as hiring an extra sales person or acquiring new facilities and equipment to expand operations, will be favoured over requests to pay higher salaries, upgrade office facilities, or buy out the shares of a business partner.

Business models

INTERACTION Building a successful new venture requires more than simply having a good idea and a potentially attractive market. It requires an appropriate business model. While existing enterprises execute a business model, new enterprises are looking for one.

The *business model canvas* helps to explain the logic and describe the rationale of how a new enterprise will create, deliver, and capture value. Many entrepreneurs spend considerable time explaining their service or product without 'validating' the level of demand or interest by prospective customers—which is essential in building business value.

The business model canvas provides a simple but effective approach to developing a model for a business (Osterwalder and Pigneur 2010). Nine building blocks of the canvas, shown in Table 15.10, provide a balanced approach to building the case for a business—beginning with a value proposition (VP) for a particular customer segment (CS) the business intends to target.

Growing the new venture

Previous discussion in the first part of the chapter identified factors influencing SME growth, so we refer you back to some of those concepts of growth (see Table 15.11).

How the new venture pursues growth will be influenced by entrepreneurial behaviour and actions and influenced by the business environment. However, it must be emphasized that the ambition and passion of the entrepreneur to pursue growth and his/her abilities to secure and manage the resources required to pursue growth are important factors in the success of high-growth ventures.

Table 15.10 Business model canvas

Building block	Key questions
Customer segment (CS)	Who is your primary customer for your business? What are their wants and needs? What are they willing to pay for?
Value proposition (VP)	What compelling things does your business provide to the customer? What needs are satisfied? e.g. convenience, novelty, uniqueness, risk or cost reduction, performance, flexibility, design, brand
Channels to market (CM)	How is your value proposition sold and delivered? Will your business directly control the channel to the customer (e.g. promotion, sales, transactions), or use partner channels (e.g. existing businesses that could also sell your product, other market intermediaries)?
Customer relations (CR)	How will your business interact with customers? What relationship does the customer expect with you and your business? How important are CRs to the VP? How will CRs be integrated into the VP and how much will it cost your business?
Revenue streams	What are customers willing to pay for your VP? What do they currently pay (what are the competitive offerings)? How will your business receive revenue?
Key resources	What resources must your business own (or control) to make the business model work? e.g. intellectual (partnerships, industry contacts), human (know-how, specialized skills), physical (location, logistics), financial (cash, lines of credit).
Key activities	What key things does your business do to deliver on the VP? e.g. superior service, transactional efficiencies, novel customer experience, new knowledge related to service or product, design, repeatable set of processes.
Key partnerships	Are you partnering to deliver your VP? Are some business activities outsourced? Can you reduce costs and increase efficiencies, enhance reputation using partners? How can you optimize partnerships to extend business capabilities, access new customers?
Cost structure	What are the key costs and cost drivers of the business? e.g. fixed vs. variable costs, economies of scale (cost advantages as you deliver more services or products) and economics of scope (e.g. use of same marketing or distribution channels to support different services or products).

Looking ahead

Entrepreneurship is now a global phenomenon across the business landscape. The appeal of entrepreneurship lies in its broad application that allows individuals and teams to pursue new opportunities, innovate, create new ventures, renew organizations, stimulate the emergence of new industries, and contribute significantly to economic development and personal prosperity.

How will the global marketplace change the way entrepreneurs create and grow their businesses?

DYNAMIC John Naisbitt, a US author and public speaker, first wrote about *megatrends* in 1982. Megatrends are major trends or movements that can influence all aspects of our lives. For entrepreneurs, understanding megatrends can provide a glimpse into future

Table 15.11 New venture start-up to scale-up

Dimension	*Start-up*	*Scale-up*
Growth	Incubation	Acceleration
Life cycle phase	Concept/ideation	Growth
Age	< 5 years	> 5 years
Size	Micro to small	Small to medium
Driver	Founder	President/CEO
Strategic posture	Entrepreneurial	Strategic
Business model	Building and proving	Repeating and scaling
Focus	Problem solving	Solution providing
Product/service	Testing market-fit	Proven market-fit
Endurance	Fragile	Robust

market opportunities and stimulate new ideas to satisfy future market needs. Megatrends challenge us to think globally, and work locally, to think strategically and beyond and build foresight. This foresight is essential for entrepreneurs in identifying new problems and finding innovative solutions that exist beyond their current line of sight. Studying and understanding these trends builds strategic leadership capacity across the entrepreneurial ecosystem for years to come.

COMPLEXITY Here are eight megatrends that we have identified (Barton 2015, Berger 2014, Dudley 2017, Schrieber 2015; see also Figure 15.7). While these eight trends are presented in isolation, it is clear that they are interdependent and influence one another. Therefore, they must all be reflected on holistically as we each, as entrepreneurs, move into the future.

1. **Technology:** this will continue to disrupt the global landscape, and change nearly every industry at an alarming rate. These transformative technologies include partial and full automation of work, 3D printing, cloud technology, autonomous vehicles, and robotics.
2. **Digitization:** 3.2 billion people, or 40 per cent of the world, are now 'online'. Fuelled by the convergence of various technologies (i.e. cloud computing, connected devices, data analytics), the way companies conduct business may be fundamentally altered. The amount of data that is accumulated each two days surpasses the amount of data we have accumulated since the dawn of time. With this wealth of knowledge, savvy companies will begin to revise their business models and use this data to optimize best business practices.
3. **Urbanization:** some experts estimate that 59 per cent of the world's population will migrate to dense urban cities. The influx of individuals moving to urban locations will intensify demands for additional infrastructure and commodities. In some cases, this will cause strain for those countries with limited access to resources.
4. **Climate considerations:** global warming is impacting the decisions we make at individual, houeshold, company, regional, national, global levels. It is unsurprising that we will continue to place an emphasis on the research, development, and use of renewable energy sources like solar and wind power. These renewable energy sources are also set to decline in price at a rapid rate.

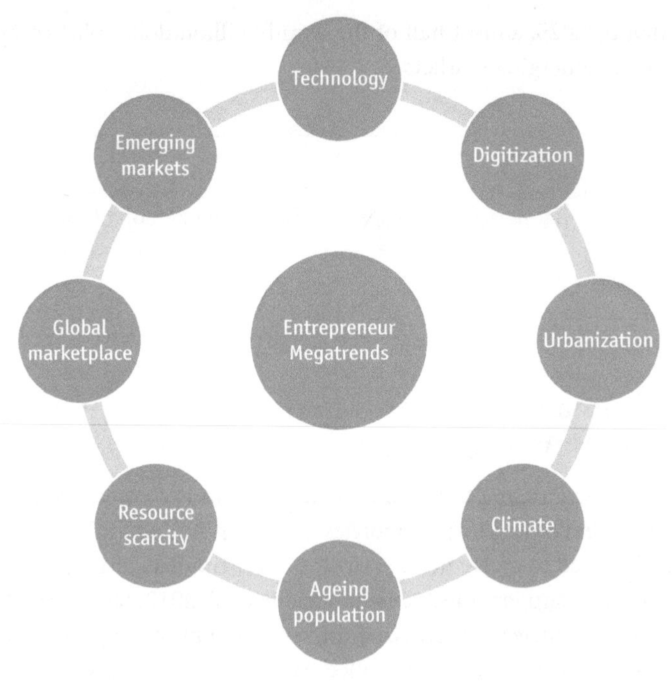

Figure 15.7 The megatrends influencing entrepreneurial venturing

5. **The ageing population:** this will continue to grow, as the proportion of the world's population over the age of 65 will double, and the number of people worldwide aged 80+ will quadruple to 400 million by 2050. This offers many opportunities to service this segment, as well as rethink the role of seniors in society. Some countries will be affected more than others as one-third of individuals in Spain, Italy, and Japan will be over the age of 65. The ageing population will undoubtedly place strain on government resources.
6. **Resource scarcity:** competition for limited resources will continue to intensify due to an increase in the world population, and an increase in global energy demands. For instance, it is anticipated that half of the world will be living in conditions with high water stress by 2030. Technologies may emerge as an advantage in some cases as the production of once finite resources are now being supported by emerging technologies.
7. **Global marketplace:** the economies of the world will remain highly interdependent through trade and financial system linkages, driving the need for stronger global policy coordination among nations and resilient supply chains for companies operating in this environment. Emerging market countries, such as Brazil, Mexico, and India, have seen conditions ease somewhat, due in part to investments made in education. Specifically, many emerging markets have rapidly expanded the number of college graduates that they produce, broadening their talent pool more than mature markets in the North.
8. **Emerging markets:** while the developed markets face an omnipresent issue with a shrinking and ageing population, companies have limited opportunity to continue their growth. Attention will be turned to emerging markets, which have an expanding population, and a growing income level. Look out for countries like China and India, but also more unassuming markets like Africa, who may become a force to be reckoned with. It

is forecast that by 2025, almost half of the world's billion dollar plus companies will be headquartered in emerging markets.

Stop and Think

Consider the challenges that these megatrends pose for the population of the future. Which of the megatrends will your entrepreneurial concept or idea help to solve? If you are yet to develop an entrepreneurial idea, what ideas do you think would be helpful?

How will policymakers respond to the changing needs of entrepreneurs, and SMEs?

STAKEHOLDERS Encouraging SME survival and growth is a common theme of government policy in the UK and other OECD countries. However, studies find little evidence of success from policies designed to create more start-ups or to stimulate SME growth by providing financing, assistance, and support mechanisms (Bridge et al. 2012, Storey and Greene 2010). These 'micro economic' policies are criticized for providing public support to entrepreneurs and enterprises that might otherwise have failed earlier or providing support to enterprises capable of surviving without such support.

Broader macroeconomic policies in support of SMEs and entrepreneurship are more favourably regarded by scholars, which include policies related to taxation, regulations, immigration, and competition (Storey and Greene 2010). Such policies have a direct influence on the economic environment facing SMEs and entrepreneurs, and do not rely on public officials attempting to favour particular groups of enterprises or 'pick winners'.

Policies to stimulate more SMEs to engage in research and development (R&D) are also common in OECD countries. Justification for such support draws on evidence of innovation as a key factor in economic growth and on expectations that a proportion of these innovative enterprises will be high-growth enterprises and contribute disproportionately to economic growth. Targeted public subsidies have been shown to trigger R&D spending, particularly among SMEs which are engaged in international business (Hottenrott and Lopes-Bento 2014).

Summary

- SMEs have characteristics that provide advantages over larger firms, which include lower cost structures and less formality and rigidity of business operations (allowing them to adapt more readily to dynamic market conditions).
- Disadvantages of SMEs compared to larger firms include 'liabilities of smallness' and not benefiting from economies of scale.
- Young, high-growth firms, often called 'gazelles', contribute disproportionately to national economies in terms of employment and contributions to GDP.
- Entrepreneurship and innovation are linked concepts. Innovation without entrepreneurial activity is deficient of the ambition, drive, and persistence often required to overcome the liabilities of newness, risk, and uncertainty that characterize innovation.

- Entrepreneurs are defined by their actions, not by sociocultural factors or the type or size of enterprise; making entrepreneurship a social phenomenon that extends across different business environments.
- Entrepreneurs are those individuals or teams able to identify the potential of an idea and display the willingness to act on it.
- Successful entrepreneurship is identified as a passion for achieving goals, opportunistic behaviour, and a relentless competitive spirit behind the desire to achieve—to create something of value.
- Entrepreneurial new venturing is the creation and formation of a new business entity—in which the entrepreneur plays the central role.
- Entrepreneurs must overcome a different set of challenges vs. SMEs that include liabilities of newness. New resources must be secured and funded, value propositions and markets acceptance must be validated, new employees recruited (if required), etc.—making its survival, let alone growth, highly uncertain. Evidence identifies the high failure rates of new ventures.
- New enterprise formation includes six common activities: opportunity identification; securing resources; management and team building; company formation; refining offering for the market; and financial feasibility.
- While SMEs have already established a business model, new ventures are seeking one. A business model explains the logic and describes the rationale of how a venture creates, delivers, and captures value.

Case study: Diving deep into entrepreneurship: how an entrepreneur is building a business in aquaponics

It sounds like a grow-op designed by Ikea. Paul Shumlich is describing the farm he's planning to build. It will contain no soil and admits no sunlight. The walls will be industrial-chic concrete, the floors spotless. Plants will grow in meticulous rows under LED lights, their roots suspended in water. Fish will swim placidly in blue pools. It's all very clean, very tasteful, very Scandinavian. It's Deepwater Farms, an aquaponics operation, and Shumlich is betting it's going to change the way residents in Calgary, Canada eat. Dressed all in black, he looks the part of the entrepreneur, but his youthful optimism and cherubic good looks drive home the fact that he's only 26. 'Local isn't just a fad', he explains 'we need a resilient food system. That's my drive'. He thinks the answer is aquaponics, a system of agriculture that few Calgarians have even heard of.

The unconventional farming method combines aquaculture (fish farming) and hydroponics (growing plants in water) in a single, closed system. Fish are kept in ponds or pools, and produce waste that is broken down into nitrites and then nitrates by micro-organisms. The waste water is sent to the plants, which absorb the nitrates and, in the process, clean the water, which is then sent back to the fish. Recirculation means that the system uses approximately 95 per cent less water than conventional farming methods. It's completely organic, and it grows plants at incredible rates, many times faster than conventional methods. The field of aquaponics is becoming well established and commercially viable.

Shumlich's interest began when he was a student running a window-washing business. It was paying his way through university, but it wasn't satisfying. 'I wanted to put time and money into something more meaningful. I wanted it to be about the triple bottom line: people, profit, planet', he says. Shumlich started scouring the Internet for ideas, and discovered aquaponics. He dived in, but at the back of his mind he wondered, 'Is this some sort of hippy technology?'

He drove down to Lethbridge College to meet an expert in aquaponics and came back convinced that he needed to start unconventional farming. The next step was rounding up a bunch of his window-washing buddies to help him build a rudimentary aquaponics system in the backyard of his parents' rental house.

They hit an immediate roadblock when they discovered that the bacteria needed to run the system would take eighteen months to mature. But Shumlich found a guy on a local advertising platform 'Kijiji.ca' who was selling his home aquaponics system, and was willing to include the bacteria. 'It was like a one-in-a-million chance', he says. With a few supplies from Home Depot, and some koi off Kijiji, the first system was ready to go. 'Stuff grew crazy quick', Shumlich says. And that's when he had his a-ha moment. 'I was in Safeway. I was buying organic produce, and I said "Why is everything grown in Mexico or California?" It was really sh–y-looking produce. I'm growing this stuff in my backyard.' He'd found his new business.

He set about building a commercial system in his grandparents' three-car garage. It took three months to clean out the space and set up the equipment. That was the easy part. The system would require constant attention, so, with the lease on his apartment set to expire, Shumlich decided to move into the garage with his plants and fish. If parenthood is defined as being available to your dependants 24/7, Shumlich was now a doting dad. He said to himself, 'If I'm still living here next winter, I'm doing something wrong.' He began making regular trips to Lethbridge to consult with the expert.

Around the same time, Shumlich began interviewing chefs in Calgary, trying to understand the market for his produce. 'I found eight ingredients that they all wanted year round and said, "Boom—here are our products"', he says. This ingredient list included various lettuces and herbs. Calgary's chefs are interested in seeing businesses like Shumlich's succeed. Local food also makes good business sense. 'We get stiffed when produce comes from the US', Hendry says. 'Anyone sending us produce from California, as soon as it's in the box, it's money for them. But because it's in transport for so long, the produce is more damaged.' This is in stark contrast to Shumlich's model, where produce and fish will be packed into reusable totes, delivered to stores, and sold to consumers the same day.

Shumlich's vision couldn't have come at a better time. Calgary Economic Development (CED) quickly took up his cause. 'What a lot of people don't realize is that this province did around $14 billion in food manufacturing sales in 2015', says Sasha Musij, of CED. 'Agriculture can help offset the downturn as we diversify into other industries that make sense for the city. There is a big appetite in Calgary for this. And Paul is at the forefront.'

That support is crucial, because the challenges are large. Legislation hasn't kept up with the growing industry. Shumlich is working with the city to change that. There's also the organic issue. Aquaponics is so new that it still isn't certified organic, and that can affect what consumers are willing to pay. And then there's the squeamishness factor. 'As a society, we have become disconnected from how food is grown, and some are grossed out that [the plants] are grown with fish, without understanding their symbiotic relationship', says Duigou. 'It's an unfortunate stigma.' The stigma is also somewhat ironic, considering that consumers often don't know how imported food has been grown. According to Bruce Martin, the general manager of Community Natural Foods, that lack of clarity has given rise to a new development. 'The public is just very interested in local—more so than organic', he says. 'I think they make the assumption that if it comes from a local farm, it will be cleaner, better.'

Source: Based on an article by Ruth Richert of Swerve, for the *Calgary Herald.* Published 3 March 2017. Reproduced with permission.

Questions

1. **What kind of entrepreneur is Paul, and what qualities does he have?**
2. **What skill development has taken place during the growth of the business?**
3. **How has the business chosen to compete and what is its competitive advantage?**

Review and discussion questions

1. New firms that show 'high-growth' potential should receive additional support from policymakers (e.g. 'picking winners' policy). Discuss this statement.
2. *Skills*: you are thinking about becoming an entrepreneur but need to understand whether you have the right skills to start up a business on your own, or whether you should create a team with broader skills. Using the content within this chapter, undertake a self-analysis of your current skills and either devise a personal development plan to gain the additional skills you might need to start a new venture, or indicate the skills you need to find additional team members.
3. *Supporting new and under-represented groups* to start a business: conduct some research on your local areas, using the Internet to look at local social entrepreneurs, enterprise support organizations, or local government to find out where areas of need or deprivation are within your region. Suggest some activities that could help people in these areas start their own businesses if they wanted to.

4. *Understanding entrepreneurs*: find a local entrepreneur to interview, or choose a famous one from the list below and use the Internet to try to understand the following:
   - What is it that they do? What role do they play?
   - What sector do they work in?
   - What businesses/ideas have they had? What connection exists between these ideas?
   - What stage of growth is their business currently at?
   - How have their values impacted on the way they conduct business?

   Suggestions of entrepreneurs to study: Jeff Bezos (Amazon), Richard Branson (Virgin), Tory Burch (Tory Burch), Arlene Dickinson (Venture Communications), Arianna Huffington (*Huffington Post*), Elon Musk (Tesla), Anita Roddick (Body Shop), JK Rowling (Harry Potter Empire), Cher Wang (HTC), Mark Zuckerberg (Facebook).

Assignments

1. Using data from the Global Entrepreneurship Monitor (GEM), compare the UK with another country of your choice regarding entrepreneurial behaviour/attitudes and the entrepreneurial ecosystem (go to the website **http://www.gemconsortium.org** and click on 'economy profiles'). What are the similarities and differences between the two countries, and how might they be explained?
2. Taking a business idea that you have, apply the business model canvas to the opportunity (e.g. using Table 15.10 as guidance). Reflecting on your completed business model canvas, would you pursue this opportunity? What additional information is required to make the opportunity more compelling?

Further reading

Drucker (2006) *this book offers key insights on innovation and entrepreneurship as championed by management guru Peter Drucker. It considers how the innovative activities of entrepreneurs has resulted in a net gain in jobs in western economies, and describes Drucker's persuasive argument that entrepreneurship has more to do with behaviour than personality. The book considers the concept of 'purposeful' innovation—which relates to the wealth-producing potential of already existing resources—and describes why and how managers must take responsibility for their contributions to society in a fast-changing marketplace.*

Harnish (2014) *founder of the globally acclaimed Entrepreneurs Organization, this book is the sequel to the bestseller the Rockefeller Habits. In this book, Harnish provides a range of tools and frameworks to help you scale up your business while navigating issues of people, strategy, execution, and cash.*

Hwang and Horowitt (2012) *Silicon Valley venture capitalists and entrepreneurs Hwang and Horowitt offer a new theory to explain the development of entrepreneurial ecosystems. Using the analogy of a rainforest, the authors draw attention to the human nature of social systems and the very human-centred approach of entrepreneurship and innovation processes, often overlooked in other texts.*

Ismail (2014) *founding executive director at Singularity University and former VP of Yahoo where he ran Brickhouse, Ismail offers essential insights into a new type of organization—the exponential organization, or ExO for short. These organizations move beyond incremental and linear gains in performance by leveraging their community, big data, algorithms, and new technologies.*

Osterwalder and Pigneur (2010) *this provides practical frameworks that can be used at all stages of growth to appraise and improve a company's business model.*

Ries (2013) *in this global bestseller, Ries applies the philosophy of the Japanese car manufacturer Toyota to the world of start-up. The premise is that we have much to learn from lean manufacturing tools and techniques when starting a business, a time when resources are scarce and time is of the essence. Ries offers a new way of thinking that places experimentation and evaluation at the heart of growing and innovating a business.*

Sarasvathy (2009) *in this groundbreaking book, Sarasvathy studied how expert entrepreneurs, those who have founded companies for fifteen years or longer, make decisions. Sarasvathy had the entrepreneurs solve a problem out loud and found that entrepreneurs used a different decision-making process to traditional thinking typically taught in the classroom.*

Wickman (2011) *provides a structured blueprint—the entrepreneurs' operating system—to encourage the development of healthy organizational approaches that drive leadership productivity, alignment, and business growth.*

Test your understanding of this chapter with online questions and answers, explore the subject further through web exercises, and use the weblinks to provide a quick resource for further research. Visit the online resources at www.oup.com/uk/wetherly_otter4e/

Useful websites

Setting up a business

British Library Business and IP Centre: www.bl.uk/business-and-ip-centre

Companies House, check company names: http://wck2.companieshouse.gov.uk

Department for Work and Pensions: www.dwp.gov.uk

HM Revenue and Customs: www.gov.uk/government/organisations/hm-revenue-customs

Startup Service: http://startups.co.uk

Startup Loans Company: www.startuploans.co.uk/about-start-up-loans-company

Becoming an entrepreneur

Global Entrepreneurship Week: http://uk.gew.co

Startup Britain: http://startupbritain.org

Entrepreneur.com: www.entrepreneur.com

Stanford Technology Ventures: http://ecorner.stanford.edu

Growing a business

Chambers of Commerce: www.britishchambers.org.uk

Department for Business Innovation and Skills: www.gov.uk/government/organisations/department-for-business-innovation-skills

Federation of Small Businesses: www.fsb.org.uk

Institute of Directors: www.iod.com

Think BIG . . . Think Business. Improvement. Growth. www.time2thinkbig.com

Studying entrepreneurship/SME growth

Global Entrepreneurship Monitor: www.gemconsortium.org

Enterprise Research Centre: www.enterpriseresearch.ac.uk

Institute for Small Business and Entrepreneurship: www.isbe.org

UK Data Archive, Small Business Survey: www.data-archive.ac.uk

Kauffman Foundation: http://www.kauffman.org

References

Adizes, I. (1979) 'Organizational passages: diagnosing and treating lifecycle problems of organizations', *Organizational Dynamics*, 8(1): 3–25

Bamiatzi, V. C. and Kirchmaier, T. (2014) 'Strategies for superior performance under adverse conditions', *International Small Business Journal*, 32(3): 259–84

Barbero, J. L., Casillas, J. C., and Feldman, H. D. (2011) 'Managerial capabilities and paths to growth as determinants of high-growth small and medium-sized enterprises', *International Small Business Journal*, 29(6): 671–94

Barrett, R. (1999) 'Industrial relations in small firms: the case of the Australian information industry', *Employee Relations*, 21(3): 211–24

Barton, D. (2015) *McKinsey Megatrends: Global Megatrends and Implications for Leaders* **https://www.cass.city.ac.uk**

Battisti, M., Deakins, D., and Perry, M. (2013) 'The sustainability of small businesses in recessionary times: evidence from the strategies of urban and rural small businesses in New Zealand', *International Journal of Entrepreneurial Behaviour and Research*, 19(1): 72–96

Berger, R. (2014) *Trends Compendium 2030* **https://www.rolandberger.com**

Bhide, A. (1994) 'How entrepreneurs craft strategies that work', *Harvard Business Review*, March–April: 150–61

Birch, D. L. (1979) 'The job generation process'. *MIT Program on Neighborhood and Regional Change* (Cambridge, MA)

Birley, S. and Stockley, S. (2000) 'Entrepreneurial Teams and Venture Growth', in D. L. Sexton and H. Landstrom (eds.), *The Blackwell Handbook of Entrepreneurship* (Malden, MA: Blackwell), 287–307

Bolton, J. E. (1971) *Small firms: Report of the Commission of Inquiry on Small Firms. Cmnd.* (London: HMSO)

Bridge, S., O'Neill, K., and Martin, F. (2012) *Understanding Enterprise: Entrepreneurship and Small Business* (New York: Palgrave Macmillan)

Burns, P. (2013) *Corporate Entrepreneurship: Innovation and Strategy in Large Organizations* (New York: Palgrave Macmillan)

Business Bunker Radio (2014) 'Creating successful and sustainable businesses', post-event blog, 5 December **http://www.kentbusinessradio.co.uk**

Cameron, K. S. and Whetten, D. A. (1981) 'Perceptions of organizational effectiveness over organizational life cycles', *Administrative Science Quarterly*, 26(4): 525–44

Carland, J. W., Hoy, F., Boulton, W. R., and Carland, J. A. C. (1984) 'Differentiating entrepreneurs from small business owners: a conceptualization', *Academy of Management Review*, 9(2): 354–59

Churchill, N. C. (1997) 'Six key phases of company growth', 'Mastering the enterprise', *Financial Times*, February, p. 3

Churchill, N. C. and Lewis, V. L. (1983) 'The five stages of small business growth', *Harvard Business Review*, 61(3): 30

Cohen, W. M. and Levinthal, D. A. (1990) 'Absorptive capacity: a new perspective on learning and innovation', *Technology, Organizations and Innovation*, 35(1): 128–52

Damanpour, F. (1991) 'Organizational innovation: a meta-analysis of effects of determinants and moderators', *Academy of Management Journal*, 34(3): 555–90

Davidsson, P., Leona., A., and Naldi, L. (2005) *Research on Small Firm Growth: A Review* (Brisbane: Queensland University of Technology)

Davis, C. (2003) 'Venture capital in Canada', in D. Cetindamar (ed.), *The Growth of Venture Capital: A Cross Cultural Comparison* (Westport, CT: Praeger), 175–206

Deakins, D. and Freel, M. (1998) 'Entrepreneurial learning and the growth process in SMEs', *Learning Organization*, 5(3): 144–55

Dean, T. J. and McMullen, J. S. (2007) 'Towards a theory of sustainable entrepreneurship: Reducing environmental degradation through entrepreneurial action', *Journal of Business Venturing*, 22(1): 50–76

Department for Business, Energy and Industrial Strategy (2016) *Business Population Estimates for the UK and Regions 2016*, BEIS/16/34 **https://www.gov.uk**

Dodge, H. R., Fullerton, S., and Robbins, J. E. (1994) 'Stage of the organizational life cycle and competition as mediators of problem perception for small businesses', *Strategic Management Journal*, 15(2): 121–34

Drucker, P. F. (1985) *Innovation and Entrepreneurship Practices and Principles* (London: Routledge).

Dudley, B (2017). *BP Energy Outlook* **https://www.bp.com**

Edison, H., Bin Ali, N., and Torkar, R. (2013) 'Towards innovation measurement in the software industry', *Journal of Systems and Software*, 86(5): 1390–1407

ERC (2016) *Boosting UK Productivity with SME Growth* **http://www.enterpriseresearch.ac.uk**

European Commission (2003) *Commission Recommendation of 6 May 2003 concerning the definition of micro, small and medium-sized enterprises*, Official Journal of the European Union, 2003-361/EC **http://ec.europa.eu**

Eurostat (2015) *Innovation Statistics*, Eurostat Statistics Explained **http://ec.europa.eu/eurostat**

Friedman, G. (2014) 'Workers without employers: shadow corporations and the rise of the gig economy', *Review of Keynesian Economics*, 2(2): 171–88

Gage, D. (2012) 'The venture capital secret: 3 out of 4 start-ups fail', *Wall Street Journal* **www.wsj.com**

Gilman, M., Raby, S., and Turpin, J. (2012) 'The BIG ten: the ten characteristics of successful SMEs, business improvement and growth initiative' (Centre for Employment, Competitiveness and Growth, University of Kent's Business School, ISBN: 978-1-902671-76-5)

Gilman, M., Raby, S., and Pyman, A. (2015) 'The contours of employee voice in SMEs: the importance of context', *Human Resource Management Journal*, 25(4): 563–79

Goss, D. (1991) *Small Business and Society* (London: Routledge)

Gregson, G. (2014) *Financing New Ventures: An Entrepreneur's Guide to Business Angel Investment* (New York: Business Expert Press)

Greiner, L. E. (1972) 'Evolution and revolution as organizations grow', *Harvard Business Review*, 50(4): 37–46

Haltiwanger, J., Miranda, J., and Jarmin, R. (2013) 'Anemic job creation and growth in the aftermath of the great recession: are home prices to blame?', Business Dynamics Statistics Briefing, July **https://www.census.gov**

Haltiwanger, John C., Jarmin, Ron, S., and Miranda, Javier (2013) 'Who creates jobs? Small versus large versus young', *Review of Economics and Statistics*, 95(2): 347–61

Hanks, S. H. and Chandler, G. (1994) 'Patterns of functional specialization in emerging high tech firms', *Journal of Small Business Management*, 32(2): 23–36

Hanks, S. H., Watson, C. J., Jansen, E., and Chandler, G. N. (1993) 'Tightening the life-cycle construct: a taxonomic study of growth stage configurations in high-technology organizations', *Entrepreneurship: Theory & Practice*, 18(2): 5–30

Hewitt-Dundas, N. (2006) 'Resource and capability constraints to innovation in small and large plants', *Small Business Economics*, 26(3): 257–77

Hilmersson, M. (2014) 'Small and medium-sized enterprise internationalization strategy and performance in times of market turbulence', *International Small Business Journal*, 32(4): 386–400

Hottenrott, H. and Lopes-Bento, C. (2014) 'International R&D collaboration and SMEs: the effectiveness of targeted R&D support schemes', *Research Policy*, 43(6): 1055–66

Industry Canada (2013) 'What share of firms are high-growth firms? Key small business statistics August 2013' **http://ic.gc.ca**

Industry Canada (2015) 'How many SMEs are there in Canada? Key small business statistics June 2015'**http://www.ic.gc.ca**

Kauffman Foundation (2008) *Entrepreneurship in American Higher Education: A Report from the Kauffman Panel on Entrepreneurship Curriculum in Higher Education*, July **http://kauffman.org**

Kobe, K. (2012) *Small Business GDP: Update 2002–2010*. Report for the Office of Advocacy, Small Business Administration, January **https://sba.gov**

Leitch, C., Hill, F., and Neergaard, H. (2010) 'Entrepreneurial and business growth and the quest for a "comprehensive theory": tilting at windmills?', *Entrepreneurship Theory and Practice*, 34(2): 249–60

Levie, J. and Lichtenstein, B. B. (2010) 'A terminal assessment of stages theory: introducing a dynamic states approach to entrepreneurship', *Entrepreneurship: Theory & Practice*, 34(2): 317–50

Lippitt, G. L. and Schmidt, W. H. (1967) 'Crises in a developing organization', *Harvard Business Review*, 45(6): 102–12

Lumpkin, G. T. and Dess, G. G. (1996) 'Clarifying the entrepreneurial orientation construct and linking it to performance', *Academy of management Review*, 21(1): 135–72

Lumpkin, G. T. and Erdogan, B. (1999) 'If not entrepreneurship, can psychological characteristics predict entrepreneurial orientation? A pilot study', in *Proceedings of the USASBE/SBIDA Annual National Conference—Sailing the Entrepreneurial Wave Into, San Diego, California* (Vol. 21)

Lundvall, B. (2010) *National Systems of Innovation: Towards a Theory of Innovation and Interactive Learning* (London: Pinter)

Martin, R. L. and Osberg, S. (2007) 'Social entrepreneurship: the case for definition', *Stanford Social Innovation Review*, 5(2): 28–39

Moule, C. (1998) 'The Regulation of Work in Small Firms', *Work, Employment and Society*, 12(4): 635–53

Ministry of Micro, Small and Medium Enterprises (2006) The Micro, Small and Medium Enterprises Development Act, No. 27 of 2006 **http://msme.gov.in**

NESTA (2009) 'The vital 6 per cent: how high-growth innovative businesses generate prosperity and jobs. Research summary' **www.nesta.org.uk**

Osterwalder, A. and Pigneur, Y. (2010) *Business Model Generation: A Handbook for Visionaries, Game Changers and Challengers* (Hoboken, NJ: Wiley)

Parker, S. C. (2004) *The Economics of Self-employment and Entrepreneurship* (Cambridge: Cambridge University Press)

Parsley, C. and Halabisky, D. (2008) *Profile of Growth Firms: A Summary of Industry Canada Research* **ic.gc.ca**

Patel, H. and Frey, C. (2015) 'How do you define innovation and make it practical and saleable to senior management?' **http://www.innovationmanagement.se**

Price, L., Rae, D., and Cini, V. (2013) 'SME perceptions of and responses to the recession', *Journal of Small Business and Enterprise Development*, 20(3): 484–502

Quinn, R. E. and Cameron, K. (1983) 'Organizational life cycles and shifting criteria of effectiveness: some preliminary evidence', *Management Science*, 29(1): 33–51

Raby, S. (2013) 'Explaining the role of human resource management in the performance of small and medium enterprises' (University of Kent, doctoral thesis)

Rainnie, A. (1989) *Industrial Relations in Small Firms: Small Isn't Beautiful* (London: Routledge)

Ram, M. (1994) *Managing to Survive: Working Lives in Small Firms* (Oxford: Blackwell)

Rammer, C., Czarnitzki, D., and Spielkamp, A. (2009) 'Innovation success of non-R&D-performers: substituting technology by management in SMEs', *Small Business Economics*, 33(1): 35–58

Rauch, A., Wiklund, J., Lumpkin, G. T., and Frese, M. (2009) 'Entrepreneurial orientation and business performance: an assessment of past research and suggestions for the future', *Entrepreneurship Theory and Practice*, 33: 761–87

Robinson, R. B., Pearce Ii, J. A., Vozikis, G. S., and Mescon, T. S. (1984) 'The relationship between stage of development and small firm planning and performance', *Journal of Small Business Management*, 22(2): 45–52

Scase, R. (1995) 'Employment relations in small firms', in P. Edwards (ed.), *Industrial Relations: Theory and Practice* (Oxford: Blackwell)

Scase, R. (2003) 'Employment relations in small firms', in P. Edwards (ed.), *Industrial Relations: Theory and Practice* (2nd edn, Oxford: Blackwell)

Schreiber, U. (2015) 'Megatrends 2015: making sense of a world in motion' **http://www.ey.com**

Schumpeter, J. A. (1934) *The Theory of Economic Development: An Inquiry into Profits, Capital, Credit, Interest, and the Business Cycle* (London: Routledge)

Smallbone, D., Leig, R., and North, D. (1995) 'The characteristics and strategies of high growth SMEs', *International Journal of Entrepreneurial Behaviour & Research*, 1(3): 44–62

Smallbone, D. and Wyer, P. (2000) 'Growth and development in the small firm', in S. Carter and D. James-Evans (eds.), *Enterprise and Small Business* (Harlow: Prentice-Hall)

Smith, K. G., Mitchell, T. R., and Summer, C. E. (1985) 'Top level management priorities in different stages of the organizational life cycle', *Academy of Management Journal*, 28(4): 799–820

Spinelli, S. and Adams, R. (2012) *New Venture Creation: Entrepreneurship for the 21st Century* (9th edn, New York: McGraw-Hill)

Steinmetz, L. L. (1969) 'Critical stages of small business growth', *Business Horizons*, 12(1): 29

Stevenson, H., and Jarillo, J. (1990) 'A paradigm of entrepreneurship: entrepreneurial management', *Strategic Management Journal*, 11: 17–27

Stinchcombe, A. L. and March, J. G. (1965) Social structure and organizations', *Advances in Strategic Management*, 17: 229–59

Stokes, D., Wilson, N., and Mador, M. (2010) *Entrepreneurship* (London: CENGAGE Learning)

Storey, D. J. (1994) *Understanding the Small Business Sector* (London: Routledge)

Storey, D. J. (2011) 'Optimism and chance: the elephants in the entrepreneurship room', *International Small Business Journal*, 29(4): 303–21

Storey, D. J. and Greene, F. J. (2010) *Small Business and Entrepreneurship* (London: Prentice-Hall)

Teece, D. J. (1998) 'Capturing value from knowledge assets: the new economy, markets for know-how and intangible assets', *California Management Review*, 40(3): 55–79

Thornberry, N. E. (2003) 'Corporate entrepreneurship: teaching managers to be entrepreneurs', *Journal of Management Development*, 22(4): 329–44

US Census Bureau (2015) *Business Dynamics Statistics* **http://www.census.gov**

US Small Business Administration (2015) *Table of Small Business Size Standards Matched to North American Industry Classification System Codes* **http://www.sba.gov**

Welsh, J. A. and White, J. F. (1981) 'A small business is not a little big business', *Harvard Business Review*, 59(4): 18–27

World Intellectual Property Organization (2015) *World Intellectual Property Indicators*, Economics and Statistics Series **http://www.wipo.int**

Chapter 16

Conclusion: Looking ahead—managing in a dynamic environment

Dorron Otter and Paul Wetherly

Learning objectives

When you have completed this chapter, you will be able to:

- Give a broad overview of the likely future trends in the business environment.
- Integrate the main predictions from the 'Looking ahead' sections of the previous chapters.
- Develop your own views as to the changing nature of the business environment.

THEMES

The following themes of this book are especially relevant to this chapter

- **DIVERSITY** Businesses are diverse, but they share the common problem that the future is uncertain. It is important that all businesses are able to try to minimize this uncertainty by looking ahead.
- **INTERNAL/EXTERNAL** Chapter 1 showed us that it was important for businesses to scan the external environment in order to anticipate change. They need to do this if their internal strategies are to be successful.
- **COMPLEXITY** Despite the environmental uniqueness of a particular business there are general features of the external environment of which all businesses need to be aware.
- **LOCAL TO GLOBAL** Globalization and technology are dramatically altering the distance between the spatial levels.
- **DYNAMIC** The one certain thing that can be said about the future is that it will be uncertain, and that change is a dynamic process.
- **INTERACTION** How will businesses manage future changes and in turn what will be their impact on the future of the business environment?
- **STAKEHOLDERS** There is an increasing recognition of the impact that individual business decisions have on wider society and a focus on the responsibility of businesses across the full range of stakeholders.
- **VALUES** Our reactions to the impact of changes depend in part on our ethical values.

Introduction

COMPLEXITY **DYNAMIC** The one thing that business managers would like to have is certainty but in the fast changing and dynamic external environment this is not possible. Therefore, managers need to be able to make decisions based on what they see as the likely conditions that will prevail in the future. While successful businesses will be the ones that are able to exploit their opportunities, they are also the ones which will be able to assess what the likely impacts from the external environment are going to be and plan to either avoid or minimize these risks if they can. Successful business strategy involves effective risk assessment and planning.

The main thrust of this book has been to show that by a careful examination of underlying political, economic, social, and technological factors we can identify important themes and features of the global business environment which can help us to better understand business behaviour in the present, as well as having a tentative stab at predicting future changes.

This chapter will bring together the main outlines of what is likely to happen within the business environment in the next few years. The structure of the book has been designed so that we would first explore the key themes in the external environment. In Chapters 1 to 8 we explored the traditional PEST factors of the political, economic, social, and technological environments and then also highlighted the legal, ethical, and natural environments which have become so important when analysing business behaviour. We then focused on what we see as being the key issues in the external environment for business, and throughout we have sought to integrate the themes that help to conceptualize the global business environment.

Each chapter ended with a short 'Looking ahead' section where we explored the things that are most likely to develop in the future in each of the key issue areas. This chapter seeks to knit together the common threads in these predictions using the general PEST framework and so look ahead to the future trends in the business environment. Having worked through the rest of the book you should be in a position to develop your own views as to the shape of the business environment in general and how this may impact and be affected by individual areas of business activity.

INTERACTION **VALUES** The nature of change in the business environment is itself often contradictory and uncertain. Change can be achingly slow and sometimes extraordinarily rapid. It is difficult to appreciate the changes that are taking place over a long time when we are most often concentrating on the 'noise' of the here and now. There are contradictions in the evidence that we see and, as Chapter 2 showed, not all people see the same evidence and draw the same conclusions.

> ***Stop and Think***
>
> Why is it difficult to make predictions in relation to the business environment?

There is a search in academic life for rational explanations for how change occurs and many of us hope that in the end, no matter how 'messy' the environmental influences might be, we will be able to explain why things have occurred and therefore attempt to predict on this basis why things might occur. Equally, there are analysts who argue that we have to accept that we are all living in an uncertain world where the information we have is imperfect, and that change will not be rational and predictable. We have also stressed in the book that while we can identify the individual changes in the business environment, in reality many of these operate at the same time and interrelate in complex ways.

In order to get a better idea of the possible future developments in the business environment, it is vital to look back into the past, and we did this in Chapter 2 when exploring the evolution of the global economic environment. While the past is not a reliable guide to the future, history does enable us to learn a lot about ourselves. Indeed, the future global business environment will be dominated by attempts to try to secure the stable path of peace and prosperity that was so difficult to achieve in the twentieth century. In order to look ahead to the future, we need to look back.

When looking ahead we can take varying positions ranging from outright optimism as to what is likely to happen to dire pessimism. It will be interesting to see where you feel you lie on this continuum.

Stop and Think

What are your hopes and fears as to the nature of the future business environment in which you will live and work?

Looking ahead: the global political environment

INTERNAL/EXTERNAL In the ten years that have passed since the first edition of this book there has been a considerable shift in attitudes to the interrelationship between the role of national and global governance and the operation of markets. Neoclassical market optimists have come under relentless attack from structuralist/institutionalist schools as well as from radical and Marxist perspectives. The battle lines over the nature of the economic environment are still firmly entrenched. We first explored this in Chapter 1 and then outlined the competing views in more detail in Chapter 2. For structuralist and radical critics, the events of the last ten years since the global economic crisis of 2008 have shown the need for economies to construct and develop supporting institutions and structures that can guide markets without succumbing to the instability and social divisions that can sometimes exist. We explored the problems and competing approaches that have been taken at the macroeconomic level in dealing with the global economic crisis in Chapter 9. The growing focus on the dangers of too little regulation in terms of top pay and the bonuses being awarded to traders in the financial sector has become a central concern amongst not just policymakers but across the wider society and we looked at the financial sector in some detail in both Chapters 3 and 5 and explored the wider issues of inequality in Chapter 12.

LOCAL TO GLOBAL While even those who argue for a pro-market approach accept the need for greater regulation of the banks, their views are that the greatest challenges facing business both globally and domestically still lie in the profligacy of governments in borrowing too much and in the imbalance between the size of the public sector in relation to the private. Within the business community there is an acknowledgement that with power comes responsibility, but there is a view that this can be achieved with responsible leadership within companies and there is a distrust of regulation. Here then the focus for political change is not at the government level but in the exercise of corporate responsibility (see Chapters 5, 7, and 11).

The battleground for the competing perspectives is fought over this central political issue of the degree and manner in which governments should intervene in the running of an economy.

What is clear is that in capitalist economic systems there is a large role for government across a range of microeconomic and macroeconomic policy areas. In terms of microeconomic management, governments seek to intervene directly and indirectly in markets in a large number of ways. Most clearly many governments take a direct role in the provision of key public services such as health, education, and welfare; although the influence of the neoclassical perspective has been seen in the wave of privatizations that have occurred in many countries, and the recent attempts to introduce market processes into areas once thought the preserve of public policy. This was a major focus of Chapter 14.

Up until the global economic crisis beginning in 2007 and then fully exploding in 2008, there had been a heady optimism that economic growth rates in both the developed countries and especially in the BRICS and other fast emerging developing countries were on a rising tide. However, with this there has been growing concern expressed about the unsustainability of rapid economic growth and a call for a reassessment of prevailing economic models especially in relation to the almost universal acceptance of the need to address global climate change. This green view of economics has grown rapidly so that now, throughout the political spectrum and increasingly within business itself, there is a call to place sustainable development at the heart of debates about the nature of the economic environment. For environmentalists, our current approaches to managing economies have ignored the rapid rate at which we have been using non-renewable resources and the environmental costs of economic activity.

Prior to the crisis there had been an ongoing debate between pro-market neoclassical economists and structuralist/institutionalist critics as to reasons why there had been these apparent success stories and the likelihood of their continuation into the future. In relation to the latter there had been calls for greater attention to be paid to having more inclusive institutions both at the national and global level to ensure a more powerful voice for developing countries. Marxist and radical critics were warning of the dangers of rising inequality and forms of crony capitalism in the developing world and polarization of societies even in the heartlands of the so-called mature democracies.

Since the crisis there has been a distinct shift in the way in which these debates are now conducted as the developed world struggles to restore the growth rates experienced in the period 1996 to 2006 and the BRICS have also encountered severe economic turbulence most notably in Brazil and South Africa which are both now mired in a toxic combination of recession, accusations of corruption, and political instability. In China the spectacular double-digit growth rates of the early part of the century have fallen and stabilized at around 6 per cent a year and is now described as 'the new normal'. For the G7 countries, economic growth rates have been declining since the 1960s and the OECD estimated that across its thirty-five members potential annual economic growth per capita is now 1 per cent. Such low levels of growth are all the more remarkable given the high level of intervention from governments in attempting to boost their economies but the austerity policies that they have been following, reliant on expansionary monetary policies and very low interest rates, do not seem to have addressed many of the fundamental structural problems of low productivity and rising inequality that we explored in Chapters 3 and 12. In fact it is argued by many structuralist critics that the failure to address seriously the power of the financial sector and the seemingly inexorable ability of the top 1 per cent to capture the majority of even the small gains in economic prosperity have left most developed countries in a weakened state and prone to future economic recessions. Across the developed world there are many people who have become disaffected with their political systems and are seeking alternatives, and this is seen as being the reason for the decision in the UK for Brexit and in the US for the firebrand language of nationalism and protectionism of President Trump. Across the EU as well there are upheavals in terms of traditional political allegiances.

Globally, the promises to replace the old Washington Consensus with a new framework of inclusive global governance do appear to be gaining ground in the form of a new 'Hangzhou Consensus' (see Mini-Case 16.1) but beneath these warm words the substance has yet to appear leading to attempts from the BRICS countries to develop their own institutions and for China to take on the mantle as the leading voice for all developing countries especially in the light of the apparent retreat of the US as the champion of global free trade (see Mini-Case 16.2). We have seen that approaches to regulation are many and varied, but there is a common desire to devise a system that recognizes the inequalities created by the expansion of markets, the problems of operating the market in that context, and the inherent instability of the market itself.

The annual meetings of the World Economic Forum that take place every year in Davos, Switzerland always provide observers of the global business environment with an insight into how the business community itself is preparing for the uncertain future. The 2017 Global Risks report highlights the five key priorities that the WEF feels will need to be addressed in order to create a conducive business environment. The first two are to address the twin economic problems of growing inequality and sluggish growth. Third, the WEF recognizes that there have been big shifts in terms of identity politics with attitudes to gender, multiculturalism, race, sexual orientation, environmental protection, and the balance between sovereignty and international cooperation all leading to surprising changes in the way in which electorates have been voting. The final two risks are the impact of both technological change and globalization in terms of polarization of societies and the need to construct effective systems of global cooperation. (http://www3.weforum.org/docs/GRR17_Report_web.pdf).

Mini-Case 16.1 Governing the global business environment

The ten years following the global financial crisis of 2008 can be seen to have resulted in a dramatic shift in terms of framing the way in which the challenges facing the global business environment have been viewed. This has been further reflected in the shifts in economic power as shown by the shift from the G8 to the G20 in terms of coordinating global cooperation with the rise in the power of the BRICS. The G20 summits that occur each year have highlighted the changes in ideas that have taken place at the domestic and global levels and the emergence of an apparent new consensus that the old Washington Consensus is broken. In recent years the annual declarations that are issued at the end of each G20 summit have clearly shown the shift to a more structuralist approach in terms of emphasizing the need to build inclusive institutions at the domestic and global level. In 2016 China hosted the G20 in the city of Hangzhou. China was able to use this opportunity not only to showcase how it had managed itself to make the transition to 'the new normal' and was seeking to build Xi Jinping's 'Chinese Dream' using its own nationally determined policy but also to bring the developing world's desire to have a greater influence to the fore. The 2016 summit was also notable for the declaration of the 'Hangzhou Consensus' emphasizing the need to reform both global and national markets but there were doubts as to the extent to which hopes can be turned into real applied policy and to which all countries agree on the detail in terms of how these policies should be implemented.

The 2017 summit in Hamburg, Germany sought to flesh out the new Hangzhou Consensus and the new agreed goals for the G20 were to be to build a 'strong, sustainable, balanced and inclusive global economy' through coordination and the three main themes through which this would be established were to be 'resilience, sustainability and responsibility'.

Resilience: labour markets

There is recognition that globalization and technology can have downsides. There is also an explicit recognition that workers' rights need to be maintained and in terms of labour markets that protection needs to be maintained through global agreements such as the UN Guiding Principles on Business and Human Rights, the International Labour Organization's Tripartite Declaration of Principles concerning multinational enterprises (MNEs) and social policy, and the OECD's MNE guidelines. There is a commitment to the abolition of child labour by 2025 and to eradicate all forms of forced labour, human trafficking, and slavery. In 2017 the amount of people defined as being in enforced slavery was 21 million producing an illegal market of $150 billion.

Resilience: trade and finance

The focus for trade policy is on greater transparency within the WTO and more careful scrutiny of the impact of global trade through organizations such as the IMF and UNCTAD. In terms of financial stability, the widespread adoption of the Basel III agreements which seek to require banks to have in place adequate capital reserve ratios are seen as providing assurance against global financial instability and there is a recognition of the need to ensure that businesses do not exploit their global reach to avoid paying their taxes and that for this there needs to be global intergovernmental cooperation.

Sustainability

In 2015 two major international agreements came into place and will form the basis of much scrutiny in the coming years. The Paris Climate Change talks did appear to end in universal agreement not only into the causes of global climate change but in a robust system of globally agreed targets to stabilize global temperatures well below the recommended 2 degree rise. In the 2017 summit the words in the final declaration had to find a delicate way of easing over the cracks of the US Trump administration's decision to take the US out of the treaty but there was optimism that despite this action at the federal level the determination of the individual states in the US and the commitments made by many US businesses would not significantly undermine the global agreement. The other major global agreement was the 2030 Sustainable Development Goals which are seen as a clear way of both defining and measuring progress in terms of bringing together the desire for inclusive with sustainable development.

Responsibility

For the G20 there is recognition that despite some African countries having started to grow rapidly many of the world's poorest are here and therefore there needs to be continuing development assistance as well as knowledge and technology transfer. International migration is also seen here as part of the global responsibility agenda and there is a recognition that business responsibility will always be undermined by corruption and that all states have a duty to root this out nationally and need to cooperate to stop illegal transfers of assets.

Looking ahead we will have to see the extent to which the commitments that have been made do materialize and progress will be monitored in the G20 meetings in Argentina in 2018, Japan in 2019, and Saudi Arabia in 2020.

Sources: http://www.g20chn.org/English/Dynamic/201609/t20160906_3396.html https://www.g20.org/Webs/G20/DE/Home/home_node.html

Question

Compare and contrast the 'Hangzhou Consensus' with the 'Washington Consensus' that we explored in Chapter 10.

Challenges for the future global political and economic environment

Looking back then across the themes and issues that have emerged in this book we can highlight four main challenges that lie ahead in terms of the global political and economic environment.

Global and national economic governance

DIVERSITY Looking ahead, a major focus will be on the development of supranational political and economic institutions to deal with the twin problems of global inequality and global economic instability (ever present without concerted global policy coordination). Dani Rodrik has pointed out what he calls the 'trilemma of globalization'. For Rodrik there is an irreconcilable conflict at the heart of the neoliberal desire to have democratic systems based on nationally determined democratic systems while also wanting a world of open markets (Rodrik 2017).

In the years since 2008 it is clear that it has been the latter dream of a form of hyper-globalization that has come under threat with different countries and regions looking to protect their own interests by pursuing their own policies. In many parts of the world it has been democracy, or at least western forms of democracy that have come under attack with moves to forms of strong leadership models as in China, Russia, India, and Turkey. In the US under the Obama administration there was a move towards Keynesian demand management at the macroeconomic level and recognition of the need to provide help for the poor through initiatives such as the Healthcare Act but still a desire to see the US as taking a leading role in restoring faith in globalization. However, it is clear that there were large sections of the US electorate who felt excluded from what they saw as a programme that simply led to vast accumulations of wealth for metropolitan elites and who were looking for someone to fight their corner. With the election of President Trump there are fears that this will usher in a form of aggressive strong leadership and a retreat from globalization under his 'Make America Great' banner and his insistence on withdrawing from multilateral trade agreements such as the Transpacific Trade Partnership (TPP), the 'reviewing' of NAFTA, and the threats to engage in defensive protectionist measures against what are seen as 'bad deals' and 'cheats'.

In the EU the austerity route has been chosen and this has meant severe hardship in the PIGS (Portugal, Ireland, Greece, and Spain) and caused severe political problems. In these countries governments might have been democratically elected but they have had little room for economic independence leading people to question the benefits of the single market.

Of course, it is the UK which did at least have the safety valve of its own independent currency that has now sought to free itself from the shackles of what those who voted for 'Brexit' felt was a straightjacket of undue interference in national sovereignty. The great British gamble is that the trilemma of globalization can be resolved with a strong independent country, pursuing its own domestic policy and yet which can have its cake and eat it by having widespread bilateral trade links outside of any formal economic bloc. The Brexit negotiators have to hope that they can minimize the costs of lost trade with the EU27 with the gains from being able to negotiate new trade deals with non-EU trade partners. It is inconceivable that there will not be trade losses with the EU27 but in 2017 it is not at all clear yet where the opportunities will lie. For British business the next few years will be highly uncertain, and all sections of British business will be affected and not just those involved in trade. While clearly Brexit optimists argue that British business will now prosper it would be fair to say that the majority opinion is that growth prospects for the UK will be lower.

In the short and medium term, it is vital that the Brexit negotiators do agree to a transitional period after the formal exit of the UK from the EU in 2019. At the time of writing all parties seem at least to agree that a sudden 'cliff-edge' departure would not be good for British business.

It is ironic that it is countries where the political and economic institutions are generally recognized as being the most conducive to ensuring growth and stability that are the ones mired in low or no growth, and it is in the emerging economies, where the institutions are not as well developed, that growth rates, although falling as a result of the global recession, are nevertheless still healthy. Here there is an increased tendency for greater South-South relationships to be developed. There are closer links now within the ASEAN and ASEAN + 3 and + 6 groupings and the BRICS have begun to operate in a concrete policy formulation way, beyond just being an acronym. At the domestic level the rhetoric is all of greater transparency, inclusive growth, and the need to develop more robust institutions as epitomized by the declaration in 2013 of Xi Jinping, the newly elected President of China, that the task for the next ten years of his tenure would be to build 'the Chinese Dream'.

It is no coincidence that the first foreign destination of Xi Jinping after his assumption of power was to visit Africa, where China has been very active in building bilateral trade links.

In the poorest parts of the world the necessary prerequisite for economic growth is political change from within and political and economic support from without. Internally, many governments are far from perfect, with abuses of human rights and widespread corruption. The danger here is that while deepening trade relationships are potentially a major catalyst for growth, if the benefits of this growth are extracted by a small elite or filtered away via corrupt deals or disappear into the profits of external business interests, then trade will not be beneficial. What is required is that internal reforms are carried out, and external advice and direct financial support might be needed in the form of infrastructure and capacity building.

We referred in Chapter 10 to Xi Jinping's speech to the WEF in 2017. It was widely reported that what was now being signalled was indeed the concrete fact that the twenty-first century was now to be an Asian century with China assuming the mantle of the leader, if not of the world as a whole, but certainly those areas of the world that will be its engines of growth in the future. For Xi, the answer to temporary economic turbulence was not a retreat from globalization but the need to assert its crucial importance. However, he was at pains to point out that the previous Washington dominated system of global governance was now indeed broken and that there needs to be a greater role for an international cooperation which includes the non-western world.

Xi Jinping's economic strategy has been based on extensive state intervention and regulation at the domestic level and looking ahead attention will be focused on the extent to which China has indeed managed a transition to this 'new normal' and the extent to which the 'Chinese Dream' based on socialism is a better system for China than trying to copy an 'American Dream' of free market capitalism. Internationally, China is now active in promoting trade links with other developing countries and building extensive trade investment deals in the far-east and beyond through its establishment of the Asian Infrastructure Investment Bank (AIIB) and the 'One Belt–One Road' initiative (case Mini-Case 16.2)

Mini-Case 16.2 The Silk Road economic belt and the twenty-first-century maritime Silk Road

In 2013 President Xi Jinping announced the launch of what originally was called the One Belt-One Road Initiative and now is shortened to Belt and Road Initiative (BRI). The BRI could be seen to be a modern form of the Marshall plan that was rolled out by the US as an investment and restructuring plan to restore the shattered economies of Western Europe after the Second World War with a view to enabling them to grow and then in turn be able to form part of the western trading system (in which of course the US was to assume the leading role). The terminology of the BRI is confusing as the 'Road' refers to a set of sea routes linking China to East Africa and the Mediterranean as well as to other countries in Indo-china and the 'Belt' refers to the resurrection of the old silk route from China and across Asia. This time though there will be more than one route and the plans are for the 'belt' to be a series of overland routes to Turkey, Russia, and Pakistan. There are many reasons that critics put forward to explain the BRI. After the global economic crisis of 2008 China was left exposed as a large part of its exports had been heavily dependent on exporting goods into western markets although for many years China had also been developing closer links with African and other South East Asian economies. The collapse in exports to western markets did result in falls in employment in many Chinese export companies and also caused problems of excess capacity in terms of key industries such as steel and cement. This was partly solved by the response of the Chinese government in sanctioning a huge increase in both local and central debt financing of large infrastructure projects and the BRI can be seen as providing another way of providing outlets for absorbing this capacity in the form of huge infrastructure projects including bridges, railways, power stations, motorways, farms and factories across the Belt. Of course while this provides an immediate short-term benefit to the Chinese economy in terms of employment and growth the longer-term hope is that by building up other developing and emerging economies across Asia and Indo-china this will increase trade as a whole in the future just at the same time that the US appears to be drawing back from expanding multilateral trade agreements in the region. For Xi Jinping the BRI complements other initiatives such as the

BRICS bank and the AIIB and shows that it is possible to have a globalization in which the interests of the developing world are indeed brought to the fore and which can bring about a coordinated and cooperative form of inclusive globalization. However, other critics argue that it can be seen as an attempt by China to now cement itself as the most powerful economic and political power in the region.

Sources: Miller 2017, State Council, the People's Republic of China 2017.

Question

What are the opportunities and threats posed by the BRI to western businesses?

Global power of big business

VALUES **STAKEHOLDERS** In the first edition of this book we predicted that:

> The issue of how best to ensure that businesses do not abuse their global market positions and operate in a globally responsible way will be very important.
>
> (Wetherly and Otter 2008)

The lessons from the recent past show that if the increasing private power of global businesses allows them to circumvent the traditional national safeguards for employees, consumers, and the wider stakeholders then there is a need for closer global political regulation.

Chapter 9 presented an optimistic view of the willingness of businesses to engage in genuine social responsibility. But in the years since 2008 the spotlight has fallen on extreme examples of irresponsibility, especially in the bonus culture that developed in the financial sector. Those that preached the virtues of the free market and argued vehemently against government regulation seemed to have no qualms in accepting huge amounts of public money to keep their banks afloat and then still were awarded their bonuses even when their banks had failed. Those that left the industry were able to soften the blows to their reputations with large redundancy payments or, in some cases, very generous pension payments.

We considered this issue of business power and responsibility in Chapter 11. It would not be in any way fair to tar all businesses with this brush and the examples of irresponsibility seem to be particularly prevalent within the very large global corporations. This would have come as no surprise to Adam Smith who warned of the dangers of monopoly power and the need for state regulation. Indeed, one of the most ironic claims made by some in the banking industry was that it was not individual or corporate acts of irresponsibility that were to blame but that it was the fault of the regulators in not anticipating that these things might occur, and they should have put in place effective regulation to stop this. To many this sounded a little like a house burglar blaming the victims of his/her crimes for leaving the doors or windows of the house open, and it would be fair to say that public opinion is not with the banks. This is reflected in the intentions of the policymaking to implement banking reform.

However, it would appear that these words have not been fully translated into actions, not least in the US and UK where the power of the financial sectors is so strong and governments are careful not to do anything that they feel might undermine the competitive advantage of the sector. Critics argue that it is not surprising that this will always tend to come down on the side of less rather than more reform, given the dominance of people with links in the industry who are advising the governments on what to do. Such irresponsible behaviour has not been confined to the banks and a common feature that unites the alleged cases of wrong doing has been the global nature of the businesses in which they occur, especially amongst corporations headquartered in developed countries. In the case of the banking sector, if regulation in one country is to work then there needs to be a global agreement or else there is the risk of banks simply moving their business elsewhere. A fear for the rest of the business community has to be that the crisis that unfolded in 2008 could easily do so once again. And in the meantime all businesses are affected by the recession that has occurred and, for small businesses in particular, the difficulty of gaining access to credit. We profiled the growing attention on tax avoidance in Chapter 1 and here the suspicion is that corporations are able to employ the brightest accountancy graduates to legally circumvent paying taxes in the countries where they are making their money by using offshore tax havens or taking advantage of the fact that different countries operate different tax rates. Companies such as Starbucks, Amazon, Google, and Apple continue to be brought before government scrutiny committees in both the US, UK, and EU accused of tax avoidance and other forms of monopoly abuse. While the defence of the companies is that they always operate within the laws of every jurisdiction in which they operate, the accusation sticks that this is because they are using every available means to find ways of avoiding the taxes. At a time when governments in the developed world are seeking to pay down their deficits and need all the money they can get, looking ahead we will see attempts to develop global coordination to curb such tax avoidance.

STAKEHOLDERS In Chapter 10 we profiled how the transnational nature of global businesses can produce a range of difficult ethical issues in relation to human rights, the environment, abuse of market power, and how to deal with regimes that are prone to graft and corruption, and that companies risk being accused of malpractice. Irrespective of the rights and wrongs of the accusations, corporations are ever mindful of the reputational damage that can occur. The rise of the use of social media means that campaign groups can quickly mobilize boycotts or generate adverse publicity, so corporations are keen to show that they are responsible citizens.

With all of these discussions of corporate excess, we must not forget that, given the institutional structure of the business environment, at least the issue of responsibility is easier to highlight and encourage within the context of active democratically accountable governments, free and inquisitive media, and a vigilant civil society to pressurize business to do the right thing. The degree to which such institutions exist elsewhere in the world is patchy and, given the fast emergence of many economies in the developing world, increasing attention will focus on the behaviour of businesses in these settings. The CSR agenda is not confined to western business environments and is, as we have seen in the case of China, at the forefront of the minds of national policymakers.

Global climate change

INTERACTION The third challenge is that posed by global warming. After the Paris Conference in 2015 there is now real optimism that an active process of decarbonization will take place across the globe. There have been significant advances in terms of alternative energy sources such as solar and wind and we are just at the beginning of a remarkable transition to electric powered automobiles with Volvo announcing that from 2019 all new models will be electric and governments setting ambitious targets for the abolition of petrol and diesel vehicles—see Mini-Case 16.3.

Businesses are changing their practices to embed principles of sustainability partly as a result of regulation but also, positively, many can identify a solid business case for these changes in that being green can also cut costs (for case studies in how businesses are responding, see http://www.wbcsd.org and http://www.forumforthefuture.org). Of course, even if these positive reasons for addressing sustainability issues did not exist there are the reputational issues involved and while a measure of 'greenwashing' may occur, nevertheless, it is clear that many businesses are now addressing the sustainability agenda.

There will continue to be pressure from environmental groups for governments to impose tighter regulations and incentives to enable a greener business approach but, equally, there will be countervailing arguments that such regulations need to be voluntary.

Moves towards more environmentally friendly ways of operating and the need to plan for mitigation and adaptation to climate change present many opportunities to develop alternative technologies and cater for more alternative lifestyles. It is clear, though, that the issue of sustainable development will impact on business behaviour and while potentially this could be seen as a threat there are also opportunities for businesses to exploit.

Stop and Think

What changes can businesses make to lessen their 'carbon footprint'? To what extent do you think that there is a business case for making these changes?

Global inequality and political instability

LOCAL TO GLOBAL **INTERACTION** Global income inequality continues to blight the progress of humanity. Across the globe there have been significant rises in the numbers of middle class consumers and we saw in Chapter 13 that this is leading to a recalibration in the structural balance of the emerging economies as they begin to trade amongst themselves and seek to target their own internal and regional markets.

While it is clear that there is still a need for aid to help the poorest of the poor, it will be providing the best environment in which poor people can develop their own business activity that is key. Initiatives such as micro-credit in the developing world and the general focus on 'bottom of the pyramid' models of business development see poor people not as passive victims but as potentially active entrepreneurs who will become the burgeoning middle classes of the future.

Political instability continues to affect many parts of the developing world and this makes it difficult for businesses. Nowhere is this more evident than in the uncertainty over energy supplies security, as these vital resources are found in many of these areas.

In Chapters 3 and 10 we did draw the distinction between countries that have been able to develop inclusive institutions—that can both produce economic growth as well as ensuring that its benefits are shared more widely—and those with extractive ones. In such countries high rates of growth are possible benefiting relatively small numbers of people and the likelihood is that they will be trading with richer developed countries. It is the case that while the BRICS have indeed been successful at producing growth, the levels of inequality and the severely distorted social structures that have developed will not be conducive to long-run development. Progress has been made in terms of education, health, and infrastructural reforms but the extreme levels of inequality in these countries can give rise to civil unrest and create powerful oligarchies resistant to wider political reform. It is important that across the global environment attention is paid to reducing inequality as a way of ensuring that growth is more equitably shared. Within these environments governments and third sector organizations, both at the national and supranational levels, have a large role to play in lifting people out of poverty.

Looking ahead: the social environment

We explored the nature of the social environment in Chapters 6, 11, and 12. In relation to the global business environment three major areas have been highlighted: the pressure of economic growth on the natural environment allied to the widening income gap between people; the implications of increases in migration; and demographic changes.

Social inequality and relative affluence

VALUES **INTERACTION** Businesses inevitably are affected by changes in the social structure as this will affect the patterns of demand. As affluence increases in much of the developed world, this has enabled businesses to target a range of high value activities and this has affected their marketing and branding strategies. There have been big shifts in the patterns of demand as the proportion of consumption has switched to services and away from basic goods.

While it is not the job of business to take responsibility for social inequality, and it is for governments to decide what levels of equality are or are not acceptable, we have seen that management decisions as to how to reward and treat employees do have a social impact, and that business in general does have to recognize its social responsibilities.

We have seen that globally there is disquiet at the growing gaps in inequality within societies, but the focus differs depending on a country's level of development.

There has been a recent surge in economic research into what people say about what makes them happy. This research harks back to a research paper published by Richard Easterlin (1974). He argued that while people with higher incomes are happier than those on lower ones, as people get richer they do not, in fact, get any happier. What seems more important to people is their relative status. We are not happy if we feel poorer than other groups. This so-called Easterlin paradox has been interpreted as proving that richer people are happier because they are richer than others, not because of the actual amount that they earn. This then brings into question the role of economic growth in developed societies.

Related to this work on happiness, is the work of Wilkinson and Pickett (2009). In their book *The Spirit Level* they use a range of indicators to show that in affluent societies with high degrees of inequality the quality of life for all people is actually lower.

> Economic growth for so long the great engine of progress has, in the rich countries, largely finished its work. Not only have measures of well-being and happiness ceased to rise with economic growth but as affluent societies have grown richer there have been long-term rises in rates of anxiety, depression and numerous other social problems.
>
> (Wilkinson and Pickett 2009: 5–6)

This ties in with the work of social psychologists such as Oliver James as well as with the views of the green critics we profiled when discussing climate change. For James (2007), in affluent societies 'affluenza' occurs with people constantly feeling that they haven't got enough as they compare themselves always to the groups above themselves. In this view of the world, the recent tendency for the concentration of wealth in the hands of an elite group of super-rich people is problematic as it will raise unrealistic expectations from the middle class and, therefore, place too much strain on resources. If 'enough is to be enough', then one way of moving towards sustainable living and increased well-being is to reduce these income disparities.

We have seen the recognition that governments do wish to curb the culture of excess pay and awards of bonuses, but at the same time there is a reluctance to risk the potential political unpopularity of such overt attempts to cut top pay. As a direct result of the public mood against what is seen as undeserved pay awards, there have been many attempts by shareholders of companies to pressure their boards to show restraint in the face of the global recession.

Of course, such concerns may only be relevant in the post-materialist developed societies and, even here, we need to be careful as there is a persistent minority of people whose incomes are still well below what could be seen as constituting an affluent lifestyle.

In the developing world it could be argued that this is the case for the majority of people and there is some way to go before 'affluenza' develops. However, as we have seen, the relative levels of inequality are even more pronounced in many of the fastest growing economies. There is not only a danger that social inequality gives rise to corruption and acts as a barrier to social mobility but there is much less evidence that the fruits of the economic growth are trickling down to the bottom of the pyramid and far too many people are being left behind.

Migration

DIVERSITY The onward march of globalization will also increase migration. While this will mean that it is important for countries to develop appropriate ways of handling the diversity of communities, businesses need to be mindful that their recruitment policies do not undermine social cohesion by using immigration as a way of driving down wages and in so doing displacing indigenous workers. Immigration brings clear economic benefits to countries, as migrant workers are often very skilled or else are prepared to work more flexibly than indigenous workers. However, unregulated immigration can impose unexpected increases in appropriate welfare provision and fuels ethnic suspicions. The inability to resolve cultural and ethnic differences can lead to tensions, and may provide the ideal environment for this to result in extreme political protests in the form of racist behaviour and actions. It is important in the future that diversity is handled effectively.

Demographic changes

DIVERSITY **INTERNAL/EXTERNAL** We have seen that in the developed world the improvement in health and living have led to big increases in life expectancy and, while this provides commercial opportunities for business to target the 'grey' market and benefit from the willingness of people to work longer (and thus benefit from their experience), it also means greater consideration must be paid to pension and healthcare provision as well as the long-term care needs of the elderly. In the UK it is estimated that the over 65s will grow by 33 per cent between 2016 and 2030 from 11.6 million to 16.4 million but that the working population will only grow by 2 per cent.

It is now increasingly argued that there is an intergenerational strain between the 'millennials' born in the decade before and in the years after 2000 and the 'baby boomers' born in the 1940s and 1950s. We have seen that despite the recession in the last ten years across the developed world, employment has held up surprisingly well, but this belies an increase in temporary and part-time work and forced self-employment. It is argued that with technological change this increase in 'the gig' economy is set to continue and so for the millennials they will be the first post-war generation to experience lower lifetime earnings compared to preceding generations (Lawrence 2016).

In the developing world the focus has shifted from seeing population as a problem to seeing it as a potential advantage, if people gain access to educational skills and training and if the entrepreneurial dynamism at the bottom of the pyramid can be unleashed. The rise in the middle classes can spread to the people at the lower ends of the pyramid and this represents a huge opportunity for businesses. What is needed for the emerging economies is to invest in their people as their key resource by directing the wealth generated from economic growth into education, health, housing, and environmental reform in the urban areas and to help raise rural incomes and diversification in rural areas.

Looking ahead: the technological environment

DYNAMIC The revolution based on new technologies has combined with the increase in globalization to create what is, for many commentators, a new paradigm of the 'network age'. The rise in robotics and autonomous systems (RAS) has led to the prospect that we are now entering into a fourth industrial age. In the old industrial age of the twentieth century production needed to be vertically integrated (all stages of the production process kept together geographically) because of the high costs of transport and communications. In this new age, it is argued, we will see an increasing horizontal organization of business activity. It is now possible for businesses to organize their activity in functional areas located in different parts of the globe, e.g. research, marketing, education and training, distribution, and production split into separate processes outsourced across the world.

What is likely to be the impact of what has now become called 'disruptive innovation'? It is clear that there will be considerable changes in terms of employment in certain industries especially in wholesaling and retail, manufacturing, administration, and transport. Estimates though on the effect overall on employment vary widely. The study of Frey and Osborne which we saw in Chapter 3 and which points to relatively high estimates of jobs threatened by automation have been challenged by the work of Amtz et al. who estimated the effect across the OECD as being more likely to be nearer 9 per cent (Amtz et al. 2016, Frey and Osborne 2013). However, it is clear that there will be future pressure on jobs and that irrespective of the quantity of jobs lost there will be an increased vulnerability for those people with a relative lack of the skills required to work with the new technologies as it is likely that while our jobs may not be replaced by automation we will have to learn to work with automated processes.

Quite clearly the spread of information and communications technology will bring about great benefits in terms of enabling people to gain access to knowledge. This will greatly help in terms of a wide range of activities, from participation in the political process and, therefore, greater transparency, through to access to research and market information. IBM has developed a supercomputer that is able to process millions of pieces of medical data to diagnose illnesses and suggest treatments that would be beyond the capabilities of human medical practitioners. The huge amounts of data that we share through our use of digital platforms and social media sites has created enormous amounts of 'big data' which can now be analysed and utilized by businesses to target specific products to individuals and, indeed, spot the potential for new ones. We are already well down the line of enabling every home in the developed world to have high-speed Internet access, and in developing economies the access to information that the Internet brings is enabling banking to develop and empowering entrepreneurs.

However, as we discussed in Chapter 3 a closer analysis of these growth rates does call for caution over technological flights of fancy. Before the recent economic turmoil growth rates in the US and Europe had been steady rather than spectacular, and where growth rates have been high, such as in South East Asia, there have been a host of other factors involved in creating the environment for growth.

INTERACTION Technology has changed the way in which businesses are organized, especially as a result of the speed with which information, goods, and people can be moved around. Biotechnology and nanotechnology mean that businesses can undertake rapid new product development and seek to build new markets, particularly in the areas of food production and health.

While it is public investment that is vital in providing the educational infrastructure for the knowledge economy, it is the private sector that is primarily responsible for translating this knowledge into product development. Across the developed countries, typically 50–60 per cent of research and development is in private companies, with universities responsible for around 15–20 per cent and public research institutions between 15–20 per cent.

Private research is even higher in the developing world. This means that there is a potential conflict between the desire of the private sector to use technology to establish competitive advantage, and the desire of the public to be both protected from unsafe technologies and to fully benefit from those that will improve the quality of our lives. Of course, the increasing reliance that businesses have on information technology and digital infrastructure means that they are constantly open to the possibility of cyberattack. There is pressure to develop open-source operating systems, and governments have to guard against the creation of monopoly power and bridge the digital divide between developed and developing countries and high and low-income groups.

It is no surprise that the main advocates of the view that we are in a qualitatively different disruptive age of technology come from the new digital industries. In the 1980s the 'masters of the universe' were the financial brokers and in the twenty-first century it is the computer geeks. The digital start-ups that have so rapidly become the behemoths of the modern corporate world are generally headed by unconventional and very young entrepreneurs who feel that they are engaged in truly changing the world, but Marxists would predict that eventually the venture of these bright young things will be snapped up and end up being concentrated in the hands of the few.

We saw in Chapter 3 that there is a fierce debate about whether the digital age is truly a fundamental change in business motivation and strategy. For technology optimists like Andersen, the digital age will create a long tail of many small entrepreneurial businesses which will spread the benefits of their enterprise widely and ensure that wealth is evenly distributed. On the other hand, there are voices of dissent. We saw that the evidence for the impact of technology on productivity is limited and that, while undoubtedly the impact of the digital age is truly amazing in terms of the gadgets that arise and the changes in lifestyle and working practices that it enables, fundamentally these are not revolutionary in the way in which electricity and running water were. The room for uncertainty is large. In 2017 in a parliamentary written answer to the UK Business and Enterprise subcommittee question as to the likely effects of RAS technologies the Secretary of State for Higher Education estimated this to be a rise in global GDP of anywhere between $1.9 and $6.4 trillion by 2025!

Furthermore, the dominance of the digital industry by such huge players as Google, Amazon, Facebook, and Apple mean that the 'head' seems to dominate in much the same way as with the old technologies, leading to concentrations of corporate wealth and power.

Mini-Case 16.3 Autonomous vehicle technology

Over thirty companies are racing to develop fully autonomous vehicles. These include the high-tech companies of Google, Apple, and Intel as well as of course car producers themselves with BMW, Honda, and Volvo to the fore. The car and vehicle industry is experiencing rapid change on many fronts and technological change is well and truly being disruptive. The rapid expansion of Uber in the provision of taxi services has shaken up the industry and prompted fierce debates. Advocates argue that Uber is a boon for customers in terms of cost and quality and for opening up new forms of flexible employment for certain groups of workers. Other argue that the benefits come at a large cost to undermining the safeguards provided by traditional taxi providers as well as the employment rights of drivers.

Uber itself is now using its profits to invest in research and development into driverless cars and the prospect of the arrival of automated vehicles has prompted a fierce debate as to its likely prevalence as well as impact. For optimists, automated vehicles hold out the prospect of much higher levels of road safety in reducing human error. It is argued that road congestion pressure will ease as driverless vehicles will move in smoother patterns, delivery costs will fall, and so there will be big gains in terms of productivity and growth. However, clearly if you are a bus, taxi, or delivery driver the future is not bright.

It has been estimated that in the US, for example, 4 million jobs will be under threat and that the degree to which such technological disruption is to be valued will crucially depend on the extent to which the costs are minimized or mitigated. The majority of drivers in these industries tend to be relatively less educated men but with caring responsibilities. Traditionally driving jobs have been a source of relatively well-paid work for such a category of workers. Inevitably if disruption is to be minimized then policymakers must prepare for the loss of livelihoods that will occur. Some people argue that at least in the short to medium term there will need to be social safety nets in the form of unemployment assistance. Others go further and argue that if there is a societal good in the onwards march of automation then the displaced victims of such automated change should have the automatic right to a universal basic income. Of course there is the hope that some people will be able to make a transition to other forms of work and for this to happen there needs to be the provision of retraining and other educational opportunities.

Source: Center for Global Policy Solutions 2017.

Question

What are the relative costs and benefits of a future of automated vehicles and who should 'pay' for the costs of the disruption caused?

COMPLEXITY This chapter has attempted to look forward to spot the main factors that will affect the future business environment. Inevitably this has taken place at a general level but, by using the PEST framework, we have been able to identify some key future developments. In the end of chapter case study, we will show how PEST factors will impact on one business in particular.

Summary

- Analysis of the underlying political, economic, social, and technological factors helps us to map the important themes and features of the business environment which can act as a guide for the future.
- The nature of the business environment is complex, and businesses need to be able to analyse the external environment, develop effective risk assessments, and then plan how to deal with these.

Case Study: The football business—the state of play in 2017

COMPLEXITY LOCAL TO GLOBAL In the previous editions of this book we showed how the football business has demonstrated the changing nature of the external environment and its effects on business strategy and structure. We charted football's move away from being an English game with amateur clubs rooted in their local communities. Football has become the most popular global sport played by millions and watched by billions. In the process, a tiny minority of footballers and their teams have become global brands, and the real business of football is about much more than what happens on the field of play. The main reason for this change has been the global television revenues that were made possible through the development of satellite and digital broadcasting, but there is a wide range of other external factors that have played their part.

Changes in the political and economic environment

INTERACTION DYNAMIC It has been television and globalization that have enabled elite football to become a global business and it is commercial television's need to earn advertising revenue that has been behind this. Changes in regulatory regimes across the world have allowed the development of commercial TV companies who quickly recognized the power of sport in general, and football in particular, with its global appeal to draw in large audiences.

The manner in which broadcasting rights have been negotiated has rapidly led to a concentration of wealth in the hands of an elite group of clubs who, in turn, are able to diversify their income streams through sponsorship deals (naming rights of stadiums, deals with kit manufacturers, corporate logos on shirts) and merchandising of branded goods from clothes to key rings. In 2017 the top three teams in terms of earnings were Manchester United who knocked Real Madrid off the top place it held for the previous twelve years and then FC Barcelona. Each of these three clubs had annual earnings of over €600 million in the 2015/16 season.

While the TV industry is regulated by governments, football is not and regulates itself through its own governing bodies, with FIFA at the global level, UEFA at the European level, and through national football associations at the national level. However, this closed world has led to constant accusations of corruption within the game with allegations and indeed prosecutions extending to the taking of bribes by officials through to illegal gambling activities of players within the game.

It is the global reach of football that has powered the huge increases in revenues. In terms of growth, gate receipts revenue is limited by ground capacity and ticket prices, although many teams are doing all they can to increase stadium size and ticket prices, but the latter is constrained by the desire to be seen to be good corporate citizens.

The price of broadcasting rights, though, is rising exponentially. The English Premier League negotiated a new deal in 2012 which boosted revenues by 70 per cent to over £5 billion over the three years to 2015/16. The bulk of this comes from domestic TV companies and here the heightened competitive environment has led to bidding wars which has resulted in a huge increase in the price paid for the rights. Increasingly, though, overseas networks also are competing for rights to the coverage and this is providing a growing source of revenue.

Similarly, there is seemingly no ceiling to the potential of global merchandising. It is estimated that Manchester United has a fan base of 200 million in China alone. Just think if it were to get each one to pay £1 for a branded item each year! The ownership of the top football clubs is a contentious issue and most commonly they are owned by wealthy private individuals or groups who made their wealth outside of football and whose primary motivation was the status that came from ownership in itself, irrespective of whether they would make any money from their investment. While at the elite level this is no longer the case, there are still too many examples of financial irresponsibility within football with short-term gains being made at the expense of long-term financial sustainability.

STAKEHOLDERS Politically, there have been questions raised about the effect this pattern of ownership has had on football and all its stakeholders with the escalating effect this has had on transfer fees and the ability of the new superstar footballers to demand large salaries. Within the global governing organizations of football, there are claims that this pattern of ownership distorts fair competition and leads to a closed rich elite which, in the long run, will damage the game. This model of ownership isn't the only one, as in some cases there are clubs where the supporters have more of a voice. To allow these different forms of control to continue and to try to create a more disciplined financial environment, the football authorities have introduced a new financial fair play rule.

While it is Europe that dominates world football in the sense of commercial revenues, FIFA is looking to boost football's prospects globally. One way it can do this is through the siting of the high-profile World Cup Finals, and it is no surprise that this took place in Brazil in 2014. The next two will be in Russia in 2018 and, controversially, Qatar in 2022.

Changes in the social environment

VALUES STAKEHOLDERS It has been the rise in the affluence of football supporters that has had the biggest influence in the game, both domestically and globally. Domestically, there has been a change in the income brackets of those that attend the game, and many supporters are keen to buy into the club merchandise by at least buying the team shirt. Globally, the rise in the middle classes has fuelled the TV-watching audiences but even poor people have access to TV sets and are able to be part of the global 'football family', which is how FIFA likes to characterize this support. Increasingly the popularity of women's football in the US is now being mirrored in more traditional football heartlands and the Women's world cup in Canada in 2015 followed by the Women's European finals in Holland attracted record attendances and TV audiences.

For some, the old values of local community have now been lost in this new commercial world. Some supporter groups are trying to counter this by developing more supporter involvement and, in some cases, direct ownership. The social landscape of football has changed.

Changes in the technological environment

DYNAMIC Of course, none of the developments above would have been able to come together were it not for the technological advancement of global television through digital and satellite. Broadcasting technology continues to develop with web streaming, HD television, and 3D, but crucially it has given the global audience immediate access to the game and all the celebrity culture that surrounds it.

Source: Deloitte 2017.

Questions

1. **Is it legitimate for the government to try to intervene in the football business?**
2. **What have been the main changes in the business environment of football that have caused the developments referred to above?**
3. **Looking ahead to the future, what are the prospects for the football business?**

Review and discussion questions

1. How has the financial crisis of 2008 and ensuing economic recession impacted on the business environment?
2. How successful have attempts to coordinate global economic policy been?
3. What are the obstacles that make it difficult for governments to try to reduce income inequalities?
4. As the second decade of the twenty-first century opens and develops do you think that businesses are becoming more socially responsible?
5. Using a company that you either work in or have knowledge of as an example, what do you think are the key aspects of the external business environment that will impact upon it in the next few years?

Assignments

1. Read the following annual reports (see relevant weblinks below):

   World Economic Forum's Global Agenda and Global Risks and at least one of the following:

   UNCTAD Trade and Development Report

   IMF World Economic Outlook

   Write a report that compares and contrasts their views as to the future of the business environment and assess the main likely factors and their impacts on business in general.
2. Write a report which analyses how you see the business environment affecting a business or business sector that you want to profile for a business magazine.
3. You are working as a business analyst for a private consultancy firm and have been asked by the local chamber of commerce to prepare a presentation which profiles an emerging economy which might provide a good place which local SMEs might want to target as part of their international strategy. Visit the World Bank's Doing Business website and select a country and then show why you feel this would be a good choice and what factors would need to be considered in doing business there.

Test your understanding of this chapter with online questions and answers, explore the subject further through web exercises, and use the weblinks to provide a quick resource for further research. Visit the online resources at www.oup.com/uk/wetherly_otter4e/

Useful websites

www.bbc.co.uk
The BBC website is a good source of information both in written archives and in terms of its 'listen again' archives. The best programmes to listen again to are the *In Business* and *Analysis* series which always contain views about the future.

www.unctad.org
This is the website of the UN Trade and Development organization, and you will find its annual report here.

www.worldbank.org
The World Bank publishes annual reports on the global environment.

http://www.doingbusiness.org
The World Bank's Doing Business website

www.imf.org
See, in particular, the annual World Economic Outlook that can be downloaded from this site.

www.wef.org
The website of the World Economic Forum

www.forumforthefuture.org.uk
This site profiles and champions the case for sustainable development.

www.technologyreview.com
This site is run by MIT in the US, one of the leading technology universities in the world.

http://www.bis.gov.uk/foresight
This is the UK government's science and technology programme to research into the future.

http://steadystate.org
A research organization that looks at ways of attaining sustainable growth

http://www.wbcsd.ch
This is the site for the World Council for Sustainable Business and on this site you can see case studies of how businesses are dealing with the sustainability agenda.

www.laborrights.org
A campaigning group for labour rights across the world

http://www.waronwant.org
The site of War on Want, a charity that campaigns against world poverty

www.ethicaltrade.org
An organization that seeks to encourage business to incorporate ethical practice

For local business information look up the web addresses of your local Chambers of Commerce.

References

Arntz, M., Gregory, T., and Zierahn, U. (2016) 'The risk of automation for jobs in OECD countries: a comparative analysis', OECD Social, Employment and Migration Working Papers, No. 189 (Paris: OECD Publishing) (accessed 26 July 2017) **http://dx.doi.org/10.1787/5jlz9h56dvq7-en**

Center for Global Policy Solutions (2017) *Stick Shift: Autonomous Vehicles, Driving Jobs, and the Future of Work* (Washington, DC: Center for Global Policy Solutions)

Deloitte (2017) 'Ahead of the curve: annual review of football finance 2017', Sports Business Group (accessed 3 August 2017) **https://www2.deloitte.com/uk/en/pages/sports-business-group/articles/annual-review-of-football-finance.html**

Easterlin, Richard A. (1974) 'Does economic growth improve the human lot?', in P. A. David and M. W. Reder (eds.), *Nations and Households in Economic Growth: Essays in Honor of Moses Abramovitz* (New York: Academic Press)

Frey C. and Osborne, M. (2013) *The Future of Employment: How Susceptible are Jobs to Computerisation* (Oxford: Oxford Martin School, University of Oxford) (accessed 14 July 2017) **http://www.oxfordmartin.ox.ac.uk/downloads/academic/The_Future_of_Employment.pdf**

James, O. (2007) *Affluenza: How to Be Successful and Stay Sane* (London: Vermillion)

Lawrence, M. (2016) *Future Proof: Britain in the 2020s* (London: Institute for Public Policy Research) (accessed 2 August 2017) **https://www.ippr.org/files/2017-07/future-proof-dec2016.pdf**

Miller, T. (2017) *China's Asian Dream: Empire Building Along the New Silk Road* (London: Zed Books)

Rodrik, D. (2017) *Straight Talk on Trade: Ideas for a Sane World Economy* (Princeton, NJ: Princeton University Press)

State Council, the People's Republic of China (2017) The Belt and Road Initiative (accessed 3 August 2017) **http://english.gov.cn/beltAndRoad**

Wetherly, P. and Otter, D. (2008) *The Business Environment* (2nd edn, Oxford: Oxford University Press)

Wilkinson, R. and Pickett, K. (2009) *The Spirit Level: Why More Equal Societies Almost Always Do Better* (London: Allen Lane)

GLOSSARY

absolute advantage if two countries produce the same range of goods one has an absolute advantage over the other if it can produce greater quantities of the goods using the same amount of resources. Adam Smith showed that where this is the case it is better for each country to specialize in the goods in which it has an absolute advantage so increasing total production. Trade could then occur so that each country would be able to increase the amount of all goods available to it (see also **comparative advantage**).

acid rain burning fossil fuels releases gases such as sulphur dioxide and nitrogen dioxide into the atmosphere. These gases are transported by prevailing winds, and combine with moisture to produce 'acid rain', devastating natural vegetation and ecological systems.

affluenza the term used to refer to the alleged tendency of people to suffer a range of mental illnesses as a result of striving to increase their incomes so that, paradoxically, higher incomes lower the quality of life.

age structure structure of the population in terms of the proportions in each age band.

ageing population falling death rates (increased longevity) result in a growing number and share of elderly in the population, and increasing average age.

agencification private or public organizations given specific mandates by government, often reporting directly to a ministry but, at the same time, often one-removed from direct governmental procedures. Context and national differences will apply to the specific status of such agencies. The increasing use of agencies has prompted other working-titles, such as 'executive-agencies', and they are often linked to what is known as 'distributed governance'.

Agenda 21 a document about sustainable development formulated at the Rio conference in 1992.

agentification the increasing use of 'professional' agencies rather than civil service-based ministries.

aggregate demand the total level of demand for all goods and services in an economy.

allocative efficiency *see* **efficiency**.

alternative scenarios a form of environmental analysis in which alternative possible futures are identified.

appropriate technology the use of technology best suited to the external environment in which business is operating. Most often used to highlight the need for developing countries to adopt 'low-tech' solutions.

austerity requires contractionary fiscal policy adjustments—cuts in public expenditure or tax increases but usually with a strong emphasis on the former—to try to ensure that government lives within its means.

basic economic problem scarcity, requiring the allocation of resources between competing wants or needs, the need to minimize resource use, and the need to ensure equitable distribution.

best value a term used both legally and managerially to quantify and qualify the 'best value' services available to the public from service providers: this was building on previous recommendations in relation to **value for money**.

BIG Ten a set of ten capabilities present in higher performing SMEs.

biodiversity the totality of species and life forms on earth.

birth rate the number of births per 1000 of the population.

Brexit is the process of the UK leaving the European Union.

bureaucracy the paid (normally) civil servants or officials and their system of public administration.

business often defined narrowly in terms of the private sector, but a broad definition includes the public and 'third' sectors. Business involves the transformation of inputs into outputs to produce goods and services for customers or users.

business class (capitalist class) social group defined by ownership and control of business.

business dominance refers to the claim that business exercises unrivalled influence in politics.

business ethics the systematic study of the theories and practice of ethics applied in business.

capacity building refers to helping organizations to develop their resources (people, buildings, etc.) so that they are better able to meet their aims.

capitalism an economic system in which the means of production are overwhelmingly privately owned and operated for profit; decisions regarding investment of capital are made privately; and where production, distribution, and the prices of goods, services, and labour are affected by the forces of supply and demand in a largely free market.

capitalist class *see* **business class**.

caretaker state refers to the main role of government being the provision of goods and services, rather than the classical role of exercising authority.

central government and local authorities most developed countries have developed public administration systems that often embrace central control and local delivery.

circular flow of income in a simple model of a market system money (or income) flows between firms and households in the form of payments for labour and commodities.

civil disobedience a tactic used by some campaigning organizations involving a willingness to break the law in order to protest a law or business action.

civil society organization (CSO) usually used as another term for pressure group—a voluntary association formed to campaign on specific issues, e.g. Greenpeace.

class social group defined by common characteristics or social position, especially occupation.

class structure a way of classifying the population according to class positions, e.g. working class and middle class.

colonialism the term is most often used in the context of the expansion of European powers across the globe from the Spanish and Portuguese conquests of South America and then the dominance of countries such as Britain, France, and Holland in North America, the Far East, and Africa. There is a fierce debate as to the effects of colonialism. Refer also to **imperialism**.

common good what is good for society as a whole, as opposed to purely private interests.

comparative advantage even if one country is better at producing all ranges of commodities compared with another, trade will still lead to overall gains in production. Here the more efficient country should specialize in the goods in which it has the greater comparative advantage and the less efficient country should specialize in the goods in which it has the smallest comparative disadvantage. In this way total production of the two countries would increase and trade will enable both countries to benefit.

competition the existence of competition is seen as being vital if businesses are to behave in an efficient manner. In reality, competition may be prevented by monopoly power and in some cases can be 'destructive'.

competition policy a major policy impacting on the EU business environment which aims to ensure that competition in the single market is not distorted by anti-competitive forces such as monopoly, oligopoly, restrictive practices, or state interference.

competition state whereas the welfare state may be seen as primarily concerned with fairness or social justice, the concept of a competition state refers to a shift of focus in favour of policies intended to enhance the competitiveness of the economy, e.g. through deregulation and tax cuts.

complements these are commodities that we buy as a result of buying another commodity, e.g. if the demand for car transport increases so will the demand for petrol.

comprador capitalists is a term used by writers in the dependency tradition to characterize what they saw as the type of capitalism that would occur in the developing world as a result of trading with the developed world. Rather than a capitalist class growing within a developing country which was based on growing domestic goods and services for domestic needs, globalization would encourage capitalists to have an outward orientation through gearing production to external markets based on a very narrow range of activities which exploited the natural resources of the country.

comprehensive performance assessment (CPA) a means by which to determine the effectiveness of public service provision.

compulsory competitive tendering introduced as an administrative mechanism to determine effective competition procedures for public services.

constitution the highest form of law and a device for limiting the power of the state; sets out the rules about making rules.

consumer sovereignty the claim that consumers, not firms, are ultimately in charge of the economic system through their spending decisions. In a free market system, it should be the consumer who has the power to decide what should be produced. If there are anxieties that this is not the case and that producers have the power, then there needs to be consumer protection.

consumerism an attitude in which consumption is seen as a prime source of personal well-being (see also **materialism**).

corporate citizenship this term views corporations as members of society with similar rights and responsibilities to citizens.

corporate responsibility (CR) a development of corporate social responsibility which broadens the focus of responsibility to relationships with internal staff and wider industry.

corporate social responsibility (CSR) the practice of corporate responsibility in relation to the stakeholders who form the social context of the business. The term is increasingly less used because of its narrow focus on methods of reporting, narrow stakeholder focus, and lack of integration into governance.

cosmopolitan society a society that is open to a wide range of cultural influences (see also **multiculturalism**).

creative destruction is the term given by Schumpeter for the process by which new inventions and innovations will constantly evolve, with the new replacing the old.

culture refers to the set of values, beliefs, and lifestyles that characterize a group or society.

death rate the number of deaths per thousand of the population.

declaration of incompatibility the courts have the power to declare any piece of legislation incompatible with the provisions of the Human Rights Act 1998. This Act brought the European Convention on Human Rights into UK law. The power of the courts is limited as a declaration of incompatibility does not affect the ongoing operation of the law. There is, however, a procedure by which the government can remove the incompatibility following such a declaration.

demand-pull inflation inflation associated with an excess demand for goods and services when the economy is at or above full employment.

democracy (see also **liberal democracy**) a political system in which political power is in the hands of the people: 'rule by the people'.

deontological ethics this theory argues that there are certain core ethical principles that apply in any situation, such as 'It is wrong to kill another person'.

dependency often used to describe the inequality of power and forms of economic domination that characterizes the relations between rich and poor countries. Dependency theory emerged from the work of André Gunder Frank and the United Nations Economic Commission on Latin America under Raul Prebisch. Reacting against theories of development and modernization that contended that poor countries would inevitably follow the stages of western economic development, dependency theorists argued that these countries faced systematic 'underdevelopment' within the world economy.

dependency culture the argument that state benefits can foster dependency on the part of recipients and undermine independence.

design, build, finance, and operate system (DBFO) a working system for developing PPP and PFI developments.

destructive competition there are areas of business activity in which unregulated competition could be harmful. Cutting costs could mean endangering health and safety to workers and consumers and so regulation is needed. There are also whole areas of business where it would be better to have only one firm (see **natural monopoly**).

devolution the sharing or giving up of power from central to local level, e.g. the establishment of a Scottish parliament.

digital era governance the means by which a government governs in all its forms and all its levels in the digital era.

diminishing returns occur when businesses face a capacity constraint. Commonly, this might be a capital or land constraint and as business tries to expand production it will find that its costs rise and productivity falls because it comes up against capacity constraints.

disposable income the amount of income that people can actually spend after all taxes, etc. have been deducted.

distributive efficiency *see* **efficiency**.

divisional structure a type of organization structure based on semi-independent operational units or divisions.

domestic division of labour the division of labour in the household, i.e. the division of unpaid domestic tasks between men and women.

dynamic gains from trade are ongoing and arise from the additional benefits of trade on top of the gains from specialization. For example, by opening up to trade a country can gain from the exposure of its domestic businesses to foreign competition as well as the ability of its domestic businesses to now sell to larger markets and, thus, benefit from potential economies of scale.

dynamic states of growth a model of growth that places the emphasis on the factors that influence the growth process.

economic growth the process of increasing the output of goods and services produced by the economy or, more strictly, the process of increasing productive capacity.

economies of scale refer to a range of circumstances in which producing and selling greater volumes of output will enable cost reductions to be made. Mini-Case 3.2 explores how containerization has enabled transport costs to be dramatically reduced.

ecosystem a community of interdependent living organisms, plants, and animals, set in the non-living components of their surroundings.

efficiency refers to the way in which the three parts of the economic problem are resolved. For a business to be efficient in an economic sense it must produce so that: customers get 'value for money' and this will happen if prices equal marginal costs (allocative efficiency); the average cost of each unit of output is minimized so that resources are being used as efficiently as possible (productive efficiency); the distribution of the output is 'fair' and creates equity (distributive efficiency). Deciding on what is equitable is very contentious. In the neoclassical perspective the free market is the best way of achieving this. Structuralist and Marxist critics argue that unregulated markets can lead to exploitation of consumers and employees and create a divided world where there is gross inequity. The Green movement argues that it is the planetary system that is being exploited and that our present prosperity endangers that of future generations.

elasticity of demand price elasticity of demand refers to the responsiveness of demand to changes in price. It determines the effect on a firm's revenue of price changes. Income elasticity of demand is the responsiveness of demand to changes in income.

emissions trading creating a market in carbon dioxide emissions whereby countries and companies receive licences to emit carbon dioxide. If the companies exceed their emission limits they must buy permits from other companies which have reduced their emissions. This creates an incentive to reduce emissions on the part of an individual company.

empirical research the gathering and use of evidence to try and prove the validity of theories.

employee protection is a term used to describe laws whose purpose is to protect the interests of employees in the workplace, such as protection against unfair dismissal.

employee voice a domain or set of practices that encourage the employee involvement in decision-making.

employer of choice an employing organization which has gained a reputation for being a good employer in the employment market. Employers of choice are characterized by competitive terms and conditions, the provision of developmental opportunities for staff, fair dealing, involving employees in decision-making, interesting work, and an interest in work–life balance.

endogenous change occurs when a variable is affected by other variables within an economic model.

enlargement the EU has grown via several waves of new entrants, although enlargement commonly refers to the 2004 accession of ten new members, largely from Eastern Europe.

enterprise 'making things happen, having ideas and doing something about them, taking advantage of the opportunities to bring about change' (SGE programme 1999: see Chapter 14 References). 'Any attempt at new business or new venture creation, such as self-employment, a new business organization, or the expansion of existing business, by an individual, teams of individuals or established businesses' (Irwin and Wilkinson 2001).

enterprise and entrepreneurship 'enterprise is a set of qualities and competencies that can be employed in different settings, whilst entrepreneurship involves the process of creating and developing new ventures' (Enterprise Insight 2005: 23: see Chapter 14 References).

entrepreneur anyone who attempts a new business or new venture creation, such as self-employment, a new business organization, social enterprise, or the expansion of an existing business by an individual, teams of individuals, to established business (DTI 2003: see Chapter 14 References).

environmental analysis the more or less systematic analysis of the business environment to assist business strategy and performance.

environmental and ecological auditing refers to processes that are analogous to financial auditing. Environmental auditing would refer generally to evaluations of processes and situations which have environmental implications to ensure compliance with regulations and implementation of environmental management systems. Ecological auditing refers to the measuring and monitoring of conditions to protect or enhance the natural environment.

environmental footprint in relation to an individual company or organization, its total environmental impact, referring to direct and indirect resource use, generation of waste and effluent, plus any other changes it imposes on the natural environment. For a whole economy, it is the land and sea area needed to provide all the energy, water, transport, food, and materials it consumes. Thus, if the population of the whole world lived at the same level as the UK, it would require three worlds to sustain it.

environmental impact assessment (EIA) is the assessment of the possible positive or negative impacts that a proposed project or course of action may have on the environment, covering the environmental, social, and economic impacts.

environmental uniqueness the recognition that each business operates in an environment that is, in some ways, unique to it.

equal opportunity the idea that people from all backgrounds should enjoy the same chances to benefit from valued opportunities, e.g. in education and employment.

equality of outcome equality between people measured in terms of outcomes such as income and wealth.

equilibrium analysis the use of demand and supply diagrams to predict the effects of changes in markets. An essential part of microeconomics.

equity *see* **efficiency**.

ethical consumerism bringing ethical considerations into spending decisions, e.g. fair trade.

ethnocentrism belief in the superiority of one's own culture over other cultures. In business, this can mean a tendency for many western global businesses to assume that the norm to aspire to is a western cultural model, and that it is western values of individualism and personal aspiration that are embedded in the supra-national bodies.

EU budget the means to fund common policies, balance the gains and losses from integration, promote cohesion, and redistribute wealth. Expenditure dominates with substantial sums allocated traditionally to the Common Agricultural Policy (CAP) and increasingly regional policy. Contributions have increased progressively necessitating new resources such as VAT and later GNP-based measures.

euro-centric view focusing on European culture or history to the exclusion of a wider view of the world; implicitly regarding European culture as pre-eminent.

European integration a process of economic association in which progressive integration requires policy harmonization and institutional changes rather than merely the removal of trade barriers.

European Monetary Union a three-stage process involving convergence of participants' economies, the establishment of a common monetary policy run by the European Central Bank, and ultimately the introduction of the single currency, the euro.

European treaties agreed by member states' governments and ratified in their parliaments, these are the legal basis for the EU and its operations, e.g. Treaty of Rome that founded the EEC, Treaty of Maastricht that formed the EU.

executive the branch of government that is concerned with implementing public policy and law.

executive dominance refers to the dominance of Parliament by the executive (government) through control of a parliamentary majority coupled with party discipline.

expert opinion a form of environmental analysis relying on expert views, often using external consultants.

external environment environmental forces that operate in the world outside the organization.

fair trade (or fairtrade) is about better prices, decent working conditions, local sustainability, and fair terms of trade for farmers and workers in the developing world. By requiring companies to pay sustainable prices (which must never fall lower than the market price), fairtrade addresses the injustices of conventional trade, which traditionally discriminates against the poorest weakest producers. It enables them to improve their position and have more control over their lives (Fairtrade Foundation https://www.fairtrade.org.uk/What-is-Fairtrade/FAQs.

federal state a state in which power is shared constitutionally between the centre and localities (as opposed to a unitary state).

feudalism refers to the type of social system which is characterized by a rigid hierarchy transmitting power and control downwards from an all-powerful monarch, supported by the landowning nobility, down to the mass of property-less peasants. In this system political and economic power is concentrated in the hands of this tiny elite.

final or finished goods and services goods and services purchased by their ultimate users.

final salary pension a form of employer-sponsored occupational pension arrangement. It is the most common type of defined benefit pension scheme. It pays former employees a pension calculated as a percentage of the salary that was being received at the date of retirement or in the final years of work prior to retirement.

fiscal policy measures that alter the level and composition of government expenditure and taxation.

first past the post (FPTP) electoral system used for parliamentary elections in the UK, in which the winning candidate in each constituency needs just to obtain more votes than any other candidate (not necessarily a majority). Criticized by supporters of proportional representation (PR).

five forces Porter's (1980) framework for analysing competitive forces in a market.

flat structure a type of organization structure or principle based on delayering, i.e. stripping out management layers.

food miles the distance food travels between producer and consumer, commonly used to highlight the impact on the environment caused by production of carbon dioxide emissions during transport.

Fordism describes the mass production assembly line techniques pioneered in the automobile industry but then adopted across manufacturing industry in the early to mid twentieth century.

foreign direct investment investment of capital by a government, company, or other organization in production and marketing operations that are located in a foreign country.

free market in a strict sense refers to a market that is free of government regulation or intervention. In practice, supporters of the free market advocate minimum government.

freedom (see **liberty**) a key political principle referring to the ability of individuals to decide for themselves how to live their own lives, often linked with arguments in favour of the 'free market'.

frictional or search unemployment arises when people find themselves, for any number of reasons, temporarily between jobs without leaving the labour market.

functional structure a type of organization structure based on functional departments, e.g. finance, marketing, HR.

gazelle another label for a 'high growth' organization.

gender pay gap the gap or difference between the average pay of men compared to women.

generalization to make a statement that is intended to be of general application.

generation gap because of cultural change people of different ages exhibit different values and lifestyles.

genetically modified organism (GMO) creation of plants, animals, and micro-organisms by unnatural manipulation of genes, perhaps taking DNA from one species and inserting it into another unrelated one. GMOs can spread and cross with naturally-occurring organisms. Proliferation in an unpredictable way may produce unknown consequences. GMOs are a form of genetic pollution.

gig economy a term that has come into use to describe temporary, flexible work provided primarily by independent freelancers or contractors, e.g. Deliveroo riders—each job they perform is a separate 'gig'. In England there are ongoing court cases about the status of individuals working in the gig economy.

glass ceiling a metaphor to refer to the under-representation of women in senior positions, especially management, above a certain level of advancement.

global financial crisis the period between 2007 and 2008 that signified a global banking collapse.

global warming the heating up of the earth's atmosphere mainly due to burning fossil fuels, leading to global climate change.

globalization the processes by which it is argued that the world economy has become more integrated. Globalization can be seen as an increase in flows across national boundaries. These include not only economic flows of trade and investment in the form of multinational companies and international finance but also the transmission and mixing of cultural influences, migration and increased communication. The benefits and drawbacks of these processes, and the extent to which they may be controlled or influenced, are the subject of much controversy.

glocalization the process of tailoring products or services to different local markets around the world.

good governance All societies need government in some form, but there may be disagreement about the form of government and its role in society. There is substantial agreement, particularly in the West, that good governance requires democracy.

good society in all societies the need for politics arises from disagreements and conflicts between people over values and interests—different views about the nature of the 'good society'.

governance the means by which a government governs in all its forms and all its levels.

government can refer to the process of governing (see also **governance**), or to those who are in government, the government of the day.

Great Depression a period of worldwide economic collapse 1929–33.

green marketing refers to the marketing of products which can be construed as having favourable environmental characteristics which can be emphasized in the marketing message to make the product more attractive to the consumer. The presumption is that the environmental characteristics highlighted in the message are genuine. Green marketing can cover changes to the product, the production process, the packaging, and the advertising.

green transport plans are produced as a matter of course by public authorities to minimize the environmental impact of the operation of the whole transport system in a town, city, or region, but green transport plans are also produced by organizations such as companies and educational institutions to minimize the environmental impact of the transport activities they generate, whether by workers, customers, or goods delivery/dispatch.

greenwash is green marketing used to deceive the consumer into thinking that an organization's products, aims, and/or policies are environmentally friendly when in reality they are not.

gross domestic product (GDP) the total output of final goods and services produced by an economy in a year.

Health and Safety Executive (HSE) the government body charged with enforcing health and safety regulations in the UK. Together with local authorities, HSE inspectors regularly examine premises to check that regulations are being fully complied with.

hierarchical structure a type of organization structure based on layers of authority with power concentrated at the top.

high-growth organizations that grow at 20 per cent or above over a period of three years.

hot money refers to inflows of foreign currency into a country simply as a result of the speculative hope that by buying a country's currency it might appreciate in value and produce a windfall profit.

ideology a set of political beliefs and values, e.g. liberalism, socialism.

immediate environment refers to those aspects of the business environment that are relevant to day-to-day decision-making and operations, e.g. the behaviour of competitors.

imperialism imperialism is a policy of extending control or authority over foreign entities as a means of acquisition and/or maintenance of empires, either through direct territorial conquest or through indirect methods of exerting control on the politics and/or economy of other countries. The essential feature of the Marxist theories of imperialism, or related theories such as dependency theory, is their focus on the economic relation between countries, rather than the formal political relationship. Imperialism thus consists not necessarily in the direct control of one country by another, but in the economic exploitation of one region by another or of a group by another.

individual freedom what it means to be free and to what extent freedom should be curtailed by laws are highly contested questions. In a basic sense freedom may be defined in terms of 'living as I choose'.

individualism no single meaning, but can refer to the idea that as individuals we make our own choices, as well as to the idea that people tend to behave in a self-interested way.

inflation the process of continually rising prices.

informal economy refers to activities, which can be paid or unpaid, which are not registered with the tax authorities. Informal paid work includes illegal tax evasion such as 'cash-in-hand' payments.

innovation the process of creating new value and/or value in new way.

institutional triangle the three decision-making bodies that implement EU laws and policies: the Council of the EU; the European Parliament; and the European Commission.

integration refers to the extent to which people from different ethnic and religious backgrounds participate as members of a common society rather than living separately.

intensification of work the process by which employers place increased pressure on employees to work longer hours and/or to expend greater effort so as to increase productivity.

intergenerational equity refers to the concept of fairness between generations, or, being as fair to our grandchildren as we are to ourselves.

intergovernmental organization (IGO) (also intergovernmentalism) an association of sovereign nation states usually for the purpose of treaty or common action, e.g. World Trade Organization (WTO).

internal environment this phrase reminds us that managers have to operate within an environment that is constituted by the organization itself, e.g. relations with other colleagues and departments.

intragenerational equity refers to the concept of fairness between different interest groups in the same generation.

intrapreneur an intrapreneur has been defined as 'a person within a large corporation who takes direct responsibility for turning an idea into a profitable finished product through assertive risk-taking and innovation' (American Heritage Directory, 3rd edn, 1992: see Chapter 14 References).

invention is the creation of a new product or process of production.

ISO 14001 an international standard of best practice for carrying out environmental management systems audits, policies, etc. It sets out a range of criteria which companies must satisfy to achieve the standard.

job creation the creation of new jobs.

job destruction the loss of jobs.

joint ventures a commercial undertaking entered into by two or more parties, usually in the short term. Joint ventures are generally governed by the Partnership Act (1890) but they differ from partnerships in that they are limited by time or by activity.

jurisdiction essentially this is the geographical scope within which a court or parliament can exercise its power. The nature of jurisdiction has changed with the rise of globalization particularly in the member states of the European Union.

just in time refers to the organization of production processes to minimize the holding of inventories, which is very expensive. The production process is organized so that parts and raw materials are delivered to the production site as nearly as possible to the time when they are actually required.

Keynesianism associated with John Maynard Keynes. A theory that paints economies as vulnerable to shocks and recessions from which there may be no quick and spontaneous recovery. Accordingly, and when necessary, governments need to assume responsibility for the management of the macroeconomy by influencing the level of aggregate demand.

Keynesian–welfare consensus broad agreement (consensus) between the main political parties and within society (in the 1950s and 1960s) that government should be responsible for managing the economy, especially to secure full employment (Keynesian), and provide a range of welfare services such as health and education (welfare).

Kyoto Protocol an international agreement linked to the United Nations Framework Convention on Climate Change, which committed its signatory parties by setting internationally binding emission reduction targets. It was adopted in Kyoto, Japan, on 11 December 1997 and entered into force on 16 February 2005.

labour market flexibility is when the labour market functions in such a way that labour resources can be utilized on a flexible basis. For example, the use of 'zero-hours' contracts which became a focus of controversy in the UK in 2013. The criticism of such flexibility is that it is beneficial to employers but disadvantageous for employees.

late industrialization after the end of the Second World War, many former colonies (see **colonialism**) gained their political independence. Amartya Sen argues that in order for these countries to develop they would need to industrialize using a different set of economic policies than that followed by the western capitalist countries.

learning organization one that consciously seeks to manage the learning and development of its workforce. Learning organizations, and the people in them, learn constantly from everything they do. Such an idea is harnessed to the target of making the organization as a whole behave in a sustainable way, rather than it just being the responsibility of the Sustainability Officer or the PR Department.

left wing has no single meaning, but generally refers to an ideological viewpoint that supports greater state involvement in business and society, and greater equality.

liberal democracy is a form of government that combines democratic procedures with forms of individual freedom and equality that have been championed in the liberal political tradition, hence 'liberal + democratic'.

liberty *see* **freedom**.

licence to operate the idea that corporations need to retain a level of public trust and legitimacy.

life cycle assessment is the assessment of the environmental impacts associated with all the stages of a product's life; from raw material extraction through to materials processing, manufacture, distribution, use, repair and maintenance, and disposal or recycling. Such a comprehensive overview improves decision-making.

lifestyle business a business based on activity enjoyed by the owner which provides a particular lifestyle and income.

Lisbon Agenda the Lisbon Summit in 2000 set the goals for the future economic development of the EU to 2010, notably that the EU should become the most competitive and dynamic knowledge-based economy in the world, capable of sustained economic growth, with more and better jobs, and greater social cohesion.

lobbying a method of political influence through advocacy and persuasion of policymakers.

locational advantage companies, especially MNCs, have the option to locate their operations in response to potential business advantages, such as cheap labour.

macroeconomics/microeconomics macroeconomics is the study of the economy in terms of the broad aggregates of employment, inflation, economic growth, trade, and the balance of payments as well as levels of inequality. Microeconomics is the study of individual product and resource markets.

macroeconomic policy is action by policymakers to improve aspects of the performance of the whole economy.

majority–minority city the phenomenon of ethnic or religious groups that are minorities in a national context coming to form a majority in a particular city.

marginality whenever we make a decision we do so 'at the margin', in other words we weigh up the advantages of the next decision to be taken against the disadvantages of not doing it. By studying these marginal costs and benefits we should not only be able to make better decisions but should be able to predict how economic actors are likely to behave.

market a system of voluntary exchange, created by the relationship between buyers and sellers.

market failure whilst markets do mostly work efficiently there are large areas in which they fail to work or else will need government support or control to enable them to do so.

market structure refers to the number and size of sellers in a market, e.g. oligopoly.

materialism an emphasis on material living standards and possessions as a prime source of well-being, e.g. that a good life means having more money (see also **consumerism**).

matrix structure introduces a horizontal principle cutting across departments, e.g. on the basis of project teams.

micro businesses is a term to describe a 'very' small business.

Millennium Development Goals eight goals that all 191 United Nations member states have agreed to try to achieve by the year 2015. The United Nations Millennium Declaration, signed in September 2000, commits the states to:

- eradicate extreme poverty and hunger;
- achieve universal primary education;
- promote gender equality and empower women;
- reduce child mortality;
- improve maternal health;
- combat HIV/AIDS, malaria, and other diseases;
- ensure environmental sustainability; and
- develop a global partnership for development.

minimum wage the national minimum wage (NMW) in the UK imposes a statutory duty on all employers to not pay below a defined minimum.

mixed economy a mix of private and public sectors, e.g. a predominantly capitalist economy with some element of public ownership of industry (nationalization).

money GDP GDP unadjusted for inflation.

monetarism an economic theory that understands inflation to be caused by an excess in the rate of growth of an economy's money supply over the rate of growth of its output of goods and services.

monetary policy measures that alter interest rates or the money supply.

money purchase pension a form of employer-sponsored occupational pension scheme, also sometimes called a 'defined contribution scheme'. Employee and employer contributions are made into separate individual pension accounts and then invested. At retirement the money in the account is used to purchase an annuity from an insurance company which pays a weekly or monthly pension for the rest of the retiree's life.

multicultural society a society in which many ethnic and religious communities coexist, as opposed to a society with a homogeneous culture.

multilevel governance governance takes place on a number of spatial scales—national, subnational, supranational.

multinational corporation (MNC) a company that has production facilities in more than one country (i.e. undertakes foreign direct investment) including securing supplies of raw materials, utilizing cheap labour sources, servicing local markets, and bypassing protectionist barriers. Multinationals may be seen as an efficient form of organization, making effective use of the world's resources and transferring technology between countries. On the other hand, some have excessive power, are beyond the control of governments (especially weak governments), and are able to exploit host countries, especially in the Third World, where they are able to operate with low safety levels and inadequate control of pollution.

narrow money refers to notes and coins in circulation and reserve balances held by commercial banks and building societies at the Bank of England.

nation state refers to the conjunction of a system of political rule (a state) and a population comprising a national community (nation).

nationalization the process of taking private sector businesses or industries into public or 'common' ownership. Related to socialist ideology public ownership can be a strategy to replace a capitalist market economy with a planned economy, but in practice has involved the creation of a 'mixed economy' in which the private sector remains the dominant element.

National Pensions Saving Scheme (NPSS) a government-sponsored pension fund proposed by the Turner Committee as a means of increasing pension savings in the UK. From 2012 all employers who do not operate an occupational pension scheme will have to contribute a sum equivalent to 3 per cent of their pay bill into NPSS accounts set up for their staff. A further 4 per cent of pay will be contributed by employees and 1 per cent as a result of tax relief. Membership will be voluntary, but new employees will be automatically enrolled.

national sovereignty the capacity of a nation to govern its own affairs: national self-determination.

natural monopoly in industries where the capital costs are very large it is often sensible to only have one firm operating so that as output expands the capital costs are spread across the output, thus lowering average costs.

natural rate of unemployment the rate of unemployment which reflects the prevailing level of competitiveness of the labour market.

neoclassical endogenous growth theory sees growth as being the result of the constant development of technology. Whilst this is driven by businesses constantly seeking to boost profits, it is also important that there is openness to trade between countries, with technology flowing across frontiers through technology transfer.

neocorporatism a system of political representation in which privileged status is accorded to business and labour, which may be seen as partners with government in formulating and implementing economic policy.

neoliberalism a label given to the revival of classical liberal ideas in the 1980s, often referred to as a free market ideology.

net job creation subtracting job losses from jobs created.

new international division of labour after the end of the Second World War and as many former colonies were gaining independence there was a belief that these developing countries would be able to specialize in labour intensive products and that the developed world would specialize in manufacturing and service activities. A global free trade system would mean that all countries would prosper and grow on the basis of this international division of labour.

New Labour a term coined by Tony Blair to distinguish the modernization of Labour party politics under his leadership, as opposed to 'old Labour'.

new public management (NPM) a general term for new management practices introduced in the public sector since the 1970s, imitating private sector management methods such as performance-related pay. A key element of the neoliberal drive to improve public sector efficiency, reflecting the theory that the public sector is intrinsically less efficient than the private sector.

New Right a label given to the character of right-wing politics in the 1980s especially in the UK and the US. No single meaning but usually refers to a combination of neoliberal and conservative ideas.

newly industrialized countries (NICs) countries which have recently increased the proportion of industrial production in their national income and of industrial exports in their trade. The NICs have been the most rapidly growing part of the world economy in the last quarter of the twentieth century. There is no standard list of NICs: they include the 'East Asian tigers', Hong Kong, South Korea, Singapore, and Taiwan, and various other countries including Brazil, China, India, Malaysia, Mexico, South Africa, and Thailand, and their number is growing.

non-democratic refers to a political system that lacks basic democratic rules and procedures, such as: competing parties, regular elections, all adults having the right to vote, freedom of speech, etc. In practice, it is more useful to think of a spectrum of political systems which are more or less democratic than a simple dichotomy between 'democratic' and 'non-democratic'. For example, some states in the EU are more democratic than others.

non-governmental organization (NGO) refers to any non-profit voluntary citizens' group which is organized on a local, national, or international level. Such groups contribute to the wider civil society through direct service to, or advocacy on behalf of, groups in need. Good international examples are Oxfam and Amnesty International.

non-profit objectives goals or aims that are not making or intending to make profit.

occupational segregation a measure of the extent to which males and females are found in different occupational groups.

old Labour a reference to traditional Labour party values and policies such as public ownership and redistribution of income, often used pejoratively by supporters of New Labour.

opportunity cost scarcity means that choices have to be made about what to produce. If you choose one thing then something else is given up and the opportunity cost is the cost of the next most desirable alternative.

organization culture the values and beliefs of an organization.

organization structure refers to the internal layout of an organization, e.g. in terms of departments and lines of accountability.

organizational design all organizations are subject to processes of conscious design intended to enhance performance, e.g. by changing the organization structure.

organizational life cycle models models that depict a common organizational growth process.

outsourcing the buying in of components, subassemblies, finished products, and services from outside suppliers rather than by supplying them internally. A firm may decide to buy in rather than supply internally because it lacks the expertise, investment capital, or physical space required to do so. It may also be able to buy in more cheaply or more quickly than manufacturing in-house.

peak organization usually in reference to the CBI and TUC, as organizations which represent the interests of business and labour as a whole.

PEST analysis a form of environmental analysis in which environmental forces are classified as political, economic, social, and technological.

pluralism a model or theory which emphasizes the dispersal and fragmentation of political influence among a large number of groups and interests in society.

politics no single definition, but may be seen as the activity that is concerned with determining the rules under which we live in society.

popular sovereignty the idea of popular rule (see also **democracy**).

portfolio investment the list of holdings in securities owned by an investor or institution. In building up an investment portfolio an institution will have its own investment analysts, while an individual may make use of the services of a merchant bank that offers portfolio management.

positive action measures to recruit from under-represented groups, e.g. through targeted advertising of job opportunities or training.

potential GDP the real GDP associated with the full employment of all an economy's resources.

poverty contested term referring to those who are poor according to some absolute or relative measure. An absolute measure has no regard to average living standards whereas a relative measure defines poverty in relation to the general living standards within the society.

Prebisch–Singer hypothesis the theory predicts that the terms of trade between primary products and manufactured goods tend to deteriorate over time. Developed independently by economists Raul Prebisch and Hans Singer in 1950, the thesis suggests that countries that export primary commodities (such as most developing countries) would be able to import less and less for a given level of exports. Prebisch went on to argue that, for this reason, developing countries should strive to diversify their economies and lessen dependence on primary commodity exports by developing their manufacturing industry. This may initially mean that such countries need to protect their domestic industries from open trade.

precautionary principle the presumption that no new technology should be introduced if there is a potential risk that the costs might outweigh the benefits even if there is no hard evidence that this may be the case.

precedent has more than one usage. In its technical legal sense, it refers to a decision of the court that can be relied upon in later cases. As noted in Chapter 6, if the precedent is found to be authoritative it will normally be followed by courts of similar or lesser standing. In the broader, less technical, sense lawyers will often refer to precedents when drafting legal documents. These precedents are documents that have been used in previous cases which can be adapted to the needs of the current client.

price elasticity of demand measures the 'responsiveness' of demand to changes in price. It is the percentage change in the quantity demanded as a result of a small percentage change in price.

private finance initiatives (PFIs) a fully developed set of rules and regulations governing the relationship between private and public sectors with targeted advice on financing.

private sector consists of all businesses in some form of private ownership.

privatization (or denationalization) the transfer of assets from the public sector to the private sector (e.g. the privatization of nationalized industries and the sale of council houses) but can include opening tax-funded services up to competition from private sector businesses, and contracting out. A main plank of neoliberal ideology.

process innovation the introduction of new methods in the production process through application of knowledge.

producer-led sometimes put forward as a criticism of public services, i.e. that they are run in the interests of the producers rather than the consumers or users.

product innovation the development of new or improved products through application of knowledge.

product market the market within which an organization competes and sells its products/services.

production possibility frontier this illustrates the potential combinations of output that a country can attain if it uses its given resources efficiently.

productive efficiency *see* efficiency.

productivity measures the rate at which inputs are converted into outputs. Productivity is rising if, for any given level of resource input, output rises. Productivity is also defined as the quantity of goods and services that people produce in a given time period.

profit the excess of total revenue over total costs. Profit is the primary motivation of private sector business.

public finance initiatives the use of public–private partnerships (PPP) for the public sector with a focus on finance.

public interest When we say that government should act in the public interest we mean it should act so as to benefit society as a whole. A 'whistle-blower' who exposes corporate wrongdoing might damage the interests of the company but be acting in the public interest (see also common good).

public–private partnerships (PPPs) a fully developed set of rules and regulations governing the relationship between private and public sectors.

public sector the public sector is made up of general government and public corporations, it comprises all activities that are controlled by government, in contrast to those that are undertaken in the private sector by households, businesses, and non-profit organizations.

public service comparator (PSC) an administrative device to ensure that a comparison is made between public and private service costs and effectiveness when considering PPPs and PFIs.

public service ethic the idea that public service managers and employees are, or should be, motivated by the desire to provide a service to the public or contribute to the public good. This is contrasted with the idea that self-interest in the form of making money governs the private sector.

race to the bottom the claim that nation states are obliged to reduce the 'burden' of regulation and taxation on business in order to attract inward investment.

real GDP GDP adjusted to strip out the effects of inflation.

recession a decline in real GDP that lasts for at least two consecutive quarters of a year.

regional development agencies (RDAs) organizations created by government to aid and focus on regional development.

regional policy a key policy area involving transfers to regions performing below the EU average and facing structural difficulties. It has increased in significance following enlargement.

relative prices the price of one good or service compared to another.

resource depletion the using up once and for all of natural resources which cannot be renewed, e.g. oil.

right to manage refers to the claim that business decisions should be in the hands of managers. An alternative idea is that employees should have more say in the running of business.

right wing has no single meaning, but generally refers to an ideological viewpoint that opposes greater state involvement in business and society, and accepts or supports inequality.

Rio conference or Rio summit a global environmental conference held in Rio de Janeiro from 3 to 14 June 1992.

rule of law means that the powers exercised by government are based in law and all citizens are equal before the law.

Schengen Agreement is a European Union-wide single state agreement for international travel purposes with no internal border controls.

secularism a secular society is one in which religion is a weak source of values and beliefs, and has been displaced by science and reason.

self-employment working for oneself rather than for an employer.

separate legal personality this is the legal device by which those who own a company are distinguished from it. Once a company is accepted as being properly formed it has an independent legal identity which gives it separate rights and responsibilities.

separation of powers a constitutional principle referring to the separation of the three main branches of government: legislative, executive, and judicial.

single market the single, common, or internal market of the EU involves the abolition of obstacles to trade among members. It embraces the four freedoms covering the movement of goods, people, capital, and services.

small and medium-sized enterprises (SMEs) a small firm the size of which is defined by local policy.

social cohesion refers to the extent to which society is held together, e.g. by shared values rather than some people feeling marginalized or excluded.

social enterprises businesses with primary social objectives whose surpluses are principally reinvested for that purpose in the business or in the community, rather than being driven by the need to maximize profit for shareholders and owners' ('Social Enterprise: a strategy for success' http://www.dti.gov.uk/socialenterprise).

social entrepreneur a specific term for someone who employs business principles and business start-up techniques for societal good and social benefit.

social justice a political principle that is concerned with the fairness of society, particularly in respect of the distribution of income.

social mobility a measure of the chances of people from different backgrounds to attain positions of high status and/or income, e.g. for working-class children to 'move up' into middle-class occupations. Often expressed in terms of whether positions at the top are 'open' or 'closed'. Social mobility may be advocated on grounds of both fairness and efficiency.

social partners usually in reference to business and labour, as partners in a shared endeavour to secure the health of business and the economy.

social responsibility obligation of an organization towards the welfare and interests of the society in which it operates.

socialism a left-wing political ideology, involving a critique of capitalism and support for state regulation and/or control of business.

sovereign the highest form or source of authority.

sovereignty a term referring to the highest form or source of authority, e.g. parliamentary sovereignty.

spatial level the territorial or geographical scale at which business or other activity takes place, e.g. local, national, global.

Stability and Growth Pact a commitment to budgetary discipline among eurozone members. It sets a ceiling of 3 per cent GDP on government borrowing, a breach of which could invoke substantial fines (up to 0.5 per cent GDP). Considered too rigid and politically unpopular, its rules were relaxed in March 2005.

stagflation a combination of economic stagnation and inflation.

stakeholder any individual or group that is affected by (and thus has a stake in) business decisions.

stakeholder analysis a form of environmental analysis based on identifying key stakeholders and assessing their interests and potential influence.

stakeholder theory the view that business has many stakeholders. These are groups who have an interest in or are affected by business. Hence, it is argued that business should take these groups into account.

state a narrow definition refers to the capacity to make and enforce rules within a defined territory backed up by coercion. In a broader sense refers to the public sector (see also **caretaker state**).

static gains from trade occur as a result of the efficiency gains from exploiting relative comparative advantages. These arise as a result of a nation's ability to specialize and trade, and are a 'one-off' gain in terms of boosting living standards amongst trading partners.

statutory maternity pay (SMP) the minimum amount of money that employers are obliged to pay employees while they are taking periods of maternity leave up to and following the birth of a baby.

structural or mismatch unemployment arises when labour is released from declining industries without the skills to be readily absorbed into new or existing industries.

subnational governance a level of political authority below or within the nation state e.g. local government.

supply chain the chain of organizations involved in transforming raw materials into goods and services for the end user.

supranational governance a level of political authority above the nation state, e.g. the EU.

sustainable development an approach to economic and social development that seeks to strike a balance between the need for economic growth, and equity between social groups and between generations, especially in terms of issues of global resource depletion and global environmental degradation.

SWOT analysis a form of internal–external environmental analysis to identify strengths, weaknesses (internal), opportunities, and threats (external).

tax resistance the claim that there is a limit to the level of taxation that voters will support to fund spending on public services. Tax resistance thus imposes a constraint on public expenditure. However, it can be argued that tax resistance has been promoted by neoliberal ideology and that it is possible to persuade voters of the need for higher taxes in order to improve public services.

technology transfer refers to technology flowing across frontiers.

Thatcherism a label given to the ideology of the Thatcher governments in Britain in the 1980s. At one level the term simply recognizes Thatcher's dominance of British politics during this period, but the ideological content is usually referred to as neoliberalism or the New Right.

transnational corporation a firm which has global presence, range of markets, production, and/or subsidiaries (see also **multinational corporation**).

treaty an international agreement between two or more nation states which becomes binding in law. The most obvious example of this is the Treaty of Rome which founded the European Economic Community, the forerunner of the European Union.

trend extrapolation a form of environmental analysis based on identifying and projecting trends, e.g. sales figures.

trickle down the idea that inequality may benefit the poorest members of society because the high rewards at the top motivate improved economic performance from which all benefit.

triple bottom line refers to the idea that, while an enterprise is normally judged by its profit and loss account ('bottom line'), it should also be judged by social and environmental criteria; also referred to as 'people, planet, profit'.

two-party system Britain is often characterized as a two-party system because the two main parties—Conservative and Labour—have dominated national politics for the last century.

unitary state a state, like the UK, in which power is concentrated at the centre, as opposed to a federal state in which power is shared between different levels of government.

upskilling is a rise in the average level of skill required.

utilitarian ethics this theory argues that something is right when it maximizes the greatest good for the greatest number.

value chain Porter sees the firm as comprising a set of horizontal functions (e.g. procurement, IT, human resources) and vertical operations, both upstream towards the market and downstream towards the sources of the resources, across which it is possible to add value by changing the way things are done (see Porter 1985, Chapter 3).

value for money (VFM) a legal and managerial term introduced to encourage local and central government to evaluate the provision of public services.

venture creation the act of creating an organization.

Washington Consensus a set of policies promulgated by many neoliberal economists as a formula for promoting economic growth in many parts of Latin America by introducing various market-oriented economic reforms which are designed to make the target economy more like that of first world countries such as the United States. It was first presented in 1989 by John Williamson, an economist from the Institute for International Economics, an international economic think tank based in Washington, DC. It is so-called because it attempts to summarize the commonly shared themes among policy advice by Washington-based institutions at the time, such as the International Monetary Fund, the World Bank, and the US Treasury Department, which were believed to be necessary for the recovery of Latin America from the financial crises of the 1980s.

welfare state refers to state expenditures on a range of public services such as education, health, housing, social services, and income support. These services have in common that they protect and enhance the welfare or well-being of citizens, and are typically seen as social rights.

work effort–bargain an agreement between employer and employee regarding the reward an employee gets from the effort they invest in the employer.

INDEX

A

B

C

D

F

G

Q

R